INTERNATIONAL TRADE AND BUSINESS: LAW, POLICY AND ETHICS

INTERNATIONAL TRADE AND BUSINESS: LAW, POLICY AND ETHICS

Second edition

Gabriël Moens and Peter Gillies

First published 2006
by Routledge·Cavendish
2 Park Square, Milton Park, Abingdon, Oxon, OX14 4RN

Simultaneously published in the USA and Canada
by Routledge·Cavendish
270 Madison Ave, New York, NY 10016

Routledge·Cavendish is an imprint of the Taylor & Francis Group,
an informa business

Printed and bound in Great Britain

British Library Cataloguing in Publication Data
A catalogue record for this book is available from the British Library

Library of Congress Cataloging in Publication Data
A catalog record for this book has been requested

ISBN10: 1-8769-0524-7
ISBN13: 978-1-8769-0524-8

PREFACE

This book deals with the core topics of international trade, which include international sales contracts, international commercial terms, carriage of goods by sea, land and air, financing of exports, regulation of imports, international commercial arbitration and the World Trade Organisation.

Every chapter offers a description and analysis of the relevant law, policies and, in some cases, ethical issues, tutorial questions and a short list of further reading. In addition, the most important international documents are reproduced in full or in part to facilitate the study of international commercial law.

International trade and business law courses are increasingly offered by most law and business schools. This increase is a response to repeated requests, by the legal and business communities, to provide courses for lawyers and business people to enable them to provide expert advice on international business practices and export trade law. In particular, *International Trade and Business: Law, Policy and Ethics* (2nd edn) is aimed at students and practitioners who are interested in international business transactions and want to gain familiarity with the law and practice of international trade law, policies and ethics. It is also hoped that it will be used by academics as their teaching and research tool on international trade and business law courses. However, the book is not limited to law since it also aims to cover trade and business policies. In addition, it deals with relevant ethical issues.

This edition is substantially revised and, as such, is very different in content from the first edition. There is a new chapter on trade in Intellectual Property written by John Selby, Lecturer in Business Law, Macquarie University. Professor Peter Gillies from Macquarie University has contributed several new chapters on The International Carriage of Goods by Air and Land (Chaper 5), Anti-dumping and Countervailing Measures Regimes (Chapter 8), International Commercial Arbitration (Chapter 10) and Enforcement of International Commercial Arbitration Awards – The New York Convention (Chapter 11). Professor Gillies and Professor Moens were responsible for the editing and revision of all other chapters in this edition. Other people who have contributed to this book include Howard Broderick (carriage of goods by sea) and Ted Tzovaras. Without their dedication and commitment this book would not have been completed. The editorial process was greatly facilitated by the excellent work of Cavendish Publishing, London who ensured that the book met the highest editorial standards. In particular, the editors are indebted to Jon Lloyd, Ewan Cooper and Jo Jacomb who provided us with superb assistance and encouragement throughout this project.

Professor Peter Gillies
Professor Gabriël A Moens

August 2005

CONTENTS

TABLE OF CASES

TABLE OF LEGISLATION

CHAPTER 1

INTERNATIONAL COMMERCIAL CONTRACTS

INTRODUCTION

The United Nations Convention on Contracts for the International Sale of Goods (Vienna Convention) came into force on 1 January 1980.[1]

It continues to be open for ratification or accession. Four States signed it (it was open for signature until 30 September 1981) and as at May 1994 a further 38 had ratified it or acceded to it. These Contracting States include Australia, Canada, China, France, Germany, Italy, the Russian Federation, Spain and the USA. Notable omissions include Japan and the UK. The list of relevant States is set out at the end of this commentary, along with a statement of declarations and reservations made by certain States pursuant to provisions in the Convention.

The Convention was adopted by a conference of 62 States convened by the Secretary General of the United Nations. These States were representative in their legal system, their geographic spread and their trading profiles.

The Convention was intended to replace the Hague Uniform Laws on International Laws (that is, the Uniform Law on International Sale of Goods of 1964, and the Uniform Law on the Formation of Contracts for the International Sale of Goods of 1964), which were adopted by the Hague Conference of 1964. The Hague Conventions were ratified by few States, being considered to be technically defective in certain aspects and Eurocentric in provenance, with, in the minds of some, an implicit bias in favour of the developed countries whose main trading interest was the export of industrial products.

The Convention, and the Hague Conventions which preceded it, were the result of decades of international discussions of, and studies on, the topic of a uniform international contract of sale law. The Vienna Convention has evolved under the aegis of the United Nations Commission on International Trade Law (UNCITRAL). The international sales contract, by its very nature, has long raised choice of law problems as well as difficult enforcement issues. The uniform international sales law movement has had, as its goal, a uniform law dealing with the international sale of goods transaction, a law that, necessarily, would be applied by the courts and tribunals of individual nations. The ultimate issues of enforcement would not be touched by such a law, which would be administered on a case-by-case municipal basis; but a uniform law would confer other benefits which could facilitate dispute resolution and, should it eventuate, litigation. The basic prospective benefit of a uniform sales law regime, of course, is that both parties can more readily know their legal rights and obligations arising from the contract, from a set of legal rules which, ideally, is expressed with comparative simplicity, is constructed without a bias towards any particular type of legal system or towards one party (buyer or seller) as opposed to another, and which is available in approved standard translations in the major languages.

---

1   The requisite number of instruments of ratification or accession were deposited by the end of 1987, with the result that the Convention came into force on 1 January 1988, pursuant to Art 99.

The Convention's broad objectives are expressed in its preamble – the Convention is predicated upon recognition that 'the development of international trade on the basis of equality and mutual benefit is an important element in promoting friendly relations among States'; and more particularly the recognition that 'the adoption of uniform rules which govern contracts for the international sale of goods and take into account the different social, economic and legal systems would contribute to the removal of legal barriers in international trade and promote the development of international trade'. The ideal and logical outcome of the process which led to the adoption of the Vienna Convention would be the universal ratification of the Convention by all States, with the result that, in the normal course (assuming its non-exclusion by the parties themselves), a common legal code of rules dealing with international sales contracts would (within the limits of its scope) be applied to international sales contracts. Buyers and sellers on the international market therefore would have a relatively simple and common uniform regime governing their contracts and their performance. The alternative would be a potentially very complex latticework of individual State sales law regimes, resort to which was dictated by the rules of private international law applying in each jurisdiction. There would (in default of agreement upon an applicable law by the parties themselves) be uncertainty at two levels: which forum's law applies, and the requirements of this law. In the typical such case, one party would benefit from having his or her own jurisdiction's law applied, and the other party would be disadvantaged by the application of a foreign and possibly poorly understood law. The Convention has not been universally adopted of course, but to the extent that it is (and the number of countries acceding to it grows steadily), the benefits of a uniform sales law regime in international sales become more widespread.

The Convention was drafted in light of common law and civil law concepts and principles, but it is intended to be a self-contained body of law to be interpreted without resort to common law or civil law precepts. Only if this approach to interpretation fails and it cannot be interpreted according to the principles on which it is based, is resort to be made to the law which would otherwise be applicable by virtue of the rules of private international law (see Art 7). The result is that, although the Convention will be applied by the courts of a given State, the courts are not to construe it in light of their own law. This canon of construction is necessary, unless the Convention is, *de facto*, to become an extension of the forum's law. This risk is particularly obvious in the case of common law States, where the typical statute becomes encrusted with judicial precedents that are pivotal in resolving issues concerning the application of the statute. To the extent that the Convention was to be thus assimilated into the law of individual States, it would lose its currency as a uniform sales regime and, once again, choice of forum would be a critical issue in respect of determining the substantive rights and obligations of the parties in dispute. The question of interpreting the Convention will be returned to below.

In the following pages, the provisions of the Convention will be reviewed and commented on.

SPHERE OF APPLICATION OF THE CONVENTION

Overview

Chapter 1 of the Convention (headed 'Sphere of Application'), that is, Arts 1–6, defines the scope of the Convention's application. A number of dimensions are important: the Convention itself must be identified by the applicable law as being applicable, or potentially so; and reference must then be made to the geography of the parties' business and the subject matter of the contract. A number of subsidiary matters must be taken into account. As well, the range of substantive issues addressed by the Convention is relatively limited. All in all, a number of tests must be satisfied before the Convention is applied. Notwithstanding this, the Convention can apply even though the parties did not contemplate this, and even in cases where neither knows of its existence. Put briefly, the Convention applies where:

(a) the contract is one for the sale of goods (certain exclusions apply);

(b) the parties have their places of business in different States;

(c) the States are Contracting States – or, in default of this, the rules of private international law lead to the application of the law of a Contracting State;

(d) the issue is one of the formation of the contract of sale and/or the rights and obligations of the parties (certain exclusions are expressed – *inter alia*, except as provided otherwise, the Convention does not deal with the validity of the contract or the effect the contract may have on the property in the goods sold);

(e) the issue is not one of the liability of the seller for death or personal injury caused by the goods to any person; and

(f) the parties have not excluded the application of the Convention in whole or in part (subject to Art 12), assuming that it is otherwise applicable.

The international element

The pivotal article in the Convention is Art 1. Article 1(1) states that:

> (1) This Convention applies to contracts of sale of goods between parties whose places of business are in different States:
>
> (a) when the States are Contracting States; or
>
> (b) when the rules of private international law lead to the application of the law of a Contracting State.

Article 1(2) provides that the fact that parties have their places of business in different States is to be disregarded whenever this fact does not appear from either the contract or from any dealings between, or from, information disclosed by the parties at any time before or at the conclusion of the contract. The effect of this is that a party in the usual case must become a willing party to an international contract for the Convention to apply.[2] This is quite different, however, from saying that the party must know of the Convention for it to apply – once the threshold tests are satisfied, the Convention applies whether or not the party had this knowledge.

---

2 Paragraph (2), *inter alia*, addresses the undisclosed foreign principal situation – see Honnold, J, *Uniform Law for International Sales under the 1980 United Nations Convention*, 3rd edn, 1999, The Hague: Kluwer Law International, p 30.

Article 1(3) provides that neither the nationality of the parties nor the civil or commercial character of the parties or of the contract is to be taken into consideration in determining the application of the Convention.

Article 1(1)(a) deals with the paradigm case, where the parties to the contract have their places of business in different Contracting States – here the Convention applies. The pivotal international element attracting the Convention is that the places of business are located in different States. It follows that the nationality (or, in the case of a company, place of incorporation/registration) of the parties is not the key to attracting the Convention under para (1)(a), nor is some other international element (such as the situation of the goods) sufficient.

So, for example, where a seller has its place of business in the USA, and contracts with a buyer with its place of business in the USA, knowing that the latter is to export the goods to a buyer in China, the contract between the first parties does not attract para (1)(a). Likewise, where a seller in the USA contracts with a buyer in the USA, and the subject matter of the contract is situated in China, the contract does not attract para (1)(a); such contract is subject to the Uniform Commercial Code (UCC). This is so whether the goods are to remain in China or be transported to a third country. A contract between a seller in the USA and a buyer in the USA, pursuant to which the seller is to deliver the goods to an address in China, does not attract para (1)(a). Such a contract will be subject to the UCC. The requirement that the international element consist in the fact that the parties have their places of business in different countries is a realistic one, because this is the case where the clear potential exists for choice of law problems and for the imposition of an unfamiliar sale of goods law on one of the parties.

The concept of 'place of business' is dealt with in Art 10. It is provided that:

(a) if a party has more than one place of business, the place of business is that which has the closest relationship to the contract and its performance, having regard to the circumstances known to or contemplated by the parties at any time before or at the conclusion of the contract; and

(b) if a party does not have a place of business, reference is to be made to that party's habitual residence.

It follows that, where a company has its headquarters in country X and a branch office in country Y, and the latter contracts, the company is deemed to have its place of business in Y.

What of the case of a transnational company that operates through subsidiary companies both in its own country of domicile and in other countries – does the subsidiary have an independent legal existence for the purposes of identifying the contracting party when applying the Convention? The Convention is silent on the matter, but most problems in this regard should disappear having regard to Art 10(a). If company X has its head office in State X, and contracts through a subsidiary company whose place of business is in State Y, the contracting party's place of business will be in State Y, because this is where the place of business most closely connected to the contract is situated.[3]

---

3   See the discussion of this issue in Honnold, *ibid*, pp 30ff; and in Roberts, J in Wilde, K and Islam, M (eds), *International Transactions – Trade and Investment, Law and Finance*, 1993, Sydney: Law Book Co, pp 33–34.

As noted, where the parties do not have their places of business in different Contracting States, the Convention may in the alternative be attracted by the operation of Art 1(1)(b). This will be so where (again) the parties have their places of business in different States and the rules of private international law lead to the application of the law of a Contracting State.

The rules of private international law vary from State to State, being a part of domestic law, but a common formulation of them in relation to international contracts would be that the parties can nominate in their contract the law to be applied; failing this, the law to which the contract has the closest connection is applied.

If the law of the forum is thus, the parties can nominate the Convention, and the Convention will then apply to their contract and any litigation concerning it. The parties can nominate the Convention directly, or they can nominate it indirectly by nominating as the applicable law the law of a country which is a Contracting State and in which Art 1(1)(b) applies (that is, it has not been the subject of a reservation under Art 95 (see below)). In this latter case, the parties may unwittingly become bound by the Convention, as where they nominate the law of an Australian State or of the USA.[4]

Alternatively, consistent with the formulation of the applicable private international law rules above, the Convention may apply pursuant to para (1)(b) because the most closely connected law is that of a Contracting State, that is a State which has the Convention as part of its law. This application will be straightforward – the parties are parties to an international contract, in the terms defined by the Convention, and the Convention states that it applies to such contracts.

It will be noted that a contract having an international element, which attracts the law of a Contracting State pursuant to its rules of private international law, but which does not answer all of the Convention tests governing the class of contracts to which it applies, will not attract the Convention. Rather, it will attract the domestic law of the forum. An instance might be a contract which is not between parties having their places of business in different States, or one which is for goods not within the Convention's definition of goods (see 'Goods – exclusions' below).

As indicated above, a Contracting State has the option under Art 95 of declaring at a prescribed time that it will not be bound by para (1)(b) of Art 1 of the Convention. A significant instance of such a reservation is that of the USA. Where the reservation is made, therefore, the domestic courts will apply the Convention in litigation concerning the conforming contract pursuant to Art 1(1)(a), that is, where the parties have their places of business in different Contracting States. Otherwise (for example, where the facts are the same but one of the States is not a Contracting State), the rules of private international law will apply. In the case of a US court, for example, this may lead to the application of the UCC in that country.

Why make the Art 95 reservation? The US position was summarised thus in 1983 in Appendix B to the *Legal Analysis accompanying the Letter of Submittal from the Secretary of State to the President*, in which the Secretary recommended to the President that the Vienna Convention be transmitted to the Senate for its advice and consent to its ratification:

---

4   See the comment by Roberts in Wilde and Islam, *ibid*, p 35.

This provision (that is, Art 1(1)(b)) would displace our own domestic law more frequently than foreign law. By its terms sub-para (1)(b) would be relevant only in sales between parties in the USA (a Contracting State) and a non-Contracting State. (Transactions that run between the USA and other contracting State are subject to the Convention by virtue of sub-para (1)(a).) Under sub-para (1)(b), when private international law points to the law of a foreign non-Contracting State, the Convention will not displace that foreign law, since sub-para (1)(b) makes the Convention applicable only when 'the rules of private international law lead to the application of the law of a Contracting State'. Consequently, when those rules point to US law, sub-para (1)(b) would normally operate to displace US law (the Uniform Commercial Code) and would not displace the law of the foreign non-Contracting States.

If US law were seriously unsuited to international transactions, there might be an advantage in displacing our law in favour of the uniform international rules provided by the Convention. However, the sales law provided by the Uniform Commercial Code is relatively modern and includes provisions that address the special problems that arise in international trade.[5]

From the USA perspective above, policy considerations justify the reservation. The application of Art 1(1)(b) would not operate to displace the law of a foreign non-Contracting State (if chosen as the law applicable to the contract). It would, however, displace the UCC in circumstances where US law was chosen as the law applicable to the contract, since the Convention would apply. Thus, foreign law would apply more frequently than would US law. This could be seen to be anomalous in litigation in a US court. Most States have not made the reservation, however, seeing the enhanced prospects of the application of the Convention (that is, under para (1)(b) in default of the application of para (1)(a)), as justifying the potential for the occurrence of this anomaly.

Goods – exclusions

The Convention does not define goods, but it is consistent with defining them as a common lawyer would define them, viz, as moveable tangibles (and thus not land or fixtures attached to it and having the status of land, and intangibles). Scope for argument as to whether a given asset fits within the concept of goods remains of course – what, for instance, is the status of a fixture immediately after severance?

Where a contract which is a mix of goods and labour is concerned, Art 3(2) adopts an approach which is familiar to a common lawyer – in essence, contracts of this type, which are predominantly for the supply of labour or other services, with the balance of the seller's obligation being to supply goods, are not contracts for the sale of goods for the purposes of the Convention. It may be assumed that a contract is predominantly one for services where the services element is more valuable than the goods element.

---

5   See the reproduction of the US documents in Kathrein, R and Magraw, D, *The Convention for the International Sale of Goods: A Handbook of Basic Materials*, 1987, Washington and Chicago: American Bar Association, Section of International Law and Practice (although the Appendices to the Legal Analysis are not included here); and likewise see Galston and Smit (eds), *International Sales: The United Nations Convention on Contracts for the International Sale of Goods*, 1984.

Article 3(1) states that contracts for the supply of goods to be manufactured or produced are to be considered sales unless the party who orders the goods undertakes to supply a substantial part of the materials necessary for such manufacture or production.

Certain things cannot be the subject of a sales contract for the purposes of the Convention. These exclusions are set out in Art 2. They are as follows:

(a) Sales of consumer goods (but note the precise definition). Consumer goods normally will not be the subject of an international sale; and in any event the consumer sale is, in many countries, regulated by extensive statutory provisions. For this reason in particular, the Convention was seen to be an inappropriate regime for their regulation.

(b) Sales by auction. These are often regulated by specific law within States, and are by their nature not negotiated sales.

(c) Sales on execution or otherwise by authority of law. These are not normal sales and could not sensibly be regulated by a typical sale of goods regime.

(d) Sales of stocks, shares, investment securities, negotiable instruments or money. Most of these are intangibles, and the sale of money *in specie* could not sensibly be regulated by a typical sale of goods regime.

(e) Sales of ships, hovercraft or aircraft. Special rules apply to these chattels (including those creating registration regimes) in municipal legal systems.

(f) Sales of electricity. Electricity is not a chattel, and a standard sale of goods regime could not sensibly be applied to a contract for its supply.

It is unclear whether the Convention applies to contracts of barter (known, *inter alia*, as counter-trade). The terms governing performance contemplate the standard transaction as being a sale for money (for example, Art 53 referring to the buyer's obligation to pay the price for the goods), but they are not obviously inconsistent with a contract of barter (the 'price' can of course be in the equivalent of money).[6]

Aspects of the contract covered by the Convention – exclusions

The Convention self-evidently is not a complete code of contract law, and therefore cannot apply to all contractual issues. For example, it does not say anything of the effect on the contract of the parties' rights or obligations because of the occurrence of a pre-contractual misrepresentation or duress, or undue influence.

Article 4 delineates the ambit of the substantive legal issues covered by it, and propounds a non-exhaustive list of matters not covered by it. According to Art 4, the Convention covers only the formation of the contract of sale (as to which see Part II of the Convention), and the rights and obligations of the seller and buyer arising from such a contract (as to which see Part III). Article 4 continues – in particular, except as otherwise expressly provided by this Convention, it is not concerned with (a) the

---

6   Honnold, *op cit*, p 53, is of the view that the Convention does not exclude barter. See too the discussion by Maskow, D, 'Obligations of the buyer' in Bianca, CM and Bonell, MJ (eds), *Commentary on the International Sales Law – the 1980 Vienna Sales Convention*, 1987, Milan: Giuffrè, pp 386–87.

validity of the contract or any of its provisions or of any usage; (b) the effect which the contract may have on the property in the goods sold.

It follows that many rules of the domestic law of a particular forum may apply to a contract's dispute which is otherwise covered by the Convention. It is possible, for example, that in a dispute concerning formation and undue influence, the Convention will apply side by side with the domestic rules of the forum, the law of which is invoked by the application of the rules of private international law.

The question of where matters relevant to the validity of a contract begin and end will depend on the domestic law of the applicable forum. For example, duress, undue influence, fraud, unconscionable dealings, mistake and misrepresentation may, in a particular case, render a contract voidable at the option of the 'innocent' party. In such a case, the complained of conduct may properly be viewed as raising an issue of validity. On the other hand, the domestic law may draw a distinction between the consequences of different sub-categories of conduct within a broader category of conduct, according to specified criteria. For instance, a distinction may be drawn between an innocent misrepresentation that does not involve a matter of substantial importance, and a fraudulent misrepresentation that does, with the law providing that the first type of misrepresentation does not render a contract voidable, while the second does.

Even if unlawful conduct by a party does not go to the validity of the contract, it may nonetheless lead to an alternative remedy outside of contract law. In a common law jurisdiction, for instance, a misrepresentation not amounting to validity may nonetheless ground a remedy in tort, or pursuant to a statute, such as one dealing with the consequences of misleading or deceptive conduct in commerce. Can the aggrieved party pursue this remedy in addition to, or in lieu of, any remedy it may have under the Convention? For example, consider a misrepresentation by the seller of goods that (a) does not make the contract voidable, but (b) does become embodied in the contract. As a result of the seller's misrepresentation, the plaintiff (buyer) is entitled to seek a Convention remedy for breach of contract; but, *prima facie*, this party can also seek a remedy in tort, or under a statutory provision in the domestic law of the forum. Does the plaintiff have a choice?

Ideally, legislation in the forum's law would attempt to regulate, in part at least, this interface between the Convention and domestic law, to resolve problems of application.[7]

In default of this (and such prescriptions could not very well cover all the problems which might arise), there will be a degree of uncertainty. How should these issues be resolved? The starting point is, of course, Art 4. Key words here are the reference to the Convention as being concerned with the formation of the agreement, and 'the rights and obligations of the seller and the buyer arising from such a contract'.[8] These words, taken with the scope of the substantive matters dealt with by

7 See, eg, the Trade Practices Act (TPA) 1974 (Australia), ss 66ff, implying certain conditions and warranties into consumer transactions (with 'consumer' having the meaning ascribed by the TPA 1974). Section 66A provides that the Convention prevails over these provisions to the extent of any inconsistency.

8 See Khoo in Bianca and Bonell, *op cit*, p 46, stressing this phrase and concluding that it is 'surely a directive to the users of the Convention to look elsewhere for solutions to other questions, viz, concerning matters other than the rights and duties created by the terms of the agreement itself, as supplemented by the Convention'.

the Convention (see Parts II and III) as noted, invite the conclusion that the Convention is concerned with relatively orthodox (conventional) issues arising between the parties. A threshold issue will be whether a contract, in the terms attracting the Convention, was formed. Thereafter, the Convention regulates, according to its terms and the terms of the agreement, matters of performance and the consequences of non-performance. If an issue is fairly within the scope of the Convention, then a domestic court should apply the Convention – to take a contrary approach would stultify it. Reference may also be made to Art 7 (considered in 'General provisions of the convention' below) dealing with the principles to be followed in interpreting the Convention.

However, even if this straightforward approach is adopted, the provisions of domestic law may be such that a question will occasionally arise as to whether the plaintiff has the option of pursuing a domestic law remedy. To repeat an example above, if a non-fundamental breach has become embodied in the agreement as a term, is the plaintiff confined to pursuing the Convention remedies for breach of contract, or can this party pursue domestic remedies that may also be grounded by such a misrepresentation? This is a problem on which the domestic law itself may waiver, dealing with a wholly domestic agreement – whether to confine the plaintiff to its contractual remedies or to allow a right of election. So, from the standpoint of the domestic court, the issue may not easily be resolved in a contest between the Convention and non-contractual domestic remedies. If the Convention is to be given full effect (again, the terms of Art 7(1) are significant here, taken together with the Art 4 injunction that the Convention is intended to regulate the rights and obligations of the parties arising from the contract), the Convention should be treated as the regime of first and only resort, in a conventional fact situation falling fairly and squarely within its scope, which does not generate an issue of validity. In this way, its goal of providing (within its terms) an exclusive, autonomous and uniform regime for the resolution of issues of formation and performance of international contracts will more readily be fulfilled.

Given the scope and complexity of the typical State's municipal law dealing with the law relevant both directly and indirectly with contracts and related issues (such as property), it is unsurprising that the Convention is limited in the range of substantive issues comprehended by it. It would not have been feasible to create a universal and exclusive regime governing all matters, including those of validity, which might arise in the context of an international contract. To reiterate, the Convention is wisely targeted at relatively conventional issues of formation and performance. As well, the great variation in the treatment of the additional matters, including validity, by the municipal legal systems of the world, would have made it very difficult to arrive at an acceptable, global code dealing with a much wider range of contractual and related issues in the context of the international sale of goods.

It has been commented that the Convention is intended to be a self-contained, uniform code of law that is to be applied uniformly, notwithstanding its implantation in many domestic legal systems. This observation must be qualified, to the extent that the courts of the States, and domestic legislation, adopt different approaches to the very basic issue of where the Convention's sphere of application ends and that of the domestic law begins. At the edges, the Vienna Convention regime will, potentially, vary in scope from State to State.

Article 4, as noted, also provides that the Convention is not concerned with the effect that the contract may have on the property in the goods sold 'except as otherwise expressly provided in this Convention'. This, likewise, was a necessary reservation – the law of property will be immensely complex from State to State, and the terms of these different regimes will vary greatly. It was not practicable to annex to the Convention a comprehensive property law code.

The fact of the agreement, and the resolution of issues of formation and performance according to the Vienna regime, will naturally bear directly upon the treatment of property rights by the domestic law of the State concerned.

Convention does not apply to liability for death or personal injury

The Convention does not apply to the liability of the seller for death or personal injury caused by the goods to any person (Art 5). These are matters best regulated by domestic law.

Exclusion of the Convention by the parties

The parties may exclude the application of the Convention or, subject to Art 12, derogate from or vary the effect of any of its provisions.

Thus, in a case where the Convention would otherwise apply, the parties may, by a term in their agreement, exclude its application in part or in whole. There is no requirement that such an exclusion be express; logically, a clear, implied intention will suffice to do this. The right of exclusion is qualified by Art 12. (In essence, according to Art 12, a Contracting State may, notwithstanding the contrary provisions of the Convention, preserve any rules in its domestic law imposing requirements that the contract or other aspects of it be in writing. Thus, if the law of the State is applicable in a given case, the requirement will apply and cannot be excluded by the parties.)

If the parties do exclude the otherwise applicable Convention in part or whole, their contract will be regulated in part or whole (depending upon the scope of the exclusions) by the law chosen by the rules of private international law. Thus, if these rules are in standard form, the parties will be permitted to choose the legal regime applicable, or the contract will be governed by the law having the closest connection with their contract.

The situation may be further complicated where the parties have agreed upon a regime of rules governing aspects of the contract's performance. In this case there will be an implied intention to exclude the Convention (and for that matter any applicable domestic law) to the extent of any inconsistency.

How is the Convention to be excluded? The obvious way is to exclude it expressly, in whole or in part. Another more oblique way of effecting exclusion is to nominate the law of a State as being the applicable law. If the State has not ratified the Convention, then this will manifest an intent to exclude it. If the State is a Contracting State, caution is needed. Simply to adopt the law of the given Contracting State will not exclude the Convention because, by virtue of ratification, this law includes the Convention. The safer course, therefore, is to adopt the domestic law of the Contracting State because this clearly excludes an adopted law like the Convention, which has its provenance in international law.[9]

GENERAL PROVISIONS OF THE CONVENTION

Articles 7ff set out provisions of general application.

Interpretation

The Convention is intended to be a self-contained law. Thus, provision has been made in Art 7 for its principles to be followed in interpreting it. As mentioned, the issue of interpretation is a critical one because of the potential for the courts of each jurisdiction to give unique and potentially conflicting interpretations as to how one article or another is to be applied. This potential for differentiation is particularly evident in the case of common law jurisdictions, with their long-standing tradition of judicial interpretation. In these cases, decisions of the courts dealing with the meaning and application of statutory provisions become precedents, which, over a long period, can come to be as significant as the original provisions themselves in delineating the law. There are numerous instances of brief, long-standing and frequently litigated provisions in statute law which have had grafted on to them countless words of judicial exegesis.

Recognising this problem, Art 7(1) provides that, in the interpretation of the Convention, regard is to be had to its international character and to the need to promote uniformity in its application and the observance of good faith in international trade. It follows that courts applying the Convention must not lose sight of the need to preserve its goals of a uniform code that is uniformly applied. The courts should be astute not to allow the principles and concepts of domestic law to condition their interpretations of the Convention, because to do this would be to assimilate it too thoroughly to domestic law and to defeat its role as a uniform international code. The interpretation should not be legalistic, and the terms of the Convention should not be treated as terms of art.

Where, notwithstanding that a given contract is governed by the Convention, a matter apparently within its general scope is not dealt with specifically by its provisions, Art 7(2) operates to maintain the status of the Convention as self-contained law and to minimise unduly hasty resort to domestic law. Article 7(2) provides that issues concerning matters governed by this Convention, which are not expressly settled in it, are to be settled in conformity with the general principles on which it is based; or, in the absence of such principles, in conformity with the law applicable by virtue of the rules of private international law. These 'general principles' include, of course, the status of the Convention as uniform law that is intended to achieve uniform application. They also include its more specific principles, as stated or implicit in its articles. Scope is allowed here for reasoning from analogy. If, however, the

---

9   See the comments in Jones, G, 'Impact of the Vienna Convention in drafting international sales contracts' (1992) 20 *International Business Lawyer* 421 at 425–26; Bonell in Bonell and Bianca, *op cit*, pp 56ff.

particular issue still cannot be resolved by the Convention, the applicable domestic law will apply. Clearly, such a resort is discouraged by Art 7, except in intractable cases.[10]

Extrinsic materials, no doubt, can be reviewed by courts in deciding issues of interpretation.[11]

Determining intent and related matters

Article 8 deals with the principles to be applied in determining the intention of the parties, and related matters. Article 8(1) approves a subjective approach to the question – statements made by, and other conduct of, a party are to be interpreted according to intent, where the other party knew or could not have been unaware what that intent was. Article 8(2) deals with cases where para (1) is not applicable, and its standpoint is one of objective assessment. Statements, etc are to be interpreted according to the understanding that a reasonable person of the same kind as the other party would have had in the same circumstances.

Article 8(3) defines what data may be reviewed in determining issues under paras (1) and (2) – due consideration is to be given to all relevant circumstances of the case, including negotiations, any practices established by the parties between themselves, usages and any subsequent conduct of the parties. Nothing resembling the common law parol evidence rule, then, applies to written contracts (unless the parties agree that the rule or some equivalent regime is to apply, as, for example, where they express their agreement to be wholly in writing).[12]

Usages

Article 9(1) provides that the parties are bound by any usage to which they have agreed and by any practice that they have established between themselves. This functions in a way analogous to the common law principle whereby terms may be implied into a contract by reference to their prior course of dealing.

Article 9(2) establishes a rebuttable presumption, that the parties have impliedly made applicable to their contract or its formation a usage of which they knew or ought reasonably to have known, and which in international trade is widely known to, and regularly observed by, parties to contracts of the type involved in the particular trade concerned. This term will assist to fill gaps in a contract in appropriate cases.

The parties can of course expressly agree upon a trade usage or analogous standardised practice in trade, such as where one or another of the International Chamber of Commerce's Incoterms is imported into the contract (see Chapter 2).

---

10 On the principles of interpretation provided for in Art 7, see Nicholas, B, 'The Vienna Convention on International Sales Law' (1989) 105 LQR 201 at 210–11; Honnold, *op cit*, pp 88ff; Roberts, *op cit*, pp 42ff.
11 See Honnold, *ibid*, pp 135ff.
12 Even here, of course, the common law courts have inevitably needed to fashion exceptions to the parol evidence rule, pursuant to which extrinsic evidence is admissible.

Requirement of writing, other requirements of form

No requirement of writing is imposed by the Convention, nor does it stipulate any other requirement of form (Art 11). A contract can be wholly or partially oral in form.

Many States, especially those belonging to the 'socialist' legal family, do impose a requirement or requirements of writing and of signature. The Convention permits a Contracting State to preserve a requirement in its domestic law that a contract be concluded in or evidenced in writing, by a declaration pursuant to Art 96. The effect of Art 12, taken with Art 96, is that the Contracting State may retain a writing/evidenced in writing requirement in relation to all or a selection of matters – the concluding of the contract itself, the variation or modification of a written contract, etc. Article 12 and Art 96 should be noted, in conjunction with Art 11 (providing generally that contracts need not be in writing or so evidenced), Art 29 (dealing with variation and modification, and again providing that writing is not required, unless the contract is in writing; and containing a provision that variation, etc be in writing – although note the estoppel-type exception), and Part II (dealing with the formation of the contract).

Article 12 provides in effect that, where a Contracting State has made an Art 96 declaration, the parties cannot overcome the effect of this by contrary agreement among themselves. Thus, if, say, the domestic law of the Contracting State, which comes to be applicable to a particular contract, requires that it be concluded in writing or so evidenced, and signed by the party to be charged, this provision will be applied by a court adjudicating a dispute between the parties.

FORMATION OF THE CONTRACT

Part II of the Convention (Arts 14–24) make provision for the formation of the contract. The concepts employed are analogous to common law concepts, although the common law authorities and concepts must not be resorted to in interpreting and applying Part II.

Offer and acceptance

Part II, broadly speaking, parallels the common law analysis of offer and acceptance in setting out a model that is to be employed in determining whether an agreement has been reached. The terms 'offer' and 'acceptance' are used (but to reiterate, they are not to be taken as being synonymous with the common law terms known by these names). In essence, for the purposes of the Convention, a contract is formed when an offer (as defined) meets with an acceptance (as defined). As it will be seen below, the Convention does not propound any other requisites for a binding contract corresponding to the common law elements of consideration; but at least where the offer is concerned, it does refer to an intention to be bound – Art 14(1).

A given fact situation may, upon examination, yield a contractual agreement but may not be readily amenable to the offer and acceptance analysis. Can it still be a contract for the purposes of the Convention? A reasoning from general principles (an approach permitted by the interpretation article, that is, Art 7(2)), should satisfy the basic requirement of Part II, that is, that an agreement has been formed. It would on occasions stultify the Convention to require a precise conformity with the offer-acceptance model.

Article 14 provides generally for the contractually significant offer. The offer must be sufficiently definite and indicate an intention to be bound in case of acceptance. It is sufficiently definite if it indicates the goods, and expressly or implicitly fixes, or makes provision for determining, the quantity and the price. This latter requirement might be thought to deviate from the common law – in the case of the common law, a failure to specify price, or a procedure for determining it, can be repaired by the implication of a term to pay a reasonable price. However, in such an event Art 55, on one view, comes to the rescue – where neither price nor a price-fixing procedure is agreed upon, and in the absence of any indication to the contrary, there is (what is in effect) an implied term that the parties have agreed that the price is the price generally charged at the time of the conclusion of the contract for such goods sold under comparable circumstances in the trade concerned.[13]

Article 14 posits as the norm the making of an offer to one or more specific persons, and provides that a proposal, other than one so addressed, is to be considered merely as an invitation to make offers (that is, in common law terms a communication falling within the concept of an invitation to treat), unless the contrary is clearly indicated by the person making the proposal. Thus, in appropriate cases an offer directed to the whole world (or at least those who will come forward), or to a class of persons, can be classed as an offer, and thus be capable of being accepted, where it was clearly the intent of the putative offeror. The result is in accordance with the common law's analysis in, for instance, one of its best known contracts decisions.[14]

Article 15(1) speaks of the offer as becoming effective when it 'reaches' the offeree (see Art 24 on the concept of 'reaches'). This provision approximates the common law requirement that the offer must be communicated (but note the extended meaning of 'reaches', which is not synonymous with 'is communicated to').

By Art 15(2), an offer, even if it is irrevocable, may be withdrawn if the withdrawal reaches the offeree before or at the same time as the offer. The concept of an irrevocable offer is described in Art 16(2). In essence, an offer is irrevocable where the offeror indicates this, expressly or impliedly (as by stating a fixed time for acceptance), or it was reasonable for the offeree to so rely on it. There is no requirement that the offeree has given consideration for the offer to be irrevocable, so at this point a clear contrast with common law principle is evident; at common law, consideration would be required (as in the case of an agreement conferring an option to purchase).

Until a contract is concluded, an offer (other than an irrevocable one) may be revoked if the revocation reaches the offeree before the latter dispatches an acceptance (Art 16(1)).

---

13 Note the comment in Nicholas, *op cit*, at 213, on the drafting quirk evident in Art 55; if it was intended to cure the problem implicitly posited in Art 14(1), ie a failure to agree upon a price or a price-fixing procedure, which problem goes to formation. Why does Art 55 make the implication of the term in question depend upon the situation being one '[w]here a contract has been validly concluded …'? Art 55 can only be allowed a full operation if the opening words in it are read as meaning 'where a contract has otherwise been validly concluded …'.

14 *Carlill v Carbolic Smoke Ball Co* [1893] 1 QB 256, where an offer made in a newspaper advertisement was determined to have contractual significance, with the result that it could be accepted by a reader unknown to the advertiser.

An offer, whether or not it is revocable, is terminated when the offeree rejects it (Art 17).

However, a counter-offer will not necessarily constitute a rejection and thus terminate the offer (contrast the common law, where a counter-offer terminates the offer, that is, it has the same effect as a more emphatic rejection). This situation is dealt with by Art 19. Its terms should be noted, but in summary it provides than an acceptance that contains additions, limitations or other modifications, is a rejection of the offer and constitutes a counter-offer. However, if the purported acceptance does propose changes, but these changes do not materially alter the terms of the offer, then this reply constitutes an acceptance (and thus a contract is formed), unless the offeror, without undue delay, objects to the discrepancy. If he does not object, a contract is formed comprising his offer and the offeree's non-material changes. Article 19(3) enunciates, non-exhaustively, a list of material alterations of the offer; they include proposals relating to price, payment, quality and quantity of goods. In aggregate, Art 19 provides for a regime quite different to that existing at common law. At common law, the offeree must accept the offer without qualification – a requirement that creates difficulties when enterprises purport to contract by an exchange of standard forms, drafted by each and differing in some of their terms. Article 19 would save purported contracts, but only where the points of difference concern non-material matters.

Acceptance is dealt with in Art 18. Article 18(1) states that a statement, or other conduct by the offeree indicating assent to the offer, is an acceptance. This parallels the common law concept. Article 18(1) does not require that the acceptance is in reliance on the offer, but this is implicit in the notion of 'assent'. As at common law, a contract cannot be unilaterally imposed upon an offeree – '[s]ilence or inactivity does not in itself amount to acceptance'. Thus, a party cannot deem another to be party to a contract if the latter does not respond to the first party's offer by a fixed term.

Acceptance was held to have occurred when a party retained a letter of offer and subsequently accepted performance from the offeror. The offeree was deemed to have accepted the terms identified in the letter of offer. The offeree did more than merely remain silent – its failure to dispute the existence of the contract after performance commenced estopped it from disputing the existence of the contract. There was in effect an acceptance by conduct. It was relevant that there had been extensive dealings between the parties on previous occasions.[15]

The acceptance becomes effective (and thus the contract is formed) at the moment the indication of assent reaches the offeror (Art 18(2)). Again, note the definition of 'reaches' in Art 24 – *inter alia*, a contractual communication such as an acceptance 'reaches' a party when it is delivered to his place of business or mailing address. It follows that actual communication to the party is not necessarily required. A person, for instance, can become party to a contract some time before he learns of the communication of the acceptance (as where the acceptance is by letter – here it reaches him when it is deposited in his letter box). The Convention does not replicate the common law's postal acceptance rule.

Article 18(2) also provides that an acceptance is not effective if the indication of assent does not reach the offeror within the time he has fixed, or, if no time is fixed,

---

15 *Filanto v Chilewich International Corporation* (1992) F. Supp 1229 789, US District Court (SD NY), referring to s 18(1).

then within a reasonable time, due account being taken of the circumstances of the transaction, including the rapidity of the means of communication employed by the offeror. An oral offer must be accepted immediately unless the circumstances indicate otherwise.

At common law, the offeror can waive the need for communication of the acceptance as a basis for formation, and instead expressly or by implication stipulate that the doing of a given act shall be both an act of acceptance and of (partial or whole) performance, at one and the same time. This position is more or less replicated by Art 18(3), which postulates, as instances of its invocation, the dispatch of goods or payment of price without notice to the offeror. In such a case, acceptance is effective at the time the act (of acceptance-performance) is performed. This act must be performed within the period of time laid down by Art 18(2). The waiver of the need for communicating acceptance can be done in the offer, or be the result of practices established between the parties, or of usage.

Article 20 deals with an ancillary matter, that is, the commencement of the period of time fixed by the offeror for acceptance; and the impact of official holidays or non-business days on the calculation of these periods.

An acceptance which reaches the offeror after the expiry of the offer period is by definition too late – the offer will have expired through the effluxion of time (see Art 18(2)). However, Art 21(1) provides, exceptionally, that a late acceptance is nevertheless effective as an acceptance if, without delay, the offeror so informs the offeree or dispatches a notice to that effect. Article 21(2) provides that, if a letter or other writing containing a late acceptance shows that it has been sent in such circumstances that, if its transmission had been normal, it would have reached the offeror in due time, the late acceptance is effective unless, without delay, the offeror orally informs the offeree that he considers his offer as having lapsed or dispatches a notice to that effect. This latter provision is, when examined, quite different to the postal acceptance rule at common law (which deems acceptance to have taken place as and when the letter of acceptance is posted, whether the letter arrives early, late or never). The rule in Art 18(2) is less likely to cause confusion than the postal acceptance rule.

An acceptance may be withdrawn if the withdrawal reaches the offeror before or at the same time that the acceptance would have become effective (Art 22). At common law, in a case comprehended by the postal acceptance rule, the acceptance would become effective and create a contract at the moment of its posting – thereafter there could not be a withdrawal of acceptance.

The time of contracting is defined by Art 23: the contract is concluded at the time when an acceptance of an offer becomes effective in accordance with the provisions of the Convention. The major such provision is Art 18(2), as noted above.

As noted, the concept of 'reaches' as applied to communications described in Part II is defined in Art 24. The concept includes communications of which, in particular circumstances, the addressee may not yet be cognisant (as where, for instance, an acceptance is delivered to the offeror's place of business; in this case it is deemed by Art 24 to have reached the offeror; and in the normal case, the contract will have been formed at this point in time – Arts 18(2), 23, 24, taken together).

If this outcome is potentially inconvenient or mischievous, the parties should agree upon an alternative regime of rules in their pre-contractual negotiations, concerning when they are to be taken to have formed a contract. The same comment may be made generally regarding the application of the formation rules. Such a variation is presumably permissible from the offeror's standpoint – by Art 14(1), the offer must, among other matters, sufficiently indicate 'the intention of the offeror to be bound in case of acceptance'. It is the offeror who is potentially most at risk in problem cases that might be hypothesised about in light of a provision like Art 24.

Consideration

Unlike the common law, the Convention does not have, as one of its pivots of formation of contract, a requirement of consideration. To the extent that the Convention is about international sales, and necessarily refers to issues of price (see, for example, Arts 14, 53ff), contracts comprehended by it will be supported, *de facto*, by consideration from both sides. But the concept of consideration does not otherwise figure in the Convention, so that there are no rules to be found in it corresponding to such common law rules as those dealing with legally insufficient consideration.

It is because consideration is not pivotal in the Convention that an offer can be irrevocable, without any requirement that the offeree has offered consideration for this benefit (see Arts 15ff). As noted above, a contract can be formed although the parties have not fixed a price (see Arts 14, 55).

Intention to create legal relations

The common law requires that the parties manifest, on an objective view, an intent to create a legally binding agreement as an element of formation. The Convention imposes no such requirement. However, as noted, Art 14 does refer to the offer as being a proposal which, *inter alia*, indicates the intention of the offeror to be bound in case of acceptance. While it is perhaps of little practical significance, given that agreements alleged to be within the purview of the Convention will be entered into in a business context, no such parallel requirement is enunciated in respect of the party accepting the offer, thus forming a contract.

SALE OF GOODS

Part III of the Convention – the major section of it – deals with the performance of the contract, remedies for breach and related matters. Before reviewing its provisions, note needs to be made of Chapter I, headed 'General provisions'. These articles deal with concepts relevant to the interpretation and application of Part III.

General provisions

Fundamental breach

Article 25 defines what amounts to a fundamental breach of contract. A breach is fundamental if it results in such detriment to the other party as substantially to deprive him of what he is entitled to expect under the contract, unless the party in breach did not foresee, and a reasonable person of the same kind and in the same circumstances would not have foreseen, such a result. The consequences of such a breach are referred to later in Part III: see, for instance, Art 49, providing that the buyer may declare the contract avoided (that is, in effect, rescinded) where the seller is responsible for a fundamental breach (note the limitations); and note the parallel article – Art 64 – vesting a parallel right in the seller.

The concept of avoiding or rescinding the contract for fundamental breach closely parallels the common law concept of rescinding a contract for breach of a condition. However, Art 25 does not replicate the common law. In particular, the usage of fundamental breach owes nothing to the concept that briefly attracted the attention of the English courts, in a development which has now been terminated.[16]

The common law in a number of jurisdictions seizes upon the concept of the condition as a basis for determining which breaches provide a basis for rescission, and the test for determining whether a term is a condition has, on one view, a partly subjective element.[17]

The focus of Art 25 is upon the nature of the breach itself rather than the term (although the more fundamental the term, in practice, the more readily will a party be able to prove that the breach is fundamental, as defined in Art 25). Also, the test is essentially objective in character (save for the exemption permitted the defendant – even here this party must fulfil the objective test of the foresight of the reasonable person). Article 25 does not define the time when the matter of fundamental breach is to be tested. At common law, the time for assessing whether a term is a condition is the time of formation.[18]

Given that Art 25 focuses on the breach, enquiry in a case where it is sought to be invoked cannot be confined to the circumstances at the time of formation, but must look as well at the circumstances as they stood at the time of breach, and at the consequences of breach. The Art 25 enquiry, therefore, cannot be tied down to the facts as they stood at any given moment; rather, it must, in the temporal sense, be potentially wide ranging.[19]

Notice of avoidance

Article 26 provides that a declaration of avoidance of the contract is effective only if made by notice to the other party. The circumstances where avoidance is permitted

---

16 For a period the English courts propounded a doctrine of fundamental breach in the context of exclusion clauses, holding that no matter how broadly the clause was drafted, it could not exclude a so called fundamental breach. The doctrine was disapproved by the House of Lords in *Suisse Atlantique Société d'Armement Maritime SA v NV Rotterdamsche Kolen Centrale* [1967] 1 AC 361, and finally repudiated by the House of Lords in *Photo Production Ltd v Securicor Transport Ltd* [1980] AC 827.

17 The condition is commonly described as a term going to the root of the contract, without which the party asserting its status as such would not have entered into the contract, with authority recognising that the plaintiff can depose as to his expectations.

18 Note, however, the famous judgment of Diplock LJ in *Hong Kong Fir Shipping Co Ltd v Kawasaki Kisen Kaisha Ltd* [1962] 2 QB 26 at 69, propounding the notion of an innominate term – a term which, given its broad nature, is not obviously classifiable as a warranty or condition – with the result that determination of whether its breach is sufficient to warrant rescission is dependent upon consideration of the seriousness of the breach, a matter which of course can only be determined by reference to the time of the breach (and of its consequences).

19 See the comments on the issue of time, in Nicholson, *op cit*, p 219.

will be noted below (as seen above, *prima facie* avoidance is permitted for fundamental breach). Given that Art 26 is in non-prescriptive terms, this notice may, it would appear, be oral or written, direct or indirect.[20]

Miscarriage in communication

Article 27 provides in substance that the dispatch of any notice, request or other communication in accordance with Part III and by means appropriate to the circumstances, is (except where Part III expressly provides otherwise) sufficient. Thereafter, the person dispatching the communication can rely upon its having been duly made. This is so notwithstanding any delay or error in its transmission. The Article avoids the need for evidence going beyond proof of dispatch. It is of course potentially productive of mischief, and in a case of importance the parties should expressly deal with the matter. To reiterate, Art 27 deals only with communications for the purposes of Part III (and not with those directed to formation of the contract).

Specific performance

Article 28 looks ahead to the provision of the specific performance remedy in later provisions (see, for example, Arts 46 and 62) and enacts a qualification on the remedy: assuming that a party is otherwise entitled to such an order, a court is not bound to enter such a judgment unless the court would do so under its own law in respect of similar contracts of sale not governed by the Convention.

The result is that, where the domestic law of the court is civil law derived, the court will more readily order specific performance; but where its law is common law derived, it is less likely to because the bias of the common law (or more particularly its equitable strand) is that, *inter alia*, specific performance of contracts for the sale of goods ought not to be awarded where damages would constitute an adequate remedy. This bias tends to be replicated in statutory provisions in the common law countries. In most cases, of course, whether the court's domestic law is civil or common law derived, the plaintiff will prefer damages where substitute goods can readily be obtained.

The law of the court may not necessarily be the law of the contract (as where a court in State A has jurisdiction, but pursuant to the rules of private international law, is applying the law of State B).[21]

Modification or termination of the contract

Article 29(2), as noted above, provides that a contract may be modified or terminated by the mere agreement of the parties. The reference to 'mere' agreement emphasises that the common law concept of consideration is not to be resorted to in applying Art 29(2).[22]

---

20 See the comments on 'Notice of Avoidance' by Date-Bah, S, in Bianca and Bonell, *op cit*, pp 224–25.
21 See Honnold, *op cit*, p 223.
22 Thus, a party who has (say) fully performed can give a valid release to a party who has only partly performed, without any requirement of fresh consideration from the latter.

Article 29(2) has also been reviewed earlier: it requires that the contract in writing which contains a provision requiring any modification or termination by agreement to be in writing, may not otherwise be modified or terminated by agreement – note the estoppel-type exception here.

Obligations of the seller

Part III Chapter II is headed 'Obligations of the seller'.

General obligations

Article 30 imposes a general obligation on the seller to deliver the goods, hand over any documents relating to them and to transfer the property in them, as required by the contract and the Convention.

The Convention, it has been seen, does not provide rules identifying when property is transferred – the property transfer rules are provided by the applicable domestic law. The parties, of course, may well make provision in their contract regarding this matter. Later provisions in the Convention deal with delivery, the handing over of documents, carriage and insurance, and the passing of risk, but they do not provide an exhaustive regime. The underlying premise is that the parties will have made specific provision regarding some of these matters, perhaps by using recognised trade terms such as the Incoterms 2000. Where these are used, they will prevail over contrary provisions in the Convention. The Convention, in this area particularly, will represent a fallback regime. It would be surprising in a negotiated international sales contract were the parties not to make very specific provision regarding such matters as delivery, carriage, insurance, the passing of risk, incidental costs, etc.

Place of delivery

Article 31 deals with the situation where the seller is not bound to deliver the goods to any other particular place (that is, where there is no agreement upon the matter). In this case, the obligation to deliver is as outlined in Art 31. For example, if the contract involves carriage of goods (it usually will), the seller must hand the goods over to the first carrier for transfer to the buyer. In cases not within this class, then, *inter alia*, where goods are to be manufactured or produced, they are to be placed at the buyer's disposal at the place of manufacture, provided that at the time of formation the parties knew that they were to be produced or manufactured at this place. In other cases, the goods are to be placed at the buyer's disposal at the place where the seller had his place of business at the time of contracting.

Needless to say, some of these fallback provisions will impose inconvenience on the buyer so that specific contractual agreement on the mode of delivery is, in practice, important.

Carrier, insurance

Article 32 deals with aspects of carriage and insurance, but takes as its premise the concept that the parties have agreed upon some, at least, of the basic details in relation to these matters (for example, by the use of an appropriate Incoterm). If the seller hands the goods over to a carrier, and the goods are not clearly identified to the contract by markings or documents, the seller must give notice to the buyer of the consignment specifying the goods (Art 32(1)). If the seller is bound to arrange for carriage, he must make the appropriate contracts according to the terms usual for such transportation (Art 31(2)). If the seller is not required to effect insurance regarding carriage, he must, at the buyer's request, provide him with the information necessary for the latter to do this (Art 31(3)).

Time for delivery

Article 33 in essence provides that the goods are to be delivered on or by the time specified, otherwise within a reasonable time after formation. The common law adopts a similar analysis.

Documents

Article 34 makes collateral provision regarding documents relating to the goods, and assumes that the contract makes provision for them. *Inter alia*, the seller can, in defined circumstances where he hands over the documents prior to the time required in the contract, cure any lack of conformity in them, although the buyer remains entitled to any damages which may be due.

Conformity of the goods and third party claims

Articles 35–44 deal with issues concerning conformity of the goods and third party claims.

Conformity of the goods – implied terms regarding quality, etc

Article 35 does not employ the usage of implied terms, but functions in a manner identical to the implied terms regime in the rules governing contracts for the sale of goods at common law and their statutory successors.

The requirements of the Convention in this regard are not identical to those of the common law's standard implied terms; in particular, no mention is made of merchantable quality, nor is there any term which (otherwise) requires that the goods supplied by a contract regulated by the Convention be at least of average quality.[23]

Article 35(1) requires that the goods be of the quantity, quality and description required by, and be contained or packaged in the manner required by the contract.

---

23 Note the criticism in this latter regard by Bianca in Bianca and Bonell, *op cit*, pp 280–81.

Article 35(2) provides that, except where the parties have agreed otherwise, the goods do not conform to the contract unless they, in essence:

(a) are fit for the purposes for which goods of the same description would ordinarily be used;

(b) are fit for any particular purpose expressly or impliedly made known by the seller at the time of contracting (except where the buyer did not rely, or it was unreasonable for him to rely, on the seller's skill or judgment);

(c) possess the qualities which the seller has held out as a sample or model; and

(d) are contained or packaged in the manner usual for such goods, otherwise in a manner adequate to preserve and protect them.

By Art 35(3) the seller is not liable under sub-paras (a)–(d) in Art 35(2) for any lack of conformity where, at the time of formation, the buyer knew or could not have been unaware of such lack of conformity. As the proviso to Art 35(2) recognises, the parties can agree that the requirements as to conformity delineated in Art 35 do not apply to their contract. Such agreement presumably may be express or implied. Can the implied term's regime in a domestic sale of goods code, including perhaps a prohibition on contracting out, be resorted to in the case of a contract governed by the Convention? If this code does not go to validity, then it should be inapplicable.[24]

The tests provided for in Art 35(3) are subjective. The phrase 'could not have been unaware' is, in context, ambiguous, but it is more demanding than the common standard objective test ('of which a reasonable person would not have been unaware').

Liability for non-conformity – time

The seller is liable for any non-conformity at the time the risk passes, although the buyer may only become aware of it at a later time (Art 36(1)). Further, the seller becomes liable for any non-conformity after risk passes when due to a breach of any of his obligations, including a breach of guarantee concerning, *inter alia*, that the goods will remain fit for their ordinary purpose, or that they will retain specified qualities (Art 36(2)).

Delivery before time due

By Art 37, the seller who delivers goods before the time due, can, up to that date, cure deficiencies in performance (as where there is a deficit in quantity or quality), provided that the buyer does not suffer unreasonable inconvenience or unreasonable expense. The buyer can still seek damages for loss.

Buyer – examination

Article 38 imposes (unusually by common law standards) a duty of examination of the goods, and regulates the time when this must occur. The goods must be examined as soon as it is practicable in the circumstances, although examination may be deferred

---

24   See generally the discussion of this issue in Honnold, *op cit*, pp 252ff.

until the goods have arrived at their destination (Art 38(1)–(2)). Article 38(3) allows examination to be deferred until the goods have reached their new destination, in a case of redirection in transit or redispatch by the buyer, provided that there was no reasonable earlier opportunity for examination and at the time of formation the seller knew or ought to have known of the possibility of such redirection or redispatch. The provision recognises that goods – especially manufactured goods – will frequently be packaged, perhaps in the form in which they will be delivered to the retailer; and shipped in containers. It recognises that goods may be resold while in transit.

Buyer: loss of right to rely on lack of conformity – time for notice

Article 39(1) requires the buyer to give notice to the seller of any lack of conformity of the goods, specifying its nature within a reasonable time after discovery or from when he should have discovered this; otherwise, the buyer loses the right to rely on this lack of conformity. By Art 39(2), the buyer in any event loses this right if this notice is not given within two years of the date on which the goods were actually handed over, unless this time limit is inconsistent with a contractual guarantee.

The relatively long period of two years is reasonable; for example, the goods may have been packaged in the form in which they are to be retailed, in which case a non-conformity issue may arise quite late. On the other hand, it does permit a long period in which latent defects may emerge and be actionable, and the seller may wish to stipulate a shorter guarantee period (if one is to be stipulated at all).

Note that the seller cannot invoke Arts 38 or 39 where the non-conformity relates to facts of which he knew or could not have been unaware, and which he did not disclose to the buyer (Art 40).

See also Art 44 – notwithstanding Art 39(1), the buyer may reduce the price pursuant to Art 50 or claim damages, except for loss of profit, if he has a reasonable excuse for his failure to give notice.[25]

Freedom from right or claim of a third party – in general and those based on industrial or other intellectual property

The seller must deliver goods free of any third party right or claim – Art 42 (which approximates the common law's implied warranties/conditions concerning good title). The situation is otherwise where the buyer has agreed to take the goods subject to such a qualification.

However, where such a right or claim is based on industrial property or other intellectual property, the situation is governed by Art 42, the terms of which should be noted. The buyer receives a parallel guarantee in this regard, but note the qualifications and ancillary provisions in Art 42.

Article 43 provides for qualifications on the application of Arts 41 and 42; and note the further qualification on the application of Art 43(1), effected by Art 44.

---

25 It will infrequently be the case that the buyer who has not given reasonable notice under Art 39(1) will have a reasonable excuse for this failure, for the purposes of Art 44: see the comments in Nicholas, *op cit*, pp 222–23; Bianca in Bianca and Bonell, *op cit*, p 238.

Remedies for breach of contract by the seller

Articles 45–52 (s III of Part III) provide for 'remedies for breach of contract by the seller'. The Convention propounds a range of possible remedies, some of them based on mandatory orders by a court after litigation while others are directed towards remedying disputes by means short of litigation. A number of them have no common law counterpart. It must also be remembered that the parties are free to negotiate their own solution to a problem, either by formal inclusion of terms in the contract or by an agreement post-contract, operating to modify the contract. (By Art 29, it will be recalled, the parties can modify the existing contract without any necessity for either one of them to supply what the common law would classify as new, legally sufficient consideration.) Where the parties agree upon a regime for resolving a difference, this would, assuming that it has contractual force, override the remedial provisions in the Convention. (If the agreed upon regime fails to do this, then, *prima facie,* the Convention would apply once more, unless its remedial provisions have been permanently excluded and one of the parties opposes their revival, in which case the appropriate municipal law will come into play.)

It will often be in the parties' interests to attempt a negotiated resolution, given the difficulties and delays of litigation, especially litigation between parties who may be a great distance apart.

Buyer's options

Article 45 sets out the buyer's remedies in a case of breach by the seller – they are the rights in Arts 46–52, and the right to seek damages as provided in Arts 74–77. The buyer is still entitled to seek damages, even as he seeks other remedies. The court or arbitral tribunal may not grant a period of grace to the seller when the buyer seeks a remedy.

Specific performance and related remedies

By Art 46(1), the buyer may seek specific performance by the seller unless the buyer has resorted to an inconsistent remedy. The scope of the specific performance remedy has been limited by Art 28, as noted above (that is, the court is not bound to order it unless it would do so pursuant to its own law). Specific performance would appear to have little role in relation to goods which are not unique and which can be readily sourced from another seller. Such an order of a court would be at the conclusion of litigation, meaning that much time would have passed since the default by the seller. In this period, the buyer ordinarily would be able to approach other suppliers. In practice, damages, if financial loss is suffered by going to another supplier, would seem to be the more obvious remedy in a case of refusal or inability on the part of the seller to supply.[26]

By Art 46(2), in a case of non-conformity between the contract and the goods amounting to a fundamental breach, the buyer may require the delivery of substitute goods (note the details). The result would, in the case of non-unique goods,

---

26   See Honnold, *op cit*, p 366.

approximate what would be obtained by specific performance. It is apt that the precondition for this remedy should be a fundamental breach to ensure that it is not invoked for a trivial non-conformity. The remedy is not paralleled in the common law.

If the goods do not conform to the contract, the buyer may require the seller to remedy the problem by repair, unless this is unreasonable in the circumstances (Art 46(3) – note the ancillary detail). The remedy, again, finds no counterpart in the common law. The reasonableness limitation is necessary, given that the seller may be at a vast distance from the buyer who has taken delivery. Distance alone, however, would not preclude its invocation, as where valuable machinery is supplied and the seller's technical expertise is not readily available in the buyer's country.

Extra time for the seller to perform obligations

The buyer may give the seller an extra period of time of reasonable length for performance of the seller's obligations (Art 47(1)). The extra period is frequently referred to in commentaries as a *Nachfrist*.[27]

It will be noted that it is the buyer's option whether to grant this extra time. If, however, the buyer does do so, then unless he receives notice from the seller that the latter will not perform in this period, the buyer may not, during the period, resort to any remedy for breach of contract. He can, however, seek damages for delay in performance (Art 47(2)).

The Art 47 *Nachfrist* can, in terms, cover a variety of acts of default such as non-conformity, but its main practical application will be in cases of non-delivery. In this latter respect, note Art 49(1)(b), providing that, in the case of non-delivery, if the seller does not deliver within the period of the Art 47 period (or declare that he will not so deliver), the buyer may declare the contract avoided (that is, at an end). The Art 47 procedure then can lay the foundation for avoidance.[28]

Seller – remedy after date of delivery

By Art 48(1), the seller may, even after the date for delivery, remedy shortcomings in his performance. Certain qualifications apply: *inter alia*, the buyer must not be subjected to unreasonable delay or inconvenience. This seller's right to cure is subject to Art 49, which deals with rescission. Among the provisions in Art 49 is that in Art 49(1)(a), which permits the buyer to avoid the contract because of a fundamental breach by the seller. The effect, according to one commentator, is that the parties need to know whether the seller is entitled to, and can indeed, cure pursuant to Art 48(1), before it can be established whether the breach is fundamental.[29]

The buyer can still seek damages, notwithstanding the seller's cure, where these are payable under the Convention (Art 48(1)). The procedure in Art 48(2), *inter alia*, permits a seller to seek the buyer's consent to a later delivery, and puts the onus on the

---

27 German law recognises a similar concept, called the 'Nachfrist'. The concept of an extra period is found elsewhere in the Convention too, such as in Art 63, providing that the buyer may be given extra time by the seller to perform his obligations.

28 Note Honnold, *op cit*, p 313, commenting that the Art 47 procedure only has teeth – courtesy of Art 49(1)(b) – in the case of non-delivery.

29 Honnold, *ibid*, p 376. See also Will in Bianca and Bonell, *op cit*, pp 349ff.

buyer to reject any such proposal.[30] Note the ancillary provisions in Art 48(3) and (4). The notice referred to there can be oral or written.

Avoidance by the buyer

Article 49 provides for avoidance of the contract by the buyer. (The effects of avoidance are set out in Art 81 – broadly, it brings the contract to an end, subject to any damages which may be due and subject to restitution being made, where this is practicable.) It is broadly comparable to the common law's termination of contract because of legally relevant fault on the part of the other party, but the details differ considerably.

As noted, the buyer may avoid because of a fundamental breach by the seller (Art 49(1)(a)); but the feasibility of a seller's cure under Art 48(1) must be considered in determining whether there has been a fundamental breach. The buyer may also avoid for non-delivery if the seller does not deliver the goods within any additional period of time fixed under Art 47(1), or declares that he will not deliver within this period.

Where goods are delivered, the buyer loses the right to avoid (that is, for fundamental breach) unless he acts in conformity with the applicable requirements of Art 49(2). Where late delivery is concerned, the buyer must avoid within a reasonable time after becoming aware of non-delivery.

In respect of breaches other than late delivery (for example, for a non-conformity of a fundamental nature), the buyer must avoid within a reasonable time after he knew, or ought to have known, of the breach. (Note, as well, the ancillary provisions concerning cases involving an Art 47(1) *Nachfrist*, and the Art 48(2) procedure – here again, the overriding requirement is for the buyer to act within a reasonable time.)

The essence of these limitations is that the buyer must avoid within a reasonable time, which will of course vary from case to case. (The complex common law rules revolving around the notion of the buyer's acceptance are not echoed in the Convention.)

Although it is not referred to in Art 49, the right of avoidance under it is clearly qualified by Art 39. This, as noted above, provides in para (1) that the buyer loses the right to rely on a lack of conformity of the goods if he does not give notice to the seller specifying this matter within a reasonable time after he has discovered it or ought to have discovered it. In any event, an over-arching two year period applies in which this notice must be given, after which the buyer cannot rely on the non-conformity (unless the contract contains an inconsistent period of guarantee): Art 39(2).[31]

Price reduction

Article 50 provides a remedy unknown at common law – the buyer's right to make a *pro rata* reduction in price where the goods do not conform. The right to reduce is

---

30 See Honnold, *ibid*, p 378, who also discusses Art 48(2) in respect of cases of proposals to cure by repair.

31 Note the comment by Will in Bianca and Bonell, *op cit*, p 365, that 'Article 39 in this context is as important a filter as it is hidden'.

qualified in cases where the seller remedies the problem under Arts 37 or 48, or if the buyer refuses to accept performance under these latter articles.

Part delivery only

Where the seller delivers part only of the goods, or part only of them conforms with the contract, Arts 46–50 apply to the missing or non-conforming part. So, for example, the contract may be avoided, in respect of this part, under Art 49: see Art 51(1). In such a case, avoidance of the entire contract is permissible only when the partial non-performance amounts to a fundamental breach (Art 41(2)).

Early delivery; excess delivery

The buyer may take or reject delivery where the goods are delivered early (Art 52(1)). The buyer has a comparable discretion in relation to the excess part of an excess delivery (although if the excess is accepted it must be paid for): Art 52(2).

The reservation of discretion in the buyer is reasonable; it may not be practicable to take an early or excess delivery.

Obligations of the buyer

Articles 53ff deal with the obligations of the buyer.

Article 53 provides compendiously that the buyer must pay and take delivery of the goods, as required by the contract and the Convention. The concept of delivery is not defined by the Convention, but a number of provisions deal with delivery – see Arts 31ff – on the place of delivery, time for delivery, and related matters.

Payment of the price

The buyer's obligation to pay the price includes ancillary matters such as complying with the laws governing the act of payment (see Art 54). Such obligations might run to, for example, payment of import duties, arrangement of foreign exchange approvals, and arranging letters of credit. The contract should deal with these matters (a shorthand way of dealing with certain of them would be to resort to the appropriate Incoterms).

Where the price is not specified nor any procedure for fixing is agreed upon, then the parties are deemed to have agreed that the price shall be that generally charged at formation for such goods sold under comparable circumstances in the trade concerned (Art 55). If the price is fixed by weight, in cases of doubt the net weight is the decisive factor (Art 56).

The place of payment should be agreed in the contract, but in default of such an agreement, payment is to be made at the seller's place of business; or, if it is to be made against the handing over of the goods or documents, at the place of handing over (Art 57(1) and note para (2)).

If the time of payment is not specified in the agreement, it is governed by the detailed regime in Art 58. Broadly, in the absence of contrary agreement the buyer is to pay when the seller places the goods or documents controlling their disposition at the buyer's disposal; and the handing over of these can be made conditional on payment (Art 58(1)). (In a case of carriage, the handing over of the goods, etc, can likewise be conditioned on payment (Art 58(2)).)

The buyer is not bound to pay until he has had an opportunity to examine them, unless the agreed upon procedures for delivery or payment are inconsistent with this (Art 58(3)). Given that contracting is often going to be at a great distance, the parties should agree in detail upon the procedures for verifying conformity, such as resort to a commercial inspection agency in the seller's country before dispatch.[32]

The buyer must pay the price without any need for request from the seller (Art 59).

Taking delivery

The buyer has a positive duty to take delivery (see Art 60). Thereby, the seller obtains a discharge from his primary obligation under the contract and avoids contingent liabilities, such as the safekeeping and retrieval of goods at a great distance. This obligation to accept delivery, of course, is qualified by other terms in the Convention where appropriate, such as where the goods are delivered too early (Art 52(1)).

Remedies for breach of contract by the buyer

The seller's remedies for breach of contract by the buyer are set out in Arts 61–65. These provisions parallel those dealing with the remedies available to the buyer (Arts 45–52) although, inevitably, the seller's regime is less complex. In most cases, the seller's remedy is to be paid the price (less any amount secured by a sale in litigation), although given that goods in the international sale will usually be transported over a considerable distance, the seller typically will have a greater interest in the buyer taking delivery than might usually be the case in a domestic sale.

Article 61 sets out the scheme of remedies: the aggrieved seller confronted with a buyer's default has resort to the remedies in Arts 62–65, and to damages pursuant to Arts 74–77. The seller is not precluded from seeking damages because he resorts to another remedy. No period of grace is to be granted to a buyer by a court or tribunal when the seller seeks a remedy.

Specific performance

The seller may require the buyer to pay the price, take delivery or perform his other obligations, unless the seller has resorted to an inconsistent remedy (Art 62). As it has been seen earlier, resort to specific performance is limited by the terms of Art 28 (providing that a court is not bound to order specific performance, unless the court would order this in respect of similar contracts of sale under its own law).

The fact that another remedy is resorted to does not necessarily mean that it is inconsistent with seeking specific performance – the alternative remedy may merely delay resort to Art 62. The giving of a *Nachfrist* under Art 63 (see 'Seller – avoiding the

---

32 See Jones, G, 'Impact of the Vienna Convention in drafting international sales contracts' (1992) 20 *International Business Lawyer* 421 at 426.

contract' below), perhaps does no more than delay resort to Art 62, should the buyer perform in terms of the *Nachfrist*.

Articles 85 and 88 – providing for the preservation of the goods by the seller, in a case of the buyer's delay in taking delivery, coupled with their sale to a third party by the seller – illustrates a remedy which is inconsistent with seeking specific performance under Art 62.

For the reasons noted in respect of specific performance by the buyer under Art 46, specific performance under Art 62 often will not be a practical remedy.

Giving the buyer extra time

The seller may fix an extra period of time of reasonable length for performance by the seller – another example of a so called *Nachfrist* (Art 63(1)). (Contrast the buyer's *Nachfrist* as provided for in the parallel Art 47.) The seller may not thereafter, during this period, resort to any remedy for breach of contract, unless the buyer gives him notice that the buyer will not perform during this period. The seller can nonetheless seek damages for delay in performance (Art 63(2)). The buyer's failure to perform within the *Nachfrist* period entitles the seller to avoid the contract under Art 64(1)(b), below.

Seller – avoiding the contract

The seller may avoid the contract pursuant to Art 64 (which parallels avoidance by the buyer under Art 49). The effects of avoidance are dealt with in Arts 81ff: essentially, the contract is terminated, subject to claims for damages and (if applicable) restitution.

The seller may avoid for fundamental breach by the buyer (Art 64(1)(a)); or avoid if the buyer does not perform within the period fixed by the Art 63 *Nachfrist* (above) (Art 64(1)(b)). The right to avoid is lost pursuant to Art 64(2) where the buyer has paid the price, unless the seller declares the contract avoided: (a) in respect of late performance; or (b) in respect of breaches other than late performance, then (in essence) within a reasonable time of becoming aware, actually or constructively, of the breach, or the expiry of the Art 63 *Nachfrist* period (note the details). These limitations set out in Art 64(2), it must be emphasised, apply only in the relatively unusual situation where the buyer has paid the price (which normally would make avoidance pointless), but the seller wishes to avoid anyhow. Such a situation might be one where the seller has found another buyer for the goods. In this case, a late and unexpected payment by the first buyer may be very inconvenient. Nonetheless, even in this case, the buyer's position merits some protection, hence the nullification of the seller's (not yet exercised) right to avoid where payment is received, albeit out of time, and the seller knows that this payment has been received.

Buyer's failure to supply specifications

The provision in Art 65 – that, where the buyer fails to supply relevant specifications for the goods, the seller may make these himself in accordance with any requirements of the buyer known to him, and thereafter perform – might be thought to be drastic and potentially productive of mischief (Art 65(2)). It is mitigated, however, by the provision in Art 65(2), that the seller who is minded to do this must inform the buyer of the details and fix a reasonable time for the buyer to specify differently (with a non-response by the buyer resulting in the seller's specification being deemed to be binding). A more prudent response by the seller in the normal case would be to avoid the contract and seek damages.[33]

Passing of risk

Overview

Articles 66–70 deal with the passing of risk. The regime differs from the common law. At common law, *prima facie* the risk passes with the title, so that the buyer becomes burdened with the risk when he acquires a title. The Convention, of course, does not deal with the passing of title (see Art 4(b)), so that different rules with a different pivot point or points needed to be devised.

These provisions regarding risk apply only where the parties have not made contrary provision in their agreement. Commonly, of course, they will deal specifically with the matter, such as by the employment of Incoterms. Considerations which were relevant in settling the Convention rules in this regard include: the fact that international contracts for the sale of goods will frequently be transacted over great distances, with the buyer being in the best position, should damage occur, to assess the damage, claim on insurance and rectify the damage if this is possible; the use of containers and of multi-modal transport; the use of one or more carriers who are independent of either party; and the appropriateness of imposing responsibility for risk on the party who is better positioned to care for the goods and to insure them.[34]

The scheme of the provisions, generally, is to identify the risk with the person who has possession or control of the goods (and who is, therefore, best placed to preserve them), and to transfer this risk when the possession or control is transferred.[35] This general principle is not a formal pivot point in every one of the risk articles.

The provisions dealing with the allocation and passing of risk defer to the preliminary one in Art 66. This provides that loss of or damage to the goods after the risk has passed to the buyer does not discharge him from his obligation to pay the price. (The only exception is where the loss, etc, is due to the act or omission of the seller.) This is realistic; the premise is that the buyer will have insurance in effect from (at least) the moment that risk passes, and the buyer taking delivery at the other end of the transit arrangements, is best placed to assess damage and to claim on his insurance.

Contracts involving carriage of goods – when risk passes

Article 67 is the most important provision in practice, dealing as it does with the contract which 'involves carriage' of the goods. Most international sales contracts will involve carriage. The terms make it clear that the arrangement is one where the seller uses a third party carrier (note the reference to the handing over to the 'first carrier').

---

33 See Nicholas, *op cit*, p 229.
34 See Honnold, *op cit*, pp 393ff.
35 See Pryles, M, 'An assessment of the Vienna Sales Convention' [1989] *Australian Mining and Petroleum Law Association Yearbook* 342.

The first type of case dealt with in Art 67(1) is that where:

(a) the contract involves carriage; and

(b) the seller is not bound to hand the goods over at a particular place.

In such a case, the risk passes to the buyer when the goods are handed over to the first carrier for transmission, etc. The buyer should therefore have insurance in effect from this point (the assumption of risk should establish an insurable interest where the jurisdiction's insurance law requires this). At the other extreme, it could have been provided that risk passes only when the goods are handed over to the buyer by the (ultimate) carrier; but as one commentator notes, the balance of convenience in long distance transactions is with allocating risk for damage during carriage to the buyer, because the latter is better placed to assess the damage, salvage the goods (if practicable) and claim on the insurer.[36]

The risk could not conveniently pass at some point during carriage because of the difficulties of proof attending the issue of whether the damage occurred before or after the passing of risk (a problem compounded by the fact of containerisation).[37]

Article 67(1) provides alternatively, in the cases of contracts involving carriage, that, where the seller is bound to hand the goods over to a carrier at a particular place, the risk does not pass to the buyer until the goods are handed over to the carrier at that place. Again, in this class of case, the time when risk passes will be able to be established with certainty.

Article 67(2) provides that, notwithstanding the provisions of Art 67(1), the risk does not pass to the buyer until the goods are clearly identified to the contract, by markings on them, notice, etc. This requires the subject goods to be abstracted from the larger bulk. It is designed to preclude the seller from falsely and conveniently claiming, in a case where in fact abstraction and identification had not occurred and where part of the goods in the larger bulk were damaged or lost, that the latter were the buyer's and thus no longer the responsibility of the seller.

Goods sold in transit – when risk passes

The *prima facie* rule in Art 68 is that the risk in respect of goods sold in transit passes to the buyer from the conclusion of the contract. The assumption is that the buyer will organise insurance covering his interest from this point. In the absence of inspection at this time, there could be later problems of proof concerning when damage or loss occurred.

The *prima facie* rule is qualified: if the circumstances so indicate, the buyer assumes the risk from the time the goods were handed over to the carrier who issued the documents embodying the contract of carriage. Nevertheless, the risk remains with the seller in both cases, where he knew or ought to have known of the damage, etc, at the time of contracting, and did not disclose this.

---

36   See Honnold, *op cit*, p 400.
37   See Nicholas in Bianca and Bonell, *op cit*, p 494.

Catch-all provision – passing of risk in other cases

In cases not covered by Arts 67 and 68 (above) and not regulated by the contract, Art 69 regulates the passing of risk.

Article 69(1) enacts the primary rule: the risk in these residual cases passes to the buyer when he takes over the goods, or, if he does not do so in due time, from the time when the goods are placed at his disposal and he commits a breach of contract by failing to take delivery. The risk in this residual class of cases, logically, is put on the party who has possession or control of the goods.

Article 69(2) enacts a qualification on the primary rule: if the buyer is bound to take over the goods at a place other than the seller's place of business (such as a warehouse), the risk passes when delivery is due and the buyer is aware that the goods are placed at his disposal at that place.

Article 69(3) enacts a precautionary provision in respect of goods that have not yet been abstracted from a larger bulk: the goods are not considered to be placed at the buyer's disposal until they are identified to the contract.

Passing of risk and fundamental breach

If the seller has committed a fundamental breach of the contract, Arts 67–69 do not impair the remedies available to the buyer on account of this breach (Art 70). A primary remedy for fundamental breach is avoidance (Art 49). So, for example, *prima facie* the buyer can avoid for a non-conformity amounting to fundamental breach, notwithstanding that the risk has passed to the buyer when he seeks to avoid.

Provisions common to the obligations of buyer and seller

Articles 71ff (Chapter V in Part III) impose obligations which (except where otherwise indicated) apply to both parties. These are cumulative upon the obligations specifically imposed upon each in the preceding articles (again, a specific provision may be to the contrary in a particular case), or otherwise supplement these.

Anticipatory breach and instalment contracts

Articles 71–73 deal with cases of anticipatory breach and related matters. The doctrine of anticipatory breach is found at common law; while the details differ, the effect of the anticipatory breach provisions parallels the role of the common law doctrine.

Article 71(1) permits a party (that is, a buyer or seller) to suspend the performance of his obligations under a concluded contract if it becomes apparent that the other party will not perform a substantial part of his obligations, because, in essence, of the latter's inability or unwillingness to perform. Lack of creditworthiness is an instance of inability. Where the seller, who is acting under para (1), has already dispatched the goods prior to the grounds for so acting becoming evident, he may prevent the handing over of the goods to the buyer (para (2)). The party suspending performance, before or after dispatch of the goods must so notify the other party and must continue with the performance if the other party provides adequate assurance of his performance (Art 71(3)). Article 71 provides for a procedure that is less drastic than avoidance for anticipatory breach as provided for in Art 72 (below), but it could still be used with undue haste. Its invocation is limited by the requirements that the other party give the appearance that he will not perform a 'substantial' part of his obligations; and further, by the requirement that notice be given to the other party (Art 71(3)).

The more drastic remedy in this category of apprehended breach of obligation is that provided for in Art 72. Article 72(1) closely parallels the common law in providing that, if prior to the date for performance of the contract it is clear that one of the parties will commit a fundamental breach[38] of the contract, the other party may declare the contract avoided (that is, terminated).[39]

If time permits, the party intending to so act must give reasonable notice to the other party in order to permit him to provide adequate assurance of his performance (Art 72(2)). Logically, if he can do this, the ground for avoidance under para (1) – anticipated fundamental breach – will not apply. Paragraph (2) is irrelevant, however, where the other party has declared that he will not perform his obligations.

Because Art 72 is more radical in its effect than Art 71, it is appropriate that the threshold for its application should be anticipated fundamental breach, as opposed to the less demanding test of an anticipated non-performance of a 'substantial' part of the obligations in Art 71.

Nonetheless, the anticipated non-performance of a substantial part of the obligations will often constitute by itself, an anticipated fundamental breach. The para (2) requirement represents a brake on the para (1) remedy, one not found at common law.

An aggrieved party could invoke the Art 71 remedy if in doubt, and then, if this proves unproductive, invoke the Art 72 remedy. He could also invoke the two concurrently.[40]

Instalment contracts are dealt with by Art 73. Paragraph (1) provides that if a failure to perform by a party (buyer or seller) in respect of any one instalment constitutes a fundamental breach with respect to that instalment, the aggrieved party can avoid the contract with respect to that instalment. The premise is that this instalment is a readily severable part of the contract, and that to permit the avoiding of the contract with respect to all future instalments would be too harsh. Paragraph (2), however, permits avoidance of the contract with respect to all future instalments, where a party's failure to perform gives the other party grounds to conclude that a fundamental breach will occur with respect to future instalments. The latter must avoid within a reasonable time. By para (3), the party who avoids in respect of any delivery (that is, under paras (1) or (2)), may, at the same time, declare it avoided in respect of prior or future deliveries if, by reason of their interdependence, those deliveries could not be used for the purposes contemplated by the parties at the time of formation. In this latter case, the instalments will not be readily severable.

Article 51 should also be noted in respect of instalment contracts. It vests remedies in a buyer in respect of part-only deliveries or non-conformity in respect of a part of

---

38 See Art 25.
39 See Arts 26, 81ff.
40 See the comment by Bennett in Bianca and Bonell, *op cit*, p 529.

the goods delivered. It is not in terms confined to instalment contracts. Article 73 is, where instalment contracts are concerned, cumulative upon Art 51.

Damages

Articles 74–77 deal with the core aspects of damages: measurement and causation (or remoteness) issues. Damages will have been awarded by reference to other provisions (for example, Arts 45(1)(b) and 61(1)(b)).

The primary provision is Art 74. It provides, first, that damages for breach of contract consist of a sum equal to the loss, including loss of profit, suffered in consequence of the breach. This measure of damages replicates the basic approach of the common law, that is, that the plaintiff is to be put in the position he would have enjoyed had the contract been duly performed.[41]

The principle is compensation; punitive damages are not provided for. The specification that damages should include profit is precautionary.

Article 74 also provides, secondly, that the damages may not exceed the loss which the party in breach foresaw or ought to have foreseen at the time of the conclusion of the contract, in light of the facts and matters of which he then knew or ought to have known, as a possible consequence of the breach of contract.

In common law language, this provision deals with remoteness of causation: it specifies the ambit of the consequences flowing from the breach, which are to be compensated – direct consequences are compensatable, but remote ones are not. The principle enunciated is broadly similar to that laid down in the leading common law decision of *Hadley v Baxendale*.[42]

There are, however, differences. *Hadley v Baxendale* broadly makes the defendant liable for those consequences of breach:

(a) which flow naturally, that is, in the normal course of things, from the breach; or (in respect of less obvious consequences);

(b) which may reasonably be assumed to have been in the contemplation of both parties at the time of formation, as the probable result of such breach.

The Convention principle posits, fundamentally, an objective test (if the subjective one is not satisfied then the objective test comes into play). The loss is limited to that which was objectively predictable as a 'possible' consequence by a reasonable person ('ought to have known' connotes reasonableness) possessed of the information which the defendant should reasonably have possessed at the time of formation. One obvious departure from the *Hadley v Baxendale* principle is the related test of eventuality governing the foresight test (the common law decision specifies foresight of probability, while Art 74 specifies foresight of possibility; clearly the latter is less demanding). It follows that the Convention will compensate more remote consequences than will *Hadley v Baxendale*. Nonetheless, these more remote

---

41   *Robinson v Harman* (1848) 1 Ex 850 at 855.
42   *Hadley v Baxendale* (1854) 9 Ex 341 at 354. Note the comment by Williams AJ in *Downs Investments Pty Ltd v Perwaja Steel SDN BHD* [2002] 462 at 484, that the article reflects the *Hadley v Baxendale* doctrine.

consequences cannot, it is submitted, be freakishly remote, because the Convention test is build around the foresight of a hypothetically reasonable defendant.

The common law authority since *Hadley v Baxendale* has clarified a related matter – the reasonable person in the defendant's shoes must have foreseen the type of loss but need not have foreseen its extent, viz the fact that the particular head of loss is greater in the quantum than the quantum contemplated is not a bar to full recovery. The Convention is silent on this point, but the key word is 'loss', which is unqualified and broad enough to yield an interpretation giving an outcome equivalent to the common law's on this issue. This approach is fortified by the reference of Art 74 to loss of profit as being compensatable – a prime issue in remoteness issues concerning contracts involving goods. Presumably, it would be enough that a loss of profit is foreseeable in terms of the remoteness test; it could not realistically be expected that the defendant seller or his hypothetical stand-in have been able to forecast the quantum of loss of profit owing to the late delivery of a machine, in order for the plaintiff buyer to recover this.

Articles 75 and 76 deal with cases where contracts are avoided by a party; and the consequential assessment of damages.

Article 75 states that, where a contract is avoided, and (within a reasonable time and in a reasonable manner) the buyer has bought replacement goods or the seller has resold the goods, the party claiming damages may recover the difference between the contract price and the price in the substitute transaction. As well, this party may claim any further damages (such as for storage expenses or loss of profit) recoverable under Art 74. The approach in Art 75 is logical; *prima facie*, the damages will approximate the difference in prices. To prevent abuse, the tests of reasonableness noted govern the plaintiff's conduct. If no direct loss results from the substitute transaction, then damages cannot be claimed under Art 75.

Article 75 applies to fungibles, as well as specific goods.[43]

Article 76 provides a mechanism for assessing damages in an avoidance case by reference to a market price benchmark (termed 'current price' in Art 76 – see the definition in para (2)). Article 76 is not applicable where there is a substitute transaction pursuant to Art 75. Broadly, the innocent party can recover damages equal to the difference between the contract price and market price at the time of avoidance (or where the plaintiff has avoided the contract after taking over). He can also seek any further damages recoverable under Art 74. If a loss has not resulted under the Art 76 regime, damages logically cannot be recovered. Article 76 can lead to an anomaly, as where the buyer in default has to pay more than the contract price because the 'current price' has gone up.

Article 77 enacts a standard mitigation principle paralleling that found in the common law. Broadly, the party seeking damages must take reasonable steps to minimise his loss; if he does not, a corresponding reduction will be applied in the assessment of damages. Article 77, therefore, qualifies the assessment of damages under Arts 74–76.

---

43 *Downs Investments Pty Ltd v Perwaja Steel SDN BHD, ibid,* at 484 – in this case scrap metal. Fungibles were described as being 'goods of which every particle or unit is indistinguishable from, or at least commercially equivalent to, every other particle or unit, eg grain flour or oil' (Benjamin's *Sale of Goods,* 2nd edn, para 117).

Interest

Article 78 provides that, if a party fails to pay the price or any other sum in arrears, the other party is entitled to interest without prejudice to a claim for damages under Art 74. The court is left to decide the interest rate.

Articles 79–80 enact certain exemptions from liability.

Frustration; force majeure; impossibility

Article 79 provides a qualified defence in cases where an impediment in prescribed terms comes into operation, impacting upon the party's ability to perform. The defence is broadly suggestive of the common law doctrine of frustration (or the overlapping concepts of impossibility, *force majeure*, etc), but many points of difference are apparent.

Frustration at common law deals with events that make the contract impossible to perform, or render its prospective performance something radically different to the parties' contemplation. The event is something that happens independently of the parties. It operates to terminate the contract with prospective effect.

The Art 79 defence is more limited. Paragraph (1) provides the defence: the party is not liable for a failure to perform any of his obligations where he proves that the failure was due to an impediment beyond his control and that he could not reasonably be expected to have taken it into account at the time of formation or to have avoided it or overcome it or its consequences.

Will a broader range of events trigger the Art 79(1) defence than will trigger the common law doctrine of frustration? Given that the consequences of the Art 79(1) doctrine (noted below) are much less drastic than the common law doctrine, this might be considered to be a reasonable conclusion. It must be stressed, however, that given that the Convention is self-contained law, the scope of Art 79(1) is not to be determined through the prism of common law principle. The very qualified nature of the defence, however, is nevertheless a factor that bears upon determining the ambit of the operative impediments.[44]

The reference to 'any one of his obligations' as opposed to 'obligations' suggests that the defence can be invoked to cover non-performance of a part of a contract, as in the case of an instalment contract, and that the defence is not an all or nothing affair.

Article 79(2) deals with the role of the defence where a party performs in whole or in part by way of a delegate.

The exemption provided by Art 79 applies only for the period during which the impediment exists (Art 79(3)). The defence, then, postpones performance, as noted; it does not terminate the contract.

Paragraph (4) requires the party who fails to perform to give notice in prescribed terms to the other party – failure to comply with the notification requirements leads to liability for damages as specified.

---

44 See Nicholas, *op cit*, p 235, seeing Art 79 as dealing with cases of impossibility. On the other hand, see Sacks, P, 'Comment on an assessment of the Vienna Convention' [1989] *Australian Mining and Petroleum Law Association Yearbook*, pp 376–77.

Article 79(5) enacts a crucial limitation on the defence: nothing in the Article prevents either party from exercising any right other than to claim damages under the Convention. The aggrieved party can, therefore, avoid the contract where ground for avoidance is made out under the Convention, although he could not sensibly be awarded specific performance of the contract during the period in which the defence is operative (this would defeat the role of Art 79). The postponement (para (3)) of the right to claim damages must be understood as making any eventual award of damages subject to a deduction for damages which would otherwise accrue because of the delay sanctioned by Art 79. Article 79(5) cannot be read as having no more effect than postponing a claim for full damages, including losses caused by the permitted period of delay – such an interpretation would nullify Art 79.

Given the limited role of Art 79 and the uncertainties inherent in determining whether an event is a requisite 'impediment', the parties should (as per long-standing commercial practice) draft their own *force majeure* clauses.[45]

The contract should also deal with common impediments to performance, such as losses during carriage and related issues like insurance (in default of specific terms – Arts 66ff deal with the passing of risk).

Obstructing/facilitating other party's performance

Article 80 enacts a precautionary provision: a party must not rely on a failure of the other party to perform, to the extent that such a failure was caused by the first party's act or omission. This clause approximates the implication at common law of a term into a contract pursuant to which each party will do what is reasonably possible to facilitate the other's performance.[46]

Effects of avoidance

Articles 81–84 deal with the consequences of avoidance or, in common law terms, termination of the contract for a reason or reasons other than due performance by each party. A key issue that needed to be addressed was, should restitution be permitted? In the case of contracts for goods especially, the possibility of restitution will more often be a live one than in some other classes of contract (such as contracts to erect a building, build a machine or supply services).

The avoidance provisions do not deal with the grounds for avoiding a contract. These are provided for elsewhere (see, in particular, Arts 49 and 64).

Avoidance does not preclude a party from seeking damages which may be due (see Art 81). Apart from this, the provisions aim at effecting an appropriate adjustment of the rights and obligations as between the parties, in a circumstance of termination.

Avoidance releases the parties from their contractual obligations, subject to any damages due (Art 81(1)). Specified legal rights and obligations continue, however: those deriving from contractual provisions for the settlement of disputes; and those

---

45 See Sacks, *ibid*, p 366; Burnett, *op cit*, p 28; Jones, *op cit* at 426.
46 A negative implied term which overlaps in part is that each party will not take steps to make the other's performance difficult or impossible.

dealing with the consequences of avoidance (para (1)). A *prima facie* right to restitution is granted to the party who has performed in part or whole – this right vests in each and every party who has at least part-performed (Art 81(2)). It is not confined to the party who has avoided. A *prima facie* right to restitution is logical. As noted, contracts for the sale of goods, in particular, are typically by their nature amenable to restitution, with goods supplied/money paid being able to be readily returned. Subject to the availability of supplementary compensation in the form of damages, where applicable, a returning of the parties to their pre-contractual positions is the obvious and sensible outcome of avoidance.

Restitution may not be sensible in all cases, however, and in some it will be physically impossible. Article 82 deals with relevant cases of this type.

The buyer cannot avoid the contract or require the seller to deliver substitute goods (as to the latter power, see Art 46(2)) if it is impossible for the buyer to make restitution of the goods substantially in the condition received (Art 82(1)). The qualifier, 'substantially', is a sensible one; the right to avoid, etc, should not be lost because of a minor change in the goods. This limitation of impossibility in para (1) does not apply, however, in cases delineated in para (2), including where the requisite impossibility is not due to the buyer's act or omission.

An apparently more controversial limitation is that enacted in Art 82(2)(c): the buyer is not precluded from avoiding the contract by the impossibility of substantial restitution if the goods have been sold in the normal course of business or have been consumed or transformed by the buyer in normal use before he discovered, or ought to have discovered, the lack of conformity (which entitles him to avoid). *Prima facie*, the buyer's remedy here would be damages – he clearly cannot avoid with a view to restitution, given that the goods have been consumed. One commentator sees the answer to this apparent problem as being that 'under Article 81 … avoidance releases the buyer from his obligation to pay the price and entitles him to recover any payments on the price …'.[47]

The buyer who loses the right to declare the contract avoided or to require the seller to deliver substitute goods (by virtue of Art 82) retains all other remedies under the contract and the Convention (Art 83). Damages will be the obvious such remedy.

The seller who is bound to refund the price, in an avoidance situation, must pay interest on it from the date of payment (Art 84(1)). (This does not preclude the seller from seeking other applicable remedies such as damages.) The corollary is that the buyer must account to the seller for all benefits derived from the goods in whole or in part: (a) if he must make restitution of them in whole or in part; or (b) if it is impossible for him to do this substantially in the condition in which they were received, but he has nevertheless avoided the contract or required the delivery of substitute goods. (Again, this does not preclude the buyer from seeking other available remedies.)

Preservation of the goods

Articles 85–88 impose certain obligations upon a party to preserve the goods and, in the ultimate resort, create a power of sale. The obligation is not dependent upon fault

---

47 See Honnold, *op cit*, p 512 and note his further comments. See also the discussion by Tallon in Bianca and Bonell, *op cit*, p 609.

being shown: the innocent party, where appropriate, must preserve the goods. The preservation regime aims to minimise the risk of damage to or loss of the goods, and hence to minimise the potential overall cost of a dispute between the parties concerning them. It has been enacted in recognition that, where many international sales contracts are concerned, the goods may be delivered at a vast distance from the supplier, and beyond the supplier's ready ability to preserve or salvage them in the event that the buyer is unable or unwilling to take delivery. It imposes the obligation of preservation on that party best able to preserve the goods, irrespective of their role in causing any contractual miscarriage, or miscarriage in transport arrangements, etc.

The preservation regime can be impinged upon by contrary agreement between the parties, and by their insurance arrangements.

The seller in possession or control of the goods must take reasonable steps to preserve the goods where there is a delay on the part of the buyer in taking delivery or in making payment in cases where delivery and payment are to take place concurrently (Art 85). The seller can retain them until the buyer reimburses them for reasonable expenses (for example, storage or insurance) (Art 85). This obligation applies even as the risk or property (or both) in the goods may have passed to the buyer.

The buyer who has received the goods must take reasonable steps to preserve them where he intends to exercise any right to reject them. Again, he is entitled to reimbursement of reasonable expenses (Art 86(1)). Further, the buyer must take reasonable steps to preserve the goods where they have been placed at his disposal at their destination, notwithstanding that he exercises a right to reject them (Art 86(2)). His obligation to take them into possession applies only if he can do this without payment of the price. His para (2) obligation does not apply if the seller or agent is present at the destination. As part of fulfilling a duty of preservation, the party may deposit them in a third party's warehouse at the (reasonable) expense of the other party (Art 87).

The goods having been secured, the ultimate question arises: if the other party will not take them over, what is to be done with them? The issue can become progressively more urgent, given ongoing insurance and storage costs, to take two possible factors. Article 85 deals with this situation by providing qualified powers of sale. By Art 85(1), the party who has to preserve the goods under Art 85 or 86 may sell them by appropriate means where there has been an unreasonable delay by the other party in taking over the goods or paying the price or costs of preservation, although reasonable notice of intention to sell must be given. If the goods are subject to rapid deterioration, etc, the party burdened under Art 85 or 86 must take reasonable steps to sell them and give notice if possible (Art 88(2)). Where the goods are sold, the vendor can take reasonable expenses and must account to the other party for the balance (Art 88(3)).

The fact that a party is burdened with a duty of preservation, or that he ultimately exercises a power of sale, does not otherwise detract from the remedies which may be available to each party. Thus, a party may on the one hand have an obligation to account to the other for the balance of the price received on a sale under Art 88, but concurrently be entitled to offsetting damages.

The Convention does not deal with the passing of property in the goods (Art 4(b)). The vesting of a power of sale in a party by Art 88 will not necessarily vest title in this party for the purposes of vesting the third party purchaser with title; these are matters for the applicable domestic law. Given the recognition of the Convention by domestic law, however, it may be supposed that, in the usual case, the legal power of sale created by the Convention, and assimilated thereby into domestic law, would adequately answer a claim that the party exercising a power of sale was not competent to vest title in the third party purchaser.

CONVENTION ON THE LAW APPLICABLE TO CONTRACTS FOR THE INTERNATIONAL SALE OF GOODS – THE HAGUE, 1986

The Convention on the Law Applicable to Contracts for the International Sale of Goods was done at The Hague in 1986. The Convention, if adopted and implemented by a State, provides for rules that determine the applicable law, when a dispute arises between the parties to a contract for the international sale of goods. The Convention is not yet in operation.

The Convention was adopted after the Vienna Convention on Contracts for the International Sale of Goods, and was formulated in light of the latter.[48] It does not prejudice the application of the latter[49] (Art 22). Similarly, it does not prevail over the application of another convention or other international agreement, provided in this latter case both parties have their place of business in States which are party to this instrument (Art 22).

The Convention determines the law applicable to contracts of sale of goods between parties having their places of business in different States; and in all other cases involving a choice between the laws of different States, unless such a choice arises solely from a stipulation by the parties as to the applicable law (even if accompanied by a choice of court of arbitration) (Art 1). In the common case, then, the Convention will apply to sales contracts between parties having their businesses in different States.

If the Convention is not applicable, then the determination of the applicable law will be guided by standard principles, such as agreement between the parties, or other principles of international private law. Ultimately, of course, where a dispute is brought before the court of a State, the State's law will determine the applicable law, whether it provides for resort to private international law, or for the application of a relevant international treaty regime, or otherwise.

Articles 3 and 4 further delineate the scope of the Convention. Essentially, it applies to contracts for the sale of goods (including ships and electricity) and not to such things as sales of stocks and other securities. It does not apply to goods bought for personal consumption (that is, personal, family or household use), although it does apply to the latter if the seller neither knew nor should have known that such was the case. The Convention applies to contracts for sale where the goods are to be used in manufacturing, unless the party that orders the goods undertakes to supply a substantial part of the materials for this process. The contract for goods and labour is

---

48 See the Preamble, noting that the Convention was agreed upon 'Bearing in mind' the Vienna Convention.
49 See Art 22 of the 1986 Hague Convention.

not within the Convention if labour is the preponderant element of the seller's obligations.

The Convention does not apply to the choice of law governing issues of contractual capacity, agency, the transfer of agency,[50] the effect of the sale on a person who is not a party, or agreements on arbitration (Art 5).

Articles 7–12 provide for the determination of the applicable law.

The paramount choice principle in the Convention is that a contract (or part of one) is governed by the law chosen by the parties, if they have chosen a law, expressly or impliedly. Such a choice can, but need not be provided for in the contract. The parties can agree after formation, as to the applicable law (such as where a dispute has arisen during performance) – if so, this will be the applicable law. Any change of law in the latter case must not be to the prejudice of a third party (Art 7).

Where Art 7 dictates choice of law, this applies to sales by auction or on a commodity or other exchange only where the law of the State where the auction takes place or the exchange is located does not prohibit such choice. If the parties to this transaction do not choose the law, or the law of the State of auction, etc, prohibits this choice, then the latter law applies (Art 9).

To the extent that the parties have not chosen the applicable law, the law applying is that of the State where the seller has its business at the time of contracting. This will not always be the case (Art 8(1). Exceptionally, the law of the buyer's State of business applies where the contract was negotiated and concluded in the presence of the parties in that State; or the contract provides expressly that the buyer must deliver the goods in that State; or the contract was concluded on terms determined mainly by the buyer and in response to a call for tenders (Art 8(2)).

Further, and exceptionally, where the contract is manifestly more closely connected with a law other than applicable by paras (1) and (2), this law of close connection applies (Art 8(3)).[51]Article 8(3) does not, however, apply where the Vienna Convention on Contracts for the International Sale of Goods provided that at the time of the contract the seller and buyer have their businesses in different States, both of which are parties to that Convention (Art 8(5)).

Article 10 provides for the applicable law governing certain issues. The law governing a contractual consent issue is that chosen by the parties in conformity with Art 10, or if this choice is invalid, then Art 8 applies (para (1)). Where the validity of the contract or a term in it is concerned, the applicable law is determined on the assumption that the contract or term is valid (para (2)). If a party contends that it did not consent to a choice of law, then it may rely upon the law of the State where it has its business, in cases where it would not be reasonable to determine the law pursuant to paras (1) and (2) (para (3)).

Subsidiary rules are provided for in Art 11, including that a contract formed between parties (directly or through an agent) in different States is valid if it satisfies the law determined by the Convention or the law of the State of formation.

The law applicable under Arts 7–9 is expressed to govern a number of matters in particular, including interpretation of the contract, the rights and obligations of the

---

50   Save as specified in Art 12.
51   Note also para (4) concerning State reservations.

parties to the contract and its performance, the time when the buyer becomes entitled to the products, fruits and income deriving from the goods, the time when risk passes to the buyer, reservation of title clauses, the consequences of non-performance and the categories of compensatable loss, and the consequences of invalidity of the contract (Art 12).

The Convention does not prevail over conventions or other international agreements which provide for the determination of the applicable law, provided that the seller and buyer have their places of business in States which are party to this Convention (Art 22). Likewise, the Convention does not prejudice the application of the Vienna Convention on Contracts for the International Sale of Goods (Art 23).

TUTORIAL QUESTIONS

1   In what major way does the sale of goods regime provided for in the Convention differ from that provided by the domestic law of your jurisdiction? On balance, which regime is superior?

2   A company, B, is incorporated, and has its head office in State X, which State has ratified the Convention. It runs a chain of bottling plants in several other States, some of which have adopted the Convention. These plants are run by subsidiary companies incorporated in these States. B approaches S, a company incorporated in State Y, which has not adopted the Convention. The approach is made to S's sales office in State X, which is not incorporated. The terms of contracts for the supply of bottling machines are agreed upon between S and B, but contracts for the supply and installation of the machines are entered into between S and each subsidiary of B. The contracts are silent as to the applicable law. There is one exception, however – one of the contracts (entered into between S and a subsidiary in a non-Contracting State) makes the 'domestic law' of State X applicable to the contract. Does the Convention apply to all of these contracts, or only some of them; and in the latter case or cases, to which is it applicable?

3   Buyer B contracts with Seller S to buy 2,000 live sheep. S's State is drought affected and the costs of feeding stock are mounting. S faxes B, proposing that 1,000 sheep be delivered one month early. B does not respond. The sheep are fully delivered one month early. B does not want to take delivery, not having the facilities, nor the need, for the sheep at this earlier time. Assuming that the Convention applies, what is the legal position of each party?

4   Buyer B and seller S enter into a contract to which the Convention applies. The goods to be supplied consist of frozen meat. B rejects the cargo tendered, contending that one separable part of the cargo (some 10%) has perished because of inadequate refrigeration. The contract is silent as to when risk passes. B claims that doubt must exist as to the whole cargo, and rejects it *in toto*. What is the legal position of each party?

What would the legal position be if the cargo was sound but B still rejected the cargo on the basis that his refrigerated premises burnt down a few days ago, and there is no alternative refrigerated space available in his small State?

5   A buyer, B, orders a large pump from S. The Convention applies to the contract. The contract specifies that the pump must pump at least x thousand litres per

minute. The pump is delivered and installed, and it is then discovered that it pumps at only 80% of the nominated capacity. This will not do for B's purposes. B has the option: either replace the pump with another full capacity pump (one has suddenly become available in B's own State); or buy a second smaller pump to make up the missing capacity. The second course of action would produce a higher aggregate expense than B contemplated when B entered into the contract. What are B's options at law?

6   Seller S ships goods to B, pursuant to a contract to which the Convention applies. The risk passes, after which time the goods suffer damage. When B takes delivery, he discovers the damage. He also discovers that, even apart from the damage, the goods do not conform to the contract and the non-conformity is such that, had B contemplated it, he would never have contracted. Examine the legal position as between the parties where (a) the goods can be repaired; and (b) they cannot be repaired.

7   Buyer B operates a theme park in State X. He contracts with S, who supplies hi-tech theme park rides to theme park operators. The contract is governed by the Convention. The machinery is very expensive, but in locations in other regions of State X previously supplied it has boosted patronage greatly, for several years. This happy outcome has boosted S's business significantly. The machinery is duly manufactured and installed. It is riddled with gremlins, and is closed for various intervals during a period of 18 months as these problems are rectified. B incurs much bad publicity and, *inter alia*, his business suffers. He incurs a heavy interest bill on the money borrowed to finance this acquisition. What is the legal position as between the parties?

8   The buyer, an Italian company, sent a purchase order form ordering goods from the seller in Brisbane. The buyer's form requested immediate shipment. The seller shipped the goods the next day and mailed an 'order confirmation form' to the buyer. The seller's order confirmation form contained the following language (in bold face type on the front of the form):

> The terms set forth on the reverse side are the only ones upon which we will accept orders. These terms supersede all prior written understandings, assurances and offers. Your attention is especially directed to the provisions concerning warranty and liability of supplier and claims procedures. Advise us immediately if anything in the acknowledgment is incorrect or is otherwise unacceptable.

The terms on the reverse of the form limited the seller's liability for breach of warranty to repair or replacement of the goods.

The delivered goods were non-conforming and the buyer is now threatening to sue. The seller claims that its liability for breach of warranty is limited by contract. Do the parties have a contract? If so, on what terms?

9   The plaintiff buyer had its place of business in Krefeld, Germany. On 18 September 1992, the buyer purchased from the defendant seller – whose place of business was located in Indiana, USA – a cutting machine to be installed in the veneer processing unit of a Russian furniture combine. After the machine had been put into operation, an accident occurred which led to the death of a worker and caused injuries to another. Subsequently, the Russian sub-purchaser demanded repair of the defective machine from the buyer, whereupon the buyer sued to recover the costs of repair from the seller. In its complaint, the buyer also

moved for a declaratory judgment from the court establishing that the seller was required to indemnify the buyer against all damage claims raised by the Russian sub-purchaser and furniture combine with respect to the accident in dispute.

Identify and discuss all relevant issues pertaining to the United Nations Convention on Contracts for the International Sale of Goods, 1980 (Vienna Convention). Note that the Vienna Convention entered into force in Germany on 1 January 1991.

10 Mr Andrew Townsend is an American manufacturer of a computer software program called 'Anglialingua', which is designed to assist non-English speaking high school students in the learning of the English language. Ms Nicole Bitterand is a French distributor of educational materials with a head office in Paris, France. Townsend meets Bitterand at a party in Brisbane, Australia, during a conference on Teaching English as a Second Language. Townsend, in conversations with Bitterand, describes his computer software program (Anglialingua) in glowing terms and points out that it has already been successfully marketed in Germany.

Bitterand agrees orally to purchase 1,000 packages of 'Anglialingua' at $200 each. Townsend undertakes to ship the packages to Paris on his return to the USA. Bitterand agrees to pay for the packages by letter of credit upon the receipt of the appropriate shipping documents.

Upon her return to Paris, Bitterand decides to contact a German importer of 'Anglialingua' to ascertain the usefulness of the program. The German importer tells Bitterand that 'Anglialingua' has not been well received in Germany because the program does not work and is overpriced. Bitterand, who did not actually see 'Anglialingua' in operation, is now very worried and comes to realise that her purchase may turn out to be a bad investment. In particular, she is afraid that 'Anglialingua' may not actually be suitable for French high school students.

Bitterand has read in *Le Monde* that you have recently attended a series of lectures on international business law at the TC Beirne School of Law at The University of Queensland, Australia. As she is confident that you are an expert on transnational business deals, she seeks your advice as to her rights.

Answer the following questions:

(i)   Does the transaction have a sufficient connection with States that have ratified the United Nations Convention on Contracts for the International Sale of Goods (Vienna Convention) so that its provisions will govern the contract?

(ii) Has a valid contract for the international sale of goods been formed? Does it matter that the contract is not in writing?

(iii) If Bitterand does not wish the contract to be governed by the Vienna Convention, can she exclude some or all of its provisions?

(iv) Does the Vienna Convention govern all the issues that might arise in this transaction?

(v)   If Bitterand refuses to accept the packages, is Townsend likely to receive specific performance? Should he request specific performance in a French court?

(vi) Assuming that a valid contract for the international sale of goods has been formed, under what circumstances would Bitterand be able to avoid the contract?

FURTHER READING

Anderson, R, 'Comment on an assessment of the Vienna Sales Convention' [1989] *Australian Mining and Petroleum Law Association Yearbook* 354.

Bianca, CM and Bonell, MJ (eds), *Commentary on the International Sales Law – The 1980 Vienna Sales Convention*, 1987, Milan: Giuffrè.

Burnett, R, *The Law of International Business Transactions*, 3rd edn, 2004, Sydney: Federation Press, Ch 1.

Corney, G, 'Obligations and remedies under the 1980 Vienna Sales Convention' (1993) *Qld Law Society* 37.

Donner, LA, 'Impact of the Vienna Sales Convention on Canada' (1992) 6 *Emory International Law R* 743.

Eiselen, S, 'Electronic commerce and the UN Convention on Contracts for the International Sale of Goods' (1999) 6 *EDI Law Review* 21.

Feltham, J, 'CIF and FOB contracts and the Vienna Convention on Contracts for the Sale of Goods' (1991) *Journal of Business Law* 413.

Govey, I and Staker, C, 'Vienna Convention takes effect in Australia next year' (June 1988) *Australian Law News* 15.

Hill, A, 'A comparative study of the United Nations Convention on the Limitation Period in the International Sale of Goods and s 2–725 of the Uniform Commercial Code' (1990) *Texas International Law J* 1.

Honnold, J, 'Uniform laws for international trade: early "care and feeding" for uniform growth' (1995) *International Trade and Business Law Journal* 1.

Honnold, J, *Uniform Law for International Sales Under the 1980 United Nations Convention*, 3rd edn, 1999, The Hague: Kluwer Law International.

Jones, G, 'Impact of the Vienna Convention in drafting international sales contracts' (1992) 20 *International Business Lawyer* 421.

Kastley, A, 'The right to require performance in international sales: towards an international interpretation of the Vienna Convention' (1988) 63 *Washington Law R* 607.

Kathrein, R and Magraw, D (eds), *The Convention for the International Sale of Goods: a Handbook of Basic Materials*, 1987, Washington and Chicago: American Bar Association, Section of International Law and Practice.

Kritzer, A, *Guide to Practical Application of the United Nations Convention on Contracts for the International Sale of Goods*, 1990, Deventer and Boston: Kluwer.

Lavers, R, 'CSIG – to use or not to use' (1993) 21 *International Business Lawyer* 10.

Lee, R, 'The UN Convention on Contracts for the International Sale of Goods – OK for the UK?' (1993) *Journal of Business Law* 131.

Lipstein, K, 'One hundred years of Hague Conferences on Private International Law' (1990) 42 *International and Comparative Law Qtly* 553 at 616–26.

Murphy, MT, 'United Nations Convention on Contracts for the International Sale of Goods: creating uniformity in international sales law' (1989) 12 *Fordham International Law J* 727.

Ndulo, M, 'The Vienna Sales Convention 1980 and the Hague Uniform Laws on International Sale of Goods 1964: a comparative analysis' (1989) 38 *International and Comparative Law Qtly* 1.

Nicholas, B, 'The Vienna Convention on International Sales Law' (1989) 105 LQR 201.

Pryles, M, 'An assessment of the Vienna Sales Convention' [1989] *Australian Mining and Petroleum Law Association Yearbook* 337.

Roberts, J, 'International sale of goods' in Wilde, K and Islam, M (eds), *International Transactions – Trade and Investment, Law and Finance*, 1993, Sydney: Law Book Co, Ch 2.

Sacks, P, 'Comment on an assessment of the Vienna Sales Convention' [1989] *Australian Mining and Petroleum Law Association Yearbook* 359.

Schlechtriem, P, *Uniform Sales Law – The UN Convention on Contracts for the International Sale of Goods*, 1986, Vienna: Manz.

Schmitthoff, C, *Export Trade – The Law and Practice of International Trade*, 10th edn, 2000, London: Sweet & Maxwell, Ch 32 (eds L D'Arcy, C Murray, B Cleave).

Strub, M, 'The Convention on the International Sale of Goods: anticipatory repudiation provisions and developing countries' (1989) 38 *International and Comparative Law Qtly* 475.

Winship, P, 'Formation of international sales contracts under the 1980 Vienna Convention' (1993) 17 *International Lawyer* 1.

Winship, P, 'Bibliography: International Sale of Goods (Symposium on International Sale of Goods Convention)' (1984) 18 *International Lawyer* 53.

http://www.cisg.law.pace.edu

APPENDIX

UNITED NATIONS CONVENTION ON CONTRACTS FOR THE INTERNATIONAL SALE OF GOODS (VIENNA SALES CONVENTION) – VIENNA, 11 APRIL 1980

The Convention entered into force on 1 January 1988 after the ratification of the USA. It culminated half a century of work to prepare uniform law for the international sales of goods.

This Convention replaces the Hague Convention Relating to a Uniform Law on the Formation of Contracts for the International Sale of Goods of 1964 and the Hague Convention Relating to a Uniform Law on the International Sale of Goods of 1964 which, because of defects, have not been widely accepted by the important trading States. The new Convention provides a balanced representation of all legal systems of the world.

United Nations Convention on Contracts for the International Sale of Goods (Vienna, 1980)

State	Signature	Ratification, Accession (a), Approval (AA), Acceptance (A), Succession (d)	Entry into force
Argentina 1/	.	19 July 1983 a	1 January 1988
Australia	.	17 March 1988 a	1 April 1989
Austria	11 April 1980	29 December 1987	1 January 1989
Belarus 1/	.	9 October 1989 a	1 November 1990
Belgium	.	31 October 1996 a	1 November 1997
Bosnia and Herzegovina	.	12 January 1994 d	6 March 1992
Bulgaria	.	9 July 1990 a	1 August 1991
Burundi	.	4 September 1998 a	1 October 1999
Canada 2/	.	23 April 1991 a	1 May 1992
Chile 1/	11 April 1980	7 February 1990	1 March 1991
China 3/	30 September 1981	11 December 1986 AA	1 January 1988
Colombia		10 July 2001 a	1 August 2002
Croatia d/	.	8 June 1998 d	8 October 1991
Cuba	.	2 November 1994 a	1 December 1995
Czech Republic a/ 7/	.	30 September 1993 d	1 January 1993
Denmark 4/	26 May 1981	14 February 1989	1 March 1990
Ecuador	.	27 January 1992 a	1 February 1993
Egypt	.	6 December 1982 a	1 January 1988
Estonia 8/	.	20 September 1993 a	1 October 1994
Finland 4/	26 May 1981	15 December 1987	1 January 1989
France	27 August 1981	6 August 1982 AA	1 January 1988
Georgia	.	16 August 1994 a	1 September 1995
Germany b/ 5/	26 May 1981	21 December 1989	1 January 1991
Ghana	11 April 1980	.	.
Greece	.	12 January 1998 a	1 February 1999
Guinea	.	23 January 1991 a	1 February 1992
Honduras	.	10 October 2002 a	1 November 2003
Hungary 1/ 6/	11 April 1980	16 June 1983	1 January 1988
Iceland 4/		10 May 2001 a	1 June 2002

State	Signature	Ratification, Accession (a), Approval (AA), Acceptance (A), Succession (d)	Entry into force
Iraq	.	5 March 1990 a	1 April 1991
Israel	.	22 January 2002 a	1 February 2003
Italy	30 September 1981	11 December 1986	1 January 1988
Kyrgyzstan	.	11 May 1999 a	1 June 2000
Latvia 1/	.	31 July 1997 a	1 August 1998
Lesotho	18 June 1981	18 June 1981	1 January 1988
Lithuania 1/	.	18 January 1995 a	1 February 1996
Luxembourg	.	30 January 1997 a	1 February 1998
Mauritania	.	20 August 1999 a	1 September 2000
Mexico	.	29 December 1987 a	1 January 1989
Mongolia	.	31 December 1997 a	1 January 1999
Netherlands	29 May 1981	13 December 1990 A	1 January 1992
New Zealand	.	22 September 1994 a	1 October 1995
Norway 4/	26 May 1981	20 July 1988	1 August 1989
Peru	.	25 March 1999 a	1 April 2000
Poland	28 September 1981	19 May 1995	1 June 1996
Republic of Korea		17 February 2004 a	1 March 2005
Republic of Moldova	.	13 October 1994 a	1 November 1995
Romania	.	22 May 1991 a	1 June 1992
Russian Federation c/ 1/	.	16 August 1990 a	1 September 1991
Saint Vincent and the Grenadines 7/	.	12 September 2000 a	1 October 2001
Serbia and Montenegro e/	.	12 March 2001 d	27 April 1992
Singapore 7/	11 April 1980	16 February 1995	1 March 1996
Slovakia a/ 7/	.	28 May 1993 d	1 January 1993
Slovenia	.	7 January 1994 d	25 June 1991
Spain	.	24 July 1990 a	1 August 1991
Sweden 4/	26 May 1981	15 December 1987	1 January 1989
Switzerland	.	21 February 1990 a	1 March 1991
Syrian Arab Republic	.	19 October 1982 a	1 January 1988
Uganda	.	12 February 1992 a	1 March 1993
Ukraine 1/	.	3 January 1990 a	1 February 1991
United States of America 7/	31 August 1981	11 December 1986	1 January 1988
Uruguay	.	25 January 1999 a	1 February 2000
Uzbekistan	.	27 November 1996 a	1 December 1997
Venezuela	28 September 1981	.	.
Zambia	.	6 June 1986 a	1 January 1988

Parties: 63

a/ The Convention was signed by the former Czechoslovakia on 1 September 1981 and an instrument of ratification was deposited on 5 March 1990, with the Convention entering into force for the former Czechoslovakia on 1 April 1991. On 28 May 1993 Slovakia, and on

30 September 1993 the Czech Republic, deposited instruments of succession, with effect from 1 January 1993, the date of succession of States.

b/ The Convention was signed by the former German Democratic Republic on 13 August 1981, ratified on 23 February 1989 and entered into force on 1 March 1990.

c/ The Russian Federation continues, as from 24 December 1991, the membership of the former Union of Soviet Socialist Republics (USSR) in the United Nations and maintains, as from that date, full responsibility for all the rights and obligations of the USSR under the Charter of the United Nations and multilateral treaties deposited with the Secretary-General.

d/ Upon succeeding to the Convention, the Republic of Croatia has decided, on the basis of the Constitutional Decision on Sovereignty and Independence of the Republic of Croatia of 25 June 1991, and the Decision of the Croatian Parliament of 8 October 1991, and by virtue of succession of the Socialist Federal Republic of Yugoslavia in respect of the territory of the Republic of Croatia, to be considered a party to the Convention with effect as from 8 October 1991, the date on which the Republic of Croatia severed all constitutional and legal connections with the Socialist Federal Republic of Yugoslavia and took over its international obligations.

e/ The former Yugoslavia had signed and ratified the Convention on 11 April 1980 and 27 March 1985, respectively. By action effected on 12 March 2001, the former Federal Republic of Yugoslavia declared the following: '[T]he Government of the Federal Republic of Yugoslavia, having considered [the Convention], succeeds to the same and undertakes faithfully to perform and carry out the stipulations therein contained as from April 27, 1992, the date upon which the Federal Republic of Yugoslavia assumed responsibility for its international relations'.

Declarations and reservations

1/ State declared, in accordance with Arts 12 and 96 of the Convention, that any provision of Art 11, Art 29 or Part II of the Convention that allows a contract of sale or its modification or termination by agreement or any offer, acceptance or other indication of intention to be made in any form other than in writing, would not apply where any party had his place of business in its territory.

2/ Upon accession, Canada declared that, in accordance with Art 93 of the Convention, the Convention will extend to Alberta, British Columbia, Manitoba, New Brunswick, Newfoundland and Labrador, Nova Scotia, Ontario, Prince Edward Island and the Northwest Territories. (Upon accession, Canada declared that, in accordance with Art 95 of the Convention, with respect to British Columbia, it will not be bound by Art 1(1)(b) of the Convention. In a notification received on 31 July 1992, Canada withdrew that declaration.) In a declaration received on 9 April 1992, Canada extended the application of the Convention to Quebec and Saskatchewan. In a notification received on 29 June 1992, Canada extended the application of the Convention to the Yukon Territory. In a notification received on 18 June 2003, Canada extended the application of the Convention to the Territory of Nunavut.

3/ Upon approving the Convention, the People's Republic of China declared that it did not consider itself bound by sub-para (b) of para (1) of Art 1 and Art 11 as well as the provisions in the Convention relating to the content of Art 11.

4/ Upon ratifying the Convention, Denmark, Finland, Norway and Sweden declared in accordance with Art 92(1) that they would not be bound by Part II of the Convention (Formation of the Contract). Upon ratifying the Convention, Denmark, Finland, Norway and Sweden declared, pursuant to Art 94(1) and 94(2), that the Convention would not apply to contracts of sale where the parties have their places of business in Denmark, Finland, Sweden, Iceland or Norway. In a notification effected on 12 March 2003, Iceland declared, pursuant to Art 94(1), that the Convention would not apply to contracts of sale or to their formation where the parties have their places of business in Denmark, Finland, Iceland, Norway or Sweden.

5/ Upon ratifying the Convention, Germany declared that it would not apply Art 1(1)(b) in respect of any State that had made a declaration that that State would not apply Art 1(1)(b).

6/ Upon ratifying the Convention, Hungary declared that it considered the General Conditions of Delivery of Goods between Organizations of the Member Countries of the Council for Mutual Economic Assistance to be subject to the provisions of Art 90 of the Convention.

7/ State declared that it would not be bound by paragraph (1)(b) of Art 1.

8/ On 9 March 2004, Estonia withdrew the reservation made upon ratification mentioned in footnote 1.

See, United Nations General Assembly A/CN.9/325, 17 May 1989, pp 4–5; Honnold, J, *Uniform Law for International Sales Under the 1980 United Nations Convention*, 1982, Deventer: Kluwer; Bianca, CM and Bonell, MJ (eds), *Commentary on the International Sales Law – The 1980 Vienna Sales Convention*, 1987, Milan: Giuffrè.

United Nations Convention on Contracts for the International Sale of Goods (Vienna Sales Convention)

Vienna, 11 April 1980

The States Parties to this Convention,

Bearing in mind the broad objectives in the resolutions adopted by the sixth special session of the General Assembly of the United Nations on the establishment of a New International Economic Order,

Considering that the development of international trade on the basis of equality and mutual benefit is an important element in promoting friendly relations among States,

Being of the opinion that the adoption of uniform rules which govern contracts for the international sale of goods and take into account the different social, economic and legal systems would contribute to the removal of legal barriers in international trade and promote the development of international trade,

Have agreed as follows:

PART I – SPHERE OF APPLICATION AND GENERAL PROVISIONS

CHAPTER I – SPHERE OF APPLICATION

Article 1

1   This Convention applies to contracts of sale of goods between parties whose places of business are in different States:

(a) when the States are Contracting States; or

(b) when the rules of private international law lead to the application of the law of a Contracting State.

2   The fact that the parties have their places of business in different States is to be disregarded whenever this fact does not appear either from the contract or from any dealings between, or from information disclosed by the parties at any time before or at the conclusion of the contract.

3   Neither the nationality of the parties nor the civil or commercial character of the parties or of the contract is to be taken into consideration in determining the application of this Convention.

Article 2

This Convention does not apply to sales:

(a) of goods bought for personal, family or household use, unless the seller, at any time before or at the conclusion of the contract, neither knew nor ought to have known that the goods were bought for any such use;

(b) by auction;

(c) on execution or otherwise by authority of law;

(d) of stocks, shares, investment securities, negotiable instruments or money;

(e) of ships, vessels, hovercraft or aircraft;
(f) of electricity.

Article 3

1 Contracts for the supply of goods to be manufactured or produced are to be considered sales unless the party who orders the goods undertakes to supply a substantial part of the materials necessary for such manufacture or production.
2 This Convention does not apply to contracts in which the preponderant part of the obligations of the party who furnishes the goods consists in the supply of labour or other services.

Article 4

This Convention governs only the formation of the contract of sale and the rights and obligations of the seller and the buyer arising from such a contract. In particular, except as otherwise expressly provided in this Convention, it is not concerned with:
(a) the validity of the contract or of any of its provisions or of any usage;
(b) the effect which the contract may have on the property in the goods sold.

Article 5

This Convention does not apply to the liability of the seller for death or personal injury caused by the goods to any person.

Article 6

The parties may exclude the application of this Convention or, subject to Article 12, derogate from or vary the effect of any of its provisions.

CHAPTER II – GENERAL PROVISIONS

Article 7

1 In the interpretation of this Convention, regard is to be had to its international character and to the need to promote uniformity in its application and the observance of good faith in international trade.
2 Questions concerning matters governed by this Convention which are not expressly settled in it are to be settled in conformity with the general principles on which it is based or, in the absence of such principles, in conformity with the law applicable by virtue of the rules of private international law.

Article 8

1 For the purposes of this Convention, statements made by and other conduct of a party are to be interpreted according to his intent where the other party knew or could not have been unaware what that intent was.
2 If the preceding paragraph is not applicable, statements made by and other conduct of a party are to be interpreted according to the understanding that a reasonable person of the same kind as the other party would have had in the same circumstances.
3 In determining the intent of a party or the understanding a reasonable person would have had, due consideration is to he given to all relevant circumstances of the case including the negotiations, any practices which the parties have established between themselves, usage's and any subsequent conduct of the parties.

Article 9

1 The parties are bound by any usage to which they have agreed and by any practices which they have established between themselves.
2 The parties are considered, unless otherwise agreed, to have impliedly made applicable to their contract or its formation a usage of which the parties knew or ought to have known and which in international trade is widely known to, and regularly observed by, parties to contracts of the type involved in the particular trade concerned.

Article 10

For the purpose of this Convention:

(a) if a party has more than one place of business, the place of business is that which has the closest relationship to the contract and its performance, having regard to the circumstances known to or contemplated by the parties at any time before or at the conclusion of the contract;

(b) if a party does not have a place of business, reference is to be made to his habitual residence.

Article 11

A contract of sale need not be concluded in or evidenced by writing and is not subject to any other requirement as to form. It may be proved by any means, including witnesses.

Article 12

Any provision of Article 11, Article 29 or Part II of this Convention that allows a contract of sale or its modification or termination by agreement or any offer, acceptance or other indication of intention to be made in any form other than in writing does not apply where any party has his place of business in a Contracting State which has made a declaration under Article 96 of this Convention. The parties may not derogate from or vary the effect of this article.

Article 13

For the purposes of this Convention, 'writing' includes telegram and telex.

PART II – FORMATION OF THE CONTRACT

Article 14

1   A proposal for concluding a contract addressed to one or more specific persons constitutes an offer if it is sufficiently definite and indicates the intention of the offeror to be bound in case of acceptance. A proposal is sufficiently definite if it indicates the goods and expressly or implicitly fixes or makes provision for determining the quantity and the price.

2   A proposal other than one addressed to one or more specific persons is to be considered merely as an invitation to make offers, unless the contrary is clearly indicated by the person making the proposal.

Article 15

1   An offer becomes effective when it reaches the offeree.

2   An offer, even if it is irrevocable, may be withdrawn if the withdrawal reaches the offeree before or at the same time as the offer.

Article 16

1   Until a contract is concluded, an offer may be revoked if the revocation reaches the offeree before he has dispatched an acceptance.

2   However, an offer cannot be revoked:

(a) if it indicates, whether by stating a fixed time for acceptance or otherwise, that it is irrevocable; or

(b) if it was reasonable for the offeree to rely on the offer as being irrevocable and the offeree has acted in reliance on the offer.

Article 17

An offer, even if it is irrevocable, is terminated when a rejection reaches the offeror.

Article 18

1   A statement made by or other conduct of the offeree indicating assent to an offer is an acceptance. Silence or inactivity does not in itself amount to acceptance.

2   An acceptance of an offer becomes effective at the moment the indication of assent reaches the offeror. An acceptance is not effective if the indication of assent does not reach the offeror within the time he has fixed or if no time is fixed within a reasonable time, due

account being taken of the circumstances of the transaction, including the rapidity of the means of communication employed by the offeror. An oral offer must be accepted immediately unless the circumstances indicate otherwise.

3 However, if, by virtue of the offer or as a result of practices which the parties have established between themselves or of usage, the offeree may indicate assent by performing an act, such as one relating to the dispatch of the goods or payment of the price, without notice to the offeror, the acceptance is effective at the moment the act is performed, provided that the act is performed within the period of time laid down in the preceding paragraph.

Article 19

1 A reply to an offer which purports to be an acceptance but contains additions, limitations or other modifications is a rejection of the offer and constitutes a counter-offer.

2 However, a reply to an offer which purports to be an acceptance but contains additional or different terms which do not materially alter the terms of the offer constitutes an acceptance, unless the offeror, without undue delay, objects orally to the discrepancy or dispatches a notice to that effect. If he does not so object, the terms of the contract are the terms of the offer with the modifications contained in the acceptance.

3 Additional or different terms relating, among other things, to the price, payment, quality and quantity of the goods, place and time of delivery, extent of one party's liability to the other or the settlement of disputes are considered to alter the terms of the offer materially.

Article 20

1 A period of time for acceptance fixed by the offeror in a telegram or a letter begins to run from the moment the telegram is handed in for dispatch or from the date shown on the letter or, if no such date is shown, from the date shown on the envelope. A period of time for acceptance fixed by the offeror by telephone, telex or other means of instantaneous communication, begins to run from the moment that the offer reaches the offeree.

2 Official holidays or non-business days occurring during the period for acceptance are included in calculating the period. However, if a notice of acceptance cannot be delivered at the address of the offeror on the last day of the period because that day falls on an official holiday or a non-business day at the place of business of the offeror, the period is extended until the first business day which follows.

Article 21

1 A late acceptance is nevertheless effective as an acceptance if without delay the offeror orally so informs the offeree or dispatches a notice to that effect.

2 If a letter or other writing containing a late acceptance shows that it has been sent in such circumstances that if its transmission had been normal it would have reached the offeror in due time, the late acceptance is effective as an acceptance unless, without delay, the offeror orally informs the offeree that he considers his offer as having lapsed or dispatches a notice to that effect.

Article 22

An acceptance may be withdrawn if the withdrawal reaches the offeror before or at the same time as time acceptance would have become effective.

Article 23

A contract is concluded at the moment when an acceptance of an offer becomes effective in accordance with the provisions of this Convention.

Article 24

For the purposes of this part of the Convention, an offer, declaration of acceptance or any other indication of intention 'reaches' the addressee when it is made orally to him or delivered by any other means to him personally, to his place of business or mailing address or, if he does not have a place of business or mailing address, to his habitual residence.

PART III – SALE OF GOODS

CHAPTER I – GENERAL PROVISIONS

Article 25

A breach of contract committed by one of the parties is fundamental if it results in such detriment to the other party as substantially to deprive him of what he is entitled to expect under the contract, unless the party in breach did not foresee and a reasonable person of the same kind in the same circumstances would not have foreseen such a result.

Article 26

A declaration of avoidance of the contract is effective only if made by notice to the other party.

Article 27

Unless otherwise expressly provided in this part of the Convention, if any notice, request or other communication is given or made by a party in accordance with this part and by means appropriate in the circumstances, a delay or error in the transmission of the communication or its failure to arrive does not deprive that party of the right to rely on the communication.

Article 28

If, in accordance with the provisions of this Convention, one party is entitled to require performance of ally obligation by the other party, a court is not bound to enter a judgment for specific performance unless the court would do so under its own law in respect of similar contracts of sale not governed by this Convention.

Article 29

1   A contract may be modified or terminated by the mere agreement of the parties.
2   A contract in writing which contains a provision requiring any modification or termination by agreement to be in writing may not be otherwise modified or terminated by agreement. However, a party may be precluded by his conduct from asserting such a provision to the extent that the other party has relied on that conduct.

CHAPTER II – OBLIGATIONS OF THE SELLER

Article 30

The seller must deliver the goods, hand over any documents relating to them and transfer the property in the goods, as required by the contract and this Convention.

Section I – Delivery of the goods and handing over of documents

Article 31

If the seller is not bound to deliver the goods at any other particular place, his obligation to deliver consists:
(a) if the contract of sale involves carriage of the goods – in handing the goods over to the first carrier for transmission to the buyer;
(b) if, in cases not within the preceding sub-paragraph, the contract relates to specific goods, or unidentified goods to be drawn from a specific stock; or to he manufactured or produced, and at the time of the conclusion of the contract the parties knew that the goods were at, or were to be manufactured or produced at, a particular place – in placing the goods at the buyer's disposal at that place;
(c) in other cases – in placing the goods at the buyer's disposal at the place where the seller had his place of business at the time of the conclusion of the contract.

Article 32

1   If the seller, in accordance with the contract or this Convention, hands the goods over to a carrier and if the goods are not clearly identified to the contract by markings on the goods, by shipping documents or otherwise, the seller must give the buyer notice of the consignment specifying the goods.

2 If the seller is bound to arrange for carriage of the goods, he must make such contracts as are necessary for carriage to the place fixed by means of transportation appropriate in the circumstances and according to the usual terms for such transportation.

3 If the seller is not bound to effect insurance in respect of the carriage of the goods, he must, at the buyer's request, provide him with all available information necessary to enable him to effect such insurance.

Article 33

The seller must deliver the goods:

(a) if a date is fixed by or determinable from the contract, on that date;

(b) if a period of time is fixed by or determinable from the contract, at any time within that period unless circumstances indicate that the buyer is to choose a date; or

(c) in any other case, within a reasonable time after the conclusion of the contract.

Article 34

If the seller is bound to hand over documents relating to the goods, he must hand them over at the time and place and in the form required by the contract. If the seller has handed over documents before that time, he may, up to that time, cure any lack of conformity in the documents, if the exercise of this right does not cause the buyer unreasonable inconvenience or unreasonable expense. However, the buyer retains any right to claim damages as provided for in this Convention.

Section II – Conformity of the goods and third party claims

Article 35

1 The seller must deliver goods which are of the quantity, quality and description required by the contract and which are contained or packaged in the manner required by the contract.

2 Except where the parties have agreed otherwise, the goods do not conform with the contract unless they:

(a) are fit for the purposes for which goods of the same description would ordinarily he used;

(b) are fit for any particular purpose expressly or impliedly made known to the seller at the time of the conclusion of the contract, except where the circumstances show that the buyer did not rely, or that it was unreasonable for him to rely, on the seller's skill and judgment;

(c) possess the qualities of goods which the seller has held out to the buyer as a sample or model;

(d) are contained or packaged in the manner usual for such goods or, where there is no such manner, in a manner adequate to preserve and protect the goods.

3 The seller is not liable under sub-paras (a) to (d) of the preceding paragraph for any lack of conformity of the goods if at the time of the conclusion of the contract the buyer knew or could not have been unaware of such lack of conformity.

Article 36

1 The seller is liable in accordance with the contract and this Convention for any lack of conformity which exists at the time when the risk passes to the buyer, even though the lack of conformity becomes apparent only after that time.

2 The seller is also liable for any lack of conformity which occurs after the time indicated in the preceding paragraph and which is due to a breach of any of his obligations, including a breach of any guarantee that for a period of time the goods will remain fit for their ordinary purpose or for some particular purpose or will retain specified qualities or characteristics.

Article 37

If the seller has delivered goods before the date for delivery, he may, up to that date, deliver any missing part or make up any deficiency in the quantity of the goods delivered, or deliver goods in replacement of any non-conforming goods delivered or remedy any lack of conformity in the goods delivered, provided that the exercise of this right does not cause the buyer unreasonable inconvenience or unreasonable expense. However, the buyer retains any right to claim damages as provided for in this Convention.

Article 38

1   The buyer must examine the goods, or cause them to he examined, within as short a period as is practicable in the circumstances.

2   If the contract involves carriage of the goods, examination may be deferred until after the goods have arrived at their destination.

3   If the goods are redirected in transit or redispatched by the buyer without a reasonable opportunity for examination by him and at the time of the conclusion of the contract the seller knew or ought to have known of the possibility, of such redirection or redispatch, examination may be deferred until after the goods have arrived at the new destination.

Article 39

1   The buyer loses the right to rely on a lack of conformity of the goods if he does not give notice to the seller specifying the nature of the lack of conformity within a reasonable time after he has discovered it or ought to have discovered it.

2   In any event, the buyer loses the right to rely on a lack of conformity of the goods if he does not give the seller notice thereof at the latest within a period of two years from the date on which the goods were actually handed over to the buyer, unless this time-limit is inconsistent with a contractual period of guarantee.

Article 40

The seller is not entitled to rely on the provisions of Articles 38 and 39 if the lack of conformity relates to facts of which he knew or could not have been unaware and which he did not disclose to the buyer.

Article 41

The seller must deliver goods which are free from any right or claim of a third party, unless the buyer agreed to take the goods subject to that right or claim. However, if such right or claim is based on industrial property or other intellectual property, the seller's obligation is governed by Article 42.

Article 42

1   The seller must deliver goods which are free from any right or claim of a third party based on industrial property or other intellectual property, of which at the time of the conclusion of the contract the seller knew or could not have been unaware, provided that the right or claim is based on industrial property or other intellectual property:

   (a) under the law of the State where the goods will be resold or otherwise used, if it was contemplated by the parties at the time of the conclusion of the contract that the goods would be resold or otherwise used in that State; or

   (b) in any other case, under the law of the State where the buyer has his place of business.

2   The obligation of the seller under the preceding paragraph does not extend to cases where:

   (a) at the time of the conclusion of the contract the buyer knew or could not have been unaware of the right or claim; or

   (b) the right or claim results from the seller's compliance with technical drawings, designs, formulae or other such specifications furnished by the buyer.

Article 43

1   The buyer loses the right to rely on the provisions of Article 41 or Article 42 if he does not give notice to the seller specifying the nature of the right or claim of the third party within a reasonable time after he has become aware or ought to have become aware of the right or claim.

2   The seller is not entitled to rely on the provisions of the preceding paragraph if he knew of the right or claim of the third party and the nature of it.

Article 44

Notwithstanding the provisions of para (1) of Article 39 and para (1) of Article 43, the buyer may reduce the price in accordance with Article 50 or claim damages, except for loss of profit, if he has a reasonable excuse for his failure to give the required notice.

Section III – Remedies for breach of contract by the seller

Article 45

1 If the seller fails to perform any of his obligations under the contract or this Convention, the buyer may:
   (a) exercise the rights provided in Articles 46–52;
   (b) claim damages as provided in Articles 74–77.
2 The buyer is not deprived of any right he may have to claim damages by exercising his right to other remedies.
3 No period of grace may he granted to the seller by a court of arbitral tribunal when the buyer resorts to a remedy for breach of contract.

Article 46

1 The buyer may require performance by the seller of his obligations unless the buyer has resorted to a remedy which is inconsistent with this requirement.
2 If the goods do not conform with the contract, the buyer may require delivery of substitute goods only if the lack of conformity constitutes a fundamental breach of contract and a request for substitute goods is made either in conjunction with notice given under Article 39 or within a reasonable time thereafter.
3 If the goods do not conform with the contract, the buyer may require the seller to remedy the lack of conformity by repair, unless this is unreasonable having regard to all the circumstances. A request for repair must be made either in conjunction with notice given under Article 39 or within a reasonable time thereafter.

Article 47

1 The buyer may fix an additional period of time of reasonable length for performance by the seller of his obligations.
2 Unless the buyer has received notice from the seller that he will not perform within the period so fixed, the buyer may not, during that period, resort to any remedy for breach of contracts. However, the buyer is not deprived thereby of any right he may have to claim damages for delay in performance.

Article 48

1 Subject to Article 49, the seller may, even after the date for delivery, remedy at his own expense any failure to perform his obligations, if he can do so without unreasonable delay and without causing the buyer unreasonable inconvenience or uncertainty of reimbursement by the seller of expenses advanced by the buyer. However, the buyer retains any right to claim damages as provided for in this Convention.
2 If the seller requests the buyer to make known whether he will accept performance and the buyer does not comply with the request within a reasonable time, the seller may perform within the time indicated in his request. The buyer may not, during that period of time, resort to any remedy which is inconsistent with performance by the seller.
3 A notice by the seller that he will perform within a specified period of time is assumed to include a request, under the preceding paragraph, that the buyer make known his decision.
4 A request or notice by the seller under para (2) or (3) of this article is not effective unless received by the buyer.

Article 49

1 The buyer may declare the contract avoided:
   (a) if the failure by the seller to perform any of his obligations under the contract or this Convention amounts to a fundamental breach of contract; or

(b) in case of non-delivery, if the seller does not deliver the goods within the additional period of time fixed by the buyer in accordance with para (1) of Article 47 or declares that he will not deliver within the period so fixed.

2   However, in cases where the seller has delivered the goods, the buyer loses the right to declare the contract avoided unless he does so:

(a) in respect of late delivery, within a reasonable time after he has become aware that delivery has been made;

(b) in respect of any breach other than late delivery, within a reasonable time:

(i)   after he knew or ought to have known of the breach;

(ii) after the expiration of any additional period of time fixed by the buyer in accordance with para (1) of Article 47, or after the seller has declared that he will not perform his obligations within such an additional period; or

(iii) after the expiration of any additional period of time indicated by the seller in accordance with para (2) of Article 48, or after the buyer has declared that he will not accept performance.

Article 50

If the goods do not conform with the contract and whether or not the price has already been paid, the buyer may reduce the price in the same proportion as the value that the goods actually delivered had at the time of the delivery bears to the value that conforming goods would have had at that time. However, if the seller remedies any failure to perform his obligation in accordance with Article 37 or Article 48 or if the buyer refuses to accept performance by the seller in accordance with those articles, the buyer may not reduce the price.

Article 51

1   If the seller delivers only a part of the goods or if only a part of the goods delivered is in conformity with the contract, Articles 46–50 apply in respect of the part which is missing or which does not conform.

2   The buyer may declare the contract avoided in its entirety only if the failure to make delivery completely or in conformity with the contract amounts to a fundamental breach of the contract.

Article 52

1   If the seller delivers the goods before the date fixed, the buyer may take delivery or refuse to take delivery.

2   If the seller delivers a quantity of goods greater than that provided for in the contract, the buyer may take delivery or refuse to take delivery of the excess quantity. If the buyer takes delivery of all or part of the excess quantity, he must pay for it at the contract rate.

CHAPTER III – OBLIGATIONS OF THE BUYER

Article 53

The buyer must pay the price for the goods and take delivery of them as required by the contract and this Convention.

Section I – Payment of the price

Article 54

The buyer's obligation to pay the price includes taking such steps and complying with such formalities as may be required under the contract or any laws and regulations to enable payment to be made.

Article 55

Where a contract has been validly concluded but does not expressly or implicitly fix or make provision for determining the price, the parties are considered, in the absence of any indication to the contrary, to have impliedly made reference to the price generally charged at the time of the conclusion of the contract for such goods sold under comparable circumstances in the trade concerned.

Article 56

If the price is fixed according to the weight of the goods, in case of doubt it is to be determined by the net weight.

Article 57

1   If the buyer is not bound to pay the price at any other particular place, he must pay it to the seller:
    (a) at the seller's place of business; or
    (b) if the payment is to be made against the handing over of the goods or of documents, at the place where the handing over takes place.
2   The seller must bear any increase in the expenses incidental to payment which is caused by a change in his place of business subsequent to the conclusion of the contract.

Article 58

1   If the buyer is not bound to pay the price at any other specific time, he must pay it when the seller places either the goods' or documents controlling their disposition at the buyer's disposal in accordance with the contract and this Convention. The seller may make such payment a condition for handing over the goods or documents.
2   If the contract involves carriage of the goods, the seller may dispatch the goods on terms whereby the goods, or documents controlling their disposition, will not be handed over to the buyer except against payment of the price.
3   The buyer is not bound to pay the price until he has had an opportunity to examine the goods, unless the procedures for delivery or payment agree upon by the parties are inconsistent with his having such an opportunity.

Article 59

The buyer must pay the price on the date fixed by or determinable from the contract and this Convention without the need for any request or compliance with any formality on the part of the seller.

Section II – Taking Delivery

Article 60

The buyer's obligation to take delivery consists:
(a) in doing all the acts which could reasonably be expected of him in order to enable the seller to make delivery; and
(b) in taking over the goods.

Section III – Remedies for breach of contract by the buyer

Article 61

1   If the buyer fails to perform any of his obligations under the contract or this Convention, the seller may:
    (a) exercise the rights provided in Articles 62–65;
    (b) claim damages as provided in Articles 74–77.
2   The seller is not deprived of any right he may have to claim damage by exercising his right to other remedies.
3   No period of grace may he granted to the buyer by a court or arbitral tribunal when the seller resorts to a remedy for breach of contract.

Article 62

The seller may require the buyer to pay the price, take delivery or perform his other obligations, unless the seller has resorted to a remedy which is inconsistent with this requirement.

Article 63

1   The seller may fix an additional period of time of reasonable length for performance by the buyer of his obligations.

2   Unless the seller has received notice from the buyer that he will not perform within the period so fixed, the seller may not, during that period, resort to any remedy for breach of contract. However, the seller is not deprived thereby of any right he may have to claim damages for delay in performance.

Article 64

1   The seller may declare the contract avoided:

   (a) if the failure by the buyer to perform any of his obligations under the contract or this Convention amounts to a fundamental breach of contract; or

   (b) if the buyer does not, within the additional period of time fixed by the seller in accordance with para (1) of Article 63, perform his obligation to pay the price or take delivery of the goods, or if he declares that he will not do so within the period so fixed.

2   However, in cases where the buyer has paid the price, the seller loses the right to declare the contract avoided unless he does so:

   (a) in respect of late performance by the buyer, before the seller has become aware that performance has been rendered; or

   (b) in respect of any breach other than late performance by the buyer, within a reasonable time:

      (i) after the seller knew or ought to have known of the breach; or

      (ii) after the expiration of any additional period of time fixed by the seller in accordance with para (1) of Article 63, or after the buyer has declared that he will not perform his obligations within such an additional period.

Article 65

1   If, under the contract, the buyer is to specify the form, measurement or other features of the goods and he fails to make such specification either on the date agreed upon or within a reasonable time after receipt of a request from the seller, the seller may, without prejudice to any other rights he may have, make the specification himself in accordance with the requirements of the buyer that may be known to him.

2   If the seller makes the specification himself, he must inform the buyer of the details thereof and must fix a reasonable time within which the buyer may make a different specification. If, after receipt of such a communication, the buyer fails to do so within the time so fixed, the specification made by the seller is binding.

CHAPTER IV – PASSING OF RISK

Article 66

Loss of or damage to the goods after the risk has passed to the buyer does not discharge him from his obligation to pay the price unless the loss or damage is due to an act or omission of the seller.

Article 67

1   If the contract of sale involves carriage of the goods and the seller is not bound to hand them over at a particular place, the risk passes to the buyer when the goods are handed over to the first carrier for transmission to the buyer in accordance with the contract of sale. If the seller is bound to hand the goods over to a carrier at a particular place, the risk does not pass to the buyer until the goods are handed over to the carrier at that place. The fact that the seller is authorised to retain documents controlling the disposition of the goods does not affect the passage of the risk.

2   Nevertheless, the risk does not pass to the buyer until the goods are clearly identified to the contract, whether by markings on the goods, by shipping documents, by notice given to the buyer or otherwise.

Article 68

The risk in respect of goods sold in transit passes to the buyer from the time of the conclusion of the contract. However, if the circumstances so indicate, the risk is assumed by the buyer from the time the goods were handed over to the carrier who issued the documents embodying the contract of carriage. Nevertheless, if at the time of the conclusion of the contract of sale the seller knew or ought to have known that the goods had been lost or damaged and did not disclose this to the buyer, the loss or damage is at the risk of the seller.

Article 69

1   In cases not within Articles 67 and 68, the risk passes to the buyer when he takes over the goods or, if he does not do so in due time, from the time when the goods are placed at his disposal and he commits a breach of contract by failing to take delivery.

2   However, if the buyer is bound to take over the goods at a place other than a place of business of the seller, the risk passes when delivery is due and the buyer is aware of the fact that the goods are placed at his disposal at that place.

3   If the contract relates to goods not then identified, the goods are considered not to be placed at the disposal of the buyer until they are clearly identified to the contract.

Article 70

If the seller had committed a fundamental breach of contract, Articles 67, 68 and 69 do not impair the remedies available to the buyer on account of the breach.

CHAPTER V – PROVISIONS COMMON TO THE OBLIGATIONS OF THE SELLER AND OF THE BUYER

Section I – Anticipatory breach and instalment contracts

Article 71

1   A party may suspend the performance of his obligations if, after the conclusion of the contract, it becomes apparent that the other party will not perform a substantial part of his obligations as a result of:

(a) a serious deficiency in his ability to perform or in his credit-worthiness; or

(b) his conduct in preparing to perform or in performing the contract.

2   If the seller has already dispatched the goods before the grounds described in the preceding paragraph become evident, he may prevent the handing over of the goods to the buyer even though the buyer holds a document which entitles him to obtain them. The present paragraph relates only to the rights in the goods as between the buyer and the seller.

3   A party suspending performance, whether before or after dispatch of the goods, must immediately give notice of the suspension to the other party and must continue with performance if the other party provides adequate assurance of his performance.

Article 72

1   If prior to the date for performance of the contract it is clear that one of the parties will commit a fundamental breach of contract, the other party may declare the contract avoided.

2   If time allows, the party intending to declare the contract avoided must give reasonable notice to the other party in order to permit him to provide adequate assurance of his performance.

3   The requirements of the preceding paragraph do not apply if the other party has declared that he will not perform his obligations.

Article 73

1   In the case of a contract for delivery of goods by instalments, if the failure of one party to perform any of his obligations in respect of any instalment constitutes a fundamental breach of contract with respect to that instalment, the other party may declare the contract avoided with respect to that instalment.

2   If one party's failure to perform any of his obligations in respect of any instalment gives the other party good grounds to conclude that a fundamental breach of contract will occur

with respect to future instalments, he may declare the contract avoided for the future, provided that he does so within a reasonable time.

3   A buyer who declares the contract avoided in respect of any delivery may, at the same time, declare it avoided in respect of deliveries already made or of future deliveries if, by reason of their interdependence, those deliveries could not be used for the purpose contemplated by the parties at the time of the conclusion of the contract.

Section II – Damages

Article 74

Damages for breach of contract by one party consist of a sum equal to the loss, including loss of profit, suffered by the other party as a consequence of the breach. Such damages may not exceed the loss which the party in breach foresaw or ought to have foreseen at the time of the conclusion of the contract, in the light of the facts and matters of which he then knew or ought to have known, as a possible consequence of the breach of contract.

Article 75

If the contract is avoided and if, in a reasonable manner and within a reasonable time after avoidance, the buyer has bought goods in replacement or the seller has resold the goods, the party claiming damages may recover the difference between the contract price and the price in the substitute transaction as well as any further damages recoverable under Article 74.

Article 76

1   If the contract is avoided and there is a current price for the goods, the party claiming damages may, if he has not made a purchase or resale under Article 75, recover the differences between the price fixed by the contract and the current price at the time of avoidance as well as any further damages recoverable under Article 74. If, however, the party claiming damages has avoided the contract after taking over the goods, the current price at the time of such taking over shall be applied instead of the current price at the time of avoidance.

2   For the purpose of the preceding paragraph, the current price is the price prevailing at the place where delivery of the goods should have been made or, if there is no current price at that place, the price at such other place as serves as a reasonable substitute, making due allowance for differences in the cost of transporting the goods.

Article 77

A party who relies on a breach of contract must take such measures as are reasonable in the circumstances to mitigate the loss, including loss of profit resulting from the breach. If he fails to take such measures, the party in breach may claim a reduction in the damages in the amount by which the loss should have been mitigated.

Section III – Interest

Article 78

If a party fails to pay the price or any other sum that is in arrears, the other party is entitled to interest on it, without prejudice to any claim for damages recoverable under Article 74.

Section IV – Exemptions

Article 79

1   A party is not liable for a failure to perform any of his obligations it he proves that the failure was due to an impediment beyond his control and that he could not reasonably be expected to have taken the impediment into account at the time of the conclusion of the contract or to have avoided or overcome it or its consequences.

2   If the party's failure is due to the failure by a third person whom he has engaged to perform the whole or part of the contract, that party is exempt from liability only if:

(a) he is exempt under the preceding paragraph; and

(b) the person whom he has so engaged would be so exempt it the provisions of that paragraph were applied to him.

3   The exemption provided by this article has effect for the period during which the impediment exists.

4   The party who fails to perform must give notice to the other party of the impediment and its effects on his ability to perform. If the notice is not received by the other party within a reasonable time after the party who fails to perform knew or ought to have known of the impediment, he is liable for damages resulting from such non-receipt.

5   Nothing in this article prevents either party from exercising any right other than to claim damages under this Convention.

Article 80

A party may not rely on a failure of the other party to perform, to the extent that such failure was caused by the first party's act or omission.

Section V – Effects of avoidance

Article 81

1   Avoidance of the contract releases both parties from their obligations under it, subject to any damages which may be due. Avoidance does not affect any provision of the contract for the settlement of disputes or any other provision of the contract governing the rights and obligations of the parties consequent upon the avoidance of the contract.

2   A party who has performed the contract either wholly or in part may claim restitution from the other party of whatever the first party has supplied or paid under the contracts. If both parties are bound to make restitution, they must do so concurrently.

Article 82

1   The buyer loses the right to declare the contract avoided or to require the seller to deliver substitute goods if it is impossible for him to make restitution of the goods substantially in the condition in which he received them.

2   The preceding paragraph does not apply:

   (a) if the impossibility of making restitution of the goods or of making restitution of the goods substantially in the condition in which the buyer received them is not due to his act or omission;

   (b) if the goods or part of the goods have perished or deteriorated as a result of the examination provided for in Article 38; or

   (c) if the goods or part of the goods have been sold in the normal course of business or have been consumed or transformed by the buyer in the course of normal use before he discovered or ought to have discovered the lack of conformity.

Article 83

A buyer who has lost the right to declare the contract avoided or to require the seller to deliver substitute goods in accordance with Article 82 retains all other remedies under the contract and this Convention.

Article 84

1   If the seller is bound to refund the price, he must also pay interest on it, from the date on which the price was paid.

2   The buyer must account to the seller for all benefits which he has derived from the goods or part of them:

   (a) if he must make restitution of the goods or part of them; or

   (b) if it is impossible for him to make restitution of all or part of the goods or to make restitution of all part of the goods substantially in the condition in which he received them, but he has nevertheless declared the contract avoided or required the seller to deliver substitute goods.

Section VI – Preservation of the goods

Article 85

If the buyer is in delay in taking delivery of the goods or, where payment of the price and delivery of the goods are to be made concurrently, if he fails to pay the price, and the seller is either in possession of the goods or otherwise able to control their disposition, the seller must take such steps as are reasonable in the circumstances to preserve them. He is entitled to retain them until he has been reimbursed his reasonable expenses by the buyer.

Article 86

1   If the buyer has received the goods and intends to exercise any right under the contract or this Convention to reject them, he must take such steps to preserve them as are reasonable in the circumstances. He is entitled to retain them until he has been reimbursed his reasonable expenses by the seller.

2   If goods dispatched to the buyer have been placed at his disposal at their destination and he exercises the right to reject them, he must take possession of them on behalf of the seller, provided that this can be done without payment of the price and without unreasonable inconvenience or unreasonable expense.

This provision does not apply if the seller or a person authorised to take charge of the goods on his behalf is present at the destination. If the buyer takes possession of the goods under this paragraph, his rights and obligations are governed by the preceding paragraph.

Article 87

A party who is bound to take steps to preserve the goods may deposit them in a warehouse of a third person at the expense of the other party provided that the expense incurred is not unreasonable.

Article 88

1   A party who is bound to preserve the goods in accordance with Article 85 or 86 may sell them by any appropriate means if there has been an unreasonable delay by the other party in taking possession of the goods or in taking them back or in paying the price or the cost of preservation, provided that reasonable notice of the intention to sell has been given to the other party.

2   If the goods are subject to rapid deterioration or their preservation would involve unreasonable expense, a party who is bound to preserve the goods in accordance with Article 85 or 86 must take reasonable measures to sell them, to the extent possible he must give notice to the other party of his intention to sell.

3   A party selling the goods has the right to retain out of the proceeds of sale an amount equal to the reasonable expenses of preserving the goods and of selling them. He must account to the other party for the balance.

PART IV – FINAL PROVISIONS

Article 89

The Secretary General of the United Nations is hereby designated as the depositary for this Convention.

Article 90

This Convention does not prevail over any international agreement which has already been or may be entered into and which contains provisions concerning the matters governed by this Convention, provided that the parties have their places of business in States parties to such agreement.

Article 91

1   This Convention is open for signature at the concluding meeting of the United Nations Conference on Contracts for the International Sale of Goods and will remain open for signature by all States at the headquarters of the United Nations, New York until 30 September 1981.

2   This Convention is subject to ratification, acceptance or approval by the signatory States.

3   This Convention is open for accession by all States which are not signatory States as from the date it is open for signature.

4   Instruments of ratification, acceptance, approval and accession are to be deposited with the Secretary General of the United Nations.

Article 92

1   A Contracting State may declare at the time of signature, ratification, acceptance, approval or accession that it will not be bound by Part II of this Convention or that it will not be bound by Part III of this Convention.

2   A Contracting State which makes it declaration in accordance with the preceding paragraph in respect of Part II or Part III of this Convention is not to be considered a Contracting State within para (1) of Article 1 of this Convention in respect of matters governed by the part to which the declaration applies.

Article 93

1   If a Contracting State has two or more territorial units in which, according to its constitution, different systems of law are applicable in relation to the matters dealt with in this Convention, it may, at the time of signature, ratification, acceptance, approval or accession, declare that this Convention is to extend to all its territorial units or only to one or more of them, and may amend its declaration by submitting another declaration at any time.

2   These declarations are to be notified to the depositary and are to state expressly the territorial units to which the Convention extends.

3   If, by virtue of a declaration under this article, this Convention extends to one or more but not all of the territorial units of a Contracting State, and if the place of business of a party is located in that State, this place of business, for the purposes of this Convention, is considered not to be in a Contracting State, unless it is in a territorial unit to which the Convention extends.

4   If a Contracting State makes no declaration under para (1) of this article, the Convention is to extend to all territorial units of that State.

Article 94

1   Two or more Contracting States which have the same or closely related legal rules on matters governed by this Convention may at any time declare that the Convention is not to apply to contracts of sale or to their formation where the parties have their places of business in those States. Such declarations may be made jointly or by reciprocal unilateral declarations.

2   A Contracting State which has the same or closely related legal rules on matters governed by this Convention as one or more non-Contracting States may at any time declare that the Convention is not to apply to contracts of sale or to their formation where the parties have their places of business in those States.

3   If a State which is the object of a declaration under the preceding paragraph subsequently becomes a Contracting State, the declaration made will, as from the date on which the Convention enters into force in respect of the new Contracting State, have the effect of a declaration made under para (1), provided that the new Contracting State joins in such declaration or makes a reciprocal unilateral declaration.

Article 95

Any State may declare at the time of the deposit of its instrument of ratification, acceptance, approval or accession that it will not he bound by sub-para (1)(b) of Article 1 of this Convention.

Article 96

A Contracting State whose legislation requires contracts of sale to be concluded in or evidenced by writing may at any time make a declaration in accordance with Article 12 that any provision of Article 11, Article 29, or Part II of this Convention, that allows a contract of sale or its modification or termination by agreement or any offer, acceptance, or other indication of intention to be made in any form other than in writing, does not apply where any party has his place of business in that State.

Article 97

1   Declarations made under this Convention at the time of signature are subject to confirmation upon ratification, acceptance or approval.

2   Declarations and confirmations of declarations are to be in writing and be formally notified to the depositary.

3   A declaration takes effect simultaneously with the entry into force of this Convention in respect of the State concerned. However, a declaration of which the depositary receives formal notification after such entry into force takes effect on the first day of the month following the expiration of six months after the date of its receipt by the depositary. Reciprocal unilateral declarations under Article 94 take effect on the first day of the month following the expiration of six months after the receipt of the latest declaration by the depositary.

4   Any State which makes a declaration under this Convention may withdraw it at any time by a formal notification in writing addressed to the depositary. Such withdrawal is to take effect on the first day of the month following the expiration of six months after the date of the receipt of the notification by the depositary.

5   A withdrawal of a declaration made under Article 94 renders inoperative, as from the date on which the withdrawal takes effect, any reciprocal declaration made by another State under that article.

Article 98

No reservations are permitted except those expressly authorised in this Convention.

Article 99

1   This Convention enters into force, subject to the provisions of para (a) of this article, on the first day of the month following the expiration of 12 months after the date of deposit of the tenth instrument of ratification, acceptance, approval or accession, including an instrument which contains a declaration made under Article 92.

2   When a State ratifies, accepts, approves or accedes to this Convention after the deposit of the tenth instrument of ratification, acceptance, approval or accession, this Convention, with the exception of the part excluded, enters into force in respect of that State, subject to the provisions of para (6) of this article, on the first day of the month following the expiration of 12 months after the date of the deposit of its instrument of ratification, acceptance, approval or accession.

3   A State which ratifies, accepts, approves or accedes to this Convention and is a party to either or both the Convention relating to a Uniform Law on the Formation of Contracts for the International Sale of Goods done at The Hague on 1 July 1964 (1964 Hague Formation Convention) and the Convention relating to a Uniform Law on the International Sale of Goods done at The Hague on 1 July 1964 (1964 Hague Sales Convention) shall at the same time denounce, as the case may be, either or both the 1964 Hague Sales Convention and the 1964 Hague Formation Convention by notifying the government of the Netherlands to that effect.

4   A State party to the 1964 Hague Sales Convention which ratifies, accepts, approves or accedes to the present Convention and declares or has declared under Article 93 that it will not be bound by Part II of this Convention shall at the time of ratification, acceptance, approval or accession denounce the 1964 Hague Sales Convention by notifying the government of the Netherlands to that effect.

5   A State party to the 1964 Hague Formation Convention which ratifies, accepts, approves or accedes to the present Convention and declares or has declared under Article 92 that it will not be bound by Part III of this Convention shall at the time of ratification, acceptance, approval or accession denounce the 1964 Hague Formation Convention by notifying the government of the Netherlands to that effect.

6   For the purpose of this article, ratifications, acceptances, approvals and accessions in respect of this Convention by States parties to the 1964 Hague Formation Convention or to the 1964 Hague Sales Convention shall not be effective until such denunciations as may be required on the part of those States in respect of the latter two conventions have themselves become effective. The depositary of this Convention shall consult with the

government of the Netherlands, as the depositary of the 1964 conventions, so as to ensure necessary co-ordination in this respect.

Article 100

1   This Convention applies to the formation of a contract only when the proposal for concluding the contract is made on or after the date when the Convention enters into force in respect of the Contracting States referred to in sub-para (1)(a) or the Contracting State referred to in sub-para (1)(b) of Article 1.

2   This Convention applies only to contracts concluded on or after the date when the Convention enters into force in respect of the Contracting States referred to in sub-para (1)(a) or the Contracting State referred to in sub-para (1)(b) of Article 1.

Article 101

1   A Contracting State may denounce this Convention, or Part II or Part III of the Convention, by a formal notification in writing addressed to the depositary.

2   The denunciation takes effect on the first day of the month following the expiration of 12 months after the notification is received by the depositary. Where a longer period for the denunciation to take effect is specified in the notification, the denunciation takes effect upon the expiration of such longer period after the notification is received by the depositary.

Done at Vienna, this day of eleventh day of April, one thousand nine hundred and eighty, in a single original, of which the Arabic, Chinese, English, French, Russian and Spanish texts are equally authentic.

In witness whereof the undersigned plenipotentiaries, being duly authorised by their respective governments, have signed this Convention.

CONVENTION ON THE LAW APPLICABLE TO CONTRACTS FOR THE INTERNATIONAL SALE OF GOODS – THE HAGUE, 22 DECEMBER 1986

The Convention has not yet entered into force.

The Convention was intended to replace the Hague Convention on the law applicable to international sales of goods, concluded on 15 June 1955. The genesis of the effort to revise the 1955 Convention is due to the completion of the Vienna Convention drafted under the auspices of the UNCITRAL. Accordingly, pursuant to a decision made by the 14th session of the Hague Conference on Private International Law in 1980, all UNCITRAL Member States, not Members of the Hague Conference, were invited to participate in the preparatory work of the present Convention.

See, Pelichet, M, *Report on the Law Applicable to International Sales of Goods*, The Hague Conference on Private International Law, preliminary document no 1, September 1982; see also *Law Applicable to Contracts for the International Sale of Goods*, draft Convention adopted by the special commission and report, written by von Mehren, AT, preliminary document no 4, August 1984 for the attention of the diplomatic conference of October 1985.

Convention on the Law Applicable to Contracts for the International Sale of Goods

The States Parties to the Present Conventions,

Desiring to unify the choice of law rules relating to contracts for the international sale of goods,

Bearing in mind the United Nations Convention on Contracts for the International Sale of Goods, concluded at Vienna on 11 April 1980,

Have agreed upon the following provisions:

CHAPTER 1 – SCOPE OF THE CONVENTION

Article 1

This Convention determines the law applicable to contracts of sale of goods:

(a) between parties having their places of business in different States;

(b) in all other cases involving a choice between the laws of different States, unless such a choice arises solely from a stipulation by the parties as to the applicable law, even if accompanied by a choice of court or arbitration.

Article 2

The Convention does not apply to:

(a) sales by way of execution or otherwise by authority of law;

(b) sales of stocks, shares, investment securities, negotiable instruments or money; it does, however, apply to the sale of goods based on documents;

(c) sales of goods bought for personal, family or household use; it does, however, apply if the seller at the time of the conclusion of the contract neither knew nor ought to leave known that the goods were bought for any such use.

Article 3

For the purposes of the Convention, 'goods' includes:

(a) ships, vessels, boats, hovercraft and aircraft;

(b) electricity.

Article 4

1   Contracts for the supply of goods to be manufacturers or produced are to be considered contracts of sale unless the party who orders the goods undertakes to supply a substantial part of the materials necessary for such manufacture or production.

2   Contracts in which the preponderant part of the obligations of the party who furnishes goods consists of the supply of labour or other services are not to be considered contracts of sale.

Article 5

The Convention does not determine the law applicable to:

(a) the capacity of the parties or the consequences of nullity or invalidity of the contract resulting from the incapacity of a party;

(b) the question whether an agent is able to bind a principal, or an organ to bind a company or body corporate or unincorporate;

(c) the transfer of ownership; nevertheless, the issues specifically mentioned in Article 12 are governed by the law applicable to the contract under the Convention;

(d) the effect of the sale in respect of any person other than the parties;

(e) agreements on arbitration or on clerics of court, even if such an agreement is embodied in the contract of sale.

Article 6

The law determined under the Convention applies whether or not it is the law of a Contracting State.

CHAPTER 2 – APPLICABLE LAW

Section 1 – Determination of the applicable law

Article 7

1   A contract of sale is governed by the law chosen by the parties. The parties' agreement on this choice must express or be clearly demonstrated by the terms of the contract and the conduct of the parties, viewed in their entirety. Such a choice may be limited to a part of the contract.

2 The parties may at any time agree to subject the contract in whole or in part to a law other that which previously governed it, whether or not the law previously governing the contract was chosen by the parties. Any change by the parties of the applicable law made after the conclusion of the contract does not prejudice its formal validity or the rights of the third parties.

Article 8

1 To the extent that the law applicable to a contract of sale has not been chosen by the parties in accordance with Article 7, the contract is governed by the law of the State where the seller has his place of business at the time of conclusion of the contract.

2 However, the contract is governed by the law of the State where the buyer has his place of business at the time of conclusion of the contract, if:

   (a) negotiations were conducted, and the contract concluded by and in the presence of the parties, in that State; or

   (b) the contract provides expressly that the seller must perform his obligation to deliver the goods in that State; or

   (c) the contract was concluded on terms determined mainly by the buyer and in response to an invitation directed by the buyer to persons invited to bid (a call for tenders).

3 By way of exception, where, in the light of the circumstances as a whole, for instance, any business relations between the parties, the contract is manifestly more closely connected with a law which is not the law which would otherwise be applicable to the contract under paras 1 or 2 of this article, the contract is governed by that other law.

4 Paragraph 3 does not apply if, at the time of the conclusion of the contract, the seller and the buyer have their places of business in States having made due reservation under Article 21, para 1, sub-para (b).

5 Paragraph 3 does not apply in respect of issues regulated in the United Nations Conventions on contracts for the International Sale of Goods (Vienna, 11 April 1980) where, at the time of the conclusion of the contract, the seller and the buyer have their places of business in different States both of which are parties to that Convention.

Article 9

A sale by auction or on a commodity or other exchange is governed by the law chosen by the parties in accordance with Article 7 to the extent to which the law of the State where the auction takes place or the exchange is located does not prohibit such choice. Failing a choice by the parties or to the extent that such choice is prohibited, the law of the State where the auction takes place or the exchange is located shall apply.

Article 10

1 Issues concerning the existence and material validity of the consent of the parties as to the choice of the applicable law are determined where the choice satisfies the requirements of Article 7, by the law chosen. If under that law the choice is invalid the law governing the contract is determined under Article 8.

2 The existence and material validity of a contract of sale or of any term thereof are determined by the law which under the Convention would govern the contract or term if it were valid.

3 Nevertheless, to establish that he did not consent to the choice of law to the contract itself or to any term thereof, a party may rely on the law of the State where he has his place of business if in the circumstances it is not reasonable to determine that issue under the law specified in the preceding paragraphs.

Article 11

1 A contract of sale concluded between persons who are in the same State is formally valid if it satisfies the requirements either of the law which governs it under the Convention or of the law of the State where it is concluded.

2 A contract of sale concluded between persons who are in different States is formally valid if it satisfies the requirements either of the law which governs it under the Convention or of the law of one of those States.

3   Where the contract is concluded by an agent, the State in which the agent acts is the relevant State for the purposes of the preceding paragraphs.

4   An act intended to have legal effect relating to an existing or contemplated contract of sale is formally valid if it satisfies the requirements either of the law which under the Convention governs or would govern the contract or of the law of the State where the act was done.

5   The Convention does not apply to the formal validity of a contract of sale where one of the parties to the contract has, at the time of its conclusion, his place of business in a State which has made the reservation provided for in Article 21, para 1, sub-para (c).

Section 2 – Scope of the applicable law

Article 12

The law applicable to a contract of sale by virtue of Articles 7, 8 or 9 governs in particular:

(a) interpretation of the contract;

(b) the rights and obligations of the parties and performance of the contract;

(c) the time at which the buyer becomes entitled to the products, fruits and income deriving from the goods;

(d) the time from which the buyer bears the risk with respect to the goods;

(e) the validity and effect as between the parties of clauses reserving title to the goods;

(f) the consequences of non-performance of the contract, including the categories of loss for which compensation may be recovered, but without prejudice to the procedural law of the forum;

(g) the various ways of extinguishing obligations, as well as prescription and limitation of actions;

(h) the consequences of nullity or invalidity of the contract.

Article 13

In the absence of all express clauses to the contrary, the law of the State where inspection of the goods takes place applies to the modalities and procedural requirements for such inspection.

CHAPTER 3 – GENERAL PROVISIONS

Article 14

1   If a party has more than one place of business, the relevant place of business is that which has the closest relationship to the contract and its performance, having regard to the circumstances known to or contemplated by the parties at any time before or at the conclusion of the contract.

2   If a party does not have a place of business, reference is to be made to his habitual residence.

Article 15

In the Convention, 'law' means the law in force in a State other than its choice of law rules.

Article 16

In the interpretation of the Convention, regard is to be held to its international character and to the need to promote uniformity in its application.

Article 17

The Convention does not prevent the application of those provisions of the law of the forum that must be applied irrespective of the law that otherwise governs the contract.

Article 18

The application of a law determined by the Convention may be refused only where such application would be manifestly incompatible with public policy (*ordre public*).

Article 19

For the purpose of identifying the law applicable under the Convention, where a State comprises several territorial units each of which has its own system of law or its own rules of law in respect of contracts for the sale of goods, any reference to the law of that State is to be construed as referring to the law in force in the territorial unit in question.

Article 20

A State within which different territorial units have their own systems of law or their own rules of law in respect of contracts of sale is not bound to apply the Convention to conflicts between the laws in force in such units.

Article 21

1 Any State may, at the time of signature, ratification, acceptance, approval or accession make any of the following reservations:

(a) that it will not apply the Convention in the cases covered by sub-para (b) of Article 1;

(b) that it will not apply para 3 of Article 8, except where neither party to the contract has his place of business in a State which has made a reservation provided for under this sub-paragraph;

(c) that, for cases where its legislation requires contracts of sale to be concluded in or evidenced by writing, it will not apply the Convention to the formal validity of the contract, where any party has his place of business in its territory at the time of conclusion of the contract;

(d) that it will not apply sub-paragraph of Article 12 in so far as that sub-paragraph relates to prescription and limitation of actions.

2 No other reservation shall be permitted.

3 Any Contracting State may at any time withdraw a reservation which it has made; the reservation shall cease to have effect on the first day of the month following the expiration of three months after notification of the withdrawal.

Article 22

1 This Convention does not prevail over any Convention or other international agreement which has been or may be entered into and which contains provisions determining the law applicable to contracts of sale, provided that such instrument applies only if the seller and buyer have their places of business in States parties to that instrument.

2 This Convention does not prevail over any international Convention to which a Contracting State is, or becomes, a party, regulating the choice of law in regard to any particular category of contracts of sale within the scope of this Convention.

Article 23

This Convention does not prejudice the application:

(a) of the United Nations Conventions on Contracts for the International Sale of Goods (Vienna, 11 April 1980);

(b) of the Conventions on the Limitation Period in the International Sale of Goods (New York, 14 June 1974), or the Protocol amending that Convention (Vienna, 11 April 1980).

Article 24

The Convention applies in a Contracting State to contracts of sale concluded after its entry into force for that State.

CHAPTER 4 – FINAL CLAUSES

Article 25

1 The Convention is open for signature by all States.

2 The Convention is subject to ratification, acceptance or approval by the signatory States.

3   The Convention is open for accession by all States which are not signatory States as from the date it is open for signature.

4   Instruments of ratification, acceptance, approval and accession shall be deposited with the Ministry of Foreign Affairs of the Kingdom of the Netherlands, depositary of the Convention.

Article 26

1   If a State has two or more territorial units in which different systems of law are applicable in relation to matters dealt with in this Convention, it may at the time of signature, ratification, acceptance, approval or accession declare that this Convention shall extend to all its territorial units or only to one or more of them and may modify this declaration by submitting another declaration at any time.

2   Any such shall be notified to the depositary and shall state expressly the territorial units to which the Convention applies.

3   If a State makes no declaration under this Article, the Convention is to extend to all territorial units of that State.

Article 27

1   The Convention shall enter into force on the first day of the month following the expiration of three months after the deposit of the fifth instrument of ratification, acceptance, approval or accession referred to in Article 25.

2   Thereafter the Convention shall enter into force:

   (a) for each State ratifying, accepting, approving or acceding to it subsequently, on the first day of the month following the expiration of three months after the deposit of its instrument of ratification, acceptance, approval or accession; for a territorial unit to which the Convention has been extended in conformity with Article 26 on the first day of the month following the expiration of three months after the notification referred to in that article.

Article 28

For each State party to the Convention on the Law Applicable to International Sales of Goods, done at The Hague on 15 June 1955, which has consented to be bound by this Convention and for which this Convention is in force, this Convention shall replace the said Convention of 1955.

Article 29

Any State which becomes a party to this Convention after the entry into force of an instrument revising it shall be considered to be a party to the Convention as revised.

Article 30

1   A State party to this Convention may denounce it by a notification in writing addressed to the depositary.

2   The denunciation takes effect on the first day of the month following the expiration of three months after the notification is received by the depositary. Where a longer period for the denunciation to take effect is specified in the notification, the denunciation takes effect upon the expiration of such longer period after the notification is received by the depositary.

Article 31

The depositary shall notify the State Members of the League Conference on Private International Law and the States which have signed, ratified, accepted, approved or acceded in accordance with Article 25, of the following:

   (a) the signatures and ratifications, acceptances, approvals and accessions referred to in Article 25;

   (b) the date on which the Convention enters into force in accordance with Article 27;

   (c) the declarations referred to in Article 26;

   (d) the reservations and the withdrawals of reservations referred to in Article 21;

   (e) the denunciations referred to in Article 30.

In witness whereof the undersigned, being duly authorised thereto, have signed this Convention.

Done at The Hague, on the twenty-second day of December 1986, in the English and French languages, both texts being equally authentic, in a single copy which shall be deposited in the archives of the government of the Kingdom of the Netherlands, and of which a certified copy shall be sent, through diplomatic channels, to each of the State Members of the Hague Conference on Private International Law as of the date of its extraordinary session of October 1985, and to each State which participated in that session.

THE UNIDROIT PRINCIPLES OF INTERNATIONAL COMMERCIAL CONTRACTS, THE PRINCIPLES OF EUROPEAN CONTRACT LAW AND THE *LEX MERCATORIA*

INTRODUCTION

It is undoubtedly true that the effort to unify and harmonise rules of international trade law has been slow. Only during the last couple of decades has there been a noticeable and measurable impetus to enhance transnational transactions by adopting harmonised rules.[1] This is particularly surprising when one realises that uniform international trade rules benefit countries and their citizens both economically and politically.[2] Perhaps the reason for the slow progress is that only since the Second World War has there been a dramatic increase in transnational commerce[3] and a reduction in State protectionism.[4] Even though general principles of international trade law (known as the *lex mercatoria*) have been around since the Middle Ages,[5] it has only been as a result of the more recent work of international and intergovernmental organisations, such as UNCITRAL,[6] UNIDROIT,[7] the Hague Conference,[8] and various private trade associations such as the International Chamber of Commerce,[9] that any documented formulation of uniform international trade rules has evolved.

Perhaps the most significant achievement with regard to the adoption of harmonised rules has been the United Nations Convention on Contracts for the International Sale of Goods (CISG) (1980)[10] to which Australia acceded on 1 April

---

1   See Waincymer, J, 'The internationalisation of Australia's Trade Law' [1995] 17 *Sydney Law Review* 298 at 299.
2   See Waincymer, *ibid* at 301.
3   See Ferrari, F, 'Defining the sphere of the application of the 1994 UNIDROIT Principles Of International Commercial Contracts' [1995] 69 *Tulane Law Review* 1225.
4   See Waincymer, *op cit* at 299.
5   See Pryles, M, Waincymer, J and Davies, M, *International Trade Law – Commentary and Materials*, 1996, Sydney: Law Book Company, p 41.
6   The United Nations Commission on International Trade Law which came into operation on 1 January 1968 and has the aim to further 'the progressive harmonisation and unification of the law of international trade'. See Art 8 of the Statute of UNCITRAL.
7   The International Institute for the Unification of Private International Law was originally established in 1926 and reorganised in 1940.
8   The Hague Conference on Private International Law was established in 1893. However, conferences were not frequently held until after the Second World War. See generally, Lipstein, K, 'One hundred years of Hague Conferences on Private International Law' (1963) 42(3) *International and Comparative Law Qtly* 553.
9   Ie, the ICC.
10 Hereinafter referred to as the 'CISG'. The Hague Conventions of 1964, ie 'The Uniform Law for the International Sale of Goods' and 'The Uniform Law on the formation of Contracts for the International Sale of Goods' were significant achievements but only attracted a few accessions when they came into force in 1972.

1989.[11] In essence, the CISG provides some international uniform rules applicable to the sale of goods, where parties have places of business in States that are Contracting States or when the rules of private international law lead to the application of the law of a Contracting State which is a party to the Convention.[12] However, whilst the CISG is in force in over 60 countries, it nevertheless has a number of limitations. For example, it is confined to the international sale of goods as distinct from other international transactions and fails to deal with issues such as validity and transfer of property. This dilemma necessitates resort to the domestic law of a State chosen by the conflict of law rules of a given forum. This, in turn, can create inconvenience and uncertainty for international traders. For example, one party at least may be unfamiliar with the applicable law, or such law, in itself, may be uncertain or impossible to interpret.

The UNIDROIT Principles of International Commercial Contracts, published by UNIDROIT in 1994, addresses a number of the limitations found in the CISG and, as will be seen, is a restatement of the principles of international trade law relevant to international commercial contracts. The next part of this chapter provides a broad overview of the use and the interpretation of the UNIDROIT Principles. Their status as an international restatement of legal principles will then be discussed followed by an examination of its most important provisions. Where relevant, the Principles will be compared with international conventions such as the CISG so as to emphasise their significance in international trade. The next part of the chapter concerns the Principles of European Contract Law (PECL), which represent another attempt to harmonise contract law. These Principles, in effect, create a blueprint for a common European Code of Contracts for the European Union. The final part of this chapter deals with the development of the *lex mercatoria*, focusing on the central list of *lex mercatoria* principles, rules and standards.

THE UNIDROIT PRINCIPLES

Overview

The UNIDROIT Principles of International Commercial Contracts[13] are the product of some 14 years of work by leading experts in the field of comparative law and international trade law from around the world.[14] The Principles set forth general rules

---

11 See the Sale of Goods (Vienna Convention) Act 1986 (Qld); the Sale of Goods (Vienna Convention) Act 1986 (NSW); the Sale of Goods (Vienna Convention) Act 1986 (SA); the Sale of Goods (Vienna Convention) Act 1986 (WA); the Sale of Goods (Vienna Convention) Act 1987 (Tas); the Sale of Goods (Vienna Convention) Act 1987 (ACT); the Sale of Goods (Vienna Convention) Act 1987 (Vic); the Sale of Goods (Vienna Convention) Act 1987 (Vic); the Sale of Goods (Vienna Convention) Act 1987 (NT). Also note that s 66A of the Trade Practices Act 1974 (Cth) provides that the CISG takes precedence over provisions of the Trade Practices Act 1974 (Cth).

12 See Art 1 of the CISG.

13 Hereinafter referred to as 'the Principles'.

14 See Bonell, MJ, 'Unification of law by non-legislative means: The UNIDROIT Draft Principles For International Commercial Contracts' (1992) 40(3) *American Journal of Comparative Law* 617 at 619 and Furmston, MP, 'UNIDROIT General Principles For International Commercial Contracts' (1996) 10 *Journal of Contract Law* 11 at 19–20 as regards members of the 'working group'.

governing 'international commercial contracts'[15] and, unlike the CISG, the Principles are not confined to the international sale of goods. On the contrary, the Comments to the Preamble[16] suggest that the concept of 'commercial' contracts should be understood as broadly as possible and it has been suggested that the Principles are flexible enough to apply to international service, leasing and licensing agreements as well as finance, banking, insurance and other transactions.[17]

As with the CISG, the Principles only apply to international, as opposed to, domestic agreements.[18] Furthermore, the Principles are, generally speaking, the same as or similar to the relevant CISG provisions.[19] This similarity is due to the fact that the CISG was one of a number of instruments examined by UNIDROIT in drafting the Principles.[20] Because of its broad similarity to the CISG, the Principles may be used to interpret not only the CISG but also to supplement the deficiencies or gaps that appear in the CISG.[21]

Of particular significance to international traders and their lawyers, the UNIDROIT Principles may be incorporated into contracts as if they were the governing law or indeed the terms of the contract[22] subject to any exclusion or modification agreed to by the parties.[23] Furthermore, the Principles may be applied by judges and arbitrators[24] so as to provide a solution to an issue when it proves impossible to establish the relevant rule of the applicable law.[25] In this regard, it has been suggested that they 'probably represent the most accurate description to date of the emerging international consensus about the rules that are most suitable to international trade law'.[26] As will be seen, the Principles may also be applied by arbitrators as the applicable law in adjudicating disputes and making awards. Lastly, as the Principles are in the nature of a restatement of the commercial law of the

---

15 See the Preamble to the Principles.
16 See Comment 2 to the Preamble. The black letter text consisting of Articles is accompanied by Comments and Illustrations so as to assist in the interpretation of the Articles. See van Houtte, H, 'The UNIDROIT Principles of International Commercial Contracts' (1996) *International Trade and Business Annual 1 at 2* and Bonell, *op cit* at 620 as to the use of the Comments and the Illustrations.
17 See Bonell, MJ, *An International Restatement of Contract Law*, 1994, Irvington, New York: Transnational Juris, p 36.
18 See Bonell, *ibid*, pp 32–33.
19 Albeit with some exceptions. See Bonell, *ibid*, p 47; Perillo, JM, 'UNIDROIT Principles of International Commercial Contracts: the black letter text and a review' [1994] 63 *Fordham Law Review* 281 at 282; Garro, AM, 'The gap-filling role of the UNIDROIT Principles in International Sales Law: some comments of the interplay between the Principles and the CISG' [1995] 69 *Tulane Law Review* 1149 at 1189.
20 See Bonell (1994), *op cit*, p 43.
21 See Art 7(1) and 7(2) of the CISG and explanations of such roles in Bonell, *ibid*, pp 110–13 and Garro, *op cit* at 1189. As regards gap filling in codes of law generally, see Kritzer, AH, *International Contract Manual – ICM Guide to UN Conventions*, Deventer and Boston: Kluwer Law and Taxation (loose-leaf) Vol 1 at 83–84.
22 See the Preamble to the Principles.
23 Note, however, that once the Principles are incorporated, some provisions cannot be excluded or modified. See Art 1.5 of the Principles.
24 Though see the discussion below as regards the non-obligatory law status of the Principles.
25 See the Preamble.
26 See Hyland, R, 'On setting forth the law of contract: a foreword' (1992) 40 *American Journal of Comparative Law* 541 at 550.

world,[27] they may additionally serve as a model for national and international legislators.[28]

Before considering the various 120 articles in the Principles, it is apt to note that the Principles cover numerous issues concerning international commercial contracts such as pre-contractual negotiation, formation, validity, interpretation, various aspects of performance, including hardship and *force majeure*, termination and remedial provisions. The Principles basically reflect concepts of contract law to be found in nearly all legal systems of the world.[29]

In interpreting the Principles, Art 1.6(1) stipulates that 'regard is to be had to their international character and to their purposes including the need to promote uniformity in their application'. Accordingly, the various articles must be interpreted in the context of themselves without cognisance or regard to any domestic law meaning or preconceived notions. As further emphasised by Comment 3 to Art 1.6, the articles must not be interpreted in a literal or strict sense but in light of the purposes of the Principles as well as the rationale(s) behind the individual articles. As evident from the Introduction to the UNIDROIT Principles, one purpose is to establish a balanced set of rules for worldwide use 'irrespective of the legal traditions and the economic and political conditions of the countries in which they are to be applied'. Other examples are the various purposes outlined in the Preamble.

In a similar vein, Art 1.6(2) stipulates that issues within the scope of the Principles but not expressly settled are, as far as possible, to be settled in accordance with their underlying general principles. Thus, gaps in the Principles that would ordinarily be addressed by rules on international commercial contracts should be *prima facie* resolved by drawing an analogy with specific articles of the Principles and their rationales.

The UNIDROIT Principles and contract law

Whilst drafted in the style of European Codes and potentially furnishing a valuable source of the *lex mercatoria*,[30] it must, at the outset, be appreciated that the Principles do not have any multinational legislative force even if the Comments to the Preamble state that they 'represent a system of rules of contract law'.[31]

As stated by Art 1.4 of the Principles: 'Nothing in these Principles shall restrict the application of mandatory rules, whether of national, international or supranational origin, which are applicable in accordance with the relevant rules of private international law.' Hence, the proper law that strictly speaking governs an international commercial contract will be determined by the rules of private international law of a particular forum, or in the case of sale of goods, the Hague Convention of the Law Applicable to Contracts for the International Sale of Goods

---

27   See Perillo, *op cit*, p 283.
28   See the Preamble to the Principles.
29   See Bonell, *op cit*, p 42.
30   See Pryles, Waincymer and Davies, *op cit*, p 41. Also see Mustill, MJ, 'The New *Lex mercatoria*: The first 25 years' (1988) 4 *Arbitration International* 86 where the concept of *lex mercatoria* is examined.
31   See the Comment to Preamble 4a.

(1986).[32] Generally speaking, the rules of private international law of most countries enable application of the domestic law of a State expressly or inferentially chosen by the parties[33] or the system of law with which the transaction has its closest and most real connection.[34] Alternatively, an international convention such as the CISG may be directly or indirectly applicable to the contract if it concerns the international sale of goods and other threshold requirements are satisfied.[35]

Whilst the courts of some forums have given limited recognition to general principles of international trade law,[36] it will normally be the case that judges are obliged to apply the proper law, as determined by rules of private international law or an applicable convention, even if parties have expressly agreed that the Principles are to govern their contract.[37] However, as suggested by the Preamble to the Principles, judges could use the Principles to assist in the interpretation of international uniform law instruments and also use the Principles to provide a solution to an issue raised when it proves impossible to establish the relevant rule of the applicable law where, for example, the law of a given State is obscure, underdeveloped or simply difficult to ascertain.[38]

Because of the increased use of arbitration and the fact that in most countries arbitrators are able to apply general principles of international commercial law,[39] the Principles will be of great benefit to parties who stipulate in their agreement that any dispute or claim arising out of or in connection with the contract shall be referred to arbitration and that the Principles shall be incorporated in and govern the contract, its interpretation and performance.[40] Arbitration is generally more attractive to international traders than court forums because it is usually less expensive than litigation and provides a speedier resolution of the conflict with confidentiality being maintained. Arbitrators may find the Principles to be a highly attractive choice of law,

---

32 Note, however, that Australia has not as yet adopted the Hague Convention.

33 As is the case, generally speaking, in Australia provided the selection of law is *bona fide* see: *Golden Acres Ltd v Qld States Pty Ltd* [1969] Qd R 378 and *Vita Food Products Inc v Unus Ship Co Ltd* [1937] AC 277 at 290–92.

34 As is the position generally in Australia under rules of private international law: see *Mendelson – Zeller Co Inc v TC Providores Pty Ltd* [1981] 1 NSWLR 566.

35 See Art 1 of the CISG and note Art 95 as to the applicability of the CISG.

36 At least in upholding the validity of arbitration awards based on the *lex mercatoria* see Ferrari, *op cit* at 1231. Also see Kirby, P in *Brown Boveri (Australia) Pty Ltd v Baltic Shipping Co (The Nadezhda Krupskaya)* [1989] 1 Lloyd's Rep 518 where principles of international trade law concerning transport rules were used to assist in interpretation.

37 See Luiz, OB, 'The UNIDROIT Principles for International Commercial Law Project: aspects of international private law' [1995] 69 *Tulane Law Review* 1209 at 1220.

38 See Perillo, *op cit* at 281.

39 See Furmston, *op cit* at 12. Also see *Channel Tunnel Group Ltd v Balfour Beatty Construction Ltd* [1992] 1 QB 656; [1993] AC 334.

40 See the recommended model clause as proposed by Brazil, P, 'UNIDROIT Principles of international commercial contracts in the context of international commercial arbitration', October 1994, paper presented at the 25th Biennial Conference of the International Bar Association, Melbourne, as extracted in Bonell, *op cit*, p 124. As regards organisations available to do arbitration and model arbitration rules, see generally Waincymer, *op cit* at 315–16.

and therefore use them in making awards because they provide an equitable solution to nearly all issues that could possibly arise in international commercial contracts.[41]

Pre-contractual negotiations

The requirement of Art 1.7 that each party must act in accordance with 'good faith and fair dealing in international trade'[42] not only applies during the life of a contract but also during pre-contractual negotiations. Such requirements in conducting negotiations generally reflect the civil law.[43] They can be contrasted with Australian or English law in that the common law does not require that negotiations be conducted in good faith where no lawyers are involved.[44]

Whilst Art 2.15(1) provides that a party is free to negotiate and is not liable for failure to reach an agreement, Art 2.15(2) nevertheless makes a party liable for losses caused to another party where the first party negotiates or breaks off negotiations in bad faith. It is bad faith, in particular, for a party to enter into or to continue negotiations when intending not to reach an agreement.[45] The Principles, therefore, censure a party who negotiates without ever intending to reach an agreement, or who initially acts *bona fide* but subsequently continues negotiations without an intention to reach an agreement. It would appear, however, that the Principles do not apply to parallel negotiations where a party also engages in negotiations with a third party where only one agreement can result.[46]

A party in breach of Art 2.15(2) is liable for 'losses caused' to the other party, though liability does not extend to lost profit which could have been made if the negotiations had not been aborted.[47] Liability would extend to expenses such as legal fees, travel expenses, translation costs and other costs arising out of the negotiations.[48] Indeed, it also has been suggested that liability may extend to the innocent party's loss of an opportunity to conclude another contract with a third party as a result of the bad faith negotiations.[49] The Principles also impose a duty not to disclose confidential information or use it improperly for a party's own purposes when such is obtained in the course of negotiations, regardless of whether a contract is subsequently concluded.[50]

Compensation for breach of confidentiality may include compensation reflecting the benefit received by the other party.[51] Compensation may also include

---

41 Arbitrators generally consider the most relevant law to be that which affords a fair or equitable solution. See Baptista, *op cit* at 1223.
42 See Art 1.7(1). Also see Art 1.7(2).
43 See van Houtte, *op cit* at 4 and Bonell (1994), *op cit*, p 80.
44 See Lord Acker in *Walfort v Miles* [1979] 2 WLR 174 and van Houtte, *op cit* at 4.
45 See Art 2.15(3).
46 See van Houtte, *op cit* at 5 and *Mine v Guinea* (1989) Yb Conn Arb, 82–87, as an example of the application of French law concerning bad faith in negotiations.
47 See Art 2.15, Comment 2.
48 van Houtte, *op cit* at 6.
49 See van Houtte, *ibid* at 6.
50 See Art 2.16.
51 See Art 2.16.

compensation for the loss suffered by the breach or for the benefit received by disclosing information to third parties.[52]

Lastly, it should be noted that even if a contract is concluded, it may be avoided where a fraudulent representation or non-disclosure occurred during the negotiation phase.[53]

Formation

The Principles generally reflect the CISG provisions concerning the formation of a contract[54] and both documents embody the concept of *favor contractus* in that they both have the aim of preserving a contract wherever possible. The Principles, however, go further than the CISG by providing in Art 2.1 that a contract may be concluded not only by the acceptance of an offer but also by the conduct of parties 'that is sufficient to show agreement'. Comment 2 to Art 2.1 explains that the sufficiency of conduct basis of formation reflects commercial practice in that contracts are often concluded after prolonged negotiations without an identifiable sequence of offer and acceptance, particularly in the case of complex transactions.

The Principles, by Art 3.2, provide, *inter alia*, that a contract is concluded by the mere agreement of the parties. Hence, unlike the common law, consideration is not an essential element.[55] An offer is effectively defined as a sufficiently definite proposal before concluding a contract that indicates the offeror's intention to be bound in the case of acceptance.[56]

The Principles provide comprehensive rules similar to the CISG as to the withdrawal of an offer;[57] revocation and irrevocability of a fixed term offer;[58] rejection of an offer;[59] methods of acceptance;[60] time for acceptance;[61] calculation of time for acceptance;[62] late acceptance and unavoidable delay in acceptance;[63] withdrawal of acceptance[64] and modified acceptance.[65]

The Principles, unlike the CISG, also provide for the situation where one party, after the conclusion of a contract, sends the other a writing that purportedly confirms

---

52 See Comment 3 to Art 2.16 and van Houtte, *op cit* at 6.
53 See Art 3.8.
54 Eg, compare Art 14(1) CISG and Art 2.2 of the Principles as to the definition of offer; also see Art 3.2 of the Principles; Art 15(1) of the CISG and Art 2.3(1) of the Principles as to effective offers; Art 2.3(2) of the Principles as to withdrawal of offer; Art 16 of the CISG and Art 2.4 as to revocation of offer; Art 17 of the CISG and Art 2.5 as to rejection of offer; Art 18 of the CISG and Art 2.6 as to the mode of acceptance.
55 Article 3.2 appears in Ch 3 concerning validity, however, it is appropriate to mention the Article at this juncture. Also see Art 5.7 as to determination of price.
56 See Art 2.2 of the Principles.
57 See Art 2.3, which reflects Art 15 of the CISG.
58 See Art 2.4, which reflects Art 16 of the CISG.
59 See Art 2.5, which is similar to Art 17 of the CISG.
60 See Art 2.6, which, in substance, reflects Art 18 of the CISG.
61 See Art 2.7, which is similar to Art 18(2) of the CISG.
62 See Art 2.8, which reflects Art 20 of the CISG.
63 See Art 2.9, which reflects Art 21 of the CISG.
64 See Art 2.10, which reflects Art 22 of the CISG.
65 See Art 2.11, which generally reflects Art 19(1), 19(2) though not 19(3) of the CISG.

the contract but in reality contains additional or different terms. In such a situation, Art 2.12 provides that such terms become part of the contract unless they materially alter the contract or the recipient of the writing, without undue delay, objects to the discrepancy.

Article 2.3 provides that no contract is concluded where, during negotiations, one party insists that the contract is not concluded until there is agreement on specific matters or in a specific form. On the other hand, a contract will result where parties intend to conclude a contract but intentionally leave a term to be agreed upon in further negotiations or to be determined by a third party.[66] The contract remains unaffected where no subsequent agreement on the term or no third party determination results, provided there is an alternative reasonable means of rendering the term in question definite having regard to the intention of the parties.[67]

The 'battle of the forms' dilemma, where either or both the parties use pre-printed standard business forms, receives innovative and sound treatment in the Principles.[68] Article 2.19(2) defines standard terms as 'provisions which are prepared in advance for general and repeated use by one party and which are actually used without negotiation with the other party'. Article 2.19(1) provides the general rule that where one party or both parties use standard terms in concluding a contract, the general rules of formation apply, subject to Arts 2.20–2.22.

Article 2.20(1) addresses 'surprising terms' and provides that no term contained in standard terms which is of such a character that the other party could not reasonably have expected it, is effective unless it has been expressly accepted by that party. By Art 2.20(2), regard is to be had to the content of a term, language and presentation in determining whether the term is a 'surprising term'. Article 2.21 however, provides that, in a case of conflict between a standard term and a term that is not a standard term, the latter prevails.

Probably the most significant rule is the Art 2.22 'knockout rule' which provides that if both parties use standard terms and reach agreement except on those terms, a contract is concluded on the basis of the agreed terms and any standard terms which are common in substance, unless one party clearly indicates in advance, or later and without undue delay informs the other party, that it does not intend to be bound by such a contract. As indicated by Comment 3 to Art 2.22, a party's assertion in advance of formation not to be bound by such standard terms should be made in a document separate to any standard term form.

Article 2.22 departs from the typical common law starting point of analysing the battle of the forms dilemma by using the 'offer-counter-offer-acceptance approach'.[69] Article 2.22 possibly provides a better approach because, as explained in Comment 3 to Art 2.22, parties often exchange pre-printed standard term forms where the terms are on the reverse side and the parties pay no attention to the terms.[70]

---

66 See Art 2.14(1).

67 See Art 2.14(2).

68 See Perillo, *op cit* at 288. Also note that no such provisions appear in the CISG.

69 See, for example, *Butler Machine Tool Co Ltd v Ex-Cell-O Corporation (England) Ltd* [1979] 1 WLR 401, where a standard order form sent in response to the seller's standard order form, but containing significantly different terms, was construed as a counter offer which was then accepted by the seller's subsequent response.

70 Also see Bonell (1994), *op cit*, p 72.

Validity

Chapter 3 of the Principles deals with validity addresses, mistake of fact or law,[71] fraud,[72] duress[73] and gross disparity.[74] The provisions in this Chapter are mandatory except in so far as they relate to the binding force of a mere agreement, initial impossibility or mistake.[75]

An innocent party may avoid a contract if grounds of invalidity exist by giving notification of avoidance[76] in accordance with the notice provision[77] within the specified time periods.[78] Avoidance takes effect retroactively,[79] and upon avoidance either party may claim restitution.[80] Because the Principles embody the *favor contractus* concept, the right to avoid may be lost or limited in specified circumstances.

Avoidance of the contract is excluded where a party entitled to avoid the contract expressly or impliedly confirms the contract after the period of time for giving notice of avoidance has begun to run.[81] The right to avoid on the grounds of mistake may be automatically lost if the other party declares itself willing to perform, or performs the contract as it was understood by the party entitled to avoid.[82] A ground of avoidance applicable only to individual terms of a contract only enables a party to exercise the right of avoidance in relation to those terms unless it is unreasonable to uphold the remaining contract.[83]

By Art 3.3, invalidity does not arise by the mere fact that at the time of the conclusion of the contract, performance was impossible or that the party was not entitled to dispose of the assets to which the contract relates. It should be noted, however, that irrespective of whether or not the contract has been avoided, the party who knew or ought to have known of the ground for avoidance is liable for damages.

Unfortunately, the Principles do not address invalidity arising from lack of capacity, authority or issues of immorality or illegality.[84] However, the Principles otherwise outshine the CISG because the CISG avoids validity issues completely.[85] Obviously, the failure of the CISG to address validity makes the Principles attractive to courts or perhaps more particularly, international arbitrators,[86] as they may be used to fill in the gaps in the CISG.

---

71 See Arts 3.14–3.17.
72 See Art 3.8.
73 See Art 3.9.
74 See Art 3.10. Gross disparity is akin to the common law doctrines of unconscionable conduct.
75 See Art 3.19.
76 See Art 3.14.
77 See Art 1.9.
78 See Art 3.15.
79 Without the need for any court declaration. See Garro, *op cit* at 1176.
80 See Art 3.17.
81 See Art 3.12.
82 See Art 3.13.
83 See Art 3.16.
84 See Art 3.1.
85 See Art 4(a) of the CISG. Also see Garro, *op cit* at 1173 who criticises the CISG in this regard.
86 See the previous discussion as to the non-binding effect of the Principles.

Interpretation

Chapter 4 of the Principles also outshines the CISG in that it provides comprehensive rules concerning the interpretation of contracts.[87] The rules concerning interpretation are based on the concept of good faith and fair dealing, and attempt to strike a neutral balance of fairness between the parties.[88]

Article 4.1 of the Principles provides the general rule that a contract shall be interpreted according to the common intention of the parties. If such an intention cannot be established, then it shall be interpreted according to the meaning that reasonable persons would give to it in the same circumstances. The subjective and reasonable persons approaches are also applied in the interpretation of a statement and the party's conduct.[89] In applying the general rules in Arts 4.1 and 4.2, Art 4.3 enables consideration to be given to preliminary negotiations, common trade meanings and usages.[90]

The *contra proferentem* rule, which requires an interpretation of unclear contract terms against the party who supplied them, appears in Chapter 4,[91] and a special rule concerning linguistic discrepancies is also provided.[92] Lastly, Art 4.8 enables an omitted term to be supplied where such a term is important for a determination of the party's rights and duties and the parties have not agreed with respect to the term.[93] None of these latter provisions appear in the CISG.

Content

Chapter 5 on Content deals with express and implied obligations, duties in performing such obligations, co-operation between the parties, quality of performance, price determination and contracts for an indefinite period.

Of particular note are the criteria in Arts 5.4 and 5.5 which help determine the extent to which a party's obligation simply involves a duty to exert its best efforts in performance of an activity, or a duty to achieve a specific result. The best efforts phenomenon, as opposed to the specific result approach, is of French origin and it has been suggested that the UNIDROIT working group thought that the adoption of such a concept would help judges and arbitrators determine liability for breach of contract.[94] As a general rule, it should be noted that Art 5.3 states that each party shall co-operate with the other party when such co-operation may reasonably be expected for the performance of that party's obligation.

---

87 The issue of interpretation is only dealt with in Arts 8 and 9 of the CISG.
88 See Bonell [1992], *op cit* at 84.
89 See Art 4.2.
90 Also note Art 1.8, which provides that parties are generally bound by their own usages or trade usages.
91 See Art 4.6 and also Arts 4.4 to 4.5 and Bonell [1992], *op cit* at 94.
92 See Art 4.7.
93 See Art 4.8.
94 See Garro, *op cit* at 117 and Perillo, *op cit* at 296.

Of particular importance is Art 5.7 which provides criteria as to the determination of price where an agreement is an open price contract.[95] Whilst Art 55 of the CISG provides one basis for price determination, the Principles by Art 5.7 provide a further four bases for price determination. The first rule in Art 5.7, reflecting Art 55 of the CISG, provides that parties are taken to have impliedly made reference to the price generally charged at the time of the conclusion of the contract (that is, formation) for such goods sold under comparable circumstances in the trade concerned, in the absence of any indication to the contrary.

Performance

Chapter 6 concerning performance is sectionalised into 'performance in general' and 'hardship'.[96] The section on performance commences with rules concerning the time of performance[97] and then addresses issues such as partial performance, order of performance, earlier performance and place of performance. As a general rule, each party bears the costs of performance of its obligations.[98]

Article 6.1.6 provides that a party is to perform a monetary obligation at the obligee's place of business. In this regard, it is analogous to Art 57 of the CISG, which requires a buyer to pay at the seller's place of business unless the contract indicates otherwise.

Article 6.1.7(1) enables payment to be made in any form used in the ordinary course of business at the place of payment, and Art 6.1.8(1) reflects commercial reality by enabling payment to be made by a transfer of funds to any of the financial institutions in which the obligee has made it known it has an account, unless the obligee has indicated a particular account. The obligor is discharged once a transfer becomes effective.[99] No similar provisions appear in the CISG.

Unlike the CISG, the Principles also address currency of payment issues;[100] the imputation of payments where an obligor has several debts owing to an obligee;[101] the imputation of non-monetary obligations;[102] duties of a party in obtaining public permissions such as export licences and impossibility of performance, and validity issues that may arise where permission is refused.[103]

The currency of payment provisions make a significant contribution to the resolutions of problems such as the fluctuation of currencies, the non-convertibility of some currencies and the failure of parties to adequately address such issues in a contract. For example, where currency is not expressed, payment must be made in the

---

95   It is not uncommon in international commercial contracts for price to be left undetermined by the parties. See Garro, *op cit* at 1179.

96   Hardship together with *force majeure* are discussed below, 'Hardship and *force majeure*'.

97   See Arts 6.1.1 and 6.1.2 which are consistent with Arts 33 and 34 (seller's obligations) and Arts 57 and 58 (buyer's obligations) of the CISG.

98   See Art 6.1.11.

99   See Art 6.1.8(2).

100 See Arts 6.1.9 and 6.1.10.

101 See Arts 6.1.12 and Perillo, *op cit* at 298.

102 See Art 6.1.13.

103 See Arts 6.1.14–6.1.17. Also see Bonell [1992], *op cit* at 53–54 and, in particular, 118 as regards draft clauses concerning public permission issues.

currency of the place where payment is to be made.[104] As noted above, this will be at the seller or obligee's place of business when the contract does not expressly or impliedly address place of payment.[105]

Where, however, currency is expressed but not as the currency of the place for payment, the monetary obligations may nevertheless still be paid in the currency of the place for payment, unless that currency is not freely convertible or the parties have agreed that payment should be made only in the currency in which the monetary obligations are expressed.[106] However, if it is impossible to make such payment in the expressed currency due, for example, to exchange regulations, then an obligee may require payment in the currency of the place for payment.[107]

Of particular note, Art 6.1.9(3) provides that payment in the currency of the place for payment is to be made according to the applicable rate of exchange prevailing when payment is due. If, however, payment is not made when due, an obligee may require payment according to the applicable rate of exchange prevailing either when payment is due or at the time of actual payment.[108] In such a situation, an obligee could quite legitimately choose the time that yields a more favourable monetary rate of exchange.

Hardship and *force majeure*

The concept of *favor contractus*, reflected expressly[109] and implicitly in the Principles,[110] is again instanced by the hardship provisions[111] and the *force majeure* (impossibility) provision.[112] For example, Art 6.2.1 (the first of the three provisions addressing hardship) stipulates that: 'Where the performance of a contract becomes more onerous for one of the parties, that party is nevertheless bound to perform its obligations subject to the following provisions on hardship.'

Whilst hardship and *force majeure* appear in different chapters, it is appropriate to consider them together as they are related concepts in that *force majeure* applies when performance becomes impossible and hardship occurs when performance becomes much more burdensome, albeit not impossible.[113]

Hardship

Hardship, by definition,[114] arises where the occurrence of events fundamentally alters the equilibrium of the contract, either because the costs of a party's performance have

---

104 See Art 6.1.10.
105 See Art 6.1.6.
106 See Art 6.1.9(1).
107 See Art 6.1.9(2).
108 See Art 6.1.9(4).
109 See Art 1.3, which reflects the maxim *'pacta sunt servanda'*.
110 See Bonell [1992], *op cit* at 65–79.
111 See Arts 6.2.1–6.2.3.
112 See Art 7.1.7 and compare Art 79 of the CISG.
113 See Garro, *op cit* at 1183–184.
114 See Art 6.2.2.

increased or because the value of the performance a party receives has diminished and:

1   the events occur or become known to the disadvantaged party after the conclusion (that is, formation) of the contract;

2   the events could not reasonably have been taken into account by the disadvantaged party at the time of the formation of the contract;

3   the events are beyond the control of the disadvantaged party; and

4   the risk of the events was not assumed by the disadvantaged party.

What amounts to a fundamental alteration of the contractual equilibrium is not defined in the black letter rules.

Comment 2 to Art 6.2.2 initially states: 'Whether an alteration is "fundamental" in a given case will of course depend upon the circumstances.' Fortunately, Comment 2 goes on to state that: 'If, however, the performances are capable of precise measurement in monetary terms, an alteration amounting to 50% or more of the cost or the value of the performance is likely to amount to a "fundamental" alteration.'

It is further indicated in the Comment that the cost of a party's performance may increase because of a dramatic rise in the price of raw materials, or as a result of the introduction of new safety regulations necessitating more expensive production procedures. The value of the performance received by a party may diminish where the market conditions have drastically changed.[115]

Article 6.2.3 provides that, in the case of hardship, the disadvantaged party is entitled to request renegotiation provided the request is made without undue delay and the hardship grounds are indicated. Where renegotiation is unsuccessful, a court or an arbitral tribunal[116] may, if reasonable, terminate the contract at a date and on terms to be fixed or adapt the contract with a view to restoring the equilibrium. As shortly explained, a renegotiation clause combined with a hardship clause should be included in international trade agreements.[117]

The ability to adapt the contract is discretionary and the courts in a given forum may refuse to modify the contract. For example, English and Belgium courts are more likely to refuse adaptation than other legal systems such as Japanese, German and Dutch forums.[118] Arbitrators may be less reluctant than judges to modify a contract whereby it would be wise to have an arbitration clause in any agreement so as to ensure a dispute goes to arbitration.[119] However, arbitrators are nevertheless inclined not to intervene in hardship situations where parties have not specifically included a hardship clause in their contract. This is especially the case where a contract is speculative and the risk of a change in circumstances is higher.[120] The last condition in the definition of hardship, namely that the risk of events must not have been assumed by the disadvantaged party, may be more easy satisfied if a hardship clause specifies what risks are or are not assumed by the parties.

---

115 See Art 6.2.2, Comment 2.
116 See Art 1.10, definition of 'court' which includes an arbitral tribunal.
117 See Bonell (1994), *op cit*, p 75, fn 120 and Perillo, *op cit* at 301.
118 See van Houtte, *op cit* at 17–18.
119 See van Houtte, *ibid* at 18.
120 See van Houtte, *ibid* at 16.

Force majeure

Under the *force majeure* provision,[121] a party's non-performance is excused if the party 'proves that the non-performance was due to an impediment beyond its control and that it could not reasonably be expected to have taken the impediment into account at the time of the conclusion of the contract or to have avoided or overcome it or its consequences.'

The requisite 'impediment' may be temporary[122] and the party seeking invocation of the provision must give notice to the other party of the impediment and the effect on its ability to perform within a reasonable time, otherwise damages liability may arise from non-receipt. Nothing in Art 7.1.7, however, prevents a party from exercising a right to terminate the contract or to withhold performance or request interest on money due.[123]

The *force majeure* provision is reminiscent of the common law doctrine of frustration which, broadly speaking, enables termination when there has been a fundamental or radical change in the surrounding circumstances and in the significance of contractual obligations.[124] However, the Principles are not to be interpreted in accordance with the common law or, for that matter, other notions of law.[125] The *force majeure* provision is in fact much more limited than the common law, whereby parties should include a *force majeure* clause in their contract such as the '*force majeure* (exemption) clause' prepared by the ICC[126] which contains a list of specific events which normally qualify as grounds for relief.[127] A party who cannot satisfy the *force majeure* provision may nevertheless be able to satisfy the less demanding hardship provisions. In this regard, the Principles again outshine the CISG because the CISG does not address hardship.[128]

Non-performance

Non-performance is defined as a failure to perform any of a party's obligations under a contract, including defective performance or late performance.[129] As with the CISG, the Principles strive to preserve a contract wherever possible. Thus, a non-performing

---

121 See Art 7.1.7 and compare Art 79 of the CISG.
122 See Art 7.1.7(2) and van Houtte, *op cit* at 18, as to temporary vis à vis definite impossibility.
123 See Art 7.1.7(4). The provision is clearer than Art 79(5) of the CISG. See Bonell (1994), *op cit*, p 112, fn 21.
124 See *Codelfa Construction Pty Ltd v State Rail Authority of NSW* (1992) 41 ALR 367.
125 See Art 1.6.
126 See Publication No 421.
127 See Bonell (1994), *op cit*, p 119.
128 By way of illustration, assume that the Suez Canal is closed again and the closure is a post-contract event not reasonably contemplated nor a risk assumed by a carrier. The carrier takes a deviation around the Cape of Good Hope which not only results in late performance (which by Art 7.1.1 is 'non-performance'), but also causes the costs of performance to increase in excess of 50% of the initial cost of performance. The *force majeure* provision would not temporarily excuse the carrier because an increase in cost or price appears to be insufficient to constitute *force majeure*. The hardship provisions would, however, arguably apply as *prima facie* the equilibrium of the contract has been fundamentally altered due to the substantial increase in costs of performance.
129 See Art 7.1.1.

party is given an opportunity to cure non-performance[130] and additional time for performance may be granted by an aggrieved party,[131] albeit an aggrieved party in either situation may still claim damages.[132] All other remedies, however, including right of termination, are suspended during the operation period of these provisions.[133]

Section 1 of Chapter 7, also addresses non-performance due to interference by a third party[134] and the withholding of performance where performance is simultaneous or consecutive.[135] The Principles prohibit the invocation of exemption clauses by a party who seeks to limit or exclude liability for non-performance or sanction a substantially different performance,[136] where to do so would be grossly unfair having regard to the purpose of the contract.[137] This latter provision reflects the underlying principle of good faith and fair dealing which is common to most of the articles in the Principles.

Remedies

The Principles, generally speaking, provide remedies found in most legal systems, and in the CISG, where a breach of contract (referred to as non-performance) occurs and is not excused by the Principles. The remedial provisions are addressed in the last three sections of Chapter 7.

Right to performance

Section 2 of Chapter 7 provides for specific performance[138] as a remedy for non-performance of monetary and non-monetary obligations.[139] The right to performance includes, where appropriate, the right to require repair, replacement or other cure of defective performance.[140]

In contrast to the CISG[141] and equitable principles of non-civil law countries, a court has no discretion in decreeing performance. By Art 7.2.4(1), a court does, however, have a discretion to impose a default penalty for non-compliance with a performance order. Such a penalty, which does not exclude any claim for damages, must be paid to the aggrieved party unless mandatory provisions of the law of the given forum provide otherwise.[142]

---

130 See Art 7.1.4, which is similar to Arts 37 and 48 of the CISG.
131 See Art 7.1.5 and compare Art 47 of the CISG, which also embodies the German *Nachfrist* concept of setting a deadline for performance by notice.
132 See Arts 7.1.4(5) and 7.1.5(2) respectively.
133 See Art 7.1.4(2) and (3) and also Art 7.1.5(2) respectively.
134 See Art 7.1.2 and Perillo, *op cit* at 302.
135 See Art 7.1.3.
136 See Art 7.1.6.
137 For further discussion, see Bonell (1994), *op cit*, pp 96–98.
138 Termed a right to performance.
139 See Arts 7.2.1 and 7.2.2 and compare Art 46 of the CISG.
140 See Art 7.2.3.
141 See Art 28 of the CISG.
142 See Art 7.2.4(2).

The right to performance in relation to non-monetary obligations is not available in the extensive list of circumstances outlined in Art 7.2.2, which range from where performance is impossible in law or in fact to where the aggrieved party has been dilatory in requesting performance. The circumstances would ordinarily be viewed by a court or an arbitrator as making specific performance inappropriate or otherwise unfair in any event.[143]

Termination and restitution

Section 3 of Chapter 7 addresses termination for actual or anticipated non-performance. Restitution upon termination is also addressed.

The most important prerequisite enabling termination is that the failure to perform an obligation amounts to a 'fundamental' non-performance.[144] Unlike the CISG,[145] Art 7.3.1(2) provides a non-exclusive list of factors to help determine whether a failure amounts to a fundamental non-performance. Factors range from the substantial deprivation of expected entitlement to a consideration of whether the non-performing party will suffer disproportionate loss if the contract is terminated. In this regard, it can be seen that the provision attempts to strike a fair balance in addressing both party's interests.

A party may also terminate for a clear anticipated fundamental non-performance[146] or where the innocent party reasonably believes that there will be a fundamental non-performance and, despite demand, no adequate assurance of performance is forthcoming within a reasonable period of time.[147]

The right to terminate must be exercised by notice[148] and a party may lose the right to terminate if notification is not given within a reasonable period of time.[149]

Termination releases both parties from their obligations but does not preclude a claim for damages for non-performance or affect any contract condition that addresses settlement of disputes or any other post-termination matter. Accordingly, an arbitration clause would be one such condition that remains unaffected. Lastly, either party may claim restitution upon termination in accordance with Art 7.3.6.[150]

---

143 Also Garro, *op cit* at 1186.
144 See Art 7.3.1.
145 See Art 25.
146 See Art 7.3.3.
147 See Art 7.3.4.
148 See Art 7.3.2 and Art 1.9 concerning 'notice'.
149 See Art 7.3.2.
150 See Art 7.3.6, Comment 2 as to restitution in kind and or money where reasonable. Also see Bonell (1994), *op cit*, p 27.

Damages

Any non-performance,[151] regardless of fault,[152] entitles the aggrieved party to damages either exclusively or in conjunction with any other remedy, unless non-performance has been excused under the Principles.[153]

The aggrieved party is entitled to full compensation for harm sustained as a result of the non-performance[154] provided harm is established with a reasonable degree of certainty.[155] Compensation may be awarded for lost opportunity[156] and, in either case, damages may be assessed in the court's discretion even if damages cannot be established with a sufficient degree of certainty.[157] It can be seen, therefore, that whilst the Principles make every effort to ensure a contract is performed, they also ensure that some avenue of assessment of damages is available in the event of non-performance.[158]

The type of harm compensatable includes any loss suffered or deprivation of gain,[159] as well as non-pecuniary harm, for instance, physical suffering or emotional distress.[160] However, the non-performing party is liable only for harm which it foresaw or could reasonably have foreseen at the time of the conclusion (that is, formation) of the contract as being likely to result from its non-performance.[161]

Where the aggrieved party has terminated the contract and has made a replacement contract, the aggrieved party may recover the difference in price between the respective contracts[162] as well as damages for future harm. Where termination occurs but no replacement contract is formed, the aggrieved party may recover the difference between the contract price and the price current at the time of termination as well as damages for any further harm.[163]

Damages are to be paid in a lump sum or, where appropriate, in instalments that may be indexed.[164] Furthermore, damages are to be assessed either in the currency in

---

151 Defined in Art 7.1.1 as a failure by a party to perform any of its obligations under the contract, including defective or late performance.

152 Contrast the requirement of fault in civil law systems (see Perillo, *op cit* at 308) though the burden of proving non-performance may depend upon whether the obligation is one of best efforts or an obligation to achieve a specific result (see Art 7.4.1, Comment 1 and Arts 5.4 and 5.5. Also see Garro, *op cit* at 1187).

153 Non-performance may be excused, eg, where an exemption clause not offending Art 7.1.6 exists or where *force majeure* arises under Art 7.1.7. See Garro, *op cit* at 1186.

154 See Art 7.4.2(1), which reflects Art 74 of the CISG. Those Articles reflect the common law position, ie the plaintiff is to be put in a position as if the contract had been performed. See *Robinson v Harman* (1848) 1 Ex 850 at 855 *per* Parke B.

155 See Art 7.4.3(1).

156 See Art 7.4.3(2).

157 See Art 7.4.3.

158 Article 7.4.3 may supplement Art 74 of the CISG. See Garro, *op cit* at 1188.

159 See Art 7.4.2(1).

160 See Art 7.4.2(2).

161 See Art 7.4.4, which broadly reflects the common law rule in *Hadley v Baxendale* (1854) 9 Ex 341 at 354.

162 See Art 7.4.5, provided the replacement contract is made within a reasonable time and in a reasonable manner.

163 See Art 7.4.6(1) and Art 7.4.6(2) which define 'current price'.

164 See Art 7.4.10.

which the monetary obligation was expressed or in the currency in which the harm was suffered, whichever is more appropriate.[165] By Art 7.4.10, interest on damages for non-performance of non-monetary obligations accrues as from the time of the non-performance.

A non-performance by way of a failure to pay money by the due time entitles the aggrieved to interest[166] on that sum whether or not the non-payment is excused, together with additional damages if the non-payment caused greater harm.[167]

Mitigation is addressed in terms familiar to all jurisdictions.[168] Unfamiliar to the common law,[169] however, is a concept of contributive harm on the part of the aggrieved party which is incorporated by Art 7.4.7.[170] According to the contributive harm principle, damages shall be reduced to reflect the extent to which an aggrieved party's act or omission, or an event for which the aggrieved party bears the risk, has contributed to the overall harm.[171]

Also unique to common law concepts but reflective of the civil law is Art 7.4.13, which upholds penalty clauses and enables a penalty sum to be reduced to a reasonable amount where it is 'grossly excessive' in comparison to the harm resulting from the non-performance and to other circumstances.[172]

THE PRINCIPLES OF EUROPEAN CONTRACT LAW

Overview

In 1976 Ole Lando, Professor of International and Comparative Commercial Law at the Copenhagen Business School came to realise that 'Europe must move beyond harmonisation in private international law and must prepare for the establishment of a body of uniform contract law'. Based upon this realisation, Lando founded the Commission on European Contract Law (CECL) with the ultimate goal to establish common principles of contract law for the countries of the European Union (EU). The CECL consisted of scholars and lawyers from every Member State in the EU and their goal was to create a comprehensive, uniform blueprint for a future European Civil Code, beginning with contract law. In 1982, the CECL commenced work on the elaboration of the Principles of European Contract law (PECL).

The PECL is divided into three parts, which were developed over the course of 19 years under the guidance of the CECL in a format similar to the American Restatement Second of Contracts. Part I of the PECL was released in the spring of 1995, covering fundamental principles of contract law as well as rules governing performance, non-performance and remedies in case of non-performance. Part II of the

---

165 See Art 7.4.12.
166 See Art 7.4.9(1) and Art 7.4.9(2) as to interest rates. Contrast Art 78 of the CISG.
167 See Art 7.4.9 generally.
168 See Art 7.4.8 and compare Art 77 of the CISG.
169 See Perillo, *op cit* at 310.
170 Compare Art 80 of the CISG.
171 See the Illustrations to Art 7.4.7 and Perillo, *op cit* at 310.
172 See Perillo, *op cit* at 313–14.

PECL was published in 1999 and covered aspects of formation, interpretation, content and validity. Part III of the PECL, released in 2002, deals with the plurality of parties, assignment of claims and debts, set-offs, and prescription.

The PECL is 'soft law', that is, not binding unless it is stated to be the law of the contract in question. Furthermore, the Principles are not connected in any way to any particular national, supranational or international law. Instead the PECL are neutral rules, which may be applied in a wide range of legal situations. The CECL envisages six instances of usage of the Principles: (i) creation of a general system of contract rules for the EU; (ii) usage as a neutral law governing a contract; (iii) application when general principles of law are set as the choice of law for the contract; (iv) a gap filler for contracts which are subject to the CISG or the UNIDROIT Principles; (v) application to contracts between public authorities and private parties; and (vi) relevancy for individuals, organisations and organs of the EU or the European Court of Justice. These situations are not exhaustive of the PECL's usage, but do define their scope reasonably well. In the following sections, the basic characteristics of the Principles are introduced, focusing on their foundations and unusual provisions.

General duties

The PECL are not mandatory as a whole, but do include some general duties, which are mandatory: good faith and fair dealing, and freedom of contract. The principle of good faith and fair dealing is a moral one, which is accepted by honourable men and women in every action they take. Good faith is an integral part of contract law in Europe; many European states have some sort of good faith and fair dealing clause in their national codes or statutes. For example, s 242 of the *Bürgerliches Gesetzbuch* provides that a debtor must perform his duty in accordance with good faith with due regard for commercial practices. This provision 'moralises' the whole of German law and is invoked to set aside unfair terms and creates the obligation of loyalty on the parties. In contrast, English law does not require any such general obligation to act in accordance with good faith, but it does require the existence of good faith called *uberrimae fidei* in specialised relationships such as that of a fiduciary. However, in an increasing number of cases, English courts have interpreted contracts by invoking good faith, thus adding the principle to English jurisprudence. Article 1:201 of the PECL requires that 'Each party must act in accordance with good faith and fair dealing', which is meant to enforce community standards of decency, fairness, and reasonableness in transactions. Article 1:201 is not confined to any specific provisions as it is broader than all the other articles.

The goal of uniformity is enhanced by the PECL in Art 1:102, which deals with freedom of contract. The principle of freedom of contract acknowledges the right of citizens and enterprises to decide with whom they will contract. However, three provisions detailed in the PECL, namely the requirements of good faith and fair dealing, and the mandatory rules established by the PECL, restrict the principle of freedom of contract. The basic principles of good faith and fair dealing, and freedom of contract are integral in establishing any form of harmonised law on contracts. This is essential to secure cross-border transactions, which in turn may lead to greater economic prosperity within the EU.

Formation

The basic requirements of formation of contract are set out in Arts 2:101 to 2:103 of the PECL. These requirements are: the intent of both parties to be legally bound without any further requirement, and the existence of an agreement which is sufficiently definite that it can be enforced or determined under the PECL. A promise may be binding if it is intended by the parties to be binding, even without acceptance by the promisee. Moreover, as the 'without any further requirement' aspect of intent indicates, no consideration is required. The absence of consideration is alien to those within the common law sphere of law, as consideration is required for a valid contract in the UK and the US.

In terms of revocation, Art 2:202 allows revocation if it reaches the offeree before the issuance of acceptance, or in the case of acceptance by conduct, before the contract is completed. However, revocation is deemed ineffective if the offer indicates it is irrevocable, the offer states a fixed time for acceptance, or if it was reasonable for the offeree to rely on the offer as being irrevocable and he has acted upon that reliance. An offer is deemed accepted in any form of statement or conduct so long as it indicates assent to the offer, but silence or inactivity is not to be considered acceptance of the offer. Late acceptance is also considered to be effective so long as the offeror notifies the offeree of his intent to consider it as such. However, an acceptance that states or implies modified terms, which would materially alter the terms of the offer, is to be considered a rejection and a counter offer. But a reply giving definite assent operates as acceptance even if it states or implies additional or different terms, provided there is no material alteration of the terms of the offer; the additional terms then become part of the offer and likewise the contract.

The modern business world has not only brought about mass production of goods and services, but has also led to the development of standardised contracts. Standardised contracts are more detailed and specific than the terms required or implied by law, but at the same time they tend to be one-sided in that they prefer the seller/offeror over the consumer/offeree. Such documents are not necessarily negotiated individually, a problem which the PECL addresses in Art 4:110, which allows avoidance of the contract in situations contrary to good faith and fair dealing, or procedural unfairness.

Validity

The PECL does not deal with contracts, the invalidity of which arises from illegality, immorality or lack of capacity. The CECL is reluctant to establish a common standard in this regard because of the existence of an extraordinary variety of such contracts in the Member States of the EU. The PECL does contain provisions dealing with impossibility, mistake, fraud and deceit. However, it does not adopt a preferred solution in situations where a contract is ineffective when, unbeknownst to the parties, it is impossible to perform because of the absence of the object contracted for or because the seller has no right to sell what he purports to sell. Under the PECL, this situation would fall under mistake, wherein both parties may avoid the contract by termination, as specific performance is impossible. A party may avoid a contract involving a mistake of fact or law which existed at the time of conclusion of the contract if the mistake was caused by information from the other party; the other party knew or should have known of the mistake or the other party knew or should have known that had the mistaken party known, it would not have entered into the contract. However, contracts may not always be avoided for mistake of law or fact: according to Art 4:103(2)(a–b), a party may not avoid the contract if in the circumstances, the mistake was inexcusable; or the risk of the mistake was assumed or in the circumstances should be borne by the party. It occurs frequently that misinformed parties enter into contracts. While freedom of contract would not bind a person to a contract unless that person was informed and specifically consents to the contract, in order to secure transactions the other party should be able to rely upon the contract unless it was conducted in bad faith, took deliberate advantage of the first party or has behaved carelessly. The only exception is fraud because the intention to deceive is deemed sufficient in order to justify avoidance of the contract by the wronged party. A party may avoid a contract when such party has been induced into the contract by the other party's fraudulent representation whether by words or conduct or fraudulent non-disclosure of any information Moreover, the party led astray by incorrect information should be allowed to avoid the contract if the second party either knew that the information was incorrect or was reckless in that it knew it did not know whether it was correct or not; or if it intended to deceive the first party.

Non-performance

In the terminology of the PECL, as well as the UNIDROIT Principles, breach of contract is known as non-performance.[173] Under the PECL, non-performance is defined as: defective performance, failure to provide goods free from rights or claims of third parties, untimely performance or a violation of an accessory duty.[174] Remedies for breach depend on whether the non-performance is excused; the default party must prove that the non-performance was due to an impediment beyond his control and that he could not have foreseen or avoided and overcome the impediment and its consequences.[175] In a situation where the impediment is excused because of an unforeseeable act beyond the control of the defaulting party, the contract will not be eliminated as such, but will give the aggrieved party the right to terminate the contract.[176] A non-performance that is not excused may give the aggrieved party the right to claim performance[177] or damages, the right to withhold his own performance, terminate the contract and/or reduce own performance.[178] The PECL does not give courts discretion to determine whether they will order specific performance, as it will be rendered if applicable, but it cannot be obtained where the performance would cause the obligor unreasonable effort or expense. In the US and England, failure to perform due to impracticability or frustration is equivalent to what the PECL refers to as non-performance.[179]

---

173 See Lando, 'Some features of the law of contracts in the third millennium', at www.cbs.dk/departments/law/staff/ol/commission_on_ecl/literature/lando01.htm.
174 See PECL, Art 8:108, Comment A.
175 See PECL, Art 9:108, Comment B(i).
176 See PECL, Arts 3:101 and 3:108.
177 Monetary damages or specific performance.
178 See PECL, Art 8:101, Comment B(i).
179 See Lando, O, 'Salient Features of the Principles of European Contract Law: A Comparison with the UCC', Fall 2001, 13 *Pace International Law Review* 339–369.

Fundamental non-performance is reason for termination of a contract and thereby releases the aggrieved party from its obligations.[180] According to Art 8:103, non-performance of an obligation is fundamental if: strict compliance with the obligation is an essential aspect of the contract; the non-performance substantially deprives the aggrieved party of what it was entitled to expect (unless the other party could not reasonably foresee the result); or the non-performance is intentional and gives the aggrieved party reason to believe that it cannot rely on the other party's future performance. The PECL allows the parties to determine whether strict compliance is required for performance of the contract, by its terms.[181]

Vis major and hardship

Throughout most of Europe, a party is bound to perform his contractual obligations even if it has become onerous for him to do so; this is the principle of *pacta sunt servanda*.[182] The principle of *rebus sic stantibus* operates as a modification of *pacta sunt servanda* in that it gives total or partial relief in the case of changed circumstances.[183] It is found in two rules within the PECL, *vis major*, which pertains to excuse due to an impediment and 'hardship', which involves merely changed circumstances.[184] The latter, *vis major*, is an exception to the rule and denotes that supervening events have occurred which make the performance of the contract impossible or quasi-impossible.[185] A corollary to *vis major* in French law is called *force majeure*, or 'act of God'. In a case of *vis major*, the defaulting party will be excused for his non-performance only if it can be shown that: his performance has become impossible in law or in fact; the obligor could not reasonably be expected to take the impossibility into account at the time of the conclusion of the contract; and that the impossibility is beyond the control of the obliging party.[186] In such situations, the contract is terminated, as there is no way to modify it so that performance, even late performance, is possible. However, the rule of *vis major* is not mandatory and the contracting parties may determine either stronger or more lenient conditions within their own agreement.[187]

Hardship generally applies to long-term contracts or contracts for a continuous supply of goods when unforeseen events make performance excessively onerous for one party. This provision is more lenient than *vis major* and operates to relieve obligors when the performance has become excessively onerous, but not impossible or quasi-impossible. Article 6:111(1) of the PECL states that a party is bound to perform even if the performance has become more onerous, whether the cost has increased or the value he receives has diminished.[188] However, if performance becomes excessively

---

180 See Lando, *op cit* at 362.
181 See Lando, *op cit* at 363.
182 See Lando, *op cit*.
183 See Lando, *op cit* at 365.
184 See Lando, *op cit*.
185 See PECL, Art 6:111, Comments A and B(i).
186 See Lando, *op cit* at 365–66.
187 See Lando, *op cit* at 366.
188 See Lando, *op cit*.

onerous, the parties are bound to enter into negotiations with the goal of adapting the contract, or may terminate it provided the conditions in Art 6:111(1)(a–c) are established. Those conditions include: unforeseeable or unknown change of circumstances; could not have taken into consideration the change of circumstances at the time of conclusion of the contract; and the risk of the change is not one which the affected party should be required to bear, according to the contract.[189] Like the *vis major* rule, hardship is not a mandatory provision of PECL contracts, but may be inserted into the terms should the parties decide to do so, and may be altered in strength as they wish.

Remedies

When there has been a non-performance, the aggrieved party should be given the greatest possible freedom to choose its remedy to fit its needs, subject only to the requirements of good faith and fair dealing. Whenever an obligation is not performed or non-performance is not excused under Art 8:108, the aggrieved party may resort to the remedy provisions set out in Art 9. Remedies may be cumulated if they are not incompatible, meaning that a party is not deprived of its right to damages by exercising its right to another remedy.[190]

In terms of the incompatibility of remedies, for example, a party cannot claim specific performance and terminate the contract at the same time, nor could a party receiving non-conforming goods exercise its right to reduce its own performance and at the same time terminate the contract.[191] A wronged party may require specific performance, reduction of the price, or may anticipatorily breach the contract.[192] When, prior to performance, it is clear that there will be a fundamental non-performance by a party, the other party may terminate the contract.[193] This right rests on the notion that a contract party cannot reasonably be expected to continue to be bound to a contract wherein the other party cannot or will not perform on time or at all.[194] The other party must be clearly unwilling or unable to perform the obligations set forth in the contract. If there are any doubts as to willingness to perform; the other party's remedy is to demand an assurance of performance.[195] Moreover, the aggrieved party may allow the non-conforming party additional time to complete performance under a *Nachfrist* provision.[196] Such a provision allows additional time to be given to the non-performing party so that it may fulfil its obligations.[197] If, instead of complete performance the performing party fulfils its promise but tenders non-conforming goods, the receiving party has the right to reduce the price.

One aspect of European and civil law that generally confuses common law practitioners is the right to price reduction. This right is described in Art 9:401, which

---

189 See PECL, Art 6:111(1)(a–c).
190 See PECL, Art 8:102.
191 See PECL, Art 8:102, Comments A and B.
192 This is not an exhaustive list.
193 See Arts 9:304 and 8:103 for full definition of fundamental non-performance.
194 See PECL, Art 9:304, Comment A.
195 See PECL, Art 9:304, Comment C.
196 See Lando, *op cit* at 363–64.
197 See PECL, Art 8:106.

states: 'A party which accepts a tender of performance not conforming to the contract may reduce the price, such reduction shall be proportional to the decrease in the value of the performance at the time this was tendered compared to the value it would have had if tendered on time.'[198] Therefore, a party which is entitled to reduce the price, and has already paid a sum which exceeds the reduced price, may recover the excess from the other party.[199] Also, an aggrieved party is entitled to a reduction in the contract price in situations when the other party's compliance is incomplete or otherwise does not conform.[200] This Article was created as an alternative to damages in situations when the aggrieved party accepts non-conforming tender of goods or services. If the aggrieved party has not accepted non-conforming tender, it must pursue restitution in Art 9:307.[201] The reduction in price must be proportionate to the decrease in the value of the performance at the time the non-conforming goods were tendered compared to the value of a conforming tender at that time.[202] In some cases, the value may be directly related to the portion of the contract performed and the price may simply be reduced.[203] A party injured by the non-conforming performance may reduce the price by withholding payment, or if it has already paid, recovering the amount of the price reduction from the non-conforming party.[204] When the aggrieved party reduces the price for non-conforming goods or services, it then cannot claim damages for the reduction in value of the performance tendered compared to the conforming goods or services. However, the party may be entitled to damages for further loss suffered because of the non-conformity according to the provisions of Art 9:501 governing damages.[205]

Assignment

Contractual claims may be sold or assigned for a loan or other type of obligation. An assignment of a claim is a transfer of a right to performance and is often a right to the payment of money.[206] However, there is no transfer of the assignor's interest, and the debtor's rights are not prejudiced by the assignment.[207] The CECL recognised the need to create a supranational rule to allow claims, especially contracts to pay money, to be transferred without the consent of the debtor in order to promote ease in international business transactions. Of course there are risks involved in a transfer without a party's consent; in this case, the risk is one of prejudice to the debtor, manifested in the possibility of serving several creditors rather than just one. Also, there is a general risk to assignees that the claim they were assigned will have been modified without its knowledge in a secret agreement between the debtor and the assignor.[208] Despite the

---

198 See PECL, Art 9:401(1).
199 See PECL, Art 9:401(2).
200 See PECL, Art 9:401, Comment A.
201 See PECL, Art 9:401, Comment A.
202 See PECL, Art 9:401(1).
203 See PECL, Art 9:401, Comment A.
204 See PECL, Art 9:401, Comment C.
205 See PECL, Art 9:401(3), Comment D.
206 See PECL, Art 11:101, Comment A.
207 See *ibid*.
208 See *ibid*.

risks involved in assigning claims, the flexibility allowed by assignment outweighs any risk because it allows the free movement of capital and securities. Moreover, the Article also includes rules on the creation of security rights over claims by methods other than assignments so not to limit the choices available to debtors and creditors.[209]

The general principles of assignment are that contract and future claims are assignable and all claims are assignable in part, the assignor of the claim being liable to the debtor for any increased costs incurred.[210] The debtor's claims under the contract are solely as against the assignor, and because assignments do not release either of the parties to the original agreement, consent is not required.[211] The first effect of assignment between assignor and assignee is transfer to the latter of all the rights to payment or other performance in respect of the assigned claim, with the assignee becoming the new holder of the claim.[212] However, the assignment in itself does not create an obligation on the debtor to perform in favour of the assignee; this obligation is governed by other provisions of the Article including Art 11:304.[213] Assigning a claim also carries with it a transfer of rights to damages and an interest for future non-performance.[214] The assignment will take effect at the time the claim is actually assigned or at a later time agreed upon by both the assignee and assignor.[215] Future claims are allowed and the assignment thereof takes place after the claim comes into existence and upon the date and time of assignment.[216] Upon assignment, the assignor warrants to the assignee that: he has the right to assign the claim; the claim exists and is not burdened by any encumbrances; and that the claim is not subject to another assignment in favour of another assignee.[217] Moreover, the assignor undertakes (warrants) to the assignee that the claim will not be modified without the consent of the assignee unless that modification is provided for within the assignment agreement. Or, if not included in the agreement, that it is a good faith action and not objectionable to the assignee.[218] These warranties exist to ensure that the assignee acquires the benefit of his bargain and are usually restricted to the assignor's rights against the debtor and undertakings (warranties) to perform any further acts necessary to perfect the assignee's title.[219]

The effects of assignment between the assignee and the debtor are enumerated in s 3 of Art 11, and generally deal with cases of contracts under which a prohibited assignment arises and the exceptions thereto. In such cases, the assignment is not effective against the debtor unless: the debtor consents; or the assignee neither knew nor ought to have known of the non-conformity; or the assignment was made under a contract for the future rights for payment of money.[220] A contract containing a no-assignment clause ought to be respected for the good commercial reasons the debtor

---

209 See *ibid.*
210 See *ibid.*
211 See *ibid.*
212 See PECL, Art 11:201, Comment A.
213 See *ibid.*
214 See PECL, Art 11:201, Comment B.
215 See PECL, Art 11:202(1).
216 See PECL, Art 11:202(2).
217 See PECL, Art 11:204(a)(i–iii).
218 See PECL, Art 11:204(b).
219 See PECL, Art 11:204, Comment A.
220 See PECL, Art 11:301(1)(a–c).

elected to include it, such as not wanting to deal with unknown creditors who may be more severe than assignors. Moreover, the debtor may not want to risk overlooking notice of assignment and paying the assignor, in which case might be the possibility of a second payment to the assignee.[221] The general rule is that assignments made in breach of a no-assignment clause are ineffective against the debtor, as his consent is required to recognise the assignment. Aside from the general provision regarding consent, there are often situations when the assignee would not know about the no-assignment clause, as it might be contained in a separate contract, in such cases Art 11:301(b)(1) allows the assignment to have effect as against the debtor when the assignee did not know about the prohibition on assignment.[222] The third exception, assignments of future money claims, is necessary where the assignment relates to a continuing stream of future debts.[223] In such an agreement, it is impossible to expect the inspection of hundreds of contracts in order to ascertain whether they all contain a no-assignment provision. This exception allows the assignment to take effect when it is made under a contract for the future payment of money claims.[224] The ability to transfer rights to performance allows fluidity and ease to transactions effected in the worlds of finance and international trade, and for that reason the presence of balanced rules of assignment is a necessary component of the PECL.

Set-off

Set-off, also known as *compensation*, describes the situation in which something, such as the amount of a debt, may be set-off against something else. For example, if A has the right to be paid $1000 by B, and B has the right to be paid $500 by A, then under set-off B can pay a single payment of $500 and the debtor-creditor situation is resolved.[225] There are four requirements necessary to set-off: mutuality; obligations of the same kind; the cross-claim must be due; and the party declaring set-off must be entitled to perform.[226] To establish mutuality, the parties must be a debtor or a creditor to the other and must be entitled to demand the other party's performance.[227]

Moreover, the obligations must be of the same kind, that is, a money claim may only be set-off by a money claim or securities for securities.[228] In order to effectuate a set-off, the cross-claim must be due, meaning that the claim the party wants to set-off is due to be paid or accepted by the other party.[229] Finally, it is sufficient to establish entitlement to perform, that the person declaring set-off is entitled to effect performance. Furthermore, a party wishing to set-off must notify the other party of this intention and must be entitled to both make and demand payment.[230] The notice need only be informal, unilateral and extrajudicial, but may also be effected

---

221 See PECL, Art 11:301, Comment A.
222 See PECL, Art 11:301, Comment B.
223 See *ibid*.
224 See *ibid*.
225 See *ibid*.
226 See PECL, Art 13:101, Comment B(1–4).
227 See PECL, Art 13:101(a–b).
228 See PECL, Art 13:101, Comment B(2).
229 See PECL, Art 13:101, Comment B(3).
230 See PECL, Survey of Chapters, p xxvii.

by contractual agreement as a default provision if any of the normal requirements for set-off are not met.[231]

If there are multiple claims or obligations, the notice of set-off is only effective if and when it specifically identifies the claim to which it pertains.[232] In order for set-off to be applicable, the claim must be ascertained, or liquid as to its existence or value, unless the set-off will not prejudice the interests of the other party.[233] The full effect of set-off is a discharge of the obligations, so far as they are co-extensive, as from the time of notice. The situations wherein set-off is not possible include: where it is excluded by agreement; when it goes against a claim which is incapable of attachment (as set-off should not deprive a person of minimum subsistence); and against a claim arising from a deliberate unlawful act such as an assault on a debtor by a disappointed creditor.[234] The concept of set-off operates prospectively under the PECL as it is a more straightforward solution than operating under the many national laws wherein set-off operates retrospectively.[235]

Conclusion

The full effect of the PECL will not be seen until the goal of a uniform European Code of Contracts is attained. A common code of contracts is the next logical step to follow European economic unity and general legal harmonisation. A uniform European law of contracts has garnered much attention, both positive and negative, in the community, and will most likely continue to do so. However, if a supranational community such as the EU is to function smoothly on a commercial level, an equally transnational law governing those relationships is required. The Principles are written in natural language, which is clear in meaning and presents a commonsense perspective on such transnational contracts. It contains basic principles of contract that are flexible and allow great freedom in contracting through its provisions concerning assignment, non-performance and set-off. Regardless of its flexibility, the PECL limits a contract by the concrete provisions of good faith and fair dealing, which cannot be excluded or limited.

The PECL, now in its complete three parts, may be used in conjunction with other transnational bodies of law such as the UNIDROIT Principles, the CISG or as basic gap fillers for national law based contracts. Even though the PECL is a 'soft law' concept, its application goes far beyond mere suggestion and may be applied in a wider range of contract situations than Member State law. On an international level, it can be used to correct deficiencies in the other Conventions governing commercial contracts.

It will take time to discover whether Ole Lando's creation of a European Contract Law will become accepted by the community as a blueprint for a European Code. However, the simplicity and common sense of the PECL provides a plan worthy of consideration on a transnational scale.

---

231 See PECL, Art 13:104, Comment B.
232 See PECL, Art 12:105(1).
233 See PECL, Art 13:102(1).
234 See PECL, Art 13:107, Comment C.
235 See *ibid*.

LEX MERCATORIA: A SPECTER OR A REALITY?

International arbitration has become *de rigueur* as a means of resolving international business disputes.[236] Its popularity is most likely due to the neutral nature of arbitration as it does not require the parties to choose a national law to govern the arbitration, but may choose to resolve the situation via national law or the general principles of the *lex mercatoria*.

The exact meaning and even the existence of *lex mercatoria* is highly contested by practitioners as well as by academics. However, its easiest definition is a simple translation of *lex mercatoria* meaning 'merchant law', a general principle of international trade law that has been used for centuries. Furthermore, it is rules or principles of a quasi-legal nature disembodied and detached from any specific jurisdiction or legal system, used often in international arbitration.[237] The concept of *lex mercatoria* has been around since the beginning of civilisation and hit its peak of use during the Middle Ages; but it went largely unused until scholars began to tout its suitability for dealing with international commercial relations soon after the Second World War.[238] *Lex mercatoria*, in modern times, has 'sprung from the soil of international trade as growth not through creation' and likewise has many definitions.[239] One of the more neatly formulated definitions comes from a Scandinavian commentator and is as follows:

> The parties to an international contract sometimes agree not to have their dispute governed by national law. Instead they submit it to the customs and usages of international trade, to the rules of law which are common to all or most of the States engaged in international trade or to those States which are connected with the dispute. Where such common rules are not ascertainable, the arbitrator applies the rule or chooses the solution that appears to him to be the most appropriate and equitable. In doing so he considers the laws of several legal systems. This judicial process, which is partly an application of legal rules and partly a selective and creative process, is here called the application of *lex mercatoria*.[240]

Despite its longevity, the *lex mercatoria* remains a shadowy principle of international law, the definition of which varies, and is contested by both scholars and practitioners. It is a system of laws based on the norms of international trade, in which the norms implicated are not always agreed upon and are constantly changing. It is because of its ever-variable nature that the *lex mercatoria* cannot be concretely described.[241] The circularity involved in defining *lex mercatoria* comes from this international purpose and its use in transnational commercial law as a general principle of law.

Lex mercatoria acts through transnational contracts that may designate the general principles of international trade law to govern the arbitration of disputes.[242] In this

---

236 See Weinberg, KS, 'Equity in international arbitration: how fair is "fair"? A study of *lex mercatoria* and amiable composition' [1994] 12 *BU Int'l LJ* 227.
237 See Highet, K, 'The enigma of the *lex mercatoria*' [1989] 63 *Tulane Law Review* 618.
238 See Maniruzzaman, AFM, 'The *lex mercatoria* and international contracts: a challenge for international commercial arbitration' [1999] 14 *Am U Int'l L Rev 657*, p 658.
239 See *ibid*, p 668.
240 See Highet, *op cit*, p 619.
241 See Weinberg, *op cit*, p 242.
242 See *ibid*.

way, the parties to the contract avoid any of the idiosyncrasies of either state's national laws or judicial systems that would destroy the neutrality of the agreement. In essence, it avoids the application of local law and the nationalisation of the contract, which would benefit the host country over the non-host country.[243] The arbitrator looks to the general principles for rules governing the situation and if there are none, he then applies the rule or solution that seems the most appropriate and equitable.[244]The pool of resources from which the arbitrator draws his solution consists of the laws of many nations; from these he draws the best solution and applies it. This is the application of *lex mercatoria*.[245] This type of arbitration is called *a-national (or transnational) arbitration* because it is not tied to any national order and thereby follows the general principles and his own opinions, which may take into account the attitude of the international commercial community.[246]

The principles of *lex mercatoria* (such as *pacta sunt servanda* and *rebus sic stantibus*) are also designated to be used as gap fillers by both The Hague and Vienna Conventions and the US' Uniform Commercial Code (UCC).[247] Beyond the basic usage of the *lex mercatoria*, the stated governing law of arbitration within a contract, the principle also exists to remove the problem of the search for the proper law to govern the contract or conflict of law. The purpose of conflict of laws rules is to enable the tribunal or arbitrator to accurately identify the national law that governs the contract, a purpose that is antithetical to that of the *lex mercatoria* which promotes the rejection of national law.[248] Furthermore, the *lex mercatoria* provides incredible flexibility in its terms and usage as well as use as gap fillers or additional answers to an arbitrator's questions.[249] However, the strongest argument for the use of *lex mercatoria* in international arbitration is the need of the international business community for systems allowing departure from national rules. This need arises, according to some, because: a national rule might have an unexpected impact on a long-term contract; national legal systems are biased; and national laws are generally meant to apply in the domestic arena, not the international forum.[250] Because of the various uses to which the *lex mercatoria* may be put, it is difficult to numerically list all of its contents but there are some basic, foundational points and some sources of law from whence *lex mercatoria* most likely has emerged.

The contents of the *lex mercatoria* may not be listed out exhaustively; such an inventory is beyond the capability of any scholar. However, the foundations of such an inventory would include a loose grouping of international laws, general trade practices and usages, and general practices as recognised by commercial nations (such as *pacta sunt servanda* and *rebus sic stantibus*, the maxim that unilateral substantial breach is grounds for termination by the other party).[251] These two concepts, *pacta sunt servanda* and substantial breach, appear to be the most concrete representations of the

---

243 See Highet, *op cit*, p 618.
244 See *ibid*, p 619.
245 See *ibid*.
246 See *ibid*.
247 See Weinberg, *op cit*, p 229.
248 See Maniruzzaman, *op cit*, p 680.
249 See Weinberg, *op cit*, p 248.
250 See *ibid*, p 251.
251 See Highet, *op cit*, p 623.

lex mercatoria, as they are universal rules which pertain to commerce.[252] At its base the *lex mercatoria* is customary law, as pertains to trade, without reference to any national law.[253] The sources of *lex mercatoria* are difficult to ascertain but that is merely because the principle has yet to mature and, moreover, because evolution of law is full of shaky circularities and *non sequiturs* on the path to a legal identity.[254]

The legal identity of *lex mercatoria* is a question of whether the rule the arbitrator chooses is a rule of law or merely common sense.[255] The determination of the legal nature of the *lex mercatoria* is best elucidated through the four tests of law: accessibility or general applicability; authoritativeness and consistency; predictability; and evident fairness.[256] The fairness of *lex mercatoria* is apparent through its use in arbitration and its essential rules of fair dealing and good faith. Furthermore, *lex mercatoria* is a general principle of international trade law, a custom, so its general applicability and accessibility are established through its recognition and use by a majority of civilised nations.[257] The element of the consistency of *lex mercatoria* is not as clear; however, the more consistent arbitral awards given will evidence the consistency of the *lex mercatoria* and accordingly its use will become predictable.[258] The more the principle is used, the stronger foundations it will have, and in time *lex mercatoria* may progress beyond its current 'soft law' status to something concrete recommended by attorneys to clients. It appears that in its current stage, *lex mercatoria* is neither fully a rule of law, nor mere common sense but a principle in transition from one phase to another.

There are aspects of the principles which have yet to be fully sorted out, such as the lack of review of *lex mercatoria* arbitration awards, and arbitrators mostly go unchecked by the judiciary because in choosing *lex mercatoria* to govern the arbitration, the parties remove the proceedings from the review of national courts.[259] In order for *lex mercatoria* to become a solid rule of law, it must be able to be reviewed by some body, as total freedom from control will breed immense unfairness, which is antithetical to its principles.[260] The progression of *lex mercatoria* is clearly not complete, and while many of its aspects appear to be rules of law, it has yet to fully develop into a true legal system.

The *lex mercatoria* is not a precise body of law with clear limits and likewise it would be inconceivable to attempt a full inventory of it. The essential rules of reason such as good faith and substantial breach are not rules *per se*, but general principles that have become universal in scope and usage. The *lex mercatoria* is not a static legal system because it changes with the norms of the international commercial community, therefore trying to identify it as any particular type of rule of law or legal system *per se* is difficult. However it is still useful, in terms of gap filling and presenting neutral principles of law to govern arbitration. The *lex mercatoria* is much like *jus cogens*, a peremptory norm of obligatory character that is so crucial that there may be no

---

252 See *ibid*.
253 See Maniruzzaman, *op cit*, p. 661
254 See Highet, *op cit*, p 625.
255 See *ibid*, p 624.
256 See *ibid*.
257 See *ibid*, p 626.
258 See *ibid*.
259 See Weinberg, *op cit*, p 251.
260 See *ibid*.

derogation.[261] It is a form of natural law of nations which, although its source is inexplicable and its contents difficult to define, serves an important need. The *lex mercatoria* may be difficult to pinpoint and fully define, but it has a purpose in the world of international commercial contracts and arbitration that cannot be denied.

The UNIDROIT Principles are a most impressive multinational promulgation of rules for international commercial contracts that have many uses. Because the Principles are not legally binding, they are easily capable of modification in the future to reflect changes in international trade practice. As already noted, Art 1.5 allows parties to exclude or derogate from, or vary the Principles, except where they are mandatory. For example, the duty of good faith and fair dealing[262] and some aspects of validity[263] cannot be excluded or limited.

In their capacity as a model for national legislators, the Principles have already influenced the drafting of recent national codifications such as the Civil Code of Quebec, the Commercial Code of Mexico and the Dutch Civil Code.[264] Indeed, countries closer to Australian shores such as Indonesia and Vietnam may derive significant use from the Principles in drafting basic contract law, particularly given the fact that the Principles are free from any political or particular jurisprudential persuasion.[265] This can only benefit Australian ties with such Asian countries, particularly given the growing economic need for trade with Asian countries.

On an international level, the Principles may play a major role in supplementing deficiencies in conventions such as the CISG. In time, they may themselves be embodied in an internationally binding convention or at least be a significant source of reference for drafting international conventions.

Because the Principles have no mandatory force of law, they will ordinarily not be recognised by court forums as the applicable law. Therefore, parties who contractually incorporate the Principles as the governing law and/or the terms of their contract, should always include an arbitration clause so as to ensure that any dispute goes to arbitration. As previously discussed, arbitrators are generally not obliged to apply a particular domestic law or convention whereby the UNIDROIT Principles should be applied as the party's choice of law in Arbitration Tribunals.

In the event of gaps in the Principles, it is submitted that a choice of law clause resembling the suggested draft in Comment 4 to Art 1.6 should be included as a matter of prudence.[266] One notable gap in the Principles, which is actually addressed in Ch IV of the CISG, is the passing of risk in relation to the international sale of goods.

Only time will tell as to whether the Principles will be universally accepted by the international trade community. They are, however, certainly worthy of consideration and are capable of universal application in all facets of their potential uses.

---

261 See Highet, *op cit*, p 626.
262 See Art 1.7.
263 See Art 3.19.
264 See Bonell [1992], *op cit* at 107.
265 See the letter of the Commonwealth Attorney General's Department (Australia) to the Secretary-General of UNIDROIT of 19 November 1993, as extracted in Bonell (1994), *op cit*, pp 108–09.
266 One suggested clause in Comment 4 to Art 1.6 is 'the contract is governed by the UNIDROIT Principles supplemented by the law of country x'.

TUTORIAL QUESTIONS

1   Professor Ulrich Magnus has argued that, in his opinion, the Principles are 'to be considered as additional general principles in the context of the CISG. The most important reason for this is that they vastly correspond both to the respective provisions of the CISG as well as to the general principles which have been derived from the CISG' (Magnus, 'General Principles of UN-Sales Law', 3 *International Trade and Business Law Annual* 34 at 54). Do you agree with his statement? Give reasons for your point of view.

2   Why are parties who wish to adopt the Principles well advised to combine their reference to the Principles with an arbitration agreement?

3   Discuss the obligations imposed on each party by Art 1.7 to act in accordance with 'good faith and fair dealing'. Does this obligation apply to pre-contractual negotiations? Compare Art 1.7 with your own civil law or common law system.

4   What are the differences, if any, between 'hardship' and *'force majeure'*?

5   In September 1989, Mr Müller, a dealer in furniture located in the former German Democratic Republic, buys stocks from Mr Volkov, situated in Bulgaria, also a former socialist country. The goods are to be delivered by Mr Volkov in December 1990. In November 1990, Mr Müller informs Mr Volkov that the goods are no longer of any use to him, claiming that after the unification of the German Democratic Republic and the Federal Republic of Germany there is no longer any market for such goods imported from Bulgaria. Is Mr Müller entitled to invoke hardship under the UNIDROIT Principles? (Question is based on UNIDROIT, *Principles of International Commercial Contracts*, Rome 1994 at 147.)

6   Discuss, compare and assess the interrelationship between the CISG and the UNIDROIT Principles of International Commercial Contracts.

FURTHER READING

Baptista, LO, 'The UNIDROIT Principles for International Commercial Law project: aspects of international private law' [1995] 69 *Tulane Law Review* 1209.

Bonell, MJ, 'Unification of law by non-legislative means: the UNIDROIT Draft Principles for International Commercial Contracts' [1992] 40 *American Journal of Comparative Law* 617.

Bonell, MJ, *An International Restatement of Contract Law – the UNIDROIT Principles of International Commercial Contracts*, 1994, Irvington, New York: Transnational Juris.

Ferrari, F, 'Defining the sphere of application of the 1994 UNIDROIT Principles of International Commercial Contracts' [1995] 69 *Tulane Law Review* 1225.

Furmston, MP, 'UNIDROIT General Principles for International Commercial Contracts' (1996) 10 *Journal of Contract Law* 11.

Garro, AM, 'The gap-filling role of the UNIDROIT Principles in International Sales Law: some comments on the interplay between the Principles and the CISG' [1995] 69 *Tulane Law Review* 1149.

Honnold, JO, *Uniform Law for International Sales Under the 1980 United Nations Convention*, 2nd edn, 1991, Deventer: Kluwer Law and Taxation Publishers.

Pryles, JM, Waincymer, J and Davies, M, *International Trade Law, Commentary and Materials*, 1996, Sydney: Law Book Company.

van Houtte, H, 'The UNIDROIT Principles of International Commercial Contracts' (1996) *International Trade and Business Law Annual* 1.

Waincymer, J, 'The internationalisation of Australia's trade laws' [1995] 17 *Sydney Law Review* 298.

APPENDIX

UNIDROIT PRINCIPLES OF INTERNATIONAL COMMERCIAL CONTRACTS – ROME, 1994 AND 2004

… The objective of the UNIDROIT Principles is to establish a balanced set of rules designed for use throughout the world irrespective of the legal traditions and the economic and political conditions of the countries in which they are to be applied.

… In offering the UNIDROIT Principles to the international legal and business communities, the Governing Council is fully conscious of the fact that the principles, which do not involve the endorsement of governments, are not a binding instrument and that in consequence their acceptance will depend upon their persuasive authority. There are a number of significant ways in which the UNIDROIT Principles may find practical application, the most important of which are amply explained in the Preamble.

Introduction of the Governing Council of UNIDROIT

Reproduced from the UNIDROIT Principles of Intentional Commercial Contracts, published by the International Institute for the Unification of Private Law (UNIDROIT), Rome, Italy, Copyright UNIDROIT 1994, by permission of UNIDROIT. Readers are reminded that the official version of the UNIDROIT Principles of International Commercial Contracts also includes the Commentary thereto. The integral edition of the English French German, Italian and Spanish versions may be ordered directly from UNIDROIT Publications, Via Panisperna 28, 00184 Italy (fax +39-6 69 94 13 94). The English version may also be ordered from Transnational Juris Publications, One Bridge Street, Irvington-on-Hudson, NY 10533 (fax: +1 (914) 591-2688).

UNIDROIT PRINCIPLES OF INTERNATIONAL COMMERCIAL CONTRACTS

Preamble – purpose of the principles

These Principles set forth general rules for international commercial contracts.

They shall be applied when the parties have agreed that their contract be governed by them.

They may be applied when the parties have agreed that their contracts be governed by general principles of law, the *lex mercatoria* or the like.

They may provide a solution to an issue raised when it proves impossible to establish the relevant rule of applicable law.

They may be used to interpret or supplement international uniform law instruments.

They may serve as a model for national and international legislators.

CHAPTER 1 – GENERAL PROVISIONS

Article 1.1 – Freedom of contract

The parties are free to enter into a contract and to determine its content.

Article 1.2 – No form required

Nothing in these Principles requires a contract to be concluded in or evidenced by writing. It may be proved by any means, including witnesses.

Article 1.3 – Binding character of contract

A contract validly entered into is binding upon the parties. It can only be modified or terminated in accordance with its terms or by agreement or as otherwise provided in these Principles.

Article 1.4 – Mandatory rules

Nothing in these Principles shall restrict the application of mandatory rules, whether of national, international or supranational origin, which are applicable in accordance with the relevant rules of private international law.

Article 1.5 – Exclusion or modification by the parties

The parties may exclude the application of these Principles or derogate from or vary the effect of any of their provisions, except as otherwise provided in the Principles.

Article 1.6 – Interpretation and supplementation of the Principles

1   In the interpretation of these Principles, regard is to be had to their international character and to their purposes including the need to promote uniformity in their application.
2   Issues within the scope of these Principles but not expressly settled by them are as far as possible to be settled in accordance with their underlying general principles.

Article 1.7 – Good faith and fair dealing

1   Each party must act in accordance with good faith and fair dealing in international trade.
2   The parties may not exclude or limit this duty.

Article 1.8 – Usages and practices

1   The parties are bound by any usage to which they have agreed and by any practices which they have established between themselves.
2   The parties are bound by a usage that is widely known to and regularly observed in international trade by parties in the particular trade concerned except where the application of such usage would be unreasonable.

Article 1.9 – Notice

1   Where notice is required it may be given by any means appropriate to the circumstances.
2   A notice is effective when it reaches the person to whom it is given.
3   For the purpose of para 2, a notice 'reaches' a person when given to that person orally or delivered at that person's place of business or mailing address.
4   For the purpose of this article, 'notice' includes a declaration, demand, request or any other communication of intention.

Article 1.10 – Definitions

In these Principles:
*   'court' includes an arbitral tribunal;
*   where a party has more than one place of business the relevant 'place of business' is that which has the closest relationship to the contract and its performance, having regard to the circumstances knows to or contemplated by the parties at any time before or at the conclusion of the contract;
*   'obliger' refers to the party who is to perform an obligation and 'obligee' refers to the party who is entitled to performance of that obligation;
*   'writing' means any mode of communication that preserves a record of the information contained therein and is capable of being reproduced in tangible form.

CHAPTER 2 – FORMATION

Article 2.1 – Manner of formation

A contract may be concluded either by the acceptance of an offer or by conduct of the parties that is sufficient to show agreement.

Article 2.2 – Definition of offer

A proposal for concluding a contract constitutes an offer if it is sufficiently definite and indicates the intention of the offeror to be bound in case of acceptance.

Article 2.3 – Withdrawal of offer
1   An offer becomes effective when it reaches the offeree.
2   An offer, even if it is irrevocable, may be withdrawn if the withdrawal reaches the offeree before or at the same time as the offer.

Article 2.4 – Revocation of offer
1   Until a contract is concluded, an offer may be revoked if the revocation reaches the offeree before it has dispatched an acceptance.
2   However, an offer cannot be revoked:
     (a) if it indicates, whether by stating a fixed time for acceptance or otherwise, that it is irrevocable; or
     (b) if it was reasonable for the offered to rely on the offer as being irrevocable and the offeree has acted in reliance of the offer.

Article 2.5 – Rejection of offer
An offer is terminated when a rejection reaches the offeror.

Article 2.6 – Mode of acceptance
1   A statement made by or other conduct of the offered assent to an offer is an acceptance. Silence or inactivity does not in itself amount to acceptance.
2   An acceptance of an offer becomes effective when the indication of assent reaches the offeror.
3   However, if, by virtue of the offer or as a result of practices which the parties have established between themselves or of usage, the offeree may indicate assent by performing an act without notice to the offeror, the acceptance is effective when the act is performed.

Article 2.7 – Time of acceptance
An offer must be accepted within the time the offeror has fixed or, if no time is fixed, within a reasonable time having regard to the circumstances, including the rapidity of the means of communication employed by the offeror. An oral offer must be accepted immediately unless the circumstances indicate otherwise.

Article 2.8 – Acceptance within a fixed period of time
1   A period of time for acceptance fixed by the offeror in a telegram or a letter begins to run from the moment the telegram is handed in for dispatch or from the date shown on the letter or, if no such date is shown, from the date shown on the envelope. A period of time for acceptance fixed by the offeror by means of instantaneous communication begins to run from the moment that offer reaches the offeree.
2   Official holidays or non-business days occurring during the period for acceptance are included in calculating the period. However, if a notice of acceptance cannot be delivered at the address of the offeror on the last day of the period because that day falls on an official holiday or a non-business day at the place of business of the offeror, the period is extended until the first business day which follows.

Article 2.9 – Late acceptance. Delay in transmission
1   A late acceptance is nevertheless effective as an acceptance if without undue delay the offeror so informs the offeree or gives notice to that effect.
2   If a letter or other writing containing a late acceptance shows that it has been sent in such circumstances that if its transmission had been normal it would have reached the offeror in due time, the late acceptance is effective as an acceptance unless without undue delay, the offeror informs the offeree that it considers the offer as having lapsed.

Article 2.10 – Withdrawal of acceptance
An acceptance may be withdraws if the withdrawal reaches the offeror before or at the same time as the acceptance would have become effective.

Article 2.11 – Modified acceptance

1   A reply to an offer which purports to be an acceptance but contains additions, limitations or other modifications is a rejection of the offer and constitutes a counter-offer.

2   However, a reply to an offer which purports to be an acceptance but contains additional or different terms which do not materially alter the terms of the offer constitutes an acceptance, unless the offeror without undue delay, objects to the discrepancy. If the offeror does not object, the terms of the contract are the terms of the offer with the modifications contained in the acceptance.

Article 2.12 – Writings in confirmation

If a writing which is sent within a reasonable time after the conclusion of the contract and which purports to be a confirmation of the contract contains additional or different terms, such terms become part of the contract, unless they materially alter the contract or the recipient, without undue delay, objects to the discrepancy.

Article 2.13 – Conclusion of contract dependent on agreement on specific matters or in a specific form

Where in the course of negotiations one of the parties insists that the contract is not concluded until there is agreement on specific matters or in a specific form, no contract is concluded before agreement is reached on those matters or in that form.

Article 2.14 – Contract with terms deliberately left open

1   If the parties intend to conclude a contract, the fact that they intentionally leave a term to be agreed upon in further negotiations or to be determined by a third person does not prevent a contract from coming into existence.

2   The existence of the contract is not affected by the fact that subsequently:
    (a) the parties reach no agreement on the terms; or
    (b) the third person does not determine the term, provided that there is an alternative means of rendering the term definite that is reasonable in the circumstances, having regard to the intention of the parties.

Article 2.15 – Negotiations in bad faith

1   A party is free to negotiate and is not liable for failure to reach an agreement.

2   However, a party who negotiates or breaks off negotiations in bad faith is liable for the losses caused to the other party.

3   It is bad faith, in particular, for a party to enter into or continue negotiations when intending not to reach an agreement with the other parts.

Article 2.16 – Duty of confidentiality

Where information is given as confidential by one party in the course of negotiations, the other party is under a duty not to disclose that information or to use it improperly for its own purposes, whether or not a contract is subsequently concluded. Where appropriate, the remedy for breach of that duty may include compensation based on the benefit received by the other party.

Article 2.17 – Merger clause

A contract in writing which contains a clause indicating that the writing completely embodies the terms on which the parties have agreed cannot be contradicted or supplemented by evidence of prior statements or agreements. However, such statements or agreements may be used to interpret the writing.

Article 2.18 – Written modification clause

A contract in writing which contains a clause requiring any modification or termination by agreement to be in writing may not be otherwise modified or terminated. However, a party may be precluded by its conduct from asserting such a clause to the extent that the other party has acted in reliance on that conduct.

Article 2.19 – Contracting under standard terms

1   Where one party or both parties use standard terms in concluding a contract, the general rules of formation apply, subject to Articles 2.20–2.22.

2 Standard terms are provisions which are prepared in advance for general and repeated use by one party and which are actually used without negotiation with the other party.

Article 2.20 – Surprising terms

1 No term contained in standard terms which is of such a character that the other party could not reasonably have expected it, is effective unless it has been expressly accepted by that party.
2 In determining whether a term is of such a character, regard is to be had to its content, language and presentation.

Article 2.21 – Conflict between standard terms and non-standard terms

In case of conflict between a standard term which is not a standard term, the latter prevails.

Article 2.22 – Battle of forms

Where both parties use standard terms and reach agreement except on those terms, a contract is concluded on the basis of the agreed terms and of any standard terms which are common in substance unless one party clearly indicates in advance, or later and without undue delay informs the other party that it does not intend to be bound by such a contract.

CHAPTER 3 – VALIDITY

Article 3.1 – Matters not covered

These Principles do not deal with invalidity arising from:

(a) lack of capacity;
(b) lack of authority;
(c) immorality or illegality.

Article 3.2 – Validity of mere agreement

A contract is concluded, modified or terminated by the mere agreement of the parties, without any further requirements.

Article 3.3 – Initial impossibility

1 The mere fact that at the time of the conclusion of the contract the performance of the obligation assumed was impossible does not affect the validity of the contract.
2 The mere fact that at the time of the conclusion of the contract a party was not entitled to dispose of the assets to which the contract relates does not affect the validity of the contract.

Article 3.4 – Definition of mistake

Mistake is an erroneous assumption relating to facts or to law existing when the contract was concluded.

Article 3.5 – Relevant mistake

1 A party may only avoid the contract for mistake if, when the contract was concluded, the mistake was of such importance that a reasonable person in the same situation as the party would not have concluded it at all if the true state of affairs had been known, and:
  (a) the other party made the same mistake, or caused the mistake, or knew or ought to have known of the mistake and it was contrary to reasonable commercial standards of fair dealing to leave the mistaken party in error; or
  (b) the other party had not at the time of avoidance acted in reliance on the contract.
2 However, a party may not avoid the contract if:
  (a) it was grossly negligent in committing the mistake; or
  (b) the mistake relates to a matter in regard to which the risk of mistake was assumed or, having regard to the circumstances, should be borne by the mistaken party.

Article 3.6 – Error in expression or transmission

An error occurring in the expression or transmission of a declaration is considered to be a mistake of the person from whom the declaration emanated.

Article 3.7 – Remedies for non-performance

A party is not entitled to avoid the contract on the ground of mistake if the circumstances on which that party relies afford, or could have afforded, a remedy for non-performance.

Article 3.8 – Fraud

A party may avoid the contract when it has been led to conclude the contract by the other partakes fraudulent representation, including language or practices, or fraudulent non-disclosure of circumstances which, according to reasonable commercial standards of fair dealing, the latter party should have disclosed.

Article 3.9 – Threat

A party may avoid the contract when it has been led to conclude the contract by the other party's unjustified threat which, having regard to the circumstances, is so imminent and serious as to leave the first party no reasonable alternative in particular, a threat is unjustified if the act or omission with which a party has been threatened is wrongful in itself, or is wrong to use it as a means to obtain the conclusion of the contract.

Article 3.10 – Gross disparity

1   A party may avoid the contract or an individual term of it if, at the time of the conclusion of the contract, the contract term unjustifiably gave the other party an excessive advantage. Regard is to be had among other factors, to:

   (a)   the fact that the other party has taken unfair advantage of the first part's dependence, economic distress or urgent needs, or of its improvidence, ignorance, inexperience or lack of bargaining skill; and

   (b)   the nature and purpose of the contract.

2   Upon the request of the party entitled to avoidance, a court may adapt the contract or term in order to make it accord with reasonable commercial standards of fair dealing.

3   A court may also adapt the contract or term upon the request of the party receiving notice of avoidance, provided that that party informs the other party of its request promptly after receiving such notice and before the other party has acted in reliance on it. The provisions of Article 3.13(2) apply accordingly.

Article 3.11 – Third persons

1   Where fraud, threat, gross disparity or a part's mistake is imputable to, or is known or ought to be known by, a third person for whose acts the other party is responsible, the contract may be avoided under the same conditions as if the behaviour or knowledge had been that of the party itself.

2   Where fraud, threat or gross disparity is imputable to a third person for whose acts the other party is not responsible, the contract may be avoided if that party knew or ought to have known of the fraud, threat or disparity, or has not at the time of avoidance acted in reliance on the contract.

Article 3.12 – Confirmation

If the party entitled to avoid the contract expressly or impliedly confirms the contract after the period of time for giving notice of avoidance has begun to run, avoidance of contract is excluded.

Article 3.13 – Loss of right to avoid

1   If a party is entitled to avoid the contract for mistake but the other party declares itself willing to perform or performs the contract as it was understood by the party entitled to avoidance, the contract is considered to have been concluded as the latter party understood it. The other party must make such a declaration or render such performance promptly after having been informed of the manner in which the party entitled to avoidance had understood the contract and before that party has acted in reliance on a notice of avoidance.

2   After such a declaration or performance, the right to avoidance is lost and any earlier notice of avoidance is ineffective.

Article 3.14 – Notice of avoidance

The right of a party to avoid the contract is exercised by notice to the other party.

Article 3.15 – Time limits

1   Notice of avoidance shall be given within a reasonable time, having regard to the circumstances, after the avoiding party knew or could not have been unaware of the relevant facts or became capable of acting freely.
2   Where an individual term of the contract may be avoided by a party under Article 3.10, the period of time for giving notice of avoidance begins to run when that term is asserted by the other party.

Article 3.16 – Partial avoidance

Where a ground of avoidance affects only individual terms of the contract, the effect of avoidance is limited to those terms unless, having regard to the circumstances, it is unreasonable to uphold the remaining contract.

Article 3.17 – Retroactive effect of avoidance

1   Avoidance takes effect retroactively.
2   On avoidance either party may claim restitution of whatever is supplied under the contract or the part of it avoided, provided that it concurrently makes restitution of whatever it has received under the contract or the part of it avoided or, if it cannot make restitution in kind, it makes an allowance for what it has received.

Article 3.18 – Damages

Irrespective of whether or not the contract has been avoided, the party who knew or ought to have known of the ground for avoidance is liable for damages so as to put the other party in the same position in which it would have been if it had not concluded the contract.

Article 3.19 – Mandatory character of the provision

The provisions of this chapter are mandatory, except in so far as they relate to the binding force of mere agreement, initial impossibility or mistake.

Article 3.20 – Unilateral declarations

The provisions of this chapter apply with appropriate adaptations to any communication of intention addressed by one party to the other.

CHAPTER 4 – INTERPRETATION

Article 4.1 – Intention of the parties

1   A contract shall be interpreted according to the common intention of the parties.
2   If such an intention cannot be established, the contract shall be interpreted according to the meaning that reasonable persons of the same kind as the parties would give to it in the same circumstances.

Article 4.2 – Interpretation of statements and other conduct

1   The statements and other conduct of a party shall be interpreted according to that part's intention if the other party knew or could not have been unaware of that intention.
2   If the preceding paragraph is not applicable, such statements and other conduct shall be interpreted according to the meaning that a reasonable person of the same kind as the other party would give to it in the same circumstances.

Article 4.3 – Relevant circumstances

In applying Articles 4.1 and 4.2, regard shall be had to all the circumstances, including:
(a)   preliminary negotiations between the parties;
(b)   practices which the parties have established between themselves;
(c)   the conduct of the parties subsequent to the conclusion of the contract;
(d)   the nature and purpose of the contract;

(e) the meaning commonly given to terms and expressions in the trade concerned;

(f) usages.

Article 4.4 – *Reference to contract or statement as a whole*

Terms and expressions shall be interpreted in the light of the whole contract or statement in which they appear.

Article 4.5 – *All terms to be given effect*

Contract terms shall be interpreted so as to give effect to all the terms rather than to deprive some of them of effect.

Article 4.6 – Contra proferentem *rule*

If contract terms supplied by one party are unclear, an interpretation against that party is preferred.

Article 4.7 – *Linguistic discrepancies*

Where a contract is drawn up in two or more language versions which are equally authoritative there is, in case of discrepancy between the versions, a preference for the interpretation according to a version in which the contract was originally drawn up.

Article 4.8 – *Supplying an omitted term*

1   Where the parties to a contract have not agreed with respect to a term which is important for a determination of their rights and duties, a term which is appropriate in the circumstances shall be supplied.

2   In determining what is an appropriate term regard shall be had, among other factors, to:

(a) the intention of the parties;

(b) the nature and purpose of the contract;

(c) good faith and fair dealing;

(d) reasonableness.

CHAPTER 5 – CONTENT

Article 5.1 – *Express and implied obligations*

The contractual obligations of the parties may be express or implied.

Article 5.2 – *Implied obligations*

Implied obligations stem from:

(a) the nature and purpose of the contract;

(b) practices established between the parties and usages;

(c) good faith and fair dealing;

(d) reasonableness.

Article 5.3 – *Cooperation between the parties*

Each party shall cooperate with the other party when such co-operation may reasonably be expected for the performance of that party's obligations.

Article 5.4 – *Duty to achieve a specific result. Duty of best efforts*

1   To the extent that an obligation of a party involves a duty to achieve a specific result, that party is bound to achieve that result.

2   To the extent that an obligation of a party involves a duty of best efforts in the performance of an activity, that party is bound to make such efforts as would be made by a reasonable person of the same kind in the same circumstances.

Article 5.5 – *Determination of kind of duty involved*

In determining the extent to which an obligation of a party involves a duty of best efforts in the performance of an activity or duty to achieve a specific result, regard shall be had, among other factors, to:

(a) the way in which the obligation is expressed in the contract;

(b) the contractual price and other terms of the contract;

(c) the degree of risk normally involved in achieving the expected result;

(d) the ability of the other party to influence the performance of the obligation.

Article 5.6 – Determination of quality of performance

Where the quality of performance is neither fixed by, nor determinable from, the contract a party is bound to render a performance of a quality that is reasonable and not less than average in the circumstances.

Article 5.7 – Price determination

1 Where a contract does not fix or make provision for determining the price, the parties are considered, in the absence of any indication to the contrary, to have made reference to the price generally charged at the time of the conclusion of the contract for such performance in comparable circumstances in the trade concerned or, if no such price is available, to a reasonable price.

2 Where the price is to be determined by one party and that determination is manifestly unreasonable, a reasonable price shall be substituted notwithstanding any contract term to the contrary.

3 Where the price is to be fixed by a third person, and that person cannot or will not do so, the price shall be a reasonable price.

4 Where the price is to be fixed by reference to factors which do not exist or have ceased to exist or to be accessible, the nearest equivalent factor shall be treated as a substitute.

Article 5.8 – Contract for an indefinite period

A contract for an indefinite period may be ended by either party by giving notice a reasonable time in advance.

CHAPTER 6 – PERFORMANCE

Section 1 – Performance in general

Article 6.1.1 – Time of performance

A party must perform its obligations:

(a) if a time is fixed by or determinable from the contract, at that time;

(b) if a period of time is fixed by or determinable from the contract, at any time within that period unless circumstances indicate that the other party is to choose a time;

(c) in any other case, within a reasonable time after the conclusion of the contract.

Article 6.1.2 – Performance at one time or in instalments

In cases under Article 6.1(b) or (c), a party must perform its obligations at one time if that performance can be rendered at one time and the circumstances do not indicate otherwise.

Article 6.1.3 – Partial performance

1 The obligee may reject an offer to perform in part at the time performance is due, whether or not such offer is coupled with an assurance as to the balance of the performance, unless the obligee has no legitimate interest in so doing.

2 Additional expenses caused to the obligor by partial performance are to be borne by the obligor without prejudice to any other remedy.

Article 6.1.4 – Order of performance

1 To the extent that the performances of the parties can be rendered simultaneously, the parties are bound to render them simultaneously unless the circumstances indicate otherwise.

2 To the extent that the performance of only one party requires a period of time, that party is bound to render its performance first, unless the circumstances indicate otherwise.

Article 6.1.5 – Earlier performance

1 The obligee may reject an earlier performance unless it has no legitimate interest in so doing.

2 Acceptability by a party of an earlier performance does not affect the time for the performance of its own obligations if that time has been fixed irrespective of the performance of the other Party's obligations.

3 Additional expenses caused to the obligee by earlier performance are to be borne by the obligor, without prejudice to any other remedy.

Article 6.1.6 – Place of performance

1 If the place of performance is neither fixed by, nor determinable from the contract, a party is to perform:

(a) a monetary obligation, at the obligates place of business;

(b) any other obligation, at its own place of business.

2 A party must bear any increase in the expenses incidental to performance which is caused by a change in its place of business subsequent to the conclusion of the contract.

Article 6.1.7 – Payment by cheque or other instrument

1 Payment may be made in any form used in the ordinary course of business at the place for payment.

2 However, an obligee who accepts, either by virtue of para 1 or voluntarily, a cheque, any other order to pay or a promise to pay, is presumed to do so only on condition that it will be honoured.

Article 6.1.8 – Payment by funds transfer

1 Unless the obligee has indicated a particular account, payment may be made by a transfer to any of the financial institutions in which the obligee has made it known that it has an account.

2 In case of payment by a transfer the obligation of the obligor is discharged when the transfer to the obligee's financial institution becomes effective.

Article 6.1.9 – Currency of payment

1 If a monetary obligation is expressed in a currency other than that of the place of payment, it may be paid by the obligor in the currency of the place for payment unless:

(a) the currency is freely convertible; or

(b) the parties have agreed that payment should be made only in the currency in which the monetary obligation is expressed.

2 If it is impossible for the obligor to make payment in the currency in which the monetary obligation is expressed, the obligee may require payment in the currency of the place for payment, even in the case referred to in para 1(b).

3 Payment in the currency of the place for payment is to be made according to the applicable rate of exchange prevailing there when payment is due.

4 However, if the obligor has not paid at the time when payment is due, the obligee may require payment according to the applicable rate of exchange prevailing either when payment is due or at the time of actual payment.

Article 6.1.10 – Currency not expressed

Where a monetary obligation is not expressed in a particular currency, payment must be made in the currency of the place where payment is to be made.

Article 6.1.11 – Costs of performance

Each party shall bear the costs of performance of its obligations.

Article 6.1.12 – Imputation of payments

1 An obligor owing several monetary obligations to the same obligee may specify at the time of payment the debt to which it intends the payment to be applied. However, the payment discharges first any expenses, then interest due and finally the principal.

2   If the obligor makes no such specification, the obligee may, within a reasonable time after payment, declare to the obligor the obligation to which it imputes the payment, provided that the obligation is due and undisputed.

3   In the absence of imputation under paras 1 or 2, payment is imputed to that obligation which satisfies one of the following criteria and in the order indicated:

(a) an obligation which is due or which is the first to fall due;

(b) the obligation for which the obligee has least security;

(c) the obligation which is the most burdensome for the obligor;

(d) the obligation which has arisen first.

If none of the preceding criteria applies, payment is imputed to all the obligations proportionally.

Article 6.1.13 – Imputation of non-monetary obligations

Article 6.1.12 applies with appropriate adaptations to the imputation of performance of non-monetary obligations.

Article 6.1.14 – Application for public permission

Where the law of a State requires a public permission affecting the validity of the contract or its performance and neither that law nor the circumstances indicate otherwise:

(a) if only one partly has its place of business in that State, that party shall take the measures necessary to obtain the permission;

(b) in any other case the party whose performance requires permission shall take the necessary measures.

Article 6.1.15 – Procedure in applying for permission

1   The party required to take the measures necessary to obtain the permission shall do so without undue delay and shall bear any expenses incurred.

2   That party shall whenever appropriate give the other party notice of the grant or refusal of such permission without undue delay.

Article 6.1.16 – Permission neither granted nor refused

1   If, notwithstanding the fact that the party responsible has taken all measures required, permission is neither granted nor refused within an agreed period or, where no period has been agreed, within a reasonable time from the conclusion of the contract, either party is entitled to terminate the contract.

2   Where the permission affects some terms only, para 1 does not apply if, having regard to the circumstances, it is reasonable to uphold the remaining contract even if the permission is refused.

Article 6.1.17 – Permission refused

1   The refusal of a permission affecting the validity of the contract renders the contract void. If the refusal affects the validity of some terms only, only such terms are void if, having regard to the circumstances, it is reasonable to uphold the remaining contract.

2   Where the refusal of a permission renders the performance of the contract impossible in whole or in part, the rules on non-performance apply.

Section 2 – Hardship

Article 6.2.1 – Contract to be observed

Where the performance of a contract becomes more onerous for one of the parties, that party is nevertheless bound to perform its obligations subject to the following provisions on hardship.

Article 6.2.2 – Definition of hardship

There is hardship where the occurrence of events fundamentally alters the equilibrium of the contract either because the cost of a party's performance has increased or because the value of the performance a party receives has diminished, and:

(a) the events occur or become known to the disadvantaged party after the conclusion of the contract;

(b) the events could not reasonably have been taken into account by the disadvantaged party at the time of the conclusion of the contract;

(c) the events are beyond the control of the disadvantaged party; and

(d) the risk of the events was not assumed by the disadvantaged party.

Article 6.2.3 – Effects of hardship

1   In case of hardship the disadvantaged party is entitled to request renegotiations. The request shall be made without undue delay and shall indicate the grounds on which it is based.

2   The request for renegotiation does not itself entitle the disadvantaged party to withhold performance.

3   Upon failure to reach agreement within a reasonable time either party may resort to the court.

4   If the court finds hardship it may, if reasonable:

(a) terminate the contract at a date and on terms to be fixed; or

(b) adapt the contract with a view to restoring its equilibrium.

CHAPTER 7 – NON-PERFORMANCE

Section 1 – Non-performance in general

Article 7.1.1 – Non-performance defined

Non-performance is failure by a party to perform any of its obligations under the contract, including defective performance or late performance.

Article 7.1.2 – Interference by the other party

A party may not rely on the non-performance of the other party to the extent that such non-performance was caused by the first party's act or omission or by another event as to which the first party bears the risk.

Article 7.1.3 – Withholding performance

1   Where the parties are to perform simultaneously, either party may withhold performance until the other party tenders performance.

2   Where the parties are to perform consecutively, the party that is to perform later may withhold its performance until the first party has performed.

Article 7.1.4 – Cure by non-performing party

1   The non-performing party may, at its own expense, cure any non-performance, provided that:

(a) without undue delay, it gives notice indicating the proposed manner and timing of the cure;

(b) cure is appropriate in the circumstances;

(c) the aggrieved party has no legitimate interest in refusing cure; and

(d) cure is effected promptly.

2   The right to cure is not precluded by notice of termination.

3   Upon effective notice of cure, rights of the aggrieved party that are inconsistent with the non-performing Party's performances are suspended until the time for cure has expired.

4   The aggrieved party may withhold performance pending cure.

5   Notwithstanding cure, the aggrieved party retains the right to claim damages for delay as well as for any harm caused or not prevented by the cure.

Article 7.1.5 – Additional period for performance

1   In a case of non-performance, the aggrieved party may by notice to the other party allow an additional period of time for performance.

2 During the additional period, the aggrieved party may withhold performance of its oval reciprocal obligations and may claim damages but may not resort to any other remedy. If it receives notice from the other party that the latter will not perform within that period, or if upon expiry of that period due performance has not been made, the aggrieved party may resort to any of the remedies that may be available under this chapter.

3 Where in a case of delay in performance which is not fundamental the aggrieved parts has given notice allowing an additional period of time of reasonable length, it may terminate the contract at the end of that period. If the additional period allowed is not of reasonable length, it shall be extended to a reasonable length. The aggrieved party may in its notice provide that if the other party fails to perform within the period allowed by the notice the contract shall automatically terminate.

4 Paragraph 3 does not apply where the obligation which has not been performed is only a minor part of the contractual obligation of the non-performing party.

Article 7.1.6 – *Exemption clauses*

A clause which limits or excludes one party's liability for non-performance or which permits one party to tender performance substantially different from what the other party reasonably expected may not be invoked if it would be grossly unfair to do so, having regard to the purpose of the contract.

Article 7.1.7 – Force majeure

1 Non-performance by a party is excused if that party proves that the non-performance was due to an impediment beyond its control and that it could not reasonably be expected to have taken the impediment into account at the time of the conclusion of the contract or to have avoided or overcome it or its consequences.

2 When the impediment is only temporary, the excuse shall have effect for such period as is reasonable having regard to the effect of the impediment on performance of the contract.

3 The party who fails to perform must give notice to the other party of the impediment and its effect on its ability to perform. If the notice is not received by the other party within a reasonable time after the party who fails to perform knew or ought to have known of the impediment, it is liable for damages resulting from such non-receipt.

4 Nothing in this article prevents a party from exercising a right to terminate the contract or to withhold performance or request interest on money due.

Section 2 – Right to performance

Article 7.2.1 – *Performance of monetary obligation*

Where a party who is obliged to pay money does not do so, the other may require payment.

Article 7.2.2 – *Performance of non-monetary obligation*

Where a party who owes an obligation other than one to pay money does not perform, the other party may require performance, unless:

(a) performance is impossible in law or fact;

(b) performance or, where relevant, enforcement is unreasonably burdensome or expensive;

(c) the parts entitled to performance may reasonably obtain performance from another source;

(d) performance is of an exclusively personal character; or

(e) the party entitled to performance does not require performance within a reasonable time after it has, or ought to have, become aware of the non-performance.

Article 7.2.3 – *Repair and replacement of defective performance*

The right to performance includes in appropriate cases the right to require repair, replacement, or other cure of defective performance. The provisions of Articles 7.2.1 and 7.2.2 apply accordingly.

Article 7.2.4 – *Judicial penalty*

1 Where the court orders a party to perform, it may also direct that this party pay a penalty if it does not comply with the order.

2   The penalty shall be paid to the aggrieved party unless mandatory provisions of the law of the forum provide otherwise. Payment of the penalty to the aggrieved party does not exclude any claim for damages.

Article 7.2.5 – Change of remedy

1   An aggrieved party who has required performance of a non-monetary obligation and who has not received performance within a period fixed or otherwise within a reasonable period of time may invoke any other remedy.

2   Where the decision of a court for performance of a non-monetary obligation cannot be enforced, the aggrieved party may invoke any other remedy.

Section 3 – Termination

Article 7.3.1 – Right to terminate the contract

1   A Party may terminate the contract where the failure of the other party to perform an obligation under the contract amounts to a fundamental performance.

2   In determining whether a failure to perform an obligation amounts to a fundamental non-performance, regard shall be had, in particular, to whether:

   (a) the non-performance substantially deprives the aggrieved party of what it was entitled to expect under the contract unless the other party did not foresee and could not reasonably have foreseen such result;

   (b) strict compliance with the obligation which has not been performed is of essence under the contract;

   (c) the non-performance is intentional or reckless;

   (d) the non-performance gives the aggrieved party reason to believe that it cannot rely on the other party's future performance;

   (e) the non-performing party will suffer disproportionate loss as a result of the preparation or performance if the contract is terminated.

3   In the case of delay, the aggrieved party may also terminate the contract if the other party fails to perform before the time allowed under Article 7.1.5 has expired.

Article 7.3.2 – Notice of termination

1   The right of a party to terminate the contract is exercised by notice to the other party.

2   If performance has been offered late or otherwise does not conform to the contract the aggrieved party will lose its right to terminate the contract unless it gives notice to the other party within a reasonable time after it has or ought to have become aware of the non-conforming performance.

Article 7.3.3 – Anticipatory non-performance

Where prior to the date for performance by one of the parties it is clear that there will be a fundamental non-performance by that party, the other party may terminate the contract.

Article 7.3.4 – Adequate assurance of due performance

A party who reasonably believes that there will be a fundamental non-performance by the other party may demand adequate assurance of due performance and may meanwhile withhold its own performance. Where this assurance is not provided within a reasonable time the party demanding it may terminate the contract.

Article 7.3.5 – Effects of termination in general

1   Termination of the contract releases both parties from their obligation to effect and to receive future performance.

2   Termination does not preclude a claim for damages for non-performance.

3   Termination does not affect any provision in the contract for the settlement of disputes or any other term of the contract which is to operate even after termination.

Article 7.3.6 – Restitution

1   On termination of contract either party may claim restitution of whatever it has supplied, provided that such party concurrently makes restitution of whatever it has received. If restitution in kind is not possible or appropriate allowance should be made in money whenever reasonable.

2   However, if performance of the contract has extended over a period of time and the contract is divisible, such restitution can only be claimed for the period after termination has taken effect.

Section 4 – Damages

Article 7.4.1 – Right to damages

Any non-performance gives the aggrieved party a right to damages either exclusively or in conjunction with any other remedies except where the non-performance is excused under these Principles.

Article 7.4.2 – Full compensation

1   The aggrieved party is entitled to full compensation for harm sustained as a result of the non-performance. Such harm includes both any loss which it suffered and any gain of which it was deprived, taking into account any gain to the aggrieved party resulting from its avoidance of cost or harm.

2   Such harm may be non-pecuniary and includes, for instance, physical suffering or emotional distress.

Article 7.4.3 – Certainty of harm

1   Compensation is due only for harm, including future harm, that is established with a reasonable degree of certainty.

2   Compensation may be due for the loss of a chance in proportion to the stability of its occurrence.

3   Where the amount of damages cannot be established with a sufficient degree of certainty, the assessment is at the discretion of the court.

Article 7.4.4 – Foreseeability of harm

The non-performing party is liable only for harm which it foresaw or could reasonably have foreseen at the time of the conclusion of the contract as being likely to result from its non-performance.

Article 7.4.5 – Proof of harm in case of replacement transaction

Where the aggrieved party has terminated the contract and has made a replacement transaction within a reasonable time and in a reasonable manner, it may recover the difference between the contract price and the price of the replacement transaction as well as damages for any further harm.

Article 7.4.6 – Proof of harm by current price

1   Where the aggrieved party has terminated the contract and has not made a replacement transaction but there is a current price for the performance contracted for, it may recover the difference between the contract price and the price current at the time the contract is terminated as well as damages for any further harm.

2   Current price is the price generally charged for goods delivered or services rendered in comparable circumstances at the place where the contract should have been performed or, if there is no current price at that place, the current price at such other place that appears reasonable to take as a reference.

Article 7.4.7 – Harm due in part to aggrieved party

Where the harm is due in part to an act or omission of the aggrieved party or to another event as to which that party bears the risk, the amount of damages shall be reduced to the extent that these factors have contributed to the harm, having regard to the conduct of the parties.

Article 7.4.8 – Mitigation of harm

1   The non-performing party is not liable for harm suffered by the aggrieved party to the extent that the harm could have been reduced by the latter party's taking reasonable steps.

2   The aggrieved party is entitled to recover any expenses reasonably incurred in attempting to reduce the harm.

Article 7.4.9 – Interest for failure to pay money

1   If a party does not pay a sum of money when it falls due, the aggrieved party is entitled to interest upon that sum from the time when payment is due to the time of payment whether or not the non-payment is excused.

2   The rate of interest shall be the average bank short term lending rate to prime borrowers prevailing for the currency of payment at the place for payment, or where no such rate exists at that place, then the same rate in the State of the currency of payment. In the absence of such a rate at either place the rate of interest shall be the appropriate rate fixed by the law of the State of the currency of payment.

3   The aggrieved party is entitled to additional damages if the non-payment caused it a greater harm.

Article 7.4.10 – Interest on damages

Unless otherwise agreed, interest on damages for non-performance of non-monetary obligations accrues as from the time of non-performance.

Article 7.4.11 – Manner of monetary redress

1   Damages are to be paid in a lump sum. However, they may be payable in instalments where the nature of the harm makes this appropriate.

2   Damages to be paid in instalments may be indexed.

Article 7.4.12 – Currency in which to access damages

Damages are to be assessed either in the currency in which the monetary obligation was expressed or in the currency in which the haven was suffered, whichever is more appropriate.

Article 7.4.13 – Agreed payment for non-performance

1   Where the contract provides that a party who does not perform is to pay a specified sum to the aggrieved party for such non-performance, the aggrieved party is entitled to that sum irrespective of its actual harm.

2   However, notwithstanding any agreement to the contrary, the specified sum may be reduced to a reasonable amount where it is grossly excessive in relation to the harm resulting from the non-performance and to the other circumstances.

CHAPTER 8 – SET-OFF

Article 8.1 – Conditions of set-off

1   Where two parties owe each other money or other performances of the same kind, either of them ('the first party') may set off its obligation against that of its obligee ('the other party') if at the time of set-off,

    (a) the first party is entitled to perform its obligation;

    (b) the other party's obligation is ascertained as to its existence and amount and performance is due.

2   If the obligations of both parties arise from the same contract, the first party may also set off its obligation against an obligation of the other party which is not ascertained as to its existence or to its amount.

Article 8.2 – Foreign currency set-off

Where the obligations are to pay money in different currencies, the right of set-off may be exercised, provided that both currencies are freely convertible and the parties have not agreed that the first party shall pay only in a specified currency.

Article 8.3 – Set-off by notice

The right of set-off is exercised by notice to the other party.

Article 8.4 – Content of notice

1 The notice must specify the obligations to which it relates.
2 If the notice does not specify the obligation against which set-off is exercised, the other party may, within a reasonable time, declare to the first party the obligation to which set-off relates. If no such declaration is made, the set-off will relate to all the obligations proportionally.

Article 8.5 – Effect of set-off

1 Set-off discharges the obligations.
2 If obligations differ in amount, set-off discharges the obligations up to the amount of the lesser obligation.
3 Set-off takes effect as from the time of notice.

CHAPTER 9 – ASSIGNMENT OF RIGHTS, TRANSFER OF OBLIGATIONS, ASSIGNMENT OF CONTRACTS

Section 1 – Assignment of rights

Article 9.1.1 – Definitions

'Assignment of a right' means the transfer by agreement from one person (the 'assignor') to another person (the 'assignee'), including transfer by way of security, of the assignor's right to payment of a monetary sum or other performance from a third person ('the obligor').

Article 9.1.2 – Exclusions

This Section does not apply to transfers made under the special rules governing the transfers:
(a) of instruments such as negotiable instruments, documents of title or financial instruments, or
(b) of rights in the course of transferring a business.

Article 9.1.3 – Assignability of non-monetary rights

A right to non-monetary performance may be assigned only if the assignment does not render the obligation significantly more burdensome.

Article 9.1.4 – Partial assignment

1 A right to the payment of a monetary sum may be assigned partially.
2 A right to other performance may be assigned partially only if it is divisible, and the assignment does not render the obligation significantly more burdensome.

Article 9.1.5 – Future rights

A future right is deemed to be transferred at the time of the agreement, provided the right, when it comes into existence, can be identified as the right to which the assignment relates.

Article 9.1.6 – Rights assigned without individual specification

A number of rights may be assigned without individual specification, provided such rights can be identified as rights to which the assignment relates at the time of the assignment or when they come into existence.

Article 9.1.7 – Agreement between assignor and assignee sufficient

1 A right is assigned by mere agreement between the assignor and the assignee, without notice to the obligor.
2 The consent of the obligor is not required unless the obligation in the circumstances is of an essentially personal character.

Article 9.1.8 – Obligor's additional costs

The obligor has a right to be compensated by the assignor or the assignee for any additional costs caused by the assignment.

Article 9.1.9 – Non-assignment clauses

1   The assignment of a right to the payment of a monetary sum is effective notwithstanding an agreement between the assignor and the obligor limiting or prohibiting such an assignment. However, the assignor may be liable to the obligor for breach of contract.

2   The assignment of a right to other performance is ineffective if it is contrary to an agreement between the assignor and the obligor limiting or prohibiting the assignment. Nevertheless, the assignment is effective if the assignee, at the time of the assignment, neither knew nor ought to have known of the agreement. The assignor may then be liable to the obligor for breach of contract.

Article 9.1.10 – Notice to the obligor

1   Until the obligor receives a notice of the assignment from either the assignor or the assignee, it is discharged by paying the assignor.

2   After the obligor receives such a notice, it is discharged only by paying the assignee.

Article 9.1.11 – Successive assignments

If the same right has been assigned by the same assignor to two or more successive assignees, the obligor is discharged by paying according to the order in which the notices were received.

Article 9.1.12 – Adequate proof of assignment

1   If notice of the assignment is given by the assignee, the obligor may request the assignee to provide within a reasonable time adequate proof that the assignment has been made.

2   Until adequate proof is provided, the obligor may withhold payment.

3   Unless adequate proof is provided, notice is not effective.

4   Adequate proof includes, but is not limited to, any writing emanating from the assignor and indicating that the assignment has taken place.

Article 9.1.13 – Defences and rights of set-off

1   The obligor may assert against the assignee all defences that the obligor could assert against the assignor.

2   The obligor may exercise against the assignee any right of set-off available to the obligor against the assignor up to the time notice of assignment was received.

Article 9.1.14 – Rights related to the right assigned

The assignment of a right transfers to the assignee:

(a)   all the assignor's rights to payment or other performance under the contract in respect of the right assigned, and

(b)   all rights securing performance of the right assigned.

Article 9.1.15 – Undertakings of the assignor

The assignor undertakes towards the assignee, except as otherwise disclosed to the assignee, that:

(a)   the assigned right exists at the time of the assignment, unless the right is a future right;

(b)   the assignor is entitled to assign the right;

(c)   the right has not been previously assigned to another assignee, and it is free from any right or claim from a third party;

(d)   the obligor does not have any defences;

(e)   neither the obligor nor the assignor has given notice of set-off concerning the assigned right and will not give any such notice;

(f)   the assignor will reimburse the assignee for any payment received from the obligor before notice of the assignment was given.

Section 2 – Transfer of obligations

Article 9.2.1 – Modes of transfer

An obligation to pay money or render other performance may be transferred from one person (the 'original obligor') to another person (the 'new obligor') either

(a) by an agreement between the original obligor and the new obligor subject to Article 9.2.3, or

(b) by an agreement between the obligee and the new obligor, by which the new obligor assumes the obligation.

Article 9.2.2 – Exclusion

This Section does not apply to transfers of obligations made under the special rules governing transfers of obligations in the course of transferring a business.

Article 9.2.3 – Requirement of obligee's consent to transfer

The transfer of an obligation by an agreement between the original obligor and the new obligor requires the consent of the obligee.

Article 9.2.4 – Advance consent of obligee

1   The obligee may give its consent in advance.
2   If the obligee has given its consent in advance, the transfer of the obligation becomes effective when a notice of the transfer is given to the obligee or when the obligee acknowledges it.

Article 9.2.5 – Discharge of original obligor

1   The obligee may discharge the original obligor.
2   The obligee may also retain the original obligor as an obligor in case the new obligor does not perform properly.
3   Otherwise the original obligor and the new obligor are jointly and severally liable.

Article 9.2.6 – Third party performance

1   Without the obligee's consent, the obligor may contract with another person that this person will perform the obligation in place of the obligor, unless the obligation in the circumstances has an essentially personal character.
2   The obligee retains its claim against the obligor.

Article 9.2.7 – Defences and rights of set-off

1   The new obligor may assert against the obligee all defences which the original obligor could assert against the obligee.
2   The new obligor may not exercise against the obligee any right of set-off available to the original obligor against the obligee.

Article 9.2.8 – Rights related to the obligation transferred

1   The obligee may assert against the new obligor all its rights to payment or other performance under the contract in respect of the obligation transferred.
2   If the original obligor is discharged under Article 9.2.5(1), a security granted by any person other than the new obligor for the performance of the obligation is discharged, unless that other person agrees that it should continue to be available to the obligee.
3   Discharge of the original obligor also extends to any security of the original obligor given to the obligee for the performance of the obligation, unless the security is over an asset which is transferred as part of a transaction between the original obligor and the new obligor.

Section 3 – Assignment of contracts

Article 9.3.1 – Definitions

'Assignment of a contract' means the transfer by agreement from one person (the 'assignor') to another person (the 'assignee') of the assignor's rights and obligations arising out of a contract with another person (the 'other party').

Article 9.3.2 – Exclusion

This Section does not apply to the assignment of contracts made under the special rules governing transfers of contracts in the course of transferring a business.

Article 9.3.3 – Requirement of consent of the other party
The assignment of a contract requires the consent of the other party.

Article 9.3.4 – Advance consent of the other party
1   The other party may give its consent in advance.
2   If the other party has given its consent in advance, the assignment of the contract becomes effective when a notice of the assignment is given to the other party or when the other party acknowledges it.

Article 9.3.5 – Discharge of the assignor
1   The other party may discharge the assignor.
2   The other party may also retain the assignor as an obligor in case the assignee does not perform properly.
3   Otherwise the assignor and the assignee are jointly and severally liable.

Article 9.3.6 – Defences and rights of set-off
1   To the extent that the assignment of a contract involves an assignment of rights, Article 9.1.13 applies accordingly.
2   To the extent that the assignment of a contract involves a transfer of obligations, Article 9.2.7 applies accordingly.

Article 9.3.7 – Rights transferred with the contract
1   To the extent that the assignment of a contract involves an assignment of rights, Article 9.1.14 applies accordingly.
2   To the extent that the assignment of a contract involves a transfer of obligations, Article 9.2.8 applies accordingly.

CHAPTER 10 – LIMITATION PERIODS

Article 10.1 – Scope of the Chapter
1   The exercise of rights governed by these Principles is barred by the expiration of a period of time, referred to as 'limitation period', according to the rules of this Chapter.
2   This Chapter does not govern the time within which one party is required under these Principles, as a condition for the acquisition or exercise of its right, to give notice to the other party or to perform any act other than the institution of legal proceedings.

Article 10.2 – Limitation periods
1   The general limitation period is three years beginning on the day after the day the obligee knows or ought to know the facts as a result of which the obligee's right can be exercised.
2   In any event, the maximum limitation period is ten years beginning on the day after the day the right can be exercised.

Article 10.3 – Modification of limitation periods by the parties
1   The parties may modify the limitation periods.
2   However they may not:
     (a) shorten the general limitation period to less than one year;
     (b) shorten the maximum limitation period to less than four years;
     (c) extend the maximum limitation period to more than fifteen years.

Article 10.4 – New limitation period by acknowledgement
1   Where the obligor before the expiration of the general limitation period acknowledges the right of the obligee, a new general limitation period begins on the day after the day of the acknowledgement.
2   The maximum limitation period does not begin to run again, but may be exceeded by the beginning of a new general limitation period under Article 10.2(1).

Article 10.5 – Suspension by judicial proceedings

1   The running of the limitation period is suspended:

(a) when the obligee performs any act, by commencing judicial proceedings or in judicial proceedings already instituted, that is recognised by the law of the court as asserting the obligee's right against the obligor;

(b) in the case of the obligor's insolvency when the obligee has asserted its rights in the insolvency proceedings; or

(c) in the case of proceedings for dissolution of the entity which is the obligor when the obligee has asserted its rights in the dissolution proceedings.

2   Suspension lasts until a final decision has been issued or until the proceedings have been otherwise terminated.

Article 10.6 – Suspension by arbitral proceedings

1   The running of the limitation period is suspended when the obligee performs any act, by commencing arbitral proceedings or in arbitral proceedings already instituted, that is recognised by the law of the arbitral tribunal as asserting the obligee's right against the obligor. In the absence of regulations for arbitral proceedings or provisions determining the exact date of the commencement of arbitral proceedings, the proceedings are deemed to commence on the date on which a request that the right in dispute should be adjudicated reaches the obligor.

2   Suspension lasts until a binding decision has been issued or until the proceedings have been otherwise terminated.

Article 10.7 – Alternative dispute resolution

The provisions of Articles 10.5 and 10.6 apply with appropriate modifications to other proceedings whereby the parties request a third person to assist them in their attempt to reach an amicable settlement of their dispute.

Article 10.8 – Suspension in case of force majeure, *death or incapacity*

1   Where the obligee has been prevented by an impediment that is beyond its control and that it could neither avoid nor overcome, from causing a limitation period to cease to run under the preceding articles, the general limitation period is suspended so as not to expire before one year after the relevant impediment has ceased to exist.

2   Where the impediment consists of the incapacity or death of the obligee or obligor, suspension ceases when a representative for the incapacitated or deceased party or its estate has been appointed or a successor has inherited the respective party's position. The additional one-year period under paragraph (1) applies accordingly.

Article 10.9 – The effects of expiration of limitation period

1   The expiration of the limitation period does not extinguish the right.

2   For the expiration of the limitation period to have effect, the obligor must assert it as a defence.

3   A right may still be relied on as a defence even though the expiration of the limitation period for that right has been asserted.

Article 10.10 – Right of set-off

The obligee may exercise the right of set-off until the obligor has asserted the expiration of the limitation period.

Article 10.11 – Restitution

Where there has been performance in order to discharge an obligation, there is no right of restitution merely because the limitation period has expired.

CHAPTER 3

AN ASSESSMENT OF INCOTERMS 2000

INTRODUCTION

The International Chamber of Commerce (based in Paris) has, since 1936, formulated and published its so called Incoterms – an abbreviation of 'international commercial terms' – and which are known officially as the 'International Rules for the Interpretation of Trade Terms'. The rules are periodically revised; changes were made in 1953, 1967, 1976, 1980, 1990 and 2000. The current Incoterms are the 2000 terms, and are referred to by the shorthand usage of 'Incoterms 2000'. The Incoterms were devised in recognition of the fact that the so called standard trade usages of CIF, FOB, etc, were not altogether uniform, with their meaning varying from one municipal legal system to the next, in matters of detail and, in some cases, at a more fundamental level. If the parties to the sales contract incorporate a particular Incoterm in their contract, the Incoterm code – which contains a detailed statement of what each trade usage means – can be referred to for a detailed interpretation of the rights and obligations created as between these parties, by their use of the given term. Thereby, uncertainty as to the precise incidents of a given term is more readily avoided. In default of this, the meaning to be attributed to a given trade term would depend upon the interpretation given to it (if one is given at all) by the applicable municipal law. The use of Incoterms (as does the use of other standard trade usages outside the Incoterm regime) also makes the process of drafting a contract more straightforward, the shorthand usage functioning as it does to incorporate a more detailed code of rights and obligations as between the parties.

The Incoterms are intended to reflect current international practice in respect of the matters covered by them, hence the periodical revision of the Incoterms. Practice evolves over time because of the impact of various factors, such as the use of containers in shipping cargo, the growing use of air carriers in moving goods, and the growing use of electronic data interchange (EDI) between parties with respect to the contract and its performance.

The Incoterms were revised in 2000 to ensure that the wording accurately reflects trade practice. As well, substantive changes were made in two areas: (1) the customs clearance and payment of duty obligations under FAS and DEQ, and (2) the loading and unloading obligations under FCA.[1]

In this chapter, the Incoterms 2000 will be reviewed. First, some preliminary matters will be noted.

---

1   International Chamber of Commerce, *Incoterms 2000*, 2000, Paris: ICC Publishing SA, p 7 (known hereafter as ICC – *Incoterms 2000*). 'FAS' is shorthand for 'Free alongside ship', 'DEQ' is 'Delivered ex-quay', and 'FCA' is 'Free carrier'.

Some preliminary matters

Incoterms – their functions

As reflected above, the Incoterms identify standard trade usages (which in turn reflect standardised trade practices or customs) and provide a detailed statement of what each term requires the parties to do. According to the Introduction to the Incoterms 2000:

> The purpose of Incoterms is to provide a set of international rules for the interpretation of the most commonly used trade terms in foreign trade. Thus, the uncertainties of different interpretations of such terms in different countries can be avoided or at least reduced to a considerable degree.[2]

As mentioned, the Incoterms, like other standard trade terms, facilitate contracting by giving the parties the option of incorporating detailed regimes of rights and obligations, by the simple use of a shorthand expression.

The Incoterms are limited in their scope, dealing as they do with nominated aspects of the delivery of goods pursuant to the international sales contract, and collateral matters – a compass expressed as being concerned with the 'carriage of goods from seller to buyer', 'export and import clearance' and 'the division of costs and risks between the parties'.[3]

Many matters are not dealt with by the Incoterms; they do not provide a general regime for the regulation of the contract. They do not, for example, regulate the passing of property in the goods, nor do they specify the consequences of a breach of contract. The rules dealing with these broader matters must be sought in the other terms of the contract, and the law of the contract (that is, the applicable municipal law, which will in the normal case be the law agreed upon by the parties).[4] Further, the Incoterms have no bearing upon the interpretation of any contract of carriage that may be entered into by a party to the sales contract.[5]

When the parties adopt as the law of their contract (directly or indirectly) the Vienna Convention on Contracts for the International Sale of Goods, and use an appropriate Incoterm, they achieve a relatively greater degree of certainty as to the regime of rules, contractual and ex-contractual, which govern the performance of their transaction. Both the Convention and the Incoterms represent standardised, internationally well recognised codes.

---

2   ICC – *Incoterms 2000, op cit*, p 5. Fundamentally, the Incoterms regime provides rules of interpretation for selected trade usages.

3   See Ramberg, J, *Guide to Incoterms 1990*, 1991, Paris: ICC Publishing SA, p 8.

4   The parties may also agree directly that the Vienna Sales Convention (see Chapter 1) should, within its compass, govern their contract; or this may come to be applied indirectly where they agree that the law of a State, which has adopted the Convention, should be the applicable law.

5   See ICC – *Incoterms 2000*, p 5, noting that the Incoterms (self-evidently, in referring to the buyer and seller) relate only to terms used in contracts of sale, and thus do not deal with terms used in contracts of carriage, including charter parties, or contracts of insurance.

Legal status of the Incoterms

The Incoterms do not possess the status of law. Unlike the Vienna Convention on Contracts for the International Sale of Goods, they have not been assimilated into the municipal law of any State. Such a process of adoption would be potentially counterproductive. The intent of the International Chamber of Commerce is to revise the Incoterms periodically (such as every decade) with a view to their amendment to reflect changing practices in the international trade of goods. Rather, they are a standardised, published and widely known code that is available for incorporation in foreign goods contracts at the option of the parties.

Incorporation of Incoterms

A preferred Incoterm will be incorporated into a contract by unambiguous reference to it: for example, 'CIF (… named place) (Incoterms 2000)' or 'Cost, insurance and freight (named place) (Incoterms 2000)'. Another comparable reference may be used, but given that numerous of the well known trade usages are found in domestic case law or legislation in municipal legal systems, the parties should refer specifically to the Incoterms.

Such a reference requires the parties (and directs a court trying a case involving the contract) to refer to the Incoterms in order to determine the rights and obligations created by the reference.

The chosen Incoterm can be modified or amplified by provision in the contract. Exceptionally, the details of a contract may be such as to negate the Incoterm chosen, as where a term requiring the seller to deliver the goods is used, but the specific provisions of the contract impose the obligation of carriage, and its ancillary incidents, upon the buyer.

Transport developments impacting upon Incoterms

The traditional trade usages were focused on marine transport (sea and inland waterway). Over the years the range of transport options has widened: the most recent major development in this respect has been of course the increasing resort to air transportation of cargo. Parallel with this development has been the use of multi-modal transportation, where different modes of transport are employed to carry the goods from seller to buyer. These developments have been reflected in the Incoterms, in their progressive revisions. Some of them, for instance, are still intended for purely marine transport (such as FAS, FOB and CIF), but there are also terms for air transport (FCA), for rail (likewise FCA) and a number for any mode of transport, including multi-modal operations (such as ExW, CPT and CIP).

The advent of containerisation (and other forms of unitisation), coupled with new methods of loading (such as roll-on/roll-off, or ro-ro loading using trucks, etc) has had implications for international trade and in turn the Incoterms. In particular, the identification of the ship's rail as the place where the costs and risks are to be divided (with the buyer assuming responsibility at the moment the cargo passes over the rail) – a feature of such traditional marine terms as CIF and FOB – has had to be supplemented with new and alternative pivot points in other trade terms for the division of risk and costs. Containerised goods, including those intended for sea transport, tend to pass out of the hands of the seller and into the (first) carrier's hands at an earlier point, such as where the goods are delivered to a freight forwarder at a freight-forwarding depot, container terminal, etc, for shipping, either in the original container or after removal and re-packing. Further, the ship's rail is irrelevant in the so called 'arrival' terms where the seller undertakes to deliver the goods to the buyer at a point in the buyer's State. These latter arrangements, imposing more comprehensive obligations on sellers, are increasingly common.

Use of intermediaries and related matters

The Incoterms (in common with the different standardised practices they represent) must take account of the use of a variety of intermediaries involved in transacting the delivery, such as a succession of carriers in multi-modal transport arrangements, freight forwarders (who may act as customs brokers), stevedores, commercial inspection agents and insurers. They must as well reflect the different types of cargo, such as general cargo (which, where sea transport is concerned, will usually be carried by the so called liner trade, that is, ships following regular schedules) and bulk cargo commodities, which will often be carried by a ship chartered by either the seller or (more commonly) the buyer.

Electronic data transmission

The Incoterms were revised in 1990 in order to recognise that a range of documents relevant to the performance of the contract are in practice being replaced to an increasing degree by so called electronic data interchange, that is, the computer-to-computer transmission of electronic messages. This electronic data interchange, or EDI, simplifies processes and reduces costs. Accordingly, the Incoterms as revised provide, where applicable (and in some cases subject to agreement), that an equivalent electronic message may replace such documents as commercial invoices, documents required for customs clearance (import or export), transport documents, and (where agreed) documents which are to be tendered in proof of delivery.[6]

The bill of lading has represented a problem for the application of electronic messages in this context. The bill of lading is of course a traditional fixture in the transport of goods by sea. The bill is issued by the ship's master to the party dispatching the cargo. It constitutes proof that the goods were delivered on board; evidences the contract to transport the goods; and functions in certain respects as a document of title. In its latter role, it is traditionally and concisely described as being the equivalent of the goods – 'the documents are the goods'. In its latter role, the bill enables the buyer to obtain delivery from the carrier at destination (upon presentation of the original bill, [7] which is sent ahead); and it also permits the buyer to sell the goods to a third party while they are in transit. (Dependent upon the contract between buyer and seller, the bill may be made non-negotiable so as to preclude this last facility of resale in transit.)

---

6   On EDI, in this context, see *Guide to the Incoterms, 1990, op cit*, pp 8–9, 31, 80–81, 144ff; Burnett, R, *The Law of International Business Transactions*, 1994, Sydney: Federation Press, pp 29–30, 84ff.
7   Note that multiple originals may be issued.

The bill is not an unqualified document of title. The transferee acquires no better a title than the transferor. The bill, that is, represents a right to possession, and thus establishes possessory title, but it does not *per se* establish legal title.

The bill of lading can be dispensed with in the maritime context, when the resale in transit facility is not required and the parties do not see any need for the delivery of the goods at destination by the carrier, to be contingent upon production of the original of the document issued by the carrier upon receipt at the place of shipment. The situation was explained thus, in the Introduction to the ICC Incoterms 1990:

> In recent years, a considerable simplification of documentary practices has been achieved. Bills of lading are frequently replaced by non-negotiable documents similar to those which are used in other modes of transport than carriage by sea. These documents are called 'sea waybills', 'liner waybills', 'freight receipts' or variants of such expressions. These non-negotiable documents are quite satisfactory to use except when the buyer wishes to sell the goods in transit by surrendering a paper document to the new buyer. In order to make this possible, the obligation of the seller to provide a bill of lading under CFR and CIF must necessarily be retained. However, when the contracting parties know that the buyer does not contemplate selling the goods in transit, they may specifically agree to relieve the seller from the obligation to provide a bill of lading, or alternatively they may use CPT and CIF where there is no obligation to provide a bill of lading.[8]

Given that the originals of these documents do not have the significance that the originals have for the bill of lading, they are more readily replaced by EDI.

Even in the case of the bill of lading, however, progress has been made towards replacing it with EDI. Provision is made for electronic bills of lading by the regime laid down in the Rules for Electronic Bills of Lading adopted in 1990 by the Comité Maritime International (CMI).[9] It was commented in the preamble to Incoterms 2000 that in spite of the particular legal nature of the bill of lading, it is expected that it will be replaced by electronic means in the near future.

The CMI scheme preserves the security of communications by resort to the so called (electronic) Private Key system (in substance, the Private Key is a unique identification number). The CMI scheme will only be used where both seller and buyer have agreed to this.

The electronic messages in this context may be sent in conformity with the international systems developed under the aegis of the United Nations known as EDIFACT (Electronic Date Interchange for Administration, Commerce and Transport) and UNCID (Uniform Rules of Conduct for Interchange of Trade Date by Teletransmission).[10]

The Incoterm categories and structure of each Incoterm

There are 13 Incoterms, and they are grouped into four categories. There are several principles underpinning this system of classification, and the subdivisions within each

---

8   ICC – *Incoterms 1990*, p 15.
9   The text is set out in the Annexes to the *Guide to the Incoterms 1990, op cit*, pp 144–45; and see the commentaries in *ibid*, pp 8–9, 31, 80–81, 144ff; and in Burnett, *op cit*, pp 84ff.
10 See *Guide to the Incoterms 1990, op cit*, p 8.

category (that is, in the individual terms themselves). Broadly, the terms are grouped according to the extent to which the seller on the one hand, or the buyer on the other, are each responsible for the delivery of the goods, and related aspects of this. More specifically, they regulate the extent of each party's responsibility (if any) for such matters as arranging for export and import clearance; arranging and paying for carriage (the main carriage, and pre- and on-carriage); and arranging and paying for insurance; and they also regulate the passing of risk. At one extreme, the ExW term imposes the minimum responsibility on the seller and a corresponding maximum liability on the buyer (the seller's delivery obligations are ended when he makes the goods available to the buyer at his premises). At the other extreme the D terms impose the maximum obligation on the seller with a corresponding diminution of responsibility on the part of the buyer, because these terms oblige the seller to deliver the goods to an agreed destination in the buyer's country. (The term that is most onerous of all where the seller is concerned is the DDP term.) The intermediate terms in categories F and C impose intermediate levels of obligation on each party; C is more onerous where the seller is concerned than is F (see below).

The E category is named thus because the sole term in this category commences with 'E', that is, ex-works. As noted, this is the term that is most beneficial to the seller.

The F terms are so named because the seller hands the goods over to the carrier free of expense and risk to the buyer. Once, however, the carrier has them, the buyer assumes the risk and expense including the expense of carriage. These contracts are known as 'shipment' contracts, with the seller fulfilling his delivery obligation in his own country. (D class contracts, in contrast, are 'arrival' contracts.) After the ExW term, the F terms are the most beneficial to the seller.

The C terms are so designated because the seller bears specified *costs*, even after delivery, at which point the general risks and costs pass to the buyer. Under C terms (and unlike the F terms), the seller is responsible for organising the main carriage. These contracts are also known as 'shipment' contracts (again, in contrast to the D, or 'arrival' contracts). The risk passes to the buyer upon this delivery to the carrier, but unlike the case in respect of the F terms, the seller is liable for the costs of carriage and (in certain cases) insurance up until the arrival of the goods at the agreed destination in the buyer's country. Nonetheless, the seller is not at risk during the main carriage: if the goods are lost or damaged during this phase, this is the buyer's burden. Because of the obligations concerning aspects of the main carriage, the C terms are relatively more burdensome for the seller than F terms. Notwithstanding that the seller has these extra obligations, his delivery obligation is, as in the case of the F, fulfilled in his own country.

The D terms are so named because the seller contracts to *deliver* the goods at an agreed destination (normally) in the buyer's country. It follows that the seller's delivery obligation is fulfilled, not at an earlier time in his own country (a characteristic of the E, F and C categories), but at the later time in the buyer's country. The D terms (known also as 'delivered' terms) are the most onerous from the seller's viewpoint. He must arrange the main carriage to the agreed destination and bear the costs and risks pertaining to and during this carriage. If the goods are lost in transit, this is the seller's problem.

D terms are becoming relatively more popular. Sellers of goods who can undertake delivery in the buyer's country are more likely to get orders for these goods.

Some of the Incoterms are designed for certain modes of transport while others are flexible. The following are for use with any mode of transport (or for multi-modal systems): ExW, FCA, CPT, CIP, DAF, DDU and DDP. FCA is to be used for air transport or rail transport; and the following are for sea or inland waterway transport – FAS, FOB, CFR, CIF, DES and DEQ.

The text of each Incoterm has been structured in a standardised format, with the seller's obligations being stated under 10 headings; and with the buyer's most closely corresponding obligations being likewise grouped under 10 headings. The obligations on each side broadly mirror those on the other side (the details of course differ). Thereby, a checklist of obligations imposed upon each party is generated. In some cases, a particular heading will be inapplicable, having regard to the particular term; in this case, the text under the heading reads 'no obligation'. Because this standard table of obligations has been used not only as between the parties, but also from one term to the next, it is relatively easy to determine the differences between each Incoterm, especially in those cases where two terms are largely identical but differ on some pivotal point.

The individual Incoterms are reviewed in the following pages.

THE E CATEGORY – 'EX-WORKS'

As noted, the E category of Incoterms has only one term – ex-works (... named place) or ExW (... named place). This term requires that the seller make the goods available at the seller's premises (as agreed upon and identified). These premises will be his works, factory, warehouse, etc. The core obligations of the seller are stated in A1 of the seller's obligations (provision of goods in conformity with the contract), and in A4, headed 'Delivery'. The seller must:

> [P]lace the goods at the disposal of the buyer at the named place of delivery, not loaded on any collecting vehicle, on the date or within the period agreed or, if no such time is agreed, at the usual time for delivery of such goods. If no specific point has been agreed within the named place, and if there are several points available, the seller may select the point at the place of delivery which best suits his purpose.

The seller has no delivery obligation beyond this point. It has been commented that the ex-works sale:

> ... is the most favourable arrangement which can be obtained by a seller desirous of conducting an export transaction as closely as possible on the lines of an ordinary sale of goods in the home market.[11]

The contract should specify, where appropriate, which party is responsible for loading the goods onto any vehicle sent by the buyer. The goods will, where applicable, need to be identified to the contract before they can be so delivered, that is, where the contract is, at formation, one for the sale of unascertained goods.

A5 provides that (subject to B5) the seller bears all risks of loss of or damage to the goods until such time as they have been placed at the buyer's disposal in accordance with A4. The provision follows the standard Incoterms scheme, that is, that risk

---

11 Schmitthoff, C, *Export Trade – The Law and Practice of International Trade*, 9th edn, 1990, London: Stevens, p 11.

normally passes from seller to buyer when the seller has performed his required act of delivery – replicating the approach of the Vienna Convention on Contracts for the International Sale of Goods.[12]

It follows that, *prima facie*, the seller has no liability for damage to or loss of the goods post-delivery. The seller will only be liable in the case where, independently of this provision in A5, or parallel provisions in the contract or the applicable law, the seller can be made legally liable for loss or damage. Such might be the case, for instance, where any required packaging (see A9) is inadequate and such a deficiency in performance amounts to breach of contract, and this breach causes damage or loss (see A9). Also, the fact that the risk passes cannot excuse the seller from liability for a non-conformity as between goods and contract (which, *inter alia*, would be a breach of A1).[13]

As A5 recognises, B5 – the parallel provision dealing with risk in the table of buyer's obligations – may operate to pass risk to the buyer prior to the seller delivering them to the buyer. This will happen where the buyer is entitled to determine the time within a stipulated period and/or the place of delivery, and he does not, as required by B7, give sufficient notice to the seller. In such a case, a failure to give notice will have the effect that the risk passes pre-delivery, that is, from the agreed date or the expiry date of any period fixed for taking delivery (provided that the goods have been appropriated to the contract) (see B5). The buyer, that is, cannot delay performing his obligations by refusing to give the required notice. If he does so delay, he is liable for the risks and costs pertaining to the goods.

The seller must assist the buyer to obtain export or import clearance (but at the buyer's expense) (A2); but consistently with the ExW scheme, the buyer must obtain at his own risk and expense any export licence, etc (B2). The arrangement of carriage from the seller's premises is of course a burden on the buyer (B3). The buyer must take delivery (B4).

The seller bears the costs, up until the time they are placed at the buyer's disposal, after which time the buyer has this burden (A6, B6). As in the case of the risks, delivery is the pivotal point for dividing costs. The buyer must pay additional costs generated by his failure to take delivery when it is duly made, or his failure to give any notice required under B7 (see B6). An obvious instance of additional costs would be storage costs.

The buyer is to give the seller a receipt upon taking delivery (see B8). The buyer is responsible for any pre-shipment inspection of the goods including inspection mandated by the authorities of the country of exportation (B9). On the other hand, the seller is responsible for the routine checking operations (for example, checking quality and weighing), which are necessary for the purpose of delivering the goods to the buyer (A9).

Note A10 and B10 concerning the obtaining of documents (or EDI equivalents) for the export/import clearance of the goods, and their intermediate transit through third countries. These are the buyer's responsibility, but the seller is to give every assistance and is entitled to be reimbursed for any expenses incurred. Likewise, under A10 the

---

12   See *Guide to Incoterms 1990, op cit*, p 44.
13   See the discussion in *ibid*, p 44.

seller is to give the buyer any necessary information, if requested, for procuring insurance.

THE F CATEGORY – FCA, FAS, FOB

As noted, an F term constitutes a contract for the international sale of goods, a shipment contract (as distinct from an arrival or D class contract). They are so designated because the seller delivers the goods to the carrier *free* of expense and risk to the buyer, whereupon the buyer assumes the risks and costs, including the cost of carriage (which will have been organised by the buyer). The seller therefore fulfils his delivery obligations in his own country. These terms are the next most beneficial to the seller after the ExW term.

Free carrier (FCA)

The free carrier (... named place) term is abbreviated FCA (... named place). FCA requires that the seller deliver the goods to the carrier nominated by the buyer, at the specified place, after having cleared them for export. Once delivery has been effected, the seller has fulfilled his delivery obligations. The term is suitable for all forms of transport and for multi-modal operations.

The term 'carrier' is defined in the preamble to the FCA terms as meaning any person who, in a contract of carriage, undertakes to perform or to procure the performance of transport by rail, road, air, sea, inland waterway or by a combination of such modes.

The seller's core obligations are set out in A1 (provision of goods in conformity with the contract); A2 (requiring him at his own risk and expense to obtain any export licence, etc, for the exportation of the goods); and A4, obliging him to deliver the goods to the nominated carrier of the buyer, at the nominated place. It is the A2 (clear for export) and A4 (deliver to carrier) terms that distinguish the FCA usage.

Under A3, the seller does not have an obligation to enter into a contract of carriage of the goods. *Prima facie*, this is the buyer's obligation (see B3, imposing the obligation on the buyer to contract at his own expense for the carriage of the goods from the named place of delivery). However, if the seller is requested by the buyer or if it is commercial practice and the buyer does not give a timely counter instruction, the seller may contract in the usual terms at the buyer's risk and expense (A3(a)). The seller has a choice in the matter (but must notify the buyer accordingly). Likewise, the seller is under no obligation to arrange insurance of the goods.

A4 – the delivery term – was revised in Incoterms 2000, in recognition of the fact that there is considerable variation in practice as to when the parties intend delivery to occur. For example, the seller may carry the goods to the buyer's premises for delivery; or the buyer may send a vehicle to the seller's premises to take delivery.

A4 provides that the seller must deliver the goods to the carrier or another person nominated by the buyer, or chosen by the seller in accordance with A3(a), at the named place on the date or within the period agreed for delivery.

Where the named place is the seller's premises, delivery is deemed to have been completed, when the goods are loaded on the transport means provided by the carrier nominated by the buyer or its agent.

If the named place is anywhere other than the seller's premises, then delivery is completed when the goods are placed at the disposal of the carrier, or other person nominated by the buyer (or chosen by the seller under A3(a)), on the seller's means of transport not unloaded.

If no specific point has been agreed within the named place, the seller may select one that best suits his purpose.

In the absence of precise instructions from the buyer, the seller may deliver the goods for carriage in such a manner as the transport mode, quantity and/or quality of the goods requires.

The reference to A3(a), as noted, is to the situation where (notwithstanding that the seller has no obligation to arrange the contract of carriage), the seller accedes to the buyer's request to arrange carriage, or arranges it pursuant to commercial practice. In such a case, the buyer is still liable for the risks and costs of carriage.

The concept of 'carrier' as noted is defined in the preamble to the statement of obligations in FCA. The delivery by the seller of the goods to a freight forwarder will satisfy his obligation under A4, when the buyer instructs him to so deliver.

The seller must (subject to B5), bear all the risks of loss of or damage to the goods until such time as they have been delivered in accordance with A4. Pursuant to B5, the buyer bears all risks of loss of, or damage to, the goods from the time of delivery under A4. The buyer also bears the risks from the agreed date or expiry date of any agreed period that arises because he fails to nominate the carrier or other person under A4, or because the nominated carrier fails to take the goods into charge at the agreed time, or because the buyer fails to give notice in accordance with B7.[14] (In these cases the goods must have been duly appropriated to the contract, that is, set aside or otherwise identified as the contract goods.)

The seller must, subject to B6, pay the costs relating to the goods until they have been delivered under A4, and pay as well applicable costs of customs and all duties, taxes and other charges payable upon export (A6). Pursuant to B6, the buyer must pay the costs relating to the goods from the time of delivery under A4. The buyer must also pay any additional costs incurred where he fails to nominate the carrier or another person under A4 or where the party nominated by the buyer fails to take charge of the goods at the agreed time, or because he has failed to give notice in accordance with B7, provided that the goods have been duly appropriated to the contract.

The seller's other obligations include giving notice to the buyer that the goods have been delivered in accordance with A4 (A7); provision of specified transport documents or the EDI equivalent (A8); performing routine checking, packaging and marking operations pre-delivery (A9); and rendering the buyer, at the latter's request, risk and expense, every assistance in obtaining any documents (or EDI equivalent) for the importation of the goods into the buyer's country, and providing necessary information, if requested, for the procuring of insurance (A10).

The buyer's other obligations include payment for the goods (B1); organising and paying for import clearance into his own country (and where applicable, transit

---

14 This provides that the buyer must give the seller sufficient notice of the name of the party designated in A4, and where necessary, specify the transport mode, the date of delivery and if required the point within the place named for delivery.

through a third country) (B2); contracting at his own expense for the carriage after the seller has fulfilled his delivery obligations – viz, in effect, taking responsibility for the main carriage and any post-carriage transport (for example, from a container terminal at his end to his premises) (B3); taking delivery (B4); accepting proof of delivery under A8 (B8); paying pre-shipment inspection except[15] when mandated by the authorities in the country of export (B9); and paying the costs incurred in the buyer's obtaining of the documents or EDI equivalents pursuant to A10 (B10).

Free alongside ship (FAS)

The free alongside ship (… named place) term is abbreviated FAS (… named place). FAS requires the seller to deliver the goods alongside the ship, that is, on the wharf or in one or more lighters. Thereupon, the risks and costs are divided. In principle, the transaction, from the seller's viewpoint, is little different from a domestic sale where he delivers goods to the premises of a domestic buyer. The seller is responsible for export clearance. (This is a reversal of the situation provided for in Incoterms 1990, which was made to recognise commercial practice.) The buyer is responsible for the main contract of carriage. By its nature, FAS is to be used only for sea and inland waterway transport.

The seller has the standard duty to supply goods in conformity with the contract (A1). He must obtain at his own risk and expense any export licence, or other official authorisation and carry out, where applicable, all customs formalities for export (A2). He does not have any obligations to arrange the contract of carriage or insurance (A3). (He will have organised and paid for pre-delivery carriage, and may have chosen to insure against the risk borne by him until delivery.)

His delivery obligation is succinctly stated in A4:

> The seller must place the goods alongside the vessel nominated by the buyer at the loading place named by the buyer at the named port of shipment on the date or within the agreed period and in the manner customary at the port.

As noted, this requires delivery on the appropriate wharf, but it is also satisfied by loading onto lighters where this is more apt. Where the ship is not alongside a wharf, the seller will have to load the goods onto lighters so that it may be transported alongside the ship. In this case the seller is liable for the costs of the lighters and of loading them, up until the time the lighter is alongside the ship. (He is not thereafter liable for the costs of loading from the lighters onto the ship – his duty is to deliver the goods alongside the ship.) The responsibility of the seller for damage and loss runs until the lighters are alongside the ship, unless the parties agree that the delivery is to be made 'free on lighter', signifying that the seller's responsibility ends once the goods pass the lighter's rail.[16]

---

15 This inspection would go beyond the routine checking required of the seller prior to delivery, by A9. Note that the mandatory inspection required by the authorities is not an expense for the buyer, consistent with the seller being responsible for export clearance. See further the situation with ExW, where this inspection is to the account of the buyer, consistently with the ExW principle that the seller's obligations are very limited – delivery to the buyer at the seller's own premises.

16 See Schmitthoff, *op cit*, p 13, discussing the use of lighters.

The seller's risks end and the buyer's begin once the goods have been delivered in accordance with A4, that is, once they have been placed alongside the ship (A5). The seller would need to insure the goods up to this point. Costs are likewise divided at the point of delivery (A6). The division of risks and costs at the point of delivery is standard in the Incoterms. Dock dues and similar charges are the seller's responsibility.[17]

The seller is to give sufficient notice to the buyer that the goods have been delivered alongside the ship (A7); provide the buyer at the seller's expense with the usual document evidencing delivery; and, if this document is not the transport document, assist the buyer to obtain the transport document (such as a bill of lading, non-negotiable sea waybill or EDI equivalent) (A8); perform routine checking obligations necessary for delivery, pack the goods as appropriate, and mark them as appropriate (A9); and assist the buyer at the latter's request, risk and expense to obtain any documents or equivalent EDI messages required for importation, or transit through a third country (A10). The seller is also to supply the buyer with the necessary information for obtaining insurance (A10).

The buyer must pay the price provided in the contract (B1). The buyer, as noted, is responsible for obtaining import clearance (B2); for organising and paying for main carriage (that is, transport after delivery) (B3); and for taking delivery in accordance with A4 (B4). The buyer, that is, must organise the loading of the goods onto the vessel after they have been placed alongside the vessel by the seller.

B5 (dealing with the transfer of risks) and B6 (on the division of costs) mirror A5 and A6, in providing that the risks and costs are transferred to the buyer upon delivery by the seller alongside the ship. B5 and B6 also provide for a pre-delivery passing of risk, where the buyer fails to give the seller sufficient notice of the vessel name, loading place and required delivery time, as required by B7 (it is assumed that one or more of these matters is not specified in the contract, or that the buyer is given a discretion – for example, to nominate delivery within a specified period – see A4 and B4). The costs and risks will pass upon the day determined to be the day by which the notice should have been given, or such other date as it identifiable by reference to the contract. Pursuant to B5 and B6, risks and costs also pass where the nominated carrier fails to arrive on time, or to take the goods. The goods must have been identified to the contract in order for there to be a pre-delivery passing of risk.

The buyer must pay the costs of pre-shipment (including that mandated by the authorities of the export country) (B9) (these do not include the routine checking operations referred to in A9). The buyer is to pay the costs of obtaining the documents or their EDI equivalents, mentioned in A10, and to reimburse the seller any expenses he incurred in this regard (B10).

Free on board (FOB)

Under free on board (... named port of shipment), or FOB (... named port of shipment), the seller's delivery obligation is concluded the instant the cargo passes

---

17 See the discussion by Schmitthoff, *op cit*, p 15, noting that in certain cases it may be advisable to deal specifically in the contract with the issue of port rates.

over the ship's rail. The passing over the rail is the point when the risks and costs are divided, with the buyer thereupon assuming both burdens. The FOB term also imposes on the seller the obligation to clear the goods for export.

The FOB is a long-standing term in mercantile usage and domestic legal systems. Its meaning varies from jurisdiction to jurisdiction in some respects, and in the common law countries it has attracted a wealth of judicial exegesis. It is a traditional marine transport term, and can only be used for sea and inland waterway transport. Its preoccupation with the ship's rail is based upon the recognition that this is equivalent to the frontier – to the line dividing the countries of export and import – of the seller's and buyer's countries respectively. Taking the ship's rail as the pivot point for the division of risks and costs is somewhat arbitrary (and potentially productive of anomaly), as reflected in the well known comment by Devlin J in an English decision dealing with the FOB term at common law:

> Only the most enthusiastic lawyer could watch with satisfaction the spectacle of liabilities shifting uneasily as the cargo sways at the end of a derrick across a notional perpendicular projecting from the ship's rail.[18]

A trade term like FOB, which pivots on the ship's rail, may be appropriate for general cargo delivered over the rail (including bulk cargo), as where a commodity is loaded *via* a conveyer belt or a chute. It is less appropriate for the roll-on/roll-off loading operation or for containerised cargo (which will be delivered at an earlier point, such as to a container terminal); in such cases FCA is more apt.[19] The preamble to Incoterms 2000 makes this point more strongly, observing that FOB is only appropriate where the goods are intended to be delivered across the ship's rail, or in any event to the ship, and not where they are to be handed over to the carrier for subsequent entry into the ship, such as when stowed in containers or loaded into trucks or wagons in roll-on/roll-off traffic. The inappropriate use of FOB can cause 'the seller to incur risks subsequent to the handing over of the goods to the carrier named by the buyer'.[20]

FOB differs from FAS; the latter, as seen above, provides for the fulfilment of the seller's delivery obligation at an earlier time (when the goods are delivered alongside the ship). The FOB term progresses towards the truly international sales contract model, in requiring the seller to obtain export clearance (in recognition that he is delivering at the notional 'frontier' of the ship's rail).

The seller has the standard duty in A1 of providing goods in conformity with the contract. A feature of FOB is the seller's obligation to obtain export clearance at his own risk and expense, as provided for in A2.

As his delivery obligation is fulfilled at the ship's rail, he does not have to arrange the contract of (main) carriage, that is, from port, nor does he have any obligation to insure the goods (although he may wish to insure them up until his risk passes, that is, upon loading) (A3). He will have to organise pre-delivery carriage and pay for this. While arranging the main contract of carriage is technically the buyer's responsibility,

---

18 *Pyrene Co Ltd v Scindia Navigation Co Ltd* [1954] 2 QB 402 at 419.
19 So observed in *Guide to Incoterms 1990, op cit,* p 69.
20 ICC–*Incoterms 2000,* p 24.

in practice it may be convenient for the seller to do this. The price of the goods can be adjusted to take account of this.[21]

In such a case the seller still completes his delivery once the goods pass over the rail, and costs (less the cost of carriage, if this has been dealt with specifically in the contract and allocated to the seller) and risks still divide at this point. Thus, even as the seller may have organised and paid for main carriage, he is not liable for the damage to, or loss of, the goods during this phase. Of course, if the parties additionally impose the risks upon the seller during main carriage, by a specific provision in the contract, the contract is not a true FOB contract, and one of the D (arrival) terms should be used instead. The seller's delivery obligation is stated in A4:

> The seller must deliver the goods on the date or within the agreed period at the named port of shipment and in the manner customary at the port on board the vessel nominated by the buyer ...

A5 and A6, in referring to the passing of the ship's rail as the key point of division for risks and costs, emphasise that delivery is effected, pursuant to A4, the moment the goods pass the rail. (A contrary interpretation is that the A4 stipulation does indeed move beyond the ship's rail as the defining moment for completion of the delivery obligation, and require delivery on board.[22] Nonetheless, A5 and A6, in dividing risks and costs at the ship's rail, are in conformity with the traditional common law concept of FOB.)[23]

The risks of loss of, or damage to, the goods are expressly transferred from seller to buyer at the time the goods pass the ship's rail at the named port of shipment (A5). The seller is not liable, therefore, for mishaps to the goods after this point; although he retains liability for any deficiency in the goods resulting from non-conformity with the contract, or inadequate packaging by him amounting to a breach of contract, etc.

The costs of delivery are also divided at the ship's rail. A6 provides that (subject to B6) the seller is to pay all costs relating to the goods until this time. It also provides that the seller (consistent with his obligation under A2) is to bear the costs of obtaining export clearance, including the costs of customs formalities, duties, taxes and other official charges incidental to this. The task of dividing the costs of loading could be difficult, given that the one party (such as a stevedore) will be responsible for the pre- and post-rail operations.[24] This is usually not necessary. As explained in *Guide to Incoterms 1990*:

> The reference in FOB A4 to 'the manner customary at the port' highlights the problem of using the passing of the ship's rail as the guiding factor in practice. The parties in these circumstances will have to follow the custom of the port regarding the actual measures to be taken in delivering the goods on board. Usually the task is performed by stevedoring companies, and the practical problem normally lies in deciding who should bear the costs of their services.[25]

---

21 See Burnett, *op cit*, pp 40–41
22 See *ibid*, pp 42–43.
23 *Ibid*, p 39, notes that given the premise that A4 requires delivery on board, the FOB Incoterm 'separates risk and delivery' (by virtue of A5). In *Guide to Incoterms 1990* it is assumed that the division of risks and costs is at the ship's rail, which is equated to delivery – *op cit*, pp 70–71.
24 Note the comment in Burnett, *op cit*, p 43.
25 See *Guide to Incoterms 1990, op cit*, p 70.

Normally, the risks (A5) and the costs (A6) are divided when the goods pass over the rail. Both A5 and A6 are expressly qualified by B5 and B6, respectively, which relate of course to the buyer's obligations. These are noted below.

The seller must give the buyer sufficient notice that the goods have been delivered on board (A7). The seller must supply to the buyer the usual document (or equivalent EDI) in proof of delivery at the seller's own expense. If this document is not the transport document, the seller must assist the buyer at the latter's request, risk and expense, to obtain a transport document (or equivalent EDI) for the contract of carriage, such as a negotiable bill of lading or a non-negotiable sea waybill (A8). The seller has the standard routine pre-delivery checking obligation, and packaging and marking obligations (A9), and must assist the buyer if required, at the latter's expense, to obtain any documents or EDI equivalents to permit the import of the goods, and (if applicable) their intermediate transit through another country (A10).

The buyer must pay the contract price (B1); obtain at his own risk and expense import clearance (and satisfy formalities for their transit through another country) (B2); organise the contract of carriage (B3) after taking delivery (and for that matter, any post-carriage contracts of transportation); and take delivery of the goods in accordance with A4 (B4).

B5 and B6 parallel A5 and A6 in recognising that the risks and costs, relating to the goods respectively, pass from seller to buyer at the time they pass the ship's rail. Accordingly, the buyer may wish to insure the goods from this point. However, the risks and costs can, pursuant to B5 and B6, be transferred earlier, that is, prior to delivery across the ship's rail. This will happen where the buyer, when required, fails to give the seller sufficient notice of the vessel name, loading point and required delivery time (see B7, on notice to the seller). The notice may be required having regard to the terms of the contract, as where one or more of these matters is left open – see A4, in particular, which envisages that the delivery may (by agreement) be either on a nominated date, or within the period stipulated. The risks and costs would be transferred, in a case where notice is not given, upon the date agreed for delivery, or at the end of the period during which notice is to be given. The buyer cannot delay his obligation to take delivery (B4) by declining to give notice. If the vessel cannot take the goods by the agreed date, risks and costs are likewise divided at the agreed date, pre-delivery. This earlier division cannot, however, operate unless and until the goods, if originally unascertained, have been identified to the contract (B5 and B6).

The buyer must accept proof of delivery in accordance with A8 (B8); pay the costs of pre-shipment inspection except where mandated by the authorities of the country of export (B9) (any such costs would not include the costs of pre-delivery checking by the seller under A9); and pay costs and charges incurred in obtaining the documents or EDI equivalents mentioned in A10 (B10).

THE C CATEGORY – CFR, CIF, CPT, CIP

As noted, the C terms are so designated because the seller bears specified *costs* even after delivery, at which point the general costs and risks have passed to the buyer. Under C terms (and contrary to the situation under the F terms), the seller is responsible for organising the contract of (main) carriage. C contracts are often referred to as shipment contracts (in contrast to the D contracts, which are known as arrival contracts – see 'The D category' below).

Cost and freight (CFR)/Cost, insurance and freight (CIF)

The twin Incoterms, cost and freight (... named port of destination) or CFR (... named port of destination), and cost, insurance and freight (... named port of destination) or CIF (... named port of destination), are identical, with one exception – CIF additionally imposes upon the seller the obligation to insure the goods during their main carriage. Given that CIF is more commonly employed, the focus of review will be on it; after which CFR will be briefly commented upon. All comments regarding CIF apply to CFR, with this one exception.

Cost, insurance and freight (CIF)

CIF is another term that, like FOB, requires the seller to deliver the goods over the ship's rail, whereupon his delivery obligation is discharged. However, the CIF seller has additional obligations (compared to the FOB seller): he must organise the main contract of carriage and effect insurance for the risks of the voyage.

The CIF seller's obligations, then, are: obtain and pay for export clearance; and transport the goods to the ship and deliver them on board, with the risks and costs being transferred to the buyer at the moment when the goods pass over the ship's rail. This division of risks and costs is qualified, however, by the two requirements:

(a) that the seller organise and pay for the main contract of carriage; and

(b) that he procure insurance to cover the risk of damage to or loss of the goods during main carriage.

Notwithstanding these qualifications, it is still appropriate to speak of his delivery obligation as being concluded at the moment the goods pass the ship's rail. The qualifications on the passing of costs are limited – the seller must pay for the main carriage and export clearance. The qualification where the passing of risks is concerned is not a true exception – certainly the CIF seller must organise insurance to cover the voyage, but he is not thereby left at risk during (or after) this phase. If there is a mishap involving the goods for which the seller has no independent liability (that is, independent of the CIF term), the buyer will need to claim on the policy, or pursue some other party.

As it was observed in relation to FOB, the 'ship's rail' class of Incoterm (like CIF) may well be appropriate for general cargo delivered over the rail (especially bulk cargo such as that delivered via a chute or conveyer belt), but it is less appropriate for the roll-on/roll-off loading operation, for containerised cargo which will be delivered at an earlier point, such as to a container terminal. In such a case FCA is more apt.[26]

CIF (and CFR) are by their nature for use only where carriage is by sea or inland waterway.

CIF is a long-standing term in mercantile usage and domestic legal systems, and can vary in its meaning from jurisdiction to jurisdiction. The Incoterm CIF is one version of it. The rationale of CIF class trade terms has been explained thus: the exporter is typically an expert in organising export clearance and carriage, and:

---

26 See *Guide to Incoterms 1990, op cit*, p 69.

... often in a position to make favourable arrangements as regards freight and insurance. In particular, they will often secure reductions in these charges when engaged in substantial or regular trade with the buyer's country, or they may be able to group several consignments to the same consignee or a number of consignments to different consignees in order to make the best use of the available shipping space; in these cases the CIF clause offers them distinct advantages.[27]

The CIF clause enables the bundling of the main carriage and insurance obligations, and their allocation to the exporter (export managers, confirming houses, manufacturers, etc). All things being equal, the cost of insurance and freight will be built into the price but at a potential saving to the buyer in time and expense.

It has often been remarked of the CIF contract at common law that, where it is concerned, 'the documents are the goods'; viz, the seller's obligation is to ship the goods from a port in his own country, with the result that the contract is a shipment and not an arrival (delivery at destination) class of contract. Where the destination is concerned, he undertakes only to tender a bill of lading. This feature is reflected in the statement by Scrutton J in an English case:

> It is not a contract that goods shall arrive, but a contract to ship goods complying with the contract of sale, to obtain, unless the contract otherwise provides, the ordinary contract of carriage to the place of destination, and the ordinary contract of insurance on that voyage, and to tender these documents against payment of the contract price.[28]

Accordingly, in the normal case the seller is still entitled to be paid upon tender of the insurance policy and the bill of lading, even if the goods are damaged or lost during main carriage.

These shipping documents – the bill of lading and the insurance policy – are the hallmarks of the traditional CIF contract. This is reflected in the following comment. The parties, although they may adapt and modify what purports to be a CIF contract, must:

> ... take care that these amendments and variations do not destroy the essential characteristics of the CIF stipulation, which are that, as the result of the transfer of the shipping documents, a direct relationship is established between the buyer on the one hand and the carrier and insurer on the other, so as to enable the buyer to make direct claims against these persons in the case of loss of, or damage to, the goods. If the parties vary this quality of the shipping documents, eg by providing that the seller shall be at liberty to tender, instead of a bill of lading, a delivery order on his agent in the port of destination or the goods themselves, the contract ceases to be a true CIF contract in the legal sense.[29]

This comment is directed to the CIF contract (or term) in its common law incidents. The use of the shorthand CIF (Incoterm 2000) imports the rules of interpretation there appended, and, as it will be seen, the negotiable bill of lading (or electronic equivalent) is optional – non-negotiable sea waybills, etc, may also be tendered (A7). In this respect, the Incoterm CIF may or may not (depending upon the precise agreement of

---

27 See Schmitthoff, *op cit*, p 35.
28 *Arnold Karberg and Co v Blythe, Green Jourdain and Co* [1915] 2 KB 379 at 388. See the comments in Schmitthoff, *op cit*, pp 34ff.
29 See Schmitthoff, *op cit*, p 36.

the parties) be synonymous with the traditional CIF contract. A bill of lading will still be used where the parties contemplate that the goods may be sold (to a third party) during transit.

Under CIF, the seller must provide goods in conformity with the contract (A1). He must obtain export clearance at his own risk and expense (A2). He must organise and pay for the carriage of the goods to the named destination; and he must obtain at his own expense cargo insurance (A3). These are also key obligations.

The insurance must be effected on terms permitting the buyer, or other person having an insurable interest, to claim directly on the policy. The insurance is to be with an insurer of good repute, and (unless agreed otherwise) it is to be in accordance with the minimum cover of the Institute Cargo Clauses (Institute of London Underwriters) or any similar set of clauses. The minimum insurance is to cover the contract price plus 10%, in the currency of the contract. The insurance is to be from the time risks are transferred to the buyer (that is, as provided for in B5, once the goods have passed over the ship's rail), until they arrive at the named port of destination. The buyer may wish to stipulate for more than minimum cover by express provision in the contract.[30]

The delivery obligation is: 'The seller must deliver the goods on board the vessel at the port of shipment on the date or within the agreed period' (A4). The seller, then, delivers the cargo to the port from which the main carriage commences. He will have arranged and paid for this main carriage (and, by definition, pre-delivery carriage will be entirely his own responsibility). Unless the contract provides otherwise, he has a discretion as to the port of shipment and choice of carrier (although note that A3 lays down some broad parameters, including that the normal route be taken). It has been commented that the CIF contract should not specify a (latest) date of delivery at the destination, because this could, on one view, be read as converting what should be a delivery contract into an arrival contract.[31] If the latter is intended, a D term should be used.

Although A4 posits the conclusion of delivery at the moment the goods are delivered 'on board', A5 and A6 make it clear that the precise moment when the delivery is effected is that moment when the goods pass over the ship's rail.

A5 specifies that, subject to the provisions of B5, the seller bears the risks of loss or damage until the goods have passed the ship's rail at the point of shipment. The seller, that is, is not liable for damage, etc, after this time, including during the voyage. An exception will be where he is independently liable for damage, etc, occurring after this time, as where the goods are later found to be non-conforming, or suffer damage because of inadequate packaging amounting to a breach of contract (see A9).

A6 divides the costs at the ship's rail (subject to B6). As noted, there are certain exceptions: the seller has to pay the costs of freight and other costs associated with organising the contract of main carriage, including the costs of loading the goods on board and any costs of unloading at the port of discharge which may be charged by regular shipping lines when contracting for carriage (see A6). The seller must also pay for export clearance (including any taxes). The seller also, as noted, pays the costs of

---

30 See *Guide to Incoterms 1990, op cit*, p 88, commenting that minimum cover is only suitable for bulk cargoes which usually do not suffer loss or damage in transit unless something happens to the ship as well as the cargo.

31 See *ibid*, p 79.

insuring the cargo during carriage. The seller must give notice to the buyer of delivery of the goods on board the vessel (A7).

The seller must at his own expense provide the buyer with the usual transport document for the agreed port of destination (A8). This may be a bill of lading – necessary if the parties contemplate the possible resale of the cargo while afloat; but A8 also recognises that something short of a bill, such as a non-negotiable sea waybill, may be employed (the parties will have to stipulate in their contract what form of documentation is to be tendered). The documents used must, at the least, permit the buyer to claim the goods from the carrier. EDI equivalents to the transport documents may be used, by agreement.[32]

The seller must carry out routine pre-delivery checking operations, pack the goods adequately, if applicable, and mark any such packaging (A9). He must assist the buyer, if requested, and, at the latter's risk and expense, obtain any documents or EDI equivalents required for importation or transit through another country (A10).

The buyer must pay the contract price (B1); obtain import clearance – the CIF contract is not an arrival contract (see B2); but he has no obligation concerning the main carriage (B3 – although he must arrange carriage from the port of destination).

The buyer must accept delivery when delivered in accordance with A4, and receive them from the carrier at the named port of destination (B4). Taking delivery over the ship's rail has the consequences earlier noted – the risks of the goods, and (with certain exception) the costs, are thereupon transferred to him. The requirement that the buyer receive them from the carrier at destination has the consequence that, if costs additional to normal freight are generated because of an undue delay in unloading, these are to the buyer's account.[33]

The seller, pursuant to A6, bears any charges for unloading at the port of destination that may be levied by regular shipping lines when contracting for carriage (as part of the seller's obligation to organise and pay for the main carriage). Otherwise, in default of contrary agreement, the buyer will pay the costs of unloading.

The risks are transferred to the buyer when the goods pass over the ship's rail (B5). The costs are likewise divided at the ship's rail (B6 – except, as noted, the seller must pay for the main carriage and export clearance; and it is the buyer's responsibility to pay for import clearance). In both cases – the division of risks and costs – the transfer of responsibility from seller to buyer can happen before delivery over the rail. This can occur when the buyer fails to give notice under B7. B7 requires the buyer, whenever he is entitled to determine the time for shipping the goods and/or the port of destination, to give the seller sufficient notice thereof. Whether he is so entitled will depend upon the contract. This is recognised in A4, which obliges the seller to deliver the goods on board the vessel at the port of shipment on the date or within the period specified (B4 imposes on the buyer the mirror obligation to take delivery thus). Naturally, there can be no such delivery unless a port of destination is specified or notified. A failure to notify a relevant matter under B7 will mean that the risks of loss/damage pass from the agreed date or the expiry date of the period fixed for shipment (B5). Responsibility

---

32　See *ibid*.
33　The parties may need to agree specifically on aspects of the unloading, and distribution of costs, in the charter party case – see the comment in *ibid*, p 83.

for costs is likewise transferred – the buyer must pay the additional costs incurred from a failure to give a B7 notice, from the agreed date or the expiry date of the period fixed for shipment. In both cases, the earlier passing of responsibility cannot occur unless the goods have (if originally unascertained) been appropriated to the contract.

The buyer must accept the transport documents or EDI equivalent, in accordance with A8, if in conformity with the contract (B8); pay, unless otherwise agreed, the costs of pre-shipment inspection except where mandated by the authorities of the country of inspection (B9) (this does not include the costs of routine pre-delivery checking by the seller, as per A9); and pay the costs of obtaining the documents or EDI equivalents mentioned in A10 (B10).

Cost and freight (CFR)

As noted, the CFR term is identical to the CIF term in the Incoterm regime, with one crucial exception. This is, that in a CFR contract the seller is not responsible for procuring insurance to cover the main carriage (see A3(b)). If he desires to be insured, the buyer must effect this. The seller must provide the buyer, upon request, with the necessary information for procuring insurance (A10).

It has been commented that the CFR term is not popular among exporters (unless their country requires insurance to be effected at home), because it 'leads to an artificial separation of the arrangements for insurance and freight, whereas the CIF stipulation, like the FOB clause, provides a natural division of responsibilities between the export merchant and the overseas buyer'.[34]

Carriage paid to (CPT)/Carriage and insurance paid to (CIP)

The twin Incoterms, carriage paid to (... named place of destination) or CPT (... named place of destination), and carriage and insurance paid to (... named place of destination) or CIP (... named place of destination), are identical with one exception: CIP imposes upon the seller the obligation to insure the goods against loss or damage during their carriage to the named destination, while CPT does not. CPT will be reviewed in some detail, following which CIP will be briefly commented upon.

The two terms, CPT and CIP, parallel the Incoterms CFR and CIF respectively. The difference between the two sets of terms is that CPT and CIP are for use with any mode of transport, and for contracts where multi-modal transport is to be employed (or for that matter several successive main carriers). On the other hand, CFR and CIF, it has been seen, are confined to marine carriers (sea or inland waterway). Accordingly, while CFR and CIF provide that delivery is completed when the goods are placed on board (with risks and costs being divided when the goods pass the ship's rail), the multi-modal terms CPT and CIP provide that delivery is completed when the goods are delivered into the custody of the carrier (or first carrier, where more than one carrier is to be used to get the goods to the named place of destination). This delivery might be at a port, where a ship is used as the carrier/first carrier, but equally it can be

---

34 See Schmitthoff, *op cit*, p 55 (referring to the C and F clauses).

to an inland point. Also, the terms CPT and CIP should be used when, even as the transport is to be by sea or inland waterway, the cargo cannot sensibly be viewed as being handed over the ship's rail, as in the case of containerised cargo, or cargo loaded by roll-on/roll-off means.[35] In such cases, delivery to the carrier will be at an earlier point, than at the ship's rail.

CPT and CIP are (like CFR and CIF) shipment contracts, where the seller undertakes not to deliver the goods to their agreed destination (which would be an arrival, or D term, contract), but to ship them (by sea, air, etc) to this destination; that is, his delivery obligations are completed at this earlier point.

Carriage paid to (CPT)

The carriage paid to (CPT) term requires the seller to organise and pay for carriage to the agreed destination named in the contract; to deliver the goods to the carrier (or first carrier, if there is more than one); and to obtain export clearance. The risks and costs divide at the point of delivery to the carrier.

The primary seller's obligations are: to provide the goods in conformity with the contract (A1); to obtain, at his own expense and risk, export clearance; (A2); to contract on usual terms, at his own expense, for the carriage of the goods to the agreed point at the named place of destination (A3) (if more than one carrier is involved, he will be obliged to organise and pay for these further transport sectors – in practice he might deal with only one party, such as a freight forwarder); and delivery. The delivery obligation is defined in A4:

> The seller must deliver the goods to the carrier contracted in accordance with A3 or, if there are subsequent carriers to the first carrier, for transport to the agreed point at the named place on the date or within the agreed period.

Delivery will take place at the place identified by the contract, for example, a container terminal.

The risks (subject to B5) are transferred from seller to buyer when the goods are delivered to the carrier (A5). Thus, the seller has no responsibility for the loss of, or damage to, the goods during carriage; this is the buyer's problem. Accordingly, the buyer would ordinarily organise insurance from the point of delivery. The seller may be liable exceptionally for post-delivery loss or damage where he has an independent legal liability for this, for example, because of a failure to pack the goods adequately, which failure causes loss or damage (see A9); and obviously the seller will still be liable for any non-conformity as between the goods and the contract, where this amounts to a breach.

The costs are also divided at the point of delivery to the carrier (A6). Certain qualifications apply: as noted, the seller will have had to pay for export clearance and for carriage to the agreed destination. The costs of carriage include any charges for unloading at the place of destination that may be included in the freight or incurred by the seller when contracting for carriage. This division of costs is subject to B6.

---

35 See *Guide to Incoterms 1990, op cit*, p 92.

The seller must give notice of delivery pursuant to A4, to the buyer (A7). He must provide the buyer at his own expense, if customary, with the usual transport documents (or, where agreed, equivalent electronic message) (A8). This document may, for example, be a negotiable bill of lading, a non-negotiable sea waybill, an air waybill or a multi-modal transport document. If the transport is by sea and the parties contemplate a resale during transit, a negotiable bill of lading will be stipulated.

The seller must pay the costs of routine pre-delivery checking operations; if appropriate, pack the goods in an adequate way; and mark any packaging (A9). He is to assist the buyer at the latter's expense to obtain any documents (or EDI equivalents) needed for import clearance and transit through another country.

The buyer has the familiar C term obligations. He must pay the contract price (B1) and take delivery when the seller has effected it under A4 (B4) (that is, when the goods have been delivered to the carrier). He has no obligation to arrange the main carriage (or, where there are several carriers, the contracts of main carriage) (B3) – this is the responsibility of the seller. While the seller, it has been seen, is responsible for export clearance, the buyer is responsible for import clearance and for any formalities governing transit through another country (B2).

Consistent with A5 and A6, the parallel B5 and B6 recognise that risks and costs are transferred at the point when the seller delivers the goods into the custody of the carrier (or first carrier). The buyer should have insurance running from this point. His obligation to bear costs does not include, of course, those covered by the seller's contract or those incurred in obtaining export clearance of carriage. Otherwise, he must pay costs incurred in transit for unloading at the place of destination, and beyond (see B6).

While normally the risks and costs are allocated upon delivery, exceptionally these may be transferred to the buyer pre-delivery. This will happen (pursuant to B5 and B6) where he does not give notice to the seller under B7 if required to do so. B7 provides that he must give sufficient notice to the seller whenever he is entitled to determine the time for dispatching the goods and/or the destination. (These options may be provided for in the contract, as reflected in A4.) If he fails to give notice under B7, he bears the risks of the goods from the agreed date or the expiry date of the period fixed for delivery (B5). Likewise, a failure to give notice means that he bears the additional costs resulting from the agreed date, etc (B6). In both cases, the earlier passing of responsibility is conditional upon the goods (if originally unascertained) being identified to the contract.

The buyer must accept the transport document in accordance with A8, if in conformity with the contract (B8); pay, unless there is a contrary agreement, the costs of pre-shipment inspection except where mandated by the authorities in the export country (B9) (the buyer does not have to pay for the seller's routine pre-delivery checking – see A9); and pay any costs incurred in obtaining the documents mentioned in A10 (B10).

Carriage and insurance paid to (CIP)

This term, it has been noted, is identical to CPT (above) with one critical exception: CIP (unlike CPT) obliges the seller to effect insurance of the cargo, on a minimum cover basis, against the risks of the carriage from the point of delivery into the custody of the carrier (or first carrier), until arrival at the agreed point at the named place of destination (A3). The insurance obligation is similar to that imposed on the seller by A3 in the CIF term (see discussion above).[36] Accordingly, B10 requires the buyer to provide the seller, upon request, with the necessary information for procuring insurance.

THE D CATEGORY – DAF, DES, DEQ, DDU, DDP

The D terms, it has been seen, are so designated because the seller contracts to deliver the goods at an agreed *destination* (normally, in the buyer's country). Therefore, the seller's delivery obligation is not fulfilled at an earlier time in his own country (a feature of the E, F and C categories) but at a later time after the conclusion of the main carriage. The D terms (also known as 'delivered' terms) are the most demanding from the seller's viewpoint. He must arrange the main carriage to the agreed destination and bear the costs and risks during this carriage. If the goods are lost in transit, this is to the seller's account rather than the buyer's (although the seller may have recourse against a third party, such as the carrier). D terms are increasingly used, as exporters who can deliver in the buyer's country are, all things being equal, more likely to get an order for their goods.

Delivered at frontier (DAF)

Delivered at frontier (… named place) (abbreviated as DAF (… named place)) can be used for any transport mode (or for multi-modal transport), but in practice it is used for road and rail deliveries and is frequently used in continental Europe trade.[37]

It imposes on the seller the obligation to deliver the goods to a named place at the specified frontier, but before the customs border of the adjacent country. In practice the precise place may be some distance from the frontier. The frontier can be that of any country, including the exporter's country. The seller arranges and pays for export clearance, and the buyer is responsible for import clearance.

The seller must provide conforming goods (A1); and organise and pay for export clearance, and likewise clearance to travel through other countries if required for delivery (A2). The seller is to organise and pay for carriage to the agreed place of delivery at the frontier (or the specified equivalent place), an obligation including paying the costs of transit, if necessary, through another country or countries (A3). If the precise delivery point is not agreed, or settled by practice, the seller may select one.

His delivery obligation is delineated in A4: 'The seller must place the goods at the disposal of the buyer on the arriving means of transport not unloaded at the named place of delivery at the frontier on the date or within the agreed period.' He will be responsible for unloading, if applicable (see A6 – this may in any event be included in the cost of freight). A comment in *Guide to Incoterms* may be noted:

> DAF may be used irrespective of the intended mode of transport, though it is more frequently used for rail carriage. The rail carriage usually continues past the border without any discharge of the goods from the railway wagon and re-loading on another

---

36 See *ibid*.
37 See Schmitthoff, *op cit*, p 59.

one. Consequently, there will be no real 'placing of the goods at the disposal of the buyer'. Instead, the seller, on the buyer's request, will provide the buyer with a through railway consignment note to the place of final destination in the country of importation ...[38]

The risks are transferred from seller to buyer upon delivery in accordance with A4 (see A5). The buyer should, therefore, consider insuring the goods from this point. The seller will be liable for loss or damage after this time only when an independent contractual or other liability may be established against him (for example, a loss caused by inadequate packaging).

Costs are likewise divided upon delivery (A6). A6 emphasises that the seller is liable for the expenses of discharge operations if applicable (as an incident of his having responsibility for carriage), and export clearance. The buyer will of course pay the costs of post-delivery carriage.

The seller is to give notice to the buyer of the dispatch of the goods to the named place at the frontier, as well as any other notice required to allow the buyer to take measures normally necessary for taking the goods (A7). The seller must provide the buyer with the usual documents (or EDI equivalents) or other evidence of delivery at the named place; provide the buyer at the latter's request, risk and expense, with a through document of transport (or, if agreed, EDI equivalent) (A8); provide pre-delivery checking operations at his own expense, and, if applicable, packaging which is appropriately marked (A9); and assist the buyer at the latter's expense to obtain the documents or EDI equivalents needed for import, etc (A10).

The buyer must pay the contract price (B1); obtain and pay for import clearance at the named point, and for any subsequent transport sector (B2); and take delivery at the named point (B4).

B5 and B6 mirror A5 and A6 in recognising the transfer of risks and division of costs upon delivery under A4. Both B5 and B6 recognise that the allocation of risks and costs can happen prior to delivery in consequence of the buyer's failure to take delivery or to give notice to the seller under B7, if required to do so. (B7 provides that, wherever he is entitled to determine the time within a stipulated period and/or the place of taking delivery, the buyer must give the seller sufficient notice thereof.) A failure to give this notice means that he bears all risks of loss, etc, from the agreed date or expiry date of the period stipulated for delivery, and in any event he is at risk from the moment of a delivery in terms of A4 (B5). If he fails to give notice under B7, or if he fails to take delivery, he bears any additional costs resulting thereby (B6). In both cases, the transfer of responsibility is conditional upon the goods having been appropriated to the contract.

The buyer is to accept the transport documents and other evidence of delivery if it is in order (B8); pay the costs of pre-shipment inspection except when mandated by the authorities in the export country (B9) (he is not liable for the seller's pre-delivery checking under A9, however); and pay the costs and charges incurred in obtaining the A10 documents or their electronic equivalents (B10).

---

38 See *Guide to Incoterms 1990*, op cit, p 105.

Delivered ex-ship (DES)

Delivered ex-ship (... named port of destination) or DES (... named port of destination) is confined to contracts involving carriage by sea or inland waterway. It requires the seller to deliver the goods to the agreed port (which usually will be in the buyer's country). The goods are to be placed by the seller at the disposal of the buyer (on the ship). The seller completes his delivery obligation at the port; thus, he must contract for (main) carriage. He must also clear the goods for export; but the buyer has responsibility for import clearance. The DES term places the seller at risk during the voyage (unlike the C class terms, such as CIF, where delivery is earlier).

The seller must provide the goods in conformity with the contract (A1); organise and pay for export clearance (and if necessary carry out customs formalities for transit through another country) (A2); and organise and pay for carriage to the agreed port of destination (A3). He has a discretion here – he can ship *via* the usual route and in a customary manner to the agreed point. If a point is not agreed or determined by practice, he may select the point that best suits his purpose. Within these parameters, he will not incur liability for breach of contract (contrast the situation where he selects an unusual and circuitous route, thereby causing economic loss to the buyer).

He delivers the goods when he places them at the disposal of the buyer on board the vessel at the usual unloading point in the named port, uncleared for import on the date or within the period stipulated, in such a way as to enable them to be removed from the vessel by unloading equipment appropriate to the situation (A4). The buyer then is responsible for unloading the goods.

Risks are (subject to B5) transferred to the buyer upon delivery (A5). The seller then is at risk during the carriage. In appropriate cases he should effect insurance. The buyer should consider insuring the goods from the time of delivery. The seller may be liable for loss of, or damage to, the goods post-delivery where there is an independent head of liability, as where damage is caused by his failure to package the goods adequately in breach of his obligation in A9.

Costs are divided upon delivery (subject to the operation of B6) (A6). Thereafter the buyer is liable. As it has been noted, the seller is liable for the costs of the carriage and export clearance (and customs clearances required for other countries, if applicable). The buyer is responsible for unloading (see B6) and for post-delivery costs. The buyer is responsible for costs incurred by his delay in unloading once the goods are at his disposal on the ship.

The seller's other obligations include giving notice to the buyer of the estimated time of arrival, etc (A7). He is to provide the buyer (at the seller's expense) with the delivery order and/or the usual transport document (for example, a negotiable bill of lading – necessary if resale while afloat is contemplated as a possibility – or non-negotiable sea waybill, or their EDI equivalent) to allow the buyer to take delivery from the carrier (A8). He is to pay the costs of routine pre-delivery checking operations, package the goods adequately, where appropriate, and mark the packaging (A9). He is to assist the buyer (at the buyer's expense) to obtain the documents or EDI equivalents which the buyer might require for import clearance, and provide the buyer, if requested, with information relevant to procuring insurance (A10).

The buyer must pay the contract price (A1); obtain and pay for import clearance (B2); and take delivery when the goods have been placed at his disposal in accordance with A4 (B4). He is not obliged to take delivery earlier than any agreed time.

The risks of loss of, or damage to, the goods are transferred to the buyer when the goods have been duly delivered (B5). Costs are divided at the same time; thus, the buyer must pay for unloading (B6). In both cases, that is, risks and costs, the transfer of responsibility to the buyer can happen pre-delivery. B7 requires him to give notice to the seller when he is entitled to determine the time within a stipulated period and/or the place of delivery. Accordingly, he bears the risks from the time the goods are placed at his disposal (such as where he delays unloading); and should he fail to give any required B7 notice, he bears the risks from the agreed date or the expiry date of the period stipulated for delivery (B5). Similarly, he must pay costs from the time of delivery (and thus is responsible for costs flowing from a failure to unload), and he is likewise liable for additional costs flowing from a failure to give any required B7 notice (B6). In both cases, the earlier division of risks and costs cannot occur until the goods have been identified to the contract, where originally unascertained.

The buyer must accept the A8 documents if they are in order (B8); pay (unless otherwise agreed) the costs of any pre-shipment inspection except when mandated by the authorities of the country of export (B9) (as noted, the seller is liable for the costs of pre-delivery checking pursuant to A9); and pay the costs of obtaining the documents or EDI equivalents mentioned in A10 (B10).

Delivered ex-quay (DEQ)

The delivered ex-quay (duty paid) (… named port of destination) or DEQ (… named port of destination) term is only for use where the main carriage is to be by ship or inland waterway. DEQ parallels DES (which has just been reviewed) but it imposes an additional obligation upon the seller, that is, the seller must make the goods available at the quay (or wharf) at the named port of destination (that is, he must unload from the ship). In summary then, the seller must deliver the goods to the quay at the named port of destination (which will usually be in the buyer's country). He must therefore organise and pay for carriage. He is at risk during this carriage. However, in contrast to Incoterms 1990, under Incoterms 2000 the seller no longer has to organise import clearance. This is now the responsibility of the buyer. The change was made in recognition of changes in customs procedures in most countries, and in recognition that it is more appropriate that the party that is domiciled in the country of importation (the buyer) should arrange clearance at his end.

The review of seller's and buyer's obligations concerning DES (immediately above) may be consulted regarding their obligations under DEQ, given the parallel nature of these terms. The qualifications on this review, to cover the distinctive features of DEQ, are as noted below.

To begin, the seller must obtain and pay for any export licence and satisfy like requirements and carry out as applicable all customs formalities for the export of the goods, and satisfy customs formalities required by any third country (or countries) (A2).

The carriage obligation on the seller is to carry the goods to the quay at the named port of destination (A3). The seller has no insurance obligation (that is, it is optional for him to insure against risks during carriage). His delivery obligation is to place the goods at the disposal of the buyer on the quay or wharf at the agreed port of destination and on the date or within the period stipulated (A4). He must therefore organise and pay for their unloading (including the use of lighters if necessary).

The division of risks and costs clauses (A5 and A6) in DEQ parallel those applying in the case of DES. The A7 terms are identical. The comments on the DES terms, above, should be noted. Applying the DEQ regime in context, the risks and costs pass at the slightly later point, that is, when the goods are made available to the buyer on the quay. Exceptionally, the division may be effected prior to delivery (that is, in the circumstances set out in B5 and B6 below).

The A1, A8, A9 and A10 obligations in DEQ are as for DES, with appropriate modifications to take account of the facts that the DEQ seller must deliver on the quay.

The buyer, pursuant to the Incoterm 2000 amendments, has the responsibility of organising import clearance. Pursuant to B2, the buyer must obtain at his own risk and expense any import licence or official authorisation or other documents, and carry out, where applicable, all customs formalities necessary for importation.

The buyer's obligations in DEQ parallel those in DES, again with the modifications needed to take account of the fact that the buyer takes delivery at the later point when the goods are on the quay. In particular, the B5 and B6 obligations in DEQ parallel those in DES (above), subject to the qualification that the buyer takes delivery on the quay. Once again, the risks and costs are divided and transferred to the buyer when the goods are placed at his disposal (in a DEQ contract – on the quay). Thereafter, he is liable for any loss/damage to the goods, or continuing costs, and thus should take them into custody promptly. The risks and costs will also be transferred, at a pre-delivery point, where the buyer fails to give a B7 notice when required to do so (see B5 and B6). The rules are as for DES. The other buyer terms (B1, B2, B3, B4, B7, B8, B9 and B10) parallel those for DES.

Delivered duty unpaid (DDU)

Delivered duty unpaid (… named place of destination) or DDU (… named place of destination) can be used for any mode of transport (or for multi-modal transport). It is the second most demanding Incoterm from the seller's viewpoint, being eclipsed in the regard only by the term delivered duty paid (DDP). DDU and DDP are identical with the one exception: the latter requires the seller to perform all of the DDU obligations plus an additional one, that is, to clear the goods for import. Below, the DDU obligations will be reviewed, following which the DDP term will be briefly reviewed.

DDU imposes on the seller the obligation to clear the goods for export, and to organise and pay for their carriage to the named destination in the country of delivery (which will be the buyer's country, or country of delivery nominated by him). The delivery is effected in the country of importation when the goods are placed at the buyer's disposal at the specified place. The buyer must organise and pay for import clearance.

The seller's obligations include providing goods in conformity with the contract (A1); obtaining, at his own expense, export clearance and satisfying customs formalities for transit through another country during carriage (A2); and organising and paying for (main) carriage of the goods to the place of destination (A3). He has some discretion in selecting the route for carriage (note the details in A3). He has no insurance obligations, but should consider insuring the goods up until the point of delivery (he is at risk until this time).

His delivery obligation is to place the goods at the disposal of the buyer (that is, at the named place of destination) on the date or within the period stipulated (A4). The parties should agree upon a precise point or delivery; in default of this the seller may select the point at the named destination that best suits his purpose (see A3).

The risks are (subject to B5) transferred from seller to buyer upon delivery (A5). The buyer should consider having insurance from this point. This term does not negate any liability which the seller may have, independently of A5, for loss or damage, such as where it is caused by inadequate packaging or marking in breach of his packaging obligations under A9.

The costs are (subject to B6) also divided upon delivery (A6). Thus, from this point on, the buyer is liable for any costs (including those resulting from his failure to take them into custody). The buyer is responsible for the costs of import clearance (see B2). The buyer, of course, is liable for post-delivery carriage.

The seller is to give notice to the buyer of the dispatch of the goods as well as any other notice required to allow him to take the goods (A7). The seller is to provide at his own expense the delivery order and/or the usual transport document (for example, a negotiable bill of lading, a non-negotiable sea waybill, etc) that the buyer may require to take delivery. If agreed, an EDI equivalent may be used. A negotiable bill of lading will be used where carriage is by sea, and the parties contemplate an in-transit resale. The seller is to pay for any routine checking operations required for delivery, to package the goods appropriately (if applicable) and to mark any such packaging (A9). He is to assist the buyer, at the latter's expense, to obtain any documents or EDI equivalents needed for the import of the goods; and to provide the buyer with any information needed to effect insurance (a matter which becomes a critical issue for the buyer upon the moment of delivery) (A10).

The buyer must of course pay the contract price (B1). He must organise import clearance and pay for this (B2). He must take delivery where this is duly tendered in accord with A4 (B4). B5 mirrors A5 in recognising that the risks of the goods are transferred to the buyer upon delivery. He should therefore consider insuring the goods from this point. Thus, if he delays taking the goods into custody, once they have been duly placed at his disposal in conformity with A4 and loss/damage results, this is to his account. Likewise, if he fails to obtain import clearance by the agreed time of delivery, he is at risk from this point (assuming the goods have been placed at his disposal). The risks will transfer to him prior to delivery where he fails to give notice, if required, under B7. B7 states that the buyer must, whenever he is entitled to determine the time within a stipulated period and/or the place of taking delivery, give the seller sufficient notice thereof. If he fails to give this notice, he must bear the risks from the agreed date or the expiry date of the period stipulated for delivery, provided the goods have been appropriated to the contract (if originally unascertained) (B5). He cannot, that is, delay taking delivery with legal impunity by failing to give a B7 notice.

The costs are likewise divided from the time the goods are placed at the buyer's disposal in accordance with A4 (B6). If he fails to obtain import clearance as required by B2 (with the result that the goods cannot be delivered); fails to take delivery when they have been placed at his disposal, in accordance with A4; or fails to give any B7 notice required (see above) – all additional costs thereby incurred are to his account, provided that the goods (if required) have been appropriated to the contract. He is, as noted, liable for all the costs of importation.

He must accept the delivery order or transport document in accordance with A8 (B8); pay, unless otherwise agreed, the costs of pre-shipment inspection except when mandated by the export country (B9) (it will be recalled that the seller has the expense of any routine pre-delivery checking (A9)); and pay for the documents or EDI equivalents mentioned in A10 (B10).

The parties can of course amend the standard DDU provisions, such as where the parties want the seller to bear some of the costs of importation, by appropriate wording – an instance envisaged in the DDU preamble.

Delivered duty paid (DDP)

The Incoterm delivered duty paid (... named place of destination) or DDP (... named place of destination) is, from the seller's viewpoint, the most demanding of all of the Incoterms. As noted in the discussion of DDU above, the DDP term is identical to DDU with one exception: the seller must, additionally, procure import clearance and pay for it (the corollary is that this obligation has been dropped from the buyer's obligations). The term is apt if the seller can readily obtain import clearance; otherwise, if the buyer can more readily effect this, DDU should be used. Also, DDU may be preferred if clearing the goods for import involves the payment of a VAT or equivalent tax which can only be deducted for tax purposes by a resident of the country of importation.[39]

The preamble to DDP notes that DDP should not be used if the seller cannot obtain, directly or indirectly, the import licence.

The seller's DDP obligations then, broadly, are to deliver the goods at the point specified in the named place of destination in the import country. He must arrange both export and import clearance and pay for these, and likewise organise and pay for the fulfilment of any customs formalities where carriage is to be through a third country or countries. He has to organise and pay for main carriage. He is at risk until the goods are delivered, and must bear the costs until this point. The buyer's main obligations are to pay the contract price and to take delivery.

The DDP provisions relating to seller's and buyer's obligations are more or less the same as those for DDU, with modifications being necessary only to take account of the transfer of responsibility for import clearance to the seller in the case of DDP. Accordingly, the commentary on the DDU term (above) may be applied to the DDP provisions, subject to this qualification. DDP obligations which have been amended to take account of the transfer of the import obligation are: A2 (requiring the seller to organise and pay for both export and import clearances); A6 (a consequential change, again identifying the cost of import clearance as being to the seller's account); A10 (again, to take account of the transfer of the import obligation); B2 (confining the buyer's obligation to render the seller, at the latter's expense, assistance in obtaining import clearance); B5 and B6 (recognising that import clearance is no longer the buyer's responsibility); and B10 (imposing on the buyer the obligation to assist the seller, at the seller's expense, to obtain any documents or EDI equivalents needed for import clearance).

---

39   See the comment in *Guide to Incoterms 1990, op cit*, p 136.

TUTORIAL QUESTIONS

1   What is the major, consistent principle governing the division of risks and costs in the Incoterms? Nominate some common situations where – pursuant to numerous of the Incoterms – this principle of allocation is displaced.

2   What are the general differences between each of the two classes of 'shipment' terms and the 'arrival' terms?

3   What terms are particularly apt for containerised cargo?

4   What terms are particularly apt for bulk cargo?

5   In the case of the FOB and CIF Incoterms, does the buyer have the right to inspect the goods before making payment? If so, can the buyer reject the goods for non-conformity with the contract after they have arrived at the port to which they are to be shipped?

6   What terms impose liability on the seller for loss in transit?

7   Goods are sold on a CIF basis. They are lost in transit. Does the buyer nonetheless have to pay for the goods?

8   Goods are shipped on a CIF basis by a buyer in State X to a seller in State Y. While they are in transit, State Y bans the importation of goods of this class. Is the buyer still obliged to pay?

9   Goods are sold on a CIF basis. The contract provides for payment on presentation of the transport documents on arrival, or in any event no later than one month from the date on the bill of lading. The ship is delayed because of an event that is independent of any fault on the part of the seller. The goods arrive three months late and well beyond the month specified. Can the buyer reject the goods because the documents are presented at a very late date?

10 Goods are sold on an FOB basis, with the buyer being required to nominate a vessel within 30 days of contract. The buyer does not nominate a vessel within this period. What is the legal position as between the parties?

11 Goods are sold on an FOB basis. By agreement between the parties, the goods are to be loaded by a stevedore at the seller's expense. They are damaged during loading once they have passed the ship's rail. Who is liable for this damage, as between the buyer and the seller?

12 What term(s) should the parties use if it is desired that the seller organise and pay for the main carriage and insure against the risks of this journey? If, where such a term is used, the goods are damaged and the insurer is unable or unwilling to pay, is the seller liable to the buyer for this damage?

13 Goods are sold on a DAF basis. The seller does not, as required by the contract, give sufficient notice to the buyer of the dispatch of the goods to the nominated place at the frontier. What are the consequences of this failure?

14 The goods are sold on a DAF basis and dispatched by the seller. The buyer does not take delivery of the goods when they have been placed at his disposal. What are the legal consequences?

15 Goods are sold on a DDU basis. What is the legal position as between the parties where the buyer purports to reject the goods for non-conformity with the contract when they are placed at his disposal at the named destination?

16 Goods are sold on an FCA basis. The seller experiences delays in obtaining export clearance. The buyer is unaware of this but neglects to notify the seller of the name of the carriers, as required by the contract. The contractual deadlines pass for both the obtaining of export clearance and the giving of the buyer's notice. Finally, the seller obtains clearance. Can the buyer reject the goods?

FURTHER READING

Burnett, R, *The Law of International Business Transactions*, 1994, Sydney: Federation Press, Ch 1, pp 29–64.

Evans, P, 'FOB and CIF Contracts' (1993) 67 *Australian Law Journal* at 844–58.

International Chamber of Commerce, *Incoterms 2000*, 2000, Paris: ICC Publishing SA.

Mo, J, *International Commercial Law*, 2003, Australia: LexisNexis Butterworths, pp 3–36.

Murray, D, 'Risk of loss of goods in transit; a comparison of the 1990 Incoterms with terms from other voices' (1991) 23 *University of Miami Inter-American Law Review* 1 at 93–131.

Ramberg, J, *Guide to Incoterms 1990*, 1991, Paris: ICC Publishing SA.

Sassoon, D, 'The origin of FOB and CIF Terms and the factors influencing their choice' (1967) *Journal of Business Law* at 32.

Sassoon, D and Merren, M, *CIF and FOB Contracts*, Vol 5, 3rd edn, 1984, London: Stevens, British Shipping Laws series.

Schmitthoff, C, *Export Trade –The Law and Practice of International Trade*, 9th edn, 1990, London: Stevens, Ch 2.

APPENDIX

INCOTERMS 2000

- ExW – Ex-Works – Title and risk pass to buyer including payment of all transportation and insurance cost from the sellerís door. Used for any mode of transportation.
- FCA – Free Carrier – Title and risk pass to buyer including transportation and insurance cost when the seller delivers goods cleared for export to the carrier. Seller is obligated to load the goods on the Buyer's collecting vehicle; it is the Buyer's obligation to receive the Seller's arriving vehicle unloaded.
- FAS – Free Alongside Ship —Title and risk pass to buyer including payment of all transportation and insurance cost once delivered alongside ship by the seller. Used for sea or inland waterway transportation. The export clearance obligation rests with the seller.
- FOB – Free On Board and risk pass to buyer including payment of all transportation and insurance cost once delivered on board the ship by the seller. Used for sea or inland waterway transportation.
- CFR – Cost and Freight – Title, risk and insurance cost pass to buyer when delivered on board the ship by seller who pays the transportation cost to the destination port. Used for sea or inland waterway transportation.
- CIF – Cost, Insurance and Freight – Title and risk pass to buyer when delivered on board the ship by seller who pays transportation and insurance cost to destination port. Used for sea or inland waterway transportation.
- CPT – Carriage Paid To – Title, risk and insurance cost pass to buyer when delivered to carrier by seller who pays transportation cost to destination. Used for any mode of transportation.
- CIP – Carriage and Insurance Paid To —Title and risk pass to buyer when delivered to carrier by seller who pays transportation and insurance cost to destination. Used for any mode of transportation.
- DAF – Delivered at Frontier – Title, risk and responsibility for import clearance pass to buyer when delivered to named border point by seller. Used for any mode of transportation.
- DES – Delivered Ex-Ship – Title, risk, responsibility for vessel discharge and import clearance pass to buyer when seller delivers goods on board the ship to destination port. Used for sea or inland waterway transportation.
- DEQ – Delivered Ex-Quay (Duty Paid) – Title and risk pass to buyer when delivered on board the ship at the destination point by the seller who delivers goods on dock at destination point cleared for import. Used for sea or inland waterway transportation.
- DDU – Delivered Duty Unpaid – Title, risk and responsibility of import clearance pass to buyer when seller delivers goods to named destination point. Used for any mode of transportation. Buyer is obligated for import clearance.
- DDU – Delivered Duty Unpaid – Seller fulfils his obligation when goods have been made available at the named place in the country of importation
- DDP – Delivered Duty Paid – Title and risk pass to buyer when seller delivers goods to named destination point cleared for import. Used for any mode of transportation.

CHAPTER 4

CARRIAGE OF GOODS BY SEA

INTRODUCTION

Where goods are carried by sea, it is generally in one of two ways. First, a ship and its crew may be chartered under a time charter or voyage charter and the goods loaded and carried by that ship. Alternatively, the cargo owner may obtain space on a general ship[1] that will carry the cargo owner's goods along with those of others from one port to another port. This chapter is concerned with the marine cargo liability regime for the latter method of carriage.[2]

Before 1903, sea carriage in Australia was governed by the common law.[3] Under the common law, the shipowner was absolutely bound to provide a seaworthy[4] ship at the start of the voyage,[5] and to proceed on the voyage with reasonable despatch[6] without unreasonable deviation[7] subject to such common law defences as act of God, act of the sovereign's enemies, inherent vice, defective packing, loss caused by sacrifice, deviation.[8]

The Carriage of Goods by Sea Act 1903 (Cth), based on the US Harter Act 1893, was the Australian Parliament's first attempt to redress a then perceived imbalance between shipowning interests (carriers) and cargo interests (shippers) under which the shipowning interests were able (under the common law which applied until the advent of this law) to introduce exclusion clauses into their terms of carriage which enabled the shipowners to exclude or limit liability for loss of or damage to cargo under virtually any circumstance.[9]

---

1   A general ship carries the goods of anyone who wants to book space on it. It is not dissimilar to a common carrier.

2   The marine cargo liability regime does not usually apply to charterparties – see, for example, Carriage of Goods by Sea Act 1991 (Cth) Schedule 1A, Art 10, r 6.

3   For a comprehensive discussion of the common law position, see Colinvaux, R (ed), *Carver's Carriage of Goods by Sea*, 13th edn, 1982, London: Steven & Sons, pp 3–20.

4   Seaworthiness means 'that the vessel – with her master and crew – is herself fit to encounter the perils of the voyage and also that she is fit to carry the cargo safely on that voyage', *Actis Steamship Co Ltd v The Sanko Steamship Co Ltd (The Acquacharm)* [1982] 1 Lloyds Rep 7, 9 *per* Lord Denning MR.

5   *Kapitoff v Wilson* (1876) 1 QBD 377; *The Europa* [1908] p 84; *Hong Kong Fir Shipping Co v Kawasaki Kisen Kaisha Ltd* [1962] 2 QB 26 *per* Diplock J at p 71.

6   *Universal Cargo Carriers Corp v Citati* [1957] 2 QB 401; *CMC (Australia) Pty Ltd v 'Socofl Stream'* [2000] FCA 1681.

7   *Thiess Brothers (Queensland) Pty Ltd v Australian Steamships Pty Ltd* [1955] 1 Lloyd's Rep 459; *F Kanematsu & Co Ltd v The Ship Shahzada* (1956) 96 CLR 477.

8   For a detailed discussion of these defences, see Colinvaux, *op cit*, pp 11–20.

9   *Paterson, Zochonis & Co Ltd v Elder Dempster & Co Ltd* [1924] AC 522.

In 1924, the Australian Parliament enacted the Sea Carriage of Goods Act, which introduced an international convention commonly known as the 'Hague Rules'[10] into Australian law.[11] The Hague Rules have been a very successful convention adopted, either formally or informally, by many countries to control international carriage of goods by sea.[12] The Hague Rules have been since updated by the Visby Protocol[13] (producing the so called Hague Visby Rules)[14] and the SDR Protocol[15] both of which have also found their way into current Australian law in the Carriage of Goods by Sea Act 1991 (Cth)[16] (COGSA) in relation to international[17] and interstate[18] carriage but not intrastate carriage[19]. The Hague Rules and the Hague Visby Rules are a compromise between the respective positions of the shipper and the shipowner as they were originally under the common law and as they came to be under the carrier formulated contracts of carriage under which much liability for loss or damage to a shipper's cargo was excluded by the shipowner.[20]

While many countries continue to use the Hague or Hague Visby Rules (or a modification of them) some countries now use the Hamburg Rules[21] as the basis of their sea carriage regime, but the latter Rules have not gained widespread acceptance.[22]

---

10 The Hague Rules is the commonly used name for the International Convention for the Unification of Certain Rules of Law Relating to Bills of Lading of 25 August 1924. The Hague Rules too drew heavily on the US Harter Act 1893.

11 As from 1 January 1925.

12 See the 'Table of Package & Kilo Limitations' published by 'Tetleys Law & Other Nonsense' at Tetley.law.mcgill.ca/maritime/table.htm for a useful summary of those countries which have adopted the Hague Rules or which use the Hague Rules (or a variant) as a basis of their sea carriage regime.

13 The Visby Protocol is the commonly used name for the Protocol amending the International Convention for the Unification of Certain Rules of Law Relating to Bills of Lading of 25 August 1924 made 23 February 1968.

14 In this chapter, the writer refers to the Hague Visby Rules as being the Hague Rules amended by both the Visby Protocol and the SDR Protocol.

15 The SDR Protocol is the commonly used name for the Protocol amending the International Convention for the Unification of Certain Rules of Law Relating to Bills of Lading of 25 August 1924 as amended by the Protocol of 23 February 1968 made at Brussels on 21 December 1979.

16 The Act applied from 31 October 1991.

17 See Carriage of Goods by Sea Act 1991 (Cth), Sched 1A, Art 10.

18 See Carriage of Goods by Sea Act 1991, s 10(1)(b)(ii), Sched 1A, Art 10, r 4. However, carriage under a non-negotiable document is not covered unless it falls within Art 10, r 5 – see COGSA, s 10(1A).

19 Intrastate carriage is regulated in New South Wales (Sea Carriage of Goods (State) Act 1921 (NSW)) and Western Australia (Sea Carriage of Goods Act 1909 (WA)) which introduce State sea carriage regimes which are similar to the Hague Rules. Interstate carriage is not regulated in the other States.

20 *Gosse Millerd Ltd v Canadian Government Merchant Marine Ltd (The Canadian Highlander)* [1929] AC 223 *per* Viscount Sumner at 236.

21 The Hamburg Rules is the commonly used name for the United National Convention on the Carriage of Goods by Sea done at Hamburg on 31 March 1978.

22 See 'Table of Package & Kilo Limitations', *op cit*. About 26 countries are signatories to the Hamburg Rules.

The continuing tension between the shipowning interests and cargo interests[23] as to whether the Hague Visby Rules or the Hamburg Rules should form the basis of Australia's liability regime resulted in the formation of the Marine Cargo Liability Working Group chaired by the Commonwealth Department of Transport and including representatives drawn from each of shipper carrier and insurer interests. The Group's brief was to see if a compromise solution could be found on possible reform of Australia's marine cargo liability arrangements, which provided fair and reasonable protection for both shippers and carriers.[24]

The Report of that Working Group,[25] which recommended that the Hague Visby Rules, continue to form the basis of Australia's Marine cargo liability regime with some modifications to those Rules, was given effect by the Carriage of Goods by Sea Amendment Act 1997 (Cth) and the Carriage of Goods by Sea Regulation 1998,[26] which introduced[27] a schedule of modifications to the Hague Visby Rules (Modified Hague Visby Rules) as Schedule 1A to COGSA.[28] Those modifications do not amend the text of the Hague Visby Rules, which are still set out in COGSA Schedule 1, but 'the text has effect ... as if it were modified in accordance with the Schedule of Modifications'.[29]

This technique of modification sits uneasily with the general principle that, in the interests of uniformity between countries, an international convention should be construed in a normal manner, appropriate for the interpretation of an international convention, unconstrained by technical rules and on broad principles of general acceptance[30] and where the need arises, regard may be had to the decisions of foreign courts.[31]

---

23 Useful summaries of the background to the current situation with respect to sea carriage regimes can be found in McNair, Sir WL, Mocatta, Sir AA, Mustill, MJ, *Scrutton on Charterparties and Bills of Lading*, 17th edn, 1971, London: Sweet & Maxwell, pp 402–09 (for early developments in the area) and for more recent developments see White, MWD (ed), *Australian Maritime Law*, 2nd edn, 2000, Sydney: The Federation Press, pp 62–68. See also, *Improving Australia's Marine Cargo Liability Regime*, Department of Transport (Cth) Information Paper, July 1996; *Report of the Marine Cargo Liability Working Group*, September 1995, Department of Transport, available at www.dotrs.gov.au/xmt/sse/Cargo Liability.

24 See *Improving Australia's Marine Cargo Liability Regime*, Department of Transport (Cth) Information Paper, July 1996.

25 *Report of the Marine Cargo Liability Working Group*, September 1995, Department of Transport, available at www.dotrs.gov.au/xmt/sse/Cargo Liability.

26 This Regulation was amended by the Carriage of Goods by Sea Regulation (No 2) 1998.

27 The modified Hague Visby Rules apply to contracts for the carriage of goods made on or after 1 July 1988 – see COGSA, s 10(1)(a).

28 In this chapter the term Modified Hague Visby Rules is used to refer to the current Australian marine cargo liability regime under COGSA.

29 Carriage of Goods by Sea Act 1991 (Cth), s 7(2).

30 *James Buchanan & Co Ltd v Babco Forwarding & Shipping (UK) Ltd* [1978] AC 141 at 152 *per* Lord Wilberforce L; *Transworld Oil (USA) Inc v Minos Compania Naviera SA (The Leni)* [1992] 2 Lloyd's Rep 48 at 52 *per* Diamond J. See also *Anglo Irish Beef Processors International v Federated Stevedores Geelong* [1997] 2 VR 676.

31 *The Hollandia* [1983] 1 AC 565 at 572; *Stag Line Ltd v Foscolo, Mango and Co Ltd* [1932] AC 328 at 350; *Kamil Export (Aust) Pty Ltd v NPL (Australia) Pty Ltd* [1996] 1 VR 538.

COMPARISON OF ASPECTS OF HAGUE RULES, HAGUE VISBY RULES, HAMBURG RULES AND THE MODIFIED HAGUE VISBY RULES IN USE IN AUSTRALIA

Application of Rules

The Hague Rules and Hague Visby Rules[32] apply to every bill of lading[33] for the carriage of goods between ports which are in two different countries[34] if:

1   the bill of lading issues in a Contracting State;[35] or

2   the carriage is from[36] a port in a Contracting State; or

3   the contract contained in or evidencing the bill of lading provides that: the Hague Rules or Hague Visby Rules (as the case may be) apply; or the law of a country which gives effect to the Hague Rules or Hague Visby Rules applies.

In Australia, the Hague Visby Rules also apply to non-negotiable sea carriage documents entered into after 31 October 1991, if the contract of carriage expressly provided for the Hague Visby Rules to govern it as if it were a bill of lading.[37]

In practice, incorporation of the Hague Rules or Hague Visby Rules by a contractual provision is not common as the carrier's superior bargaining power allows the carrier to set the terms and conditions of carriage and the carrier will often contractually exclude liability for loss or damage to the cargo in any situation where the Hague or Hague Visby Rules do not have compulsory application. In addition, particularly on short-haul routes, such as the trans-Tasman route, for the convenience of both carrier and shipper, non-negotiable documents such as sea waybills have come into common use. These non-negotiable documents need not be subject to the Hague Visby Rules[38] and, once again, the carrier is in a position to exempt itself completely from liability for loss or damage to cargo.

The Hamburg Rules apply to all contracts of carriage by sea between two different States if:

1   the port of lading, as provided for in the contract of carriage by sea, is located in a Contracting State;

---

32   Article 10.

33   The Hague Rules and Hague Visby Rules have no compulsory application to sea carriage documents other than bills of lading such as sea waybills, mates receipts, non-negotiable receipts and the like. However, the contract of carriage could contractually incorporate them.

34   The rules can apply to carriage from one port in a country to another port in that country if they are contractually incorporated into the contract of carriage or if they are incorporated by the domestic legislation of that country – Art 10(c).

35   A Contracting State is a country that is a signatory to the Hague Rules or the Hague Visby Rules.

36   Only outbound carriage from a Contracting State is covered by the Hague Rules or Hague Visby Rules unless:
   • the contract for carriage for inbound cargo to that Contracting State provides for those Rules to apply; or
   • the country from which the goods are carried is itself a Contracting State; or
   • the bill of lading for the carriage is issued in a Contracting State.

37   COGSA, s 10(1)(b)(iii).

38   Unless they are contractually incorporated.

2 the port of discharge, as provided for in the contract of carriage by sea, is located in a Contracting State;

3 one of the optional ports of discharge in the contract of carriage by sea is the actual port of discharge, and such port is located in a Contracting State;

4 the bill of lading or other document evidencing the contract of carriage by sea is issued in a Contracting State; or

5 the bill of lading or other document evidencing the contract of carriage by sea provides that the Convention or the legislation of any State giving effect to the Convention are to govern the contract.[39]

The Hamburg Rules cover all sea cargo carriage whether under bills of lading or not, except gratuitous carriage and charter parties.[40] A contract of carriage by sea is defined under the Rules as:

> ... any contract whereby the carrier undertakes against payment of freight to carry goods by sea from one port to another; however a contract which involves carriage by sea and also carriage by some other means is deemed to be a contract of carriage by sea for the purposes of this Convention only insofar as it relates to the carriage by sea.[41]

So, unlike the Hague Rules and the Hague Visby Rules, the Hamburg Rules apply to:

1 contracts of carriage by sea for both inward and outward cargo; and

2 both negotiable and non-negotiable contracts of carriage.

The Hamburg Convention is potentially more difficult to circumvent as it applies uniformly to nearly all such contracts for carriage. If the Hamburg Rules were to become widely used, from a shipper's point of view, there would be no need for the shipper to concern itself with whether the cargo is an import or an export cargo, or whether it is carried under a bill of lading or under a sea waybill – the same rules would always apply. However, there can be conflict of law issues in applying liability rules to both inbound and outbound cargo. If the country where the cargo is shipped on board and the country where the cargo is delivered, each applies its own laws both to inbound cargo and outbound cargo, then if those laws are not identical, it is distinctly possible to have two competing marine cargo liability regimes applying to the same carriage and cargo. This is unfortunately a real possibility today as some nations, including Australia, are using modified marine cargo liability regimes which are specific to their own countries rather than giving uniform effect to a widely accepted international convention.[42]

In Australia, the Modified Hague Visby Rules modify the application of the Hague Visby Rules in Australia from 1 July 1998.[43] From that date, the Rules apply to:

---

39 Article 2, r 1.

40 Article 2, r 3.

41 Article 1, r 6.

42 These modified regimes tend to use the Hague Visby Rules modified by the inclusion of some provisions taken from the Hamburg Rules.

43 Carriage of Goods by Sea Regulation 1998 (Cth), s 2.1.

1 'sea carriage documents relating to the carriage of goods from ports in Australia to ports outside Australia regardless of the form in which the sea carriage document is issued'.[44]

2 'the carriage of goods by sea from ports outside Australia to ports in Australia' unless by agreement or by law, either the Hague Rules, the Hague Visby Rules or the Hamburg Rules already apply to that carriage.[45]

3 A sea carriage document[46] for the carriage of goods by sea from a port in one State or Territory to a port in another State or Territory.[47]

4 Sea carriage documents under the Modified Hague Visby Rules include not only bills of lading[48] but also other negotiable documents of carriage which are similar to bills of lading and which evidence or contain the contract of carriage[49] and non-negotiable bills of lading.[50] In addition, non-negotiable sea carriage documents such as sea waybills, consignment notes[51] and the like are covered.[52]

The Modified Hague Visby Rules also extend the application of the Rules into electronic sea carriage documentation.[53] When the Modified Hague Visby Rules require a document to be in writing, this is taken to include 'electronic mail, electronic data interchange, facsimile transmission, and entry in a database maintained on a computer system'.[54]

Elimination of the Vita Food Gap

The Hague Rules were usually incorporated into a bill of lading for an outbound carriage of goods from a Hague Rules country by way of a legislative requirement[55] that any such bill of lading must contain a clause (the clause paramount) which provided that the bill of lading has effect subject to the provisions of the Hague Rules, that is, they were given the status of contractual terms, and not the status of legal

---

44 Carriage of Goods by Sea Act 1991 (Cth), Sched 1A, Art 10, r 1.
45 Carriage of Goods by Sea Act 1991 (Cth), Sched 1A, Art 10, rr 2 and 3.
46 The Modified Hague Visby Rules only apply to interstate carriage where:
   • the document of carriage is a bill of lading; or
   • the interstate carriage is being done under a non-negotiable document; and
      (1) either the cargo is to be carried onwards by sea to, or have been carried onwards by sea from, a port outside Australia;
      (2) or the cargo has been declared to the carrier as international cargo.
47 Carriage of Goods by Sea Act 1991 (Cth), Sched 1A, Art 10, r 4.
48 Carriage of Goods by Sea Act 1991 (Cth), Sched 1A, Art 1, r 1(g)(i).
49 Carriage of Goods by Sea Act 1991 (Cth), Sched 1A, Art 1, r 1(g)(ii).
50 Carriage of Goods by Sea Act 1991 (Cth), Sched 1A, Art 1, r 1(g)(iii).
51 See Carriage of Goods by Sea Act 1991 (Cth), Sched 1A, Art 1, r 1(aa) which defines a consignment note.
52 Carriage of Goods by Sea Act 1991 (Cth), Sched 1A, Art 1, r 1(g)(iv) and rule.
53 Carriage of Goods by Sea Act 1991 (Cth), Sched 1A, Art 1A.
54 Carriage of Goods by Sea Act 1991 (Cth), Sched 1A, Art 1, r 1(h).
55 See, eg, Sea Carriage of Goods Act 1924 (Cth), s 6.

enactments having the force of law.[56] The Hague Rules were accordingly interpreted by the Courts using the usual principles of contract interpretation.[57]

This method of incorporation using the clause paramount gave rise to the so called Vita Food Gap.[58] In essence, if the clause paramount was omitted from the bill of lading for shipment out of a Hague Rules country, and if the choice of law clause elected the jurisdiction of a country which either did not apply the Hague Rules or did not apply them to that voyage, then the Hague Rules would not apply.[59]

The Carriage of Goods by Sea Act 1991 closed this gap[60] by giving the Hague Visby Rules (now the Modified Hague Visby Rules) 'the force of law in Australia'.[61]

Application of Rules to third parties

There was a problem with the application of the Hague Rules to third parties as was highlighted by *Scruttons v Midland Silicones*.[62] In this case, the Court found that stevedores were not parties to the contract of carriage and could not rely upon the limitations of liability in the Hague Rules, that is, the Rules only dealt with contractual liability and not tortious or other liability of third parties.[63] This case made it clear that

---

56 Section 6 of the Sea Carriage of Goods Act 1924 provided that 'every bill of lading or similar document of title issued in the Commonwealth which contains or is evidence of any contract to which the Rules apply, shall contain an express statement that it is to have effect subject to the provisions of the Rules as applied by this Act'.

57 *Vita Food Products Inc v Unus Shipping Co Ltd* [1939] AC 277.

58 The Vita Food Gap took its name from the case of *Vita Food Products Inc v Unus Shipping Co Ltd* [1939] AC 277. The bills of lading were issued in Newfoundland. Newfoundland law required all bills of lading to contain a clause paramount that the bill is subject to the Hague Rules. The bills were issued without this clause paramount and also stated that they were subject to English law. The cargo was damaged and the question before the court was whether the carrier could rely upon the exemption from liability clauses in the bill of lading. The action was taken in the courts in Nova Scotia. The Privy Council *per* Lord Wright found that the carrier could rely on the exemption clause. It found that if the bill had been governed by Newfoundland law, then the Hague Rules would have applied; but as they were not, the bills were not subject to the Hague Rules and were not illegal under Newfoundland law or under any other relevant law. The bills were enforceable in accordance with their terms. Even if the bills were illegal in Newfoundland, they were still enforceable in Nova Scotia.

59 Of course, this may be a breach of s 6 of the Sea Carriage of Goods Act 1924, but that does not affect the validity of the contract of carriage.

60 See s 8 of COGSA 1991.

61 An example of how the Vita Good Gap closes by giving the Rules the force of law can be seen in *The Hollandia* [1983] 1 AC 565. That case involved a shipment from Scotland in a Dutch vessel with the bill of lading being governed by Dutch law. At that time, the UK had the Hague Visby Rules while the Dutch had the Hague Rules governing carriage of goods by sea. The liability limits are lower under the Hague Rules. The English court found that, if they gave effect to the jurisdiction clause, it would introduce lower carriers' liability limits than those which were available under the Hague Visby Rules, which had the force of law. Accordingly, the jurisdiction clause was a clause reducing the carriers' liability as defined by Art 3, r 8 of the Hague Visby Rules and, as such, it was invalid. As the jurisdiction clause was invalid, the appropriate jurisdiction was looked at on a *forum conveniens* basis, and England was found to be the appropriate forum.

62 [1962] AC 446.

63 This case followed the earlier case of *Adler v Dickson* [1955] 1 QB 158, where a passenger was able to successfully sue the captain and bosun of the vessel 'Himalaya' as a result of an accident involving the operation of the ship's gangway.

the Hague Rules, being contract based, only related to contractual liability, and a shipper could circumvent the Hague Rules and obtain full recovery for its loss if negligence could be established against a third party such as a stevedore or a negligent crew member who was sued in tort rather than in contract.

The shipowners responded to the *Scruttons* decision with the so called 'Himalaya' clause. This was a clause inserted in a bill of lading which originally provided[64] that the carrier's employees and agents could also rely on the limitations of liability under the Hague Rules which were available to the carrier. After the *Scruttons* decision, the Himalaya clause was broadened to give the same protection to sub-contractors. Over the years, the Himalaya clause has been very successful,[65] and it is now adopted almost universally by carriers in their carriage documentation.

Even though the Himalaya clause has been so successful, the Visby Protocol incorporated amendments into the Hague Rules which also addressed this issue. Article 4 *bis* provides that:

1) The defences and limits of liability provided for in this Convention shall apply in any action against the carrier in respect of loss or damage to goods covered by a contract of carriage whether the action be founded in contract or in tort.

2) If such an action is brought against a servant or agent of the carrier (such servant or agent not being an independent contractor), such servant or agent shall be entitled to avail himself of the defences and limits of liability which the carrier is entitled to invoke under this Convention.

These amendments to the Hague Rules introduced by the Visby Protocol only protect servants or agents of the carrier. A Himalaya clause must still be used to protect independent contractors, as the Hague Visby Rules do not deal with them. The Visby Protocol does not give the carrier any greater protection than the carrier already obtains through appropriate wording on its bill of lading.

The Hague Visby Rules have the force of law.[66] It was initially considered that this Rule applied to limit liability in tort, even where there is no corresponding contractual right available, for example, where a shipper contracts with a carrier or freight forwarder and then seeks to sue the actual carrier.[67] However, *The Captain Gregos*[68] seems to indicate that this Rule may only apply to limit liability in tort if the carrier could be sued either in contract or in tort in respect of the loss, and tort was elected. If, on the other hand, there is no contractual liability, then there will be no limitation on tortious liability.[69]

The Hamburg Rules contain similar provisions to those in the Hague Visby Rules. Article 7, rr 1 and 2 of the Hamburg Rules provide that:

---

64 After *Adler v Dickson, ibid*.
65 See, eg, *New Zealand Shipping Co Limited v AM Satterthwaite & Co Ltd 'The Eurymedon'* [1975] AC 154; *The New York Star* [1981] WLR 138.
66 Carriage of Goods by Sea Act 1991 (Cth), s 8.
67 This was the view of Anthony Diamond QC in 'The Hague Visby Rules' [1987] *Lloyd's Maritime & Commercial Law Quarterly* 225.
68 *Compania Portorafti Commerciale SA v Ultramara Panama Inc (The Captain Gregos)* [1990] Lloyd's Rep 310.
69 This is the view in the above case and is also the view taken by Professor Treitel in [1984] *Lloyd's Maritime & Commercial Law Quarterly* 304.

1) The defences and limits of liability provided for in this Convention apply in any action against the carrier in respect of loss or damage to the goods covered by the contract of carriage by sea, as well as of delay in delivery whether the action is founded in contract, in tort or otherwise.

2) If such an action is brought against a servant or agent of the carrier, such servant or agent, if he proves that he acted within the scope of his employment, is entitled to avail himself of the defences and limits of liability which the carrier is entitled to invoke under this Convention.

The Rule is very similar in wording to the Hague Visby Rule and it may well be that, as with the Hague Visby Rules, the limitation provisions will not apply where it is possible for the shipper to proceed in tort against someone other than the carrier with whom the shipper has no direct contractual relationship.

As with the Hague Visby Rules, there is no mention of independent contractors, so a carrier will still need to use a Himalaya clause if they are to receive the benefit of the carrier's limitations of liability.

Non-contractual liability of the carrier to consignee

The Modified Hague Visby Rules are not an exclusive code dealing with a carrier's liability for loss or damage to goods,[70] and a carrier may still be liable at common law even though excepted from liability under the Modified Hague Visby Rules.

Can a consignee (to whom the risk in goods has passed under the sale contract) sue in tort even though, at the time of the loss, the consignee had no property in the goods (because it had not yet passed from the shipper) or interest under the contract of carriage (as the rights under the contract had not yet transferred)?[71]

In the UK, a consignee in this situation may be left without a right to recovery. The House of Lords in *Leigh & Sillavan Ltd v Aliakmon Shipping Co Ltd (The Aliakmon)*,[72] and the Privy Council in *Candlewood Navigation Corporation Ltd v Mitsui OSK Lines Ltd (The Mineral Transporter)*,[73] both denied recovery to CFR buyers and time charterers respectively on the grounds that they had no proprietary interest in the goods when they were damaged. If these decisions are followed in Australia, then parties who accept risk in the goods without legal ownership or possession amounting to bailment or custody may be denied recovery. So buyers who accept a delivery order in lieu of a

---

70 *Shipping Corp of India Ltd v Gamlen Chemical Co (A'asia) Pty Ltd* (1980) 147 CLR 142 at 152–53 *per* Stephen J, at 157–59 *per* Mason and Wilson JJ; 32 ALR 609; 55 ALJR 88.

71 These situations can arise with goods sold under CIF or CFR contracts.

72 [1986] AC 785 (following the rule in *Cattle v Stockton Waterworks Co* (1875) LR 10 QB 453 that only a person with a proprietary interest in a ship or cargo can recover economic loss in negligence). See *Margarine Union v Cambray Prince Steamship Co Ltd (The Wear Breeze)* [1969] 1 QB 219; Powles J, 'Title to sue, problems of consignees and others' [1987] JBL 313; Tettenborn AM, 'The carrier and the non-owning consignee – an inconsequential immunity' [1987] JBL 12.

73 [1986] AC 1. See also *The Aramis* [1987] 2 Lloyd's Rep 58, where consignees were held by the Commercial Court of Queen's Bench to have an implied contract entitling them to sue the carriers.

bill of lading, a common practice in respect of unascertained goods, where damage occurs before the delivery order is passed on to them,[74] may have no remedy.

However, it is by no means certain that the UK position will be followed in Australia[75] as pure economic loss is recoverable in Australian courts.[76]

Interaction with Trade Practices Act 1974

The Modified Hague Rules,[77] prevail over the provisions of the Trade Practices Act 1974, Pt V Div 2 to the extent of any inconsistency.[78] However, those implied conditions and warranties in consumer transactions[79] which are imposed by the Trade Practices Act 1974 will apply if neither the Modified Hague Rules nor the Hague Rules or Hague Visby Rules apply to the contract of sea carriage in question

COGSA and the Trade Practices Act 1974, Pt V Div 2 also prevail over any inconsistent State or Territory laws.[80] However, intrastate carriage of goods by sea will be governed by the Trade Practices Act 1974 and the equivalent State Fair Trading Acts.[81]

Multi-modalism

Unlike the Hague Visby Rules, the Hamburg Rules have been drafted with an eye to multi-modalism. Article 1, r 6, which defines a 'contract of carriage by sea', excludes coverage by the Hamburg Rules (where the contract has a non-sea leg of carriage) of that non-sea leg of carriage. However, the Hamburg Rules do not give clear guidance as to how the Rules are to operate where multi-modal transport is involved. It is not clear whether the Hamburg Rules apply when the carrier takes possession of the goods from the shipper at some point prior to the goods being delivered to the port of loading, or when the carrier continues to have responsibility for the goods and for their delivery to the ultimate destination after the goods have been discharged from the vessel at the port of discharge.[82]

---

74 See Powles J, 'Title to sue, problems of consignees and others' [1987] JBL 313 at 317.
75 In *J Gadsden Pty Ltd v Australian Coastal Shipping Commission* [1977] 1 NSWLR 575 [31 FLR 157], consignees suing on bailment and in negligence were successful.
76 See *Caltex Oil (Aust) Pty Ltd v The Dredge 'Willemstad'* (1976) 136 CLR 529. See also Davies, M and Lawson, G, 'Limiting shipowner's liability for economic loss' (1988) 16 ABLR 271; Davies, M, 'The elusive carrier: whom do I sue and how?' (1991) 19 ABLR 230.
77 Carriage of Goods by Sea Act 1991 (Cth), s 8.
78 *Ibid*, s 18.
79 Trade Practices Act 1974 (Cth), Pt V, Div 2.
80 Commonwealth Constitution, s 109.
81 *Wallis v Downard-Pickford (North Queensland) Pty Ltd* (1994) 179 CLR 388.
82 While Art 4, r 1 provides that 'the responsibility of the carrier for the goods under this Convention covers the period during which the carrier is in charge of the goods at the port of loading, during the carriage and at the port of discharge', Art 4, r 2 provides that the carrier is deemed to be in charge of the goods from the time it has taken over the goods from the shipper. If the carrier takes possession prior to the goods arriving at the port, the carrier is clearly in charge of the goods, but do the Rules apply to this period? It seems not, but the question appears to be open to interpretation.

Deck cargo

Neither the Hague Rules nor the Hague Visby Rules apply to deck cargo[83] unless the shipper and the carrier agree:

1 that the goods will be carried on deck;
2 that the goods will be carried under the Hague Rules or Hague Visby Rules; and
3 the goods are then actually carried on deck.

As a result, the way is open for the carrier to exclude liability absolutely where goods are carried as deck cargo, and this, in fact, happens in practice. The carrier also commonly inserts a provision in the bill of lading under which the carrier is given liberty to stow the cargo above or below deck at the carrier's discretion.[84]

If the parties agree to carry the goods on deck, then no liability will accrue to the carrier. However, where the goods are carried on deck without the express agreement of the shipper, then a question arises as to whether the liberty clause commonly found in a bill of lading would give the carrier a right to carry the goods on deck and then to claim an exemption from liability.

A carrier may wish to carry the goods on deck for a number of reasons, for example:

1 where the carrier moves the goods to the deck to ensure the safety of the cargo[85] when there seems no doubt that the liberty clause would be valid and the carrier exempt from liability;
2 where the cargo is carried on the deck purely for the convenience of the carrier and not out of any necessity. Here it seems that the liberty clause may not amount to a statement that the goods were to be carried as deck cargo and the goods will continue to be covered by the Hague Rules;[86]
3 if the goods are carried on deck because they cannot otherwise be carried by the vessel (for example, if too big to be carried below decks or if some legislative requirement mandates that they be carried above deck), then the liberty clause may well be valid.[87]

The difficulty with the Hague Rules and Hague Visby Rules is that, even where goods are customarily carried on deck, a statement that the goods are to be carried on deck is still required. If not, and if the carrier cannot fall back on the liberty clause, then carrying the goods as deck cargo may be a deviation outside the terms of the carriage contract, in which case the carrier may become liable for the full value of the cargo as the carrier will not be able to limit its liability under the Hague Rules or Hague Visby Rules.[88]

---

83 See definition of 'goods' in Art 1(c) of the Rules, which excludes 'cargo which, by the contract of carriage, is stated as being carried on deck and is so carried'.
84 Sometimes known as the 'liberty' clause.
85 Here the carrier would be carrying out its duty under Art 3, r 2 to properly care for the cargo.
86 *Svenska Traktor Akt v Maritime Agencies (Southampton)* [1953] 2 Lloyd's Rep 124.
87 The carrier would be complying with its duty under Art 3, r 2.
88 *Svenska Traktor Aktiebolaget v Maritime Agencies (Southampton) Ltd* [1953] 2 Lloyd's Rep 124, 129–30.

However, the Modified Hague Visby Rules do include deck cargo as being goods covered under those Rules,[89] provided that at or before the time of booking, the skipper tells the carrier of any specific storage requirements for the goods and the carrier agrees in writing. If the carrier carries goods as deck cargo contrary to express agreement, the carrier will remain liable.[90]

The Hamburg Rules apply to all cargo, whether carried on or below deck.[91] However, while the carrier cannot exclude liability for deck cargo under the Hamburg Rules, as a trade-off the carrier is given an express right to carry cargo on deck if:

1   the shipper agrees;

2   it is the usage of the trade; or

3   it is required by law.[92]

An important provision in the Hamburg Rules is whether or not carriage of the goods on deck is a usage of the particular trade. In particular, container cargo is often carried on deck. Is this 'usage of the particular trade'? It may well be. If so, then the carrier can limit its liability in accordance with the limitation provisions set out in Art 6 of the Hamburg Rules.

There were very good reasons for the exclusion of deck cargo at the turn of the century when the Hague Rules were being formulated. These days, however, very large numbers of containers are carried as deck cargo and, even though deck cargo does involve special risks, in view of the volume of container cargo now carried this way, it does not seem unreasonable that some remedy should be available to a shipper where cargo is carried on deck. The Modified Hague Visby Rules and the Hamburg Rules do address this issue.

Live animals

Carriage of live animals is outside the coverage of both the Hague Rules and the Hague Visby Rules.[93] The Modified Hague Visby Rules make no change to this position.[94] Carriers commonly insert exclusion clauses in the contract of carriage denying liability completely in respect of such carriage.

The definition of goods in the Hamburg Rules specifically provides[95] that goods include 'live animals', so a shipper may recover against the carrier under the Hamburg Rules where such loss or damage is suffered.

---

89   Article 2, r 2 of the Modified Rules.
90   Article 2, r 4, Sched 1A.
91   Hamburg Rules, Art 1, r 5.
92   Article 9.
93   See definition of goods in Art 1(c).
94   The Report of the Working Group noted that 'This was agreed by the Working Group not to be an issue: live animals can remain outside the liability regime'. This is primarily because live animals are habitually carried by way of charterparty.
95   Article 1, r 5.

Nautical fault and negligent management

Both the Hague Rules and the Hague Visby Rules contain[96] a lengthy list of excepted perils that, should they occur, will exempt a carrier from liability. Most of these exceptions are based on the common law defences available to sea carriers and/or the principle that the carrier should be exempt from liability if the loss occurred without any fault or negligence on its part.

However, Art 4, r 2(a) sets out the so called 'nautical fault' and 'negligent management' defences. It provides that 'neither the carrier nor the ship shall be responsible for loss or damage arising or resulting from act, neglect or default of the master, mariner, pilot, or the servants of the carrier[97] in the navigation or the management of the ship'.[98]

The original rationale for this exemption appears to be that, at the turn of the century, vessels were sailing into uncharted or poorly charted areas and maritime adventures were potentially very hazardous. The master of the vessel was out of contact for long periods and, in effect, the shipowner was risking his ship and cargo owners their cargo. The master was out of the effective control of the shipowner as the master was out of contact for long periods. This is not the situation today. While sea carriage today still presents risks, the carriage of goods is considerably less hazardous than it was.

Shippers have for some time been agitating for removing this exemption as:

1 the reason for its creation no longer substantially exists;

2 the exemption is contrary to the general principles of negligence;

3 the exemption is unique to sea carriage and is not found in other carriage regimes and hence detracts from uniformity.

As Anthony Diamond QC stated:[99]

3) Much ingenuity has been devoted to trying to justify these exceptions but, it is submitted, there has not been any argument which really gets off the ground. It is difficult to see why negligence in navigating a ship should have different legal consequences than any other kind of negligence. As to negligence in the management of the ship, this exception requires the court to ascertain whether the negligent management occurred before or after the voyage began. If it occurred before the beginning of the voyage, the shipowner is liable for failing to exercise due diligence. If afterwards, it is necessary to decide whether the negligence was in managing the ship or in looking after the cargo. ... The exceptions of negligent navigation and negligent management of the ship are distinctly out of place in a regime based on a duty of care.

---

96 Art 4, r 20.

97 The immunity does not extend to the carrier's own personal acts, neglect or default. See *Lennard's Carrying Co Ltd v Asiatic Petroleum Co Ltd* [1915] AC 705; *Leval & Co Ltd v Colonial Steamships* [1961] 1 Lloyd's Rep 560.

98 The exemption is only from management acts and decisions relating to the ship. It does not extend to negligent 'management' of the cargo. See *Maxine Footwear Co Ltd v Canadian Government Merchant Marine Ltd* [1959] AC 589.

99 Diamond, A, 'Responsibility for loss of, or damage to, cargo on a sea transit', *op cit*, p 11.

The Hamburg Rules make such a change. Article 5, r 1 states:

> 4) The carrier is liable for loss resulting from loss of or damage to the goods, as well as from delay in delivery, if the occurrence which caused the loss, damage or delay took place while the goods were in his charge as defined in Article 4, unless the carrier proves that he, his servants or agents took all measures that could reasonably be required to avoid the occurrence and its consequences.

This rule effectively does away with the nautical fault and negligent management defence, as a carrier could not demonstrate in those situations that all reasonably required measures were taken by the carrier's servant or agent.

The Hamburg Rules are an improvement over the Hague Rules and the Hague Visby Rules in this area from the viewpoints of equity and uniformity. However, there are policy considerations to consider with this exemption, as their implementation would see a substantial shift in the amount of risk assumed by the carrier and the cargo owner.[100] For this reason, when the Working Group considered the issue they concluded:

> The carrier view was that the existing mechanism allocates liability efficiently, while shipper interests viewed nautical fault as an issue of principle, questioning its relevance with radar, GPS etc – the overriding issue was that of fairness.

> The insurer view was that nautical fault was all about risk management, but acknowledged that nautical fault is not equitable. Insurer interests note that all losses have to be paid for over time, whichever side of the shipper/carrier divide they fall. It was desirable to keep the costs of dividing them to a minimum.

> The Working Group could not find strong supporting evidence that the existing liability regime regarding Nautical Fault or Basis of Liability has caused major practical problems for shippers. Nevertheless, it was agreed that, providing there is clear international support for such a move by Australia's major trading partners, Australia also should support abolition or partial abolition of the nautical defence, at least in respect of act, neglect or default in the management of the ship as a basis for an exemption from liability.

Fire

The fire exemption is another provision unique to the Hague and Hague Visby Rules. Article 4, r 2(b) provides that 'neither the carrier nor the ship shall be responsible for loss or damage arising or resulting from fire, unless caused by the actual fault or privity of the carrier'.[101]

As with the nautical fault exception, it seems a curious anomaly today to have a defence based on fire caused by the negligence of the carrier's servants or agents, and the tide of opinion may be turning against maintaining such special case exemptions.[102]

---

100 See Makins, B, 'Sea carriage of goods liability: which route for Australia? The case for the Hague Visby Rules and the SDR Protocol', 14th International Trade Law Conference, Canberra, 16 October 1987, Australian Government Publishing Service, 1988.

101 Article 4, r 2(b).

102 However, it is worth noting that the Working Party in its Report stated that 'Provisions regarding fire were not an issue'.

The Hamburg Rules do away with this exemption. They provide that:

4(a) The carrier is liable:

    (i) for loss of or damage to the goods or delay in delivery caused by fire, if the claimant proves that the fire arose from fault or neglect on the part of the carrier, his servants or agents;

    (ii) for such loss, damage or delay in delivery which is proved by the claimant to have resulted from the fault or neglect of the carrier, his servants or agents, in taking all measures that could reasonably be required to put out the fire and avoid or mitigate its consequences;

  (b) In case of fire on board the ship affecting the goods, if the claimant or the carrier so desires, a survey in accordance with shipping practices must be held into the cause and circumstances of the fire, and a copy of the surveyor's report shall be made available on demand to the carrier and the claimant.[103]

While the Hamburg Rules remove the fire defence, they place the onus of proof of the negligence on the shipper,[104] unlike the general formulation of liability set out in Art 5, r 1, where the onus is placed on the carrier to show that it took all measures reasonably required to avoid the occurrence and its consequences.

When does carriage begin and end?

Both the Hague Rules and the Hague Visby Rules do not generally cover goods during the period they are in the port prior to their being shipped, on board the vessel or after they have been unloaded. The general rule in Australia (following the UK approach) is that the rules apply from tackle to tackle;[105] that is, from when the tackle is hooked on to the goods until the tackle is removed from the goods on delivery.[106]

The application of the Hague Rules and the Hague Visby Rules can be extended by agreement between the parties[107] to cover cargo while on the dock or while being transferred to another vessel during the original voyage.[108] The Rules might also apply to that period if it could be shown that it was the custom to do so.

However, it is generally the case that carriers operating under the Hague or Hague Visby Rules provide only 'tackle to tackle' coverage and exclude liability for the period during which the goods are being loaded or off-loaded.[109] In addition, by the use of a Himalaya clause, the carrier also contracts out of liability on behalf of the stevedoring company. The result is that, when the goods are on the docks before loading or after

---

103 Article 5, r 4.

104 Article 5, r 4(a).

105 Sometimes also referred to as 'hook to hook'.

106 *Pyrene v Scindia* [1954] 2 QB 402.

107 *Pyrene v Scindia* [1954] 2 QB 402; *Falconbridge Nickel Mines Ltd v Chimo Shipping Ltd* [1969] 2 Lloyd's Rep 277.

108 But see *Captain v Far East Steamship Co* [1979] 1 Lloyd's Rep 595, 602, where it was held that the Hague Rules did not apply where two bills of lading were issued for two voyages and the goods were stored on the dock for a lengthy period during which the damage occurred while awaiting transhipment by water. This case was distinguished in *Mayhew Foods v OCL* [1984] 1 Lloyd's Rep 317 where only one bill of lading was issued for the voyage and the cargo owner was not made aware of the transshipment. The court held that the goods were covered by the Hague Visby Rules for the whole voyage including transfers. See also *The Anders Maersk* [1986] 1 Lloyd's Rep 483.

109 The *Bunga Teratsai; Nissho Iwai Ltd v Malaysian International Shipping Corp* (1989) 167 CLR 219.

unloading, at the times when there is a significant risk of loss or damage,[110] both the carrier and the stevedore will often have no responsibility to the shipper as they have contracted out of liability.

The Hamburg Rules extend coverage beyond tackle to tackle. Article 4, r 1 provides that:

> The responsibility of the carrier for the goods under this Convention covers the period during which the carrier is in charge of the goods at the port of loading, during the carriage and at the port of discharge.

So, instead of 'tackle to tackle' coverage, the Hamburg Rules cover from 'port to port'; that is, they include the period during which the carrier is in charge of the goods at the port. Goods during this period are actually in the custody of a stevedore – usually an independent entity to the carrier although sometimes with close links. Is it reasonable for a carrier to be responsible for the actions of an independent contractor? The answer would appear to be 'yes'. The shipper engages the carrier to move the goods from one place to another, leaving all arrangements, including loading and unloading and sub-contracting of the carriage, up to the carrier. It does not seem unreasonable for the carrier to be responsible for the loss or damage to the cargo during this period. The carrier, of course, may have its own remedies against the third party who caused the loss or damage to the cargo.

Like the Hamburg Rules, under the Modified Hague Visby Rules, a carrier is deemed to be in charge of the goods:

1   from the time they are delivered to the carrier, to servant or agent within the limits of a port or wharf;[111] and

2   until the goods are delivered to, or placed at the disposal of, the consigner within the limits of the port or wharf of destination.[112]

However, there may be some doubt as to what duty the carrier owes to the shipper during those phases of carriage when the goods are at the port terminal but not yet loaded, or when they are at the port terminal awaiting collection. The primary rules[113] relating to the care of the cargo remain unchanged and those rules have traditionally been interpreted so as to apply only to 'tackle to tackle' coverage.[114] In addition, Art 7 of the Modified Hague Visby Rules seems to expressly reserve to the carrier a right to exclude liability for the custody, care and handling of the goods before loading and after discharge.

---

110 See submission by NSW Shippers Association to the Australian Department of Transport entitled 'Implementation of Hamburg Rules', March 1994.

111 The Modified Hague Visby Rules allow for the limits of a port or wharf to be fixed by the Chief Executive Officer of Customs – see Carriage of Goods by Sea Act 1991 (Cth), Sched 1A, Art 1, rr 4 and 5. The limits of overseas ports are to be fixed by the local laws of that country – Carriage of Goods by the Sea Act 1991 (Cth), Sched 1A, Art 1, r 6.

112 Carriage of Goods by Sea Act 1991 (Cth), Sched 1A, Art 1, r 3.

113 Hague Visby Rules, Art 3, r 2 under which the carrier must 'properly and carefully load, handle, stow, carry, keep, care for and discharge the goods carried', and Art 2, r 1 under which the carrier is subject to the responsibilities set out in the Rules in relation to 'the loading, handling, storage, carriage, custody, care and discharge' of the goods.

114 See Lewins, K, 'Are the 1998 amendments to COGSA holding water' (2000) 28 ABLR 422 at 423, 424.

Delay

Neither the Hague Rules nor the Hague Visby Rules deal with delay. The common law imposes a duty on the carrier to deliver the goods within a reasonable time if that is within the reasonable contemplation of the parties,[115] but this can be overridden by contractual provisions to the contrary. The carrier is free to deny liability for any economic loss caused by delay in the contract of carriage, and it is common to see such clauses in bills of lading. If the delay causes physical damage to the goods, the Hague Rules and Hague Visby Rules will apply as Art 3, r 2 imposes a duty of care on the carrier in the handling of the cargo.

The 'loss or damage' referred to is not confined to physical loss or damage[116] but may include other losses.[117] In order for loss or damage to arise or result from an excepted peril,[118] the loss or damage and the peril must have some kind of causal connection but the peril need not be the direct or physical cause; it is sufficient if it has some kind of causal relation with the loss.[119]

The Hamburg Rules expressly give the shipper rights against the carrier in respect of delay. Article 5 provides that:

1) The carrier is liable for loss resulting from loss of or damage to the goods, as well as from delay in delivery, if the occurrence which caused the loss, damage or delay took place while the goods were in his charge as defined in Article 4, unless the carrier proves that he, his servants or agents took all measures that could reasonably be required to avoid the occurrence and its consequences.

2) Delay in delivery occurs when the goods have not been delivered at the port of discharge provided for in the contract of carriage by sea within the time expressly agreed upon or, in the absence of such agreement, within the time which it would be reasonable to require of a diligent carrier, having regard to the circumstances of the case.

The Hamburg rules impose a special limit on recoverable damages, where delay is concerned, of 'two and a half times the freight payable for the goods delayed, but not exceeding the total freight payable under the contract of carriage of goods by sea'.[120] However, if the delay period exceeds 60 days, the shipper may treat the goods as lost.[121]

While the Hamburg Rules give a shipper some benefits (as opposed to a contractual denial of liability for loss from delay under the Hague and Hague Visby Rules), it also raises some difficulties. First, it is difficult to understand the reasoning behind the differing method of calculating the limitation of liability for delay. From the

---

115 *Renton v Palmyra Trading Corp* [1957] AC 149; *The Makedonia* [1962] 1 Lloyd's Rep 316.

116 *Adamastos Shipping Co Ltd v Anglo-Saxon Petroleum Co Ltd* [1959] AC 133 at 157.

117 See, eg, *Marifortuna Naviera SA v Government of Ceylon* [1970] 1 Lloyd's Rep 247 (expenses due to delay). *Eridania SpA v Rudolf A Oetker (The Fjord Wind)* [2000] 2 Lloyd's Rep 191, CA (any loss).

118 Under amended Hague Rules 1979, Art 4(2).

119 *Frank Hammond Pty Ltd v Huddart Parker Ltd* [1956] VLR 496 at 498; [1956] ALR 1215 *per* Gavan Duffy J.

120 Article 6, r 1(b).

121 Article 5, r 3.

shipper's point of view, a loss is a loss – whether it is caused by loss of, or damage to, the goods or by delay. So why not the same limitation amount?

Secondly, can the carrier specify in the contract of carriage that the delivery period will be 12 months (or some other excessively long period) and thereby avoid any liability for delay until that date is reached? If so, does this mean the shipper cannot claim for loss of the goods until 60 days after the long transport period? Does the delivery time stop running for strikes by the carrier's employees?

Thirdly, given that the Hamburg Rules are supposed to take into account multi-modal transport, how will this provision apply where multi-modal transport is involved? Does delay in another mode of carriage have to be taken into account?

Another difficulty of interpretation posed by the Hamburg Rules is in respect of the application of the 60 day period in Art 5, r 3. Does the consignee have to abandon the goods to claim them as lost? If so, who owns the goods? If the carriage document is a bill of lading, then how can the bill of lading remain a negotiable document?

Under the Modified Hague Visby Rules, a carrier (including its servants or agents) is liable for loss caused by delay[122] unless the delay was excusable and the carrier took all measures reasonably required to avoid the delay and its consequences[123] while the carrier is 'in charge of the goods'.[124]

An excusable delay is one that was:

1   caused by a deviation authorised by the shipper concerned, or by any special term in the contract of carriage; or

2   caused by circumstances beyond the reasonable control of the carrier or its servants or agents; or

3   reasonably necessary to comply with an express or implied warranty; or

4   reasonably necessary for the safety of the ship or its cargo; or

5   for the purposes of saving human life or aiding a ship in distress; or

6   reasonably necessary for the purposes of obtaining medical or surgical aid for a person on board; or

7   caused by barratrous conduct of the master or crew;[125] or caused by industrial action which is not substantially caused by, or contributed to by, the unreasonable conduct of the carrier.[126]

Under Art 4A, r 5, conduct of servants or agents is only taken to be that of the carrier if the servants or agents engage in the conduct with the carrier's express or implied authority. As with the Hamburg Rules, the quantum of damages for delay is limited to the lesser of:

---

122 'Delay' is defined in Art 4, r 2 as being non-delivery within the time allowed for in the contract, or if the contract does not specify any particular time, within the time that a reasonable shipper would reasonably allow for delivery (as defined in Art 1, r 2) of goods by a diligent carrier at the particular port in question.

123 Article 4A, r 1(a) and (b), Sched 1A.

124 Article 1, r 3 defines when a carrier is in charge of the goods.

125 Carriage of Goods by Sea Act 1991 (Cth), Sched 1A, Art 4A, r 3.

126 Carriage of Goods by Sea Act 1991 (Cth), Sched 1A, Art 4A, r 4.

1   two and a half times the freight payable for the goods delayed; or

2   the total amount payable as freight for all of the goods shipped by the shipper concerned under the contract of carriage concerned.[127]

Time bars

Under the Hague Rules and the Hague Visby Rules, the time bar for taking action[128] against the carrier is one year after the goods were or should have been delivered.[129] If suit is not taken within that time, the carrier and the ship are discharged from all liability 'in respect of loss or damage', that is, the claim is extinguished.[130] However, the usual time limit prescribed by the limitation of actions legislation applies if the carrier takes action against the shipper for freight.[131] For example, in *The Aries*[132] the carrier was able to claim successfully against the shipper for freight,[133] but the shipper's claim against the carrier was time-barred under the Hague Visby Rules.

The one year limitation period for the shipper to take action for loss or damage to cargo remains in the Modified Hague Visby Rules.[134]

The Hamburg Rules provide for a longer time bar period that applies equally to both shipper and courier. Article 20, r 1 provides that:

> Any action relating to carriage of goods under this Convention is time-barred if judicial or arbitral proceedings have not been instituted within a period of two years.

Containerisation and package or unit limitations

While cargo has always been consolidated, containerisation originated in America in the mid-1950s.[135] As a result, the Hague Rules did not deal with this important industry development and the effect of containerisation on the package or unit limitation.

---

127 Carriage of Goods by Sea Act 1991 (Cth), Sched 1A, Art 4A, r 6.

128 This refers to the issue of proceedings and not to their service upon the defendant. See *Van Leer Australia Pty Ltd v Palace Shipping KK* (1981) 34 ALR 3.

129 Article 3, r 6.

130 *Aries Tanker Corporation v Total Transport (The Aries)* [1977] 1 Lloyd's Rep 334; *J Gadsen Pty Ltd v Australian Coastal Shipping Commission* [1977] 1 NSWLR 575; *Australian Shipping Commission v Kooragang Cement Pty Ltd* [1988] VR 29, 31, 35; *The Nordglimt* [1988] QB 183; *Transpetrol Ltd v Ekali Shipping Co Ltd (The Aghia Marina)* [1989] 1 Lloyd's Rep 62–67.

131 See, for example, Limitation of Actions Act 1974 (Qld), s 10, which prescribes a limitation period of six years for a suit in contract.

132 *Aries Tanker Corp v Total Transport Ltd* [1977] 1 Lloyd's Rep 334.

133 As the carrier sued within the period allowed by the Statute of Limitations when suing on a simple contract, as it is only the shipper who has the time bar under the Hague Rules or Hague Visby Rules imposed on it.

134 The Working Group did consider a possible extension of time in which to make a claim to two years as under the Hamburg Rules but, in their Report, the Working Group noted that there were arguments both ways and to leave the time bar period unchanged at one year. See pp 25–26 of the Report.

135 See generally Kendall, LC, *The Business of Shipping*, 2nd edn, 1986, London: Chapman & Hall.

As a result, the meaning of the words 'package or unit' in the Hague Rules have led to confusion.[136] The courts in different countries have given differing interpretations to this phrase. The only Australian authority in this area is *PS Chellaram & Co v China Ocean Shipping Co*,[137] a case on the original Hague Rules where Carruthers J adopted the 'functional package' test: that the package or unit is determined by reference to the physical nature of the packaging of the goods, particularly the unit in which the shipper packaged the goods.[138]

In 1968, when the Visby Protocol was being finalised, containerisation was becoming widespread and by 1978, when the Hamburg Rules were being finalised, containerisation was a well developed and widely used method of carriage of cargo. So both the Visby Protocol and the Hamburg Rules deal with how the package or unit limitation in the Rules applies to containers and other consolidated cargos.

The Hague Visby Rules provide:

> Where a container, pallet or similar article of transport is used to consolidate goods, the number of packages or units enumerated in the bill of lading as packed in such article of transport shall be deemed the number of packages for units for the purpose of this paragraph as far as these packages or units are concerned. Except as aforesaid, such article of transport shall be considered the package or unit.[139]

So under the Hague Visby Rules, one looks to the description of the goods on the bill of lading rather than the physical nature of the packaging of the goods. If the number of packages or units are specified, they will each be considered a package or unit, otherwise the container, pallet or the like will be considered the package or unit.[140] So if the bill of lading, for example, specifies on its face that it is 'one container containing 20 cartons of ...' then the carton is the unit. However, if it says 'one container of ...', then the container itself becomes the unit.[141]

The Hamburg Rules use a similar formulation to the Hague Visby Rules. Article 6, r 2 provides that:

> For the purpose of calculating which amount is the higher in accordance with para 1(a) of this article, the following rules apply:
>
> 1) Where a container, pallet or similar article of transport is used to consolidate goods, the package or other shipping units enumerated in the bill of lading, if issued, or otherwise in any other document evidencing the contract of carriage by sea, as packed in such article of transport, are deemed packages or shipping units. Except as aforesaid, the goods in such article of transport are deemed one shipping unit.

---

136 Article 4, r 5.
137 [1989] 1 Lloyd's Rep 413.
138 The decision of Carruthers J was reversed by the NSW Court of Appeal but on other grounds – *China Ocean Shipping Co v PS Chellaram and Co*, unreported, Court of Appeal NSW, no CA762/88.
139 Article 4, r 5(c) Hague Visby Rules. The Modified Hague Visby Rules make no change to the position under the Hague Visby Rules. See also *River Gurara (owners of Cargo lately laden on board) v Nigerian National Shipping Line Ltd* [1997] 3 WLR 1128.
140 *El Greco (Australia) Pty Ltd v Mediterranean Shipping Company SA* [2003] FCA 588.
141 This seems to rule out the 'functional package' test favoured by the Court in *China Ocean Shipping Co v PS Chellaram & Co*. See note 135.

2) In cases where the article of transport itself has been lost or damaged, that article of transport, if not owned or otherwise supplied by the carrier, is considered one separate shipping unit.

The Hamburg Rules seems to allow for three possibilities. If the bill of lading:

1 does not detail the contents of the container, the container is one shipping unit;

2 specifies the contents individually, then each of the specified packages is a unit; and

3 specifies certain packages plus general cargo in the container, then each package is a unit and the general cargo is another unit.

The Hamburg Rules follow the Hague Visby Rules; that is, the wording on the face of the bill of lading or other document of carriage will be examined and will be determinative of the package or shipping unit. While this removes the uncertainty of the original Hague Rule formulation, there is still ambiguity where an entry in a bill of lading reads 'said to contain'. For example, if an entry reads 'one container said to contain 50 electric motors', what then is the appropriate shipping unit? It could be arguably either the container or the 50 electric motors.[142]

Jurisdiction/arbitration

The Hague Rules and the Hague Visby Rules are silent on jurisdiction and arbitration. As documents of carriage are habitually prepared by the carrier, the carrier generally has the advantage of choosing a forum for arbitration or litigation that is convenient to itself. That forum is often inconvenient to the shipper, which may find itself having to take action in an unfamiliar jurisdiction to seek redress, even though the rules themselves are uniform. The burden of proof and the interpretation of the rules can differ from country to country. The carrier can forum shop to have its bill of lading interpreted by courts of a country giving the most favourable interpretations.

While the Hague Rules and the Hague Visby Rules do not deal with jurisdiction, in Australia, s 11 of the COGSA[143] provides:

11 Construction and jurisdiction

(1) All parties to:

(a) a sea carriage document relating to the carriage of goods from any place in Australia to any place outside Australia;

(b) a non-negotiable document of a kind mentioned in sub-paragraph 10(1)(b)(iii), relating to such a carriage of goods;

are taken to have intended to contract according to the laws in force at the place of shipment.

(2) An agreement (whether made in Australia or elsewhere) has no effect so far as it purports to:

(a) preclude or limit the effect of sub-section (1) in respect of a bill of lading or a document mentioned in that sub-sections; or

---

142 *El Greco (Australia) Pty Ltd v Mediterranean Shipping Company SA* [2003] FCA 588.

143 Prior to COGSA, the Sea Carriage of Goods Act 1924, s 9, contained a provision to like effect with respect to the Hague Rules.

(b) preclude or limit the jurisdiction of a court of the Commonwealth or of a State or Territory in respect of a bill of lading or a document mentioned in subsection (1); or

(c) preclude or limit the jurisdiction of a court of the Commonwealth or of a State or Territory in respect of:

(i) a sea carriage document relating to the carriage of goods from any place outside Australia to any place in Australia; or

(ii) a non-negotiable document of a kind mentioned in sub-paragraph 10(1)(b)(iii), relating to such a carriage of goods;

(3) An agreement, or a provision of an agreement, that provides for the resolution of a dispute by arbitration is not made ineffective by sub-section (2) (despite the fact that it may preclude or limit the jurisdiction of a court) if, under the agreement or provision, the arbitration must be conducted in Australia.

So, even though there was no jurisdiction clause in the rules, the problems this caused in overseas jurisdictions[144] were not apparent here because the jurisdiction of the Australian courts could not be ousted. The wording of this section (prior to the Carriage of Goods by Sea Amendments Act 1997 (Cth) did have the consequence that arbitration clauses in contracts of carriage were deemed to be ousters of jurisdiction of the Australian courts and were therefore void. However, in respect of cargo inbound to Australia, the Australian courts may have to interpret the contract of carriage subject to the governing law of another jurisdiction.[145]

The Hamburg Rules specifically deal with jurisdiction. Article 21 provides that a plaintiff (who apparently can be either the carrier or the shipper) can bring an action in the Courts of:

1   the place of the defendant's business (or, if none, habitual residence);

2   the place where the contract was made;

3   the port of loading;

4   the port of discharge;

5   the agreed place in the contract; or

6   the place where the vessel has been arrested.

There is some doubt as to whether the insertion of these provisions on jurisdiction is an improvement over the Hague and Hague Visby Rules. As can be seen from *The Eleftheria*,[146] the courts were able to formulate a satisfactory solution to the jurisdiction problem. In Australia, the courts have had the benefit of a statutory jurisdiction provision,[147] so the Hamburg Rules provisions on jurisdiction make no significant improvement in the Australian context.

---

144 *The Eleftheria* [1969] 1 Lloyd's Rep 237.

145 Note that it does not necessarily follow that if the law of a particular country was the proper law of the contract, there was a submission to the law of that country – *Dunbee Ltd v Gilmen and Co (Australia) Pty Ltd* [1968] 2 Lloyd's Rep 394.

146 [1969] 1 Lloyd's Rep 237.

147 Section 9 of the Sea Carriage of Goods Act 1924, and s 11 of the COGSA 1991.

Indeed, the Hamburg Rules may be a backward step. There is some ambiguity in terms such as 'agency' and 'residence'. It is also difficult to see why r 5 has been inserted – it apparently covers the same ground as Art 21, r 1(d). The Hamburg Rules may once again muddy the waters that had been cleared up by judicial interpretation of the Hague Rules.

Liability under the Hague and the Hamburg Rules

The basis of the carrier's liability under the Hague and Hague Visby Rules is a breach of the carrier's duties which are set out in Art 3, which provide that:

1   The carrier shall be bound before and at the beginning of the voyage to exercise due diligence to:
     (a) make the ship seaworthy;
     (b) properly man, equip and supply the ship; and
     (c) make the holds, refrigerating and cool chambers, and all other parts of the ship in which goods are carried, fit and safe for their reception, carriage and preservation.
2   Subject to the provisions of Article 4, the carrier shall properly and carefully load, handle, stow, carry, keep, care for and discharge the goods carried.

This duty to exercise due diligence to provide a seaworthy vessel is non-delegable[148] and is not subject to the carrier's defences in Art 4, r 2, that is, if the carrier fails to provide a seaworthy vessel at the commencement of the voyage, then it cannot rely on the usual defences if the cargo is lost or damaged.

The duty of seaworthiness imposed by the Hague and Hague Visby Rules is something greater than the tortious duty of care.[149] However, the duty to care for the cargo is closer to the tortious duty (except the nautical fault and fire exemptions in Art 4, r 2), but there have been problems interpreting the word 'properly'[150] in 'properly man, equip and supply the ship', and it may be that the obligation is something more than a duty to take reasonable care.[151]

The Hague Rules liability provisions create some anomalies. First, a ship can be seaworthy for the purpose of carriage of certain types of cargo but not for others. As a result, the owner of one cargo for which the vessel was unseaworthy could obtain full recovery, whereas another cargo owner may not, as the vessel was seaworthy for that cargo. Secondly, the carrier's duty is only to exercise due diligence to make the vessel seaworthy at the commencement of the voyage defined on the bill of lading. A ship will commonly stop at a number of ports *en route*. If the ship is seaworthy (or if due diligence has been exercised) at the time of loading of the first shipper's cargo, but it is no longer seaworthy at a port *en route* where a second shippers' cargo is loaded, then when both cargoes are unloaded at the destination port, only the second shipper will be able to recover.

---

148 *The Muncaster Castle* [1961] Lloyd's Rep 57; *The Amstelslot* [1963] 2 Lloyd's Rep 223.
149 *Ibid*.
150 *Albacora SRL v Westcott and Lawrence Line* [1966] 2 Lloyd's Rep 37.
151 *Shipping Corp of India Ltd v Gamlen Chemical Co (Australasia) Pty Ltd* (1980) 147 CLR 142 at 150.

The Hamburg Rules, in Art 5, make a significant change to the basis of liability. Article 5, r 1 provides that:

> The carrier is liable for loss resulting from loss of or damage to the goods, as well as from delay in delivery, if the occurrence which caused the loss, damage or delay took place while the goods were in his charge as defined in Article 4, unless the carrier proves that he, his servants or agents took all measures that could reasonably be required to avoid the occurrence and its consequences.

Under the Hamburg Rules, there is no distinction between the duty imposed on the carrier in relation to the vessel and the duty imposed on the carrier in relation to cargo – in either case the duty is to take 'all measures that could reasonably be required to avoid the occurrence and its consequences'.

This duty imposed by the Hamburg Rules is a continuing duty on the carrier to maintain the vessel in a seaworthy state throughout the voyage rather than just at the commencement of the voyage. The nautical fault and fire exemptions in relation to the cargo are effectively removed by the Hamburg Rules, as in these situations the shipowner could not demonstrate that all reasonable measures were taken to avoid the occurrence. It also places the onus of proof on the carrier to establish that it exercised due diligence, unlike the Hague Rules and Hague Visby Rules where the onus was on the shipper to establish that there had been a breach of Art 3 of those Rules. The rationale behind this reversal of the onus of proof is that the shipper is in a very difficult position in being able to prove a want of due diligence, whereas the carrier should be in a better position to establish, positively, due diligence.

While the duty on the carrier under the Hamburg Rules has the merit of being uniform, a question that remains unanswered is just what is the standard of care; is it the 'negligence' standard or something more, as it is under the Hague and Hague Visby Rules?[152]

The Hamburg Rules apparently impose a significantly greater level of liability on the carrier. However, whether the duty of care imposed is any greater than the usual negligence standard remains to be seen.

Limitation of liability

The rationale behind the introduction of limitation of liability was to encourage investment in shipping.[153] The rationale now for retaining the limitation is that it enables the carrier to calculate risks, to establish uniform and cheaper freight rates and to protect itself from risks associated with the carriage of undisclosed, high value cargo. On the other hand, from the shipper's point of view, the liability limitations should be set high enough to give the carrier sufficient incentive to care properly for the cargo.

Under the Hague Rules, Art 4, r 5 provides that the carrier's liability is limited to '£100 per package or unit'. Article 9 provides that 'the monetary units mentioned in

---

152 *The Muncaster Castle* [1961] Lloyd's Rep 57; *Albacora SRL v Westcott and Lawrence Line* [1966] 2 Lloyd's Rep 37.
153 Wilson, JF, 'Basic carrier liability and the right of limitation' in Mankabady, S (ed), *The Hamburg Rules On The Carriage of Goods by Sea*, 1978, Leyden/Boston: AW Sijthoff, pp 137, 146.

these rules are to be taken to be gold value'. Until recently in Australia this was taken to be a package or unit limitation of $200 in today's currency. This significantly limits the carrier's liability as inflationary pressures have made $200 (£100) significantly less in real terms then it was in 1924.

However, the New South Wales Court of Appeal in *Brown Boveri (Aust) Pty Ltd v Baltic Shipping Co Ltd*[154] found that the Hague Rules limit is the market value today of the amount of gold contained in 100 gold sovereigns in the year 1924.[155]

The Hague Visby Rules incorporate the Special Drawing Right (SDR) Protocol, which provides that:

> Unless the nature and value of such goods have been declared by the shipper before shipment and inserted in the bill of lading, neither the carrier nor the ship shall in any event be or become liable for any loss or damage to or in connection with the goods in an amount exceeding 666.67 units of account per package or unit or two units of account per kilogram weight of the goods lost or damaged, whichever is the higher.[156]

The unit of account under the Hague Visby Rules is the SDR as defined by the International Monetary Fund. The effect of the introduction of the Hague Visby Rules has been to reduce the liability limit under the Hague Rules (as defined by the NSW Court of Appeal in *Brown Boveri*).

Under the Hamburg Rules, the liability limits are increased by about 20% over the limits set down in the Hague Visby Rules. Article 6, r 1(a) provides that:

> The liability of the carrier for loss resulting from loss of or damage to goods according to the provisions of Article 5 is limited to an amount equivalent to 835 units of account per package or other shipping unit or 2.5 units of account per kilogramme gross weight of the goods lost or damaged, whichever is the higher.

So, while the Hamburg Rules significantly lift the liability limits imposed under the Hague Visby Rules, they are still less than the limitation amount imposed under the Hague Rules (after *Brown Boveri*).

Unlimited liability

Although the Hague Rules have no specific provision dealing with the circumstances in which a carrier may be deprived of its right to limit its liability under the rules, the courts deprive carriers of the right to limit their liability in some circumstances. In particular, a deviation from the agreed course of the contract may deprive a carrier of its right to limit its liability under those rules.[157]

In Australia, in *JI Case (Australia) Pty Ltd v Tasman Express Line Ltd (The Canterbury Express)*,[158] Carruthers J found that a carrier was not entitled to the benefit of

---

154 *The Nadezhda Krupskaya* (1989) 15 NSWLR 448; [1989] 1 Lloyd's Rep 518.

155 In 1989, when *Brown Boveri* was decided, that value was in excess of $11,000.

156 Article 4, r 5(a).

157 *Wibau Maschinen Fabric Hartman SA v Mackinnon Mackenzie and Co* [1989] 2 Lloyd's Rep 494, where Hirst J found that a carrier who deviated from the agreed course of the contract by carrying on deck containers which were supposed to be carried underdeck was unable to rely upon the protection of Art 4, r 5 of the Hague Rules.

158 (1990) 102 FLR 59.

contractual exclusion clauses in a bill of lading as it had deviated from the agreed course of the contract by interfering with the goods during their discharge from the ship. The reasoning behind this is that, at common law, a carrier impliedly promises that the carriage will be performed without unjustified deviation and where such a deviation occurs, the shipper can treat the contract as at an end and take action against the carrier outside the contract.[159]

Unlike the Hague Rules, the Hague Visby Rules have the force of law, and it seems unlikely that an unjustified deviation under the Hague Visby Rules would have the effect of depriving the carrier of exclusions and limitations imposed by force of law. However, the Hague Visby Rules in Art 4, r 5(e) provide that:

> Neither the carrier nor the ship shall be entitled to the benefit of the limitation of liability provided for in this paragraph if it is proved that the damage resulted from an act or omission of the carrier done with intent to cause damage, or recklessly and with knowledge that damage would probably result.

So the Visby Protocol amends the Hague Rules by inserting a specific provision depriving the carrier of the right to limit liability if the carrier's conduct falls within this reckless or wilful conduct exemption. There is a similar provision in the Hamburg Rules, Art 8, r 1:

> The carrier is not entitled to the benefit of the limitation of liability provided for in Article 6 if it is proved that the loss, damage or delay in delivery resulted from an act or omission of the carrier done with the intent to cause such loss, damage or delay, or recklessly and with knowledge that such loss, damage or delay would probably result.

The New South Wales Court of Appeal considered a very similar provision in the Warsaw Convention (a convention relating to the carriage of goods by air enacted under the Civil Aviation (Carrier's Liability) Act 1959) as amended by the Hague Protocol.[160] In that case – *SS Pharmaceutical Pty Ltd v Qantas Airways Ltd*,[161] the Court of Appeal adopted a subjective approach (as did Rogers CJ at first instance) in interpreting the phrase 'recklessly and with knowledge that damage would probably result'. It is likely this reasoning would be persuasive.

Arguments against the introduction of the Hamburg Rules

Since the possible implementation of the Hamburg Rules was signalled, the Australian carriers have summoned a formidable array of arguments against their introduction. The major arguments against adoption of the Hamburg Rules seem to be:

1   the existing system works well, has been in force for over 70 years and the rules and the positions of each party are well understood (the status quo argument);

2   the Hamburg Rules are not compatible with the rules in force in the countries which are Australia's major trading partners (the compatibility argument); and

3   introduction of a new carriage regime will mean substantial litigation because of the uncertainty of the rules (the uncertainty argument).

---

159 *Ibid* at 74.
160 Article 25 in Sched 2 of that Act.
161 [1991] 1 Lloyd's Rep 288 – on appeal. Case at first instance before Rogers CJ (SCNSW), *SS Pharmaceutical Pty Ltd v Qantas Airways Ltd* (1989) 92 FLR 244.

The status quo argument

As to the status quo argument, it is certainly true that, thanks to some 70 years of litigation, the Hague Rules have come to be well understood. However, there continue to be problems with those rules and with the Hague Visby Rules. Certainly, from the point of view of the carrier, there appear to be considerable advantages continuing to operate under the existing rules. But there appear to be substantial problems with the Hague Visby Rules from the point of view of the shipper.

The carriers argue that the interests of the shipper are covered by insurance and that, therefore, it is of little importance to increase the liability of the carrier or to change the carriage regime, as any problems in the existing system are adequately addressed by cargo insurance. This view is supported by cargo insurance interests.

The shipper argues that its primary requirement is that the goods be delivered on time to the consignee in good condition. This is how the shipper builds up and maintains the trading links between itself and its customer. The shipper's most important consideration is to preserve that trading link. Having the goods arrive late or not at all, or to arrive in a damaged condition, will not improve the consignor's trading relationship with the consignee, no matter that the consignee is compensated by insurance – it was the goods the consignee really wanted, not the fall-back of insurance.

Regardless of insurance cover, loss or damage that occurs during this transportation period has a potentially significant impact on the shipper's trade relationship with the consignee, and there appears to be little incentive for the carrier or its subcontractors to improve their cargo handling procedures during this period. Any remedy in tort the shipper may have because of a breach of the duty of care by the stevedore or agent of the carrier will usually come within the ambit of the carrier's Himalaya clause. Remedies against the carrier are, of course, limited by the bill of lading and the Hague Visby Rules.

Even when the shipper has remedies against the carrier, there is a significant degree of unevenness in the potential for recovery by the shipper. The shipper must first identify where the loss occurred and then see if he comes within the Hague Rules or whether the loss occurred during the period the rules did not apply.

Conversely, with the Hamburg Rules, the rules are defined in such a way that they have considerably wider application. They will, in many cases, include deck cargo. They will include live animals. They apply to virtually all contracts of carriage by sea.

Under the Hamburg Rules it does not matter whether the goods are transported by way of a negotiable or a non-negotiable instrument – either attracts the same rules and is dealt with the same way. The rules cover a longer period – so called 'port to port' coverage. So, if the loss occurs during the period in 'which the carrier is in charge of the goods at the port of loading, during the carriage and at the port of discharge', then the shipper will have rights of recovery not presently available under the Hague Visby Rules.

The Hamburg Rules, on their face, appear to treat cargo owning interests more equitably, on balance, than either the Hague Rules or the Hague Visby Rules. The shipper (and for that matter, the shipper's insurer) know that once cargo has been delivered into the hands of the carrier at the port of discharge, the same rules will apply to all those goods until the carrier delivers those goods at the port of discharge.

The coverage of the Hamburg Rules – in the scope of goods covered by the rules, the types of instruments of carriage covered by the rules and period of time during which the goods are covered by the rules – all seem more equitable than the existing Hague Rules or the Hague Visby Rules.

It may be many decades before the law relating to carriage of goods by sea conducted under the Hamburg Rules would again have the certainty it has today under the Hague Visby Rules. Lord Diplock noted this in a seminar in 1976.

> So, while there has been no real criticism of the Hague Rules, there has been I think a consensus of criticism of the changes suggested in the UNCTAD/UNCITRAL draft; criticisms because basically these changes will increase the number of recourse actions and also because of the vagueness of the phrases used leading to great uncertainty and doubt as to what the subjective position of the judge will be in the various jurisdictions. They will render useless all that expensive jurisprudence accumulated over 50 years upon the meanings of the phrases in the Hague Rules, and for many years after a new and vague criterion has been set down there will be all the expense incurred again while the uncertainty continues to exist.

Compatibility

Carriers contend that the Hamburg Rules are not 'compatible' with the Hague and Hague Visby Rules. As no other major trading partner of Australia is an adherent of the Hamburg Rules, if Australia were to adopt those rules there would be problems because of the incompatibility of the Hamburg Rules with the Hague Rules and Hague Visby Rules. It is certainly true that the Hamburg Rules differ from the Hague Visby Rules, but are they 'incompatible'? If so, of course, they would not meet the object laid down by the legislation in s 31(1)(c) of COGSA 1991.

The *Macquarie Dictionary* defines 'compatible' as:

1)   capable of existing together in harmony; and
2)   capable of orderly, efficient integration with other elements in a system.

An analysis by James L Roberts shows that 50% of the Hamburg Rules are common to the Hague Rules or Hague Visby Rules. The Hamburg Rules have also borrowed from the Warsaw Convention, which is a convention that has been in use now in many countries for many years. Surely then, there is sufficient compatibility between the Hamburg Rules and the Hague Visby Rules to mean that the trade between the nations will not be unduly hindered. Trade is, after all, possible between countries that use the Hague Visby Rules and countries that have no rules or different rules; why then should the Hamburg Rules be incompatible.

It is suggested that the Hamburg Rules, in the broader sense of the word, are 'compatible with arrangements existing in countries that are major trading partners of Australia', in that the Hamburg Rules:

1   have about half their content in common with the Hague Visby Rules;
2   have part of their content based on conventions dealing with air and/or road carriage with which Australia's major trading partners are familiar; and
3   will not make it impossible or unduly difficult for trade to take place between Australia (under the Hamburg Rules) and other countries that adhere to the Hague Rules or the Hague Visby Rules.

TUTORIAL QUESTIONS

1   A general ship departs:

1.1   Sydney, Australia for Southampton, UK with general cargo. Amongst the cargo are two containers in each of which there are 400 television sets, each set individually packed in its own carton. Two bills of lading issue to the shipper one for each container. Each bill states on its face that there has been shipped on board for the 400 cartons.
- What law governs the carriage?
- What is the limitation amount?

1.2   Southampton for Sydney as above.
- What law governs the carriage?
- What is the limitation amount?

1.3   Shanghai for Sydney as above.
- What law governs the carriage?
- What is the limitation amount?

1.4   Sydney for Auckland with, amongst other cargo of other shippers, 400 cartons of DVD players on board. The shipowner and shipper of the DVD players agree in Sydney, on the telephone, that neither a bill of lading nor a charter party will be issued.
- What is the contract?
- What law applies?
- Suppose the 400 cartons occupy the whole ship, what is the contract and what law applies?

2   Precision Tools Ltd is a New York based manufacturer of specialist machines. It contracts with MetalFabricators Ltd, a Sydney company, for the international sale of a roll forming machine.

The contract of sale calls for a documentary sale, CIF Sydney. The machine is loaded in a container and shipped on board the vessel 'Sahara' at New York under a bill of lading issued by ArcticLine on 1 April 2003 for delivery to Sydney. The bill of lading incorporates the Hague Visby Rules and is a port-to-port bill marked to 'seller or order'. The bill, on its face, states that 'one container, containing one roll forming machine', has been received on board as container cargo for shipment from New York to Sydney.

The bill of lading contained a Himalaya clause, extending the benefit of defences and immunities conferred by the bill of lading upon the carrier to independent contractors employed by the carrier.

On 1 May 2003, the machine was in the custody and control of stevedores engaged by the carrier to unload it and store it pending collection by the consignee. The stevedores were transporting it to the warehouse when it fell and was damaged beyond repair. The buyer begins legal proceedings against the carrier in a Sydney court alleging that the damage was caused by the negligence of the servants and agents of the carrier, namely the stevedores.

Comment on all aspects of the buyer's case, in particular, whether the buyer can recover damages from the carrier.

3   A load of chilled pork was shipped from Brisbane to Japan, CIF Osaka. Before the cargo was shipped or the bill of lading issued, the ship's agent promised the shipper orally that the cargo would arrive in Osaka by 30 November 2003. The cargo was shipped on board in reefer on 10 November. A bill of lading incorporating the Hague Visby Rules was issued by the carrier to the shipper.

Problem one: en route to Japan the vessel called in at several ports as the carrier found cargo for the vessel. As a result, the vessel did not arrive in Japan until 10 January 2004.

On 1 January 2004, a new Japanese law took effect and import duty became payable on pork imported into Japan on or after that date. The market for imported pork had deteriorated substantially as a result of this.

What rights are available to the shipper?

Problem two: A few weeks before the vessel arrived in Japan, the Japanese government prohibited the importation of overseas pork due to the outbreak of a disease ('mad pig disease') believed to be carried by pigs. Upon arrival in Japan, the pork was confiscated and destroyed by Japanese customs.

What rights, if any, does the holder of the bill of lading have?

Problem three: *En route* to Japan, the vessel breaks down and spends two weeks in Hong Kong while necessary repairs are effected. As a result, the vessel arrives in Osaka after a new import duty is in place. Had the vessel not broken down, the pork would have been unloaded before the import duty came into effect.

Advise the shipper.

4   Is a sea waybill issued for trans-Tasman carriage from Sydney to Napier NZ subject to the Carriage of Goods by Sea Act 1991 (Cth)?

5   In what circumstances does the Trade Practices Act 1974 apply to carriage of goods by sea?

6   How do the Hague Visby Rules and Hamburg Rules protect the master and crew?

7   A normal commercial shipment leaves:

- Sydney for Brisbane under waybills. Do the Hague/Visby Rules apply?
- Brisbane to Townsville. Do the Hague Visby Rules apply?

8   What are the advantages and disadvantages of sea waybills?

9   Who may sue the carrier under a sea waybill? How?

10 SCA Ltd, a Sydney-based company, issues a booking note to carry underdeck the container of a shipper, Widget Ltd, also of Sydney, to Halifax, NS, Canada. The container is, however, loaded on the deck of the vessel 'Hobart' and a bill of lading that is issued by SCA Ltd states on its face that the container is carried on deck.

The 'Hobart' is owned by XXXX Co Ltd of Liberia and under time charter to SCA Ltd.

The bill of lading contains:

- a superseding clause (that is, a clause which provides that the bill of lading supersedes all prior agreements or freight engagements for the shipment and that the terms of the bill of lading are binding on the shipper); and
- a demise clause (that is, a clause which states that unless the bill is owned by or chartered by demise to the party which issued the bill of lading, the ship owner or demise charterer is the carrier).

The contents of the container are damaged when the container leaks during the voyage at the time of very heavy rains.

Advise Widget Ltd as to its rights under the law and what proceedings, if any, it should take against whom.

What limits do the modified Hague Visby Rules put on the measure of damages?

11 Shins Ltd purchased 10,000 hides from Fibrasa Brasileira SA (Fibrasa) CFR, Cabedelo, Brazil, (180 days). The booking note invoked Australian law. The hides were shipped from Cabedelo to Melbourne under a bill of lading issued by the time charterer, Kimberley Line, and signed by it 'for the master', which invoked US law. (Brazil is not party to the Hague, the Hague Visby or the Hamburg Rules.) 3,500 hides were damaged during the voyage by the fault of the carrier. The consignee sues the time charterer, the ship and the shipowner in the Federal Court of Australia at Melbourne. What judgment should be rendered by the Federal Court of Australia as to:

- the applicable law?
- which parties, if any, were responsible?
- the measure of damages, if any?
- what interest, if any, and from what date payment should commence if interest is to be paid?

12 Compare and contrast:

- the Hague Visby Rules to the Hague Rules;
- the Hamburg Rules to the Hague Visby Rules;
- the Modified Hague Visby Rules to the Hamburg Rules.

13 Do the Hamburg rules provide the carrier with the same exculpatory exception as the Hague Rules for peril of the sea and error in navigation and management of the ship? Explain.

14 Explain the Himalaya Clause.

15 A ship leaves San Francisco, USA for Melbourne on the liner trade. At sea the master is ordered by the owner to go to Auckland to load a lucrative cargo and carry it to Melbourne. The voyage thus takes 14 days instead of seven days. Two days before arrival in Melbourne, the ship meets a very unexpected and very heavy storm that damages cargo; both underdeck cargo and cargo stored on deck. The underdeck cargo was stated on the bill of lading as carried on deck and agreed to be carried on deck by the shipper, and carrier and was subject to a clause that the carrier took no responsibility for deck cargo.

- What are the ship owner's obligations?
- What would the situation be if the deck cargo was improperly carried on deck?
- If the ship left London rather than San Francisco, would that make any difference?

16 Suppose the:

- Hague Visby Rules were incorporated by reference into the bill of lading. Would that change the previous three answers?
- Hamburg Rules were incorporated by reference into the bill of lading. Would that change the first three answers?

FURTHER READING

Astle, WE, *The Hamburg Rules*, 1981, London: Fairway Publications.

Attorney General's Department in conjunction with Department of Transport and Communications, *Discussion Paper: Proposals for Reform of Australian Bills of Lading Legislation*, August 1993.

Bauer, RB, 'Conflicting liability regimes: Hague Visby v Hamburg Rules – a case by case analysis' (1993) 24 *J Maritime L* 53.

Beatson, J and Cooper, JJ, 'Rights of suit in respect of carriage of goods by sea' [1991] *Lloyd's MCLQ* 196.

Berlingieri, F, 'Uniformity in maritime law and implementation of international conventions' (1987) 18 *J Maritime L* 317.

Berlingieri, F, 'Uniformity of the law of carriage of goods by sea: the 1990s' (1990) CMI, II, 110–77.

Butler, DA and Duncan, WD, *Maritime Law in Australia*, 1991, Sydney: Legal Books.

Carr, IM, 'The scope of application of Hamburg Rules and Hague Visby Rules: a comparison' [1992] 6 ICCLR.

Chandler, GF, 'A comparison of COGSA, the Hague Visby Rules and the Hamburg Rules' (1984) 15 *J Maritime L* 233.

Cooper, R, 'The Hamburg Rules and the carriage of goods by sea', dissertation for LLM, 1981, University of Queensland.

Davies, M, 'Carriage of goods by sea' (1991) ABusLR 57.

Department of Transport and Communication, *Australian Marine Cargo Liability: a Discussion Paper*, September 1987 (1988) 159 Parliamentary Debates (H of R) 980.

Department of Transport and Communication, *Carriage of Goods by Sea Act 1991: Possible Implementation of the Hamburg Rules*, December 1993, Issues Paper.

Diplock, 'Conventions and morals – limitation clauses in international maritime conventions' (1970) 1 *J Maritime L* 525.

European Institute of Maritime and Transport Law, *The Hamburg Rules: A Choice for the EEC?*, 18–19 November 1993, International Colloquium.

Goldie, CWH, 'Effect of the Hamburg Rules on shipowners' liability insurance' (1993) *J Maritime L* 111.

Hannah, F, 'Which rules for Australian maritime trade? The controversy continues', proceedings of MLAANZ 20th Annual Conference, 6–11 November 1993, Melbourne, Australia.

Hetherington, S, 'Bills of lading: do they have a future? Freight forwarders bills of lading', paper presented at University of Sydney Faculty of Law, 17 August 1993.

Honnold, J, 'Ocean carriers and cargo: clarity and fairness – Hague or Hamburg' (1993) 24 *J Maritime L* 75.

Kimball, JD, 'Owner's liability and the proposed reunion of the Hague Rules' (1975) *J Maritime L* 217.

Kindred, HM, 'From Hague to Hamburg: international regulation of carriage of goods by sea' (1984) 7 *Dalhousie LJ* 585.

Koh Soan Kwong, P, *Carriage of Goods by Sea*, 1986, Singapore: Butterworths.

Luddeke, CF and Johnson, A, *A Guide to the Hamburg Rules: From Hague to Hamburg via Visby*, 1991, London: Lloyd's.

Mendelsohn, AI, 'Why the US did not ratify the Visby Amendments' (1992) 23 *J Maritime L* 29.

Mustill, LJ, 'Ships are different – or are they' [1993] *Lloyd's MCLQ* 433.

Myburgh, P, 'Bits, bytes and bills of lading: EDI and New Zealand maritime law' [1993] NZLJ 324.

New Zealand Department of Transport, *Maritime Discussion Paper*, January 1992.

O'Hare, CW, 'Shipping documentation for the carriage of goods and the Hamburg Rules' (1978) 52 ALJ 415.

Ramberg, J, 'Freedom of contract: maritime law' [1992] *Lloyd's MCLQ* 178.

Ramberg, J, 'Freedom of contract in maritime law' [1993] *Lloyd's MCLQ* 145.

Reynolds, F, 'The Hague Rules, the Hague Visby Rules and the Hamburg Rules' (1990) 7 *Marine Lawyers Association of Australia and New Zealand Journal* 16.

Sturley, JF, 'Changing liability rules and marine insurance: conflicting empirical evidence arguments about Hague, Visby and Hamburg in a vacuum of empirical evidence' (1993) 24 *J Maritime L* 119.

Sweeney, JC, 'The UNCITRAL Draft Convention on Carriage of Goods by Sea Parts 1–5' (1975) 7 *J Maritime L* 69–125, 327–50; (1977) 8 *J Maritime L* 167–94.

Sweeney, JC, 'UNCITRAL and the Hamburg Rules' (1991) 22 *J Maritime L* 511.

Tetley, W, 'The Hamburg Rules – a commentary' [1979] *Lloyd's MCLQ* 1.

'COGSA, Hague Visby and Hamburg' (1984) 15 *J Maritime L* 233.

Thompson, SM, 'The Hamburg Rules: should they be implemented in Australia and New Zealand?' (1992) 4 *Bond LR* 168.

UNCTAD, *The Economic and Commercial Implications of the Entry into Force of the Hamburg Rules and the Multi-modal Convention*, 1991, New York: United Nations.

Wilde, DM and Wilde, KC, *International Transactions*, 1993, Sydney: The Law Book Co.

Yancey, BW, 'The carriage of goods: Hague, COGSA, Visby and Hamburg' (1983) 57 *Tulane Law Review* 1238.

Details of cargo carrying regimes of various nations (as at 25 March 1994)

Country	Limitation	Hague	Hague Visby	Hamburg	SDR
Algeria		*			
Angola		*			
Antigua and Barbuda			*		
Argentina	400 pesos gold				3
Australia			*	*	3
Austria					4
Bahamas		*			
Bangladesh					*
Barbados		*			*
Belgium			*	2	
Belize		*			
Bermuda			*		
Bolivia		*			
Botswana					*
Brazil	Commercial Code 1850 applies, Article 102, 103				4
Burkina Faso				*	
Cameroon United Rep				*	
Canada			*		3
Cape Verde Islands				*	
Chile					*
China (PRC)	Maritime Code			7	7
Colombia	Not signatory: Commercial Code applies parts of Hague Rules				
Croatia		*			
Cuba		*			
Cyprus		*			
Denmark			*	2	4
Dominican Rep		*			4
Ecuador			*		4
Egypt, Arab Rep of					*
Estonia		*			
Fiji	Gold value	*			
Finland			*	2	4
France			*	2	3
Gambia		*			
Germany			*		4
Ghana		*			4
Gibraltar				2	
Goa		*			
Greece	8,000 Drachmas (National law equivalent)			*	*
Grenada		*			
Guinea		*			*
Guyana		*			*
Holy See			*	*	4
Hong Kong				2	
Hungary		*			*

Country	Limitation	Hague	Hague Visby	Hamburg	SDR
India	Gold value				
Indonesia	Commercial Code		6		
Iran		*			
Ireland	100	*			
Isle of Man					
Israel	pgf	*			
Italy			*	2	
Ivory Coast		*			
Jamaica		*			
Japan	1 June 1993		*	*	5
Kenya		*			*
Kingdom of Serbia			*		
Kiribati		*			
Korea	Commercial Code			8	
Kuwait		*			
Lebanon			*		*
Lesotho					*
Liberia	Maritime law			*	
Luxemburg			*	*	
Madagascar		*		*	4
Malagasy Rep		*			
Malawi					*
Malay, Fed States of	*				
Malay, Non-Fed State of		*			
Malaysia	Gold value except Sabah, Sarawak R850				4
Mauritania			*		
Mauritius		*			
Mexico	Contractual limitation				4
Monaco		*			
Morocco					*
Mozambique		*			
Naura		*			
Netherlands	pgf		*	*	
New Zealand	NZ$200				3
Nigeria	Gold value	*			*
North Borneo		*			
Norway			*	2	4
Pakistan	Gold value				4
Palestine		*			
Panama					4
Papua New Guinea	*				
Paraguay			*		
Peru	Gold value	*			
Philippines	USA COGSA Limit US$500		*		4
Poland			*	2	
Portugal	Esc12,000	*		*	4

Country	Limitation	Hague	Hague Visby	Hamburg	SDR
Romania		*			*
Sao Tome and Principe		*			
Sarawak		*			
Senegal		*			*
Seychelles		*			
Sierra Leone		*			*
Singapore	S$1,563.65p/4.69kg		*	*	4
Slovakia					4
Solomon Islands		*			
Somalia		*			
South Africa	pgf				
Spain	161 pesetas			*	1
Sri Lanka			*		
St Christopher and Nevis		*			
St Lucia		*			
St Vincent and the Grenadines		*			
Sweden			*	*	4
Switzerland	1pgf = 0.27095 francs			*	1
Syria, Arab Rep of				*	*
Taiwan	NT$9,000 (Applies USA COGSA)				
Tanzania					*
Tanganyika		*			
Thailand	Not signatory				
Timor					
Timores		*			
Togo					
Tonga			*		
Trinidad and Tobago		*			
Tunisia					*
Turkey		*			
Tuvalu		*			
Uganda					*
United Kingdom			*	2	
Uruguay			*		
USA	$500	*			4
USSR	R250				
Venezuela	Contractual limit				4
Yugoslavia	D40,000	*			
Zaire			*		4
Zambia					*

Notes

* Denotes adoption.
1 SDR Protocol applies national currency.
2 Applies a limitation of 666.67 SDRs per package or 2 SDRs per kg.
3 These nations have made legislative provision, or are believed to be considering a provision that will trigger adoption of the Hamburg Rules in the future.
4 These nations have signed but have not yet ratified or acceded to the Hamburg Rules.

5   Under the Japanese COGSA 1994, a carrier's liability shall be limited by a bigger amount calculated by the following two methods of calculation:

(a)   666.67 SDR as per the package or unit;

(b)   2 x SDR per kg.

From the above (a) and (b), until the weight of 333.335 kg (666.67/2 = 333.335) a fixed figure of (a) 666.67 SDR shall be applied, but from the weight in excess of 333.335, (b) shall be applied as in the following list:

Kg	SDR				
333.335	666.67	400	800	500	
1,000	600	1,200	700	1,400	800
1,600	900	1,800	1,000	2,000	2,000
4,000	3,000	6,000	4,000	8,000	5,000
10,000	10,000	20,000			

6   Indonesian commercial code applies the Hague Rules unless specific agreement provides for the Hague Visby Rules.

7   On 1 July 1993, the new Chinese Maritime Code came into effect. This Code, whilst adopting some Hamburg Rules principles, has substantially adopted Hague Visby Rules principles. Effectively adopts SDR.

8   On 1 July 1993, Korea's Revised Commercial Code came into effect. The Code substantially adopts the Hague Visby Rules.

Hague Rules

The full name of this Convention is International Convention for the Unification of Certain Rules of Law Relating to Bills of Lading, Brussels, 25 August 1924.

Some nations have adopted these rules into their national law, but with variations to the rules.

Some nations that originally ratified or acceded to the Hague Rules have renounced the Hague Rules and adopted either Hague Visby, or Hague Visby with the SDR Protocol.

Hague Visby Rules

The 1968 Visby amendments to the Hague Rules came into force in 1977.

The full name of this Convention is Protocol to Amend the International Convention for the Unification of Certain Rules of Law Relating to Bills of Lading , Brussels, 23 February 1968.

Hamburg Rules

This is the United Nations Convention on the Carriage of Goods by Sea, Hamburg, 1978. The Convention achieved 20 ratifications and accessions on 31 October 1991.

SDR Protocol

This Protocol came into effect on 4 February 1984.

The full name of this Convention is Protocol Amending the International Convention for the Unification of Certain Rules of Law Relating to Bills of Lading (25 August 1924, as amended by the Protocol of 23 February 1968, Brussels, 21 December 1979).

The main effect of this Protocol is to substitute SDRs for poincare gold francs (pgf).

10,000 pgf became 666.67 SDRs per package or 2 SDRs per kg. But some nations have specified a currency conversion rate that applies instead.

Gold value

This has now been established by a number of courts to be today's value of the quantity of gold contained in 100 gold sovereigns specified in the Hague Rules.

PGF

These are poincare gold French francs per kilo.

INTERNATIONAL CONVENTION FOR THE UNIFICATION OF CERTAIN RULES OF LAW RELATING TO BILLS OF LADING (THE HAGUE RULES) – BRUSSELS, 25 AUGUST 1924

The Convention entered into force on 2 June 1931.

The government of Belgium reports that the following ratifications (r), accessions (a) or notifications of succession (s) have been deposited with it:

Algeria	(a)	13 April 1964
Angola	(a)	2 February 1952
Antigua and Barbuda	(a)	2 December 1930
Argentina	(a)	19 April 1961
Australia	(a)	4 July 1955
Bahamas	(a)	2 December 1930
Barbados	(a)	2 December 1930
Belgium	(r)	2 June 1930
Belize	(a)	December 1930
Bolivia	(a)	28 May 1982
Cameroon	(a)	2 December 1930
Cape Verde	(a)	2 February 1952
Cuba	(a)	25 July 1977
Cyprus	(a)	2 December 1930
Denmark	(a)	1 July 1938
Dominican Republic	(a)	2 December 1930
Ecuador	(a)	23 March 1977
Egypt	(a)	29 November 1933
Fiji	(a)	10 October 1970
Finland	(a)	1 July 1939
France	(r)	4 January 1937
Gambia	(a)	2 December 1930
Germany, Federal Republic of	(r)	1 July 1939
Ghana	(a)	2 December 1930
Grenada	(a)	2 December 1930
Guinea-Bissau	(a)	2 February 1952
Guyana	(a)	2 December 1930
Hungary	(r)	2 June 1930
Iran	(a)	26 April 1966
Ireland	(a)	30 January 1962
Israel	(a)	5 September 1959
Italy	(r)	7 October 193S
Ivory Coast	(a)	15 December 1961
Jamaica	(a)	2 December 1930
Japan	(r)	2 July 1957
Kenya	(a)	2 December 1930
Kiribati	(a)	2 December 1930
Kuwait	(a)	25 July 1969
Lebanon	(a)	19 July 1975
Madagascar	(a)	13 July 1965
Malaysia	(a)	2 December 1930
Mauritius	(a)	24 August 1970

Monaco	(a)	15 May 1931
Mozambique	(a)	2 February 1952
Nauru	(a)	4 July 1955
Netherlands	(a)	18 August 1956
Nigeria	(a)	2 December 1930
Norway	(a)	1 July 1938
Palestine	(a)	2 December 1930
Papua New Guinea	(a)	4 July 1955
Paraguay	(a)	22 November 1967
Peru	(a)	29 October 1964
Poland	(r)	26 October 1936
Portugal	(a)	24 December 1931
Macao	(a)	2 February 1952
Romania	(r)	4 August 1937
Sabah, North Borneo	(a)	2 December 1930
Sao Tome and Principe	(a)	2 February 1952
Sarawak	(a)	3 November 1931
Senegal	(a)	14 February 1978
Seychelles	(a)	2 December 1930
Sierra Leone	(a)	2 December 1930
Singapore	(a)	2 December 1930
Solomon Islands	(a)	2 December 1930
Somalia	(a)	2 December 1930
Spain	(r)	2 June 1930
Sri Lanka	(a)	2 December 1930
St Christopher-Nevis	(a)	2 December 1930
St Lucia	(a)	2 December 1930
St Vincent	(a)	2 December 1930
Sweden	(a)	1 July 1938
Switzerland	(a)	28 May 1954
Syrian Arab Republic	(a)	1 August 1974
Timor	(a)	2 December 1952
Tonga	(a)	2 December 1930
Trinidad and Tobago	(a)	2 December 1930
Turkey	(a)	4 July 1955
Tuvalu	(a)	2 December 1930
United Kingdom of Great Britain and Northern Ireland including Jersey, Guernsey and Isle of Man	(r)	2 June 1930
British overseas territories: Bermuda, Falkland Islands and Dependencies, Gibraltar, Hong Kong, Turk and Caicos Islands and Cayman Islands, British Virgin Islands, Monserrat, British Antarctic Territories, Anguilla	(a)	2 December 1930
Ascension, St Helena	(a)	November 1931
United Republic of Tanzania	(a)	3 December 1962
United States of America	(r)	29 June 1937
Yugoslavia	(r)	17 April 1959
Zaire	(a)	17 July 1967

International Convention for the Unification of Certain Rules of Law Relating to Bills of Lading

Signed at Brussels, 25 August 1924

Article 1

In this Convention the following words are employed with the meanings set out below:

(a) 'Carrier' includes the owner of the vessel or the charterer who enters into a contract of carriage with a shipper.

(b) 'Contract of carriage' applies only to contracts of carriage covered by a bill of lading or any similar document of title, in so far as such document relates to the carriage of goods by sea; it also applies to any bill of lading or any similar document as aforesaid issued under or pursuant to a charterparty from the moment at which such instrument regulates the relations between a carrier and a holder of the same.

(c) 'Goods' includes goods, wares, merchandise, and articles of every kind whatsoever except live animals and cargo which by the contract of carriage is stated as being carried on deck and is so carried.

(d) 'Ship' means any vessel used for the carriage of goods by sea.

(e) 'Carriage of goods' covers the period from the time when the goods are loaded on to the time they are discharged from the ship.

Article 2

Subject to the provisions of Article 6, under every contract of carriage of goods by sea the carrier, in relation to the loading, handling, stowage, carriage, custody, care, and discharge of such goods shall be subject to the responsibilities and liabilities, and entitled to the rights and immunities hereinafter set forth.

Article 3

1   The carrier shall be bound before and at the beginning of the voyage to exercise due diligence to:

(a) make the ship seaworthy;

(b) properly man, equip, and supply the ship;

(c) make the holds, refrigerating and cool chambers, and all other parts of the ship in which goods are carried, fit and safe for their reception, carriage, and preservation.

2   Subject to the provisions of Article 4, the carrier shall properly and care fully load, handle, stow, carry, keep, care for, anti discharge the goods carried.

3   After receiving the goods into his charge, the carrier or the master or agent of the carrier shall, on demand of the shipper, issue to the shipper a bill of lading showing among other things:

(a) the leading marks necessary for identification of the goods as the same are furnished in writing by the shipper before the loading of such goods starts, provided such marks are stamped or otherwise shown clearly upon the goods if uncovered, or on the eases or coverings in which such goods are contained, in such a manner as should ordinarily remain legible until the end of the voyage;

(b) either the number of packages or pieces, or the quantity, or weight, as the case may be, as furnished in writing by the shipper;

(c) the apparent order and condition of the goods.

Provided that no carrier, master, or agent of the carrier shall be bound to state or show in the bill of lading any marks, number, quantity, or weight which he has reasonable grounds for suspecting not accurately to represent the goods actually received or which he has had no reasonable means of checking.

4   Such a bill of lading shall be *prima facie* evidence of the receipt by the carrier of the goods as therein described in accordance with para 3(a), (b) and (c).

5   The shipper shall be deemed to have guaranteed to the carrier the accuracy at the time of shipment of the marks, number, quantity, and weight, as furnished by him, and the shipper shall indemnify the carrier against all loss, damages, and expenses arising or

resulting from inaccuracies in such particulars. The right of the carrier to such indemnity shall in no way limit his responsibility and liability under the contract of carriage to any person other than the shipper.

6 Unless notice of loss or damage and the general nature of such loss or damage be given in writing to the carrier or his agent at the port of discharge before or at the time of the removal of the goods into the custody of the person entitled to delivery thereof under the contract of carriage, such removal shall be *prima facie* evidence of the delivery by the carrier of the goods as described in the bill of lading.

If the loss or damage is not apparent, the notice must be given within three days of the delivery.

The notice in writing need not be giver it the state of the goods has at the time of their receipt been the subject of joint survey or inspection.

In any event, the carrier and the ship shall be discharged from all liability in respect of loss or damage unless suit is brought within one year after delivery of the goods or the date when the goods should have been delivered.

In the ease of any actual or apprehended loss or damage the carrier and the receiver shall give all reasonable facilities to each other for inspecting and tallying the goods.

7 After the goods are loaded, the bill of lading to be issued by the carrier master, or agent of the carrier to the shipper shall, if the shipper so demands, be a 'shipped' bill of lading, provided that if the shipper shall have previously taken up any document of title to such goods, he shall surrender the same as against the issue of the 'shipped' bill of lading. At the option of the carrier such document of title may be noted at the port of shipment by the carrier, master, or agent with the name or names of the ship or ships upon which the goods have been shipped and the date or dates of shipment, and when so noted, if it shows the particulars mentioned in para 3 of Article 3, it shall for the purpose of this article be deemed to constitute a 'shipped' bill of lading.

8 Any clause, covenant, or agreement in a contract of carriage relieving the carrier or the ship from liability for loss or damage to or in connection with goods arising from negligence, fault, or failure in the duties and obligations provided in this article, or lessening such liability otherwise than as provided in this convention, shall be null and void and of no effect. A benefit of insurance in favour of the carrier or similar clause shall be deemed to be a clause relieving the carrier from liability.

Article 4

1 Neither the carrier nor the ship shall be liable for loss or damage arising or resulting from unseaworthiness unless caused by want of due diligence on the part of the carrier to make the ship seaworthy and to secure that the ship is properly manned, equipped, and supplied and to make the holds, refrigerating and cool chambers, and all other parts of the ship in which goods are carried fit and safe for their reception, carriage, and preservation in accordance with the provisions of para 1 of Article 3. Whenever loss or damage has resulted from unseaworthiness, the burden of proving the exercise of due diligence shall be on the carrier or other person claiming exemption under this article.

2 Neither the carrier nor the ship shall be responsible for loss or damage arising or resulting from:

(a) Act, neglect, or default of the master, mariner, pilot, or the servants of the carrier in the navigation or in the management of the ship.

(b) Fire, unless caused by the actual fault or privity of the carrier.

(c) Perils, dangers, and accidents of the sea or other navigable water.

(d) Act of God.

(e) Act of war.

(f) Act of public enemies.

(g) Arrest or restraint of princes, rulers, or people or seizure under legal process.

(h) Quarantine restrictions.

(i) Act or omission of the shipper or owner of the goods, his agent, or representative.

(j) Strikes or lockouts or stoppage or restraint of labour from whatever cause, whether partial or general.

(k) Riots and civil commotions.

(l) Saving or attempting to save life or property at sea.

(m) Wastage in bulk or weight or any other loss or damage arising from inherent defect, quality, or vice of the goods.

(n) Insufficiency of packing.

(o) Insufficiency or inadequacy of marks.

(p) Latent defects not discoverable by due diligence.

(q) Any other cause arising without the actual fault or privity of the carrier, or without the fault or neglect of the agents or servants of the carrier, but the burden of proof shall be on the person claiming the benefit of this exception to show that neither the actual fault or privity of the carrier nor the fault or neglect of the agents or servants of the carrier contributed to the loss or damage.

3   The shipper shall not be responsible for loss or damage sustained by the carrier or the ship arising or resulting from any cause without the act, fault, or neglect of the shipper, his agents, or his servants.

4   Any deviation in saving or attempting to save life or property at sea or any reasonable deviation shall not be deemed to be an infringement or breach of this convention or of the contract of carriage, and the carrier shall not be liable for any loss or damage resulting therefrom.

5   Neither the carrier nor the ship shall in any event be or become liable for any loss or damage to or in connection with goods in an amount exceeding £100 sterling per package or unit or the equivalent of that sum in other currency unless the nature and value of such goods have been declared by the shipper before shipment and inserted in the bill of lading.

This declaration if embodied in the bill of lading shall be *prima facie* evidence but shall not be binding or conclusive on the carrier.

By agreement between the carrier, master, or agent of the carrier and the shipper another maximum amount than that mentioned in this paragraph may be fixed, provided that such maximum shall not be less than the figure above named.

Neither the carrier nor the ship shall be responsible in any event for loss or damage to, or in connection with, goods if the nature or value thereof has been knowingly misstated by the shipper in the bill of lading.

6   Goods of an inflammable, explosive, or dangerous nature to the shipment whereof the carrier, master, or agent of the carrier has not consented with knowledge of their nature and character may at any time before discharge be landed at any place or destroyed or rendered innocuous by the carrier without compensation, and the shipper of such goods shall be liable for all damages and expenses directly or indirectly arising out of or resulting from such shipment. If any such goods shipped with such knowledge and consent shall become a danger to the ship or cargo, they may in like manner be landed at any place or destroyed or rendered innocuous by the carrier without liability on the part of the carrier except to general average, if any.

Article 5

A carrier shall be at liberty to surrender in whole or in part all or any of this rights and immunities, or to increase any of his responsibilities and liabilities under this convention provided such surrender or increase shall be embodied in the bill of lading issued to the shipper.

The provisions of this convention shall not be applicable to charter parties, but if bills of lading are issued in the case of a ship under a charter party they shall comply with the terms of this convention. Nothing in these rules shall be held to prevent the insertion in a bill of lading of any lawful provision regarding general average.

Article 6

Notwithstanding the provisions of the preceding articles, a carrier, master, or agent of the carrier and a shipper shall in regard to any particular goods be at liberty to enter into any agreement in any terms as to the responsibility and liability of the carrier for such goods, and as to the rights and immunities of the carrier in respect of such goods, or concerning his obligation as to seaworthiness so far as this stipulation is not contrary to public policy, or concerning the care or diligence of his servants or agents in regard to the loading, handling, stowage, carriage, custody, care, and discharge of the goods carried by sea, provided that in this case no bill of lading has been or shall be issued and that the terms agreed shall be embodied in a receipt which shall be a non-negotiable document and shall be marked as such.

Any agreement so entered into shall have full legal effect:

Provided that this article shall not apply to ordinary commercial shipments made in the ordinary course of trade, but only to other shipments where the character or condition of the property to be carried or the circumstances, terms, and conditions under which the carriage is to be performed are such as reasonably to justify a special agreement.

Article 7

Nothing herein contained shall prevent a carrier or a shipper from entering into any agreement stipulation, condition, reservation, or exemption as to the responsibility and liability of the carrier or the ship for the loss or damage to, or in connection with, the custody and care and handling of goods prior to the loading on, and subsequent to the discharge from, the ship on which the goods are carried by sea.

Article 8

The provision of this convention shall not affect the rights and obligations of the carrier under any statute for the time being in force relating to the limitation of the liability of owners of seagoing vessels.

Article 9

The monetary units mentioned in this convention are to be taken to be gold value.

Those Contracting States in which the pound sterling is not a monetary unit reserve to themselves the right of translating the sums indicated in this convention in terms of pound sterling into terms of their own monetary system in round figures.

The national laws may reserve to the debtor the right of discharging his debt in national currency according to the rate of exchange prevailing on the day of the arrival of the ship at the port of discharge of the goods concerned.

Article 10

The provisions of this convention shall apply to all bills of lading issued in any of the Contracting States.

Article 11

After an interval of not more than two years from the day on which the convention is signed, the Belgian government shall place itself in communication with the governments of the high contracting parties which have declared themselves prepared to ratify the convention, with a view to deciding whether it shall be put into force. The ratifications shall be deposited at Brussels at a date to be fixed by agreement among the said governments. The first deposit of ratifications shall be recorded in a *procès-verbal* signed by the representatives of the powers which take part therein and by the Belgian Minister for Foreign Affairs.

The subsequent deposits of ratifications shall be made by means of a written notification, addressed to the Belgian government and accompanied by the instrument of ratification.

A duly certified copy of the *procès-verbal* relating to the first deposit of ratifications, of the notifications referred to in the previous paragraph, and also of the instruments of ratification accompanying them, shall he immediately sent by the Belgian government through the diplomatic channel to the powers who have signed this convention or who have acceded to it. In the cases contemplated in the preceding paragraph, the said government shall inform them at the same time of the date on which it received the notification.

Article 12

Non-signatory States may accede to the present convention whether or not they have been represented at the international conference at Brussels.

A State which desires to accede shall notify its intention in writing to the Belgian government, forwarding to it the document of accession, which shall be deposited in the archive of the said government.

The Belgian government shall immediately forward to all the States which have signed or acceded to the convention a duly certified copy of the notification and of the act of accession, mentioning the date on which it received the notification.

Article 13

The high contracting parties may at the time of signature, ratification, or accession declare that their acceptance of the present convention does not include any or all of the self-governing dominions, or of the colonies, overseas possessions, protectorates, or territories under their sovereignty or authority, and they may subsequently accede separately on behalf of any self-governing dominion, colony, overseas possession, protectorate, or territory excluded in their declaration. They may also denounce the convention separately in accordance with its provisions in respect of any self-governing dominion, or any colony, overseas possession, protectorate, or territory under their sovereignty or authority.

Article 14

The present convention shall take effect, in the case of the States which have taken part in the first deposit of ratifications, one year after the date of the *procès-verbal* recording such deposit. As respects the States which ratify subsequently or which accede, and also in cases in which the convention is subsequently put into effect in accordance with Article 13, it shall take effect six months after the notifications specified in para 2 of Article 11, and para 2 of Article 12, have been received by the Belgian government.

Article 15

In the event of one of the Contracting States wishing to denounce the present convention, the denunciation shall be notified in writing to the Belgian government, which shall immediately communicate a duly certified copy of the notification to all the other States informing them of the date on which it was received.

The denunciation shall only operate in respect of the State which made the notification, and on the expiry of one year after the notification has reached the Belgian government.

Article 16

Any one of the Contracting States shall have the right to call for a fresh conference with a view to considering possible amendments.

A State which would exercise this right should notify its intention to the other States through the Belgian government. which would make arrangements for convening the conference.

Done at Brussels, in a single copy, 25 August 1924.

Protocol of signature

In proceeding to the signature of the international convention for the unification of certain rules in regard to bills of lading, the undersigned plenipotentiaries have agreed on the present Protocol which shall have the same force and the same scope as if these provisions were inserted in the text of the convention to which they relate.

The high contracting parties may give effect to this convention either by giving it the force of law or by including in their national legislation in a form appropriate to that legislation, the rules adopted under this convention.

They may reserve the right:

1   To prescribe that in the cases referred to in para 2(c)–(p) of Article 4, the holder of a bill of lading shall be entitled to establish responsibility for loss or damage arising from the personal fault of the carrier or the fault of his servants which are not covered by para (a).

2   To apply Article 6 in so far as the national coasting trade is concerned to all classes of goods without taking account of the restriction set out in the last paragraph of that article.

Done at Brussels, in a single copy, 25 August 1924.

ANNEX

Reservations and declarations

Australia

... Now therefore, I, Sir William Joseph Slim, the Governor General in and over the Commonwealth of Australia acting with the advice of the Federal Executive Council and in the exercise of all powers me thereunto enabling do by these presents accede in the name and on behalf of Her Majesty in respect of the Commonwealth of Australia and the Territories of Papua and Norfolk Island and the Trust Territories of New Guinea and Nauru to the convention aforesaid subject to the following reservations, namely:

(a) The Commonwealth of Australia reserves the right to exclude from the operation of legislation passed to give effect to the convention the carriage of goods by sea which is not carriage in the course of trade or commerce with other countries or among the States of Australia.

(b) The Commonwealth of Australia reserves the right to apply Article 6 of the convention in so far as the national coasting trade is concerned to all classes of goods without taking account of the restriction set out in the last paragraph of that article.

Belgium

In proceeding to the deposit of the ratifications of His Majesty the King of the Belgians, the Belgian Minister for Foreign Affairs declared, in accordance with the provisions of Article 13 of the convention, that these ratifications extend only to Belgium and do not apply to the Belgian Congo and Ruanda-Urundi, Territories under mandate.

Denmark

This accession is subject to the proviso that the other Contracting States do not object to the application of the provisions of the convention being limited in the following manner with regard to Denmark:

1   Under the Danish Navigation Law of 7 May 1937, bills of lading and similar documents may continue to be made out, for national coasting trade, in accordance with the provisions of that Law without the provisions of the convention being applied to them or to the legal relationship which is thereby established between the carrier and the holder of the document.

2   Maritime carriage between Denmark and other Nordic States, whose navigation laws contain similar provisions, shall be considered as equivalent to national coasting trade for the purposes mentioned in para 1 – if a provision to that effect is decreed pursuant to the last paragraph of Article 122 of the Danish Navigation Law.

3   The provisions of the International Conventions on the Transport of Passengers and Baggage by Rail and on the Traffic of Goods by Rail, signed at Rome on 23 November 1933, shall not be affected by this convention.

Egypt

We have resolved hereby to accede to the said convention and undertake to cooperate in its application.

Egypt is, however, of the opinion that the convention does not in any part apply to national coasting trade. Consequently, it reserves to itself the right freely to regulate the national coasting trade by its own law.

In witness whereof ...

France

... In proceeding to this deposit, the Ambassador of France at Brussels declares, in accordance with Article 13 of the above-mentioned convention, that the French government's acceptance of the convention does not include any of the colonies, overseas possessions, protectorates or territories under its sovereignty or authority.

Ireland

... subject to the following declarations and reservations:

1   In relation to the carriage of goods by sea in ships carrying goods from any port in Ireland to any other port in Ireland or to a port in the UK, Ireland will apply Article 6 of the convention as though the Article referred to goods of any class instead of to particular goods, and as though the proviso in the third paragraph of the said article were omitted;

2   Ireland does not accept the provisions of the first paragraph of Article 9 of the convention.

Ivory Coast

The government of the Republic of the Ivory Coast, in acceding to the said convention, specifies that:

1   For the application of Article 9 of the convention, concerning the value of the monetary units used, the limit of liability shall be equal to the exchange value in CFA francs, one gold pound being equal to two pounds sterling in notes, at the rate of exchange prevailing at the arrival of the ship at the port of discharge.

2   It reserves the right to regulate, by specific provisions of national law, the system of limitation of liability to be applied to maritime carriage between two ports in the Republic of the Ivory Coast.

Japan

(at time of signature)

Subject to the reservations formulated in the note relative to this treaty and appended to my letter dated 25 August 1925 to HE the Minister for Foreign Affairs of Belgium.

At the moment of proceeding to the signature of the International Convention for the Unification of Certain Rules Relating to Bills of Lading, the undersigned, plenipotentiary of Japan, makes the following reservations:

(a) To Article 4:

Japan reserves to itself until further notice the acceptance of the provisions in (a) of para 2 of Article 4.

(b) Japan is of the opinion that the convention does not in any part apply to national coasting trade: consequently there should be no occasion to make it the object of provisions in the Protocol. However, if it be not so, Japan reserves to itself the right freely to regulate the national coasting trade by its own law.

(at time of ratification)

… The government of Japan declares:

1   that it reserves to itself the application of the first paragraph of Article 9 of the convention;

2   that it maintains reservation (b) formulated in the note annexed to the letter of the Ambassador of Japan to the Minister for Foreign Affairs of Belgium, of 25 August 1925, concerning the right freely to regulate the national coasting trade by its own law; and

3   that it withdraws reservation (a) in the above-mentioned note, concerning the provisions in (a) of para 2 of Article 4 of the convention.

Kuwait

… subject to the following reservation: the maximum amount for liability for any loss or damage to or in connection with goods referred to in Article 4, para 5, to be raised to £250 instead of £100.

This reservation was rejected by France and Norway.

In a note of 30 March 1971, received by the Belgian government on 30 April 1971, the government of Kuwait declares that the amount of '£250' should be replaced by '250 Kuwait Dinars'.

Netherlands

… Desiring to exercise the option of accession reserved to non-signatory States under Article 12 of the International Convention for the Unification of Certain Rules Relating to Bills of Lading, with protocol of signature, concluded at Brussels on 25 August 1924, we have resolved hereby definitively to accede, in respect of the Kingdom in Europe, to the said convention, with protocol of signature, and undertake co operate in its application, while reserving the right by legal enactment:

1   to prescribe that in the cases referred to in para 2(c)–(p) of Article 4 of the convention, the holder of a bill of lading shall be entitled to establish responsibility for loss or damage arising from the personal fault of the carrier or the fault of his servants which are not covered by para (a).

2   To apply Article 6 in so far as the national coasting trade is concerned to all classes of goods without taking account of the restriction set out in the last paragraph of that article; and subject to the following:

(a) accession to the convention is subject to the exclusion of the first paragraph of Article 9 of the convention;

(b) Netherlands law may limit the possibilities of furnishing evidence to the contrary against the bill of lading.

In witness whereof …

Norway

… The accession of Norway to the International Convention for the Unification of Certain Rules Relating to Bills of Lading, signed at Brussels on 25 August 1924, and to the protocol of signature annexed thereto, is subject to the proviso that the other Contracting States do not object to the application of the provisions of the convention being limited in the following manner with regard to Norway:

1   Under the Norwegian Navigation Law of 7 May 1937, bills of lading and similar documents may continue to be made out, for national coasting trade, in accordance with the provisions of that law without the provisions of the convention being applied to them or to the legal relationship which is thereby established between the carrier and the holder of the document.

2   Maritime carriage between Norway and other Nordic States, whose navigation laws contain similar provisions, shall be considered as equivalent to national coasting trade for the purpose mentioned in para 1 – if a provision to that effect is decreed pursuant to the last paragraph of Article 122 of the Norwegian Navigation Law.

3   The provisions of the International Conventions on the Transport of Passengers and Baggage by Rail and on the Traffic of Goods by Rail, signed at Rome on 23 November 1933, shall not be affected by this convention.

Switzerland

… In accordance with the second paragraph of the protocol of signature, the federal authorities reserve the right to give effect to this international act by including in Swiss legislation, in a form appropriate to that legislation, the rides adopted under this convention.

United Kingdom of Great Britain and Northern Ireland

(*at time of signature*)

… I declare that His Britannic Majesty's government adopt the last reservation in the additional Protocol of the Bills of Lading Convention. I further declare that my signature applies only to Great Britain and Northern Ireland. I reserve the right of each of the British Dominions, Colonies, Overseas Possessions and Protectorates, and of each of the territories over which His Britannic Majesty exercises a mandate to accede to this convention under Article 13.

(*at time of ratification*)

… In accordance with Article 13 of the above-named convention, I declare that the acceptance of the convention given by His Britannic Majesty in the instrument of ratification deposited this day extends only to the United Kingdom of Great Britain and Northern Ireland and does not apply to any of His Majesty's Colonies or Protectorates, or territories under suzerainty or mandate.

United Republic of Tanzania

The government of the Republic of Tanganyika has requested the government of Belgium to circulate the following remarks concerning Tanganyika's relation to the International Convention for the unification of certain rules of Law relating to Bills of Lading, done at Brussels, 25 August 1924.

Tanganyika acceded to the convention by instrument dated 16 November 1962. As the convention had been applied to the territory of Tanganyika prior to its independence, Tanganyika was given the opportunity to declare that it considered the convention in force as to its territory from the date of independence, rather than having to wait the normal six month period provided for in Article 11 of the convention. While Tanganyika availed itself of this opportunity of having the convention in force from the day of its independence, by virtue of the instrument of 16 November 1962, this in no way should be considered as indicating that Tanganyika considered itself bound by the UK accession to the convention which had applied to the territory of Tanganyika prior to independence. It is the position of Tanganyika that it has adhered to the convention of its own volition and did not inherit, or consider itself in any way bound, by the obligations of the government of the UK vis à vis the convention.

United States of America

… and whereas, the Senate of the USA by their resolution of 1 April (legislative day 13 March), 1935 (two thirds of the Senators present concurring therein), did advise and consent to the ratification of the said convention and protocol of signature thereto, 'with the understanding, to be made part of such ratification, that, notwithstanding the provisions of Article 4, s 5, and the first paragraph of Article 9 of the convention, neither the carrier nor the ship shall in any event be or become liable within the jurisdiction of the USA for any loss or damage to or in connection with goods in an amount exceeding $500.00, lawful money of the USA, per package or unit unless the nature and value of such goods have been declared by the shipper before shipment and inserted in the bill of lading'.

And whereas, the Senate of the USA by their resolution of 6 May 1937 (two thirds of the Senators present concurring therein), did add to and make a part of their aforesaid resolution of 1 April 1935, the following understanding:

That should any conflict arise between the provisions of the convention and the provision of the Act of 16 April 1936, known as the 'Carriage of Goods by Sea Act', the provisions of said Act shall prevail.

Now, therefore, be it known that I, Franklin D Roosevelt, President of the USA, having seen and considered the said convention and protocol of signature, do hereby in pursuance of the aforesaid advice and consent of the Senate, ratify and confirm the same and every article and clause thereof, subject to the two understandings herein above recited and made part of this ratification.

THE AMENDED HAGUE RULES

Article 1

In this convention the following words are employed, with the meanings set out below:

(a) 'Carrier' includes the owner or the charterer who enters into a contract of carriage with a shipper.

(b) 'Contract of carriage' applies only to contracts of carriage covered by a bill of lading or any similar document of title, in so far as such document relates to the carriage of goods by sea, including any bill of lading or any similar document as aforesaid issued under or pursuant to a charter party from the moment at which such bill of lading or similar document of title regulates the relations between a carrier and a holder of the same.

(c) 'Goods' includes goods, wares, merchandise, and articles of every kind whatsoever except live animals and cargo which by the contract of carriage is stated as being carried on deck and is so carried.

(d) 'Ship' means any vessel used for the carriage of goods by sea.

(e) 'Carriage of goods' covers the period from the time when the goods are loaded on to the time they are discharged from the ship.

Article 2

Subject to the provisions of Article 6, under every contract of carriage of goods by sea the carrier, in relation to the loading, handling, stowage, carriage, custody, care and discharge of such goods, shall be subject to the responsibilities and liabilities, and entitled to the rights and immunities hereinafter set forth.

Article 3

1   The carrier shall be bound before and at the beginning of the voyage to exercise due diligence to:

    (a) Make the ship seaworthy.

    (b) Properly man, equip and supply the ship.

    (c) Make the holds, refrigerating and cool chambers, and all other parts of the ship in which goods are carried, fit and safe for their reception, carriage and preservation.

2   Subject to the provisions of Article 4, the carrier shall properly and carefully load, handle, stow, carry, keep, care for, and discharge the goods carried.

3   After receiving the goods into his charge the carrier or the master or agent of the carrier shall, on demand of the shipper, issue to the shipper a bill of lading showing among other things:

    (a) The leading marks necessary for identification of the goods as the same are furnished in writing by the shipper before the loading of such goods starts, provided such marks are stamped or otherwise shown clearly upon the goods if uncovered, or on the cases or coverings in which such goods are contained, in such a manner as should ordinarily remain legible until the end of the voyage.

    (b) Either the number of packages or pieces, or the quantity, or weight, as the case may be, as furnished in writing by the shipper.

    (c) The apparent order and condition of the goods.

Provided that no carrier, master or agent of the carrier shall be bound to state or show in the bill of lading any marks, number, quantity, or weight which he has reasonable ground for suspecting not accurately to represent the goods actually received, or which he has had no reasonable means of checking.

4   Such a bill of lading shall be *prima facie* evidence of the receipt by the carrier of the goods as therein described in accordance with para 3(a), (b) and (c). However, proof to the contrary shall not be admissible when the bill of lading has been transferred to a third party acting in good faith.

5   The shipper shall be deemed to have guaranteed to the carrier the accuracy at the time of shipment of the marks, number, quantity and weight, as furnished by him, and the shipper shall indemnify the carrier against all loss, damages and expenses arising or resulting from inaccuracies in such particulars. The right of the carrier to such indemnity shall in no way limit his responsibility and liability under the contract of carriage to any person other than the shipper.

6   Unless notice of loss or damage and the general nature of such loss or damage be given in writing to the carrier or his agent at the port of discharge before or at the time of the removal of the goods into the custody of the person entitled to delivery thereof under the contract of carriage, or, if the loss or damage be not apparent, within three days, such removal shall be *prima facie* evidence of the delivery by the carrier of the goods as described in the bill of lading.

The notice in writing need not be given if the state of the goods has, at the time of their receipt, been the subject of joint survey or inspection.

Subject to para 6 *bis* the carrier and the ship shall in any event be discharged from all liability whatsoever in respect of the goods, unless suit is brought within one year of their delivery or of the date when they should have been delivered. This period may, however, be extended if the parties so agree after the cause of action has arisen.

In the case of any actual or apprehended loss or damage the carrier and the receiver shall give all reasonable facilities to each other for inspecting and tallying the goods.

6 *bis* An action for indemnity against a third person may be brought even after the expiration of the year provided for in the preceding paragraph if brought within the time allowed by the law of the court seized of the case. However, the time allowed shall be not less than three months, commencing from the day when the person bringing such action for indemnity has settled the claim or has been served with process in the action against himself.

7   After the goods are loaded the bill of lading to be issued by the carrier, master, or agent of the carrier, to the shipper shall, if the shipper so demands, be a 'shipped' bill of lading, provided that if the shipper shall have previously taken up any document of title to such goods, he shall surrender the same as against the issue of the 'shipped' bill of lading, but at the option of the carrier such document of title may be noted at the port of shipment by the carrier, master, or agent with the name or names of the ship or ships upon which the goods have been shipped and the date or dates of shipment, and when so noted, if it shows the particulars mentioned in para 3 of Article 3, shall for the purpose of this article be deemed to constitute a 'shipped' bill of lading.

8   Any clause, covenant, or agreement in a contract of carriage relieving the carrier or the ship from liability for loss or damage to, or in connection with, goods arising from negligence, fault, or failure in the duties and obligations provided in this article or lessening such liability otherwise than as provided in this convention, shall be null and void and of no effect. A benefit of insurance in favour of the carrier or similar clause shall be deemed to be a clause relieving the carrier from liability.

Article 4

1   Neither the carrier nor the ship shall be liable for loss or damage arising or resulting from unseaworthiness unless caused by want of due diligence on the part of the carrier to make the ship seaworthy, and to secure that the ship is properly manned, equipped and supplied, and to make the holds, refrigerating and cool chambers and all other parts of the ship in which goods are carried fit and safe for their reception carriage and preservation in accordance with the provisions of para 1 of Article 3. Whenever loss or damage has resulted from unseaworthiness the burden of proving the exercise of due diligence shall be on the carrier or other person claiming exemption under this article.

2   Neither the carrier nor the ship shall be responsible for loss or damage arising or resulting from:

(a) Act, neglect or default of the master, mariner, pilot, or the servants of the carrier in the navigation or in the management of the ship.

(b) Fire, unless caused by the actual fault or privity of the carrier.

(c) Perils, dangers and accidents of the sea or other navigable waters.

(d) Act of God.

(e) Act of war.

(f) Act of public enemies.

(g) Arrest or restraint of princes, rulers or people, or seizure under legal process.

(h) Quarantine restrictions.

(i) Act or omission of the shipper or owner of the goods, his agent or representative.

(j) Strikes or lock outs or stoppage or restraint of labour from whatever cause, whether partial or general.

(k) Riots and civil commotions.

(l) Saving or attempting to save life or property at sea.

(m) Wastage in bulk or weight or any other loss or damage arising from inherent defect, quality or vice of the goods.

(n) Insufficiency of packing.

(o) Insufficiency or inadequacy of marks.

(p) Latent defects not discoverable by due diligence.

(q) Any other cause arising without the actual fault or privity of the carrier, or without the fault or neglect of the agents or servants of the carrier, but the burden of proof shall be on the person claiming the benefit of this exception to show that neither the actual fault or privity of the carrier nor the fault or neglect of the agents or servants of the carrier contributed to the loss or damage.

3   The shipper shall not be responsible for loss or damage sustained by the carrier or the ship arising or resulting from any cause without the act, fault or neglect of the shipper, his agents or his servants.

4   Any deviation in saving or attempting to save life or property at sea or any reasonable

deviation shall not be deemed to be an infringement or breach of this convention or of the contract of carriage, and the carrier shall not be liable for any loss or damage resulting therefrom.

5   (a) Unless the nature and value of such goods have been declared by the shipper before shipment and inserted in the bill of lading, neither the carrier nor the ship shall in any event be or become liable for any loss or damage to or in connection with the goods in an amount exceeding 666.67 units of account per package or unit or two units of account per kg of gross weight of the goods lost or damaged, whichever is the higher.

  (b) The total amount recoverable shall be calculated by reference to the value of such goods at the place and time at which the goods are discharged from the ship in accordance with the contract or should have been so discharged.

The value of the goods shall be fixed according to the commodity exchange price, or, if there be no such price, according to the current market price, or, if there be no commodity exchange price or current market price, by reference to the normal value of goods of the same kind and quality.

  (c) Where a container, pallet or similar article of transport is used to consolidate goods, the number of packages or units enumerated in the bill of lading as packed in such article of transport shall be deemed the number of packages or units for the purpose of this paragraph as far as these packages or units are concerned. Except as aforesaid such article of transport shall be considered the package or unit.

  (d) The unit of account mentioned in this article is the Special Drawing Right as defined by the International Monetary Fund. The amounts mentioned in sub-para (a) of this paragraph shall be converted into national currency on the basis of the value of that currency on a date to be determined by the law of the court seized of the case.

The value of the national currency, in terms of the Special Drawing Right, of a State which is a member of the International Monetary Fund, shall be calculated in accordance with the method of valuation applied by the International Monetary Fund in effect at the date in question for its operations and transactions. The value of the national currency, in terms of the Special Drawing Right, of a State which is not a member of the International Monetary Fund, shall be calculated in a manner determined by that State.

Nevertheless, a State which is not a member of the International Monetary Fund and whose law does not permit the application of the provisions of the preceding sentences may, at the time of ratification of the protocol of 1979 or accession thereto or at any time thereafter, declare that the limits of liability provided for in this convention to be applied in its territory shall be fixed as follows:

    (i) in respect of the amount of 666.67 units of account mentioned in sub-para (a) of para 5 of this article, 10,000 monetary units;

    (ii) in respect of the amount of 2 units of account mentioned in sub-para (a) of para 5 of this article, 30 monetary units.

The monetary unit referred to in the preceding sentence corresponds to 65.5 mg of gold of millesimal fineness 900. The conversion of the amounts specified in that sentence into the national currency shall be made according to the law of the State concerned.

The calculation and the conversion mentioned in the preceding sentences shall be made in such a manner as to express in the national currency of the State as far as possible the same real value for the amounts in sub-para (a) of para 5 of this article as is expressed there in units of account.

States shall communicate to the depositary the manner of calculation or the result of the conversion as the case may be, when depositing an instrument of ratification of the protocol of 1979 or of accession thereto and whenever there is a change in either.

  (e) Neither the carrier nor the ship shall be entitled to the benefit of the limitation of liability provided for in this paragraph if it is proved that the damage resulted from an act or omission of the carrier done with intent to cause damage, or recklessly and with knowledge that damage would probably result.

  (f) The declaration mentioned in sub-para (a) of this paragraph, embodied in the bill of lading, shall be *prima facie* evidence, but shall not be binding or conclusive on the carrier.

(g) By agreement between the carrier, master or agent of the carrier and the shipper other maximum amounts than those mentioned in sub-para (a) of this paragraph may be fixed, provided that no maximum amount so fixed shall be less than the appropriate maximum mentioned in that sub-paragraph.

(h) Neither the carrier nor the ship shall be responsible in any event for loss or damage to, or in connection with, goods if the nature or value thereof has been knowingly misstated by the shipper in the bill of lading.

6   Goods of an inflammable, explosive or dangerous nature to the shipment whereof the carrier, master or agent of the carrier has not consented with knowledge of their nature and character, may at any time before discharge be landed at any place, or destroyed or rendered innocuous by the carrier without compensation and the shipper of such goods shall be liable for all damages and expenses directly or indirectly arising out of or resulting from such shipment. If any such goods shipped with such knowledge and consent shall become a danger to the ship or cargo, they may in like manner be landed at any place, or destroyed or rendered innocuous by the carrier without liability on the part of the carrier except to general average, if any.

Article 4 bis

1   The defences and limits of liability provided for in this convention shall apply in any action against the carrier in respect of loss or damage to goods covered by a contract of carriage whether the action be founded in contract or in tort.

2   If such an action is brought against a servant or agent of the carrier (such servant or agent not being an independent contractor) such servant or agent shall be entitled to avail himself of the defences and limits of liability which the carrier is entitled to invoke under this convention.

3   The aggregate of the amounts recoverable from the carrier, and such servants and agents, shall in no case exceed the limit provided for in this convention.

4   Nevertheless, a servant or agent of the carrier shall not be entitled to avail himself of the provisions of this article, if it is proved that the damage resulted from an act or omission of the servant or agent done with intent to cause damage or recklessly and with knowledge that damage would probably result.

Article 5

A carrier shall be at liberty to surrender in whole or in part all or any of his rights and immunities or to increase any of his responsibilities and obligations under this convention, provided such surrender or increase shall be embodied in the bill of lading issued to the shipper. The provisions of this convention shall not be applicable to charterparties, but if bills of lading are issued in the case of a ship under a charterparty they shall comply with the terms of this convention. Nothing in these rules shall be held to prevent the insertion in a bill of lading of any lawful provision regarding general average.

Article 6

Notwithstanding the provisions of the preceding articles, a carrier master or agent of the carrier and a shipper shall in regard to any particular goods be at liberty to enter into any agreement in any terms as to the responsibility and liability of the carrier for such goods, and as to the rights and immunities of the carrier in respect of such goods, or his obligation as to seaworthiness, so far as this stipulation is not contrary to public policy, or the care or diligence of his servants or agents in regard to the loading, handling, stowage, carriage, custody, care and discharge of the goods carried by sea, provided that in this case no bill of lading has been or shall be issued and that the terms agreed shall be embodied in a receipt which shall be a non-negotiable document and shall be marked as such.

Any agreement so entered into shall have full legal effect.

Provided that this article shall not apply to ordinary commercial shipments made in the ordinary course of trade, but only to other shipments where the character or condition of the property to be carried or the circumstances, terms and conditions under which the carriage is to be performed are such as reasonably to justify a special agreement.

Article 7

Nothing herein contained shall prevent a carrier or a shipper from entering into any agreement, stipulation, condition, reservation or exemption as to the responsibility and liability of the carrier or the ship for the loss or damage to, or in connection with, the custody and care and handling of goods prior to the loading on, and subsequent to the discharge from the ship on which the goods are carried by sea.

Article 8

The provisions of this convention shall not affect the rights and obligations of the carrier under any statute for the time being in force relating to the limitation of the liability of owners of sea going vessels.

Article 9

This convention shall not affect the provisions of any international convention or national law governing liability for nuclear damage.

Article 10

The provisions of this convention shall apply to every bill of lading relating to the carriage of goods between ports in two different States if:

(a) the bill of lading is issued in a Contracting State; or

(b) the carriage is from a port in a Contracting State; or

(c) the contract contained in or evidenced by the bill of lading provides that the rules of this convention or legislation of any State giving effect to them are to govern the contract whatever may be the nationality of the ship, the carrier, the shipper, the consignee, or any other interested person.

Each Contracting State shall apply the provisions of this convention to the Bills of Lading mentioned above.

This article shall not prevent a Contracting State from applying the rules of this convention to bills of lading not included in the preceding paragraphs.

THE HAMBURG RULES

PART I – GENERAL PROVISIONS

Article 1 – Definitions in this convention

1   'Carrier' means any person by whom or in whose name a contract of carriage of goods by sea has been concluded with a shipper.

2   'Actual carrier' means any person to whom the performance of the carriage of the goods, or of part of the carriage, has been entrusted by the carrier, and includes any other person to whom such performance has been entrusted.

3   'Shipper' means any person by whom or in whose name or on whose behalf a contract of carriage of goods by sea has been concluded with a carrier, or any person by whom or in whose name or on whose behalf the goods are actually delivered to the carrier in relation to the contract of carriage by sea.

4   'Consignee' means the person entitled to take delivery of the goods.

5   'Goods' includes live animals; where the goods are consolidated in a container, pallet or similar article of transport or where they are packed, 'goods' includes such article of transport or packaging if supplied by the shipper.

6   'Contract of carriage by sea' means any contract whereby the carrier undertakes against payment of freight to carry goods by sea from one port to another, however, a contract which involves carriage by sea and also carriage by some other means is deemed to be a contract of carriage by sea for the purposes of this convention only in so far as it relates to the carriage by sea.

7   'Bill of lading' means a document which evidences a contract of carriage by sea and the taking over or loading of the goods by the carrier, and by which the carrier undertakes to

deliver the goods against surrender of the document. A provision in the document that the goods are to be delivered to the order of a named person, or to order, or to bearer, constitutes such an undertaking.

8 'Writing' includes, *inter alia*, telegram and telex.

Article 2 – Scope of application

1 The provisions of this convention are applicable to all contracts of carriage by sea between two different States, if:
   (a) the port of loading as provided for in the contract of carriage by sea is located in a Contracting State; or
   (b) the port of discharge as provided for in the contract of carriage by sea is located in a Contracting State; or
   (c) one of the optional ports of discharge provided for in the contract of carriage by sea is the actual port of discharge and such port is located in a Contracting State; or
   (d) the bill of lading or other document evidencing the contract of carriage by sea is issued in a Contracting State; or
   (e) the bill of lading or other document evidencing the contract of carriage by sea provides that the provisions of this convention or the legislation of any State giving effect to them are to govern the contract.

2 The provisions of this convention are applicable without regard to the nationality of the ship, the carrier, the actual carrier, the shipper, the consignee or any other interested person.

3 The provisions of this convention are not applicable to charterparties. However, where a bill of lading is issued pursuant to a charterparty, the provisions of the convention apply to such a bill of lading if it governs the relation between the carrier and the holder of the bill of lading, not being the charterer.

4 If a contract provides for future carriage of goods in a series of shipments during an agreed period, the provisions of this convention apply to each shipment. However, where a shipment is made under a charterparty, the provisions of para 3 of this article apply.

Article 3 – Interpretation of the convention

In the interpretation and application of the provisions of this convention regard shall be had to its international character and to the need to promote uniformity.

PART II – LIABILITY OF THE CARRIER

Article 4 – Period of responsibility

1 The responsibility of the carrier for the goods under this convention covers the period during which the carrier is in charge of the goods at the port of loading, during the carriage and at the port of discharge.

2 For the purpose of para 1 of this article, the carrier is deemed to be in charge of the goods:
   (a) from the time he has taken over the goods from:
       (i) the shipper, or a person acting on his behalf; or
       (ii) an authority or other third party to whom, pursuant to law or regulations applicable at the port of loading, the goods must be handed over for shipment;
   (b) until the time he has delivered the goods:
       (i) by handing over the goods to the consignee; or
       (ii) in cases where the consignee does not receive the goods from the carrier, by placing them at the disposal of the consignee in accordance with the contract or with the law or with the usage of the particular trade, applicable at the port of discharge; or
       (iii) by handing over the goods to an authority or other third party to whom, pursuant to law or regulations applicable at the port of discharge, the goods must be handed over.

3   In paras 1 and 2 of this article, reference to the carrier or to the consignee means, in addition to the carrier or the consignee, the servants or agents, respectively of the carrier or the consignee.

Article 5 – Basis of liability

1   The carrier is liable for loss resulting from loss of or damage to the goods, as well as from delay in delivery, if the occurrence which caused the loss, damage or delay took place while the goods were in his charge as defined in Article 4, unless the carrier proves that he, his servants or agents took all measures that could reasonably be required to avoid the occurrence and its consequences.

2   Delay in delivery occurs when the goods have not been delivered at the port of discharge provided for in the contract of carriage by sea within the time expressly agreed upon or, in the absence of such agreement, within the time which it would be reasonable to require of a diligent carrier, having regard to the circumstances of the case.

3   The person entitled to make a claim for the loss of goods may treat the goods as lost if they have not been delivered as required by Article 4 within 60 consecutive days following the expiry of the time for delivery according to para 2 of this article.

4   (a)   The carrier is liable:

       (i)   for loss of or damage to the goods or delay in delivery caused by fire, if the claimant proves that the fire arose from fault or neglect on the part of the carrier, his servants or agents;

      (ii)   for such loss, damage or delay in delivery which is proved by the claimant to have resulted from the fault or neglect of the carrier, his servants or agents, in taking all measures that could reasonably be required to put out the fire and avoid or mitigate its consequences.

   (b)   In case of fire on board the ship affecting the goods if the claimant or the carrier so desires, a survey in accordance with shipping practices must be held into the cause and circumstances of the fire, and a copy of the surveyor's report shall be made available on demand to the carrier and the claimant.

5   With respect to live animals, the carrier is not liable for loss damage or delay in delivery resulting from any special risks inherent in that kind of carriage. If the carrier proves that he has complied with any special instructions given to him by the shipper respecting the animals and that, in the circumstances of the case, the loss, damage or delay in delivery could be attributed to such risks, it is presumed that the loss, damage or delay in delivery was so caused, unless there is proof that all or a part of the loss, damage or delay in delivery resulted from fault or neglect on the part of the carrier, his servants or agents.

6   The carrier is not liable, except in general average, where loss damage or delay in delivery resulted from measures to save life or from reasonable measures to save property at sea.

7   Where fault or neglect on the part of the carrier, his servants or agents combines with another cause to produce loss, damage or delay in delivery, the carrier is liable only to the extent that the loss, damage or delay in delivery is attributable to such fault or neglect, provided that the carrier proves the amount of the loss, damage or delay in delivery not attributable thereto.

Article 6 – Limits of liability

1   (a)   The liability of the carrier for loss resulting from loss of or damage to goods according to the provisions of Article 5 is limited to an amount equivalent to 835 units of account per package or other shipping unit or 2.5 units of account per kg of gross weight of the goods lost or damaged, whichever is the higher.

   (b)   The liability of the carrier for delay in delivery according to the provisions of Article 5 is limited to an amount equivalent to two and a half times the freight payable for the goods delayed, but not exceeding the total freight payable under the contract of carriage of goods by sea.

   (c)   In no case shall the aggregate liability of the carrier under both sub-paras (a) and (b) of this paragraph, exceed the limitation which would be established under sub-para (a) of this paragraph for total loss of the goods with respect to which such liability was incurred.

2   For the purpose of calculating which amount is the higher in accordance with para 1(a) of this article, the following rules apply:

    (a) Where a container, pallet or similar article of transport is used to consolidate goods, the package or other shipping units enumerated in the bill of lading, if issued, or otherwise in any other document evidencing the contract of carriage by sea, as packed in such article of transport are deemed packages or shipping units. Except as aforesaid the goods in such article of transport are deemed one shipping unit.

    (b) In cases where the article of transport itself has been lost or damaged, that article of transport, if not owned or otherwise supplied by the carrier, is considered one separate shipping unit.

3   Unit of account means the unit of account mentioned in Article 26.

4   By agreement between the carrier and the shipper, limits of liability exceeding those provided for in para 1 may be fixed.

Article 7 – Application to non-contractual claims

1   The defences and limits of liability provided for in this convention apply in any action against the carrier in respect of loss or damage to the goods covered by the contract of carriage by sea, as well as of delay in delivery whether the action is founded in contract, in tort or otherwise.

2   If such an action is brought against a servant or agent of the carrier, such servant or agent, if he proves that he acted within the scope of his employment, is entitled to avail himself of the defences and limits of liability which the carrier is entitled to invoke under this convention.

3   Except as provided in Article 8, the aggregate of the amounts recoverable from the carrier and from any persons referred to in para 2 of this article shall not exceed the limits of liability provided for in this convention.

Article 8 – Loss of right to limit responsibility

1   The carrier is not entitled to the benefit of the limitation of liability provided for in Article 6 if it is proved that the loss, damage or delay in delivery resulted from an act or omission of the carrier, done with the intent to cause such loss, damage or delay, or recklessly and with knowledge that such loss, damage or delay would probably result.

2   Notwithstanding the provisions of para 2 of Article 7, a servant or agent of the carrier is not entitled to the benefit of the limitation of liability provided for in Article 6, if it is proved that the loss, damage or delay in delivery resulted from an act or omission of such servant or agent, done with the intent to cause such loss, damage or delay, or recklessly and with knowledge that such loss, damage or delay would probably result.

Article 9 – Deck cargo

1   The carrier is entitled to carry the goods on deck only if such carriage is in accordance with an agreement with the shipper or with the usage of the particular trade or is required by statutory rules or regulations.

2   If the carrier and the shipper have agreed that the goods shall or may be carried on deck, the carrier must insert in the bill of lading or other document evidencing the contract of carriage by sea a statement to that effect. In the absence of such a statement, the carrier has the burden of proving that an agreement for carriage on deck has been entered into; however, the carrier is not entitled to invoke such an agreement against a third party, including a consignee, who has acquired the bill of lading in good faith.

3   Where the goods have been carried on deck contrary to the provisions of para 1 of this article or where the carrier may not under para 2 of this article invoke an agreement for carriage on deck, the carrier, notwithstanding the provisions of para 1 of Article 5, is liable for loss of or damage to the goods, as well as for delay in delivery, resulting solely from the carriage on deck, and the extent of his liability is to be determined in accordance with the provisions of Article 6 or Article 8 of this Convention, as the case may be.

4   Carriage of goods on deck contrary to express agreement for carriage under deck is deemed to be an act or omission of the carrier within the meaning of Article 8.

Article 10 – Liability of the carrier and actual carrier

1   Where the performance of the carriage or part thereof has been entrusted to an actual carrier, whether or not in pursuance of a liberty under the contract of carriage by sea to do so, the carrier nevertheless remains responsible for the entire carriage according to the provisions of this convention. The carrier is responsible, in relation to the carriage performed by the actual carrier, for the acts and omissions of the actual carrier and of his servants and agents acting within the scope of their employment.

2   All the provisions of this convention governing the responsibility of the carrier also apply to the responsibility of the actual carrier for the carriage performed by him. The provisions of paras 2 and 3 of Article 7 and of para 2 of Article 8 apply if an action is brought against a servant or agent of the actual carrier.

3   Any special agreement under which the carrier assumes obligations not imposed by this convention or waives rights conferred by this convention affects the actual carrier only if agreed to by him expressly and in writing. Whether or not the actual carrier has so agreed, the carrier nevertheless remains bound by the obligations or waivers resulting from such special agreement.

4   Where and to the extent that both the carrier and the actual carrier are liable, their liability is joint and several.

5   The aggregate of the amounts recoverable from the carrier, the actual carrier and their servants and agents shall not exceed the limits of liability provided for in this convention.

6   Nothing in this article shall prejudice any right of recourse as between the carrier and the actual carrier.

Article 11 – Through carriage

1   Notwithstanding the provisions of para 1 of Article 10, where a contract of carriage by sea provides explicitly that a specified part of the carriage covered by the said contract is to be performed by a named person other than the carrier, the contract may also provide that the carrier is not liable for loss, damage or delay in delivery caused by an occurrence which takes place while the goods are in the charge of the actual carrier during such part of the carriage. Nevertheless, any stipulation limiting or excluding such liability is without effect if no judicial proceedings can be instituted against the actual carrier in a court competent under para 1 or 2 of Article 21. The burden of proving that any loss, damage or delay in delivery has been caused by such an occurrence rests upon the carrier.

2   The actual carrier is responsible in accordance with the provisions of para 2 of Article 10 for loss, damage or delay in delivery caused by an occurrence which takes place while the goods are in his charge.

PART III – LIABILITY OF THE SHIPPER

Article 12 – General rule

The shipper is not liable for loss sustained by the carrier or the actual carrier, or for damage sustained by the ship, unless such loss or damage was caused by the fault or neglect of the shipper, his servants or agents. Nor is any servant or agent of the shipper liable for such loss or damage unless the loss or damage was caused by fault or neglect on his part.

Article 13 – Special rules on dangerous goods

1   The shipper must mark or label in a suitable manner dangerous goods as dangerous.

2   Where the shipper hands over dangerous goods to the carrier or an actual carrier, as the case may be, the shipper must inform him of the dangerous character of the goods and, if necessary, of the precautions to be taken. If the shipper fails to do so and such carrier or actual carrier does not otherwise have knowledge of their dangerous character:

   (a) the shipper is liable to the carrier and any actual carrier for the loss resulting from the shipment of such goods; and

   (b) the goods may at any time be unloaded, destroyed or rendered innocuous, as the circumstances may require, without payment of compensation.

3   The provisions of para 2 of this article may not be invoked by any person if during the carriage he has taken the goods in his charge with knowledge of their dangerous character.

4   If, in cases where the provisions of para 2, sub-para (b) of this article do not apply or may not be invoked, dangerous goods become an actual danger to life or property, they may be unloaded, destroyed or rendered innocuous, as the circumstances may require, without payment of compensation except where there is an obligation to contribute in general average or where the carrier is liable accordance with the provisions of Article 5.

PART IV – TRANSPORT DOCUMENTS

Article 14 – Issue of bill of lading

1   When the carrier or the actual carrier takes the goods in his charge, the carrier must, on demand of the shipper, issue to the shipper a bill of lading.

2   The bill of lading may be signed by a person having authority from the carrier. A bill of lading signed by the master of the ship carrying the goods is deemed to have been signed on behalf of the carrier.

3   The signature on the bill of lading may be in handwriting printed in facsimile, perforated, stamped, in symbols, or made by any other mechanical or electronic means, if not inconsistent with the law of the country where the bill of lading is issued.

Article 15 – Contents of bill of lading

1   The bill of lading must include, *inter alia*, the following particulars:

(a) the general nature of the goods, the leading marks necessary for identification of the goods, an express statement, if applicable, as to the dangerous character of the goods, the number of packages or pieces, and the weight of the goods or their quantity otherwise expressed, all such particulars as furnished by the shipper;

(b) the apparent condition of the goods;

(c) the name and principal place of business of the carrier;

(d) the name of the shipper;

(e) the consignee if named by the shipper;

(f) the port of loading under the contract of carriage by sea and the date on which the goods were taken over by the carrier at the port of loading;

(g) the port of discharge under the contract of carriage by sea;

(h) the number of originals of the bill of lading, if more than one;

(i)   the place of issuance of the bill of lading;

(j)   the signature of the carrier or a person acting on his behalf;

(k) the freight to the extent payable by the consignee or other indication that freight is payable by him;

(l)   the statement referred to in para 3 of Article 23;

(m) the statement, if applicable, that the goods shall or may be carried on deck;

(n) the date or the period of delivery of the goods at the port of discharge if expressly agreed upon between the parties; and

(o) any increased limit or limits of liability where agreed in accordance with para 4 of Article 6.

2   After the goods have been loaded on board, if the shipper so demands, the carrier must issue to the shipper a 'shipped' bill of lading which, in addition to the particulars required under para 1 of this article, must state that the goods are on board a named ship or ships, and the date or dates of loading. If the carrier has previously issued to the shipper a bill of lading or other document of title with respect to any of such goods, on request of the carrier, the shipper must surrender such document in exchange for a 'shipped' bill of lading. The carrier may amend any previously issued document in order to meet the shipper's demand for a 'shipped' bill of lading if, as amended, such document includes all the information required to be contained in a 'shipped' bill of lading.

3   The absence in the bill of lading of one or more particulars referred to in this article does not affect the legal character of the document as a bill of lading provided that it nevertheless meets the requirements set out in para 7 of Article 1.

Article 16 – Bills of lading: reservations and evidentiary effect

1   If the bill of lading contains particulars concerning the general nature, leading marks, number of packages or pieces, weight or quantity of the goods which the carrier or other person issuing the bill of lading on his behalf knows or has reasonable grounds to suspect do not accurately represent the goods actually taken over or, where a 'shipped' bill of lading is issued, loaded, or if he had no reasonable means of checking such particulars, the carrier or such other person must insert in the bill of lading a reservation specifying these inaccuracies, grounds of suspicion or the absence of reasonable means of checking.

2   If the carrier or other person issuing the bill of lading on his behalf fails to note on the bill of lading the apparent condition of the goods, he is deemed to have noted on the bill of lading that the goods were in apparent good condition.

3   Except for particulars in respect of which and to the extent to which a reservation permitted under para 1 of this article has been entered:

(a) the bill of lading is *prima facie* evidence of the taking over or, where a 'shipped' bill of lading is issued, loading, by the carrier of the goods as described in the bill of lading; and

(b) proof to the contrary by the carrier is not admissible if the bill of lading has been transferred to a third party, including a consignee, who in good faith has acted in reliance on the description of the goods therein.

4   A bill of lading which does not, as provided in para 1, sub-para (k) of Article 15, set forth the freight or otherwise indicate that freight is payable by the consignee or does not set forth demurrage incurred at the port of loading payable by the consignee, is *prima facie* evidence that no freight or such demurrage is payable by him. However, proof to the contrary by the carrier is not admissible when the bill of lading has been transferred to a third party, including a consignee, who in good faith has acted in reliance on the absence in the bill of lading of any such indication.

Article 17 – Guarantees by the shipper

1   The shipper is deemed to have guaranteed to the carrier the accuracy of particulars relating to the general nature of the goods, their marks, number, weight and quantity as furnished by him for insertion in the bill of lading. The shipper must indemnify the carrier against the loss resulting from inaccuracies in such particulars. The shipper remains liable even if the bill of lading has been transferred by him. The right of the carrier to such indemnity in no way limits his liability under the contract of carriage by sea to any person other than the shipper.

2   Any letter of guarantee or agreement by which the shipper undertakes to indemnify the carrier against loss resulting from the issuance of the bill of lading by the carrier, or by a person acting on his behalf, without entering a reservation relating to particulars furnished by the shipper for insertion in the bill of lading, or to the apparent condition of the goods, is void and of no effect as against any third party, including a consignee, to whom the bill of lading has been transferred.

3   Such letter of guarantee or agreement is valid as against the shipper unless the carrier or the person acting on his behalf, by omitting the reservation referred to in para 2 of this article, intends to defraud a third party, including a consignee, who acts in reliance on the description of the goods in the bill of lading. In the latter case, if the reservation omitted relates to particulars furnished by the shipper for insertion in the bill of lading, the carrier has no right of indemnity from the shipper pursuant to para 1 of this article.

4   In the case of intended fraud referred to in para 3 of this article, the carrier is liable, without the benefit of the limitation of liability provided for in this convention, for the loss incurred by a third party, including a consignee, because he has acted in reliance on the description of the goods in the bill of lading.

Article 18 – Documents other than bills of lading

Where a carrier issues a document other than a bill of lading to evidence the receipt of the goods to be carried, such a document is *prima facie* evidence of the conclusion of the contract of carriage by sea and the taking over by the carrier of the goods as therein described.

PART V – CLAIMS AND ACTIONS

Article 19 – Notice of loss, damage or delay

1 Unless notice of loss or damage, specifying the general nature of such loss or damage, is given in writing by the consignee to the carrier not later than the working day after the day when the goods were handed over to the consignee, such handing over is *prima facie* evidence of the delivery by the carrier of the goods as described in the document of transport or, if no such document has been issued, in good condition.

2 Where the loss or damage is not apparent, the provisions of para 1 of this article apply correspondingly if notice in writing is not given within 15 consecutive days after the day when the goods were handed over to the consignee.

3 If the state of the goods at the time they were handed over to the consignee has been the subject of a joint survey or inspection by the parties, notice in writing need not be given of loss or damage ascertained during such survey or inspection.

4 In the case of any actual or apprehended loss or damage the carrier and the consignee must give all reasonable facilities to each other for inspecting and tallying the goods.

5 No compensation shall be payable for loss resulting from delay in delivery unless a notice has been given in writing to the carrier within 60 consecutive days after the day when the goods were handed over to the consignee.

6 If the goods have been delivered by an actual carrier, any notice given under this article to him shall have the same effect as if it had been given to the carrier, and any notice given to the carrier shall have effect as if given to such actual carrier.

7 Unless notice of loss or damage, specifying the general nature of the loss or damage, is given in writing by the carrier or actual carrier to the shipper not later than 90 consecutive days after the occurrence of such loss or damage or after the delivery of the goods in accordance with para 2 of Article 4, whichever is later, the failure to give such notice is *prima facie* evidence that the carrier or the actual carrier has sustained no loss or damage due to the fault or neglect of the shipper, his servants or agents.

8 For the purpose of this article, notice given to a person acting on the carrier's or the actual carrier's behalf, including the master or the officer in charge of the ship, or to a person acting on the shipper's behalf is deemed to have been given to the carrier, to the actual carrier or to the shipper, respectively.

Article 20 – Limitation of actions

1 Any action relating to carriage of goods under this convention is time-barred if judicial or arbitral proceedings have not been instituted within a period of two years.

2 The limitation period commences on the day on which the carrier has delivered the goods or part thereof or, in cases where no goods have been delivered, on the last day on which the goods should have been delivered.

3 The day on which the limitation period commences is not included in the period.

4 The person against whom a claim is made may at any time during the running of the limitation period extend that period by a declaration in writing to the claimant. This period may be further extended by another declaration or declarations.

5 An action for indemnity by a person held liable may be instituted even after the expiration of the limitation period provided for in the preceding paragraphs if instituted within the time allowed by the law of the State where proceedings are instituted. However, the time allowed shall not be less than 90 days commencing from the day when the person instituting such action for indemnity has settled the claim or has been served with process in the action against himself.

Article 21 – Jurisdiction

1 In judicial proceedings relating to carriage of goods under this convention, the plaintiff, at his option, may institute an action in a court which, according to the law of the State where the court is situated, is competent and within the jurisdiction of which is situated one of the following places:

   (a) the principal place of business or, in the absence thereof, the habitual residence of the defendant; or

(b) the place where the contract was made provided that the defendant has there a place of business, branch or agency through which the contract was made; or

(c) the port of loading or the port of discharge; or

(d) any additional place designated for that purpose in the contract of carriage by sea.

2 (a) Notwithstanding the preceding provisions of this article, an action may be instituted in the courts of any port or place in a Contracting State at which the carrying vessel or any other vessel of the same ownership may have been arrested in accordance with applicable rules of the law of that State and of international law. However, in such a case, at the petition of the defendant, the claimant must remove the action, at his choice, to one of the jurisdictions referred to in para 1 of this article for the determination of the claim, but before such removal the defendant must furnish security sufficient to ensure payment of any judgment that may subsequently be awarded to the claimant in the action.

(b) All questions relating to the sufficiency or otherwise of the security shall be determined by the court of the port or place of the arrest.

3 No judicial proceedings relating to carriage of goods under this convention may be instituted in a place not specified in para 1 or 2 of this article. The provisions of this paragraph do not constitute an obstacle to the jurisdiction of the Contracting States for provisional or protective measures.

4 (a) Where an action has been instituted in a court competent under para 1 or 2 of this article or where judgment has been delivered by such no new action may be started between the same parties on the same grounds unless the judgment of the court before which the first action was instituted is not enforceable in the country in which the new proceedings are instituted;

(b) for the purpose of this article the institution of measures with a view to obtaining enforcement of a judgment is not to be considered as the starting of a new action;

(c) for the purpose of this article, the removal of an action to a different court within the same country, or to a court in another country, in accordance with para 2(a) of this article, is not to be considered as the starting of a new action.

5 Notwithstanding the provisions of the preceding paragraphs, an agreement made by the parties, after a claim under the contract of carriage by sea has arisen, which designates the place where the claimant may institute an action, is effective.

Article 22 – Arbitration

1 Subject to the provisions of this article, parties may provide by agreement evidenced in writing that any dispute that may arise relating to carriage of goods under this convention shall be referred to arbitration.

2 Where a charterparty contains a provision that disputes arising thereunder shall be referred to arbitration and a bill of lading issued pursuant to the charterparty does not contain a special annotation providing that such provision shall be binding upon the holder of the bill of lading, the carrier may not invoke such provision as against a holder having acquired the bill of lading in good faith.

3 The arbitration proceedings shall, at the option of the claimant be instituted at one of the following places:

(a) a place in a State within whose territory is situated:

(i) the principal place of business of the defendant or, in the absence thereof, the habitual residence of the defendant; or

(ii) the place where the contract was made, provided that the defendant has there a place of business, branch or agency through which the contract was made; or

(iii) the port of loading or the port of discharge; or

(b) any place designated for that purpose in the arbitration clause or agreement.

4 The arbitrator or arbitration tribunal shall apply the rules of this convention.

5 The provisions of paras 3 and 4 of this article are deemed to be part of every arbitration clause or agreement, and any term of such clause or agreement which is inconsistent therewith is null and void.

6 Nothing in this article affects the validity of an agreement relating to arbitration made by the parties after the claim under the contract of carriage by sea has arisen.

PART VI – SUPPLEMENTARY PROVISIONS

Article 23 – Contractual stipulations

1 Any stipulation in a contract of carriage by sea, in a bill of lading, or in any other document evidencing the contract of carriage by sea is null and void to the extent that it derogates, directly or indirectly, from the provisions of this convention. The nullity of such a stipulation does not affect the validity of the other provisions of the contract or document of which it forms a part. A clause assigning benefit of insurance of the goods in favour of the carrier, or any similar clause, is null and void.

2 Notwithstanding the provisions of para 1 of this article, a carrier may increase his responsibilities and obligations under this convention.

3 Where a bill of lading or any other document evidencing the contract of carriage by sea is issued, it must contain a statement that the carriage is subject to the provisions of this convention which nullify any stipulation derogating therefrom to the detriment of the shipper or the consignee.

4 Where the claimant in respect of the goods has incurred loss as a result of a stipulation which is null and void by virtue of the present article, or as a result of the omission of the statement referred to in para 3 of this article, the carrier must pay compensation to the extent required in order to give the claimant compensation in accordance with the provisions of this convention for any loss of or damage to the goods as well as for the delay in delivery. The carrier must, in addition, pay compensation for costs incurred by the claimant for the purpose of exercising his right, provided that costs incurred in the action where the foregoing provision is invoked are to be determined in accordance with the law of the State where proceedings are instituted.

Article 24 – General average

1 Nothing in this convention shall prevent the application of provisions in the contract of carriage by sea or national law regarding the adjustment of general average.

2 With the exception of Article 20, the provisions of this convention relating to the liability of the carrier for loss of or damage to the goods also determine whether the consignee may refuse contribution in general average and the liability of the carrier to indemnify the consignee in respect of any such contribution made or any salvage paid.

Article 25 – Other conventions

1 This convention does not modify the rights or duties of the carrier, the actual carrier and their servants and agents, provided for in international conventions or national law relating to the limitation of liability of owners of seagoing ships.

2 The provisions of Articles 21 and 22 of this convention do not prevent the application of the mandatory provisions of any other multilateral convention already in force at the date of this convention relating to matters dealt with in the said articles, provided that the dispute arises exclusively between parties having their principal place of business in States members of such other convention. However, this paragraph does not affect the application of para 4 of Article 22 of this convention.

3 No liability shall arise under the provisions of this convention for damage caused by a nuclear incident if the operator of a nuclear installation is liable for such damage:

(a) under either the Paris Convention of 29 July 1960 on Third Party Liability in the Field of Nuclear Energy as amended by the Additional Protocol of 28 January 1964 or the Vienna Convention of 21 May 1963 on Civil Liability for Nuclear Damage; or

(b) by virtue of national law governing the liability for such damage, provided that such law is in all respects as favourable to persons who may suffer damage as either the Paris or Vienna Conventions.

4 No liability shall arise under the provisions of this convention for any loss of or damage to or delay in delivery of luggage for which the carrier is responsible under any international convention or national law relating to the carriage of passengers and their baggage by sea.

5   Nothing contained in this convention prevents a Contracting State from applying any other international convention which is already in force at the date of this convention and which applies mandatorily to contracts of carriage of goods primarily by a mode of transport other than transport by sea. This provision also applies to any subsequent revision or amendment of such international convention.

Article 26 – Unit of account

1   The unit of account referred to in Article 6 of this convention is the Special Drawing Right as defined by the International Monetary Fund. The amounts mentioned in Article 6 are to be converted into the national currency of a State according to the value of such currency at the date of judgment or the date agreed upon by the parties. The value of a national currency, in terms of the Special Drawing Right, of a Contracting State which is a member of the International Monetary Fund is to be calculated in accordance with the method of valuation applied by the International Monetary Fund in effect at the date in question for its operations and transactions. The value of a national currency in terms of the Special Drawing Right of a Contracting State which is not a member of the International Monetary Fund is to be calculated in a manner determined by that State.

2   Nevertheless, those States which are not members of the International Monetary Fund and whose law does not permit the application of the provisions of para 1 of this article may, at the time of signature, or at the time of ratification, acceptance, approval or accession or at any time thereafter, declare that the limits of liability provided for in this convention to be applied in their territories shall be fixed as: 12,500 monetary units per package or other shipping unit or 37.5 monetary units per kg of gross weight of the goods.

3   The monetary unit referred to in para 2 of this article corresponds to 65.5 mg of gold of millesimal fineness 900. The conversion of the amounts referred to in para 2 into the national currency is to be made according to the law of the State concerned.

4   The calculation mentioned in the last sentence of para 1 and the conversion mentioned in para 3 of this article is to be made in such a manner as to express in the national currency of the Contracting State as far as possible the same real value for the amounts in Article 6 as is expressed there in units of account. Contracting States must communicate to the depositary the manner of calculation pursuant to para 1 of this article, or the result of the conversion mentioned in para 3 of this article, as the case may be, at the time of signature or when depositing their instruments of ratification, acceptance, approval or accession, or when availing themselves of the option provided for in para 2 of this article and whenever there is a change in the manner of such calculation or in the result of such conversion.

CHAPTER 5

THE INTERNATIONAL CARRIAGE OF GOODS BY AIR AND LAND

INTERNATIONAL TRANSPORT OF GOODS BY AIR

Overview

The international transportation of goods by air is regulated by a mix of international and domestic law. When a cause of action is brought in a given State's jurisdiction, potentially both international law as implemented by domestic law, and domestic law[1] will govern its resolution. This chapter reviews the international law of principal relevance.

The Warsaw Convention and associated treaties are at the heart of the international regime regulating the international transportation of goods by air. The Warsaw Convention was signed at Warsaw in 1929. It was amended by The Hague Protocol of 1955. Most States which have ratified the 1929 Convention have also ratified The Hague Protocol, so in the following analysis the Warsaw Convention as amended by the Hague Protocol, will be discussed. Numerous other treaties also impact upon the Warsaw regime, such as the Guadalajara Convention 1961, and the Montreal Additional Protocol No 4, 1975. Each of these instruments amends the Convention. Many of the States that have acceded to the original Convention and its 1955 amendments have not ratified these latter instruments. Certain parts of them will be referred to in the following pages – to reiterate, the principal focus in the following pages will be on the Warsaw Convention as amended by the 1955 Hague Convention.

The Montreal Convention of 1999 (Convention for the Unification of Certain Rules for International Carriage by Air) will be increasingly significant in the future, as States accede to it. It came into operation in late 2003, after the last of the required minimum of 30 countries ratified it. This Convention replaces Warsaw, although it draws upon its provisions to a considerable extent. It will be discussed below.

In order that an international treaty may provide a source of legal obligations within a State, the State must, once it has ratified the treaty, implement it in domestic law. Many States have adopted the Warsaw-Hague regime, and implemented it into domestic law.[2] Once implemented in domestic law, the regime functions as an independent legislative code. Thus, potentially, it can operate by way of exception to the general law requirement in common law countries that only a party that is privy to a contract can sue on this contract.

---

1   Regarding matters which are not sought to be regulated by the Warsaw Convention – see, eg, *Gatewhite Ltd v Iberia Lineas Aeras de Espana SA* [1990] 1 QB 326 at 334 (*per* Gatehouse J), observing that there was nothing in the Convention precluding the owner of cargo which has been lost or damaged during air carriage, from exercising its common law right to sue the carrier in its own name. Likewise, see the comment by Lord Hope with whom the other Law Lords concurred, in *Abnett v British Airways plc* [1997] 2 Lloyd's Rep 76 at 82, that the Convention 'is a partial harmonisation, directed to the particular issues with which it deals'.

2   Eg, in Australia the Warsaw-Hague-Guadalajara regime has been implemented by the Civil Aviation (Carriers' Liability) Act 1959 (Cth). The text of the treaties is set out in schedules to the Act.

As it will be seen below ('The Warsaw Convention applies to "international carriage"'), the Warsaw Convention only applies to 'international carriage' as defined in Art 1 of the Warsaw Convention (an article which has survived amendment by the various supplementary instruments, and is reproduced in the Montreal Convention 1999, which may eventually displace Warsaw entirely). This carriage, according to Warsaw, must be between two States that have ratified and implemented Warsaw (with one exception).[3] It follows that if the two States in question have implemented the original Convention, but only one has implemented one or more of the amending instruments, the courts in both will apply the original Convention, that is, they will apply the lowest common denominator version of Warsaw.

If one of them has not applied the Convention, then the air carriage is not between two States which are party to Warsaw. Accordingly, this carriage is not international carriage as defined by Art 1, for the purpose of attracting the Warsaw Convention's operation. Thus, Warsaw will not apply. Instead the law of the contract will apply (that is, the relevant domestic law of the State with jurisdiction).

Other international treaties also deal with international aviation. For example, the Chicago Convention on International Civil Aviation 1944, and supplementary treaties, deals with the regulation of international air space for civil purposes, and related matters. It will not be examined, as it is not directly relevant to the international transportation of goods.

The Warsaw Convention sought to achieve two broad objectives. The first was to secure international uniformity in respect of key rules governing the carriage of goods and passengers and their baggage. This chapter deals with those articles in the Convention relating to the transportation of goods in international trade. The quest for uniformity has been stymied considerably, by the proliferation of subsequent treaties which, if adopted by a given State or States, function to amend the original treaty. Many combinations of the Warsaw treaty and the amending treaties have been adopted by various States, with the result that there are, in effect, numerous Warsaw regimes. Clearly, the rules governing these topics have been ripe for a general reformulation, with a view to again securing a consistent common international regime governing them. The Montreal Convention of 1999 reformulated these rules, and in time, depending upon the extent of its adoption, it will install a uniform regime. As noted, it came into operation in late 2003, but many countries have yet to ratify it.

The second objective of Warsaw was to limit the liability of carriers for the loss of or damage to goods, the injury or death of passengers, and the loss or damage of their baggage. The Convention was adopted at a time when the civil aviation industry was much less safe, and a failure to enact limits on liability, both in terms of the substantive rules and monetary limits on compensation, may well have stifled its development. If there is a criticism of the current monetary limits on damages, it is that they are far too low, that is, they unduly favour the airlines over their customers. Further, given the dramatic improvements in the safety of airline operations, it may be argued that this rationale for Warsaw – limiting the liability of air carriers to promote the development of civil aviation – is no longer valid.

---

3   Ie, in the unusual case where the carriage is between two places in the territory of the one State which has ratified Warsaw, but involving an agreed stopping place within another State, whether or not the latter has acceded to Warsaw. This also qualifies as 'international carriage' for Warsaw, so that the treaty will apply to the carriage.

The Warsaw Convention (as amended by Hague), in its application to the international transport of goods, focuses on the concept of 'international carriage' (as a basis for delimiting the scope of its operation), air waybills, the liability of carriers and limits on this liability (in essence the carrier is deemed liable for loss of or damage to goods, although certain defences are permitted, and monetary claims are capped), and certain aspects of the legal position of the consignor and consignee.

The Warsaw Convention

The Warsaw Convention applies to 'international carriage'

The Warsaw Convention applies to 'all international carriage of persons, baggage or cargo performed by aircraft for reward'. It also applies to the gratuitous air transport performed by an air transport undertaking (Art 1(1)).

The concept of 'international carriage' is defined in Art 1(2). First, carriage is international if the place of departure and of destination are each in a separate Contracting State (whether or not there has been a break in carriage). So, for example, the transport of goods from Sydney to Auckland would fall within Warsaw. Carriage from a Contracting to a non-Contracting State would not qualify. Secondly, carriage is international if the place of departure and destination are within the same Contracting State, provided that there is an agreed stopping place within another State, whether or not the latter is a Contracting State. (Again, this is so whether or not there has been a break in carriage.) Thus, carriage from Seattle to Chicago via Calgary would be international. Carriage in other circumstances is not within Warsaw.

Carriage by successive carriers is deemed, for present purposes, to be one undivided carriage if it has been regarded by the parties as a single operation, whether the contract is one or a series of contracts, and does not cease to be international merely because one contract or a series is to be performed within the one State (para (2)). Where carriage is multi-model, the Convention only applies to the carriage by air, provided this carriage satisfies the tests of internationality delineated in Art 1 (Art 31).

Air waybills

A key element in the Warsaw regime is the air waybill. The air waybill is not mandatory in every case under Warsaw, but one must be produced in defined cases. If there is none, or if the air waybill is defective or lost, the validity of the contract of carriage is unaffected, and Warsaw will still apply in situations where its operation is not contingent upon there being an air waybill, but not otherwise (see Art 5(1)). In particular, if there is no bill, the carrier will not be able to rely upon the provisions in the Convention limiting its liability (Art 9).

The air waybill will be made out by the consignor of the goods. The consignor must make out and hand over to the carrier a bill, if the carrier requires this. Conversely, the consignor has the right to require the carrier to accept an air waybill. Thus, either party can stipulate its creation and use (Art 5(1)).

The air waybill is to be made out in three parts by the consignor and handed over with the cargo. The first part is to be marked 'for the carrier' and signed by the consignor. The second part is to be marked 'for the consignee' and signed by both consignor and carrier and is to accompany the cargo. The third part is to be signed by the carrier and handed to the consignor after the cargo has been accepted (Art 6(1)). The bill then will document the carriage process through to delivery.

The bill must contain certain matters, including places of departure and destination, and any agreed stopping place, which demonstrate the international character of the carriage (as defined in Art 1). It is also to contain a notice to the consignor as to the potential applicability of the Warsaw Convention and its limitation, in most cases, of the carrier's liability (Art 8).

The nature of the air waybill is not defined in the treaty. It may be viewed broadly as an air transport document which has certain features as stipulated by the treaty, which bear upon the legal rights and liabilities of the parties to the carriage of goods. It documents the stages in the carriage.[4]

Its role is documenting the contract of carriage (where, as in most cases the carriage is for reward) and its performance is apparent from Arts 6 and 7. Further, it is *prima facie* evidence of the conclusion of the contract of carriage, of receipt of the cargo, and of the conditions of carriage. Statements in the bill relating to the weight, dimensions, etc, of the cargo are *prima facie* evidence of facts stated, although certain other statements are not evidence (see Art 11). It must be accompanied by relevant documents such as those needed to clear customs (Art 16).

In the absence of the air waybill, or in the absence of a warning in the bill as to the limitation of the carrier's liability as specified in Art 8, the carrier loses the benefit of the capping of liability for loss or damage to goods specified in Art 22(2) (Art 9). In short, the bill functions to warn the consignor of limits on its rights under Warsaw.

Subject to its contractual liabilities, the consignor has the right to withdraw the cargo at the airport of departure or destination, or redirect delivery, etc, provided that it does not exercise this right of disposition in such a way as to prejudice the carrier or other consignors, and must pay any expenses associated with exercising this right. If it becomes impossible to carry out the orders of the consignor, the carrier must inform it promptly. If the carrier acts on these instructions without requiring the production of that part of the bill delivered to the consignor, the carrier will be liable for any loss thereby caused to the person in lawful possession of this part (although the carrier's right of recovery against the consignor is not prejudiced). The consignor loses the right of disposition where the consignee's rights begin, except where the latter refuses to accept delivery or cannot be communicated with (Art 12).

The carrier is to give notice to the consignee of the arrival of the cargo. The consignee can then require the carrier to hand over the bill and cargo (subject to payment of any charges due). The consignor can take legal action under the contract of

---

4   One description of the air waybill is that it is 'a document which is made out by the consignor, or on his behalf, and which is evincive of the air transport contract established between the consignor and the carrier and according to which transportation must be performed on the carriers' routes. It is also effectively a standard form contract, because the customer cannot in reality negotiate its terms. The document justifies the right of disposition, and can be used as a transport invoice since the costs, expenses and incidental charges are clearly marked. It is also used as a customs declaration when other documents are not required. It may serve as an insurance policy when the consignor wants additional insurance': see *Air Canada v Demond* (1990) 96 NSW (2d) 256 at 259, *per* Palmeter CJCC, relying upon Magdelenat, J, Air Canada Regulations and Claims (1983).

carriage against the carrier if the goods do not arrive within seven days of the date when they should have arrived, or if the carrier admits the loss of the cargo (Art 13).[5]

The consignor's right of disposition (Art 12), and the consignee's rights under Art 14, do not affect the relations between consignor and consignee. However, these provisions can be varied by express provisions in the contract (Art 15).

The air waybill issued under Warsaw is not *per se* negotiable, but nothing in the treaty prevents the issue of such a bill (Art 15). Negotiability would have to be provided for by another (domestic) law.

The consignor must attach to the air waybill such documents as are necessary to conform with customs requirements and those of other authorities before the cargo can be delivered to the consignee, and is liable for any loss resulting from failure to do so (except where the carrier is liable for the problem). The carrier can take these documents at face value and is not required to inquire into the correctness of facts asserted in these documents (Art 16).

Where the consignor of goods is not the owner (as where the consignor is a freight forwarder), and the owner is not named in the air waybill, the owner nonetheless can sue for damages for damage to goods during air carriage. The owner was entitled to sue in its own name and nothing in the Warsaw Convention precluded the owner from doing this.[6]

The unamended Warsaw Convention requires further details to be in the air waybill than does the amended Convention, including the name and address of the 'first carrier' (such as a freight forwarder) (unamended Convention Art 8(e)). It has been held in an Australian case dealing with the unamended Convention, and following US authority, that if the air waybill in substance complies with Warsaw, it will be valid and thus the carrier will be able to avail itself of the cap on liability, that is, no particular wording is needed for an air waybill to be valid.[7] These decisions are also relevant to the construction of the amended Convention, in respect of its own (more limited) stipulations as to what must appear in an air waybill (see Art 8 in conjunction with Art 9, which precludes the carrier from relying on the Convention to cap damages for mishaps involving cargo in a case where the air waybill has not been made out).

The carrier's liability

The carrier is presumptively liable for damage to cargo or baggage. This is provided for in Art 18, which provides for liability for the loss of or damage to any registered

---

5   The rights given by Arts 12 and 13 can be enforced by the consignor and consignee each in their own name, whether acting in their own interests or those of another, provided that either carries out any contractual obligations: Art 14.

6   *Gatewhite Ltd v Iberia Lineas Aereas de Espana SA* [1990] 1 QB 326 at 334 (Gatehouse J).

7   *Emery Air Freight Corporation v Merck Sharpe and Dohme (Aust) Pty Ltd* [1999] NSWCA 415 at 419, 431(17 November 1999), a majority decision of the Supreme Court of New South Wales, dealing with a dispute between an Australian and US parties (unreported – available at www.austlii.edu.au). It had been alleged that the bill did not contain identification of the place of departure, or agreed stopping place, and name and address of the first carrier (here, a freight forwarder), as required by Art 8(b), (c) and (e). The court by majority held that the bill did identify the place of departure, that the agreed stopping place could be identified from readily available timetables, and that where a freight forwarder contracts as the principal and states its name and address on the bill, is to be treated as having identified itself as the 'first carrier' – at 10ff, 33.

baggage or cargo if this took place during the carriage by air. 'Carriage by air' denotes the period when the cargo 'was in charge of' the carrier, whether at an airport or on board an aircraft (or where the landing was outside an airport, in any place whatsoever).

That cargo can still be 'during air carriage' although it is on the ground, having regard to the extended concept of air carriage provided for in Art18, is illustrated in a case where the airline was made liable for damage to the goods while they were on pallets on the tarmac awaiting loading.[8] In this case, the air carrier was 'in charge' of the cargo, in that it had physical possession of the cargo (the means of physical control coupled with an intent to exercise that control). Cargo stolen in the course of a robbery which was in the import cargo warehouse at an airport while awaiting customs clearance, was determined in an English case still to be in the charge of the carrier, and thus stolen 'during air carriage'.[9]

Where Art 18 is relied upon to recover damages on account of the destruction of the cargo, the claimant must point to some causative event other than destruction *per se*, for which the airline can be made liable. Thus, the mere fact that a cargo of fruit perishes during air carriage does not make the airline presumptively liable. This was the holding in an English case where there was no undue delay on the part of the airline. Delivery of the goods in damaged condition, after they have been loaded in good condition, clearly imposed a burden on the carrier, and the carrier would be liable provided that the damage was consistent with their being some causative event. But if there is no such event apparent on the evidence, there is no basis for imposing liability upon the carrier. Evidence established that mould inherent in the fruit had been a big factor in its deterioration, and that further, being an organic cargo, it would have been best if it had been refrigerated (the contract did not contemplate that it would be).[10]

The carrier is also liable for loss resulting from delay in the carriage by air (Art 19). Again, liability is presumed.

This period of carriage by air does not extend to any carriage by another mode performed outside the airport, except where the carriage takes place in the performance of the contract for air transport for the purpose of loading, delivery or transhipment. In this latter case, the carrier's liability is presumed (Art 18(3)). To illustrate, if the carrier hands over the cargo at the airport to an independent contractor retained by the consignor, transport thereafter will not be a 'carriage by air' and thus the carrier will not incur liability for any subsequent damage. On the other hand, if a carrier undertakes to transport the goods by air from an airport in one State to an airport in another State, and it offloads the cargo at an airport in the second State and completes the transport by road to the designated airport of delivery within this State, the second road stage of the carriage will be part of the carriage by air.[11]

---

8   *SS Pharmaceutical Co Ltd v Qantas Airways Ltd* (1988) 22 NSWLR 734.
9   *Thomas Cook Group Ltd v Air Malta Co Ltd* [1997] 2 Lloyd's Law Rep 399. See the parallel case of *Swiss Bank Corporation v Brink's MAT Ltd* [1986] 2 Lloyd's Rep 79.
10 *Winchester Fruit Ltd v American Airlines Inc* [2002] 2 Lloyd's Law Rep 265 at 272ff.
11 *Hill & Delamain (Hong Kong) Ltd v Manobar Gangaram Ahuja* [1994] 1 HKLR 353 (the carrier chose to fly into an airport in the State where the cargo was to be delivered, and to transport the cargo from that airport to the nearby airport where delivery was to be made).

The liability of the carrier for the loss, destruction of or damage to goods, or delay in delivery, is presumed by the Convention. Thus, the party claimant need prove no more than the foundation facts – no fault needs to be proven on the part of the carrier. However, the carrier has certain defences, the onus of proof of which will be upon it.

The carrier is not liable if it can prove that it took all necessary measures to avoid the damage or that it was impossible to take such measures (Art 20). Likewise, if the carrier can prove that the injured party negligently caused or contributed to its own loss, the court may relieve the carrier from liability or reduce this liability (that is, by reducing damages) (Art 21).

Where a person who is not the agent of the consignee, falsely represents to the carrier that it is and supplies the air waybill number and the carrier negligently hands the cargo over to this party, the carrier is liable to compensate the consignee.[12]

Capping the carrier's liability

In the event that the carrier is found to be liable in damages, the Convention operates to impose a monetary limit on these damages. Damages are limited to two hundred and fifty francs per kilogram of cargo (Art 22(2)(a)). 'Franc' is given a defined meaning.[13]

If damages are capped they can be derisory, and far below the actual loss. For example, in a 1999 Australian case the cap would have contained damages to AU$12,000, although the actual loss was assessed at $375,000.[14]

This limit does not apply when the consignor, at the time of handing over the cargo, has made a special declaration of interest in delivery at destination, nominating a monetary value, and if necessary has paid an additional sum for carriage. If the carrier accepts transportation on these terms, it is liable to pay the declared sum (provided it does not exceed the actual loss)[15] (Art 22(2)(a)). In effect, the consignor will be paying insurance to enjoy a higher limit (the alternative is to independently insure the goods). In practice, airlines may undertake in a standard form contract to pay an amount greater than the Warsaw cap in a case where a special declaration has not been made. (Article 23 envisages that such a contractual term will be binding on the airline.)

The court can in addition to damages award the costs of litigation (unless the airline agreed within six months of the loss, to pay an amount at least equal to the damages awarded) (Art 22(4)).

A contractual provision which tends to relieve the carrier of liability or to fix a lower limit than that specified in the Convention is null and void, but this provision is

---

12 *Air Canada v Demond* (1999) 96 NSW (2d) 256, where the airline succeeded in recovering the amount paid to the consignee, from the party which had induced it to hand over the cargo.

13 A franc is a currency unit consisting of 65.5 milligrams of gold of millesimal fineness 900. The sum thus derived is to be converted into national currencies in round figures. This franc is also known as a poincare franc.

14 *Emery Air Freight Corporation v Merck Sharpe and Dohme (Aust) Pty Ltd, op cit.*

15 See *Williams Dental Co Ltd v Air Express International* 824 F Supp 435 (1993) United States District Court (SDNY), for an instance where the declared value was above the market value, with the result that damages were limited to market value.

to be severed from the contract and does not nullify its whole. This prohibition on limitation clauses does not apply to those governing loss or damage resulting from an inherent quality defect in the cargo (Art 23).

The caps on damages specified in Art 22 do not apply if the claimant can prove that the damage resulted from an act or omission of the carrier (or its servant or agent acting within the scope of employment) done with intent to cause damage, or recklessly and with knowledge that damage would probably result (Art 25). These tests are demanding. The claimant must prove actual intention, that is, that the actor had the purpose of bringing out the defined harm. Alternatively, it must be proven that the actor had subjective recklessness and further averted to the probability that damage would result. An event may be said to be probable if there is a substantial chance of it happening.

An airline can be found to have acted recklessly in relation to rain damage to cargo sitting on pallets on the tarmac in boxes, with an umbrella symbol indicating the need to protect them from water, on the basis that recklessness can be inferred on the part of its employees, although their identities cannot be ascertained.[16] Article 25 in its terms requires that this recklessness be subjective, something which has been confirmed in the cases.[17]

Where the employee of an airline steals the cargo, can the airline evade the cap pursuant to Art 22 on the basis that it was not acting with intent to cause damage, or recklessly, because the servant was not acting in the scope of employment? A case decided on a like provision in the unamended Warsaw Convention (which referred to 'wilful misconduct', which has since been interpreted to mean intentionally or recklessly) decided that the employee was acting in the scope of employment in this situation. This was because 'it was clearly part of his duty to take reasonable care of the package during the operation of loading and stowing it on the aircraft'.[18]

The servants or agents of a carrier, if sought to be made personally liable, likewise can avail themselves of the monetary caps specified in Art 22, except where it is proven that they acted intentionally or recklessly in relation to the damage (Art 25A).

Other provisions relevant to the carrier's liability

Where a person takes delivery of the cargo, absence of complaint is *prima facie* evidence that the cargo has been delivered in good condition and in accordance with the document of carriage. The person who has a complaint must complain to the carrier by certain timelines (Art 26).

An action for damages must be brought, at the option of the plaintiff, in a Contracting State. Subject to this, the action must be brought either in the jurisdiction where the carrier is ordinarily resident or has its principal place of business, or has an office where the contract was made. Alternatively, the action can be brought at the place of destination (Art 28). A limitation provision applies – the action must be

---

16 *SS Pharmaceutical Co Ltd v Qantas Airways Ltd* (1988) 22 NSWLR 734 at 750.

17 *Ibid* at 749–50, *per* Rogers CJ Comm D, citing *Goldman v Thai Airways International Ltd* [1983] 1 WLR 1186, and noting that French courts have held that objective recklessness suffices.

18 *Rustenburg Platinum Mines Ltd v South African Airways* [1977] 1 Lloyd's Rep 564 at 576 (Ackner J).

brought within two years from the date or scheduled date of arrival at the destination, or from the date when the carriage stopped (Art 29).

Where the carriage is performed by successive carriers and is international for the purposes of the Convention (see Art 1), each carrier is bound by the Convention and is deemed to be a party to the contract in respect of its segment of the carriage (Art 30).

The Guadalajara Convention

The Guadalajara Convention, or more fully the Convention Supplementary to the Warsaw Convention for the Unification of Certain Rules Relating to International Carriage by Air Performed by a Person other than the Contracting Carrier, was signed at Guadalajara in 1961. It is one of a number of supplementary treaties which, if adopted by a State that is party to the Warsaw Convention, operates in its jurisdiction in effect to amend the Convention. Technically, it does not undertake an amendment of the Warsaw text; rather, Guadalajara is to be read alongside Warsaw, amplifying (and where there is a clash, overriding) the Warsaw Convention.

The Guadalajara Convention sets out its objective in its Preamble. The States signatory to the Warsaw Convention note that the latter does not contain particular rules relating to international carriage by air, performed by a person who is not a party to the agreement for carriage, and that it is desirable to formulate such rules. Accordingly, the Guadalajara Convention formulates rules. It deals, for example, with the situation where the consigning manufacturer contracts with a freight company to transport goods by air to another country, and the freight company then contracts with an airline to transport the goods to the required destination. The airline is not party to the original contract for carriage. For certain purposes, the 1961 treaty assimilates it to the position of the freight company, in so far as rights and liabilities under Warsaw are concerned.

The Guadalajara treaty deals with both goods and passenger transport, as does Warsaw. In the analysis below, the focus will be solely on the 1961 treaty's operation in relation to the transport of cargo.

Guadalajara draws a distinction between the contracting carrier, who as principal, makes an agreement for carriage governed by the Warsaw Convention with a consignor or with a person acting on its behalf (in the above example, the freight forwarder), and the actual carrier (in the above example, the airline company). The latter is a person other than the contracting carrier, who by virtue of authority from the contracting carrier, performs the whole or part of the carriage contemplated, but who is not with respect to such part a successive carrier within the meaning of the Warsaw Convention.[19] Such authority is presumed in the absence of proof to the contrary (Art I) [20].

---

19 See the Warsaw Convention, Arts 1 and 31. Article 1(3) deems carriage to be performed by several successive carriers to be one undivided carriage if the parties have regarded it as a single operation, whether agreed upon by one contract or a succession of contracts. Note also Art 30, providing that in the case of carriage to be performed by various successive carriers, each carrier who accepts cargo is subject to the Convention and deemed to be one of the parties to the contract of carriage in so far as the contract deals with that part of the carriage performed under its supervision.

20 Thus, the party who wishes to establish that there was no such authority has the burden of proving this, once the foundation facts giving rise to the presumption of authority have been established.

If the actual carrier performs the whole or part of the carriage, both it and the contracting carrier are subject to the Warsaw Convention, except as otherwise provided in Guadalajara. The contracting carrier is liable for the whole of the carriage, and the actual carrier for that segment of the carriage performed by it (Art II).

The contracting carrier is further liable for the acts of the actual carrier and its servants and agents done within the scope of employment. Paralleling this vicarious liability, the actual carrier is liable for the acts of the contracting carrier and its servants and agents acting within the scope of employment (Art III).

In accordance with the assimilation of the position of the actual carrier to that of the contract carrier, the actual carrier, if found to be liable for the loss of or damage to the goods, has the benefit of the same caps on damages provided for in Art 22 of the Warsaw Convention. The actual carrier cannot be made liable for damages in excess of the caps, where a consignor has made a special declaration of value, unless the actual carrier has agreed to this (that is, to carry the goods on this basis) (Art III(2)).

A complaint made regarding the loss of or damage to goods consigned under Warsaw will have the same effect whether made to the contracting or actual carrier (Art IV). A servant or agent of an actual carrier shall, if he proves that he acted in the scope of employment, be able to invoke the limits on liability applicable to his employer, except where the Warsaw Convention prevents this (Art V).

Where the loss or damage occurs in the actual carriage, the total amount of damages recoverable from the actual and contracting carriers and their servants and agents cannot exceed the highest amount that could be awarded against either (Art VI). It follows that the parties can, after the loss or damage comes to light, arrive at an agreement setting aside Warsaw-Guadalajara in respect of these matters.

The plaintiff has the option of bringing its action against either carrier or against both together or separately. If only one is sued, it can join the other carrier in proceedings as a co-defendant (Art VII).

Actions must be brought in a jurisdiction permitted by Art 28 of the Warsaw Convention, or in a court having jurisdiction at a place where the actual carrier is ordinarily resident or has its principal place of business (Art VIII).

Contractual provisions seeking to relieve either carrier of liability under the Guadalajara Convention (in conjunction with Warsaw), or to fix a lower limit than that prescribed, are null and void, but such nullity does not nullify the entire agreement. This provision relating to limitation clauses does not affect the validity of clauses directed to limit or sterilise liability for loss or damage arising from the inherent defect in the quality of the cargo, that is, the parties can protect themselves against this liability. Finally, any contractual provision entered into before the damage occurred, seeking to set aside the operation of the Convention in relation to matters of jurisdiction or applicable law is null and void (Art IX).[21]

The Montreal Additional Protocol 1975

The Montreal Additional Protocol of 1975, if adopted by a given State, makes certain amendments to the Warsaw Convention. The Warsaw Convention, as amended,

---

21   Except that in contracts to carry cargo, private arbitration clauses are permitted.

provides in Art 5 for the delivery of an air waybill (as does the unamended Convention). It further provides, however, that any other means that would preserve a record of the carriage to be performed may, with the consent of the consignor, be substituted for the delivery of an air waybill. It provides that, if these alternative means are used, the carrier must, if requested by the consignor, deliver to the consignor a receipt for the cargo permitting identification of the consignment and access to the information contained in the record preserved by such other means. Where it is impossible to use at points of transit and destination these other means of recording the transaction, Art 22 does not permit the carrier to refuse to accept the cargo for carriage (para (3)).

This amendment sanctions, *inter alia*, electronic records of carriage.

The Convention as amended by Montreal No 4, also substitutes the original 250 franc limit on claims for loss, etc, of cargo, with a monetary limit of 17 Special Drawing Rights (SDRs) converted into the national currency of the State having jurisdiction. These amendments have been reproduced in the Montreal Convention of 1999, and are discussed below.

The Montreal Convention 1999

The Montreal Convention for the Unification of Certain Rules for International Carriage by Air 1999, is intended to replace the Warsaw Convention, as amended by the Hague Protocol of 1955 and supplemented by the Guadalajara Convention of 1961. The framers of the Montreal Convention recognised that the original purpose of the Warsaw Convention, to unify certain rules relating to international air transport of passengers, baggage and cargo, had been to an extent defeated by the large number of subsequent amending or supplementary treaties, which in various combinations had been adopted by the various States. The result has been a range of varying Warsaw-based regimes. Montreal is intended to replace all of them. One of the expressed goals in the Preamble to Montreal 1999, is to 'modernise and consolidate the Warsaw Convention and related instruments'. It reproduces much of the original text, as amended (in particular) by The Hague Protocol of 1955 and supplemented by the Guadalajara Convention. To the extent that Warsaw States ratify the Montreal Convention and implement its terms in their domestic law, it will gradually displace the latter as the main source of rules on international air transport. The Convention came into operation on 4 November 2003, after the last of the required minimum 30 countries ratified it.

Montreal 1999 deals with the transportation of passengers, baggage and cargo. Only its role in respect of cargo is considered below.

The Montreal Convention 1999 applies to 'international carriage'

The Montreal Convention 1999 applies to the 'international carriage' of cargo (and passengers and goods) (Art 1). The relevant provision delineating 'international carriage', and therefore the scope of the Convention, is identical to that in the Warsaw Convention (see above, 'The Warsaw Convention applies to "international carriage"').

Air waybills

Article 4 of Montreal 1999 specifies that in respect of cargo, an air waybill shall be delivered. Unlike Warsaw, it provides in the alternative that any other means that preserves a record of the carriage to be performed may be substituted for the delivery of an air waybill. In the latter case, the consignor must deliver to the consignor a cargo receipt identifying the consignment and access to the information contained in this alternate record. (Warsaw makes production of an airway bill mandatory where the carrier requires it, and also provides that the carrier must accept one if produced by the consignor.)

As is the case in Warsaw (see 'The Warsaw Convention – Air waybills' above), the non-supply of an air waybill, or non-conformity with provisions in the Convention governing its contents, does not affect the validity or existence of the contract of carriage, which remains subject to the rules of the Convention including those relating to limitation of liability (Art 9).

The provisions governing the contents of the air waybill parallel those in Warsaw, although there are slight differences. The consignor is to make out the bill in three parts. The obligations on each party in relation to their part are the same as specified by Warsaw (see Montreal, Art 7; Warsaw, Art 6).

As in the case of Warsaw, the nature of the air waybill is not defined in Montreal 1999. Again, it may be viewed as an air transport document which has certain features stipulated by the Convention, which bear upon the legal rights and liabilities of the parties to the carriage of goods.

As in the case of Warsaw, the consignor is required, if necessary, to meet the formalities of customs and like authorities (Art 16, which is in substance the same as Warsaw, Art 16).

The consignor is responsible for the correctness of the particulars and statements relating to the cargo inserted in the air waybill or like transportation record, and must indemnify the carrier in respect of loss suffered because of error in this regard (Art 10, which is similar to Art 10 of Warsaw, except that the latter does not refer to an alternative documentary record, as this is not part of the Warsaw regime). The carrier in turn must indemnify the consignor against loss resulting from any error inserted in the alternative transport record by it (Art 10(3)).

Article 11 parallels Art 11 of Warsaw, in providing that the air waybill (and in the case of Montreal) 'or cargo receipt' is *prima facie* evidence of the conclusion of the contract, of the acceptance of the cargo and of the condition of carriage mentioned therein. Likewise, any statements in the bill or cargo receipt relating to other specified matters such as weight and dimensions of the cargo are *prima facie* evidence; while those relating to quality, volume and condition are not evidence against the carrier except where they have been checked in the presence of the consignor or relate to the apparent condition of the cargo (Art 11(2)).

As in Warsaw, the Montreal Convention provides that the consignor has a right of disposition of cargo, subject to certain qualifications, such as by redirecting delivery (Art 12, paralleling Art 12 of the Warsaw Convention).

Articles 13–16 of Montreal parallel Arts 14–16 of Warsaw, dealing with the delivery of cargo, the enforcement of the rights of the consignor and consignee, the relations of consignor and consignee or mutual relations of third parties, and the formalities of the customs and like authorities.

The carrier's liability

The carrier is presumptively liable for the destruction, or loss of or damage to, the cargo provided that the event which caused this loss took place during the 'carriage by air' (Art 18(1), paralleling Art 18 of Warsaw).

The carrier is not liable if it proves that the harm was caused by an inherent defect of quality in the cargo, defective packing by a person other than the carrier or a delegate, or an act of war or armed conflict (Art 18(2)).

The definition of the term 'carriage by air' for the purpose of imposing liability upon the carrier for loss, etc, of the cargo, parallels Warsaw to the extent that this consists of the period during which the cargo is 'in the charge of the carrier' (Art 18(3), which is similar to Warsaw, Art 18(2) – see above, 'The Warsaw Convention – The carrier's liability'). Montreal also parallels Warsaw in providing that the period of carriage by air does not extend to any carriage by air or otherwise performed outside an airport, except where this carriage takes place in the performance of the contract of carriage by air for the purpose of loading, delivery or transhipment. In this latter case, it is presumed that the harm resulted from an event during carriage by air (Art 18(4) paralleling Warsaw, Art 18(2)).

However, Montreal 1999 goes further than Warsaw at this point, in adding that if the carrier, without the consignor's consent, substitutes carriage by another mode of transport (which will be land or sea) for the whole or part of a carriage intended by the agreement between the parties to be a carriage by air, such carriage by another mode is deemed to be within the period of carriage by air (Art 18A(4)). It follows that even if the consignor has not consented to the substitution (and indeed, may have no knowledge of it), it is still affected by the caps on the carrier's liability imposed by Montreal.[22]

Montreal 1999 imposes presumptive liability upon the carrier for damage resulting from delay in delivery, but additionally provides a defence of proof by the carrier that it took all reasonable steps to avoid the damage or that it was impossible to take such measures (Art 19).

As in the case of Warsaw, Montreal provides a defence to the carrier consisting of proof that the plaintiff by its own negligence contributed to the loss suffered – Montreal additionally provides a like defence in a case where the plaintiff's other wrongful act or omission has contributed to the loss. This contribution may require the court to wholly or partially exonerate the carrier (Art 20).

Capping the carrier's liability

The Montreal Convention caps the damages otherwise payable by the carrier pursuant to the Convention. The capping regime is similar but not identical to the Warsaw regime (for the latter, see 'The Warsaw Convention – Capping the carrier's liability' above).

---

22 See the comment by Chuah, J, *Law of International Trade*, 2nd edn, 2001, London: Sweet & Maxwell, p 30. Of course, the Warsaw-Montreal type regime is susceptible to the criticism that the imposition of caps on the carrier's liability is outmoded, given that air travel is now infinitely safer than it was in the 1920s.

Where damages for loss, destruction, damage or delay in respect of cargo are concerned, the carrier's liability is limited to 17 SDRs per kilogram, unless the consignor has made at the time the package is handed over to the carrier, a special declaration of interest in delivery at destination nominating a value for the cargo, and has paid any supplementary sum required. The carrier in this case will have to pay the agreed sum, unless it proves that the damage actually suffered is less (Art 22(3)). This provision parallels the Warsaw figure, except that the monetary unit specified for each kilogram differs.

SDRs are defined in Art 23. The SDR referred to is the SDR as defined by the International Monetary Fund (IMF). Where a court orders damages, conversion of the SDR into the relevant national currency is to be made according to the value of such currencies in terms of the SDR at the date of judgment. The value of the currency is to be determined in accordance with the method of valuation applied by the IMF for its operations and transactions. Where a State party is not a member of the IMF, the value of its national currency shall be calculated in a manner determined by that State.

Nevertheless, those States which are not members of the Fund can adhere to the old Warsaw formula (250 monetary units per kilogram, with each unit corresponding to 65.5 milligrams of gold of millesimal fineness 900, which sums may be converted into the national currency according to the law of the State concerned) (Art 23(2)).

Provision is made for the five yearly review of the monetary limits (Art 24).

The carrier loses the benefit of capping if the plaintiff proves that the damage resulted from an act or omission of the carrier or its delegates done with intent to cause damage, or recklessly and with knowledge that such damage would probably result. In the case of a delegate, it must be proven that they were acting within the scope of employment (Art 22(5), paralleling Warsaw, Art 25). In addition to damages, the court can award the costs of litigation (Art 22(6), similar to Warsaw, Art 22(4)).

Other provisions relevant to the carrier's liability

A carrier can contract for higher limits of liability than those provided by the Convention, or for no limits whatsoever (Art 25). Provisions seeking to relieve the carrier of liability or to set a lower limit than that prescribed by the Convention are null and void (Art 26). The carrier can refuse to contract for carriage, or waive defences under the Convention, or to stipulate contractual terms not in conflict with the Convention (Art 27).

If a servant or agent is liable under the Convention, they can if they prove that they acted within the scope of employment, avail themselves of the conditions and liability limits that the carrier can invoke under the Convention (Art 30).

Receipt of cargo without complaint is *prima facie* evidence of delivery in good condition and in accordance with the document of carriage or other record. Complaint must be made promptly after discovery of damage as specified (Art 31).

The provision relating to the jurisdiction for legal actions under the Convention is similar to that in Warsaw (Montreal, Art 32; Warsaw, Art 28, save that the former refers to the place of domicile of the carrier, and the latter to its place of residence).

The parties to the contract of carriage can stipulate that any dispute arising from it shall be submitted to arbitration (Art 34). A time limitation of two years is imposed upon the bringing of actions for damages (Art 35).

Where the carriage is performed by successive carriers and is international for the purposes of the Convention (see Art 1), each carrier is bound by the Convention and is deemed to be party to the contract in respect of its segment of carriage (Art 30, paralleling Art 30 of the Warsaw Convention). In the case of cargo, the consignor will have a right of action against the first carrier, and the consignee a right of action against the last carrier, and further, each may take action against the carrier that performed the carriage during which the loss was suffered. These carriers are jointly and severally liable (Art 36(3)).

Where the carriage is partly performed by air and partly by another mode, the provisions of the Convention apply to the air segment only, subject to Art 18(4) (Art 38, which is similar to Warsaw, Art 31).

Any contract or contractual clause entered into before the damage occurred, by which the parties purport to set aside the operation of the Convention in respect of the applicable law or stipulation as to jurisdiction, are null and void (Art 49). The parties, that is, are bound by the Convention, but can after the damage has occurred, voluntarily agree to decide their dispute by reference to another law, or try it in a jurisdiction other than one permitted by the Convention.

The position of the actual carrier which is not party to the contract of carriage with the consignor

The Montreal Convention in substance incorporates (in Arts 38–48) the provisions of the Guadalajara Convention of 1961, which deals with the liability of the person who performs the whole or part of an international carriage by air, without being a party to the contract for this carriage. The differences are slight.[23] The provisions in both instruments draw a distinction between this person (the 'actual carrier') and the 'contracting carrier'. For example, a freight company may be the contractor, but retain an airline company to carry the goods on its behalf. In essence, these regimes assimilate the position of the actual carrier to that of the contract carrier, for the purpose of the Convention in question. Thus the actual carrier has the burdens of the contracting carrier, but also the benefits (such as the capping of liability and defences to liability). This regime also deals with the position of the delegates of each class of carrier, and rights and liabilities as between each carrier. The Guadalajara regime is discussed above at 'The Guadalajara Convention'.

INTERNATIONAL CARRIAGE OF GOODS BY RAIL

Overview

Aspects of the international carriage of goods by rail are regulated by the Convention Concerning International Carriage of Goods by Rail, known by the acronym of COTIF.[24] The Convention was agreed upon at Berne in 1980 and came into effect in

---

23   They are textual rather than substantive.
24   The acronym is from the French title of the Convention, ie, Convention relative aux transports internationaux ferroviares.

1985. Its Member States are predominantly European, but include members from the Middle East and Africa. COTIF includes (in Appendix B) the Uniform Rules Concerning the Contract for International Carriage of Goods by Rail (CIM).[25] The latter rules were adopted as an independent Convention in 1980, which has since been abrogated in favour of Appendix B.

COTIF has to be implemented as part of domestic law, in order for the COTIF rules to be enforceable in the courts of a Member State.

COTIF deals with the carriage of passengers and luggage, as well as goods. The rules relating to the carriage of goods (those in CIM) will be the focus of the following commentary.

The Convention provides, in Arts 1ff, for the establishment of an intergovernmental organisation known as the Intergovernmental Organisation for International Carriage by Rail, or OTIF. The aim of the organisation is to establish a uniform system of law applicable to the carriage of passengers, luggage and goods in international through traffic between Member States, and to facilitate the application and development of this system.

Provision is made for OTIF organs, viz, the General Assembly, Administrative Committee, Revision Committee, Committee for the Carriage of Dangerous Goods, and Central Office for International Carriage by Rail. The Assembly consists of representatives of Member States. Provision is made for the arbitration of disputes between Members concerning COTIF.

Appendix A of COTIF contains the Uniform Rules for International Carriage of Passengers and Luggage by Rail (CIV). Appendix B, as noted, contains CIM dealing with the carriage of cargo.

International carriage of goods by rail – the CIM regime

International carriage by rail – when CIM applies

The CIM rules apply, broadly speaking, to the carriage of goods by international rail operations. More specifically, the rules apply to 'all consignments of goods for carriage under a through consignment note made out for a route over the territories of at least two States exclusively over lines of service included in the list provided for in Articles 3 and 10 [of COTIF] …' (Art 1(1)). The railway line, that is, must be one that is entered in a list maintained by the central office administering COTIF. Such lines may only be listed with the approval of the relevant Member States. Transit must be over the territory of at least two States, which is of course intrinsic to the concept of an international carriage.

The expression 'station' covers facilities other than railway stations, such as shipping ports (Art 2(1)).

Where a journey commences and sends in the one State, but transits the territory of another State *en route*, it is not within CIM where the lines or service over which the transit occurs are exclusively operated by the railway of the State of departure; or of

---

25 Convention internationale concernant le transport des merchandises.

the States or railways concerned have agreed not to regard such consignments as international (Art 2(1)).

Certain articles are not acceptable for carriage, including postal articles in a State where the postal authority has a monopoly (see Art 4). Carriage charges are subject to certain rules, such as that they must be duly published in each State, and they must be applied to all users on the same conditions (although there are certain exceptions here) (Art 6).

It is recognised that the CIM rules may not cover all aspects of dispute centring upon the international carriage of goods by rail. In the absence of relevant CIM rules, national law (viz, the domestic law of the State with jurisdiction) applies (Art 10).

The contract of carriage

The contract of carriage is deemed to come into existence when the forwarding railway has accepted the goods for carriage along with an assignment note (below) Acceptance is established by the stamping of the note (or other accounting machine entry on it) showing the date of acceptance. The note then becomes evidence of the making and content of the contract (Art 11).[26]

The consignment note; performance of the contract of carriage

The consignment note is the transport document, performing a role similar to that of a bill of lading or an air waybill. It is the responsibility of the consignor to present a note duly completed. The railway is to prescribe a standard form of note, which must include a duplicate for the consignor (Art 12). The note is to contain prescribed details, including the name of the destination station, the name and address of the consignee, the description of the goods, a detailed list of documents required by customs and like authorities,[27] and the name and address of the consignor (Art 13). The consignor may stipulate in the note the route to be followed (Art 14(1)).

The charges (including carriage, customs duties) are payable by the consignor or consignee, as prescribed by the rules. If the consignor is to pay all or part of the charges, this must be indicated on the consignment note by one of the prescribed phrases. Any charges which the consignor has not undertaken to pay are payable by the consignee, although such liability does not crystallise until the consignee has obtained possession of the consignment note (Art 15).

The consignment note may include a declaration of a special interest in delivery, with the value of the goods being stated. This will attract a higher charge calculated for the whole route, in accordance with the tariffs of the forwarding railway (Art 16). The purpose of this declaration of value is potentially to increase the amount of compensation for the loss of, or damage to, the goods otherwise payable under the

---

26 Note, however, para (4) – where the loading of the goods is the duty of the consignor, the details in the note relating to the mass of the goods or number of packages shall only be evidence against the railway when the detail in question has been verified by the latter and certified in the note.

27 The consignor must also attach to the consignment note the documents needed for the completion of formalities required by customs and other authorities before delivery of the goods: Art 25.

rules, in a case where the party making the interest is of the opinion that the cap imposed by the rules is lower than the value of the goods.

The consignor may make the goods subject to a cash on delivery payment not exceeding their value at the time of acceptance at the forwarding station. The railway is then obliged to collect this payment from the consignee prior to delivery, and is liable to pay compensation for the actual loss resulting from any default in this regard (Art 17).

The consignor is responsible for the correctness of particulars entered in the consignment note (Art 18).

Where the railway accepts goods for carriage, which goods show obvious signs of damage, it may require this condition to be entered on the note. The railway may also require appropriate packaging of the goods, where this is necessary, to protect them from damage (Art 19).

The loading of the goods at the forwarding station is the duty of the consignor or the railway, according to the provisions in force at this station, unless the rules or a special agreement between the parties in the consignment note provide otherwise. If the consignor is to load, it must comply with certain requirements, including the load limit (Art 20).

The railway has the right to verify that the consignment corresponds with the particulars recorded in the consignment note by the consignor and that provisions relating to the carriage have been complied with (Art 22).

Articles deal with such matters as ascertainment of weight and number of packages (Art 22), overloading (Art 23), and surcharges in defined cases, such as overloading (Art 25).

Customs and related formalities are to be completed by the railway or its agent (Art 26).

Provisions in the rules govern the transit period. This is as specified either by agreement between the railways involved in the carriage, or by the international tariffs applicable from the forwarding to the destination station. Such periods must not exceed those stipulated in the rules, such as that providing that, where a whole wagonload is concerned, the transit time must not exceed 24 hours for each 400 kilometres or fraction thereof (Art 27).

The railway is obliged to deliver the goods and the consignment note to the consignee at the destination station. In return, the railway is to be given a receipt and any amount chargeable against the consignee by the railway. The delivery can be at another place (such as a siding) where the provisions in force at the station or any agreement provide for this. After arrival at the station, the consignee can require the railway to deliver the goods to it. If the goods are lost or have not arrived after the required time, the consignee can assert in its own name any rights which it may have against the railway by reason of the contract of carriage. The consignee may refuse to accept the goods where an examination, for which he has asked to establish alleged loss or damage, has not been made (Art 29).

Modifying the contract of carriage

The rules permit the consignor to modify the contract after it has been formed (something not ordinarily permitted by contract law). The consignor is given the right to give orders, *inter alia*, for the goods to be withdrawn at the forwarding station, for the goods to be stopped in transit, for delivery to be delayed, for the goods to be delivered to a person other than the consignee shown on the consignment note, and for the goods to be delivered at a station other than the destination station shown on the note. The right to modify is lost where, *inter alia*, the consignee has taken possession of the note, or has accepted the goods (Art 30).

The consignee also can modify the contract. Where the consignor has not undertaken to pay the carriage charges in the country of destination, and has not inserted in the note, 'Consignee not authorised to give subsequent orders', the consignee may order, *inter alia*, that the goods be stopped in transit, or that delivery be delayed, or that they be delivered to a person other than the named consignee. The consignee loses this right to modify disposition of the goods where, *inter alia*, it has taken possession of the consignment note, or has accepted the goods. If the consignee orders delivery to another person, the latter cannot modify the contract of carriage (Art 32).

Circumstances preventing carriage or delivery

The carrier may, subject to certain conditions (such as asking for instructions if appropriate), modify the route, seeking further instructions where circumstances prevent carriage. Extra charges thus incurred are payable to the railway (Art 33).

If circumstances prevent delivery, the railway is to seek instructions from the consignor without delay. If the consignee refuses the goods, the consignor shall be entitled to give instructions even if it is unable to produce the duplicate of the consignment note (Art 34).

Responsibility and liability of the railway

The railway, which has accepted the goods for carriage, is liable for the carriage over the entire route up to delivery. Succeeding carriers, when they take over the goods, become party to the contract of carriage and assume the obligations imposed by it (Art 35).

There is a presumption of liability on the part of the carrier for the total or partial loss of, or damage to, the goods between the acceptance for carriage and the time of delivery, and for any loss flowing from the stipulated transit period being exceeded (Art 35). Accordingly, the railway is liable in damages unless it can prove[28] one of the defences provided for in the rules.

These defences include: that the loss resulted from fault on the part of the person entitled (such as the consignee), an order given by the person entitled (where there was no fault on the part of the railway), inherent vice of the goods (decay, etc), or circumstances which the railway could not have avoided, and the consequences of which it was unable to prevent. The railway is relieved where the loss arises from such special risk as carriage in an open wagon under the conditions applicable or under an agreement between the parties noted on the consignment note, or where it arises from inadequate packing, or defective loading by the consignor when the latter carries out

---

28   See Art 37 imposing the burden of proof.

loading pursuant to the applicable conditions or agreement referred to in the note, or from the nature of certain goods which renders them inherently liable to total or partial loss or damage, etc (Art 36).

The person entitled may, without furnishing further proof, consider the goods lost when they have not been delivered to the consignee or are not being held at its disposal after the expiry of 30 days from the expiry of the transit period (Art 39).

Provision is made for wastage in transit. For example, where the goods are of a type which are generally subject to wastage in transit by the sole fact that they are being carried, the railway is not liable for wastage of less than 2% of the mass for liquid goods or goods consigned in moist condition (Art 41).

The railway is not liable for losses occurring in rail-sea traffic, where it proves that the loss occurred during transit by sea because of, *inter alia*, the act, neglect or default on the part of the master or mariner of the ship. The States nominating the line for inclusion in the list of lines attracting the rules must have included a suitable note in these terms, allowing this provision to be invoked (Art 48).

The railway is liable for its servants and any other persons it employs to perform the carriage, except where the delegate makes out consignment notes, etc, which the railway is under no obligation to render (Art 50).

Where the person entitled (such as the consignee) accepts the goods, any claim against the railway arising from loss, damage or delay is extinguished. However, the right to claim is not lost in exceptional cases, such as where the loss was partial and this loss was ascertained before the goods were accepted; or the loss or damage was not apparent and was not ascertained until after acceptance, provided that the claimant thereafter acts promptly and fulfils certain requirements (Art 57).

Capping damages

Damages for the total or partial loss of goods are capped by Art 40. Damages are to be calculated by reference to the commodity exchange quotation (if applicable), or the current market price, or if there is no such quotation or price, then according to the normal value of goods of the same kind and quality at the time and place of acceptance for delivery. Whatever this sum may be, it must not exceed 17 units of account per kilogram of gross mass short.[29] The railway is also liable to refund such sums as carriage charges and customs duties, where it has received these (Art 40).

The equivalent cap applies where the goods are damaged. Where the railway is liable for damage to goods (as distinct from their total or partial loss), the railway must pay compensation equivalent to the percentage loss in value of the goods (to the exclusion of all other damages). This amount is to be calculated by applying to the value of the goods, as defined in Art 40, the percentage of loss in value noted at the place of destination. This compensation is not to exceed the amount payable in case of total loss (where the whole value of the consignment has been lost), or the amount which would have been payable for partial loss (where only part of the value of the

---

29 See Art 7. The units of account referred to are Special Drawing Rights as defined by the International Monetary Fund, converted into the relevant national currency (viz, that of the State with jurisdiction). Where a State is not a member of the IMF an alternative measure is provided for – the unit of account is three gold francs as defined.

consignment has been lost) (Art 42). In short, where the damage is not total, the railway must pay an appropriate part of the overall amount which would have been payable under Art 40.

Compensation for a delay in delivery is capped at four times the carriage charges (Art 43).

The railway cannot invoke the caps on damages provided in the preceding articles where it is proved by the claimant that the loss or damage resulted from an act or omission on the part of the railway, done with intent to cause such damage, or recklessly and with knowledge that such loss or damage will probably result (Art 44). As noted, the railway is liable for the acts of its delegates whom it employs to perform the carriage (Art 50).

Where the consignee or other person has made a declaration of interest in delivery, and has stated the value of the goods (and paid the applicable extra charge) pursuant to Art 16, this becomes the amount payable by way of compensation (or in the case of a loss falling short of total loss, the basis of the *pro rata* calculation of damages) (Art 46). In this case the damages caps do not apply.

Miscellaneous

Articles 52ff deal with procedural aspects of claims for compensation, and other matters. Claims must be within limitation periods specified in the rules (Art 58). Provision is made for the recovery of contributions from other railways by a railway that has paid compensation. For example, where a railway has compensated a claimant, but another railway has taken part in the carriage, and this latter railway has caused the loss, the latter is liable to pay the whole of the first railway's loss. Where there are succeeding carriers, and it cannot be established during which railway's carriage the loss occurred, the loss is to be equally apportioned among the carriers (Art 60).

INTERNATIONAL CARRIAGE OF GOODS BY ROAD

The Convention for the Contract for the International Carriage of Goods by Road, known as CMR,[30] was done at Geneva in 1956. It formulates uniform rules for the international carriage of goods by road. A number of European countries have ratified and implemented the Convention.

The Convention deals with a range of matters, including formation and performance of the contract of carriage, consignment notes, and the liability of the carrier and caps on this liability.

Any stipulation in the contract of carriage that derogates from the provision of the Convention is null and void, such as one shifting the burden of proof (Art 41).

---

30   Convention relative au contrat de transport international des merchandises par route.

International carriage by road

The Convention is expressed to apply to 'every contract for the carriage of goods by road in vehicles for reward'. The place of taking over the goods and the place designated for delivery, as specified in the contract, must be situated in two different countries, at least one of which is a Contracting State (that is, a State which has adopted the Convention). The vehicle in question is to be a motor vehicle. Certain carriages are excluded, such as that performed under an international postal convention (Art 1). Thus, provided the journey involves at least one Contracting State, it is within the Convention.

The Convention applies to the whole of the carriage even where part of it is by another mode, such as sea or rail, provided that the goods remain in the vehicle. However, if it is proved that any loss, damage or delay in delivery of the goods that occurs during the other transport mode was not caused by the road carrier, the Convention does not govern the liability of this carrier (Art 2).

In an English case, goods were carried by air from Singapore to Paris, and from Paris to the intended destination of Dublin, by road. They were stolen during the road journey. The sender contracted with the one carrier, an airline, for the carriage from Singapore to Dublin. The contract permitted carriage by road during the second leg, at the election of the airline. The court found that the contract was not one undivided contract for carriage by air. Rather, the second leg involved the performance of a contract to transport by road and was within CMR. Where the air carrier is given the right or discretion to complete a segment by road, the latter transit is within CMR.[31]

The carrier is liable for the acts of its servants and agents when they are acting within the scope of employment (Art 3).

The contract of carriage

The contract of carriage is confirmed by the making out of a consignment note. The contract is not dependent upon there being a note, or the regularity of its contents (Art 3). The note is expressed to be *prima facie* evidence of the contract and certain other matters (Art 9).

Although the absence of a note does not affect the validity of the contract, its absence has other consequences, as noted below. For example, it is relevant to the exercise of the sender's right to stop the goods in transit (Art 12), and it is pivotal in imposing liability on a successive carrier (Arts 34 and 35).[32]

The note parallels a bill of lading or an air waybill. It documents the contract of carriage and its performance. This note is to be made out in three original copies, signed by the sender and the carrier. The first is to be handed to the sender, the second is to accompany the goods, and the third is to be retained by the carrier (Art 6). The contents are prescribed. They include such matters as date and place of making, details of the sender and carrier, the place of taking over of the goods and delivery, details of the consignee, a description of the goods and method of packing, their weight, charges

---

31 *Quantum Corp Inc v Plane Trucking Ltd* [2002] 2 Lloyd's Rep 25 at 39.
32 See *Gefco UK Ltd v Mason* [1998] 2 Lloyd's Rep 585 at 590.

relating to carriage, instructions for customs and other authorities, and a statement that the carriage is subject to the Convention (notwithstanding any clause to the contrary). The note is also to contain other details, if applicable, such as a statement that transhipment is not allowed, the charges payable by the sender, the amount of 'cash on delivery' charges, the agreed time limit for carriage, and a list of documents to be handed to the carrier (Art 6).

A party may make a declaration of the value of the goods and the amount representing special interest in delivery (Art 6). If a value is declared, this may increase the amount payable by the carrier in the event of the loss of or damage to the goods (see 'The carrier's liability' below).

The sender must attach any documents needed for customs or other formalities to the note or otherwise place them at the carrier's disposal (Art 11).

The sender is responsible for all expenses, loss and damage suffered by the carrier sustained by the latter by reason of the inaccuracy of certain particulars in the consignment note, such as the name and address of the sender (Art 7).

When it takes over the goods, the carrier is to check such matters as the accuracy of statements in the consignment note as to the number of packages and their marks, and the apparent condition of the goods and packaging. Where the carrier has no reasonable means of checking these matters, it shall enter its reservations on the note (Art 8).

The consignment note is *prima facie* evidence of the making of the contract, its conditions and receipt of the goods by the carrier. If it contains no specific reservations by the carrier, it shall be presumed unless the carrier proves the contrary, that the goods and packaging appeared to be in good condition when taken over and that the number of packages, etc, corresponded with the details in the note (Art 9).

The carrier is liable for damage to persons, equipment or other goods, and for any expenses due to defective packaging, unless the defect was apparent or made known to the carrier at the time when it took over the goods and it made no reservations concerning it (Art 10).

The sender has a right of disposition in relation to the goods after delivery to the carrier, such as by asking the carrier to stop the goods in transit, or to change the place of delivery or the consignee. This right is extinguished when the sent copy of the note is handed to the consignee or when the consignee has taken delivery. (The consignor can, however, by an entry in the note, give a right of disposition to the consignee from the time when the note is drawn up.) The exercise of this right is subject to certain conditions, such as that the change in delivery is possible at the time when instructions are received and that it will not interfere with the carrier's normal operations (Art 12).

After the arrival of the goods at the place designated for delivery, the consignee can require the carrier to deliver the goods to it along with the second consignment note. If the goods have been lost or have not arrived after the stipulated time,[33] the carrier can enforce the contract of carriage in its own name. The consignee must pay

---

33 Article 19 makes provision for this. This will be any time agreed by the parties, or when there is no such agreement, delivery has not occurred within a reasonable time having regard to the circumstances.

the charges shown as due on the note. If there is dispute regarding these, the carrier may withhold delivery unless security is furnished (Art 13).

The carrier must seek instructions from the person entitled to dispose of the goods, should it become impossible to carry out the contract in accordance with the terms of the consignment note. If this is not possible, the carrier can take such steps as seem to it to be in the best interests of the person entitled to dispose of the goods (Art 14). Likewise, where circumstances prevent delivery after the goods have arrived at the designated place of delivery, the carrier is to seek instructions from the sender (Art 15).

The carrier has certain other rights, including the right to sell the goods without waiting for instructions, if they are perishable or their condition warrants such a course, where storage expenses would be out of proportion to the value of the goods (Art 16).

An umbrella contract for the regular haulage of discrete consignments of goods in the future was found by an English court to be within the CMR regime. The CMR was not limited to contracts to carry existing and unascertained goods.[34]

The carrier's liability

The Convention provides for a presumption of liability on the part of the carrier, where goods are lost, damaged or delayed in transit; for defences on the part of the carrier; and for a cap on the carrier's liability in damages, subject to certain exceptions. In this regard the Convention parallels those dealing with the international carriage of goods by other transport modes.

The carrier's liability is for loss of or damage to goods occurring between the time when it takes over the goods and the time of delivery, as well as for delay in delivery (Art 17). This liability is presumed, and the onus is then on the carrier[35] to establish one of the defences provided for.

These defences include that the loss or delay was caused by the wrongful act or neglect of the claimant; or by inherent vice in the goods; or through circumstances which the carrier could not avoid and the consequences of which it was unable to prevent.[36] The carrier is also relieved of liability where there was a special inherent risk resulting from the use of open unsheeted vehicles where their use was specified in the consignment note; or lack of or defective packaging; or where the nature of the goods exposes them to loss or damage such as through breakage, decay, or normal waste (Art 17).

The carrier cannot avail itself of one of these defences where the loss has been caused by the defective condition of the vehicle used, or the wrongful conduct of the person supplying the vehicle (Art 17).

The carrier is liable for any loss resulting from a delay in transport when the time taken exceeds the agreed time, or if there is no agreement, a period which is reasonable in the circumstances (Art 19).

---

34 *Gefco UK Ltd v Mason, op cit.*
35 Article 18.
36 See, for example, *GL Cicatiello SRL v Anglo European Shipping Services Ltd* [1994] 1 Lloyd's Rep 678, where the court found that the carrier had proven this defence. The truck and cargo had been stolen by a band of armed robbers after the driver stopped at a service station on a motorway.

The carrier who neglects to collect a 'cash on delivery' charge from the consignee as required by the note, must make good this loss (although it can take action against the consignee) (Art 21).

The carrier cannot use any defence provided or any provision which shifts the burden of proof, if the damage has been caused by its wilful misconduct or default[37] or that of its servant or agent acting in the scope of employment (Art 29).

An issue arose in an English case as to whether an apparent carrier, one of a succession of carriers involved in transporting the goods, could escape liability under CMR on the basis that it had written on the CMR consignment note that it was an 'agent only'. The sender was not given a photocopy of the note, as amended in this manner. The court found on the facts the reality was that the apparent carrier had accepted responsibility for delivery as a carrier and not a mere forwarder. Accordingly, its role was governed by the CMR rules.[38]

Capping the carrier's liability

Where goods being carried under the contract are lost or damaged, their value is to be determined by reference to the commodity exchange price, if applicable, otherwise the market price or the normal value of goods of the same kind and quality (Art 23(2)). Compensation is capped at 25 francs[39] per kilogram of gross weight short (Art 23(3)). If the loss is less than this figure, then the actual loss will be compensated. The cap, that is, is a maximum. It may be overly generous for manufactured goods, but excessively generous for a commodity like coal. The carrier must also refund carriage charges, customs duties and other charges, in proportion to the loss, that is, total or partial (Art 23).

The 25 franc gold cap on damages may be less than the actual value of the goods in a particular case. The person with an interest may declare a special interest in delivery prior to formation of the contract of carriage (which declaration will be entered in the consignment note), and nominate a value for the goods and pay any applicable surcharge for what in effect will be insurance (see Arts 23(6), 26). A like declaration may be made in relation to late delivery, with a sum payable for lateness being nominated. Should such a declaration be made, the claimant will, in the event of loss or damage, receive the sum declared even if it exceeds that specified for in Art 23(3) (that is, 25 gold francs per kilogram) (Art 24). If the goods are damaged and not lost, the compensation in a case of declaration of special interest is the corresponding proportion of the sum declared (Art 25).

Where a declaration has been made in respect of delayed delivery, the claimant is entitled to the sum nominated (Art 26).

---

37 Ie, where the carrier acts intentionally, or recklessly (in the sense that it knew that the harm was a probable outcome of its conduct, although it was not intended).

38 *Aqualon (UK) Ltd v Vallana Shipping Corp* [1994] 1 Lloyd's Rep 669 at 675ff. It was noted by Mance J that even had the sender been alerted to the amendment it would not put the sender on notice that the defendant was rejecting its role as carrier.

39 'Franc' means a gold franc weighing 10/31 of a gram and being of millesimal fineness 900 (Art 23(3)).

The carrier cannot avail itself of the cap on damages where the loss has been caused by its own wilful misconduct or default, or that of its servants or agents acting in the scope of employment (Art 29).

Conduct causing loss is to be characterised as 'wilful misconduct or default' when the party has either acted with an inaction to do something which it knows to be wrong, or recklessly, in that the party is aware that a loss may result from its act although it does not care whether loss will result or not.[40] In an English case where a lorry driver parked unattended in a street, following which the truck and its load were stolen, the driver was found on the facts not to have been responsible for wilful misconduct. The driver did not intentionally act wrongly, nor did he consciously take a risk which he knew he ought not to have taken.[41] On the other hand, a driver was found to have been responsible for wilful misconduct where he ignored an express instruction to the carrier to deliver the goods only to the one address as advised, and instead delivered the goods to another party, thereby causing their loss. The driver had delivered them to an unmarked truck on the roadside. The driver was experienced. It was found that he must have known that he was exposing the goods to risk when he delivered them to a person without making any attempt to establish their identity.[42]

Where, under domestic law, the loss, damage or delay gives rise to an extra-contractual claim (such as breach of bailment or negligence), the carrier can avail itself of the provisions in the Convention which exclude its liability or cap the damages payable (Art 28).

In assessing the loss caused by the loss, damage or delay in delivery, the loss of profits on resale is to be factored in.[43]

Other matters

Where the consignee takes delivery of the goods without checking them or sending the carrier a reservation as to loss or damage, which must be done no later than delivery, or within seven days of delivery in the case of loss or damage which is not apparent, the taking of delivery is *prima facie* evidence that the goods have been received in the condition described in the consignment note. No compensation is payable for damage unless a written reservation is sent within 21 days of delivery (Art 30).

The general period of limitation on claims under the rules is one year, with a three year period in the case of wilful misconduct or default (Art 32).

The contract of carriage may contain an arbitration clause. If so, the tribunal is to apply the Convention (Art 33).

Where the transport is performed by successive road carriers, each is responsible for the whole operation, and each becomes a party to the contract of carriage by reason of acceptance of the goods and the consignment note (Art 34). Provisions deal with the

---

40   *National Semiconductors (UK) Ltd v UPS Ltd* [1996] 2 Lloyd's Rep 212 at 214.
41   *Ibid* at 215.
42   *Laceys Footwear (Wholesale) Ltd v Bowler International Freight Ltd* [1997] 2 Lloyd's Rep 369 at 376ff.
43   *Ibid* at 377.

liability of each successive carrier in a case of loss, damage or delay. For example, if a carrier is responsible for the loss, it is solely liable to compensate the carrier whether paid by itself or another carrier. In appropriate cases, a carrier that pays compensation is entitled to contribution from another carrier or carriers (for example, where liability is joint because it cannot be determined to which carrier liability is attributable) (Art 37). Of course, the cap (if applicable) may preclude recovery of much of the loss, including this component. The principle is very relevant where the cap does not apply because, for example, of wilful misconduct or default on the part of the carrier.

TUTORIAL QUESTIONS

1   What are the rationales for the Warsaw Convention and equivalent regimes? Do they still apply?

2   State A has ratified and implemented the Warsaw Convention of 1929, and the Hague Convention of 1955. State B has adopted and implemented the Warsaw Convention of 1929 and the Montreal Convention of 1999. A consignor delivers cargo to a carrier in State A, for delivery in State B. The cargo disappears *en route*. What law governs the carrier's liability?

3   The facts are as above, except that State B has implemented only the Montreal Convention 1999. What law governs liability?

4   The facts are as above in 2, except that State A has not adopted the Warsaw Convention, and it has ratified but not implemented the Montreal Convention. What law governs liability?

5   Australia and New Zealand have ratified and implemented the Warsaw Convention. A consignor in Sydney, Australia, delivers cargo to an air carrier for delivery in Hamilton, New Zealand. The carrier flies the cargo to Auckland, New Zealand, and then transports it by road to Hamilton. The cargo disappears in the journey between Auckland and Hamilton. Is the carrier's liability capped?

6   State A and State B have each implemented the Warsaw Convention, the amending Hague Convention of 1955, and the Montreal Protocol No 4. A consignor delivers goods to a carrier in A for transport to B. The carrier gets the consignor to fill out a document headed 'air waybill'. The document does not contain a warning that the carrier's liability is capped. The goods are lost in transit. Can the carrier avail itself of the cap?

7   A carrier delivers the cargo to the nominated airport. The carrier uses another airline as its contractor in loading and unloading cargo. While this contractor is unloading the cargo, one of its employees steals it. Can the carrier avail itself of the Warsaw limits on its liability?

8   A carrier issues an air waybill. The consignor makes a special declaration as to value. The bill contains a fine print clause limiting the carrier's liability to twice the cap imposed by Warsaw, in cases where a special declaration is made. Can the carrier avail itself of this limit?

9   An airline contracts with a sender to carry goods by air from State A to airport Y in State B. Both States are party to the Warsaw Convention as amended by the 1955 Hague Protocol, and CMR. The airline lands the cargo at airport X in State B, and contracts with a road carrier to carry the goods to airport Y. The lorry

driver parks the truck and leaves it unattended while he makes a phone call. The cargo is stolen, along with the truck. The statutory caps in each of the Warsaw Convention and CMR leave the sender out of pocket. Examine the liability of the airline and the road carrier. Would it make a difference if the contract between the sender and the airline expressly gave the airline a discretion as to mode of performance in either of State A or State B?

FURTHER READING

Batra, J, 'Modernisation of the Warsaw System – Montreal 1999' (2000) 65 *J of Air Law and Commerce* 429.

De Leon and Eyskens, 'The Montreal Convention: analysis of some aspects of the attempted modernisation and consolidation of the Warsaw System' (2001) 66 *J of Air Law and Commerce* 1155.

Dempsey, P, 'Pennies from heaven: breaking through the liability ceiling of Warsaw' (1997) 22 *Annals of Air and Space Law* 267.

Heinonen, J, 'The Warsaw Convention Jurisdiction and the internet' (2000) 65 *J of Air Law and Commerce* 453.

Lowenfeld, A and Mendelsohn, A, 'The United States and the Warsaw Convention' (1967) 80:3 *Harvard Law R* 497.

Maulawicz, A, 'The liability regime of the international air carrier' (1979) 4 *Annals of Air and Space Law* 122.

Mendelsohn, A and Lieux, R, 'The Warsaw Convention Article 28, the doctrine of *forum non conveniens*, and the foreign plaintiff' (2003) 68 *J of Air Law and Commerce* 75.

Muller-Rostin, W, 'The Montreal Convention of 1999: uncertainties and inconsistencies' (2000) *The Aviation Q* 218.

Tomkins, G, 'The future for the Warsaw Convention liability system' (1999) *The Aviation Q* 38.

APPENDIX

CONVENTION FOR THE UNIFICATION OF CERTAIN RULES RELATING TO INTERNATIONAL CARRIAGE BY AIR (WARSAW CONVENTION) – WARSAW, 1929

CHAPTER I – SCOPE AND DEFINITIONS

Article 1

1   This Convention applies to all international carriage of persons, luggage or goods performed by aircraft for reward. It applies equally to gratuitous carriage by aircraft performed by an air transport undertaking.

2   For the purpose of this Convention the expression 'international carriage' means any carriage in which, according to the contract made by the parties, the place of departure and the place of destination, whether or not there be a break in the carriage or a transshipment, are situated either within the territories of two high Contracting parties, or within the territory of a single high Contracting party, if there is an agreed stopping place within a territory subject to the sovereignty, suzerainty, mandate or authority of another power, even though that power is not a party to this Convention. A carriage without such an agreed stopping place between territories subject to the sovereignty, suzerainty, mandate or authority of the same high Contracting party is not deemed to be international for the purposes of this Convention.

3   A carriage to be performed by several successive air carriers is deemed, for the purposes of this Convention, to be one undivided carriage, if it has been regarded by the parties as a single operation, whether it had been agreed upon under the form of a single contract or of a series of contracts, and it does not lose its international character merely because one contract or a series of contracts is to be performed entirely within a territory subject to the sovereignty, suzerainty, mandate or authority of the same high Contracting party.

Article 2

1   This convention applies to carriage performed by the State or by legally constituted public bodies provided it falls within the conditions laid down in Article 1.

2   This convention does not apply to carriage performed under the terms of any international postal convention.

CHAPTER II – DOCUMENTS OF CARRIAGE

Section 1 – Passenger ticket

Article 3 [omitted]

Section 2 – Luggage ticket

Article 4 [omitted]

Section 3 – Air consignment note

Article 5

1   Every carrier of goods has the right to require the consignor to make out and over to him a document called an 'air consignment note'; every consignor has the right to require the carrier to accept this document.

2   The absence, irregularity or loss of this document does not affect the existence or the validity of the contract of carriage which shall, subject to the provisions of Article 9, be none the less governed by the rules of this Convention.

Article 6

1   The air consignment note shall be made out by the consignor in three original parts and be handed over with the goods.

2   The first part shall be marked 'for the carrier', and shall be signed by the consignor. The second part shall be marked 'for the consignee', it shall be signed by the consignor and by

the carrier and shall accompany the goods. The third part shall be signed by the carrier and handed by him to the consignor after the goods have been accepted.

3   The carrier shall sign on acceptance of the goods.

4   The signature of the carrier may be stamped; that of the consignor may be printed or stamped.

5   If, at the request of the consignor, the carrier makes out the air consignment note, he shall be deemed, subject to proof to the contrary, to have done so on behalf of the consignor.

Article 7

The carrier of goods has the right to require the consignor to make out separate consignment notes when there is more than one package.

Article 8

The air consignment note shall contain the following particulars:

(a) the place and date of its execution;

(b) the place of departure and of destination;

(c) the agreed stopping places, provided the carrier may reserve the right to alter the stopping places in case of necessity, and that if he exercises that right the alteration shall not have the affect of depriving the carriage of its international character;

(d) the name and address of the consignor;

(e) the name and address of the first carrier;

(f) the name and address of the consignee, if the case so requires;

(g) the nature of the goods;

(h) the number of the packages, the method of packing and the particular marks or numbers upon them;

(i) the weight, the quantity and the volume or dimensions of the goods;

(j) the apparent condition of the goods and of the packing;

(k) the freight, if it has been agreed upon, the date and place of payment, and the person who is to pay it;

(l) if the goods are sent for payment on delivery, the price of the goods, and, if the case so requires, the amount of the expenses incurred;

(m) the amount of the value declared in accordance with Article 22(2);

(n) the number of parts of the air consignment note;

(o) the document handed to the carrier to accompany the air consignment note;

(p) the time fixed for the completion of the carriage and a brief note of the route to be followed, if these matters have been agreed upon;

(q) a statement that the carriage is subject to the rules relating to liability established by this Convention.

Article 9

If the carrier accepts goods without an air consignment note having been made out, or if the air consignment note does not contain all the particulars set out in Article 8(a) to (i) inclusive and (q), the carrier shall not be entitled to avail himself of the provisions of this Convention which exclude or limit his liability.

Article 10

1   The consignor is responsible for the correctness of the particulars and statements relating to the goods which he inserts in the air consignment note.

2   The consignor will be liable for all damage suffered by the carrier or any other person by reason of the irregularity, incorrectness or incompleteness of the said particulars and statements.

Article 11

1   The air consignment note is *prima facie* evidence of the conclusion of the contract, of the receipt of the goods and of the conditions of carriage.

2   The statements in the air consignment note relating to the weight, dimensions and packing of the goods, as well as those relating to the number of packages, are *prima facie* evidence of the facts stated; those relating to the quantity, volume and condition of the goods do not constitute evidence against the carrier except so far as they both have been, and are stated in the air consignment note to have been, checked by him in the presence of the consignor, or relate to the apparent condition of the goods.

Article 12

1   Subject to his liability to carry out all his obligations under the contract of carriage, the consignor has the right to dispose of the goods by withdrawing them at the aerodrome of departure or destination, or by stopping them in the course of the journey on any landing, or by calling for them to be delivered at the place of destination or in the course of the journey to a person other than the consignee named in the air consignment note, or by requiring them to be returned to the aerodrome of departure. He must not exercise this right of disposition in such a way as to prejudice the carrier or other consignors and he must repay any expenses occasioned by the exercise of this right.

2   If it is impossible to carry out the orders of the consignor the carrier must so inform him forthwith.

3   If the carrier obeys the orders of the consignor for the disposition of the goods without requiring the production of the part of the air consignment note delivered to the latter, he will be liable, without prejudice to his right of recovery from the consignor, for any damage which may be caused thereby to any person who is lawfully in possession of that part of the air consignment note.

4   The right conferred on the consignor ceases at the moment when that of the consignee begins in accordance with Article 13. Nevertheless, if the consignee declines to accept the consignment note or the goods, or if he cannot be communicated with, the consignor resumes his right of disposition.

Article 13

1   Except in the circumstances set out in the preceding article, the consignee is entitled, on arrival of the goods at the place of destination, to require the carrier to hand over to him the air consignment note and to deliver the goods to him, on payment of the charges due and on complying with the conditions of carriage set out in the air consignment note.

2   Unless it is otherwise agreed, it is the duty of the carrier to give notice to the consignee as soon as the goods arrive.

3   If the carrier admits the loss of the goods have not arrived at the expiration of seven days after date on which they ought to have arrived, the consignee is entitled to put into force against the carrier the rights which flow from the contract of carriage.

Article 14

The consignor and the consignee can respectively enforce all the rights given them by Articles 12 and 13, each in his own name, whether he is acting in his own interest or in the interest of another, provided that he carries out the obligations imposed by the contract.

Article 15

1   Articles 12, 13 and 14 do not affect either the relations of the consignor or the consignee with each other or the mutual relations of third parties whose rights are derived either from the consignor or from the consignee.

2   The provisions of Articles 12, 13 and 14 can only be varied by express provision in the air consignment note.

Article 16

1   The consignor must furnish such information and attach to the air consignment note such documents as are necessary to meet the formalities of Customs, *Octroi* or police before the goods can be delivered to the consignee. The consignor is liable to the carrier for any damage occasioned by the absence, insufficiency or irregularity of any such information or documents, unless the damage is due to the fault of the carrier or his agents.

2   The carrier is under no obligation to enquire into the correctness or sufficiency of such information or documents.

CHAPTER III – LIABILITY OF THE CARRIER

Article 17

The carrier is liable for damage sustained in the event of the death or wounding of a passenger or any other bodily injury suffered by a passenger, if the accident which caused the damage so sustained took place on board the aircraft or in the course of any of the operations of embarking or disembarking.

Article 18

1   The carrier is liable for damage sustained in the event of the destruction or loss of, or of damage to, any registered luggage or any goods, if the occurrence which caused the damage so sustained took place during the carriage by air.

2   The carriage by air within the meaning for the preceding paragraph comprises the period during which the luggage or goods are in charge of the carrier, whether in an aerodrome or on board an aircraft, or, in the case of a landing outside an aerodrome, in any place whatsoever.

3   The period of the carriage by air does not extend to any carriage by land, by sea or by river performed outside an aerodrome. If, however, such a carriage takes place in the performance of a contract for carriage by air, for the purpose of loading, delivery or trans-shipment, any damage is presumed, subject to proof to the contrary, to have been the result of an event which took place during the carriage by air.

Article 19

The carrier is liable for damage occasioned by delay in the carriage by air of passengers, luggage or goods.

Article 20

1   The carrier is not liable if he proves that he and his agents have taken all necessary measures to avoid the damage or that it was impossible for him or them to take such measures.

2   In the carriage of goods and luggage, the carrier is not liable if he proves that the damage was occasioned by negligent pilotage or negligence in the handling of the aircraft or in navigation and that, in all other respects, he and his agents have taken all necessary measures to avoid the damage.

Article 21

If the carrier proves that the damage was caused by or contributed to by the negligence of the injured person, the court may, in accordance with the provisions of its own law, exonerate the carrier wholly or partly from his liability.

Article 22

1   In the carriage of passengers, the liability of the carrier for each passenger is limited to the sum of 125,000 francs. Where, in accordance with the law of the court seised of the case, damages may be awarded in the form of periodical payments, the equivalent capital value of the said payment shall not exceed 125,000 francs. Nevertheless, by special contract, the carrier and the passenger may agree to a higher limit of liability.

2   In the carriage of registered luggage and of goods, the liability of the carrier is limited to a sum of 250 francs per kg, unless the consignor has made, at the time when the package was handed over to the carrier, a special declaration of the value at delivery and has paid a supplementary sum if the case so requires. In that case, the carrier will be liable to pay a sum not exceeding the declared sum, unless he proves that the sum is greater than the actual value to the consignor at delivery.

3   As regards objects of which the passenger takes charge himself the liability of the carrier is limited to 5000 francs per passenger.

4   The sums mentioned above shall be deemed to refer to the French franc consisting of 65.5 mg gold of millesimal fineness 900. These sums may be converted into any national currency in round figures.

Article 23

Any provision tending to relieve the carrier of liability or to fix a lower limit than that which is laid down in this Convention shall be null and void, but the nullity of any such provision does not involve the nullity of the whole contract, which shall remain subject to the provisions of this Convention.

Article 24

1. In the cases covered by Articles 18 and 19, any action for damages, however founded, can only be brought subject to the conditions and limits set out in this Convention.
2. In the cases covered by Article 17, the provisions of the preceding paragraph also apply, without prejudice to the questions as to who are the persons who have the right to bring suit and what are their respective rights.

Article 25

1. The carrier shall not be entitled to avail himself of the provisions of this Convention which exclude or limit his liability, if the damage is caused by his wilful misconduct or by such default on his part as, in accordance with the law of the court seised of the case, is considered to be equivalent to wilful misconduct.
2. Similarly, the carrier shall not be entitled to avail himself of the said provisions, if the damage is caused as aforesaid by any agent of the carrier acting within the scope of his employment.

Article 26

1. Receipt by the person entitled to delivery of luggage or goods without complaint is *prima facie* evidence that the same have been delivered in good condition and in accordance with the document of carriage.
2. In the case of damage, the person entitled to delivery must complain to the carrier forthwith after the discovery of the damage, and, at the latest, within three days from the date of receipt in the case of luggage and seven days from the date of receipt in the case of goods. In the case of delay, the complaint must be made at the latest within 14 days from the date on which the luggage or goods have been placed at his disposal.
3. Every complaint must be made in writing upon the document of carriage or by separate notice in writing dispatched within the times aforesaid.
4. Failing complaint within the times aforesaid, no action shall lie against the carrier, save in the case of fraud on his part.

Article 27

In the case of the death of the person liable, an action for damages lies in accordance with the terms of this Convention against those legally representing his estate.

Article 28

1. An action for damages must be brought, at the option of the plaintiff, in the territory of one of the high Contracting parties, either before the court having jurisdiction where the carrier is ordinarily resident, or has his principal place of business, or has an establishment by which the contract has been made or before the court having jurisdiction at the place of destination.
2. Questions of procedure shall be governed by the law of the court seised of the case.

Article 29

1. The right to damages shall be extinguished if an action is not brought within two years, reckoned from the date of arrival at the destination, or from the date on which the aircraft ought to have arrived, or from the date on which the carriage stopped.
2. The method of calculating the period of limitation shall be determined by the law of the court seised of the case.

Article 30

1. In the case of carriage to be performed by various successive carriers and falling within the definition set out in the third paragraph of Article 1, each carrier who accepts passengers,

luggage or goods is subjected to the rules set out in this Convention, and is deemed to be one of the Contracting parties to the contract of carriage in so far as the contract deals with that part of the carriage which is performed under his supervision.

2   In the case of carriage of this nature, the passenger or his representative can take action only against the carrier who performed the carriage during which the accident or the delay occurred, save in the case where, by express agreement, the first carrier has assumed liability for the whole journey.

3   As regards luggage or goods, the passenger or consignor will have a right of action against the first carrier, and the passenger or consignee who is entitled to delivery will have a right of action against the last carrier, and further, each may take action against the carrier who performed the carriage during which the destruction, loss, damage or delay took place. These carriers will be jointly and severally liable to the passenger or to the consignor or consignee.

Chapter IV – Provisions to combined carriage

Article 31

1   In the case of combined carriage performed partly by air and partly by any other mode of carriage, the provisions of the Convention apply only to the carriage by air, provided that the carriage by air falls within the terms of Article 1.

2   Nothing in this convention shall prevent the parties in the case of combined carriage from inserting in the document of air carriage conditions relating to other modes of carriage, provided that the provisions of this Convention are observed as regards the carriage by air.

Chapter V – General and final provisions

Article 32

Any clause contained in the contract and all special agreements entered into before the damage occurred by which the parties purport to infringe the rules laid down by this Convention, whether by deciding the law to be applied, or by altering the rules as to jurisdiction, shall be null and void. Nevertheless, for the carriage of goods arbitration clauses are allowed, subject to this convention, if the arbitration is to take place within one of the jurisdictions referred to in the first paragraph of Article 28.

Article 33

Nothing contained in this Convention shall prevent the carrier either from refusing to enter into any contract of carriage, or from making regulations which do not conflict with the provisions of this Convention.

Article 34

This Convention does not apply to international carriage by air performed by way of experimental trial by air navigation undertakings with the view to the establishment of a regular line of air navigation, nor does it apply to carriage performed in extraordinary circumstances outside the normal scope of an air carrier's business.

Article 35

The expression 'days' when used in this convention means current days not working days.

Articles 36–41 [omitted]

UNIFORM RULES CONCERNING THE CONTRACT FOR INTERNATIONAL CARRIAGE OF GOODS BY RAIL (CIM) 1980

TITLE I – GENERAL PROVISIONS

Article 1 – Scope

1   Subject to the exceptions provided for in Article 2, the Uniform Rules shall apply to all consignments of goods for carriage under a through consignment note made out for a route over the territories of at least two States and exclusively over lines or services included in the list provided for in Articles 3 and 10 of the Convention.

2   In the Uniform Rules the expression 'station' covers: railway stations, ports used by shipping services and all other establishments of transport undertakings, open to the public for the execution of the contract of carriage.

Article 2 – Exceptions from scope

1   Consignments between sending and destination stations situated in the territory of the same State, which pass through the territory of another State only in transit, shall not be subject to the Uniform Rules:
    (a) if the lines or services over which the transit occurs are exclusively operated by a railway of the State of departure; or
    (b) if the States or the railways concerned have agreed not to regard such consignments as international.

2   Consignments between stations in two adjacent States and between stations in two states in transit through the territory of a third State shall, if the lines over which the consignments are carried are exclusively operated by a railway of one of those three States, be subject to the internal traffic regulations applicable to that railway if the sender, by using the appropriate consignment note, so elects and where there is nothing to the contrary in the laws and regulation of any of the States concerned.

Article 3 – Obligation to carry

1   The railway shall be bound to undertake all carriage of any goods in complete wagon-loads, subject to the terms of the Uniform Rules, provided that:
    (a) the sender complies with the Uniform Rules, the supplementary provisions and the tariffs;
    (b) carriage can be undertaken by the normal staff and transport resources which suffice to meet usual traffic requirements;
    (c) carriage is not prevented by circumstances which the railway cannot avoid and which it is not in a position to remedy.

2   The railway shall not be obliged to accept goods of which the loading, trans-shipment or unloading requires the use of special facilities unless the stations concerned have such facilities at their disposal.

3   The railway shall only be obliged to accept goods the carriage of which can take place without delay; the provisions in force at the forwarding station shall determine the circumstances in which goods not complying with that condition must be temporarily stored.

4   When the competent authority decides that:
    (a) a service shall be discontinued or suspended totally or partially,
    (b) certain consignments shall be refused or accepted only subject to conditions,
    these measures shall, without delay, be brought to the notice of the public and the railways; the latter shall inform the railways of the other States with a view to their publication.

5   The railways may, by joint agreement, concentrate goods traffic between certain places on specified frontier points and transit countries. These measures shall be notified to the central office. They shall be entered by the railways in special lists, published in the manner laid down for international tariffs, and shall come into force one month after the date of notification to the central office.

6   Any contravention of this article by the railway may constitute a cause of action for compensation for loss or damage caused.

Article 4 – Articles not acceptable for carriage

1 The following shall not be accepted for carriage:

(a) articles the carriage of which is prohibited in any one of the territories in which the articles would be carried;

(b) articles the carriage of which is a monopoly of the postal authorities in any one of he territories in which the articles would be carried;

(c) articles which, by reason of their dimensions, their mass, or their packaging, are not suitable for the carriage proposed, having regard to the installations or rolling stock of any one of the railways which would be used;

(d) substances and articles which are not acceptable for carriage under the regulations concerning the international carriage of dangerous goods by rail (RID), Annex I to the Uniform Rules, subject to the exceptions provided for in Article 5, para 2.

Article 5 – Articles acceptable for carriage subject to conditions

1 The following shall be acceptable for carriage subject to conditions:

(a) Substances and articles acceptable for carriage subject to the conditions laid down in the RID or in the agreements and tariff clauses provided for in para 2.

(b) Funeral consignments, railway rolling stock running on its own wheels, live animals and consignments the carriage of which presents special difficulties by reason of their dimensions, their mass or their packaging: subject to the conditions laid down in the supplementary provision; these may derogate from the Uniform Rules.

Live animals must be accompanied by an attendant provided by the consignor. Nevertheless, an attendant shall not be required when the international tariffs permit or when the railways participating in the carriage so permit at the consignor's request; in such cases, unless there is an agreement to the contrary, the railway shall not be liable for any loss or damage resulting from any risk which the attendant was intended to avert.

2 Two or more States, by agreement, or two or more railways, by tariff clauses, may jointly determine the conditions with which certain substances or articles not acceptable for carriage under the RID must comply if they are nevertheless to be accepted. States or railways may, in the same manner, make the conditions for acceptance laid down in the RID less rigorous. Such agreements and tariff clauses must be published and notified to the central office which will bring them to the notice of the States.

Article 6 – Tariffs, private agreements [omitted]

Article 7 – Unit of account. Rate of exchange or of acceptance of foreign currency

1 The unit of account referred to in the Uniform Rules shall be the Special Drawing Right as defined by the International Monetary Fund.

The value in Special Drawing Right of the national currency of a State which is a Member of the International Monetary fund shall be calculated in accordance with the method of valuation applied by the International Monetary Fund for its own operations and transactions.

2 The value in Special Drawing Right of the national currency of a State which is not a member of the International Monetary Fund shall be calculated by the method determined by that State.

The calculation must express in the national currency a real value approximating as closely to that which would result from the application of para 1.

3 In the case of a State which is not a member of the International Monetary Fund and whose legislation does not permit the application of para 1 or para 2 above, the unit of account referred to in the Uniform Rules shall be deemed to be equal to three gold francs.

The gold franc is defined as 10/31 of a gram of gold of millesimal fineness 900.

The conversion of the gold franc must express in the national currency a real value approximating as closely to that which would result from the application of para 1.

4 Within three months after the entry into force of the Convention and each time that a change occurs in their method of calculation or in the value of their national currency in relation to the unit of account, States shall notify the central office of their method of

calculation in accordance with para 2, or the results of the conversion in accordance with para 3.

The central office shall notify the States of this information.

5   The railway shall publish the rates at which:

(a)   it converts sums expressed in foreign currencies but payable in domestic currency (rates of conversion);

(b)   It accepts payment in foreign currencies (rates of acceptance).

Article 8 – Special provisions for certain types of transport

1   In the case of the haulage of privately owned wagons, special provisions are laid down in the regulations concerning the international haulage of private owners' wagons by rail (RIP), Annex II to the Uniform Rules.

2   In the case of the carriage of containers, special provisions are laid down in the regulations concerning the international carriage of containers by rail (RICo), Annex III to the Uniform Rules.

3   In the case of express parcels traffic, railways may, by tariff clauses, agree on special provisions in accordance with the regulations concerning the international carriage of express parcels by rail (RIEx), Annex IV to the Uniform Rules.

4   Two or more States, by special agreement, or two or more railways by supplementary provisions or by tariff clauses, may agree on terms derogating from the Uniform Rules for the following types of consignments:

(a)   consignments under cover of a negotiable document;

(b)   consignments to be delivered only against return of the duplicate of the consignment note;

(c)   consignments of newspapers;

(d)   consignment intended for fairs or exhibitions;

(e)   consignment of loading tackle and of equipment for protection of goods in transit against heat or cold;

(f)   consignments over all or part of the route under cover of consignment notes which are not used for charging and billing;

(g)   consignments sent under cover of an instrument suitable for automatic data transmission.

Article 9 – Supplementary provision

1   Two or more States or two or more railways may make supplementary provisions for the execution of the Uniform Rules. They may not derogate from the Uniform Rules unless the latter expressly so provide.

2   The supplementary provisions shall be put into force and published in the manner required by the laws and regulations of each State. The central office shall be notified of the supplementary provisions and of their coming into force.

Article 10 – National law

1   In the absence of provisions in the Uniform Rules, supplementary provisions or international tariffs, national law shall apply.

2   'National law' means the law of the State in which the person entitled asserts his rights, including the rules relating to conflict of laws.

TITLE II – MAKING AND EXECUTION OF THE CONTRACT OF CARRIAGE

Article 11 – Making of the contract of carriage

1   The contract of carriage shall come into existence as soon as the forwarding railway has accepted the goods for carriage together with the consignment note. Acceptance is established by the application to the consignment note and, where appropriate, to each additional sheet, of the stamp of the forwarding station, or accounting machine entry, showing the date of acceptance.

2   The procedure laid down in para 1 must be carried out immediately after all the goods to which the consignment note relates have been handed over for carriage and – where the provisions in force at the forwarding station so require – such charges as the consignor has undertaken to pay have been paid or a security deposited in accordance with Article 15, para 7. The procedure shall be carried out in the presence of the consignor if he so requests.

3   When the stamp has been affixed or the accounting machine entry has been made, the consignment note shall be evidence of the making and content of the contract.

4   Nevertheless, when the loading of the goods is the duty of the consignor in accordance with tariffs or agreements existing between him and the railway, and provided that such agreements are authorised at the forwarding station, the particulars in the consignment note relating to the mass of the goods or to the number of packages shall only be evidence against the railway when that weight or number of packages has been verified by the railway and certified in the consignment note. If necessary these particulars may be proved by other means.

If it is obvious that there is no actual deficiency corresponding to the discrepancy between the mass or number of packages and the particulars in the consignment note, the latter shall not be evidence against the railway. This shall apply in particular when the wagon is handed over to the consignee with the original seals intact.

5   The railway shall certify receipt of the goods and the date of acceptance for carriage by affixing the date stamp to or making the accounting machine entry on the duplicate of the consignment note before returning the duplicate to the consignor. The duplicate shall not have effect as the consignment note accompanying the goods, nor as a bill of lading.

Article 12 – Consignment note

1   The consignor shall present a consignment note duly completed. A separate consignment note shall be made out for each consignment. One and the same consignment note may not relate to more than a single wagon load. The supplementary provisions may derogate from these rules.

2   The railways shall prescribe, for both *petite vitesse* and *grande vitesse* traffic, a standard form of consignment note, which must include a duplicate for the consignor. The choice of consignment note by the consignor shall indicate whether the goods are to be carried by *petite vitesse* or by *grande vitesse*. A request for *grande vitesse* over one part of the route and *petite vitesse* over the remainder will not be allowed except by agreement between all the railways concerned.

In the case of certain traffic, notably between adjacent countries, the railways may prescribe, in the tariffs, the use of a simplified form of consignment note.

3   The consignment note must be printed in two or where necessary in three languages, at least one of which shall be one of the working languages of the organisation.

International tariffs may determine the language in which the particulars to be filled in by the consignor in the consignment note shall be entered. In the absence of such provisions, they must be entered in one of the official languages of the State of departure and a translation in one of the working languages of the organisation must be added unless the particulars have been entered in one of those languages. The particulars entered by the consignor in the consignment note shall be in Roman lettering, save where the supplementary provisions or international tariffs otherwise provide.

Article 13 – Wording of the consignment note

1   The consignment note must contain:
(a) the name of the destination station;
(b) the name and address of the consignee; only one individual or legal person shall be shown as consignee;
(c) the description of the goods;
(d) the mass, or failing that, comparable information in accordance with the provisions in force at the forwarding station;
(e) the number of packages and a description of the packing in the case of consignments in less than wagon loads, and in the case of complete wagon loads comprising one or more packages, forwarded by rail-sea and requiring to be trans-shipped;

(f) the number of the wagon and also, for privately owned wagons, the tare, in the case of goods where the loading is the duty of the consignor,

(g) a detailed list of the documents which are required by Customs or other administrative authorities and are attached to the consignment note or shown as held at the disposal of the railway at a named station or at an office of the Customs or of any other authority;

(h) the name and address of the consignor; only one individual or legal person shall be shown as the consignor; if the provisions in force at the forwarding station so require, the consignor shall add to his name and address his written, printed or stamped signature.

The provisions in force at the forwarding station shall determine the meanings of the terms 'wagon load' and 'less than wagon load' for the whole of the route.

2   The consignment note must, where appropriate, contain all the other particulars provided for in the Uniform Rules. It shall not contain other particulars unless they are required or allowed by the laws and regulations of a State, the supplementary provisions or the tariffs, and are not contrary to the Uniform Rules.

3   Nevertheless, the consignor may insert in the consignment note in the space set apart for the purpose, but as information for the consignee, remarks relating to the consignment, without involving the railway in any obligation or liability.

4   The consignment note shall not be replaced by other documents or supplemented by documents other than those prescribed or allowed by the Uniform Rules, the supplementary provisions or the tariffs.

Article 14 – Route and tariffs applicable

1   The consignor may stipulate in the consignment note the route to be followed, indicating it by reference to frontier points or frontier stations and where appropriate, to transit stations between railways. He may only stipulate frontier points and frontier stations which are open to traffic between the forwarding and destination places concerned.

2   The following shall be regarded as routing instructions:

(a) designation of stations where formalities required by Customs or other administrative authorities are to be carried out, and of stations where special care is to be given to the goods (attention to animals, re-icing, etc);

(b) designation of the tariffs to be applied, if this is sufficient to determine the stations between which the tariffs requested are to be applied;

(c) instructions as to the payment of the whole or a part of the charges up to X (X indicating by name the point at which the tariffs of adjacent countries are applied).

3   Except in the cases specified in Article 3, paras 4 and 5, and Article 33, para 1, the railway may not carry the goods by a route other than that stipulated by the consignor unless both:

(a) the formalities required by Customs or other administrative authorities, as well as the special care to be given to the goods, will in any event be carried out at the stations indicated by the consignor; and

(b) the charges and the transit periods will not be greater than the charges and transit periods calculated according to the route stipulated by the consignor.

Sub-para (a) shall not apply to consignments in less than wagon loads if one of the participating railways is unable to adhere to the route chosen by the consignor by virtue of the routing instructions arising from its arrangements for the international carriage of consignments in less than wagon loads.

4   Subject to the provisions of para 3, the charges and transit periods shall be calculated according to the route stipulated by the consignor or, in the absence of any such indication, according to the route chosen by the railway.

5   The consignor may stipulate in the consignment note which tariffs are to be applied. The railway must apply such tariffs if the conditions laid down for their application have been fulfilled.

6   If the instructions given by the consignor are not sufficient to indicate the route or tariffs to be applied, or if any of those instructions are inconsistent with one another, the railway shall choose the route or tariffs which appear to it to be the most advantageous to the consignor.

7   The railway shall not be liable for any loss or damage suffered as a result of the choice made in accordance with para 6, except in the case of wilful misconduct or gross negligence.

8   If an international tariff exists from the forwarding to the destination station and if, in the absence of adequate instructions from the consignor, the railway has applied that tariff, the railway shall, at the request of the person entitled, refund him the difference between the carriage charges thus applied and those which the application of other tariffs would have produced over the same route, when such difference exceeds four units of account per consignment note.

   The same shall apply if, in the absence of adequate instructions from the consignor, the railway has applied consecutive tariffs, even though there is an international tariff offering a more advantageous charge, all other conditions being the same.

Article 15 – Payment of charges

1   The charges (carriage charges, supplementary charges, Customs duties and other charges incurred from the time of acceptance for carriage to the time of delivery) shall be paid by the consignor or the consignee in accordance with the following provisions.

   In applying these provisions, charges which, according to the applicable tariff, must be added to the standard rates or special rates when calculating the carriage charges, shall be deemed to be carriage charges.

2   A consignor who undertakes to pay a part or all of the charges shall indicate this on the consignment note by using one of the following phrases:

   (a) (i)   'carriage charges paid', if he undertakes to pay carriage charges only;

      (ii) 'carriage charges paid including ...', if he undertakes to pay charges additional to those for carriage; he shall give an exact description of those charges; additional indications, which may relate only to the supplementary charges or other charges incurred from the time of acceptance for carriage until the time of delivery as well as to sums collected either by Customs or other administrative authorities shall not result in any division of the total amount of any one category of charges (eg the total amount of Customs duties and of other amounts payable to Customs, value added tax being regarded as a separate category);

      (iii) 'carriage charges paid to X' (X indicating by name the point at which the tariffs of adjacent countries are applied), if he undertakes to pay carriage charges to X;

      (iv) 'carriage chargers paid to X including ...' (X indicating by name the point at which the tariffs of adjacent countries are applied), if he undertakes to pay charges additional to those for carriage to X, but excluding all charges relating to the subsequent country or railway; the provisions of (ii) shall apply analogously;

   (b) 'all charges paid', if he undertakes to pay all charges (carriage charges, supplementary charges, Customs duties and other charges);

   (c) 'charges paid not exceeding ...', if he undertakes to pay a fixed sum; save where the tariffs otherwise provide, this sum shall be expressed in the currency of the country of departure.

   Supplementary and other charges which, according to the provisions in force at the forwarding station, are to be calculated for the whole of the route concerned, and the charge for interest in delivery laid down in Article 16, para 2, shall always be paid in full by the consignor in the case of payment of the charges in accordance with (a)(iv).

3   The international tariffs may, as regards payment of charges, prescribe the exclusive use of certain phrases set out in para 2 of this Article or the use of other phrases.

4   The charges which the consignor has not undertaken to pay shall be deemed to be payable by the consignee. Nevertheless, such charges shall be payable by the consignor if the consignee has not taken possession of the consignment note nor asserted his rights under Article 28, para 4, nor modified the contract of carriage in accordance with Article 31.

5   Supplementary charges, such as charges for demurrage and standage, warehousing and weighing, which arise from an act attributable to the consignee or from a request which he has made, shall always be paid by him.

6   The forwarding railway may require the consignor to prepay the charges in the case of goods which in its opinion are liable to undergo rapid deterioration or which, by reason of their low value or their nature, do not provide sufficient cover for such charges.

7   If the amount of the charges which the consignor undertakes to pay cannot be ascertained exactly at the time the goods are handed over for carriage, such charges shall be entered in a charges note and a settlement of accounts shall be made with the consignor not later than 30 days after the expiry of the transit period. The railway may require as security a deposit approximating to the amount of such charges, for which a receipt shall be given. A detailed account of charges drawn up from the particulars in the charges note shall be delivered to the consignor in return for the receipt.

8   The forwarding station shall specify, in the consignment note and in the duplicate, the charges which have been prepaid, unless the provisions in force at the forwarding station provide that those charges are only to be specified in the duplicate. In the case provided for in para 7 of this article, these charges are not to be specified either in the consignment note or in the duplicate.

Article 16 – Interest in delivery

1   Any consignment may be the subject of a declaration of interest in delivery. The amount declared shall be shown in figures in the consignment note in the currency of the country of departure, in another currency determined by the tariffs or in units of account.

2   The charge for interest in delivery shall be calculated for the whole of the route concerned, in accordance with the tariffs of the forwarding railway.

Article 17 – Cash on delivery and disbursements

1   The consignor may make the goods subject to a cash on delivery payment not exceeding their value at the time of acceptance at the forwarding station. The amount of such cash on delivery payment shall be expressed in the currency of the country of departure; the tariffs may provide for exceptions.

2   The railway shall not be obliged to pay over any amount representing a cash on delivery payment unless the amount in question has been paid by the consignee. That amount shall be placed at the consignor's disposal within 30 days of payment by the consignee; interest at 5% per annum shall be payable from the date of the expiry of that period.

3   If the goods have been delivered, wholly or in part, to the consignee without prior collection of the amount of the cash on delivery payment, the railway shall pay the consignor the amount of any loss or damage sustained up to the total amount of the cash on delivery payment without prejudice to any right of recovery from the consignee.

4   Cash on delivery consignment shall be subject to a collection fee laid down in the tariffs; such fee shall be payable notwithstanding cancellation or reduction of the amount of the cash on delivery payment by modification of the contract of carriage in accordance with Article 30, para 1.

5   Disbursements shall only be allowed if made in accordance with the provisions in force in force at the forwarding station.

6   The amounts of the cash on delivery payment and of disbursements shall be entered in figures on the consignment note.

Article 18 – Responsibility for particulars furnished in the consignment note

The consignor shall be responsible for the correctness of the particulars inserted by, or for, him, in the consignment note. He shall bear all the consequences in the event of those particulars being irregular, incorrect, incomplete, or not entered in the allotted space. If that space is insufficient, the consignor shall indicate therein the place in the consignment note where the rest of the particulars are to be found.

Article 19 – Condition, packing and marking of goods

1   When the railway accepts for carriage goods showing obvious signs of damage, it may require the condition of such goods to be indicated in the consignment note.

2   When the nature of the goods is such as to require packing, the consignor shall pack them in such a way as to protect them from total or partial loss and from damage in transit and to avoid risk of injury or damage to persons, equipment or other goods.

Moreover the packing shall comply with the provisions in force at the forwarding station.

3   If the consignor has not complied with the provisions of para 2, the railway may either refuse the goods or require the sender to acknowledge in the consignment note the absence of packing or the defective condition of the packing, with an exact description thereof.

4   The consignor shall be liable for all the consequences of the absence of packing or defective condition of packing and shall in particular make good any loss or damage suffered by the railway from this cause. In the absence of any particulars in the consignment note, the burden of proof of such absence of packing or defective condition of the packing shall rest upon the railway.

5   Save where the tariffs otherwise provide, the consignor of a consignment amounting to less than a wagon load shall indicate on each package or on a label approved by the railway in a clear and indelible manner which will avoid confusion and correspond exactly with the particulars in the consignment note:

(a)   the name and address of the consignee;

(b)   the destination station.

The details required under (a) and (b) above shall also be shown on each article or package comprised in a wagon load forwarded by rail/sea and requiring to be trans-shipped.

Old markings or labels shall be obliterated or removed by the consignor.

6   Save where the supplementary provisions or the tariffs otherwise provide, goods which are fragile or may become scattered in wagons and goods which may taint or damage other goods shall be carried only in complete wagon loads, unless packed or fastened together in such a manner that they cannot become broken or lost, or taint or damage other goods.

Article 20 – Handing over of goods for carriage and loading of goods

1   The handing over of goods for carriage shall be governed by the provisions in force at the forwarding station.

2   Loading shall be the duty of the railway or the consignor according to the provisions in force at the forwarding station, unless otherwise provided in the Uniform Rules or unless the consignment note includes a reference to a special agreement between the consignor and the railway.

When the loading is the responsibility of the consignor, he shall comply with the load limit. If different load limits are in force on the lines traversed, the lowest load limit shall be applicable to the whole route. The provisions laying down load limit shall be applicable to the whole route. The provisions laying down load limits shall be published in the same manner as tariffs. If the consignor so requests, the railway shall inform him of the permitted load limit.

3   The consignor shall be liable for all the consequences of defective loading carried out by him and shall, in particular, make good any loss or damage suffered by the railway through this cause. Nevertheless, Article 15 shall apply to the payment of costs arising from the reloading of goods in the event of defective loading. The burden of proof of defective loading shall rest upon the railway.

4   Unless otherwise provided in the Uniform Rules, goods shall be carried in covered wagons, open wagons, sheeted open wagons or specially equipped wagons according to the international tariffs. If there are no international tariffs, or if they do not contain any provisions on the subject, the provisions in force at the forwarding station shall apply throughout the whole of the route.

5   The affixing of seals to wagons shall be governed by the provisions in force at the forwarding station.

The consignor shall indicate in the consignment note the number and description of the seals affixed to the wagons by him.

Article 21 – Verification

1   The railway shall always have the right to verify that the consignment corresponds with the particulars furnished in the consignment note by the consignor and that the provisions relating to the carriage of goods accepted subject to conditions have been complied with.

2   If the contents of the consignment are examined for this purpose, the consignor or the consignee, according to whether the verification takes place at the forwarding station or the destination station, shall be invited to be present. Should the interested party not attend, or should the verification take place in transit, it shall be carried out in the presence of two witnesses not connected with the railway, unless the laws or regulations of the State where the verification takes place provide otherwise. The railway may not, however, carry out the verification in transit unless compelled to do so by operational necessities or by the requirements of the Customs or of other administrative authorities.

3   The result of the verification of the particulars in the consignment note shall be entered therein. If verification takes place at the forwarding station, the result shall also be recorded in the duplicate of the consignment note if it is held by the railway.

If the consignment does not correspond with the particulars in the consignment note or if the provisions relating to the carriage of goods accepted subject to conditions have not been complied with, the costs of the verification shall be charged against the goods, unless paid at the time.

Article 22 – Ascertainment of weight and number of packages

1   The provisions in force in each state shall determine the circumstances in which the railway must ascertain the mass of the goods or the number of packages and the actual tare of the wagons.

The railway shall enter in the consignment note the results ascertained.

2   If weighing by the railway, after the contract of carriage has been made, reveals a difference, the mass ascertained by the forwarding station or, failing that, the mass declared by the consignor, shall still be the basis for calculating the carriage charges:

(a) if the difference is manifestly due to the nature of the goods or to atmospheric conditions; or

(b) the weighing takes place on a weighbridge and does not reveal a difference exceeding 2% of the mass ascertained by the forwarding station or, failing that, of that declared by the consignor.

Article 23 – Overloading

1   When overloading of a wagon is established by the forwarding station or by an intermediate station, the excess load may be removed from the wagon even if no surcharge is payable. Where necessary the consignor or, if the contract of carriage has been modified in accordance with Article 31, the consignee shall be asked without delay to give instructions concerning the excess load.

2   Without prejudice to the payment of surcharges under Article 24, the excess load shall be charged for the distance covered in accordance with the carriage charges applicable to the main load. If the excess load is unloaded, the charge for unloading shall be determined by the tariffs of the railway which carries out the unloading.

If the person entitled directs that the excess load be forwarded to the same destination station as the main load or to another destination station, or directs that it be returned to the forwarding station, the excess load shall be treated as a separate consignment.

Article 24 – Surcharges

1   Without prejudice to the railway's entitlement to the difference in carriage charges and to compensation for any possible loss or damage, the railway may impose:

(a) a surcharge equal to one unit of account per kg of gross mass of the whole package;

(i) in the case of irregular, incorrect or incomplete description of substances and articles not acceptable for carriage under the RID;

(ii) in the case of irregular, incorrect or incomplete description of substances and articles which under the RID are acceptable for carriage subject to conditions, or in the case of failure to observe such conditions;

(b) a surcharge equal to five units of account per 100 kg of mass in excess of the load limit, where the wagon has been loaded by the consignor;

(c) a surcharge equal to twice the difference;

(i) between the carriage charge which should have been payable from the forwarding station to the destination station and that which had been charged, in the case of irregular, incorrect or incomplete description of goods other than those referred to in (a), or in general where the description of the consignment would enable it to be carried at a lower tariff than the one that is actually applicable;

(ii) between the carriage charge for the mass declared and that for the ascertained mass, where the mass declared is less than the real mass.

When a consignment is composed of goods charged at different rates and their mass can be separately determined without difficulty, the surcharge shall be calculated on the basis of the rates respectively applicable to such goods if this method of calculation results in a lower surcharge.

2   Should there be both an underdeclaration of mass and overloading in respect of one and the same wagon, the surcharges payable in respect thereof shall be cumulative.

3   The surcharges shall be charged against the goods irrespective of the place where the facts giving rise to the surcharges were established.

4   The amount of the surcharges and the reason for imposing them must be entered in the consignment note.

5   No surcharge shall be due in the case of:

(a) an incorrect declaration of mass, if the railway is bound to weigh the goods under the provisions in force at the forwarding station;

(b) an incorrect declaration of mass, or overloading, if the consignor has requested in the consignment note that the railway should weigh the goods;

(c) overloading arising in the course of carriage from atmospheric conditions if it is proved that the load on the wagon did not exceed the load limit when it was consigned;

(d) an increase in mass during carriage, without overloading, if it is proved that the increase was due to atmospheric conditions;

(e) an incorrect declaration of mass, without overloading, if the difference between the mass indicated in the consignment note and the ascertained mass does not exceed 3% of the declared mass;

(f) overloading of a wagon when the railway has neither published nor informed the consignor of the load limit in a way which would enable him to observe it.

Article 25 – Documents for completion of administrative formalities, custom seals

1   The consignor must attach to the consignment note the documents necessary for the completion of formalities required by Customs or other administrative authorities before delivery of the goods. Such documents shall relate only to goods which are the subject of one and the same consignment note, unless otherwise provided by the requirements of Customs or of other administrative authorities or by the tariffs.

However, when these documents are not attached to the consignment note or if they are to be provided by the consignee, the consignor shall indicate in the consignment note the station, the Customs office or the office of any other authority where the respective documents will be made available to the railway and where the formalities must be completed. If the consignor will himself be present or be represented by an agent when the formalities required by Customs or other administrative authorities are carried out, it will suffice for the documents to be produced at the time when those formalities are carried out.

2   The railway shall not be obliged to check whether the documents furnished are sufficient and correct.

3   The consignor shall be liable to the railway for any loss or damage resulting from the absence or insufficiency of or any irregularity in such documents, save in the case of fault by the railway. The railway shall, where it is at fault, be liable for any consequences arising from the loss, non-use or misuse of the documents referred to in the consignment note and accompanying it or deposited with the railway; nevertheless, any compensation shall not exceed that payable in the event of loss of the goods.

4   The consignor must comply with the requirements of Customs or of other administrative authorities with respect to the packing and sheeting of the goods. If the consignor has not packed or sheeted the goods in accordance with those requirements the railway shall be entitled to do so; the resulting costs shall be charged against the goods.

5   The railway may refuse consignments when the seals affixed by Customs or other administrative authorities are damaged or defective.

Article 26 – Completion of administrative formalities

1   In transit, the formalities required by Customs or other administrative authorities shall be completed by the railway. The railway may, however, delegate that duty to an agent.

2   In completing such formalities, the railway shall be liable for any fault committed by itself or by its agent; nevertheless, any compensation shall not exceed that payable in the event of loss of the goods.

3   The consignor, by so indicating in the consignment note, or the consignee by giving orders as provided for in Article 31, may ask:

(a)   to be present himself or to be represented by an agent when such formalities are carried out, for the purpose of furnishing any information or explanations required;

(b)   to complete such formalities himself or to have them completed by an agent, in so far as the laws and regulations of the State in which they are to be carried out so permit;

(c)   to pay Customs duties and other charges, when he or his agent is present at or completes such formalities, in so far as the laws and regulations of the State in which they carried out permit such payment.

Neither the consignor, nor the consignee who has the right of disposal, nor the agent of either may take possession of the goods.

4   If, for the completion of the formalities, the consignor designated a station where the provision in force do not permit of their completion, or if he has stipulated for the purpose any other procedure which cannot be followed, the railway shall act in the manner which appears to it to be the most favourable to the interests of the person entitled and shall inform the consignor of the measures taken.

If the consignor, by an entry in the consignment note, has undertaken to pay charges including Customs duty, the railway shall have the choice of completing Customs formalities either in transit or at the destination station.

5   Subject to the exception provided for in the second sub-para of para 4, the consignee may complete Customs formalities at the destination station if that station has a Customs office and the consignment note requests Customs clearance on arrival, or, in the absence of such request, if the goods arrive under Customs control. The consignee may also complete these formalities at a destination station that has no Customs officer if the national laws and regulations so permit or it the prior authority of the railway and the Customs authorities has been obtained. If the consignee exercises any of these rights, he shall pay in advance the amounts chargeable against the goods.

Nevertheless, the railway may proceed in accordance with para 4 if the consignee has not taken possession of the consignment note within the period fixed by the provisions in force at the destination station.

Article 27 – Transit periods

1   The transit periods shall be specified either by agreement between the railways participating in the carriage, or by the international tariffs applicable from the forwarding station to the destination station. For certain special types of traffic and on certain routes, these periods may also be established on the basis of transport plans applicable between the railways concerned; in that case they must be included in international tariffs or special agreements which, where appropriate, may provide for derogations from §§3 to 9 below.

Such periods shall not in any case exceed those which would result from the application of the following paragraphs.

2   In the absence of any indication in regard to the transit periods as provided for in para 1, and subject to the following paras, the transit periods shall be as follows:

   (a) for wagon load consignments:

      (i) by *grande vitesse*: period for despatch – 12 hours; period for carriage, for each 400 km or fraction thereof – 24 hours;

      (ii) by *petite vitesse*: period for despatch – 24 hours; period for carriage, for each 300 km or fraction thereof – 24 hours;

   (b) for less than wagon load consignments:

      (i) by *grande vitesse*: period for despatch – 12 hours; period for carriage, for each 300 km or fraction thereof – 24 hours;

      (ii) by *petite vitesse*: period for despatch – 24 hours; period for carriage, for each 200 km or fraction thereof – 24 hours;

All these distances shall relate to the kilometric distances contained in the tariffs.

3   The period for carriage shall be calculated on the total distance between the forwarding station and the destination station. The period for despatch shall be counted only one, irrespective of the number of systems traversed.

4   The railway may fix additional transit periods of specified duration in the following cases:

   (a) consignments handed in for carriage, or to be delivered, at places other than stations;

   (b) consignments to be carried:

      (i) by a line or system not equipped to deal rapidly with consignments;

      (ii) by a junction line connecting two lines of the same system or of different systems;

      (iii) by a second line;

      (iv) by lines of different gauge;

      (v) by sea or inland navigable waterway;

      (vi) by road if there is no rail link;

   (c) consignments charged at reduced rates in accordance with special or exceptional internal tariffs;

   (d) exceptional circumstances causing an exceptional increase in traffic or exceptional operating difficulties.

5   The additional transit period provided for in para 4 (a) to (c) shall be shown in the tariffs or in the provisions duly published in each State.

Those provided for in para 4 (d) must be published and may not come into force before their publication.

6   The transit period shall run from midnight next following acceptance of the goods for carriage. In the case, however, of traffic consigned *grande vitesse* the period shall start 24 hours later if the day which follows the day of acceptance for carriage is a Sunday or a statutory holiday and if the forwarding station is not open for *grande vitesse* traffic on that Sunday or statutory holiday.

7   Except in the case of any fault by the railway, the transit period shall be extended by the duration of the period necessitated by:

   (a) verification or ascertainment in accordance with Article 21 and Article 22, para 1, which reveals differences from the particulars shown in the consignment note;

   (b) completion of the formalities required by Customs or other administrative authorities;

   (c) modification of the contract of carriage under Articles 30 or 31;

   (d) special care to be given to the goods;

   (e) the trans-shipment or reloading of any goods loaded defectively by the consignor;

   (f) any interruption of traffic temporarily preventing the commencement or continuation of carriage.

The reason for and the duration of such extensions shall be entered in the consignment note. If necessary proof may be furnished by other means.

8   The transit period shall be suspended for:

   (a) *petite vitesse*, on Sundays and statutory holidays;

   (b) *grande vitesse*, on Sundays and certain statutory holidays when the provisions in force in any State provide for the suspension of domestic railway transit periods on those days;

(c) *grande vitesse* and *petite vitesse*, on Saturdays when the provisions in force in any State provide for the suspension of domestic railway transit periods on those days.

9   When the transit period ends after the time at which the destination station closes, the period shall be extended until two hours after the time at which the station next opens.

In addition, in the case of *grande vitesse* consignments, if the transit period ends on a Sunday or a holiday as defined in para 8(b) the period shall be extended until the same time on the next working day.

10 The transit period is observed if, before its expiry:

(a) in cases where consignments are to be delivered at a station and notice of arrival must be given, such notice is given and the goods are held at the disposal of the consignee;

(b) in cases where consignments are to be delivered at a station and notice of arrival need not be given, the goods are held at the disposal of the consignee;

(c) in the case of consignments which are to be delivered at places other than stations, the goods are placed at the disposal of the consignee.

Article 28 – Delivery

1   The railway shall hand over the consignment note and deliver the goods to the consignee at the destination station against a receipt and payment of the amounts chargeable to the consignee by the railway.

Acceptance of the consignment note obliges the consignee to pay to the railway the amounts chargeable to him.

2   It shall be equivalent to delivery to the consignee if, in accordance with the provisions in force at the destination station:

(a) the goods have been handed over to Customs or *Octroi* authorities at their premises or warehouses, when these are not subject to railway supervision;

(b) the goods have been deposited for storage with the railway, with a forwarding agent or in a public warehouse.

3   The provisions in force at the destination station or the terms of any agreements with the consignee shall determine whether the railway is entitled or obliged to hand over the goods to the consignee elsewhere than at the destination station, whether in a private siding, at his domicile or in a railway depot. If the railway hands over the goods, or arranges for them to be handed over in a private siding, at his domicile or in a depot, delivery shall be deemed to have been effected at the time when they are so handed over. Save where the railway and the user of a private siding have agreed otherwise, operations carried out by the railway on behalf of and under the instructions of that user shall not be covered by the contract of carriage.

4   After the arrival of the goods at the destination station, the consignee may require the railway to hand over the consignment note and deliver the goods to him.

If the loss of the goods is established or if the goods have not arrived on the expiry of the period provided for in Article 39, para 1, the consignee may assert, in his own name, any rights against the railway which he may have acquired by reason of the contract of carriage.

5   The person entitled may refuse to accept the goods, even when he has received the consignment note and paid the charges, so long as an examination for which he has asked in order to establish alleged loss or damage has not been made.

6   In all other respects, delivery of goods shall be carried out in accordance with the provisions in force at the destination station.

Article 29 – Correction of charges

1   In case of incorrect application of a tariff or of error in the calculation or collection of charges, overcharges shall be repaid by the railway and undercharges paid to the railway only if they exceed four units of account per consignment note. The repayment shall be made as a matter of course.

2   If the consignee has not taken possession of the consignment note, the consignor shall be obliged to pay to the railway any amounts undercharged. When the consignment note has been accepted by the consignee or the contract of carriage modified in accordance with

Article 31, the consignor shall be obliged to pay any undercharge only to the extent that it relates to the costs which he has undertaken to pay by an entry in the consignment note. Any balance of the undercharge shall be paid by the consignee.

3 Sums due under this Article shall bear interest at 5% per annum from the day of receipt of the demand for payment or from the day of the claim referred to in Article 53 or, if there has been no such demand or claim, from the day on which legal proceedings are instituted.

If, within a reasonable period allotted to him, the person entitled does not submit to the railway the supporting documents required for the amount of the claim to be finally settled, no interest shall accrue between the expiry of the period laid down and the actual submission of such documents.

TITLE III – MODIFICATION OF THE CONTRACT OF CARRIAGE

Article 30 – Modification by the consignor

1 The consignor may modify the contract of carriage by giving subsequent orders:
  (a) for the goods to be withdrawn at the forwarding station;
  (b) for the goods to be stopped in transit;
  (c) for delivery of the goods to be delayed;
  (d) for the goods to be delivered to a person other than the consignee shown in the consignment note;
  (e) for the goods to be delivered at a station other than the destination station shown in the consignment note;
  (f) for the goods to be returned to the forwarding station;
  (g) for the consignment to be made subject to a cash on delivery payment;
  (h) for a cash on delivery payment to be increased, reduced or cancelled;
  (i) for charges relating to a consignment which has not been prepaid to be debited to him, or for charges which he has undertaken to pay in accordance with Article 15, para 2 to be increased.

The tariffs of the forwarding railway may provide that orders specified in (g) to (i) are not acceptable.

The supplementary provisions or the international tariffs in force between the railways participating in the carriage may provide for the acceptance of orders other than those listed above.

Orders must not in any event have the effect of splitting the consignment.

2 Such orders shall be given to the forwarding station by means of a written declaration in the form laid down and published by the railway. The declaration shall be reproduced and signed by the consignor in the duplicate of the consignment note which shall be presented to the railway at the same time. The forwarding station shall certify that the order has been received by affixing its date stamp on the duplicate note below the declaration made by the consignor and the duplicate shall then be returned to him.

If the consignor asks for a cash on delivery payment to be increased, reduced or cancelled, he shall produce the document which was delivered to him. Where the cash on delivery payment is to be increased or reduced, such document shall be returned to the consignor after correction; in the event of cancellation it shall not be returned. Any order given in a form other than that prescribed shall be null and void.

3 If the railway complies with the consignor's orders without requiring the production of the duplicate, where this has been sent to the consignee, the railway shall be liable to the consignee for any loss or damage caused thereby. Nevertheless, any compensation shall not exceed that payable in the event of loss of the goods.

4 The consignor's right to modify the contract of carriage shall, notwithstanding that he is in possession of the duplicate of the consignment note, be extinguished in cases where the consignee:
  (a) has taken possession of the consignment note;
  (b) has accepted the goods;

(c) has asserted his rights in accordance with Article 28, para 4;

(d) is entitled, in accordance with Article 31, to give orders as soon as the consignment had entered the Customs territory of the country of destination.

From that time onwards, the railway shall comply with the orders and instructions of the consignee.

Article 31 – Modification by the consignee

1   When the consignor has not undertaken to pay the charges relating to carriage in the country of destination, and has not inserted in the consignment note the words 'Consignee not authorised to give subsequent orders', the consignee may modify the contact of carriage by giving subsequent orders:

(a) for the goods to be stopped in transit;

(b) for delivery of the goods to be delayed;

(c) for the goods to be delivered in the country of destination to a person other than the consignee shown in the consignment note;

(d) for the goods to be delivered in the country of destination at a station other than the destination station shown in the consignment note, subject to contrary provisions in international tariffs;

(e) for formalities required by Customs or other administrative authorities to be carried out in accordance with Article 26, para 3.

The supplementary provisions or the international tariffs in force between the railways participating in the carriage may provide for the acceptance of orders other than those listed above.

Orders must not in any case have the effect of splitting the consignment. The consignee's orders shall only be effective after the consignment has entered the Customs territory of the country of destination.

2   Such orders shall be given either to the destination station or to the station of entry into the country of destination, by means of a written declaration in the form laid down and published by the railway.

Any order given in a form other than that prescribed shall be null and void.

3   The consignee's right to modify the contract of carriage shall be extinguished in cases where he has:

(a) taken possession of the consignment note;

(b) accepted the goods;

(c) asserted his rights in accordance with Article 28, para 4;

(d) designated a person in accordance with para 1(c) and that person has taken possession of the consignment note or asserted his rights in accordance with Article 28, para 4.

4   If the consignee has given instructions for delivery of the goods to another person, that person shall not be entitled to modify the contract of carriage.

Article 32 – Execution of subsequent orders

1   The railway may not refuse to execute orders given under Articles 30 or 31 or delay doing so save where:

(a) it is no longer possible to execute the orders by the time they reach the station responsible for doing so;

(b) compliance with the orders would interfere with normal railway operations;

(c) a change of destination station would contravene the laws and regulations of a State, and in particular the requirements of the Customs or of other administrative authorities;

(d) in the case of a change of destination station, the value of the goods will not, in the railway's view, cover all the charges which would be payable on the goods on arrival at the new destination, unless the amount of such charges is paid or guaranteed immediately.

The person who has given the orders shall be informed as soon as possible of any circumstances which prevent their execution.

If the railway is not in a position to foresee such circumstances, the person who has given the orders shall be liable for all the consequences of starting to execute them.

2   The charges arising from the execution of an order, except those arising from any fault by the railway, shall be paid in accordance with Article 15.

3   Subject to para 1, the railway shall, in the case of any fault on its part, be liable for the consequences of failure to execute an order or failure to execute it properly. Nevertheless, any compensation shall not exceed that payable in the event of loss of the goods.

Article 33 – Circumstances preventing carriage

1   When circumstances prevent the carriage of goods, the railway shall decide whether it is preferable to carry the goods as a matter of course by modifying the route or whether it is advisable in the consignor's interest to ask him for instructions and at the same time give him any relevant information available to the railway.

Save fault on its part, the railway may recover the carriage charges applicable to the route followed and shall be allowed the transit periods applicable to such route.

2   If it is impossible to continue carrying the goods, the railway shall ask the consignor for instructions. It shall not be obliged to do so in the event of carriage being temporarily prevented as a result of measures taken in accordance with Article 3, para 4.

3   The consignor may enter in the consignment note instructions to cover the event of circumstances preventing carriage. If the railway considers that such instructions cannot be executed, it shall ask for fresh instructions.

4   The consignor, on being notified of circumstances preventing carriage, may give his instructions either to the forwarding station or to the station where the goods are being held. If those instructions change the consignee or the destination station or are given to the station where the goods are being held, the consignor must enter them in the duplicate of the consignment note and present this to the railway.

5   If the railway complies with the consignor's instructions without requiring the production of the duplicate, when this has been sent to the consignee, the railway shall be liable to the consignee for any loss or damage caused thereby. Nevertheless, any compensation shall not exceed that payable in the event of loss of the goods.

6   If the consignor, on being notified of a circumstance preventing carriage, fails to give within a reasonable time instructions which can be executed, the railway shall take action in accordance with the provisions relating to circumstances preventing delivery, in force at the place where the goods have been held up. If the goods have been sold, the proceeds of sale, less any amounts chargeable against the goods, shall be held at the disposal of the consignor. If the proceeds are less than those costs, the consignor shall pay the difference.

7   When the circumstances preventing carriage cease to obtain before the arrival of instructions from the consignor, the goods shall be forwarded to their destination without waiting for such instructions; the consignor shall be notified to that effect as soon as possible.

8   When the circumstances preventing carriage arise after the consignee has modified the contract of carriage in accordance with Article 31, the railway shall notify the consignee. Paragraphs 2, 6, 7 and 9 shall apply analogously.

9   Save fault on its part, the railway may raise demurrage or standage charges if circumstances prevent carriage.

10 Article 32 shall apply to carriage undertaken in accordance with Article 33.

Article 34 – Circumstances preventing delivery

1   When circumstances prevent delivery of the goods, the destination station shall without delay notify the consignor through the forwarding station, and ask for his instructions. The consignor shall be notified direct, either in writing, by telegram or by teleprinter, if he has so requested in the consignment note; the costs of such notification shall be charged against the goods.

2   If the circumstances preventing delivery cease to obtain before the arrival at the destination station of instructions from the consignor the goods shall be delivered to the

consignee. The consignor shall be notified without delay be registered letter; the costs of such notification shall be charged against the goods.

3   If the consignee refuses the goods, the consignor shall be entitled to give instructions even if he is unable to produce the duplicate of the consignment note.

4   The consignor may also request, by an entry in the consignment note, that the goods be returned to him as a matter of course in the event of circumstances preventing delivery. Unless such request is made, his express consent is required.

5   Unless the tariffs otherwise provide, the consignor's instructions shall be given through the forwarding station.

6   Except as otherwise provided for above, the railway responsible for delivery shall proceed in accordance with the provisions in force at the place of delivery. If the goods have been sold, the proceeds of sale, less any costs chargeable against the goods, shall be held at the disposal of the consignor. If such proceeds are less than those costs, the consignor shall pay the difference.

7   When the circumstances preventing delivery arise after the consignee has modified the contract of carriage in accordance with Article 31, the railway shall notify the consignee. Paragraphs 1, 2 and 6 shall apply analogously.

8   Article 32 shall apply to carriage undertaken in accordance with Article 34.

TITLE IV – LIABILITY

Article 35 – Collective responsibility of railways

1   The railway which has accepted goods for carriage with the consignment note shall be responsible for the carriage over the entire route up to delivery.

2   Each succeeding railway, by the very act of taking over the goods with the consignment note, shall become a party to the contract of carriage in accordance with the terms of that document and shall assume the obligations arising therefrom, without prejudice to the provisions of Article 55, para 3, relating to the railway of destination.

Article 36 – Extent of liability

1   The railway shall be liable for loss or damage resulting from the total or partial loss of, or damage to, the goods between the time of acceptance for carriage and the time of delivery and for the loss or damage resulting from the transit period being exceeded.

2   The railway shall be relieved of such liability if the loss or damage or the exceeding of the transit period was caused by a fault on the part of the person entitled, by an order given by the person entitled other than as a result of a fault on the part of the railway, by inherent vice of the goods (decay, wastage, etc) or by circumstances which the railway could not avoid and the consequences of which it was unable to prevent.

3   The railways shall be relieved of such liability when the loss or damage arises from the special risks inherent in one or more of the following circumstances:

(a) carriage in open wagons under the conditions applicable thereto or under an agreement made between the consignor and the railway and referred to in the consignment note;

(b) absence or inadequacy of packing in the case of goods which by their nature are liable to loss or damage when not packed or when not properly packed;

(c) loading operations carried out by the consignor or unloading operations carried out by the consignee under the provisions applicable thereto or under an agreement made between the consignor and the railway and referred to in the consignment note, or under an agreement between the consignee and the railway;

(d) defective loading, when loading has been carried out by the consignor under the provisions applicable thereto or under an agreement made between the consignor and the railway and referred to in the consignment note;

(e) completion by the consignor, the consignee or an agent of either, of the formalities required by Customs or other administrative authorities;

(f) the nature of certain goods which renders them inherently liable to total or partial loss or damage, especially through breakage, rust, interior and spontaneous decay, desiccation or wastage;

(g) irregular, incorrect or incomplete description of articles not acceptable for carriage or acceptable subject to conditions, or failure on the part of the consignor to observe the prescribed precautions in respect of articles acceptable subject to conditions;

(h) carriage of live animals;

(i) carriage which, under the provisions applicable or under an agreement made between the consignor and the railway and referred to in the consignment note, must be accompanied by an attendant, if the loss or damage results from any risk which the attendant was intended to avert.

Article 37 – Burden of proof

1   The burden of proving that the loss, the damage or the exceeding of the transit period was due to one of the causes specified in Article 36, para 2 shall rest upon the railway.

2   When the railway establishes that, having regard to the circumstances of a particular case, the loss or damage could have arisen from one or more of the special risks referred to in Article 36, para 3, it shall be presumed that it did so arise. The person entitled shall, however, have the right to prove that the loss or damage was not attributable either wholly or partly to one of those risks.

This presumption shall not apply in the case referred to in Article 36, para 3(a) if an abnormally large quantity has been lost or if a package has been lost.

Article 38 – Presumption in case of reconsignment

1   When a consignment dispatched in accordance with the Uniform Rules has been reconsigned subject to the same rules and partial loss or damage has been ascertained after the reconsignment, it shall be presumed that it occurred during the latest contract of carriage if the consignment remained in the care of the railway and was reconsigned in the same condition as it arrived at the station from which it was reconsigned.

2   This presumption shall also apply when the contract of carriage prior to the reconsignment was not subject to the Uniform Rules, if the rules would have applied in the case of a through consignment from the original forwarding station to the final destination station.

Article 39 – Presumption of loss of goods

1   The person entitled may, without being required to furnish further proof, consider the goods lost when they have not been delivered to the consignee or are not being held at his disposal within 30 days after the expiry of the transit periods.

2   The person entitled may, on compensation for the lost goods, make a written request to be notified without delay should the goods be recovered within one year after the payment of compensation. The railway shall give a written acknowledgement of such request.

3   Within 30 days after receipt of such notification, the person entitled may require the goods to be delivered to him at any station on the route. In that case, he shall pay the charges in respect of carriage from the forwarding station to the station where delivery is effected and shall refund the compensation received, less any costs which may have been included therein. Nevertheless, he shall retain his rights to claim compensation for exceeding the transit period provided for in Articles 43 and 46.

4   In the absence of the request mentioned in para 2 or of any instructions given within the period specified in para 3, or if the goods are recovered more than one year after the payment of compensation, the railway shall dispose of them in accordance with the laws and regulations of the State having jurisdiction over the railway.

Article 40 – Compensation for loss

1   In the event of total or partial loss of the goods, the railway must pay, to the exclusion of all other damages, compensation calculated according to the commodity exchange quotation or, if there is no such quotation, according to the current market price, or if there is neither such quotation nor such price, according to the normal value of goods of the same kind and quality at the time and place at which the goods were accepted for carriage.

2   Compensation shall not exceed 17 units of account per kg of gross mass short, subject to the limit provided for in Article 45.

3   The railway shall in addition refund carriage charges, Customs duties and other amounts incurred in connection with carriage of the lost goods.

4   When the calculation of compensation requires the conversion of amounts expressed in foreign currencies, conversion shall be at the rate of exchange applicable at the time and place of payment of compensation.

Article 41 – Liability for wastage in transit

1   In respect of goods which, by reason of their nature, are generally subject to wastage in transit by the sole fact of carriage, the railway shall only be liable to the extent that the wastage exceeds the following allowances, whatever the length of the route:

   (a) Two per cent of the mass for liquid goods or goods consigned in a moist condition, and also for the following goods:

      bark; leather; whole or ground bones; liquorice root; coal and coke; fresh mushrooms; grated or ground dye-woods; peat and turf; fats; putty or mastic; fresh fish; dried roots; fresh, dried or cooked fruit; salt; furs; animal sinews; hide cuttings; soap and solidified oils; hides; cut tobacco; hog bristles; fresh tobacco leaves; hops; fresh vegetables; horns and hooves; wool; horsehair.

   (b) One per cent of the weight for all other dry goods.

2   The limitation of liability provided for in para 1 may not be invoked if, having regard to the circumstances of a particular case, it is proved that the loss was not due to cause which would justify an allowance.

3   Where several packages are carried under a single consignment note, the wastage in transit shall be calculated separately for each package if its mass on despatch is shown separately in the consignment note or can otherwise be ascertained.

4   In the event of total loss of the goods, no deduction for wastage in transit shall be made in calculating the compensation payable.

5   This Article shall not derogate from Articles 36 and 37.

Article 42 – Compensation for damage

1   In case of damage to goods, the railway must pay compensation equivalent to the loss in value of the goods, to the exclusion of all other damages. The amount shall be calculated by applying to the value of the goods as defined in Article 40 the percentage of loss in value noted at the place of destination.

2   The compensation may not exceed:

   (a) if the whole consignment has lost value through damage, the amount which would have been payable in case of total loss;

   (b) if only part of the consignment has lost value through damage, the amount which would have been payable had that part been lost.

3   The railway shall in addition refund the amounts provided for in Article 40, para 3, in the proportion set out in para 1.

Article 43 – Compensation for exceeding the transit period

1   If loss or damage has resulted from the transit period being exceeded, the railway shall pay compensation not exceeding three times the carriage charger.

2   In case of total loss of the goods, the compensation provided for in para 1 shall not be payable in addition to that provided for in Article 40.

3   In case of partial loss of the goods, the compensation provided for in para 1 shall not exceed three times the carriage charges in respect of that part of the consignment which has not been lost.

4   In case of damage to the goods, not resulting from the transit period being exceeded, the compensation provided for in para 1 shall, where appropriate, be payable in addition to that provided for in Article 40.

5   In no case shall the total of compensation payable under para 1 together with that payable under Articles 40 and 42 exceed the compensation which would be payable in the event of total loss of the goods.

6   The railway may provide, in international tariffs or in special agreements for other forms of compensation than those provided for in para 1 when, in accordance with Article 27, para 1, the transit period has been established on the basis of transport plans.

If, in this case, the transit periods provided for in Article 27, para 2 are exceeded, the person entitled may demand either the compensation provided for in para 1 above or that determined by the international tariff or the special agreement applied.

Article 44 – Compensation in case of wilful misconduct or gross negligence

When the loss, damage or exceeding of the transit period, or the failure to perform or failure to perform properly the railway's additional services provided for in the Uniform Rules, has been caused by wilful misconduct or gross negligence on the part of the railway, full compensation for the loss or damage proved shall be paid to the person entitled by the railway.

In case of gross negligence, liability shall, however, be limited to twice the maxima specified in Articles 25, 26, 30, 32, 33, 40, 42, 43, 45 and 46.

Article 45 – Limitation of compensation under certain tariffs

When the railway agrees to special conditions of carriage through special or exceptional tariffs, involving a reduction in the carriage charge calculated on the basis of the general tariffs, it may limit the amount of compensation payable to the person entitled in the event of loss, damage or exceeding of the transit period, provided that such limit is indicated in the tariff.

When the special conditions of carriage apply only to part of the route, the limit may only be invoked if the event giving rise to the compensation occurred on that part of the route.

Article 46 – Compensation in case of interest in delivery

In case of a declaration of interest in delivery, further compensation for loss or damage proved may be claimed, in addition to the compensation provided for in Articles 40, 42, 43 and 45, up to the amount declared.

Article 47 – Interest on compensation

1   The person entitled may claim interest on compensation payable, calculated at 5% per annum, from the date of the claim referred to in Article 53 or, if no such claim has been made, from the day on which legal proceedings are instituted.

2   Interest shall only be payable if the compensation exceeds four units of account per consignment note.

3   If, within a reasonable period allotted to him, the person entitled does not submit to the railway the supporting documents required for the amount of the claim to be finally settled, no interest shall accrue between the expiry of the period laid down and the actual submission of such documents.

Article 48 – Liability in respect of rail-sea traffic

1   In rail-sea transport by the services referred to in Article 2, para 2 of the convention each State may, by requesting that a suitable note be included in the list of lines or services to which the Uniform Rules apply, indicate that the following grounds for exemption from liability will apply in their entirety in addition to those provided for in Article 36.

The carrier may only avail himself to these grounds for exemption if he proves that the loss, damage or exceeding of the transit period occurred in the course of the sea journey between the time when the goods were loaded on board the ship and the time when they were discharged from the ship.

The grounds for exemption are as follows:

(a) act, neglect or default on the part of the master, a mariner, pilot or the carrier's servants in the navigation or management of the ship;

(b) unseaworthiness of the ship, if the carrier proves that the unseaworthiness is not attributable to lack of due diligence on his part to make the ship seaworthy, to ensure that it is properly manned, equipped and supplied or to make all parts of the ship in which the goods are loaded fit and safe for their reception, carriage and protection;

(c) fire, if the carrier proves that it was not caused by his act or fault, or that of the master, a mariner, pilot or the carrier's servants;

(d) perils, dangers and accidents of the sea or the navigable waters;

(e) saving or attempting to save life or property at sea;

(f) the loading of goods on the deck of the ship, if they are so loaded with the consent of the consignor given in the consignment note and are not in wagons.

The above grounds for exemption in no way affect the general obligations of the carrier and, in particular, his obligation to exercise due diligence to make the ship seaworthy, to ensure that it is properly manned, equipped and supplied and to make all parts of the ship in which the goods are loaded fit and safe for their reception, carriage and protection.

Even when the carrier can rely on the foregoing grounds for exemption, he shall nevertheless remain liable if the person entitled proves that the loss, damage or exceeding of the transit period is due to a fault of the carrier, the master, a mariner, pilot or the carrier's servants, fault other than provided for under (a).

2   Where one and the same sea route is served by several undertakings included in the list referred to in Articles 3 and 10 of the convention, the regime of liability applicable to that route shall be the same for all those undertakings.

In addition, where such undertakings have been included in the list at the request of several States, the adoption of this regime shall be the subject of prior agreement between those States.

3   The measures taken under this Article shall be notified to the central office. They shall come into force at the earliest at the expiry of a period of 30 days from the date of the letter by which the central office notifies them to the other States.

Consignments already in transit shall not be affected by such measures.

Article 49 – Liability in case of nuclear incidents

The railway shall be relieved of liability under the Uniform Rules for less or damage caused by a nuclear incident when the operator of a nuclear installation or another person who is substituted for him is liable for the loss or damage pursuant to a State's laws and regulations governing liability in the field of nuclear energy.

Article 50 – Liability of the railway for its servants

The railway shall be liable for its servants and for any other persons whom it employs to perform the carriage. If, however, such servants and other persons, at the request of an interested party, make out consignment notes, make translations or render other services which the railway itself is under no obligation to render, they shall be deemed to be acting on behalf of the person to whom the services are rendered.

Article 51 – Other actions

In all cases to which the Uniform Rules apply, any action in respect of liability on any grounds whatsoever may be brought against the railway only subject to the conditions and limitations laid down in the rules. The same shall apply to any action brought against those servants and other persons for whom the railway is liable under Article 50.

TITLE V – ASSERTION OF RIGHTS

Article 52 – Ascertainment of partial loss or damage

1   When partial loss of, or damage to, goods is discovered or presumed by the railway or alleged by the person entitled, the railway must without delay, and if possible in the presence of the person entitled, draw up a report stating, according to the nature of the loss or damage, the condition of the goods, their mass and, as far as possible, the extent of the loss or damage, its cause and the time of its occurrence.

A copy of the report must be supplied free of charge to the person entitled.

2   Should the person entitled not accept the findings in the report, he may request that the condition and mass of the goods and the cause and amount of the loss or damage be ascertained by an expert appointed either by the parties or by a court. The procedure to be followed shall be governed by the laws and regulations in the State in which such ascertainment takes place.

Article 53 – Claims

1   Claims relating to the contract of carriage shall be made in writing to the railway specified in Article 55.

2   A claim may be made by persons who have the right to bring an action against the railway under Article 54.

3   To make the claim, the consignor must produce the duplicate of the consignment note. Failing this, he must produce an authorisation from the consignee or furnish proof that the consignee has refused to accept the consignment. To make the claim, the consignee must produce the consignment note if it has been handed over to him.

4   The consignment note, the duplicate and any other documents which the person entitled thinks fit to submit with the claim shall be produced either in the original or as copies, the copies to be duly authenticated if the railway so requires. On settlement of the claim, the railway may require the production, in the original form, of the consignment note, the duplicate or the cash on delivery voucher so that they may be endorsed to the effect that settlement has been made.

Article 54 – Persons who may bring an action against the railway

1   An action for the recovery of a sum paid under the contract of carriage may only be brought by the person who made the payment.

2   An action in respect of the cash on delivery payments provided for in Article 17 may only be brought by the consignor.

3   Other actions arising from the contract of carriage may be brought:
(a) by the consignor, until such time as the consignee has:
(i)   taken possession of the consignment note;
(ii) accepted the goods; or
(iii) asserted his rights under Article 28, para 4 or Article 31;
(b) by the consignee, from the time when he has:
(i)   taken possession of the consignment note;
(ii) accepted the goods;
(iii) asserted his rights under Article 28, para 4; or
(iv) asserted his rights under Article 31 provided that the right of action shall be extinguished from the time when the person designated by the consignee in accordance with Article 31, para 1(c) has taken possession of the consignment note, accepted the goods, or asserted his rights under Article 28, para 4.

4   In order to bring an action, the consignor must produce the duplicate of the consignment note. Failing this, in order to bring an action under para 3(a) he must produce an authorisation from the consignee or furnish proof that the consignee has refused to accept the consignment. In order to bring an action, the consignee shall produce the consignment note if it has been handed over to him.

Article 55 – Railways against which an action may be brought

1   An action for the recovery of a sum paid under the contract of carriage may be brought against the railway which has collected that sum or against the railway on whose behalf it was collected.

2   An action in respect of the cash on delivery payments provided for in Article 17 may only be brought against the forwarding railway.

3   Other actions arising from the contact of carriage may be brought against the forwarding railway, the railway of destination or the railway on which the event giving rise to the proceedings occurred. Such actions may be brought against the railway of destination even if it has received neither the goods nor the consignment note.

4   If the plaintiff can choose between several railways, his right to choose shall be extinguished as soon as he brings an action against any one of them.

5   An action may be brought against a railway other than those specified in paras 1, 2 and 3 when instituted by way of counterclaim or by way of exception to the principal claim based on the same contract of carriage.

Article 56 – Competence

Actions brought under the Uniform Rules may only be instituted in the competent court of the State having jurisdiction over the defendant railway, unless otherwise provided in agreements between States or in acts of concession. When a railway operates independent railway systems in different States, each system shall be regarded as a separate railway for the purposes of this article.

Article 57 – Extinction of right of action against the railway

1   Acceptance of the goods by the person entitled shall extinguish all rights of action against the railway arising from the contract in case of partial loss, damage or exceeding of the transit period.

2   Nevertheless, the right of action shall not be extinguished:

(a) in the case of partial loss or of damage, if:

(i) the loss or damage was ascertained before the acceptance of the goods in accordance with Article 52 by the person entitled;

(ii) the ascertainment which should have been carried out under Article 52 was omitted solely through the fault of the railway;

(b) in the case of loss or damage which is not apparent and is not ascertained until after acceptance of the goods by the person entitled, provided that he:

(i) asks for ascertainment in accordance with Article 52 immediately after discovery of the loss or damage and not later than seven days after the acceptance of the goods;

(ii) and, in addition, proves that the loss or damage occurred between the time of acceptance for carriage and the time of delivery;

(c) in cases where the transit period has been exceeded, if the person entitled has, within 60 days, asserted his rights against one of the railways referred to in Article 55, para 3;

(d) if the person entitled furnishes proof that the loss or damage was caused by wilful misconduct or gross negligence on the part of the railway.

3   If the goods have been reconsigned in accordance with Article 38, para 1 rights of action in case of partial loss or of damage, arising from one of the previous contracts of carriage, shall be extinguished as if there had been only one contract of carriage.

Article 58 – Limitation of action

1   The period of limitation for an action arising from the contract of carriage shall be one year. Nevertheless, the period of limitation shall be two years in the case of an action:

(a) to recover a cash on delivery payment collected by the railway from the consignee;

(b) to recover the proceeds of a sale affected by the railway;

(c) for loss or damage caused by wilful misconduct;

(d) for fraud;

(e) arising from one of the contracts of carriage prior to the reconsignment in the case provided for in Article 38, para 1.

2   The period of limitation shall run:

(a) in actions for compensation for total loss, from the thirtieth day after the expiry of the transit period;

(b) in actions for compensation for partial loss, for damage or for exceeding the transit period, from the day when delivery took place;

(c) in actions for payment or refund of carriage charges, supplementary charges, other charges or surcharges, or for correction of charges in case of a tariff being wrongly applied or of an error in calculation or collection:

(i) if payment has been made, from the day of payment;

(ii) if payment has not been made, from the day when the goods were accepted for carriage if payment is due from the consignor, or from the day when the consignee took possession of the consignment note if payment is due from him;

(iii) in the case of sums to be paid under a charge note, from the day on which the railway submits to the consignor the account of charges provided for in Article 15, para 7; if no such account has been submitted, the period in respect of sums due to the railway shall run from the 30th day following the expiry of the transit period;

(d) in an action by the railway for recovery of a sum which has been paid by the consignee instead of by the consignor or *vice versa* and which the railway is required to refund to the person entitled, from the day of the claim for a refund;

(e) in actions relating to cash on delivery as provided for in Article 17, from the 30th day following the expiry of the transit period;

(f) in actions to recover the proceeds of a sale, from the day of the sale;

(g) in actions to recover additional duty demanded by Customs or other administrative authorities, from the day of the demand made by such authorities;

(h) in all other cases, from the day when the right of action arises.

The day indicated for the commencement of the period of limitation shall not be included in the period.

3   When a claim is presented to a railway in accordance with Article 53 together with the necessary supporting documents, the period of limitation shall be suspended until the day that the railway rejects the claim by notification in writing and returns the documents. If part of the claim is admitted, the period of limitation shall recommence in respect of that part of the claim still in dispute. The burden of proof of receipt of the claim or of the reply and of the return of the documents shall rest on the party who relies on those facts.

The period of limitation shall not be suspended by further claims having the same object.

4   A right of action which has become time-barred may not be exercised by way of counter claim or relied upon by way of exception.

5   Subject to the foregoing provisions, the suspension and interruption of periods of limitation shall be governed by national law.

TITLE VI – RELATIONS BETWEEN RAILWAYS

Article 59 – Settlement of accounts between railways

1   Any railway which has collected, either at the time of forwarding or on arrival, charges or other sums due under the contract of carriage must pay to the railways concerned their respective shares.

The methods of payment shall be settled by agreements between railways.

2   Subject to its rights of recovery against the consignor, the forwarding railway shall be liable for carriage and other charges which it has failed to collect when the consignor has undertaken to pay them in accordance with Article 15.

3   Should the railway of destination deliver the goods without collecting charges or other sums due under the contract of carriage, it shall be liable for them to the railways which have taken part in the carriage and to the other parties concerned.

4   Should one railway default in payment and such default be confirmed by the central office at the request of one of the creditor railways, the consequences thereof shall be borne by all the other railways which have taken part in the carriage in proportion to their shares of the carriage charges.

The right of recovery against the defaulting railway shall not be affected.

Article 60 – Recourse in case of loss or damage

1   A railway which has paid compensation in accordance with the Uniform Rules, for total or partial loss or for damage, has a right of recourse against the other railways which have taken part in the carriage in accordance with the following provision:

(a) the railway which has caused the loss or damage shall be solely liable for it;

(b) when the loss or damage has been caused by more than one railway, each shall be liable for the loss or damage it has caused; if such distinction cannot be made, the compensation shall be apportioned between those railways in accordance with (c);

(c) if it cannot be proved that the loss or damage has been caused by one or more railways in particular, the compensation shall be apportioned between all the railways which have taken part in the carriage, except those which can prove that the loss or damage was not caused on their lines; such apportionment shall be in proportion to the kilometric distances contained in the tariffs.

2   In the case of the insolvency of any one of the railways, the unpaid share due from it shall be apportioned among all the other railways which have taken part in the carriage, in proportion to the kilometric distances contained in the tariffs.

Article 61 – Recourse in case of exceeding the transit period

1   Article 60 shall apply where compensation is paid for exceeding the transit period. If this has been caused by more than one railway, the compensation shall be apportioned between such railways in proportion to the length of the delay occurring on their respective lines.

2   The transit periods specified in Article 27 shall be apportioned in the following manner:
    (a) where two railways have taken part in the carriage;
        (i)   the period for despatch shall be divided equally;
        (ii) the period for transport shall be divided in proportion to the kilometric distances contained in the tariffs;
    (b) where three or more railways have taken part in the carriage;
        (i)   the period for despatch shall be divided equally between the forwarding railway and the railway of destination;
        (ii) the period for transport shall be divided between all the railways: one-third in equal shares, the remaining two-thirds in proportion to the kilometric distances contained in the tariffs.

3   Any additional periods to which a railway may be entitled shall be allocated to that railway.

4   The interval between the time when the goods are handed over to the railway and commencement of the period for despatch shall be allocated exclusively to the forwarding railway.

5   Such apportionment shall only apply if the total transit period has been exceeded.

Article 62 – Procedure for recourse

1   The validity of the payment made by the railway exercising one of the rights of recourse under Articles 60 and 61 may not be disputed by the railway against which the right of recourse is exercised, when compensation has been determined by a court and when the latter railway duly served with notice, has been afforded an opportunity to intervene in the proceedings. The court seised of the main proceedings shall determine what time shall be allowed for such notification and for intervention in the proceedings.

2   A railway exercising its right of recourse must take proceedings by one and the same action against all the railways concerned with which it has not reached a settlement, failing which it shall lose its right of recourse in the case of those against which it has not taken proceedings.

3   The court shall give its decision in one and the same judgment on all recourse claims brought before it.

4   The railways against which such action has been brought shall have no further right of recourse.

5   Recourse proceedings may not be joined with proceedings for compensation taken by the person entitled on the basis of the contract of carriage.

Article 63 – Competence for recourse

1   The courts of the country in which the railway against which the recourse claim has been made, has its headquarters shall have exclusive competence for all recourse claims.

2   When the action is to be brought against several railways, the plaintiff railway shall be entitled to choose the court in which it will bring the proceedings from among those having competence under para 1.

Article 64 – Agreements concerning recourse

By agreement, railways may derogate from the provisions concerning reciprocal rights of recourse set out in Title VI, apart from that contained in Article 62, para 5.

Articles 65–66 [omitted]

CARRIAGE OF GOODS BY ROAD ACT 1965

SCHEDULE

Convention on the Contract for the International Carriage of Goods by Road

CHAPTER I – SCOPE OF APPLICATION

Section 1

Article 1

1 This Convention shall apply to every contract for the carriage of goods by road in vehicles for reward, when the place of taking over of the goods and the place designated for delivery, as specified in the contract, are situated in two different countries, of which at least one is a Contracting country, irrespective of the place of residence and the nationality of the parties.

2 For the purposes of this Convention, 'vehicles' means motor vehicles, articulated vehicles, trailers and semi-trailers as defined in Article 4 of the Convention on Road Traffic dated 19 September 1949.

3 This Convention shall apply also where carriage coming within its scope is carried out by States or by governmental institutions or organisations.

4 This Convention shall not apply:
   (a) to carriage performed under the terms of any international postal convention:
   (b) to funeral consignments;
   (c) to furniture removal.

5 The Contracting parties agree not to vary any of the provisions of this Convention by special agreements between two or more of them, except to make it inapplicable to their frontier traffic or to authorise the use in transport operations entirely confined to their territory of consignment notes representing a title to the goods.

Article 2

1 Where the vehicle containing the goods is carried over part of the journey by sea, rail, inland waterways or air, and, except where the provisions of article 14 are applicable, the goods are not unloaded from the vehicle, this Convention shall nevertheless apply to the whole of the carriage. Provided that to the extent that it is proved that any loss, damage or delay in delivery of the goods which occurs during the carriage by the other means of transport was not caused by an act or omission of the carrier by road, but by some event which could only have occurred in the course of and by reason of the carriage by that other means of transport, the liability of the carrier by road shall be determined not by this Convention but in the manner in which the liability of the carrier by the other means of transport would have been determined if a contract for the carriage of the goods alone had been made by the sender with the carrier by the other means of transport in accordance with the conditions prescribed by law for the carriage of goods by that means of transport. If, however, there are no such prescribed conditions, the liability of the carrier by road shall be determined by this Convention.

2 If the carrier by road is also himself the carrier by the other means of transport, his liability shall also be determined in accordance with the provisions of para 1 of this article, but as if, in his capacities as carrier by road and as carrier by the other means of transport, he were two separate persons.

CHAPTER II – PERSONS FOR WHOM THE CARRIER IS RESPONSIBLE

Article 3

For the purposes of this Convention the carrier shall be responsible for the acts and omissions of his agents and servants and of any other persons of whose services he makes use for the performance of the carriage, when such agents, servants or other persons are acting within the scope of their employment, as if such acts or omissions were his own.

Article 4

The contract of carriage shall be confirmed by the making out of a consignment note. The absence, irregularity or loss of the consignment note shall not affect the existence or the validity of the contract of carriage which shall remain subject to the provisions of this Convention.

Article 5

1   The consignment note shall be made out in three original copies signed by the sender and by the carrier. These signatures may be printed or replaced by the stamps of the sender and the carrier if the law of the country in which the consignment note has been made out so permits. The first copy shall be handed to the sender, the second shall accompany the goods and the third shall be retained by the carrier.

2   When the goods which are to be carried have to be loaded in different vehicles, or are of different kinds or are divided into different lots, the sender or the carrier shall have the right to require a separate consignment note to be made out for each vehicle used, or for each kind or lot of goods.

Article 6

1   The consignment note shall contain the following particulars:
(a) the date of the consignment note and the place at which it is made out;
(b) the name and address of the sender;
(c) the name and address of the carrier;
(d) the place and the date of taking over of the goods and the place designated for delivery;
(e) the name and address of the consignee;
(f) the description in common use of the nature of the goods and the method of packing, and, in the case of dangerous goods, their generally recognised description;
(g) the number of packages and their special marks and numbers;
(h) the gross weight of the goods or their quantity otherwise expressed;
(i) charges relating to the carriage (carriage charges, supplementary charges, customs duties and other charges incurred from the making of the contract to the time of delivery);
(j) the requisite instructions for Customs and other formalities;
(k) a statement that the carriage is subject, notwithstanding any clause to the contrary, to the provisions of this Convention.

2   Where applicable, the consignment note shall also contain the following particulars:
(a) a statement that trans-shipment is not allowed;
(b) the charges which the sender undertakes to pay;
(c) the amount of 'cash on delivery' charges;
(d) a declaration of the value of the goods and the amount representing special interest in delivery;
(e) the sender's instructions to the carrier regarding insurance of the goods;
(f) the agreed time limit within which the carriage is to be carried out;
(g) a list of the documents handed to the carrier.

3   The parties may enter in the consignment note any other particulars which they may deem useful.

Article 7

1   The sender shall be responsible for all expenses, loss and damage sustained by the carrier by reason of the inaccuracy or inadequacy of:
(a) the particulars specified in Article 6, para 1, (b), (d), (e), (f), (g), (h) and (j):
(b) the particulars specified in Article 6, para 2;

(c) any other particulars or instructions given by him to enable the consignment note to be made out or for the purpose of their being entered therein .

2   If, at the request of the sender, the carrier enters in the consignment note the particulars referred to in para 1 of this article, he shall be deemed, unless the contrary is proved, to have done so on behalf of the sender.

3   If the consignment note does not contain the statement specified in Article 6, para 1(k) the carrier shall be liable for all expenses, loss and damage sustained through such omission by the person entitled to dispose of the goods.

Article 8

1   On taking over the goods, the carrier shall check:

(a) the accuracy of the statements in the consignment note as to the number of packages and their marks and numbers; and

(b) the apparent condition of the goods and their packaging.

2   Where the carrier has no reasonable means of checking the accuracy of the statements referred to in para 1(a) of this Article, he shall enter his reservations in the consignment note together with the grounds on which they are based. He shall likewise specify the grounds for any reservations which he makes with regard to the apparent condition of the goods and their packaging. Such reservations shall not bind the sender unless he has expressly agreed to be bound by them in the consignment note.

3   The sender shall be entitled to require the carrier to check the gross weight of the goods or their quantity otherwise expressed. He may also require the contents of the packages to be checked. The carrier shall be entitled to claim the cost of such checking. The result of the checks shall be entered in the consignment note.

Article 9

1   The consignment note shall be *prima facie* evidence of the making of the contract of carriage, the conditions of the contract and the receipt of the goods by the carrier.

2   If the consignment note contains no specific reservations by the carrier, it shall be presumed, unless the contrary is proved, that the goods and their packaging appeared to be in good condition when the carrier took them over and that the number of packages. their marks and numbers corresponded with the statements in the consignment note.

Article 10

The sender shall be liable to the carrier for damage to persons, equipment or other goods, and for any expenses due to defective packing of the goods, unless the defect was apparent or known to the carrier at the time when he took over the goods and he made no reservations concerning it.

Article 11

1   For the purposes of the Customs or other formalities which have to be completed before delivery of the goods, the sender shall attach the necessary documents to the consignment note or place them at the disposal of the carrier and shall furnish him with all the information which he requires.

2   The carrier shall not be under any duty to enquire into either the accuracy or the adequacy of such documents and information. The sender shall be liable to the carrier for any damage caused by the absence, inadequacy or irregularity of such documents and information, except in the case of some wrongful act or neglect on the part of the carrier.

3   The liability of the carrier for the consequences arising from the loss or incorrect use of the documents specified in and accompanying the consignment note or deposited with the carrier shall be that of an agent, provided that the compensation payable by the carrier shall not exceed that payable in the event of loss of the goods.

Article 12

1   The sender has the right to dispose of the goods, in particular by asking the carrier to stop the goods in transit, to change the place at which delivery is to take place or to deliver the goods to a consignee other than the consignee indicated in the consignment note.

2 This right shall cease to exist when the second copy of the consignment note is handed to the consignee or when the consignee exercises his right under Article 13, para 1; from that time onwards the carrier shall obey the orders of the consignee.

3 The consignee shall, however, have the right of disposal from the time when the consignment note is drawn up, if the sender makes an entry to that effect in the consignment note.

4 If, in exercising his right of disposal, the consignee has ordered the delivery of the goods to another person, that other person shall not be entitled to name other consignees.

5 The exercise of the right of disposal shall be subject to the following conditions:

(a) that the sender or, in the case referred to in para 3 of this article, the consignee who wishes to exercise the right produces the first copy of the consignment note on which the new instructions to the carrier have been entered and indemnifies the carrier against all expenses, loss and damage involved in carrying out such instructions;

(b) that the carrying out of such instructions is possible at the time when the instructions reach the person who is to carry them out and does not either interfere with the normal working of the carrier's undertaking or prejudice the senders or consignees of other consignments;

(c) that the instructions do not result in a division of the consignment.

6 When, by reason of the provisions of para 5(b) of this article, the carrier cannot carry out the instructions which he receives, he shall immediately notify the person who gave him such instructions.

7 A carrier who has not carried out the instructions given under the conditions provided for in this article, or who has carried them out without requiring the first copy of the consignment note to be produced, shall be liable to the person entitled to make a claim for any loss or damage caused thereby.

Article 13

1 After arrival of the goods at the place designated for delivery, the consignee shall be entitled to require the carrier to deliver to him, against a receipt, the second copy of the consignment note and the goods. If the loss of the goods is established or if the goods have not arrived after the expiry of the period provided for in Article 19, the consignee shall be entitled to enforce in his own name against the carrier any rights arising from the contract of carriage.

2 The consignee who avails himself of the rights granted to him under para 1 of this article shall pay the charges shown to be due on the consignment note, but in the event of dispute on this matter the carrier shall not be required to deliver the goods unless security has been furnished by the consignee.

Article 14

1 If for any reason it is or becomes impossible to carry out the contract in accordance with the terms laid down in the consignment note before the goods reach the place designated for delivery, the carrier shall ask for instructions from the person entitled to dispose of the goods in accordance with the provisions of Article 12.

2 Nevertheless, if circumstances are such as to allow the carriage to be carried out under conditions differing from those laid down in the consignment note and if the carrier has been unable to obtain instructions in reasonable time from the person entitled to dispose of the goods in accordance with the provisions of Article 12, he shall take such steps as seem to him to be in the best interests of the person entitled to dispose of the goods.

Article 15

1 Where circumstances prevent delivery of the goods after their arrival at the place designated for delivery, the carrier shall ask the sender for his instructions. If the consignee refuses the goods the sender shall be entitled to dispose of them without being obliged to produce the first copy of the consignment note.

2 Even if he has refused the goods, the consignee may nevertheless require delivery so long as the carrier has not received instructions to the contrary from the sender.

3 When circumstances preventing delivery of the goods arise after the consignee, in exercise of his rights under Article 12, para 3, has given an order for the goods to be delivered to

another person, paras 1 and 2 of this article shall apply as if the consignee were the sender and that other person were the consignee.

Article 16

1   The carrier shall be entitled to recover the cost of his request for instructions and any expenses entailed in carrying out such instructions, unless such expenses were caused by the wrongful act or neglect of the carrier.

2   In the cases referred to in Article 11, para 1, and in Article 15, the carrier may immediately unload the goods for account of the person entitled to dispose of them and thereupon the carriage shall be deemed to be at an end. The carrier shall then hold the goods on behalf of the person so entitled. He may however entrust them to a third party, and in that case he shall not be under any liability except for the exercise of reasonable care in the choice of such third party. The charges due under the consignment note and all other expenses shall remain chargeable against the goods.

3   The carrier may sell the goods, without awaiting instructions from the person entitled to dispose of them. if the goods are perishable or their condition warrants such a course, or when the storage expenses would be out of proportion to the value of the goods. He may also proceed to the sale of the goods in other cases if after the expiry of a reasonable period he has not received from the person entitled to dispose of the goods instructions to the contrary which he may reasonably be required to carry out.

4   If the goods have been sold pursuant to this article, the proceeds of sale, after deduction of the expenses chargeable against the goods, shall be placed at the disposal of the person entitled to dispose of the goods. If these charges exceed the proceeds of sale, the carrier shall be entitled to the difference.

5   The procedure in the case of sale shall be determined by the law or custom of the place where the goods are situated.

Chapter IV – Liability of the Carrier

Article 17

1   The carrier shall be liable for the total or partial loss of the goods and for damage thereto occurring between the time when he takes over the goods and the time of delivery, as well as for any delay in delivery.

2   The carrier shall however be relieved of liability if the loss, damage or delay was caused by the wrongful act or neglect of the claimant, by the instructions of the claimant given otherwise than as the result of a wrongful act or neglect on the part of the carrier, by inherent vice of the goods or through circumstances which the carrier could not avoid and the consequences of which he was unable to prevent.

3   The carrier shall not be relieved of liability by reason of the defective condition of the vehicle used by him in order to perform the carriage, or by reason of the wrongful act or neglect of the person from whom he may have hired the vehicle or of the agents or servants of the latter.

4   Subject to Article 18, paras 2 to 5, the carrier shall be relieved of liability when the loss or damage arises from the special risks inherent in one or more of the following circumstances:

(a) use of open unsheeted vehicles, when their use has been expressly agreed and specified in the consignment note;

(b) the lack of, or defective condition of packing in the case of goods which, by their nature, are liable to wastage or to be damaged when not packed or when not properly packed;

(c) handling, loading, stowage or unloading of the goods by the sender, the consignee or persons acting on behalf of the sender or the consignee;

(d) the nature of certain kinds of goods which particularly exposes them to total or partial loss or to damage, especially through breakage, rust, decay, desiccation, leakage, normal wastage, or the action of moth or vermin;

(e) insufficiency or inadequacy of marks or numbers on the packages;

(f) the carriage of livestock.

5   Where under this article the carrier is not under any liability in respect of some of the factors causing the loss, damage or delay, he shall only be liable to the extent that those factors for which he is liable under this article have contributed to the loss, damage or delay.

Article 18

1   The burden of proving that loss, damage or delay was due to one of the causes specified in Article 17, para 2, shall rest upon the carrier.

2   When the carrier establishes that in the circumstances of the case, the loss or damage could be attributed to one or more of the special risks referred to in Article 17, para 4, it shall be presumed that it was so caused. The claimant shall however be entitled to prove that the loss or damage was not, in fact, attributable either wholly or partly to one of these risks.

3   This presumption shall not apply in the circumstances set out in Article 17, para 4(a), if there has been an abnormal shortage, or a loss of any package .

4   If the carriage is performed in vehicles specially equipped to protect the goods from the effects of heat, cold, variations in temperature or the humidity of the air. the carrier shall not be entitled to claim the benefit of Article 17, para 4(d), unless he proves that all steps incumbent on him in the circumstances with respect to the choice, maintenance and use of such equipment were taken and that he complied with any special instructions issued to him.

5   The carrier shall not be entitled to claim the benefit of Article 17, para 4(f), unless he proves that all steps normally incumbent on him in the circumstances were taken and that he complied with any special instructions issued to him.

Article 19

Delay in delivery shall be said to occur when the goods have not been delivered within the agreed time limit or when? failing an agreed time limit, the actual duration of the carriage having regard to the circumstances of the case, and in particular, in the case of partial loads, the time required for making up a complete load in the normal way, exceeds the time it would be reasonable to allow a diligent carrier.

Article 20

1   The fact that goods have not been delivered within thirty days following the expiry of the agreed time limit, or, if there is no agreed time limit, within 60 days from the time when the carrier took over the goods, shall be conclusive evidence of the loss of the goods, and the person entitled to make a claim may thereupon treat them as lost.

2   The person so entitled may, on receipt of compensation for the missing goods, request in writing that he shall be notified immediately should the goods be recovered in the course of the year following the payment of compensation. He shall be given a written acknowledgment of such request.

3   Within the 30 days following receipt of such notification, the person entitled as aforesaid may require the goods to be delivered to him against payment of the charges shown to be due on the consignment note and also against refund of the compensation he received less any charges included therein but without prejudice to any claims to compensation for delay in delivery under Article 23 and, where applicable, Article 26.

4   In the absence of the request mentioned in para 2 or of any instructions given within the period of 30 days specified in para 3, or if the goods are not recovered until more than one year after the payment of compensation, the carrier shall be entitled to deal with them in accordance with the law of the place where the goods are situated.

Article 21

Should the goods have been delivered to the consignee without collection of the cash on delivery charge, which should have been collected by the carrier under the terms of the contract of carriage, the carrier shall be liable to the sender for compensation not exceeding the amount of such charge without prejudice to his right of action against the consignee.

Article 22

1   When the sender hands goods of a dangerous nature to the carrier, he shall inform the carrier of the exact nature of the danger and indicate, if necessary, the precautions to be

taken. If this information has not been entered in the consignment note, the burden of proving, by some other means, that the carrier knew the exact nature of the danger constituted by the carriage of the said goods shall rest upon the sender or the consignee.

2   Goods of a dangerous nature which, in the circumstances referred to in para 1 of this article, the carrier did not know were dangerous, may, at any time or place, be unloaded, destroyed or rendered harmless by the carrier without compensation; further, the sender shall be liable for all expenses, loss or damage arising out of their handing over for carriage or of their carriage.

Article 23

1   When, under the provisions of this Convention, a carrier is liable for compensation in respect of total or partial loss of goods, such compensation shall be calculated by reference to the value of the goods at the place and time at which they were accepted for carriage.

2   The value of the goods shall be fixed according to the commodity exchange price or, if there is no such price, according to the current market price or, if there is no commodity exchange price or current market price, by reference to the normal value of goods of the same kind and quality.

3   Compensation shall not, however, exceed 25 francs per kg of gross weight short. 'Franc' means the gold franc weighing 10/31 of a gramme and being of millesimal fineness 900.

4   In addition, the carriage charges, Customs duties and other charges incurred in respect of the carriage of the goods shall be refunded in full in case of total loss and in proportion to the loss sustained in case of partial loss, but no further damages shall be payable.

5   In the case of delay, if the claimant proves that damage has resulted therefrom the carrier shall pay compensation for such damage not exceeding the carriage charges.

6   Higher compensation may only be claimed where the value of the goods or a special interest in delivery has been declared in accordance with Articles 24 and 26.

Article 24

The sender may, against payment of a surcharge to be agreed upon, declare in the consignment note a value for the goods exceeding the limit laid down in Article 23, para 3, and in that case the amount of the declared value shall be substituted for that limit.

Article 25

1   In case of damage, the carrier shall be liable for the amount by which the goods have diminished in value, calculated by reference to the value of the goods fixed in accordance with Article 23, paras 1, 2 and 4.

2   The compensation may not, however, exceed:
    (a) if the whole consignment has been damaged the amount payable in the case of total loss;
    (b) if part only of the consignment has been damaged, the amount payable in the case of loss of the part affected.

Article 26

1   The sender may, against payment of a surcharge to be agreed upon. fix the amount of a special interest in delivery in the case of loss or damage or of the agreed time-limit being exceeded, by entering such amount in the consignment note .

2   If a declaration of a special interest in delivery has been made, compensation for the additional loss or damage proved may be claimed, up to the total amount of the interest declared, independently of the compensation provided for in Articles 23, 24 and 25.

Article 27

1   The claimant shall be entitled to claim interest on compensation payable. Such interest, calculated at 5% per annum, shall accrue from the date on which the claim was sent in writing to the carrier or, if no such claim has been made, from the date on which legal proceedings were instituted.

2   When the amounts on which the calculation of the compensation is based are not expressed in the currency of the country in which payment is claimed, conversion shall be at the rate of exchange applicable on the day and at the place of payment of compensation.

Article 28

1   In cases where, under the law applicable, loss, damage or delay arising out of carriage under this Convention gives rise to an extra-contractual claim, the carrier may avail himself of the provisions of this Convention which exclude his liability or which fix or limit the compensation due.

2   In cases where the extra-contractual liability for loss. damage or delay of one of the persons for whom the carrier is responsible under the terms of Article 3 is in issue, such person may also avail himself of the provisions of this Convention which exclude the liability of the carrier or which fix or limit the compensation due.

Article 29

1   The carrier shall not be entitled to avail himself of the provisions of this chapter which exclude or limit his liability or which shift the burden of proof if the damage was caused by his wilful misconduct or by such default on his part as, in accordance with the law of the court or tribunal seised of the case, is considered as equivalent to wilful misconduct.

2   The same provision shall apply if the wilful misconduct or default is committed by the agents or servants of the carrier or by any other persons of whose services he makes use for the performance of the carriage, when such agents, servants or other persons are acting within the scope of their employment. Furthermore, in such a case such agents, servants or other persons shall not be entitled to avail themselves, with regard to their personal liability, of the provisions of this chapter referred to in para 1.

CHAPTER V – CLAIMS AND ACTIONS

Article 30

1   If the consignee takes delivery of the goods without duly checking their condition with the carrier or without sending him reservations giving a general indication of the loss or damage, not later than the time of delivery in the case of apparent loss or damage and within seven days of delivery, Sundays and public holidays excepted, in the case of loss or damage which is not apparent, the fact of his taking delivery shall be *prima facie* evidence that he has received the goods in the condition described in the consignment note. In the case of loss or damage which is not apparent the reservations referred to shall be made in writing.

2   When the condition of the goods has been duly checked by the consignee and the carrier, evidence contradicting the result of this checking shall only be admissible in the case of loss or damage which is not apparent and provided that the consignee has duly sent reservations in writing to the carrier within seven days, Sundays and public holidays excepted, from the date of checking.

3   No compensation shall be payable for delay in delivery unless a reservation has been sent in writing to the carrier, within 21 days from the time that the goods were placed at the disposal of the consignee.

4   In calculating the time limits provided for in this Article the date of delivery, or the date of checking, or the date when the goods were placed at the disposal of the consignee, as the case may be, shall not be included.

5   The carrier and the consignee shall give each other every reasonable facility for making the requisite investigations and checks.

Article 31

1   In legal proceedings arising out of carriage under this Convention, the plaintiff may bring an action in any court or tribunal of a Contracting country designated by agreement between the parties and, in addition, in the courts or tribunals of a country within whose territory

    (a) the defendant is ordinarily resident, or has his principal place of business, or the branch or agency through which the contract of carriage was made,

    (b) the place where the goods were taken over by the carrier or the place designated for delivery is situated,

    and in no other courts or tribunals.

2   Where in respect of a claim referred to in para 1 of this Article an action is pending before a court or tribunal competent under that paragraph, or where in respect of such a claim a judgment has been entered by such a court or tribunal no new action shall be started between the same parties on the same grounds unless the judgment of the court or tribunal before which the first action was brought is not enforceable in the country in which the fresh proceedings are brought.

3   When a judgment entered by a court or tribunal of a Contracting country in any such action as is referred to in para 1 of this Article has become enforceable in that country, it shall also become enforceable in each of the other Contracting States, as soon as the formalities required in the country concerned have been complied with. The formalities shall not permit the merits of the case to be re-opened.

4   The provisions of para 3 of this Article shall apply to judgments after trial, judgments by default and settlements confirmed by an order of the court, but shall not apply to interim judgments or to awards of damages, in addition to costs against a plaintiff who wholly or partly fails in his action.

5   Security for costs shall not be required in proceedings arising out of carriage under this Convention from nationals of Contracting countries resident or having their place of business in one of those countries.

Article 32

1   The period of limitation for an action arising out of carriage under this Convention shall be one year. Nevertheless, in the case of wilful misconduct, or such default as in accordance with the law of the court or tribunal seised of the case, is considered as equivalent to wilful misconduct, the period of limitation shall be three years. The period of limitation shall begin to run:

(a) in the case of partial loss, damage or delay in delivery, from the date of delivery;

(b) in the case of total loss, from the 30th day after the expiry of the agreed time limit or where there is no agreed time limit from the 60th day from the date on which the goods were taken over by the carrier;

(c) in all other cases, on the expiry of a period of three months after the making of the contract of carriage.

The day on which the period of limitation begins to run shall not be included in the period.

2   A written claim shall suspend the period of limitation until such date as the carrier rejects the claim by notification in writing and returns the documents attached thereto. If a part of the claim is admitted the period of limitation shall start to run again only in respect of that part of the claim still in dispute. The burden of proof of the receipt of the claim, or of the reply and of the return of the documents, shall rest with the party relying upon these facts. The running of the period of limitation shall not be suspended by further claims having the same object.

3   Subject to the provisions of para 2 above, the extension of the period of limitation shall be governed by the law of the court or tribunal seised of the case. That law shall also govern the fresh accrual of rights of action.

4   A right of action which has become barred by lapse of time may not be exercised by way of counterclaim or set off.

Article 33

The contract of carriage may contain a clause conferring competence on an arbitration tribunal if the clause conferring competence on the tribunal provides that the tribunal shall apply this Convention.

CHAPTER VI – PROVISIONS RELATING TO CARRIAGE PERFORMED BY SUCCESSIVE CARRIERS

Article 34

If carriage governed by a single contract is performed by successive road carriers, each of them shall be responsible for the performance of the whole operation, the second carrier and each succeeding carrier becoming a party to the contract of carriage, under the terms of the consignment note, by reason of his acceptance of the goods and the consignment note.

Article 35

1   A carrier accepting the goods from a previous carrier shall give the latter a dated and signed receipt. He shall enter his name and address on the second copy of the consignment note. Where applicable, he shall enter on the second copy of the consignment note and on the receipt reservations of the kind provided for in Article 8, para 2.

2   The provisions of Article 9 shall apply to the relations between successive carriers .

Article 36

Except in the case of a counterclaim or a set off raised in an action concerning a claim based on the same contract of carriage, legal proceedings in respect of liability for loss, damage or delay may only be brought against the first carrier, the last carrier or the carrier who was performing that portion of the carriage during which the event causing the loss, damage or delay occurred; an action may be brought at the same time against several of these carriers.

Article 37

A carrier who has paid compensation in compliance with the provisions of this Convention, shall be entitled to recover such compensation, together with interest thereon and all costs and expenses incurred by reason of the claim, from the other carriers who have taken part in the carriage, subject to the following provisions:

(a)   the carrier responsible for the loss or damage shall be solely liable for the compensation whether paid by himself or by another carrier;

(b)   when the loss or damage has been caused by the action of two or more carriers, each of them shall pay an amount proportionate to his share of liability; should it be impossible to apportion the liability, each carrier shall be liable in proportion to the share of the payment for the carriage which is due to him;

(c)   if it cannot be ascertained to which carriers liability is attributable for the loss or damage, the amount of the compensation shall be apportioned.

Article 38

If one of the carriers is insolvent, the share of the compensation due from him and unpaid by him shall be divided among the other carriers in proportion to the share of the payment for the carriage due to them.

Article 39

1   No carrier against whom a claim is made under Articles 37 and 38 shall be entitled to dispute the validity of the payment made by the carrier making the claim if the amount of the compensation was determined by judicial authority after the first mentioned carrier had been given due notice of the proceedings and afforded an opportunity of entering an appearance.

2   A carrier wishing to take proceedings to enforce his right of recovery may make his claim before the competent court or tribunal of the country in which one of the carriers concerned is ordinarily resident, or has his principal place of business or the branch or agency through which the contract of carriage was made. All the carriers concerned may be made defendants in the same action.

3   The provisions of Article 31, paras 3 and 4, shall apply to judgments entered in the proceedings referred to in Articles 37 and 38.

4   The provisions of Article 32 shall apply to claims between carriers. The period of limitation shall, however, begin to run either on the date of the final judicial decision fixing the amount of compensation payable under the provisions of this Convention, or, if there is no such judicial decision, from the actual date of payment.

Article 40

Carriers shall be free to agree among themselves on provisions other than those laid down in Articles 37 and 38.

CHAPTER VII – NULLITY OF STIPULATIONS CONTRARY TO THE CONVENTION

Article 41

1   Subject to the provisions of Article 40, any stipulation which would directly or indirectly derogate from the provisions of this Convention shall be null and void. The nullity of such a stipulation shall not involve the nullity of the other provisions of the contract.

2   In particular, a benefit of insurance in favour of the carrier or any other similar clause, or any clause shifting the burden of proof shall be null and void.

[Chapter VIII of the Convention is not reproduced. This deals with the coming into force of the Convention, the settlement of disputes between the high Contracting parties and related matters.]

PROTOCOL OF SIGNATURE

1   This Convention shall not apply to traffic between the United Kingdom of Great Britain and Northern Ireland and the Republic of Ireland.

IATA INTERCARRIER AGREEMENT ON PASSENGER LIABILITY

Whereas: The Warsaw Convention system is of great benefit to international air transportation; and

Noting that: The Convention's limits of liability, which have not been amended since 1955, are now grossly inadequate in most countries and that international airlines have previously acted together to increase them to the benefit of passengers;

The undersigned carriers agree

1   To take action to waive the limitation of liability on recoverable compensatory damages in Article 22 para 1 of the Warsaw Convention as to claims for death, wounding or other bodily injury of a passenger within the meaning of Article 17 of the Convention, so that recoverable compensatory damages may be determined and awarded by reference to the law of the domicile of the passenger.

2   To reserve all available defences pursuant to the provisions of the Convention; nevertheless, any carrier may waive any defence, including the waiver of any defence up to a specified monetary amount of recoverable compensatory damages, as circumstances may warrant.

3   To reserve their rights of recourse against any other person, including rights of contribution or indemnity, with respect to any sums paid by the carrier.

4   To encourage other airlines involved in the international carriage of passengers to apply the terms of this Agreement to such carriage.

5   To implement the provisions of this Agreement no later than 1 November 1996 or upon receipt of requisite government approvals, whichever is later.

6   That nothing in this Agreement shall affect the rights of the passenger or the claimant otherwise available under the Convention.

7   That this Agreement may be signed in any number of counterparts, all of which shall constitute one Agreement. Any carrier may become a party to this Agreement by signing a counterpart hereof and depositing it with the Director General of the International Air Transport Association (IATA).

8   That any carrier party hereto may withdraw from this Agreement by giving twelve (12) months' written notice of withdrawal to the Director General of IATA and to the other carriers parties to the Agreement.

Signed this   day of   199

INTERCARRIER AGREEMENT ON PASSENGER LIABILITY

EXPLANATORY NOTE

The Intercarrier Agreement is an 'umbrella accord'; the precise legal rights and responsibilities of the signatory carriers with respect to passengers will be spelled out in the applicable Conditions of Carriage and tariff filings.

The carriers signatory to the Agreement undertake to waive such limitations of liability as are set out in the Warsaw Convention (1929), The Hague Protocol (1955), the Montreal Agreement of 1966, and/or limits they may have previously agreed to implement or were required by Governments to implement.

Such waiver by a carrier may be made conditional on the law of the domicile of the passenger governing the calculation of the recoverable compensatory damages under the Intercarrier Agreement. But this is an option. Should a carrier wish to waive the limits of liability but not insist on the law of the domicile of the passenger governing the calculation of the recoverable compensatory damages, or not be so required by a governmental authority, it may rely on the law of the court to which the case is submitted.

The Warsaw Convention system defences will remain available, in whole or in part, to the carriers signatory to the Agreement, unless a carrier decides to waive them or is so required by a governmental authority.

AGREEMENT ON MEASURES TO IMPLEMENT THE IATA INTERCARRIER AGREEMENT

I   Pursuant to the IATA Intercarrier Agreement of 31 October 1995, the undersigned carriers agree to implement said Agreement by incorporating in their conditions of carriage and tariffs, where necessary, the following:

  1   [CARRIER] shall not invoke the limitation of liability in Article 22(1) of the Convention as to any claim for recoverable compensatory damages arising under Article 17 of the Convention.

  2   [CARRIER] shall not avail itself of any defence under Article 20(1) of the Convention with respect to that portion of such claim which does not exceed 100,000 SDRs [unless option II(2) is used].

  3   Except as otherwise provided in paras 1 and 2 hereof, [CARRIER] reserves all defences available under the Convention to any such claim. With respect to third parties, the carrier also reserves all rights of recourse against any other person, including without limitation, rights of contribution and indemnity.

II   At the option of the carrier, its conditions of carriage and tariffs also may include the following provisions:

  1   [CARRIER] agrees that subject to applicable law, recoverable compensatory damages for such claim may be determined by reference to the law of the domicile or permanent residence of the passenger.

  2   [CARRIER] shall not avail itself of any defence under Article 20(1) of the Convention with respect to that portion of such claims which does not exceed 100,000 SDRs, except that such waiver is limited to the amounts shown below for the routes indicated, as may be authorised by governments concerned with the transportation involved.

  [Amounts and routes to be inserted]

  3   Neither the waiver of limits nor the waiver of defences shall be applicable in respect of claims made by public social insurance or similar bodies however asserted. Such claims shall be subject to the limit in Article 22(1) and to the defences under Article 20(1) of the Convention. The carrier will compensate the passenger or his dependents for recoverable compensatory damages in excess of payments received from any public social insurance or similar body.

III Furthermore, at the option of a carrier, additional provisions may be included in its conditions of carriage and tariffs, provided they are not inconsistent with this Agreement and are in accordance with applicable law.

IV Should any provision of this Agreement or a provision incorporated in a condition of carriage or tariff pursuant to this Agreement be determined to be invalid. illegal or unenforceable by a court of competent jurisdiction, all other provisions shall nevertheless remain valid, binding and effective.

V

1 This Agreement may be signed in any number of counterparts, all of which shall constitute one Agreement. Any carrier may become party to this Agreement by signing a counterpart hereof and depositing it with the Director General of the International Air Transport Association (IATA).

2 Any carrier party hereto may withdraw from this Agreement by giving twelve (12) months' written notice of withdrawal to the Director General of IATA and to the other carriers Parties to the Agreement.

3 The Director General of IATA shall declare this Agreement effective on 1 November 1996, or such later date as all requisite Government approvals have been obtained for this Agreement and the IATA Intercarrier Agreement of 31 October 1995.

Signed this   day of   199

CHAPTER 6

FINANCING EXPORTS: LETTERS OF CREDIT

INTRODUCTION

The expressions 'documentary credit' and 'letter of credit' are used interchangeably to refer to the most frequent and most secure facility for financing international trade. The security aspect of a documentary credit rests upon the fact that it represents an undertaking by the bank issuing the documentary credit at the request of its customer (usually the buyer of goods), to pay the beneficiary (usually the seller of goods), a specified amount on condition that the beneficiary presents to the bank stipulated documents. These documents evidence, among other things, the shipment of goods within a prescribed period of time. The bank thus acts as an intermediary between the buyer and the seller, satisfying the competing interests between them, and removes the risk of each party to the commercial transaction. While the bank guarantees payment to the seller for the goods, it protects the buyer by ensuring that no payment is made to the seller until the latter has shipped the goods, delivered the relevant documents, and otherwise complied with the prescribed conditions.

Hence, a letter of credit is a conditional promise issued by the issuing bank to pay a specified amount in the stated currency, within the prescribed time limit and against stipulated documents. These documents are specified to the bank by its customer, namely the buyer, who applies for the issuing of a letter of credit. Letters of credit are popular instruments in international trade because they substitute the financial standing of a bank for that of an individual or firm. The popularity of letters of credit derives from the fact that a seller can be confident that, provided he can meet the requirements stipulated in the letter, he will receive prompt payment. Also, a buyer who is able to offer the security of payment by a letter of credit is usually in a better bargaining position than a buyer offering an alternative method of payment. A letter of credit is described in *Voest-Alpine International Corporation v Chase Manhattan Bank*[1] as follows:

> A typical letter of credit transaction ... involves three separate and independent relationships – an underlying sale of goods contract between buyer and seller, an agreement between a bank and its customer (buyer) in which the bank undertakes to issue a letter of credit, and the bank's resulting engagement to pay the beneficiary (seller) providing that certain documents presented to the bank conform with the terms and conditions of the credit issued on its customer's behalf. Significantly, the bank's payment obligation to the beneficiary is primary, direct and completely independent of any claims which may arise in the underlying sale of goods transaction.

A letter of credit is the most frequently used method of financing international trade because of its autonomy. As appears from the above quotation, a documentary credit transaction is separate from and independent of the underlying contract for the sale of goods or other relevant transaction that it is financing. The bank is obliged to make payment to the seller under the letter of credit upon delivery by the seller of the

---

1   (1983) 707 F 2d 680, 682.

stipulated documents, provided these documents comply with the terms and conditions contained in the letter of credit. The bank is not concerned with the underlying contract and whether the terms thereof have been complied with. This autonomous character of the letter of credit has made it 'the lifeblood of commerce', because the mercantile practice is to treat rights under it 'as being equivalent to cash in hand'.[2]

Typically, the buyer accepts the seller's offer in respect of the sale of goods including the requirement that payment be made under a letter of credit. The buyer then instructs his bank, namely the issuing bank, to issue a letter of credit in favour of the seller as beneficiary. Next, the issuing bank in accordance with the buyer's instructions issues a letter of credit to the beneficiary and for such purpose instructs a correspondent bank (located in the seller's country) to act as an advising bank. In turn, the advising bank informs the seller/beneficiary that a letter of credit is opened in his favour and that payment will be made conditional upon the presentation of the stipulated documents by the seller to the advising bank (or another bank nominated for payment purposes) by a specified date. Finally, the beneficiary presents the documents to that bank and thereupon receives payment. Thus, a request for the issue of a letter of credit is made by the buyer, while settlement usually takes place in the seller's country.

Often the seller may require as an additional term of payment that the documentary credit be confirmed, that is, guaranteed by the advising bank located in his country. In such case, the advising bank will also be acting as a confirming bank. A request to confirm a letter of credit will usually be made by the beneficiary (seller) if he doubts the creditworthiness of the issuing bank or if that bank is located in a country subject to political or economic turmoil. A confirmed letter of credit provides the seller with increased security because the confirming bank would be obliged to make the specified payment if the issuing bank is prevented from honouring the letter of credit. For example, the issuing bank would be prevented from making payment if the government of the country in which that bank is located imposes currency restrictions between the time of the issuing of the letter of credit and the time the documents are delivered to the bank by the beneficiary. Thus, it is often good commercial practice for the seller to require the buyer to arrange for the confirmation of the letter of credit by a bank located in the beneficiary's country.

There are, therefore, usually four parties to the documentary credit transaction, namely:

1   the applicant of the letter of credit (buyer/importer);
2   the issuing bank in the applicant's country;
3   the correspondent bank in the seller's country acting as advising and/or confirming bank; and
4   the beneficiary of the documentary credit (seller/exporter).

---

2   *Intraco Ltd v Notis Shipping Corp of Liberia* (*The Bhoja Trader*) [1981] 2 Lloyd's Rep 256 at 257 (Donaldson LJ). A similar reference to 'the lifeblood of commerce' has been made by Kerr LJ in *RD Harbottle (Mercantile) Ltd v National Westminster Bank Ltd* [1978] QB 146 at 155; Griffiths LJ in *Power Curber International Ltd v National Bank of Kuwait SAK* [1981] 2 Lloyd's Rep 394 at 400; Stevenson LJ in *United City Merchants (Investments) Ltd v Royal Bank of Canada* [1982] QB 208 at 222; and Hirst J in *Hong Kong and Shanghai Banking Corp v Kloeckner and Co AG* [1989] 2 Lloyd's Rep 323, 330.

The universal use of commercial credit has resulted in the standardisation of the banking practice relating to documentary credit by the establishment and publication of the *Uniform Customs and Practice for Documentary Credits* (commonly referred to as the UCP) by the International Chamber of Commerce (ICC). The current version of the UCP is contained in ICC publication No 500, which entered into force on 1 January 1994. The UCP 500 sets out the rules by which banks will process letter of credit transactions. It also defines the rights and responsibilities of all parties to the credit. The UCP 500 is used by most banks throughout the world. Its use has resulted in documentary credits achieving the highest degree of uniformity. Article 2 defines a documentary credit as follows:

> For the purposes of these articles, the expressions 'documentary credit(s)' and 'standby letter(s) of credit' (hereinafter referred to as 'credit(s)'), mean any arrangement, however named or described, whereby a bank (the 'issuing bank') acting at the request and on the instruction of a customer (the 'applicant') or on its own behalf:
>
> (i)   is to make a payment to or to the order of a third party (the 'beneficiary'), or is to accept and pay bills of exchange (draft(s)) drawn by the beneficiary; or
>
> (ii)   authorises another bank to effect such payment, or to accept and pay such bills of exchange (draft(s)); or
>
> (iii)   authorises another bank to negotiate,
>
> against stipulated document(s), provided that the terms and conditions of the credit are complied with.

For the purposes of these articles, branches of a bank in different countries are considered another bank.

This definition envisages three forms which the issuing bank's obligation to make payment may take. First, the bank may undertake to pay cash against the tender of documents. This type of 'cash credit' is frequently used in continental Europe and South America. Secondly, the bank may undertake to accept (that is, to guarantee) a bill of exchange for the amount to be drawn on it by the seller and to be accompanied by the stipulated documents. This form of documentary credit is commonly used in the UK, Australia and most other Commonwealth countries, and in the USA. Thirdly, the bank may undertake to negotiate (that is to give value for) a bill of exchange for the amount to be drawn on it by the seller on the buyer and to be accompanied by the stipulated documents. This type of documentary credit is frequently used in South East Asia.

In accordance with Art 1, the UCP provisions have no application to a documentary credit unless they are expressly incorporated into the text of such credit. These provisions are, however, usually incorporated by banks in their standard forms of instructions and in their letters of credit. Consequently, the UCP provisions are practically universally imposed upon customers of banks and upon the beneficiaries of letters of credit. For this reason, it is essential when dealing with letters of credit to have a thorough understanding and knowledge of the UCP provisions and judicial decisions dealing with them.

BASIC FORMS AND TYPES OF DOCUMENTARY CREDIT

Basic forms of documentary credit

There are two basic forms of documentary credit, namely irrevocable credit and revocable credit. The quality of a documentary credit being 'irrevocable' or 'revocable' refers to the obligation of the issuing bank to the beneficiary. The quality of the credit being confirmed or unconfirmed, on the other hand, refers to the obligation of the advising bank to the beneficiary. Pursuant to Art 6(b) of the UCP 500 the letter of credit 'should clearly indicate whether it is revocable or irrevocable'. In cases governed by the UCP, a letter of credit is deemed to be irrevocable unless the issuing bank clearly indicates that it is revocable (Art 6(c)).

Revocable and unconfirmed credits

A revocable credit can be amended or cancelled by the issuing bank at any time without prior notice to the beneficiary (Art 8(a)). A bank will thus not be liable to the beneficiary (exporter) for revocation of the revocable credit before the transaction is completed. The standard form of instructions by the buyer to the issuing bank in respect of a revocable letter of credit usually contains an express provision to the effect that the bank may revoke the credit at any time during its currency. Because of its revocable nature, such credit cannot be confirmed by a correspondent or advising bank, which will usually advise that the notification 'is merely an advice of opening of the (subject credit) and is not a confirmation of the same'[3] and that therefore the credit is subject to cancellation or modification at any time without notice. As such, the revocable credit fails to provide adequate security for the beneficiary exporter.

Irrevocable and unconfirmed credits

An irrevocable credit constitutes a legally binding undertaking by the issuing bank to make payment. It cannot be amended or cancelled with the consent of the beneficiary or the issuing bank (Art 9(d)(i)). Thus, if the seller wishes to amend any of the provisions of the credit, he must request the buyer to instruct the issuing bank to that effect.

Being an unconfirmed irrevocable credit, the correspondent bank acts merely as an advising bank when notifying the beneficiary that the credit has been opened. It does not itself undertake to make payment under the credit and is therefore under no obligation to honour documents presented by the beneficiary (Art 7(a)). The only recourse open to the beneficiary is against the buyer's bank acting as the issuing bank. Because the issuing bank is usually a foreign bank, located in the country of the buyer, an unconfirmed irrevocable credit is inappropriate where the buyer's country is politically unstable or where there are in that country restrictions on foreign exchange or other transfer risks.

---

3   *Cape Asbestos Co v Lloyd's Bank* [1921] WN 274.

Confirmed irrevocable credit

A confirmed irrevocable credit gives the beneficiary the highest degree of assurance that he will be paid for his goods. It provides him with the greatest security, particularly where the confirming bank to the irrevocable credit is the seller's own bank. By adding its confirmation to the credit, the correspondent, advising bank thereby undertakes to honour the documents that conform with the terms and conditions of the credit and are presented within the prescribed time limit. In this case, the beneficiary has recourse not only against the issuing bank in respect of its undertaking, but also separate and independent recourse against the confirming bank in respect of its independent promise of payment under the documentary credit. With a confirmed irrevocable credit, the exporter removes any political and transfer risks that may prevail in the buyer's country. The confirmed irrevocable credit imposes on the confirming bank an absolute obligation to pay and provides the seller with an absolute assurance of payment. In the words of Jenkins LJ in *Hamzeh Malas and Sons v British Imex Ltd*:[4]

> It seems to me plain enough that the opening of a confirmed letter of credit constitutes a bargain between the banker and the vendor of the goods, which imposes upon the banker an absolute obligation to pay, irrespective of any dispute there may be between the parties as to whether the goods are up to the contract or not … A vendor of goods selling against a confirmed letter of goods is selling under the assurance that nothing will prevent him from receiving the price. That is no mean advantage when goods manufactured in one country are being sold in another.

The whole commercial purpose for which the system of confirmed irrevocable documentary credits has been created in international trade, is to give to the seller an assured right to be paid before he relinquishes control over the goods that does not permit of any dispute with the buyer as to the performance of the contract of sale being used as a ground for non-payment or reduction or deferment of payment. One established exception is where the seller fraudulently presents to the confirming bank documents that contain material representations of fact that to his knowledge are untrue. The fact that the documents had been taken up before any fraud was notified would not change the fact that when it was sought to enforce the consequent payment obligation, the claimant would be dishonestly seeking to use the process of the courts to carry out a fraud. The relevant time for considering this question is the time when payment falls due and is claimed and refused. If the party claiming the payment had negotiated the relevant documents in good faith, the issuing bank cannot excuse his refusal to pay on the ground that at some earlier time the negotiating bank was a mere agent for collection on behalf of the seller, and allege against him fraud or forgery on the part of the beneficiary of the letter of credit.[5]

Types of letters of credit

Documentary credits are classified into various types depending on the way in which the credit is made available to the beneficiary. The different types of credit include

---

4   [1958] 2 QB 127.
5   *Banco Santander v Bayfern Limited* [1999] Lloyd's Rep Bank 239.

sight credit, deferred payment credit, acceptance credit, red clause credit, revolving credit, negotiation credit, standby letter of credit, transferable credit, and back-to-back credit.

Article 10(a): 'available for payment on sight ... against presentation of documents', represented compliance with this Article. This Article requires a clear indication whether they were available by sight payment or deferred payment; those words together with the words, 'upon receipt at our counter in X (city) we shall pay you', were directed to the time at which the obligation of payment arises and were not intended to specify the place of payment.

Both Arts 9 and 10 demonstrate that there is a condition precedent to the beneficiary's right to payment, but neither is framed in terms of an obligation owed to the beneficiary to deal with the documents in a particular way.[6]

Sight credit

Sight credit is the most commonly used type of credit. It provides for payment to be made to the beneficiary immediately after presentation of the stipulated documents and on condition that the submitted documents comply with the terms and conditions of the credit. Following presentation of the documents, the issuing bank (or its correspondent bank) will carefully examine the documents to ensure that these comply strictly with the terms and conditions contained in the letter of credit. Following satisfactory examination of the documents, the bank then pays to the beneficiary the proceeds of the credit. It is simply a process of payment against documents.

Deferred payment credit

Under a deferred payment credit, provision is made in the letter of credit itself for payment to be made by the bank at a future, determinable time, for example, 90 days after the issuing of the bill of lading. In effect, this type of credit enables the buyer (importer) to make payment for the goods after obtaining the prescribed documents. The time given to the buyer to make payment could be used by him to resell the goods and use the proceeds of any such sale to provide for payment under the deferred payment credit by the due date.

Article 9(b)(ii) UCP 500 deals with a deferred payment undertaking. The authority given by the issuing bank to the confirming bank in a deferred payment letter of credit is to pay at maturity. Hence, under a deferred payment credit, the confirming bank that has paid 'on the maturity date(s) determinable in accordance with the stipulations of the credit' will be entitled to reimbursement by the issuing bank. The right to reimbursement is expressly addressed in Art 10(d) and Art 14(a). The consideration for the confirming banks' undertaking to pay at maturity is that if and when payment is made, the issuing bank will reimburse it.[7] Article 14(a) in effect establishes that the issuing bank cannot complain about conforming documents presented under the credit in order to dispute the confirming and/or nominating bank's right to incur the deferred payment obligation. But that obligation remains to pay at maturity with

---

6   *Chailease Finance Corporation v Credit Agricole Indosuez* [2000] 1 Lloyd's Rep 348.
7   *Banco Santander v Bayfern Limited* [1999] Lloyd's Rep Bank 239.

the right to be reimbursed once payment is made.[8] The consequent obligation to reimburse is to reimburse once payment has been made at maturity. However, if at that time fraud is established, the confirming bank has no obligation to pay and the issuing bank is not obliged to reimburse.[9]

Acceptance credit

In the case of an acceptance credit, the beneficiary (seller) draws a bill of exchange either on the issuing bank, the confirming bank, or on the buyer, or even sometimes on another bank depending on the terms of the credit. An acceptance credit provides for payment on the date on which the bill of exchange matures. Following the tendering of conforming documents in accordance with the terms and conditions of the credit, the bill of exchange is accepted by the bank.

The purpose of an acceptance credit is to give the buyer (importer) time to make payment. Thus, if the buyer can resell the goods before payment falls due, he can use the proceeds to meet the bill of exchange and thereby avoid the necessity of borrowing funds to finance the transaction. However, if the exporter as beneficiary of the bill requires payment before the maturity date, he may negotiate the accepted bill to his own bank to be discounted. The readiness of the exporter's bank to discount the bill will depend on the standing of the accepting bank.

Negotiation credit

A negotiation credit empowers the beneficiary to draw a bill of exchange on the issuing bank, or on any other drawee stipulated in the credit. However, Art 9(a)(iv) of the UCP 500 states that a letter of credit 'should not be issued available by draft(s) on the applicant'. The beneficiary may then present the bill to a bank for negotiation, together with the original letter of credit and the documents stipulated therein. Usually a negotiation credit permits negotiation by any bank, although the negotiation may be limited to specified banks. The bill of exchange may either be a sight or a time draft. The main advantage of a negotiation credit lies in the fact that the beneficiary is not limited to receive payment of the credit from the advising bank, but may obtain payment from any bank of his choice by drawing a bill of exchange that is guaranteed by the issuing bank. Thus, negotiation involves the 'giving of value for draft(s) and/or document(s) by the bank authorised to negotiate' (Art 10(b)(ii)).

Article 9(a)(iv) indicates that an irrevocable credit constitutes a definite undertaking of the issuing bank 'to pay without recourse to drawers and/or *bona fide* holders, draft(s) drawn by the beneficiary ... under the credit.'[10] Article 10(b)(i) reinforces the idea that no bank other than the one nominated by the issuing bank is authorised to make payment. Due to the fact that issuing banks and confirming banks 'pay' rather than 'negotiate', the reference in Art 9(a)(iv) to payment without recourse refers to the action that the authorised negotiating bank must complete in order to qualify as a negotiating bank. If that bank fulfils this action, it secures the rights of a negotiating bank, specifically to be reimbursed without recourse by the issuing bank.

---

8   *Ibid*.
9   *Ibid*.
10   Dolan, JF, 'Negotiation letters of credit', *Banking Law Journal*, May 2002.

Article 10(b)(ii), which states that 'Mere examination of the documents without giving of value does not constitute a negotiation', disapproves of the practice of some banks to delay payment until the issuing bank remits payment. Thus, although Art 10(b)(ii) defines negotiation as 'the giving of value for draft(s) and/or documents by the bank authorised to negotiate', the mere examination of documents without giving of value does not constitute negotiation. Giving 'value' is essential for negotiation, but is not sufficient to constitute negotiation. This definition does not concentrate on the more common term 'negotiation under reserve'. This is where present value is given in exchange for the draft, but it is given with recourse. This means that the value given is nothing more than a loan or credit advance against the receipt of collection.[11]

Red clause credit

Under a 'red clause' credit, the seller is able to obtain an advance from the correspondent/advising bank prior to the presentation of the prescribed documents by the seller. The red clause, which derives its name from the fact that it was formerly written in red ink, authorises the advising bank to advance a part of the credit amount to the seller for the delivery of the merchandise. Such advance, which will be delivered under the documentary credit, is frequently intended to finance the manufacture or purchase of the goods by the seller. On receiving the advance, the beneficiary (seller) must give a receipt (for example, a warehouse receipt) and an undertaking to present the prescribed documents within the period of validity of the credit. This type of credit is used very often in the Australian wool trade. The clause may simply read, for example: 'red clause A$50,000 permitted'. Such clause means that, with the issuing bank assuming liability for the transaction, the advising bank is authorised to advance the beneficiary A$50,000 prior to the presentation of the documents.

Although the advance is paid out by the advising bank, it is the issuing bank that assumes liability. If the seller fails to present the prescribed documents in time and fails to refund the advance, the advising bank will debit the issuing bank with the amount of the advance, together with interest thereon. The issuing bank, in turn, will have recourse against the buyer (importer), who therefore bears the ultimate risk for the advance and the interest thereon.

A red clause 'permits the beneficiary to receive temporary advances from the opening or confirming bank to enable him to make purchases and shipment of the goods described in the credit, said advances to be repaid with interest out of the proceeds of the beneficiary's drafts and ultimately drawn under the credit'.[12]

Additionally, another definition of a red clause is 'a Documentary Credit with a special condition incorporated into it that authorises the confirming bank or any other nominated bank to make advances to the beneficiary before presentation of the documents'.[13]

---

11   Rosenblith, RM, 'To negotiate or not to negotiate – does it make a difference?', *International Financial Services Association Network*, Vol 11, N 9, September 2000.

12   *Feinberg v Central Asia Capital Corp*, (1997) 974 F Supp 822 (Eastern District of PA) citing Dolan, JF, *The Law of Letters of Credit, Glossary of Letter of Credit Terms*, 3rd edn, 1996, Boston, Mass: Warren, Gorham & Lamont, G-23.

13   *Ibid* citing del Busto, C, *ICC Guide To Documentary Credit Operations For The UCP 500*, 1994, Paris: ICC Publishing, p 49.

Revolving credit

A revolving credit is used commonly where the buyer (importer) is a regular customer of the seller (exporter), or where the buyer receives goods from the exporter in instalments at specified intervals. In such cases, provisions may be made under a revolving credit to cover the value of each instalment as it is delivered. For example, a revolving credit may contain a clause which reads: 'credit amount A$100,000, revolving 11 times up to a total amount of A$1,200,000'. After utilisation of the first A$100,000, the next portion becomes automatically available, up to the total of A$1,200,000. Frequently, a revolving clause will also stipulate the dates of individual instalments, in which case it may, for example, read:

> Credit amount A$100,000, revolving every month for the same amount for the first time in January 1996, for the last time in November 1996, maximum amount payable under this credit A$1,200,000.

A revolving credit may be cumulative or non-cumulative. As the expressions suggest, in the case of cumulative revolving credit, amounts from unused or incompletely used portions may be carried forward and utilised in a subsequent period. In the case of a non-cumulative revolving credit, non-utilised instalments or balances may not be added to later instalments.

The main advantage of a revolving credit is that it avoids banking charges and clerical costs to the importer, which would otherwise be incurred if a separate letter of credit were issued in respect of each transaction in a series of similar, or instalment, transactions.

A revolving credit should not be confused with an 'evergreen clause' in a letter of credit. An 'evergreen clause', if incorporated in the letter, has the effect of automatically extending the credit for another fixed period from the expiration date, unless the bank notifies the beneficiary by registered mail that it has elected not to renew the credit.

Standby credit

Standby letters of credit are in effect bank guarantees that, because of their documentary character, unlike ordinary bank guarantees, are governed by the UCP. They are principally used in the USA, where they take the place of guarantees, which, under most state laws, may not be issued by banks. However, the use of this type of credit is increasing in continental Europe, England, and Australia. Standby credit may be used to guarantee performance of services as well as payment by a party. For example, a standby credit may guarantee the payment of bills payable after sight, the repayment of a bank advance, the payment for goods delivered, the delivery of goods in accordance with a contract, and the fulfilment of contracts for work and materials.

The principal difference between the standby letter of credit and an ordinary letter of credit is that in the case of the latter, but not the former, the documents which the beneficiary has to tender normally relate to an underlying sales transaction. In the case of a standby letter of credit, the required documents may be of any description. For example, the prescribed document may merely be a demand for payment by the beneficiary; or it may be a statement or a certification by the beneficiary to the effect that the other party is in default. It is for this reason that a standby letter of credit is often equated to a bank guarantee or, because of the documents required thereunder, a documentary bank guarantee.

By virtue of Art 1, the UCP applies to standby letters of credit. Although Art 1 states that its provisions apply to the standby letter of credit 'to the extent to which they may be applicable', the UCP is not specific about its inapplicability to a standby letter of credit. If a letter of credit is not intended to pay for a particular, simultaneous sale and shipment of goods, then the parties should consider incorporating ISP 98 instead of UCP 500. The ISP 98 is a document adopted by the International Chamber of Commerce.

Transferable credit

The transferable credit is used mainly to enable the beneficiary (known in Art 48 as the 'first beneficiary') to transfer the whole or part of the credit to his supplier ('second beneficiary') of goods or raw materials. Indeed, the seller (beneficiary) may only be able to sell goods to the buyer (importer) that have previously been manufactured or produced by the beneficiary. The manufacture of goods requires the beneficiary to obtain components or raw materials from his supplier. Thus, in effect, the beneficiary becomes a 'middleman' in that he owes money to his supplier, but is himself owed money by the buyer (importer), who applies for the issuing of a letter of credit. A transferable credit enables the beneficiary, who receives payment from his own buyer under a documentary credit, to transfer the whole or part of his claim under that credit to his own supplier. In this manner, the beneficiary can carry out transactions with only a limited outlay of his own funds or capital.

Typically, the procedure would be as follows. The beneficiary requires as a term of his contract with his own buyer (importer or applicant for the credit), that the buyer provide an irrevocable transferable credit in his favour. Upon the beneficiary receiving confirmation of the issuing of the transferable credit, he may then instruct the bank to transfer the credit to his own supplier as second beneficiary. The transfer takes the form of the issuing of a fresh, or second, credit separate from the original (transferable) credit. In other words, the original (transferable) credit itself is not, in fact, physically transferred to the transferee.

Following notification of such transfer (that is, of the issuing of the second credit), the supplier will dispatch the goods to his own buyer (first beneficiary), and upon presentation of the prescribed documents, he will receive the agreed payment from the confirming or advising bank. The documents are then forwarded to the transferee bank upon receipt of which it will debit the beneficiary's account. The beneficiary then delivers to the transferring bank his own invoice made out to the buyer, receives in exchange the invoice of his supplier, and is credited with the amount of his own invoice. Finally, the transferring bank forwards to the issuing bank all the prescribed documents including the beneficiary's invoice. The difference between the amount debited and the amount credited to the beneficiary's account represents his profit. To ensure that the identity of the supplier does not become known to the buyer, the middleman will require of his supplier that none of the prescribed documents (other than the invoice which will be substituted with the beneficiary's own invoice) contain any indication of the supplier's identity. Similarly, to prevent the buyer's identity from becoming known to the supplier, the beneficiary will ensure that the transferable letter of credit does not stipulate any documents that contain the buyer's name.

In order to meet the objective of the transferable credit, it is essential that the terms and conditions of the transferred credit be identical to those of the original credit except for the following:

1   the amount of the credit and the unit price may be reduced;

2   the expiry date may be brought forward;

3   the period of shipment may be shortened provided that the original credit does not specify a particular date for shipment;

4   the first beneficiary may require additional documents which remain in his keeping; and

5   the first beneficiary has the right to substitute his own invoice for that of the supplier/second beneficiary.

Thus, the beneficiary is not only able to trade with a limited outlay of his own funds, but is able to do so while preventing the buyer and supplier from knowing each other's identity and from receiving knowledge of his profit margin.

To make credit transferable, it is essential that the issuing bank expressly designates the credit to have such quality. It may be so expressed by the use of the word 'transferable'. Terms such as 'divisible', 'fractionable', 'assignable', and 'transmissible' do not render the credit transferable (Art 48(b)). Without an expressed quality of transferability, the advising bank is not authorised to extend the cover provided by the credit by making finance available thereunder to any person satisfying the conditions of the credit; it is bound to make payment under the credit on tender of the stipulated documents to the named beneficiary only. This is because, unlike a bill of exchange, a letter of credit is not a negotiable instrument and therefore may not be transferred unless the parties thereto (the issuing bank and the applicant) have so agreed.

Comprehensive provisions for the regulation of transferable credits is made under Art 48 of the UCP 500 which, pertinently, states:

(a)   A transferable credit is a credit under which the beneficiary (first beneficiary) may request the bank authorised to pay, incur a deferred payment undertaking, accept or negotiate (the 'transferring bank'), or in the case of a freely negotiable credit, the bank specifically authorised in the credit as a transferring bank, to make the credit available in whole or in part to one or more other beneficiary(ies) (second beneficiary(ies)).

(b)   A credit can be transferred only if it is expressly designated as 'transferable' by the issuing bank. Terms such as 'divisible', 'fractionable', 'assignable', and 'transmissible' do not render the credit transferable. If such terms are used they shall be disregarded.

(c)   The transferring bank shall be under no obligation to effect such transfer except to the extent and in the manner expressly consented to by such bank.

Paragraph (f) deals with bank charges. Paragraph (g) provides that a transferable credit can be transferred only once, but 'a retransfer to the first beneficiary does not constitute a prohibited transfer'. Paragraph (g) also makes provision for fractions of a transferable credit, the aggregate of which will be considered as constituting only one transfer of the credit. Paragraph (i) gives the first beneficiary the right to substitute his own invoices in exchange for those of the second beneficiary. Finally, para (j) entitles the first beneficiary of a transferable credit to request that the credit be transferred to a second beneficiary in the same country or in another country.

Thus, Art 48 'regulates the condition on which a transferable letter of credit could be transferred'. Such credit could be transferred only on the terms and conditions of the original credit subject to certain specified exceptions.[14]

Back-to-back credit

In the case of a back-to-back credit, a confirmed letter of credit opened by the buyer (applicant for the credit) in favour of the beneficiary, known as 'overriding credit', is used by the latter as security for the opening by him of a second credit in favour of his own supplier. This arrangement may be repeated where the same goods are sold or resold by several sellers (middlemen), as in the case of string contracts. In such case, each seller will use the credit in his favour as security for the credit which he needs to open in favour of his own seller, right through the chain of contracts until the first buyer in the chain opens a credit in favour of the original supplier. The back-to-back arrangement may involve different banks for each of the parties concerned, although it is preferable to have the whole operation conducted by one bank. It is essential that, save in relation to prices, the terms of each of the credits in a chain of back-to-back credits be identical.

Assignment of proceeds under a documentary credit

If a documentary credit is not transferable and the beneficiary is unable to obtain a back-to-back credit, he may nonetheless finance his own purchase in order to effect a sale of goods, by assigning to his supplier the proceeds of the credit issued by his buyer (applicant for the credit) in his favour. In such case, the bank acting on the instructions of the beneficiary of the credit transmits to the assignee (the supplier) a declaration in which it undertakes to pay him a specified sum out of funds that have become available under the documentary credit.

Article 49 of the UCP 500 provides that the fact that a credit is not stated to be transferable shall not affect the beneficiary's right to assign any proceeds thereunder 'in accordance with the provisions of the applicable law'. The applicable law in Australia, as in England, is that dealing with the assignment of choses in action. As a letter of credit is a chose in action, it is capable to be assigned without the consent of either the buyer or the issuing bank. In this context, all the beneficiary needs to do is to satisfy the legal requirement relating to the assignment of choses in action or debts. In respect of the requirements of the credit itself, it is necessary that the condition relating to the tendering of documents as stipulated in the letter of credit be complied with. Such condition, being an obligation, is incapable of assignment and therefore can only be discharged by the beneficiary of the letter of credit, and not by the supplier/assignee. The latter's dependence on the beneficiary for the satisfaction of the condition relating to the tendering of documents constitutes a risk to which a supplier is exposed under an assignment of credit, and which renders the credit of limited security worth. The supplier does not receive payment until after the credit has been honoured and yet has no assurance that the beneficiary will present the documents in time and in conformity with the provisions of the credit.

---

14   *FH Bertling Ltd v Tube Developments Ltd* [1999] 2 Lloyd's Rep 55.

The UCP distinguishes between transfer of a letter of credit and assignment of proceeds. Transfer effectuates a more complete change. The transferee is effectively substituted for the original beneficiary. After transfer, the transferee must present the draft and documentation to cause payment. Such transfer may be made to a new substituted beneficiary only if the letter of credit is expressly designated as transferable by the issuing bank.

An assignment of proceeds changes only the party entitled to receive payment of proceeds. In spite of assignment, only the named beneficiary may draw the draft in favour of an assignee. These assignments are commonplace.[15] In *Nassar v Florida Fleet Sales*[16] the plaintiff, whose business involved the exportation of cars, was also the sole proprietor of Insearch Marketing and Trading Company, which was located in Texas. After the Gulf War in August 1991, Al-Jazira Trading Company, Kuwait Company, entered into a contract with the Kuwait government. This contract consisted of Al-Jazira supplying 100 armoured General Motors trucks to be used at the initial meeting of the Member States of the Gulf Co-operation Council in Kuwait. Al-Jazira entered into an agreement with Insearch in the amount of $3,036,625. Next, Insearch sought out a sub-contractor and entered into a similar agreement with Florida Fleet Sales. The agreed purchase price for the trucks was $2,286,995. The agreement also specified shipping the trucks by an ocean freighter.

The payment under agreement between Insearch and Al-Jazira was effectuated through a letter of credit issued by National Bank of Kuwait (NBK), with NBK in New York serving as the US advising and confirming bank. NBK issued the letter of credit by telex on 7 October 1991. NBK New York advised Insearch of the letter of credit on 8 October 1991.

Under its terms, the letter of credit was to function as follows: upon meeting certain conditions specified in the letter of credit, involving the presentation of documents describing vehicles and bills of lading from shipment, the first beneficiary, Insearch, would be permitted to be paid in the form of a draw on the letter of credit. NBK New York, as advising and confirming bank, would assure the conditions had been met and make payments to Insearch. The letter of credit was irrevocable.

Fundamental principles

There are two fundamental principles governing letters of credit, namely:

1 the doctrine of strict compliance; and

2 the autonomy of the credit.

Pursuant to the autonomy principle, a letter of credit is a separate and independent transaction from the contract of sale or other transaction on which it is based. According to the doctrine of strict compliance, a bank is entitled to reject documents that do not strictly conform with the terms and conditions of the credit. These two principles will be discussed under separate headings below.

---

15 *Algemene Bank Nederland NV v Soysen Tarim Urunleri Dis Ticaret Ve Sanayi AS* (1990) 748 F Supp 177 (SDNY).
16 (1999) 79 F Supp 2d 284, 293 (SDNY).

The doctrine of strict compliance

The doctrine of strict compliance requires that the prescribed documents that are tendered by the beneficiary strictly conform with the terms and conditions of the credit. There is no obligation on the bank to honour non-conforming documents. In the words of Lord Sumner in *Equitable Trust Co of New York v Dawson Partners Ltd*: 'There is no room for documents which are almost the same, or which will do just as well. Business could not proceed securely on any other lines.'[17]

In that case, the defendants bought vanilla beans from a seller in Batavia (Jakarta) in respect of which they instructed the plaintiff bank to open a confirmed letter of credit in favour of the seller. The documents required to be tendered under the letter of credit included a certificate of quality to be issued 'by experts who are sworn brokers'. The advising bank incorrectly informed the seller that the requisite certificate was to be issued 'by expert who is sworn broker'. The error occurred because of an incorrect decoding of the message sent by private and secret telegraphic code of the advising bank which used the same symbols for both the singular and plural of words. The seller fraudulently shipped rubbish (with only 1% of vanilla beans) and managed to extract a certificate from a sworn broker. The plaintiff bank, having accepted the tender of documents and having honoured the letter of credit, sought to be reimbursed by the buyer who refused to accept the documents. The plaintiff bank was successful at first instance but lost on appeal in the Court of Appeal, and in the House of Lords, where it was held that the plaintiff bank was not entitled to be reimbursed by the buyer because, in making available finance on the certificate of one expert instead of at least two experts, the plaintiff bank had acted contrary to the instructions of its customer. Lord Sumner reasoned as follows:[18]

> The bank's branch abroad, which knows nothing officially of the details of the transaction thus financed, cannot take upon itself to decide what will do well enough and what will not. If it does as it is told, it is safe; if it declines to do anything else, it is safe; if it departs from the conditions laid down, it acts at its own risk. The documents tendered were not exactly the documents which the defendants had promised to take up, and *prima facie* they were right in refusing to take them.

In determining whether the documents conform strictly with the terms of the credit, the bank is only concerned with what appears on the face of the documents. It does not need to look behind the documents. It is not concerned with the underlying transaction. This is made clear by Art 4 of the UCP 500 which states that: 'In credit operations all parties concerned deal with documents, and not with goods, services and/or other performances to which the documents may relate.' In *Instituto Nacional de Comercializacion Agricola v Continental Illinois National Bank and Trust Co*,[19] the court decided that a buyer had no cause of action for negligent misrepresentation against the confirming bank, which negligently confirmed that documents submitted by the beneficiary of the credit complied with its terms and conditions. The court decided that a letter of credit transaction is not even amenable to the tort of negligent misrepresentation and that, in any event, the confirming bank has no duty of care to the customer, but only to the issuing bank.

---

17 [1926] 27 Lloyd's Rep 49 at 52.
18 *Ibid* at 52.
19 (1988) 858 F 2d 1264.

The strictness of the doctrine of strict compliance is well illustrated in *SH Rayner and Co v Hambros Bank Ltd*.[20] There, a bank received instructions from a customer/buyer to open a confirmed credit in favour of the plaintiff seller in respect of a cargo of 'coromandel groundnuts'. The bank opened the credit and notified the plaintiff that it was available against invoice and bills of lading of 'coromandel groundnuts'. The plaintiff presented bills of lading for 'machine-shelled groundnut kernels' accompanied by an invoice for 'coromandel groundnuts'. The bank refused payment on the ground of non-compliance and the plaintiff sued the bank on the credit. At the trial, there was evidence that 'machine-shelled groundnut kernels' were universally understood in the trade to be identical with 'coromandel groundnuts'. In these circumstances, the trial judge gave judgment for the plaintiff. On appeal, the Court of Appeal reversed the trial judge's decision. In rejecting the central submission for the seller that the bank ought to be affected with the knowledge prevailing in the relevant trade that the two expressions referred to the same thing, MacKinnon LJ stated that 'it is quite impossible to suggest that a banker is to be affected with knowledge of the customs and customary terms of every one of the thousands of trades for whose dealings he may issue letters of credit'.[21]

Goddard LJ took it a step further, so that even if the bank had knowledge of the customary term, it was bound to comply strictly and literally with the terms of its mandate. He stated:[22]

> It does not matter whether the terms imposed by the person who requires the bank to open the credit seem reasonable or unreasonable. The bank is not concerned with that. If it accepts the mandate to open the credit, it must do exactly what its customer requires it to do. If the customer says: 'I require a bill of lading "for coromandel groundnuts",' the bank is not justified, in my judgment, in paying against a bill of lading for anything except coromandel groundnuts, and it is no answer to say: 'You know perfectly well that "machine-shelled groundnut" kernels are the same as "coromandel groundnuts".' For all the bank knows, its customer may have a particular reason for wanting 'coromandel groundnuts' in the bill of lading.

If the documents fail to conform appropriately, the issuing bank would be acting wrongfully by honouring the letter of credit. The obligation to honour the credit only under certain conditions does not usually appear in the agreements, but is incorporated in the UCP. The UCP requires the issuing bank to examine 'all documents with reasonable care to ascertain that they appear on their face to be in accordance with the terms and conditions of the credit. Documents which appear on their face to be inconsistent with one another will be considered as not appearing on their face to be in accordance with the terms and conditions of the credit.'

No case law supports dishonour when the descriptions in the documents required by the letter of credit conform entirely, and the additional information does not create an inconsistency with the required descriptions unless one is familiar with trade usages.

In *Axxess*, the commercial invoice for a shipment of batteries presented to the issuer contained additional information, but conformed with the requirements of

---

20 [1943] 1 KB 37.
21 *Ibid* at 41.
22 *Ibid* at 42–43.

the letter of credit. The invoices specifically contained additional columns with the headings 'unit price' and 'unit'. After the issuer remitted payment, the applicant received the batteries and realised that the shipment contained fewer batteries than it had contracted for. The applicant then brought a lawsuit against the issuer for improperly releasing the funds in breach of its application agreement with the issuer. The court held that while the application agreement itself did not establish the issuer's obligation to honour the letter of credit under certain conditions only, the letter itself did expressly incorporate the UCP and therefore the issuer was required by Art 13 to examine all the documents with reasonable care to ascertain that they appeared on their face to be in accordance with the terms and conditions of the credit. Further, the court held that the additional information in the invoice upon which the applicant relied did not create an inconsistency with the letter of credit.[23]

Article 14 addresses the issuing bank's and the beneficiary's rights when the beneficiary provides 'discrepant documents' in a payment demand. Under this Article, the standard of strict compliance applies to the beneficiary's duty to provide the documentation that the letter of credit requires, which means that 'even slight discrepancies in compliance with the terms of the letter of credit justify refusal to pay'.[24]

The issuing bank is entitled to have a motion to dismiss granted if it properly refused a payment demand that was not in strict compliance.[25]

The issuer may not be held liable for performance of the underlying contract, however, as this would again ignore the cardinal tenet of letter of credit law, namely the independence of the letter of credit from the underlying goods or services.[26]

Precisely because a letter of credit involves dealing in documents rather than the underlying goods or services, there has been 'rigorous insistence' by the courts that documents presented comply with the letter of credit requirements. This statement was made by a case in 1978 and was disagreed with in a 2000 case called *Voest-Alpine Trading Co v Bank of China*. This case provides that these rulings retreat from rigorous insistence on compliance with the letter of credit requirements. They simply recognise that variance between documents specified and documents submitted is not terminal if there is no possibility that the documents could mislead the paying bank to its detriment.

Voest-Alpine Trading Company also holds that the doctrine of strict compliance ensures banks will be able to act quickly, enhancing the letter's fluidity; literal compliance is essential to protect the bank's right of indemnity from its customer.[27]

Under the UCP, banks are required to scrutinise closely the documents presented to them and accept only documents that comply precisely with the letter of credit.[28]

---

23 *Axxess, Inc v Rhode Island Hospital Trust National Bank* (1991) 15 UCC Rep Serv 2d 1011 (USDC Mass).
24 *Creaciones Con Idea SA de CV v MashreqBank PSC* (1999) 51 F Supp 2d 423 (SDNY).
25 *Kostroma Ltd v Standard Chartered Bank* (1997) 237 AD 2d 220 (NYS).
26 *Flagship Cruises Ltd v New England Merchants National Bank of Boston* (1978) 569 F 2d 699 (1st Cir).
27 *Voest-Alpine Trading Co v Bank of China* (2000) 167 F Supp 2d 940 (SD Tex).
28 *Brenntag International Chemicals Inc v Norddeutsche Landesbank GZ* (1999) 70 F Supp 2d 399 (SDNY).

Time for accepting/rejecting tender of documents

Both at common law and under Art 13(a) of the UCP the bank has an obligation to examine the documents with reasonable care to ascertain whether they appear on their face to be in accordance with the terms and conditions of the credit. Pursuant to Art 13(b), 'The issuing bank, the confirming bank, if any, or a nominated bank acting on their behalf, shall each have a reasonable time, not to exceed seven banking days following the day of receipt of the documents, to examine the documents and determine whether to take up or refuse the documents and to inform the party from which it received the documents accordingly'. Although the bank has a maximum of seven banking days in which to examine the document, the bank has an obligation to proceed with such examination with reasonable promptness. If it decides to refuse the documents, it must give notice to that effect without delay to the remitting bank or the beneficiary as the case may be (Art 14(d)(i)). If it delays in deciding whether to refuse the documents, it will be precluded from claiming that the documents are not in accordance with the terms and conditions of the credit (Art 14(e)).

Article 14(d) establishes the procedure for an issuing bank to refuse a payment demand supported by discrepant documents. The issuing bank must give notice of the refusal decision within seven days. Such notice must state all discrepancies in respect of which the bank refuses the documents. If the issuing bank fails to comply with this refusal procedure, then it 'shall be precluded from claiming that the documents are not in compliance with the terms and conditions of the letter of credit.[29]

The term 'reasonable time' cannot be equated with 'without delay'. What the beneficiary is interested in is the time between the bank's receipt of the documents and his receipt of notice that they have been rejected.

By using the words 'reasonable time' the UCP did not intend to fix time limits. What is a reasonable time limit must depend on the facts of each case, judged as necessary by contemporary banking practice. The danger is that a flexible standard would be converted into something more rigid if the courts attempted to preach in any general way about what is or is not a reasonable time. The need for flexibility is obvious: transactions vary widely in their size, complexity and sensitivity; banks vary considerably in size and so the availability of staff to process transactions of this kind in one bank may be very different from those available to do so in another.[30]

Appearance and not substance of documents is critical

The bank is only concerned with ascertaining that the documents appear on their face to conform with the terms and conditions of the credit. It is entitled to treat as non-conforming documents that appear on their face to be ambiguous or inconsistent with one another (Art 13(a)). The situation is the same at common law. Hence, the position of the bank and the extent of the application of the doctrine of strict compliance remain unchanged even where the provisions of the UCP 500 are not incorporated in a documentary credit. This is clear from a judgment of the Privy Council on appeal from

---

29   *Creaciones Con Idea SA de CV v MashreqBank PSC* (1999) 51 F Supp 2d 423 (SDNY).
30   *Seaconsar Far East Ltd v Bank Markazi Jomhouri Islami Iran* [1999] 1 Lloyd's Rep 36 CLC.

the Court of Appeal in Singapore in *Gian Singh and Co Ltd v Banque de l'Indochine*.[31] The judgment of their Lordships was delivered by Lord Diplock who stated:[32]

> The duty of the issuing bank, which it may perform either by itself, or by its agent, the notifying bank, is to examine documents with reasonable care to ascertain that they appear on their face to be in accordance with the terms and conditions of the credit. The express provision to this effect in Article 7 of the Uniform Customs and Practice for Documentary Credits [being Article 15 of the UCP 1983 Revision] does no more than re-state the duty of the bank at common law. In business transactions financed by documentary credits, banks must be able to act promptly on presentation of the documents. In the ordinary case visual inspection of the actual documents presented is all that is called for. The bank is under no duty to take any further steps to investigate the genuineness of a signature which, on the face of it, purports to be the signature of the person named or described in the letter of credit.

The principle that the bank is only concerned with the appearance of the tendered documents and not with their substance is further reinforced by Art 15 of the UCP 500, which provides as follows:

> Banks assume no liability or responsibility for the form, sufficiency, accuracy, genuineness, falsification or legal effect of any document(s), or for the general and/or particular conditions stipulated in the document(s) or superimposed thereon; nor do they assume any liability or responsibility for the description, quantity, weight, quality, condition, packing, delivery, value or existence of the goods represented by any document(s), or for the good faith of acts and/or omissions, solvency, performance or standing of the consignors, the carriers, the forwarders, the consignees or the insurers of the goods, or any other person whomsoever.

In accordance with Art 22 of the UCP 500, banks will usually accept a document bearing a date of issuance prior to that of the credit, subject to such document being presented within the time limits set out in the credit.

Ambiguous terms interpreted by bank

It is clear that, if the bank is confronted with an ambiguity when examining the tendered documents, it is entitled to reject the tender and refuse to make payment under the letter of credit. The bank may, however, give an interpretation to the ambiguous term that will render the documents in conformity with the terms and conditions of the credit. Assuming that in such case the bank were wrong in its interpretation and that, therefore, on a proper interpretation of the ambiguous term, the documents do not comply with the terms and conditions of the credit, the question would then arise whether the bank is in breach of its obligations or whether it is entitled to be reimbursed in respect of the payment made under the credit.

This question is answered by the Privy Council in an appeal from the Supreme Court of New South Wales in *Commercial Banking Co of Sydney Ltd v Jalsard Pty Ltd*.[33] In that case, the buyer (the respondent) contracted to purchase a quantity of battery-operated Christmas lights from a seller in Taiwan to be shipped to Sydney in two

---

31 [1974] 1 WLR 1234.
32 *Ibid* at 1238–39.
33 [1973] AC 279.

consignments. The buyer requested the bank (the appellant) to issue a letter of credit to authorise the seller to draw upon the bank's correspondent in Taiwan for a sum to cover invoice, costs FOB of the two shipments. The documents required to be tendered under the credit included a packing list certifying the quantity of the goods exported. Later, in accordance with the buyer's instructions, the bank amended the letter of credit by adding to the documents required a 'certificate of inspection'.

In due course, the documents were tendered by the seller and handed over by the bank to the buyer against reimbursement of the purchase price of the goods. The documents included 'certificates of inspection' in relation to the two shipments, issued by two firms of surveyors in Taiwan each certifying that the surveyors had supervised the packing of the boxes for checking the quantity and condition of the contents. On arrival in Sydney, the goods were found to be of defective quality and substantially unsaleable. The defects were not discoverable by visual inspection but only by physical testing. The buyer brought an action against the bank claiming damages for breach of contract for accepting tendered documents, namely the certificates of inspection, which did not comply with the terms of the letter of credit. The buyer contended that 'certificate of inspection' meant a document certifying the condition and quality of the goods inspected and not merely the condition and quantity of such goods. The buyer succeeded in his action in the Supreme Court of New South Wales.

In reversing the judgment of the Supreme Court, the Judicial Committee held that the minimum requirement implicit in the ordinary meaning of the words 'certificate of inspection' was 'that the goods the subject matter of the inspection have been inspected, at any rate visually, by the person issuing the certificate'. If it is intended that a particular method of inspection should be adopted or that particular information as to the result of the inspection should be recorded, this, in their Lordship's view, would not be implicit in the words 'certificate of inspection' by themselves, but would need to be expressly stated.[34] His Lordship then went on to deal specifically with the question posed earlier.[35]

It is a well established principle in relation to commercial credits that if the instructions given by the customer to the issuing banker as to the documents to be tendered by the beneficiary are ambiguous or are capable of covering more than one kind of document, the banker is not in default if he acts upon a reasonable meaning of the ambiguous expression or accepts any kind of document which fairly falls within the wide description used.[36] There is good reason for this. By issuing the credit, the banker does not only enter into a contractual obligation to his own customer, the buyer, to honour the seller's drafts if they are accompanied by the specified documents. By confirming the credit to the seller through his correspondent at the place of shipment he assumes a contractual obligation to the seller that his drafts on tender to the correspondent bank will be accepted if accompanied by the specified documents, and a contractual obligation to his correspondent bank to reimburse it for accepting the seller's drafts. The banker is not concerned as to whether the documents for which the buyer has stipulated serve any useful commercial purpose or as to why the customer called for tender of a document of a particular description. Both the

---

34   *Ibid* at 285.
35   Ibid at 285–86.
36   See *Midland Bank Ltd v Seymour* [1955] 2 Lloyd's Rep 147.

issuing banker and his correspondent bank have to make quick decisions as to whether a document that has been tendered by the seller complies with the requirements of a credit at the risk of incurring liability to one or other of the parties to the transaction if the decision is wrong. Delay in deciding may in itself result in a breach of his contractual obligations to the buyer or to the seller. This is the reason for the rule that where the banker's instructions from his customer are ambiguous or unclear he commits no breach of his contract with the buyer if he has construed in a reasonable sense, even though upon the closer consideration which can be given to questions of construction in a court of law, it is possible to say that some other meaning is to be preferred.[37]

Irrelevant discrepancies

Not all discrepancies would entitle a bank to reject the tender of documents. Slight discrepancies must be disregarded if the instructions in the tendered documents, notwithstanding such irregularity, make sense and have the same meaning as the related documents. Indeed, the UCP 500 itself makes allowance for irrelevant or immaterial irregularities. For example, Art 39(b) permits under-shipment or over-shipment within a tolerance of 5% provided there is no contrary stipulation in the credit. It is impossible to provide any guidelines that will assist in determining what discrepancies are and are not relevant. It is a matter of applying good commercial sense in each case. In the words of Schmitthoff:[38]

> If the tendered documents are ambiguous, the tender is, in principle, a bad tender. But the bank, when examining the tendered documents, should not insist on the rigid and meticulous fulfilment of the precise wording in all cases. If, 'properly read and understood', the words in the instructions and in the tendered documents have the same meaning, if they correspond though not being identical, the bank should not reject the documents. ... But the margin allowed to the bank in interpreting the documents is very narrow and the bank will be at risk if it does not insist on strict compliance.

An illustration of an irrelevant discrepancy is provided in *M Golodetz and Co Inc v Czarnikow-Rionda Co Inc, The Galatia*.[39] There, buyers of sugar in India opened a letter of credit in favour of their supplier in respect of goods to be shipped in *The Galatia* which was to load in Kandla, India. When the vessel was partly loaded, fire broke out and a large quantity of the sugar already on board was damaged by the fire as well as by the water used to extinguish the fire. The damaged sugar was discharged and a note was typed on the bill of lading stating '[c]argo covered by this bill of lading has been discharged Kandla view damaged by fire and/or water used to extinguish for which general average declared'.[40] The confirming bank refused to take up the bill of lading on the ground that the note typed on the bill made it a claused bill. Such view accorded with the commercial view that every bill that contains a notation or clausing

---

37   *Credit Agricole Indosuez v Muslim Commercial Bank* [2000] 1 Lloyd's Rep 275 (Court of Appeal).
38   Schmitthoff, CM, *The Law and Practice of International Trade*, 9th edn, 1990, London: Stevens, p 411.
39   [1980] 1 WLR 495.
40   *Ibid* at 498.

is automatically to be regarded as a claused bill. The Court of Appeal preferred the legal view and held that the bill was a clean bill because the note on it referred to an event that had occurred after the goods were loaded in good order and condition.

Another illustration of an irrelevant discrepancy which also related to a bill of lading is found in *Westpac Banking Corporation v South Carolina National* Bank,[41] which was decided by the Privy Council on appeal from the Court of Appeal in New South Wales. In that case, Commonwealth Steel Co Ltd agreed to sell 400 truck side frames and 200 truck bolsters to National Railway Utilisation Corporation of Charlestown, South Carolina. The buyers requested South Carolina National Bank (SCNB) to open an irrevocable letter of credit in favour of the seller. The credit was available on presentation of 'shipped' bills of lading. Except as otherwise expressly stated, the letter of credit incorporated the UCP (1974 Revision). The credit was advised to the seller by Westpac Banking Corporation (Westpac). The bills tendered by the seller to Westpac were in the form 'received for shipment'. On the face of each of the bills were the words 'shipped on board' and 'freight pre-paid' and the intended vessel was stated to be *Columbus America*. The advising bank, Westpac, accepted the bills of lading and negotiated an accompanying bill of exchange drawn on SCNB. However, the latter, as the issuing bank, rejected the bills of lading. In the New South Wales Court of Appeal and in the Privy Council, SCNB relied on the contention that the bills were internally inconsistent in that on their face they stated to be in the nature of both 'shipped on board' and 'received for shipment'. The argument was accepted by the Court of Appeal but rejected by the Privy Council. The judgment of their Lordships was delivered by Lord Goff who stated:[42]

> Their Lordships approached the matter as follows. First, they are unable to accept the proposition that the words 'shipped on board' make the bill internally inconsistent. True, it is that the bill is on a 'received for shipment' form and for that reason refers to *Columbus America* as the intended vessel; but there is nothing inconsistent in a document which states that the specified goods have been received for shipment on board a named vessel and have in fact been shipped on board that vessel ... True, this bill of lading was, in form, a 'received for shipment' bill; but with the words 'shipped on board' forming part of the stencilled wording inserted in the bill and present at the time of its signature and issue, it was plain on the face of the bill that it stated that the goods had at that time been shipped on board the intended ship, *Columbus America*, at the intended port of loading, Melbourne, and it followed that the set of bills presented to SCNB was a set of on board ocean bills of lading as required by the letter of credit.

Thus, mere technical or irrelevant discrepancies as distinct from discrepancies that go to the substance of the documents may not be relied upon to reject tendered documents.

Pursuant to Art 14(c) of the UCP 500, 'If the issuing bank determines that the documents appear on their face not to be in compliance with the terms and conditions of the credit, it may in its sole judgment approach the applicant for a waiver of the discrepancy(ies)'. The bank's decision to seek a waiver from its customer (applicant for the credit) does not, however, extend the maximum period of seven banking days available to the bank to examine the submitted documents. When the documents do not strictly conform to the letter of credit conditions, the issuer may request express

41   [1986] 1 Lloyd's Rep 311.
42   *Ibid* at 315–16.

waiver from applicant. 'Waiver' is an intentional relinquishment of a known right with both knowledge of its existence and an intention to relinquish it. Thus, a party cannot waive discrepancies in a letter of credit unless it is aware of them at the time of the waiver.

In *Oei v Citibank NA*,[43] the applicant for a letter of credit sued the issuing and advising banks for their alleged wrongful honour of a letter of credit. The District Court held that 'absent evidence that applicant knew of substantial discrepancies in documents submitted by beneficiary, or at least that discrepancies of such a magnitude existed, applicant could not waive them'.

In *Marsala International Trading Co v Comerica Bank Inc*, Barracuda Bicycle purchased bicycles from Marsala, a supplier located in Taiwan. On 10 March 1995, Barracuda applied for and received a letter of credit from Comerica for Marsala's benefit. This agreement required Marsala to submit specific documentation containing a signed statement that an unpaid balance still existed, the original bill of lading, invoices and copies of the truckers' bills of lading. Comerica, acting as advising bank, sent an advice of credit to Marsala, stating to read the terms carefully. If Marsala could not comply with the terms of the credit, it should let the applicant know to arrange for an amendment. Marsala knew its documents did not conform under the terms of the letter of credit. It suggested that Barracuda apply to Comerica for an amendment waiving the submission of certain documents. This was completed as requested. Comerica contacted Barracuda to inquire whether the discrepancies would be waived.

Barracuda's response was that it would try to reach an agreement with Marsala, but that it did not waive the discrepancies. Barracuda refused to waive the discrepancies and instructed Comerica not to issue payment under any terms, except the ones stated in the letter of credit. Comerica refused payment to Marsala. The letter of credit expired prior to Marsala submitting conforming documents. Marsala filed a suit against Comerica alleging that Barracuda had previously waived the discrepancies in the required documents and that Comerica was obliged to pay Marsala once it received the letter. The district court and now the Court of Appeals held that plaintiff was entitled to payment under the letter of credit issued by Comerica.

Because many presentments of documents are defective, it is not unusual for issuing banks to request waivers from the customers when the beneficiary presents such documents. Additionally, when the customer has waived the discrepancies that preclude payment, the bank has no further obligation to examine or investigate the transactions between the customer and the beneficiary. To require or allow a bank to take further action before it issues payment would undermine the policy underlying letters of credit that the bank issuing payment is entitled to rely strictly on the documents before it.[44]

If the issuing bank determines that the documents appear on their face to be non-compliant with the terms and conditions of the credit, it may, according to Art 14 of the UCP 500, in its own judgment approach the applicant for a waiver of the discrepancy(ies).

---

43 (1997) 957 F Supp 492 (SDNY).
44 *Marsala International Trading Co v Comerica Bank Inc* (1998) 976 P 2d 275 (Col CA).

The requirement of linkage of documents

Article 37(c) of the UCP 500 stipulates that: 'The description of the goods in the commercial invoice must correspond with the description in the credit. In all other documents, the goods may be described in general terms not inconsistent with the description of the goods in the credit.' Thus, although the goods must be described in the commercial invoice in the same way in which they are described in the letter of credit, their description in other documents, for example, the transport and insurance documents, need not correspond with the description in the credit. An example of the application of this rule is provided by *Courtaulds North America Inc v North Carolina National Bank*,[45] which was decided under the UCP (1973 Revision). In this case, the bank issued an irrevocable letter of credit on behalf of its customer, Adastra Knitting Mills. It undertook to pay orders to pay for up to US$135,000 covering shipments of '100% acrylic yarn'. Courtaulds' commercial invoice described the goods as 'imported acrylic yarn', but the packing lists attached to the invoices described the goods as '100% acrylic yarn'. The bank refused to pay because it found a discrepancy between the letter of credit and the commercial invoice. The bank's refusal was condoned by the Court of Appeal for the 4th Circuit. Courtaulds also argued unsuccessfully that the packing lists, which were stapled to the invoice, were part of the invoice and that, therefore, the description of the goods in the invoice corresponded with the description of the goods in the letter of credit. On this issue, the court ruled that packing lists, even if attached to the commercial invoice, are not part of the invoice.

The issue of the description of the goods in documents and its consistency with the description of the goods in the credit is, however, different from the requirement of linkage of documents. A genuine discrepancy of documents will exist where the documents cannot be properly linked together and, therefore, may not relate to the same goods. The linkage requirement is expressly provided by Art 13(a) of the UCP 500, which in part states that 'documents which appear on their face to be inconsistent with one another will be considered as not appearing on their face to be in accordance with the terms and conditions of the credit'.

What is required is that all documents tendered to the bank clearly and unequivocally relate to the same goods. It is not necessary that, as in the case of the commercial invoice, each document comprehensively describes the goods, but that each unambiguously makes reference to the same goods. It is in this manner that the documents to be tendered are said to be linked together. A case in point is *Banque de l'Indochine et de Suez SA v JH Rayner (Mincing Lane) Ltd*.[46] In that case, a bank in Djibouti, acting as issuing bank, opened an irrevocable credit which was advised and confirmed by the plaintiff bank. The credit related to the sale of sugar by the defendants to the buyers on whose instructions the credit was opened in favour of the defendants. The defendants tendered the documents under the credit and requested payment of the amount due thereunder, approximately one million dollars. After examining the documents, the plaintiff bank considered that the tender was defective because of discrepancies between the documents. The defendants disputed that the

---

45   528 F 2d 802 (1975) (4th Circ).

46   [1983] QB 711. The judgment of Parker J, the first instance judge, which was affirmed by the Court of Appeal, is reported at 713–22; and the judgments of the Court of Appeal are reported at 726–34.

tender was defective. Following discussions between the parties, the plaintiff bank proceeded to pay, advising that such payment was 'effected under reserve due to the discrepancies', which the plaintiff bank went on to list. The last of the listed discrepancies was directed to an alleged absence of linkage, stating that: '(4) Certificates of weight, quality, packing and certificates of origin and EUR1 certificates cannot be related to remaining documents or to letter of credit.'

The issuing bank having refused to accept the documents, the plaintiff bank sought to recover from the defendants the payment it had made 'under reserve'. In dealing with the issue of linkage, Parker J stated:[47]

> I have no doubt that as long as the documents can be plainly seen to be linked with each other, are not inconsistent with each other or with the terms of the credit, do not call for enquiry and between them state all that is required in the credit, the beneficiary is entitled to be paid.

His Honour then went on to consider the specific discrepancies in the documents that gave rise to inconsistencies and, therefore, lack of linkage both between the documents themselves and between the documents and the credit. For this and other reasons, his Honour considered that the tender was bad and found for the plaintiff bank.

In respect to linkage, Parker J's reasoning and decision were affirmed by the Court of Appeal. In particular, Sir John Donaldson MR stated:

> I approach this aspect of the appeal [that is the linking of documents] on the same basis as did the judge, namely that the banker is not concerned with why the buyer has called for particular documents (*Commercial Banking Co of Sydney Ltd v Jalsard Pty Ltd* [1973] AC 279), that there is no room for documents which are almost the same, or which will do just as well, as those specified, *Equitable Trust Co of New York v Dawson Partners Ltd* (1926) 27 Lloyd's Rep 49, that whilst the bank is entitled to put a reasonable construction upon any ambiguity in its mandate, if the mandate is clear there must be strict compliance with that mandate (*Jalsard's case* [1973] AC 279), that documents have to be taken up or rejected promptly and without opportunity for prolonged enquiry (*Hansson v Hamel and Horley Ltd* [1922] 2 AC 36) and that a tender of documents which properly read and understood call for further enquiry or are such as to invite litigation are a bad tender (*M Golodetz and Co Inc v Czarnikow-Rionda Co Inc* [1980] 1 WLR 495).

His Lordship then dealt with the subject documents and found that the inconsistencies were such that the documents were not on their face linked to each other and to the commercial invoice. Interestingly, he also considered that the reference in the certificate of origin to 'nv Markhor or substitute' was inconsistent with the reference appearing in the other documents to 'nv Markhor' and considered that the words 'or substitute' could be referring to a different vessel and, therefore, the reference could be to a different parcel of sugar which was the subject of the sale. This aspect of the judgment has been criticised by Schmitthoff[48] who considers that the requirement of linkage in this respect was applied by the court too strictly.

In *North American Foreign Trading Corp v Chiao Tung Bank*,[49] North American Foreign Trading Corp (NAFT) was in the business of importing electronic equipment.

---

47   *Ibid* at 72.
48   Schmitthoff, *op cit*, pp 415–16.
49   (1997) WL 193197 (SDNY).

The issue in this case concerned a particular transaction in which it purchased about $1.8 million in telephones and answering machines from Huston Electronics Co., which required payment by letters of credit. The seller was required to present certain documents to a bank in Zurich in order to receive payment on these letters of credit. Chiao Tung Bank was a negotiating bank between NAFT and Huston. Chiao Tung would make payments to Huston, obtain the required documentation from Huston and remit the documentation to Zurich Bank to obtain reimbursement pursuant to the letters of credit. Chiao Tung was essentially the negotiating bank that paid the $1.8 million to Huston and sought reimbursement from the Zurich Bank. The Zurich Bank denied payment to Chiao Tung claiming that it failed to provide all of the documentation required for reimbursement under the letters of credit. Specifically, Chiao Tung did not submit certain 'inspection certificates'. Chiao Tung argued that it relied upon the fact that Zurich Bank had made payment on over forty prior negotiations where inspection certificates had not been provided. On these occasions, payment was made because the documents were eventually turned over or because NAFT waived the requirement. NAFT declined to waive the requirement for this particular transaction. One of the carriers was instructed by Huston to seize the remaining goods. This prompted NAFT to file suit.

Courts in the United States have recognised that equitable principles of estoppel and waiver are applicable to letter of credit transactions and, therefore, an issuing bank may by its conduct waive the right to insist on the application of the doctrine of strict compliance. Several recent cases relate to this issue. The Eleventh Circuit held that bank's prior one-time acceptance of discrepant documents did not constitute a waiver of right to demand conforming documents in future transactions.[50] The Seventh Circuit rejected the argument that the bank's failure to mention the particular form of documentary discrepancy in past transactions served to estop the bank from insisting on strict conformity in subsequent transactions.[51] The New York Appellate Division held that the fact that the defendant may have waived strict compliance in the past does not justify an inference of a waiver of any discrepancies that might arise at some future point under such another letter.[52]

The Eleventh Circuit rationalised these holdings as follows: it would severely hamper large institutions dealing in complex international transactions, if a single failure to apply the strict compliance standard under a letter of credit were to result in the loss of the right to demand conforming documents in subsequent transactions with the same beneficiary. If courts were to permit a sophisticated party who has ignored the rule of strict compliance to recover, great damage would be done to the utility of letters of credit. This utility springs from the ability of the parties to these transactions to rely on the clearly defined rules that govern them.

A beneficiary that fails to submit proper documentation to an issuing bank should not be permitted to obtain recovery by means of an unjust enrichment claim.

---

50   *Banco General Runinahui v Citibank International* (1996) 97 F 3d 480 (11th Cir).
51   *Occidental Fire & Cas Co of NC v Continental Bank* (1990) 918 F 2d 1312 (7th Cir).
52   *Alparqatas v Century Bus Credit Corp* (1992) 183 A 2d 491 (NY App Div).

Payment under reserve

If a bank finds the tendered documents to be clearly defective, it will reject the documents. Where, however, the position is not clear, the bank may still wish to accommodate the beneficiary and accept them subject to certain protective measures. In such a case, the bank may make 'payment under reserve', that is, on condition that if the documents are rejected by any subsequent recipient, for instance, by the issuing bank or the buyer, the bank will be entitled to reimbursement by the beneficiary of the amount paid by the bank under reserve. Provision for payment under reserve is made by Art 14(f) of the UCP 500 as follows:

> If the remitting bank draws the attention of the issuing bank and/or confirming bank, if any, to any discrepancy(ies) in the document(s) or advises such banks that it has paid, incurred a deferred payment undertaking, accepted draft(s) or negotiated under reserve or against an indemnity in respect of such discrepancy(ies), the issuing bank and/or confirming bank, if any, shall not be thereby relieved from any of their obligations under any provision of this article. Such reserve or indemnity concerns only the relations between the remitting bank and the party towards whom the reserve was made, or from whom, or on whose behalf, the indemnity was obtained.

The UCP provisions do not, however, define the expression 'payment under reserve'. Nor has any such expression been judicially defined in any complete or absolute manner. The meaning of such expression may for that reason vary from case to case depending on the meaning which the parties intended to give to such expression, having regard to all the facts and circumstances surrounding the subject transaction and, in particular, giving rise to the making of the payment 'under reserve'. It will be recalled that payment under reserve was made by the plaintiff bank in *Banque de l'Indochine et de Suez SA v JH Rayner (Mincing Lane) Ltd*,[53] discussed above in the context of the linkage of documents requirement. In that case the court of first instance and the Court of Appeal, having reached the view that certain discrepancies alleged by the plaintiff bank were valid grounds for rejecting the tendered documents, then examined the meaning of the expression 'under reserve'. Parker J considered that in the absence of any established custom, the meaning of such expression had to be determined in the light of the surrounding circumstances, or as it is also called, 'the factual matrix', namely:

1   that the remitting bank genuinely believed that there were one or more discrepancies justifying non-payment;
2   that the beneficiary believed that the bank was wrong and that it was entitled to payment under the credit; and
3   that both parties hoped that, notwithstanding the alleged discrepancies that were disputed by the beneficiary, the issuing bank would take up the documents and reimburse the remitting bank.

Other relevant facts were that the confirming bank proceeded to effect payment in order to resolve the beneficiary's cash flow problems, and that the beneficiary was considered by the confirming bank to be a reputable, valued and creditworthy customer.

---

53   [1983] QB 711.

In the Court of Appeal, Kerr LJ dealt with the 'commercial reality of the situation'.[54] The reality was that, while holding opposite views, both the confirming bank and the beneficiary hoped that, whichever of them was right, neither the issuing bank nor the buyer would raise any objection to the documents. It was with this hope uppermost in its mind that the confirming bank agreed to pay, but only 'under reserve'. But, in so agreeing, the bank could not, in his Lordship's view, be taken to have agreed to become involved in legal proceedings, if the documents were rejected, by having to sue the beneficiary to recover the money, and establishing the defect of the tendered documents, or by suing the issuing bank on the ground that the tender was in fact good. In his Lordship's view the proper approach was as follows:[55]

> What the parties meant, I think, was that payment was to be made under reserve in the sense that the beneficiary would be bound to repay the money on demand if the issuing bank should reject the documents, whether on its own initiative or on the buyer's instructions. I would regard this as a binding agreement made between the confirming bank and the beneficiary by way of a compromise to resolve the impasse created by the uncertainty of their respective legal obligations and rights.

A commercial view of the meaning of the expression 'under reserve' was also adopted by Sir John Donaldson MR who expounded his reasoning by imputing a dialogue between the parties as follows:[56]

Merchant: These documents are sufficient to satisfy the terms of the letter of credit and certainly will be accepted by my buyer. I am entitled to the money and need it.

Bank: If we thought that the documents satisfied the terms of the letter of credit, we would pay you at once. However, we do not think that they do and we cannot risk paying you and not being paid ourselves. We are not sure that your buyer will authorise payment, but we can of course ask.

Merchant: But that will take time and meanwhile we will have a cash flow problem.

Bank: Well the alternative is for you to sue us and that will take time.

Merchant: What about you paying us without prejudice to whether we are entitled to payment and then you seeing what is the reaction of your correspondent bank and our buyer?

Bank: That is all right, but if we are told that we should not have paid, how do we get our money back?

Merchant: You sue us.

Bank: Oh no, that would leave us out of our money for a substantial time. Further, it will involve us in facing in two directions. We should not only have to sue you, but also to sue the issuing bank in order to cover the possibility that you might be right. We cannot afford to pay on those terms.

---

54 *Ibid* at 733.
55 *Ibid.*
56 *Ibid* at 727–28.

| **Merchant:** | All right. I am quite confident that the issuing bank and my buyer will be content that you should pay, particularly since the documents are in fact in order. You pay me and if the issuing bank refuses to reimburse you for the same reason that you are unwilling to pay, we will repay you on demand and then sue you. But we do not think that this will happen. |
| **Bank:** | We agree. Here is the money under reserve. |

This dialogue gives rise to the agreement, referred to by Kerr LJ in his judgment (and quoted above), made between the plaintiff bank and the beneficiary. In this agreement, they made a commitment to resolve their dispute as to the compliance, or otherwise, of intended documents.

Seller's right of recovery against the buyer in case of non-conforming documents

It will be recalled that in accordance with the principle of autonomy, the credit is separate and independent from the underlying contract of sale. Assume that a seller has been refused payment by a bank under a documentary credit on the ground that the documents tendered by the seller failed to comply with the terms and conditions of the credit. The question for consideration is whether the seller, in those circumstances, is entitled to claim payment against the buyer personally under the separate contract of sale in respect of which the documentary credit was issued.

This question came for consideration before Bingham J in the English Commercial Court in *Shamster Jute Mills Ltd v Sethia (London) Ltd*.[57] In that case, pursuant to a contract, the plaintiff seller sold to the defendant buyer 200 tonnes of Jute yarn for a specified price. Payment was to be by irrevocable and confirmed letter of credit at sight. The buyer opened letters of credit to cover four monthly shipments under the contract. The credit was to be available by the seller's drafts drawn on the buyer, accompanied by specified documents. A number of consignments were shipped for which documents were presented and payment made under the relevant letter of credit. Subsequently, Oriental Credit Ltd of London (Oriental) opened a further irrevocable letter of credit in favour of the seller that did not appear in this case to be confirmed. The sellers submitted the documents to their own bank, namely Sonali Bank (Sonali) in Dhaka, asking that the documents be negotiated and paid. Although Sonali agreed to negotiate the documents, it did so 'under reserve' as there were a number of specified discrepancies that were not acceptable to Sonali. The documents were then transmitted to Sonali's London branch with instructions to present to Oriental. Oriental, having been presented with the documents, informed the buyer of the discrepancies. The buyer refused to accept the documents and as a result the seller brought an action against the buyer to recover the contract price or damages for non-acceptance. Bingham J held that the sellers, having failed to comply with the terms of the credit, could not recover against the buyers personally. His Honour approached the matter as follows:[58]

> The parties are right to agree in the present case that the letter of credit is, on Lord Denning's classification in *Alan*, conditional payment. The sellers never agreed that

---

57   [1987] 1 Lloyd's Rep 388.
58   *Ibid* at 392, col 2.

they would only look to Oriental Credit for payment whatever happened. Nor is the credit to be regarded as no payment at all but only a means by which payment may be obtained, a form of collateral security. But to speak of a letter of credit as conditional payment of the price does not perhaps make very clear what the condition is or how it works. If the buyer establishes a credit which conforms or is to be treated as conforming with the sale price, he has performed his part of the bargain so far. If the credit is honoured according to its terms, the buyer is discharged even though the credit terms differ from the contract terms: that was the *Alan* case. If the credit is not honoured according to its terms because the bank fails to pay, the buyer is not discharged because the condition has not been fulfilled. That was the *Nigerian Sweets* case. This makes good sense: 'for the buyers promised *to pay* by letter of credit, not to provide by a letter of credit a source of payment which did *not* pay [as Stephenson LJ put it in the *Alan* case at 329 and 220G].'

If the seller fails to obtain payment because he does not and cannot present the documents which under the terms of the credit, supplementing the terms of the contract, are required, the buyer is discharged: that was the *Ficom* case. In the ordinary case, therefore, of which the present is an example, the due establishment of the letter of credit fulfils the buyer's payment obligations unless the bank which opens the credit fails for any reason to make payment in accordance with the credit terms against documents duly presented. I know of no case where a seller who has failed to obtain payment under a credit because of failure on his part to comply with its terms has succeeded in recovering against the buyer personally. If this were an available road to recover, many of the familiar arguments about discrepancies in documents would be unnecessary. Bearing in mind the likelihood that buyers will (as here) sell unto sub-buyers such a result would, I think, throw the course of international trade into some confusion. It must in my view follow that the sellers here, not having complied with the credit terms, cannot recover against the buyers personally.

Although dismissing the seller's claim, his Honour noted the harshness of the result because the seller, who appeared to have set out to perform the contract in an honest, efficient and businesslike way, had parted with the goods and had received no payment from anyone.

THE PRINCIPLE OF AUTONOMY OF THE LETTER OF CREDIT

The principle

The essential feature of a documentary credit is its independence of any underlying transactions, such as the contract of sale, and the contract between the issuing bank and the buyer as applicant of the credit. This fundamental principle is given expression in Art 3 of the UCP 500, which reads as follows:

(a) Credits, by their nature, are separate transactions from the sales or other contract(s) on which they may be based and banks are in no way concerned with or bound by such contract(s), even if any reference whatsoever to such contract(s) is included in the credit. Consequently, the undertaking of a bank to pay, accept and pay draft(s) or negotiate and/or to fulfil any other obligation under the credit, is not subject to claims or defences by the applicant resulting from his relationships with the issuing bank or the beneficiary.

(b) A beneficiary can in no case avail himself of the contractual relationships existing between the banks or between the applicant and the issuing bank.

The autonomy principle is supported by the maxim, incorporated in Art 4, that the bank deals in documents and not in goods. The absoluteness of the bank's undertaking, in the form of a credit issued in favour of the seller as beneficiary, has been firmly upheld by the courts. These have frequently refused to interfere with such undertaking by making restraining orders that would prevent compliance. The leading Australian case is *Wood Hall Ltd v Pipeline Authority*,[59] in which Stephen J indicated that the autonomy principle is necessary to ensure that letters of credit remain as good as cash. The obligation of the issuing bank is described well in *Maurice O'Meara Co v National Park Bank of New York*.[60] In this case, the issuing bank refused to pay on a letter of credit that covered a shipment of newsprint paper. Its refusal was based on the ground that there was a reasonable doubt regarding the quality of the newspaper print. The court, in holding for the plaintiff, restated the autonomy principle when it decided that the bank 'was absolutely bound to make the payment under the letter of credit, irrespective of whether it knew, or had reason to believe, that the paper was not of the tensile strength contracted for'. In *Hamzeh Malas and Sons v British Imex Industries Ltd*,[61] where the Court of Appeal refused to grant an injunction, Lord Jenkins stated:[62]

> It seems to be plain enough that the opening of a confirmed letter of credit constitutes a bargain between the banker and the vendor of the goods, which imposes upon the banker an absolute obligation to pay, irrespective of any dispute there may be between the parties as to whether the goods are up to contract or not.

There is this to be remembered, too: a vendor of goods selling against a confirmed letter of credit is selling under the assurance that nothing will prevent him from receiving the price. That is of no mean advantage when goods manufactured in one country are being sold in another.

The quality of autonomy of the documentary credit provides it with attributes similar to those of a bill of exchange. In each case, the instrument is separate from and independent to the underlying transaction. The parties to the instrument are not concerned with any dispute arising out of the underlying transaction. The obligation under the instrument is absolute and is not capable of any defence (save in the case of fraud which will be discussed in 'The fraud exception' below) and entitles the beneficiary thereunder to obtain summary judgment. An application for summary judgment (save in the case of fraud) cannot be resisted by any defence or cross-claim. The analogy with the bill of exchange was noted by Lord Denning MR in *Power Curber International Ltd v National Bank of Kuwait SAK*:[63]

> It is vital that every bank which issues a letter of credit should honour its obligations. The bank is in no way concerned with any dispute that the buyer may have with the seller. The buyer may say that the goods are not up to contract. Nevertheless the bank must honour its obligations. The buyer may say that he has a cross-claim in a large amount. Still the bank must honour its obligations. A letter of credit is like a bill of exchange given for the price of goods. It ranks as cash and must be honoured. No set off or counterclaim is allowed to detract from it: see *Nova (Jersey) Knit Ltd v Kammgarn*

---

59   (1979) 141 CLR 443 at 457.
60   (1925) 239 NY 386, 146 NE 636, 639.
61   [1958] 2 QB 127.
62   *Ibid* at 129.
63   [1981] 1 WLR 1233 at 1241.

Spinnerei GmbH.[64] All the more so with a letter of credit. Whereas a bill of exchange is given by buyer to seller, a letter of credit is given by a bank to the seller with the very intention of avoiding anything in the nature of a set off or counterclaim.

That case concerned an action brought by an American seller (Power Curber) against the National Bank of Kuwait (NBK), claiming under an irrevocable letter of credit issued by NBK. Power Curber had sold to a Kuwaiti distributor machinery, which was duly delivered to the Kuwaiti buyer. However, the latter apparently on the basis of a large counterclaim against Power Curber obtained from a court in Kuwait a provisional attachment order against NBK that prevented NBK from paying under the credit notwithstanding its willingness to do so. NBK operated a branch in London, hence Power Curber's decision to commence proceedings in England. The matter came at first instance before Parker J who gave summary judgment against NBK but imposed a stay upon the execution of the judgment. Power Curber appealed against the stay and NBK cross-appealed against the judgment. The Court of Appeal dismissed the cross-appeal and allowed the appeal. In upholding the bank's obligation to pay under the irrevocable letter of credit, the court held that such obligation was not affected by the Kuwaiti court's provisional attachment order. In this context, Lord Denning MR observed that the order for 'provisional attachment' operated against NBK's head office in Kuwait, but not against its branch office in London. That branch was subject to the orders of the English courts.[65]

Thus, in the absence of fraud, summary judgment will be granted in respect of claims made under letters of credit. Similarly, in the absence of fraud no injunction would be granted to restrain a bank from honouring its obligations under a letter of credit. In *Bolivinter Oil SA v Chase Manhattan Bank NA and Others*,[66] an application was made for an injunction restraining the defendant bank from making payment pursuant to an irrevocable letter of credit. The application was based on disputes between the parties over the performance of the underlying contract. The judge at first instance refused to grant the injunction and an appeal against such refusal was dismissed. In his judgment, Sir John Donaldson MR stated:[67]

> Judges who are asked, often at short notice and *ex parte*, to issue an injunction restraining payment by a bank under an irrevocable letter of credit or performance bond or guarantee should ask whether there is any challenge to the validity of the letter, bond or guarantee itself. If there is not or if the challenge is not substantial, *prima facie* no injunction should be granted and the bank should be left free to honour its contractual obligation, although restrictions may well be imposed upon the freedom of the beneficiary to deal with the money after he has received it. The wholly exceptional case where an injunction may be granted is where it is proved that the bank knows that any demand for payment already made or which may thereafter be made will clearly be fraudulent. But the evidence must be clear, both as to the fact of fraud and as to the bank's knowledge. It would certainly not normally be sufficient that this rests upon the uncorroborated statement of the customer, for irreparable damage can be done to a bank's credit in the relatively brief time which must elapse between the granting of such an injunction and an application by the bank to have it discharged.

---

64 [1977] 1 WLR 713, where summary judgment was given to a plaintiff as holder in due course of bills of exchange.
65 [1981] 1 WLR 1233 at 1241.
66 [1984] 1 WLR 392.
67 *Ibid* at 393.

'The independence principle protects only the distribution of proceeds of the letter of credit ... and does not address claims respecting the underlying contract'.[68] This fundamental principle governing letters of credit extends to the relationship between the issuing bank and the confirming bank that is brought into the transaction not by the buyer-applicant but by the issuing bank, and as a consequence a buyer-applicant may not sue the confirming bank.[69]

'Fraud in the transaction' theory means that the bank would not be bound by a claim which is fraudulent in nature but which complied on its face to the letter of credit. The theory of fraud in the transaction is the only method by which a bank might protect itself from a false and fraudulent claim on a letter of credit. While the UCP does not specifically disallow a defence of fraud in the transaction, it also does not specifically provide for it either. If the UCP is silent on this matter, the UCC (in an American context) would apply. The UCC provides that the bank *may* honour the draft despite the existence of fraud. The American legislature also gave the bank the option of not honouring a sight draft where there is fraud in the transaction.[70]

The fraud exception will now be considered in detail in the next section of this chapter.

The fraud exception

Fraud is the only exception to the absolute obligation of a bank to pay under a letter of credit; this obligation is founded on the principle of autonomy of letters of credit. Not surprisingly, a mere allegation of fraud is insufficient to affect the bank's obligation to make payment under a credit. Indeed, although an allegation of fraud made by a buyer may be based on a genuine belief or suspicion, such belief or suspicion may itself be ill-founded. It is clear that something more than an allegation of fraud is required. However, it is far from clear what degree of evidence of fraud is required, and what knowledge of such fraud the beneficiary and/or the bank must have for the fraud exception to be available.

The fraud exception can be traced back to the American case of *Szteijn v J Henry Schroder Banking Corporation*.[71] In that case, the issuing bank opened an irrevocable credit covering a shipment of bristles. The seller shipped crates containing rubbish, but managed to procure and tender documents that were regular on their face. The buyer, having discovered the fraud, made an application for an injunction restraining the issuing bank from accepting the documents and making payment under the credit. The bank made an application to strike out the action on the ground that it did not disclose a cause of action. The strike out application was dismissed by Shientag J who held that:[72]

> ... where the seller's fraud has been called to the bank's attention before the drafts and documents have been presented for payment, the principle of the independence of the

---

68   *Demczyk v Mutual Life Insurance Co (in re Graham Square)* (1997) 126 F 3d 823 (6th Cir).
69   *International Trade Relationship and Export v Citibank* (2000) WL 343899 (SDNY).
70   *Prairie State Bank v Universal Bonding Insurance Company* (1998) 953 P 2d 1047 (Kan App).
71   (1941) 31 NYS 2d 631 (NY Sup Ct).
72   *Ibid* at 634.

bank's obligation under the letter of credit should not be extended to protect the unscrupulous seller.

Szteijn was distinguished by Megarry J in *Discount Records Ltd v Barclays Bank Ltd and Another*.[73] That case was concerned with an application for an injunction restraining the defendant bank from paying a draft pursuant to an irrevocable credit opened at the plaintiff's request to enable the purchase of certain goods. The plaintiff's evidence was that on arrival the cartons containing the goods were found to be empty or half empty, or filled with rubbish or containing, mostly, goods not ordered. Megarry J dismissed the application for an injunction holding that the evidence of the alleged fraud had yet to be established and the draft might be in the hands of a holder in due course. In this context he stated that, 'I would be slow to interfere with bankers' irrevocable credits, and not least in the sphere of international banking, unless a sufficiently grave cause is shown'.[74]

If a bank has no knowledge of the fraud at the time when it makes payment or negotiates the letter of credit, assuming the relevant tendered documents appear regular on their face, it will not be liable to its principal if it is later discovered that the documents were forged. Such liability is precluded by Art 15 of the UCP 500, which provides, in its relevant part, that 'banks assume no liability or responsibility for the form, sufficiency, accuracy, genuineness, falsification or legal effect of any document(s)'. Even if the provisions of the UCP are not incorporated in the letter of credit, the position at common law is the same and the bank would not be liable.[75]

The relevant time for considering the bank's state of knowledge in relation to any forgery or other relevant fraud is when payment falls due and is refused by the bank.[76] If the party claiming payment has negotiated the documents in good faith with the remitting bank, the issuing bank cannot excuse refusal to honour the credit on the ground that at some earlier time the remitting bank was a mere agent for collection on the part of the seller and allege against the beneficiary fraud or forgery.[77]

It will be recalled that in *Bolivinter Oil SA v Chase Manhattan Bank NA and Others*,[78] Sir John Donaldson MR stated that the evidence of fraud must be clear, both as to the fact of fraud and as to the bank's knowledge.[79] The evidentiary requirement was further elaborated by Hirst J in *Tukan Timber Ltd v Barclays Bank plc*,[80] where his Honour stated:[81]

> We would expect the court to require strong corroborative evidence of the allegation, usually in the form of contemporaneous documents, particularly those emanating from the seller. In general, for the evidence of fraud to be clear, we would also expect the seller to have been given an opportunity to answer the allegation and to have

73 [1975] 1 WLR 315.
74 *Ibid* at 320.
75 *Woods v Thiedemann* (1862) 1 H and C 478; *Ulster Bank v Synott* (1871) 5 IREq 595; *Basse and Selve v Bank of Australasia* (1904) 90 LT 618; *Guaranteed Trust Co of New York v Hannay and Co* [1918] 2 KB 623.
76 *European Asian Bank AG v Punjab and Sind Bank* (No 2) [1983] 1 WLR 642.
77 *Ibid* at 658.
78 [1984] 1 WLR 392.
79 *Ibid* at 393.
80 [1987] 1 Lloyd's Rep 171.
81 *Ibid* at 175.

failed to provide any, or any adequate answer in circumstances where one could properly be expected.

If, therefore, the bank has received corroborative evidence of fraud that includes some contemporaneous documents emanating from the buyer, and the seller has not given a satisfactory answer to the allegations, the bank will be entitled (and probably ought) to refuse payment under the credit.

What if the bank is furnished with such strong corroborative evidence, but there is no evidence showing that the beneficiary (seller) knew of the fraud? Although one would have thought that in such a hypothetical situation the fraud exception would apply, the House of Lords took an opposite view in *United City Merchants (Investments) Ltd v Royal Bank of Canada (The American Accord)*.[82] In that case, a Peruvian company ('the buyers') agreed to buy from English sellers ('the sellers') a plant for the manufacture of glass fibres ('the goods') at a specified price FOB London for shipment to Callao. Payment was to be in London by confirmed irrevocable transferable credit on presentation of specified documents. The buyers' bank, which acted as the issuing bank, appointed Royal Bank of Canada ('the confirming bank') to advise and confirm the credit to the sellers. This was duly done. The credit was expressed to be subject to the UCP and to be available by sight drafts on the issuing bank against delivery, *inter alia*, of a full set of 'on board' bills of lading evidencing receipt for shipment of the goods from London to Callao on or before a specified date which was subsequently extended to 15 December 1976.

It was intended by the loading brokers acting on behalf of the carriers that the goods be shipped on a vessel belonging to the carriers, namely the *American Legend* which was due to arrive at an agreed substituted destination on 10 December 1976. The arrival of *American Legend* at such destination was cancelled and another vessel, *American Accord*, was substituted by the loading brokers even though its date of arrival was scheduled for 16 December 1976, that is, one day after the latest date of shipment required by the documentary credit. The goods were in fact loaded on board *American Accord* on 16 December 1976, but the loading brokers who issued bills of lading as agents for the carriers issued in the first instance a set of 'received for shipment' bills of lading dated 15 December 1976, which they handed over to the sellers in return for payment of the freight.

On presentation of the shipping documents to the confirming bank on 17 December, that bank raised various objections including the fact that the bills of lading did not bear any dated 'on board' notations. The bills of lading were returned to the brokers who then issued a fresh set bearing the notation that was untrue: 'these goods are actually on board 15 December 1976. EH Munday and Co (Freight Agents) Ltd as agents.' The amended bills of lading and all other relevant documents were presented to the confirming bank on 22 December 1976. The confirming bank again refused payment, this time on the ground that they had information in their possession that suggested that shipment was not effected as it appeared on the bills of lading. At the trial, it was found that an employee of the loading brokers had acted fraudulently in issuing the bills of lading bearing a false date. The trial judge also found that the sellers (and their transferee) were not privy to any fraud and had acted in good faith without knowledge of the false date that appeared on the bills of lading when tendering the documents to the confirming bank.

The leading judgment was delivered by Lord Diplock, with whom the other Law Lords agreed. Having referred to the general principle governing the contractual obligations of the confirming bank and the seller, his Lordship went on as follows:[83]

> To this general statement of principle ... there is one established exception: that is, where the seller, for the purpose of drawing on the credit, fraudulently presents to the confirming bank documents that contain, expressly or by implication, material representations of fact that to his knowledge are untrue. Although there does not appear among the English authorities any case in which this exception has been applied, it is well established in the American cases of which the leading or 'landmark' case is *Szteijn v J Henry Schroder Banking Corp* (1941) 31 NYS 2d 631. This judgment of the New York Court of Appeals was referred to with approval by the English Court of Appeal in *Edward Owen Engineering Ltd v Barclays Bank International Ltd* [1978] QB 159, though this was actually a case about a performance bond ... The exception for fraud on the part of the beneficiary seeking to avail himself of the credit is a clear application of the maxim *ex turpi causa non oritur actio* or if plain English is to be preferred 'fraud unravels all'. The courts will not allow their process to be used by a dishonest person to carry out a fraud.

The instant case, however, does not fall within the fraud exception. Mocatta J found the sellers to have been unaware of the inaccuracy of Mr Baker's notation of the date at which the goods were actually on board *American Accord*. What rational ground can there be for drawing any distinction between apparently conforming documents that, unknown to the seller, in fact contain a statement of fact that is inaccurate, where the inaccuracy was due to inadvertence by the maker of the document, and the like documents where the same inaccuracy had been inserted by the maker of the documents with intent to deceive, among others, the seller/beneficiary himself? *Ex hypothesi*, we are dealing only with a case in which the seller/beneficiary claiming under the credit *has* been deceived, for if he presented documents to the confirming bank with knowledge that this apparent conformity with the terms and conditions of the credit was due to the fact that the documents told a lie, the seller/beneficiary would himself be a party to the misrepresentation made to the confirming bank by the lie in the documents and the case would come within the fraud exception.

In summary, the House of Lords held that the fraud exception which entitles a banker to refuse to pay under a letter of credit does not extend to fraud to which a seller or beneficiary under the credit was not a party.

There is no Australian judicial authority that deals comprehensively with the fraud exception. However, it appears from one case, namely *Hortico (Australia) Pty Ltd v Energy Equipment Co (Australia) Pty Ltd*[84] that the fraud exception may be more extensively applied. Although that case was concerned with an instrument, the true character of which was a performance bond, Young J made reference to and applied the principles governing letters of credit.[85] In dealing with a submission on fraud in respect of the exercise of the power, Young J stated:[86]

---

83 *Ibid* at 183.
84 [1985] 1 NSWLR 545.
85 For instance his Honour followed *Discount Records Ltd v Barclays Bank Ltd* [1975] 1 WLR 315 and *Edward Owen Engineering Ltd v Barclays Bank International Ltd* [1978] QB 159.
86 *Ibid* at 554.

[I]t is probably true to say that there is a wide general principle of equity that whenever a person unconscionably makes use of a statutory or contractual power for an improper purpose, that equity may step in and restrain the exercise of that power ... However, equity intervenes in such a case in the exercise of its discretion. As I have said, with commercial transactions such as the present, the courts have consistently taken a 'hands-off' approach and it does not seem to me that anything short of actual fraud would warrant this court in intervening, though it may be that in some cases ... the unconscionable conduct may be so gross as to lead to exercise of the discretionary power.

From the passage quoted above, it would seem that, at least in the State of New South Wales, there is a second basis or exception to the principle of autonomy of letters of credit, namely, that of unconscionable conduct. If that is correct, the quality of letters of credit being equivalent to cash would be exposed to a substantial risk of erosion that will adversely affect the standing of banks and ultimately international trade in Australia. For, unlike the fraud exception, which is rarely capable of being established, unconscionable conduct provides very fertile ground for successful applications for injunctions restraining banks from making payment under letters of credit.

The Mareva injunction

Apart from the fraud exception, a buyer against whose account the payment of a letter of credit may be debited could prevent the bank making payment by obtaining a Mareva injunction[87] against the seller/beneficiary which would have the effect of freezing the funds held by the bank for the benefit of, and payable to, the beneficiary. The principles relating to the grant of the Mareva injunction affecting the payment under a letter of credit were discussed by the Court of Appeal in *Etablissement Esefka International Anstaff v Central Bank of Nigeria*.[88] The fundamental principle relating to the grant of a Mareva injunction remains that it is to be granted only where there is a danger of the money being taken out of the jurisdiction so that, if the plaintiff succeeded, he was not likely to get his money.[89] That a *Mareva* injunction may be imposed upon the fruits of the letter of credit was made authoritatively clear by the Court of Appeal in *Intraco Ltd v Notis Shipping Corp*,[90] where Donaldson LJ stated:[91]

The learned judge went on to say that this did not prevent the court, in an appropriate case, from imposing a Mareva injunction upon the fruits of the letter of credit or guarantee. Again we agree. It is a natural corollary of the proposition that a letter of credit or bank guarantee is to be treated as cash that when the bank pays and cash is received by the beneficiary, it should be subject to the same restraints as any other of his cash assets. *in rem*

Similarly, in *Z Ltd v A-Z and AA – LL*[92] the Court of Appeal held that the Mareva injunction was an established feature of English law which should be granted where it appeared likely that the plaintiff would recover judgment against the defendant for a

---

87 So named after *Mareva Compania Naviera SA v International Bulkcarriers SA* [1975] 2 Lloyd's Rep 509.
88 [1979] 1 Lloyd's Rep 455.
89 *Ibid* at 448, col 2; 449, cols 1 and 2.
90 [1981] 2 Lloyd's Rep 256.
91 *Ibid* at 258.
92 [1982] 1 QB 558.

certain or approximate sum, and there were reasons to believe that the defendant had assets within the jurisdiction to meet the judgment, wholly or in part, but might deal with them so that they were not available or traceable when judgment was given against him. It was further held that a Mareva injunction operated *in rem* and took effect from the moment it was pronounced on every asset of the defendant that it covered. If such assets included the defendant's bank account, upon the relevant bank receiving notice of the Mareva injunction, the defendant's instructions to the bank as its customer regarding that account were automatically revoked and the injunction made it unlawful for the bank to honour the defendant's cheques. Confirming the availability of a Mareva injunction to prevent payment under a letter of credit, Lord Denning said that: 'The injunction does not prevent payment under a letter of credit or under a bank guarantee, but it may apply to the proceeds as and when received by the defendant.'[93]

Nonetheless, it is thought that the courts will normally refuse to issue a Mareva injunction against a bank restraining it from making payment under a letter of credit unless, of course, the fraud exception is established.

CONCLUSION

Documentary credit is by far the most universally used method of payment in foreign trade transactions. Through the bank acting as an intermediary between the buyer and the seller, the competing interests between these two parties are balanced. The exporter achieves security of payment before parting with the goods and delivering the prescribed documents. Also, if a credit is confirmed, the exporter never needs to sue outside his own jurisdiction. He may also use the security of the credit to raise money from his own bank. The overseas buyer also has his interest secured: the negotiating bank ensures that the documents of title representing the goods and other related documents tendered by the seller comply strictly with the requirements of the purchaser before making payment under the credit to the seller. Furthermore, the importer may benefit from a letter of credit transaction in cases where the issuing bank provides liquidity without requiring immediate reimbursement.

Appropriately, the legal principles governing letters of credit as well as the provisions of the UCP 500 have maintained a balance between the respective rights and obligations of the exporter and the overseas buyer, while promoting and protecting the interests of the issuing, advising and confirming banks.

Further, the courts have continuously promoted the sanctity of the principle of autonomy of letters of credit by admitting only one exception to such principle, namely the fraud exception. Even then, the courts have not been prepared to allow the operation of the fraud exception unless there was clear evidence of fraud which required not only the knowledge of the bank at the time a claim for payment was made, but also that the beneficiary had been privy to such fraud.

Erosion of the principle of autonomy, either by allowing a broader application of the fraud exception or by introducing other exceptions, for example, one based on unconscionable conduct which was referred to by Young J in *Hortico (Australia) Pty Ltd*

---

93 *Ibid* at 574.

v Energy Equipment Co (Australia) Pty Ltd[94] may adversely affect international trade in Australia and its traditional trading partners. In this respect, it is apt to quote Lord Denning LR in the *Power Curber International Ltd v National Bank of Kuwait SAK*:[95]

> If the court of any of the countries should interfere with the obligations of one of its banks (by ordering it not to pay under a letter of credit) it would strike at the very heart of that country's international trade. No foreign seller would supply goods to that country on letters of credit – because he could no longer be confident of being paid. No trader would accept a letter of credit issued by a bank of that country if it might be ordered by its courts not to pay.

TUTORIAL QUESTIONS

1   The Deflatable Toy Co, located in South Bend, Indiana (buyer) was the purchaser of a consignment of deflatable plastic toys, manufactured by Toyworld, Brisbane, Australia (seller). Payment for each shipment of toys was made by a confirmed irrevocable letter of credit (LC) issued in favour of Toyworld. In the final shipment to be made under the LC, Toyworld sent a draft to the confirming bank accompanied by a bill of lading showing the various goods shipped, including deflatable Pineapple Men. The confirming bank paid Toyworld, as the documentation conformed with that required by the LC.

In fact the bill of lading was inaccurate. Because of a manufacturing fault the deflatable Pineapple Men had been removed from the container after the manufacturer's customs broker had made up the shipping documents. According to the seller, it was too late to amend the shipping documents. It advised the purchaser of the change in the shipment and contended that the purchaser was fully aware that the bill of lading did not accurately reflect the contents of the container.

When the issuing bank advised Deflatable Toy Co that it had received the documents, the buyer informed the bank that it regarded the bill of lading as fraudulent and it requested that the LC should not be honoured. When the issuing bank refused the buyer's request, the buyer applied for a court order to prevent payment under the LC.

Give judgment. Under what circumstances are banks entitled to refuse payment under the LC?

(Consult *Inflatable Toy Co Pty Ltd v State Bank of New South Wales* (1994) 34 NSWLR 243.)

2   An exporter of goods and the purchaser of those goods may adopt the letter of credit as the method of payment.

Discuss (i) the nature of this method of payment; (ii) the circumstances in which this method would be appropriately used; (iii) the manner in which this method of payment addresses an exporter's concerns in relation to (a) obtaining maximum security of payment for the goods supplied, and (b) minimising delay

---

94   [1985] 1 NSWLR 545.
95   [1981] 1 WLR 1233 at 1241.

in payment for the goods supplied. Refer in your answer to relevant provisions of the UCP and relevant case law.

3   The Forgan Smith Bank Ltd, an Australian bank, received a cable from an English company, Better Living Ltd, requesting that an irrevocable letter of credit be opened in favour of Furniture Unlimited and Co, who have their Head Office in Brisbane, Queensland. Better Living Ltd instructed the Forgan Smith Bank that the letter of credit be for 'A$25,000 against commercial invoice, certificate of inspection, clean shipped bill of lading covering 500 computer desks made from Tasmanian oak'. The bill of lading presented to the Forgan Smith Bank by Furniture Unlimited referred to '500 Tasmanian desks'. The Forgan Smith Bank refused to pay on this letter of credit. Furniture Unlimited and Co sued the Forgan Smith Bank for failing to honour its letter of credit.

     Was the bank correct in denying payment on this letter of credit? Discuss the scope of the doctrine of strict compliance. Refer in your answer to relevant cases.

4   Assume that a letter of credit opened by the buyer does not conform with the underlying contract. In what circumstances will such letter of credit bind the buyer and seller? Consult *Alan v El Nasr Import and Export* [1972] 2 QB 189.

FURTHER READING

Burnett, R, *The Law of International Business Transactions*, 1994, Annandale: The Federation Press, pp 132–87.

Roberts, JL, 'International payments' in Wilde, KCDM and Islam, MR, *International Transactions: Trade and Investment, Law and Finance*, 1993, North Ryde: The Law Book Co, pp 74–84.

Schaffer, R, Earle, B and Agusti, F, *International Business Law and Its Environment*, 2nd edn, 1993, St Paul, Minneapolis: West Publishing Co, pp 182–209.

Schmitthoff, CM, *The Law and Practice of International Trade*, 9th edn, 1990, London: Stevens, pp 379–452.

Van Houtte, H, *The Law of International Trade*, 1995, London: Sweet & Maxwell, pp 257–311.

APPENDIX

ICC UNIFORM CUSTOMS AND PRACTICE FOR DOCUMENTARY CREDITS

1993 Revision in force as of 1 January 1994.

A General provisions and definitions

Article 1 – Application of UCP

The Uniform Customs and Practice for Documentary Credits, 1993 Revision, ICC publication no 500, shall apply to all documentary credits (including to the extent to which they may be applicable, standby letter(s) of credit) where they are incorporated into the text of the credit. They are binding on all parties thereto, unless otherwise expressly stipulated in the credit.

Article 2 – Meaning of credit

For the purposes of these articles, the expressions 'documentary credit(s)' and 'standby letter(s) of credit' (hereinafter referred to as 'credit(s)'), mean any arrangement, however named or described, whereby a bank (the 'issuing bank') acting at the request and on the instructions of a customer (the 'applicant') or on its own behalf:

(i)   is to make a payment to or to the order of a third party (the 'beneficiary'), or is to accept and pay bills of exchange (draft(s)) drawn by the beneficiary; or

(ii) authorises another bank to effect such payment, or to accept and pay such bills of exchange (draft(s)); or

(iii) authorises another bank to negotiate;

against stipulated document(s), provided that the terms and conditions of the credit are complied with.

For the purposes of these articles, branches of a bank in different countries are considered another bank.

Article 3 – Credits v contracts

(a) Credits, by their nature, are separate transactions from the sales or other contract(s) on which they may be based and banks are in no way concerned with or bound by such contract(s), even if any reference whatsoever to such contract(s) is included in the credit. Consequently, the undertaking of a bank to pay, accept and pay draft(s) or negotiate and/or to fulfil any other obligation under the credit, is not subject to claims or defences by the applicant resulting from his relationships with the issuing bank or the beneficiary.

(b) A beneficiary can in no case avail himself of the contractual relationships existing between the banks or between the applicant and the issuing bank.

Article 4 – Documents v goods/services/performances

In credit operations all parties concerned deal with documents, and not with goods, services and/or other performances to which the documents may relate.

Article 5 – Instructions to issue/amend credits

(a) Instructions for the issuance of a credit, the credit itself, instructions for an amendment thereto, and the amendment itself, must be complete and precise.

In order to guard against confusion and misunderstanding, banks should discourage any attempt:

(i)   to include excessive detail in the credit or in any amendment thereto;

(ii) to give instructions to issue, advise or confirm a credit by reference to a credit previously issued (similar credit) where such previous credit has been subject to accepted amendment(s), and/or unaccepted amendment(s).

(b) All instructions for the issuance of a credit and the credit itself and, where applicable, all instructions for an amendment thereto and the amendment itself, must state precisely the document(s) against which payment, acceptance or negotiation is to be made.

B Form and notification of credits

Article 6 – Revocable v irrevocable credits

(a) A credit may be either (i) revocable or (ii) irrevocable.

(b) The credit, therefore, should clearly indicate whether it is revocable or irrevocable.

(c) In the absence of such indication the credit shall be deemed to be irrevocable.

Article 7 – Advising bank's liability

(a) A credit may be advised to a beneficiary through another bank (the 'advising bank') without engagement on the part of the advising bank, but that bank, if it elects to advise the credit, shall take reasonable care to check the apparent authenticity of the credit which it advises. If the bank elects not to advise the credit, it must so inform the issuing bank without delay.

(b) If the advising bank cannot establish such apparent authenticity it must inform, without delay, the bank from which the instructions appear to have been received that it has been unable to establish the authenticity of the credit and if it elects nonetheless to advise the credit it must inform the beneficiary that it has not been able to establish the authenticity of the credit.

Article 8 – Revocation of a credit

(a) A revocable credit may be amended or cancelled by the issuing bank at any moment and without prior notice to the beneficiary.

(b) However, the issuing bank must:

   (i) reimburse another bank with which a revocable credit has been made available for sight payment, acceptance or negotiation – for any payment, acceptance or negotiation made by such bank – prior to receipt by it of notice of amendment or cancellation, against documents which appear on their face to be in compliance with the terms and conditions of the credit;

   (ii) reimburse another bank with which a revocable credit has been made available for deferred payment, if such a bank has, prior to receipt by it of notice of amendment or cancellation, taken up documents which appear on their face to be in compliance with the terms and conditions of the credit.

Article 9 – Liability of issuing and confirming banks

(a) An irrevocable credit constitutes a definite undertaking of the issuing bank, provided that the stipulated documents are presented to the nominated bank or to the issuing bank and that the terms and conditions of the credit are complied with:

   (i) if the credit provides for sight payment – to pay at sight;

   (ii) if the credit provides for deferred payment – to pay on the maturity date(s) determinable in accordance with the stipulations of the credit;

   (iii) if the credit provides for acceptance:

      (a) by the issuing bank – to accept draft(s) drawn by the beneficiary on the issuing bank and pay them at maturity; or

      (b) by another drawee bank – to accept and pay at maturity draft(s) drawn by the beneficiary on the issuing bank in the event the drawee bank stipulated in the credit does not accept draft(s) drawn on it, or to pay draft(s) accepted but not paid by such drawee bank at maturity;

   (iv) if the credit provides for negotiation – to pay without recourse to drawers and/or *bona fide* holders, draft(s) drawn by the beneficiary and/or document(s) presented under the credit. A credit should not be issued available by draft(s) on the applicant. If the credit nevertheless calls for draft(s) on the applicant, banks will consider such draft(s) as an additional document(s).

(b) A confirmation of an irrevocable credit by another bank ('the confirming bank') upon the authorisation or request of the issuing bank, constitutes a definite undertaking of the confirming bank, in addition to that of the issuing bank, provided that the stipulated documents are presented to the confirming bank or to any other nominated bank and that the terms and conditions of the credit are complied with:

    (i) if the credit provides for sight payment – to pay at sight;

    (ii) if the credit provides for deferred payment – to pay on the maturity date(s) determinable in accordance with the stipulations of the credit;

    (iii) if the credit provides for acceptance:

        (a) by the confirming bank – to accept draft(s) drawn by the beneficiary on the confirming bank and pay them at maturity; or

        (b) by another drawee bank – to accept and pay at maturity draft(s) drawn by the beneficiary on the confirming bank, in the event the drawee bank stipulated in the credit does not accept draft(s) drawn on it, or to pay draft(s) accepted but not paid by such drawee bank at maturity;

    (iv) if the credit provides for negotiation – to negotiate without recourse to drawers and/or *bona fide* holders, draft(s) drawn by the beneficiary and/or document(s) presented under the credit. A credit should not be issued available by draft(s) on the applicant. If the credit nevertheless calls for draft(s) on the applicant, banks will consider such draft(s) as an additional document(s).

(c) (i) If another bank is authorised or requested by the issuing bank to add its confirmation to the credit but is not prepared to do so, it must so inform the issuing bank without delay.

    (ii) Unless the issuing bank specifies otherwise in its authorisation or request to add confirmation, the advising bank may advise the credit to the beneficiary without adding its confirmation.

(d) (i) Except as otherwise provided by Article 48, an irrevocable credit can neither be amended nor cancelled without the agreement of the issuing bank, the confirming bank, if any, and the beneficiary.

    (ii) The issuing bank shall be irrevocably bound by an amendment(s) issued by it from the time of the issuance of such amendment(s). A confirming bank may, however, choose to advise an amendment to the beneficiary without extending its confirmation and if so must inform the issuing bank and the beneficiary without delay.

    (iii) The terms of the original credit (or a credit incorporating previously accepted amendment(s)) will remain in force for the beneficiary until the beneficiary communicates his acceptance of the amendment to the bank that advised such amendment. The beneficiary should give notification of acceptance or rejection of amendment(s). If the beneficiary fails to give such notification, the tender of documents to the nominated bank or issuing bank, that conform to the credit and to not yet accepted amendment(s), will be deemed to be notification of acceptance by the beneficiary of such amendment(s) and as of that moment the credit will be amended.

    (iv) Partial acceptance of amendments contained in one and the same advice of amendment is not allowed and consequently will not be given any effect.

Article 10 – Types of credit

(a) All credits must clearly indicate whether they are available by sight payment, by deferred payment, by acceptance or by negotiation.

(b) (i) Unless the credit stipulates that it is available only with the issuing bank, all credits must nominate the bank (the 'nominated bank') which is authorised to pay, to incur a deferred payment undertaking, to accept draft(s) or to negotiate. In a freely negotiable credit, any bank is a nominated bank.

       Presentation of documents must be made to the issuing bank or the confirming bank, if any, or any other nominated bank.

    (ii) Negotiation means the giving of value for draft(s) and/or document(s) by the bank authorised to negotiate. Mere examination of the documents without giving of value does not constitute a negotiation.

(c) Unless the nominated bank is the confirming bank, nomination by the issuing bank does not constitute any undertaking by the nominated bank to pay, to incur a deferred payment undertaking, to accept draft(s), or to negotiate. Except where expressly agreed to by the nominated bank and so communicated to the beneficiary, the nominated bank's receipt of and/or examination and/or forwarding of the documents does not make that bank liable to pay, to incur a deferred payment undertaking, to accept draft(s), or to negotiate.

(d) By nominating another bank, or by allowing for negotiation by any bank, or by authorising or requesting another bank to add its confirmation, the issuing bank authorises such bank to pay, accept draft(s) or negotiate as the case may be, against documents which appear on their face to be in compliance with the terms and conditions of the credit and undertakes to reimburse such bank in accordance with the provisions of these articles.

Article 11 – Teletransmitted and pre-advised credits

(a) (i) When an issuing bank instructs an advising bank by an authenticated teletransmission to advise a credit or an amendment to a credit, the teletransmission will be deemed to be the operative credit instrument or the operative amendment, and no mail confirmation should be sent. Should a mail confirmation nevertheless be sent, it will have no effect and the advising bank will have no obligation to check such mail confirmation against the operative credit instrument or the operative amendment received by teletransmission.

(ii) If the teletransmission states 'full details to follow' (or words of similar effect) or states that the mail confirmation is to be the operative credit instrument or the operative amendment, then the teletransmission will not be deemed to be the operative credit instrument or the operative amendment. The issuing bank must forward the operative credit instrument or the operative amendment to such advising bank without delay.

(b) If a bank uses the services of an advising bank to have the credit advised to the beneficiary, it must also use the services of the same bank for advising an amendment(s).

(c) A preliminary advice of the issuance or amendment of an irrevocable credit (pre-advice), shall only be given by an issuing bank if such bank is prepared to issue the operative credit instrument or the operative amendment thereto. Unless otherwise stated in such preliminary advice by the issuing bank, an issuing bank having given such pre-advice shall be irrevocably committed to issue or amend the credit, in terms not inconsistent with the pre-advice, without delay.

Article 12 – Incomplete or unclear instructions

If incomplete or unclear instructions are received to advise, confirm or amend a credit, the bank requested to act on such instructions may give preliminary notification to the beneficiary for information only and without responsibility. This preliminary notification should state clearly that the notification is provided for information only and without the responsibility of the advising bank. In any event, the advising bank must inform the issuing bank of the action taken and request it to provide the necessary information.

The issuing bank must provide the necessary information without delay. The credit will be advised, confirmed or amended, only when complete and clear instructions have been received and if the advising bank is then prepared to act on the instructions.

C Liabilities and responsibilities

Article 13 – Standard for examination of documents

(a) Banks must examine all documents stipulated in the credit with reasonable care, to ascertain whether or not they appear, on their face, to be in compliance with the terms and conditions of the credit. Compliance of the stipulated documents on their face with the terms and conditions of the credit, shall be determined by international standard banking practice as reflected in these articles. Documents which appear on their face to be inconsistent with one another will be considered as not appearing on their face to be in compliance with the terms and conditions of the credit.

Documents not stipulated in the credit will not be examined by banks. If they receive such documents, they shall return them to the presenter or pass them on without responsibility.

(b) The issuing bank, the confirming bank, if any, or a nominated bank acting on their behalf, shall each have a reasonable time, not to exceed seven banking days following the day of receipt of the documents, to examine the documents and determine whether to take up or refuse the documents and to inform the party from which it received the documents accordingly.

(c) If a credit contains conditions without stating the document(s) to be presented in compliance therewith, banks will deem such conditions as not stated and will disregard them.

Article 14 – Discrepant documents and notice

(a) When the issuing bank authorises another bank to pay, incur a deferred payment undertaking, accept draft(s), or negotiate against documents which appear on their face to be in compliance with the terms and conditions of the credit, the issuing bank and the confirming bank, if any, are bound:

    (i) to reimburse the nominated bank which has paid, incurred a deferred payment undertaking, accepted draft(s), or negotiated,

    (ii) to take up the documents.

(b) Upon receipt of the documents the issuing bank and/or confirming bank, if any, or a nominated bank acting on their behalf, must determine on the basis of the documents alone whether or not they appear on their face to be in compliance with the terms and conditions of the credit. If the documents appear on their face not to be in compliance with the terms and conditions of the credit, such banks may refuse to take up the documents.

(c) If the issuing bank determines that the documents appear on their face not to be in compliance with the terms and conditions of the credit, it may in its sole judgment approach the applicant for a waiver of the discrepancy(ies). This does not, however, extend the period mentioned in sub-Article 13(b).

(d) (i) If the issuing bank and/or confirming bank, if any, or a nominated bank acting on their behalf, decides to refuse the documents, it must give notice to that effect by telecommunication or, if that is not possible, by other expeditious means, without delay but no later than the close of the seventh banking day following the day of receipt of the documents. Such notice shall be given to the bank from which it received the documents, or to the beneficiary, if it received the documents directly from him.

    (ii) Such notice must state all discrepancies in respect of which the bank refuses the documents and must also state whether it is holding the documents at the disposal of, or is returning them to, the presenter.

    (iii) The issuing bank and/or confirming bank, if any, shall then be entitled to claim from the remitting bank refund, with interest, of any reimbursement which has been made to that bank.

(e) If the issuing bank and/or confirming bank, if any, fails to act in accordance with the provisions of this article and/or fails to hold the documents at the disposal of, or return them to the presenter, the issuing bank and/or confirming bank, if any, shall be precluded from claiming that the documents are not in compliance with the terms and conditions of the credit.

(f) If the remitting bank draws the attention of the issuing bank and/or confirming bank, if any, to any discrepancy(ies) in the document(s) or advises such banks that it has paid, incurred a deferred payment undertaking, accepted draft(s) or negotiated under reserve or against an indemnity in respect of such discrepancy(ies), the issuing bank and/or confirming bank, if any, shall not be thereby relieved from any of their obligations under any provision of this article. Such reserve or indemnity concerns only the relations between the remitting bank and the party towards whom the reserve was made, or from whom, or on whose behalf, the indemnity was obtained.

Article 15 – Disclaimer on effectiveness of documents

Banks assume no liability or responsibility for the form, sufficiency, accuracy, genuineness, falsification or legal effect of any document(s), or for the general and/or particular conditions stipulated in the document(s) or superimposed thereon; nor do they assume any liability or responsibility for the description, quantity, weight, quality, condition, packing, delivery, value or existence of the goods represented by any document(s), or for the good faith or acts and/or omissions, solvency, performance or standing of the consignors, the carriers, the forwarders, the consignees or the insurers of the goods, or any other person whomsoever.

Article 16 – Disclaimer on the transmission of messages

Banks assume no liability or responsibility for the consequences arising out of delay and/or loss in transit of any message(s), letter(s) or document(s), or for delay, mutilation or other error(s) arising in the transmission of any telecommunication. Banks assume no liability or responsibility for errors in translation and/or interpretation of technical terms, and reserve the right to transmit credit terms without translating them.

Article 17 – Force majeure

Banks assume no liability or responsibility for the consequences arising out of the interruption of their business by Acts of God, riots, civil commotions, insurrections, wars or any other causes beyond their control, or by any strikes or lockouts. Unless specifically authorised, banks will not, upon resumption of their business, pay, incur a deferred payment undertaking, accept draft(s) or negotiate under credits which expired during such interruption of their business.

Article 18 – Disclaimer for acts of an instructed party

(a) Banks utilising the services of another bank or other banks for the purpose of giving effect to the instructions of the applicant do so for the account and at the risk of such applicant.

(b) Banks assume no liability or responsibility should the instructions they transmit not be carried out, even if they have themselves taken the initiative in the choice of such other bank(s).

(c) (i) A party instructing another party to perform services is liable for any charges, including commissions, fees, costs or expenses incurred by the instructed party in connection with its instructions.

(ii) Where a credit stipulates that such charges are for the account of a party other than the instructing party, and charges cannot be collected, the instructing party remains ultimately liable for the payment thereof.

(d) The applicant shall be bound by and liable to indemnify the banks against all obligations and responsibilities imposed by foreign laws and usages.

Article 19 – Bank-to-bank reimbursement arrangements

(a) If an issuing bank intends that the reimbursement to which a paying, accepting or negotiating bank is entitled, shall be obtained by such bank (the 'claiming bank'), claiming on another party (the 'reimbursing bank'), it shall provide such reimbursing bank in good time with the proper instructions or authorisation to honour such reimbursement claims.

(b) Issuing banks shall not require a claiming bank to supply a certificate of compliance with the terms and conditions of the credit to the reimbursing bank.

(c) An issuing bank shall not be relieved from any of its obligations to provide reimbursement if and when reimbursement is not received by the claiming bank from the reimbursing bank.

(d) The issuing bank shall be responsible to the claiming bank for any loss of interest if reimbursement is not provided by the reimbursing bank on first demand, or as otherwise specified in the credit, or mutually agreed, as the case may be.

(e) The reimbursing bank's charges should be for the account of the issuing bank. However, in cases where the charges are for the account of another party, it is the responsibility of the issuing bank to so indicate in the original credit and in the reimbursement authorisation. In cases where the reimbursing bank's charges are for the account of another party they shall be collected from the claiming bank when the credit is drawn under. In cases where the credit is not drawn under, the reimbursing bank's charges remain the obligation of the issuing bank.

D Documents

Article 20 – Ambiguity as to the issuers of documents

(a) Terms such as 'first class', 'well-known', 'qualified', 'independent', 'official', 'competent', 'local' and the like, shall not be used to describe the issuers of any document(s) to be presented under a credit. If such terms are incorporated in the credit, banks will accept the relative document(s) as presented, provided that it appears on its face to be in compliance with the other terms and conditions of the credit and not to have been issued by the beneficiary.

(b) Unless otherwise stipulated in the credit, banks will also accept as an original document(s), a document(s) produced or appearing to have been produced:

(i) by reprographic, automated or computerised systems;

(ii) as carbon copies;

provided that it is marked as original and, where necessary, appears to be signed.

A document may be signed by handwriting, by facsimile signature, by perforated signature, by stamp, by symbol, or by any other mechanical or electronic method of authentication.

(c) (i) Unless otherwise stipulated in the credit, banks will accept as a copy(ies), a document(s) either labelled copy or not marked as an original – a copy(ies) need not be signed.

(ii) Credits that require multiple document(s) such as 'duplicate', 'two-fold', 'two copies' and the like, will be satisfied by the presentation of one original and the remaining number in copies except where the document itself indicates otherwise.

(d) Unless otherwise stipulated in the credit, a condition under a credit calling for a document to be authenticated, validated, legalised, visaed, certified or indicating a similar requirement, will be satisfied by any signature, mark, stamp or label on such document that on its face appears to satisfy the above condition.

Article 21 – Unspecified issuers or contents of documents

When documents other than transport documents, insurance documents and commercial invoices are called for, the credit should stipulate by whom such documents are to be issued and their wording or data content. If the credit does not so stipulate, banks will accept such documents as presented, provided that their data content is not inconsistent with any other stipulated document presented.

Article 22 – Issuance date of documents v credit date

Unless otherwise stipulated in the credit, banks will accept a document bearing a date of issuance prior to that of the credit, subject to such document being presented within the time limits set out in the credit and in these articles.

Article 23 – Marine/ocean bill of lading

(a) If a credit calls for a bill of lading covering a port to port shipment, banks will, unless otherwise stipulated in the credit, accept a document, however named, which:

(i) appears on its face to indicate the name of the carrier and to have been signed or otherwise authenticated by: the carrier or a named agent for or on behalf of the carrier; or the master or a named agent for or on behalf of the master.

Any signature or authentication of the carrier or master must be identified as carrier or master, as the case may be. An agent signing or authenticating for the carrier or master must also indicate the name and the capacity of the party, ie carrier or master, on whose behalf that agent is acting; and

(ii) indicates that the goods have been loaded on board, or shipped on a named vessel.

Loading on board or shipment on a named vessel may be indicated by pre-printed wording on the bill of lading that the goods have been loaded on board a named vessel or shipped on a named vessel, in which case the date of issuance on, the bill of lading will be deemed to be the date of loading on board and the date of shipment.

In all other cases loading on board a named vessel must be evidenced by a notation on the bill of lading which gives the date on which the goods have been loaded on board, in which case the date of the on board notation will be deemed to be the date of shipment.

If the bill of lading contains the indication 'intended vessel', or similar qualification in relation to the vessel, loading on board a named vessel must be evidenced by an on board notation on the bill of lading which, in addition to the date on which the goods have been loaded on board, also includes the name of the vessel on which the goods have been loaded, even if they have been loaded on the vessel named as the 'intended vessel'.

If the bill of lading indicates a place of receipt or taking in charge different from the port of loading, the on board notation must also include the port of loading stipulated in the credit and the name of the vessel on which the goods have been loaded, even if they have been loaded on the vessel named in the bill of lading. This provision also applies whenever loading on board the vessel is indicated by pre-printed wording on the bill of lading; and

(iii) indicates the port of loading and the port of discharge stipulated in the credit, notwithstanding that it:

- indicates a place of taking in charge different from the port of loading, and/or a place of final destination different from the port of discharge; and/or
- contains the indication 'intended' or similar qualification in relation to the port of loading and/or port of discharge, as long as the document also states the ports of loading and/or discharge stipulated in the credit; and

(iv) consists of a sole original bill of lading or, if issued in more than one original, the full set as so issued; and

(v) appears to contain all of the terms and conditions of carriage, or some of such terms and conditions by reference to a source or document other than the bill of lading (short form/blank back bill of lading); banks will not examine the contents of such terms and conditions; and

(vi) contains no indication that it is subject to a charterparty and/or no indication that the carrying vessel is propelled by sail only; and

(vii) in all other respects meets the stipulations of the credit.

(b) For the purpose of this article, trans-shipment means unloading and reloading from one vessel to another vessel during the course of ocean carriage from the port of loading to the port of discharge stipulated in the credit.

(c) Unless trans-shipment is prohibited by the terms of the credit, banks will accept a bill of lading which indicates that the goods will be trans-shipped, provided that the entire ocean carriage is covered by one and the same bill of lading.

(d) Even if the credit prohibits trans-shipment, banks will accept a bill of lading which:

- indicates that trans-shipment will take place as long as the relevant cargo is shipped in container(s), trailer(s) and/or 'Lash' barge(s) as evidenced by the bill of lading, provided that the entire ocean carriage is covered by one and the same bill of lading; and/or
- incorporates clauses stating that the carrier reserves the right to trans-ship.

Article 24 – Non-negotiable sea waybill

(a) If a credit calls for a non-negotiable sea waybill covering a port to port shipment, banks will, unless otherwise stipulated in the credit, accept a document, however named, which:

(i) appears on its face to indicate the name of the carrier and to have been signed or otherwise authenticated by:

- the carrier or a named agent for or on behalf of the carrier; or
- the master or a named agent for or on behalf of the master;

Any signature or authentication of the carrier or master must be identified as carrier or master, as the case may be. An agent signing or authenticating for the carrier or master must also indicate the name and the capacity of the party, ie carrier or master, on whose behalf that agent is acting, and

(ii) indicates that the goods have been loaded on board, or shipped on a named vessel.

Loading on board or shipment on a named vessel may be indicated by pre-printed wording on the non-negotiable sea waybill that the goods have been loaded on board a named vessel or shipped on a named vessel, in which case the date of issuance of the non-negotiable sea waybill will be deemed to be the date of loading on board and the date of shipment.

In all other cases loading on board a named vessel must be evidenced by a notation on the non-negotiable sea waybill which gives the date on which the goods have been loaded on board, in which case the date of the on board notation will be deemed to be the date of shipment.

If the non-negotiable sea waybill contains the indication 'intended vessel', or similar qualification in relation to the vessel, loading on board a named vessel must be evidenced by an on board notation on the non-negotiable sea waybill which, in addition to the date on which the goods have been loaded on board, includes the name of the vessel on which the goods have been loaded, even if they have been loaded on the vessel named as the 'intended vessel'.

If the non-negotiable sea waybill indicates a place of receipt or taking in charge different from the port of loading, the on board notation must also include the port of loading stipulated in the credit and the name of the vessel on which the goods have been loaded, even if they have been loaded on a vessel named in the non-negotiable sea waybill. This provision also applies whenever loading on board the vessel is indicated by pre-printed wording on the non-negotiable sea waybill; and

(iii) indicates the port of loading and the port of discharge stipulated in the credit, notwithstanding that it:

- indicates a place of taking charge different from the port of loading, and/or a place of final destination different from the port of discharge; and/or

- contains the indication 'intended' or similar qualification in relation to the port of loading and/or port of discharge, as long as the document also states the ports of loading and/or discharge stipulated in the credit; and

(iv) consists of a sole original non-negotiable sea waybill, or if issued in more than one original, the full set as so issued; and

(v) appears to contain all of the terms and conditions of carriage, or some of such terms and conditions by reference to a source or document other than the non-negotiable sea waybill (short form/blank back non-negotiable sea waybill); banks will not examine the contents of such terms and conditions; and

(vi) contains no indication that it is subject to a charter party and/or no indication that the carrying vessel is propelled by sail only; and

(vii) in all other respects meets the stipulations of the credit.

(b) For the purpose of this article, trans-shipment means unloading and reloading from one vessel to another vessel during the course of ocean carriage from the port of loading to the port of discharge stipulated in the credit.

(c) Unless trans-shipment is prohibited by the terms of the credit, banks will accept a non-negotiable sea waybill which indicates that the goods will be trans-shipped, provided that the entire ocean carriage is covered by one and the same non-negotiable sea waybill.

(d) Even if the credit prohibits trans-shipment, banks will accept a non-negotiable sea waybill which:

(i) indicates that trans-shipment will take place as long as the relevant cargo is shipped in container(s), trailer(s) and/or 'Lash' barge(s) as evidenced by the non-negotiable sea waybill, provided that the entire ocean carriage is covered by one and the same non-negotiable sea waybill; and/or

(ii) incorporates clauses stating that the carrier reserves the right to trans-ship.

Article 25 – Charterparty bill of lading

(a) If a credit calls for or permits a charterparty bill of lading, banks will, unless otherwise stipulated in the credit, accept a document, however named, which:

(i) contains any indication that it is subject to a charterparty; and

(ii) appears on its face to have been signed or otherwise authenticated by:

- the master or a named agent for or on behalf of the master; or

- the owner or a named agent for or on behalf of the owner.

Any signature or authentication of the master or owner must be identified as master or owner as the case may be. An agent signing or authenticating for the master or owner must also indicate the name and the capacity of the party, ie master or owner, on whose behalf that agent is acting; and

(iii) does or does not indicate the name of the carrier; and

(iv) indicates that the goods have been loaded on board or shipped on a named vessel.

Loading on board or shipment on a named vessel may be indicated by pre-printed wording on the bill of lading that the goods have been loaded on board a named vessel or shipped on a named vessel, in which case the date of issuance of the bill of lading will be deemed to be the date of loading on board and the date of shipment.

In all other cases loading on board a named vessel must be evidenced by a notation on the bill of lading which gives the date on which the goods have been loaded on board, in which case the date of the on board notation will be deemed to be the date of shipment; and

(v) indicates the port of loading and the port of discharge stipulated in the credit; and

(vi) consists of a sole original bill of lading or, if issued in more than one original, the full set as so issued; and

(vii) contains no indication that the carrying vessel is propelled by sail only; and

(viii) in all other respects meets the stipulations of the credit.

(b) Even if the credit requires the presentation of a charterparty contract in connection with a charterparty bill of lading, banks will not examine such charterparty contract, but will pass it on without responsibility on their part.

Article 26 – Multi-modal transport document

(a) If a credit calls for a transport document covering at least two different modes of transport (multi-modal transport), banks will, unless otherwise stipulated in the credit, accept a document, however named, which:

(i) appears on its face to indicate the name of the carrier or multi-modal transport operator and to have been signed or otherwise authenticated by:

• the carrier or multi-modal transport operator or a named agent for or on behalf of the carrier or multi-modal transport operator; or

• the master or a named agent for or on behalf of the master.

Any signature or authentication of the carrier, multi-modal transport operator or master must be identified as carrier, multi-modal transport operator or master, as the case may be. An agent signing or authenticating for the carrier, multi-modal transport operator or master must also indicate the name and the capacity of the party, ie carrier, multi-modal transport operator or master, on whose behalf that agent is acting; and

(ii) indicates that the goods have been dispatched, taken in charge or loaded on board.

Dispatch, taking in charge or loading on board may be indicated by wording to that effect on the multi-modal transport document and the date of issuance will be deemed to be the date of dispatch, taking in charge or loading on board and the date of shipment. However, if the document indicates, by stamp or otherwise, a date of dispatch, taking in charge or loading on board, such date will be deemed to be the date of shipment; and

(iii) indicates the place of taking in charge stipulated in the credit which may be different from the port, airport or place of loading, and the place of final destination stipulated in the credit which may be different from the port, airport or place of discharge; and/or contains the indication 'intended' or similar qualification in relation to the vessel and/or port of loading and/or port of discharge; and

(iv) consists of a sole original multi-modal transport document or, if issued in more than one original, the full set as so issued; and

(v) appears to contain all of the terms and conditions of carriage, or some of such terms and conditions by reference to a source or document other than the multi-modal transport document (short form/blank back multi-modal transport document); banks will not examine the contents of such terms and conditions; and

(vi) contains no indication that it is subject to a charterparty and/or no indication that the carrying vessel is propelled by sail only; and

(vii) in all other respects meets the stipulations of the credit.

(b) Even if the credit prohibits trans-shipment, banks will accept a multi-modal transport document which indicates that trans-shipment will or may take place, provided that the entire carriage is covered by one and the same multi-modal transport document.

Article 27 – Air transport document

(a) If a credit calls for an air transport document, banks will, unless otherwise stipulated in the credit, accept a document, however named, which:

  (i) appears on its face to indicate the name of the carrier and to have been signed or otherwise authenticated by:

   • the carrier; or

   • a named agent for or on behalf of the carrier.

   Any signature or authentication of the carrier must be identified as carrier. An agent signing or authenticating for the carrier must also indicate the name and the capacity of the party, ie carrier, on whose behalf that agent is acting; and

  (ii) indicates that the goods have been accepted for carriage; and

  (iii) where the credit calls for an actual date of dispatch, indicates a specific notation of such date, the date of dispatch so indicated on the air transport document will be deemed to be the date of shipment.

   For the purpose of this article, the information appearing in the box on the air transport document (marked 'For Carrier Use Only' or similar expression) relative to the flight number and date will not be considered as a specific notation of such date of dispatch.

   In all other cases, the date of issuance of the air transport document will be deemed to be the date of shipment; and

  (iv) indicates the airport of departure and the airport of destination stipulated in the credit; and

  (v) appears to be the original for consignor/shipper even if the credit stipulates a full set of originals, or similar expressions; and

  (vi) appears to contain all of the terms and conditions of carriage, or some of such terms and conditions, by reference to a source or document other than the air transport document; banks will not examine the contents of such terms and conditions; and

  (vii) in all other respects meets the stipulations of the credit.

(b) For the purpose of this article, trans-shipment means unloading and reloading from one aircraft to another aircraft during the course of carriage from the airport of departure to the airport of destination stipulated in the credit.

(c) Even if the credit prohibits trans-shipment, banks will accept an air transport document which indicates that trans-shipment will or may take place, provided that the entire carriage is covered by one and the same air transport document.

Article 28 – Road, rail or inland waterway transport documents

(a) If a credit calls for a road, rail, or inland waterway transport document, banks will, unless otherwise stipulated in the credit, accept a document of the type called for, however named, which:

  (i) appears on its face to indicate the name of the carrier and to have been signed or otherwise authenticated by the carrier or a named agent for or on behalf of the carrier and/or to bear a reception stamp or other indication of receipt by the carrier or a named agent for or on behalf of the carrier.

   Any signature, authentication, reception stamp or other indication of receipt of the carrier, must be identified on its face as that of the carrier. An agent signing or authenticating for the carrier, must also indicate the name and the capacity of the party, ie carrier, on whose behalf that agent is acting; and

  (ii) indicates that the goods have been received for shipment, dispatch or carriage or wording to this effect. The date of issuance will be deemed to be the date of shipment unless the transport document contains a reception stamp, in which case the date of the reception stamp will be deemed to be the date of shipment; and

  (iii) indicates the place of shipment and the place of destination stipulated in the credit; and

  (iv) in all other respects meets the stipulations of the credit.

(b) In the absence of any indication on the transport document as to the numbers issued, banks will accept the transport document(s) presented as constituting a full set. banks will accept as original(s) the transport document(s) whether marked as original(s) or not.

(c) For the purpose of this article, trans-shipment means unloading and reloading from one means of conveyance to another means of conveyance, in different modes of transport, during the course of carriage from the place of shipment to the place of destination stipulated in the credit.

(d) Even if the credit prohibits trans-shipment, banks will accept a road, rail, or inland waterway transport document which indicates that trans-shipment will or may take place, provided that the entire carriage is covered by one and the same transport document and within the same mode of transport.

Article 29 – Courier and post receipts

(a) If a credit calls for a post receipt or certificate of posting, banks will, unless otherwise stipulated in the credit, accept a post receipt or certificate of posting which:

   (i) appears on its face to have been stamped or otherwise authenticated and dated in the place from which the credit stipulates the goods are to be shipped or dispatched and such date will be deemed to be the date of shipment or dispatch; and

   (ii) in all other respects meets the stipulations of the credit.

(b) If a credit calls for a document issued by a courier or expedited delivery service evidencing receipt of the goods for delivery, banks will, unless otherwise stipulated in the credit, accept a document, however named, which:

   (i) appears on its face to indicate the name of the courier/service, and to have been stamped, signed or otherwise authenticated by such named courier/service (unless the credit specifically calls for a document issued by a named courier/service, banks will accept a document issued by any courier/service); and

   (ii) indicates a date of pick-up or of receipt or wording to this effect, such date being deemed to be the date of shipment or dispatch; and

   (iii) in all other respects meets the stipulations of the credit.

Article 30 – Transport documents issued by freight forwarders

Unless otherwise authorised in the credit, banks will only accept a transport document issued by a freight forwarder if it appears on its face to indicate:

(i) the name of the freight forwarder as a carrier or multi-modal transport operator and to have been signed or otherwise authenticated by the freight forwarder as carrier or multi-modal transport operator; or

(ii) the name of the carrier or multi-modal transport operator and to have been signed or otherwise authenticated by the freight forwarder as a named agent for or on behalf of the carrier or multi-modal transport operator.

Article 31 – 'On deck', 'shipper's load and count', name of consignor

Unless otherwise stipulated in the credit, banks will accept a transport document which:

(i) does not indicate, in the case of carriage by sea or by more than one means of conveyance including carriage by sea, that the goods are or will be loaded on deck. Nevertheless, banks will accept a transport document which contains a provision that the goods may be carried on deck, provided that it does not specifically state that they are or will be loaded on deck; and/or

(ii) bears a clause on the face thereof such as 'shipper's load and count' or 'said by shipper to contain' or words of similar effect; and/or

(iii) indicates as the consignor of the goods a party other than the beneficiary of the credit.

Article 32 – Clean transport documents

(a) A clean transport document is one which bears no clause or notation which expressly declares a defective condition of the goods and/or the packaging.

(b) Banks will not accept transport documents bearing such clauses or notations unless the credit expressly stipulates the clauses or notations which may be accepted.

(c) Banks will regard a requirement in a credit for a transport document to bear the clause 'clean on board' as complied with if such transport document meets the requirements of this article and of Articles 23, 24, 25, 26, 27, 28 or 30.

Article 33 – Freight payable/prepaid transport documents

(a) Unless otherwise stipulated in the credit, or inconsistent with any of the documents presented under the credit, banks will accept transport documents stating that freight or transportation charges (hereafter referred to as 'freight') have still to be paid.

(b) If a credit stipulates that the transport document has to indicate that freight has been paid or prepaid, banks will accept a transport document on which words clearly indicating payment or prepayment of freight appear by stamp or otherwise, or on which payment or prepayment of freight is indicated by other means. If the credit requires courier charges to be paid or prepaid banks will also accept a transport document issued by a courier or expedited delivery service evidencing that courier charges are for the account of a party other than the consignee.

(c) The words 'freight prepayable' or 'freight to be prepaid' or words of similar effect, if appearing on transport documents, will not be accepted as constituting evidence of the payment of freight.

(d) Banks will accept transport documents bearing reference by stamp or otherwise to costs additional to the freight, such as costs of, or disbursements incurred in connection with, loading, unloading or similar operations, unless the conditions of the credit specifically prohibit such reference.

Article 34 – Insurance documents

(a) Insurance documents must appear on their face to be issued and signed by insurance companies or underwriters or their agents.

(b) If the insurance document indicates that it has been issued in more than one original, all the originals must be presented unless otherwise authorised in the credit.

(c) Cover notes issued by brokers will not be accepted, unless specifically authorised in the credit.

(d) Unless otherwise stipulated in the credit, banks will accept an insurance certificate or a declaration under an open cover pre-signed by insurance companies or underwriters or their agents. If a credit specifically calls for an insurance certificate or a declaration under an open cover, banks will accept, in lieu thereof, an insurance policy.

(e) Unless otherwise stipulated in the credit, or unless it appears from the insurance document that the cover is effective at the latest from the date of loading on board or dispatch or taking in charge of the goods, banks will not accept an insurance document which bears a date of issuance later than the date of loading on board or dispatch or taking in charge as indicated in such transport document.

(f) (i) Unless otherwise stipulated in the credit, the insurance document must be expressed in the same currency as the credit.

    (ii) Unless otherwise stipulated in the credit, the minimum amount for which the insurance document must indicate the insurance cover to have been effected is the CIF (cost, insurance and freight (... 'named port of destination')) or CIP (carriage and insurance paid to (... 'named place of destination')) value of the goods, as the case may be, plus 10%, but only when the CIF or CIP value can be determined from the documents on their face. Otherwise, banks will accept as such minimum amount 110% of the amount for which payment, acceptance or negotiation is requested under the credit, or 110% of the gross amount of the invoice, whichever is the greater.

Article 35 – Type of insurance cover

(a) Credits should stipulate the type of insurance required and, if any, the additional risks which are to be covered. Imprecise terms such as 'usual risks' or 'customary risks' shall not be used; if they are used, banks will accept insurance documents as presented, without responsibility for any risks not being covered.

(b) Failing specific stipulations in the credit, banks will accept insurance documents as presented, without responsibility for any risks not being covered.

(c) Unless otherwise stipulated in the credit, banks will accept an insurance document which indicates that the cover is subject to a franchise or an excess (deductible).

Article 36 – All risks insurance cover

Where a credit stipulates 'insurance against all risks', banks will accept an insurance document which contains any 'all risks' notation or clause, whether or not bearing the heading 'all risks', even if the insurance document indicates that certain risks are excluded, without responsibility for any risk(s) not being covered.

Article 37 – Commercial invoices

(a) Unless otherwise stipulated in the credit, commercial invoices;
 (i) must appear on their face to be issued by the beneficiary named in the credit (except as provided in Article 48); and
 (ii) must be made out in the name of the applicant (except as provided in sub-Article 48(h)); and
 (iii) need not be signed.
(b) Unless otherwise stipulated in the credit, banks may refuse commercial invoices issued for amounts in excess of the amount permitted by the credit. Nevertheless, if a bank authorised to pay, incur a deferred payment undertaking, accept draft(s), or negotiate under a credit accepts such invoices, its decision will be binding upon all parties, provided that such bank has not paid, incurred a deferred payment undertaking, accepted draft(s) or negotiated for an amount in excess of that permitted by the credit.
(c) The description of the goods in the commercial invoice must correspond with the description in the credit. In all other documents, the goods may be described in general terms not inconsistent with the description of the goods in the credit.

Article 38 – Other documents

If a credit calls for an attestation or certification of weight in the case of transport other than by sea, banks will accept a weight stamp or declaration of weight which appears to have been superimposed on the transport document by the carrier or his agent unless the credit specifically stipulates that the attestation or certification of weight must be by means of a separate document.

E Miscellaneous provisions

Article 39 – Allowances in credit amount, quantity and unit price

(a) The words 'about', 'approximately', 'circa' or similar expressions used in connection with the amount of the credit or the quantity or the unit price stated in the credit are to be construed as allowing a difference not to exceed 10% more or 10% less than the amount or the quantity or the unit price to which they refer.
(b) Unless a credit stipulates that the quantity of the goods specified must not be exceeded or reduced, a tolerance of 5% more or 5% less will be permissible, always provided that the amount of the drawings does not exceed the amount of the credit. This tolerance does not apply when the credit stipulates the quantity in terms of a stated number of packing units or individual items.
(c) Unless a credit which prohibits partial shipments stipulates otherwise, or unless sub-Article (b) above is applicable, a tolerance of 5% less in the amount of the drawing will be permissible, provided that if the credit stipulates the quantity of the goods, such quantity of goods is shipped in full, and if the credit stipulates a unit price, such price is not reduced. This provision does not apply when expressions referred to in sub-Article (a) above are used in the credit.

Article 40 – Partial shipments/drawings

(a) Partial drawings and/or shipments are allowed, unless the credit stipulates otherwise.
(b) Transport documents which appear on their face to indicate that shipment has been made on the same means of conveyance and for the same journey, provided they indicate the same destination, will not be regarded as covering partial shipments, even if the transport documents indicate different dates of shipment and/or different ports of loading, places of taking in charge, or dispatch.

(c) Shipments made by post or by courier will not be regarded as partial shipments if the post receipts or certificates of posting or courier's receipts or dispatch notes appear to have been stamped, signed or otherwise authenticated in the place from which the credit stipulates the goods are to be dispatched, and on the same date.

Article 41 – Instalment shipments/drawings

If drawings and/or shipments by instalments within given periods are stipulated in the credit and any instalment is not drawn and/or shipped within the period allowed for that instalment, the credit ceases to be available for that and any subsequent instalments, unless otherwise stipulated in the credit.

Article 42 – Expiry date and place for presentation of documents

(a) All credits must stipulate an expiry date and a place for presentation of documents for payment, acceptance, or with the exception of freely negotiable credits, a place for presentation of documents for negotiation. An expiry date stipulated for payment, acceptance or negotiation will be construed to express an expiry date for presentation of documents.

(b) Except as provided in sub-Article 44(a), documents must be presented on or before such expiry date.

(c) If an issuing bank states that the credit is to be available 'for one month', 'for six months', or the like, but does not specify the date from which the time is to run, the date of issuance of the credit by the issuing bank will be deemed to be the first day from which such time is to run. Banks should discourage indication of the expiry date of the credit in this manner.

Article 43 – Limitation on the expiry date

(a) In addition to stipulating an expiry date for presentation of documents, every credit which calls for a transport document(s) should also stipulate a specified period of time after the date of shipment during which presentation must be made in compliance with the terms and conditions of the credit. If no such period of time is stipulated, banks will not accept documents presented to them later than 21 days after the date of shipment. In any event, documents must be presented not later than the expiry date of the credit.

(b) In cases in which sub-Article 40(b) applies, the date of shipment will be considered to be the latest shipment date on any of the transport documents presented.

Article 44 – Extension of expiry date

(a) If the expiry date of the credit and/or the last day of the period of time for presentation of documents stipulated by the credit or applicable by virtue of Article 43 falls on a day on which the bank to which presentation has to be made is closed for reasons other than those referred to in Article 17, the stipulated expiry date and/or the last day of the period of time after the date of shipment for presentation of documents, as the case may be, shall be extended to the first following day on which such bank is open.

(b) The latest date for shipment shall not be extended by reason of the extension of the expiry date and/or the period of time after the date of shipment for presentation of documents in accordance with sub-Article (a) above. If no such latest date for shipment is stipulated in the credit or amendments thereto, banks will not accept transport documents indicating a date of shipment later than the expiry date stipulated in the credit or amendments thereto.

(c) The bank to which presentation is made on such first following business day must provide a statement that the documents were presented within the time limits extended in accordance with sub-Article 44(a) of the Uniform Customs and Practice for Documentary Credits, 1993 Revision, ICC publication no 500.

Article 45 – Hours of presentation

Banks are under no obligation to accept presentation of documents outside their banking hours.

Article 46 – General expressions as to dates for shipment

(a) Unless otherwise stipulated in the credit, the expression 'shipment' used in stipulating an earliest and/or a latest date for shipment will be understood to include expressions such as, 'loading on board', 'dispatch', 'accepted for carriage', 'date of post receipt', 'date of pick-up', and the like, and in the case of a credit calling for a multi-modal transport document the expression 'taking in charge'.

(b) Expressions such as 'prompt', 'immediately', 'as soon as possible', and the like should not be used. If they are used, banks will disregard them.

(c) If the expression 'on or about' or similar expressions are used, banks will interpret them as a stipulation that shipment is to be made during the period from five days before to five days after the specified date, both end days included.

Article 47 – Date terminology for periods of shipment

(a) The words 'to', 'until', 'till', 'from' and words of similar import applying to any date or period in the credit referring to shipment will be understood to include the date mentioned.

(b) The word 'after' will be understood to exclude the date mentioned.

(c) The terms 'first half', 'second half' of a month shall be construed respectively as the 1st to the 15th, and the 16th to the last day of such month, all dates inclusive.

(d) The terms 'beginning', 'middle', or 'end' of a month shall be construed respectively as the 1st to the 10th, the 11th to the 20th, and the 21st to the last day of such month, all dates inclusive.

F Transferable credit

Article 48 – Transferable credit

(a) A transferable credit is a credit under which the beneficiary (first beneficiary) may request the bank authorised to pay, incur a deferred payment undertaking, accept or negotiate (the 'transferring bank'), or in the case of a freely negotiable credit, the bank specifically authorised in the credit as a transferring bank, to make the credit available in whole or in part to one or more other beneficiary(ies) ('second beneficiary(ies)).

(b) A credit can be transferred only if it is expressly designated as 'transferable' by the issuing bank. Terms such as 'divisible', 'fractionable', 'assignable', and 'transmissible' do not render the credit transferable. If such terms are used they shall be disregarded.

(c) The transferring bank shall be under no obligation to effect such transfer except to the extent and in the manner expressly consented to by such bank.

(d) At the time of making a request for transfer and prior to transfer of the credit, the first beneficiary must irrevocably instruct the transferring bank whether or not he retains the right to refuse to allow the transferring bank to advise amendments to the second beneficiary(ies). If the transferring bank consents to the transfer under these conditions, it must, at the time of transfer, advise the second beneficiary(ies) of the first beneficiary's instructions regarding amendments.

(e) If a credit is transferred to more than one second beneficiary(ies), refusal of an amendment by one or more second beneficiary(ies) does not invalidate the acceptance(s) by the other second beneficiary(ies) with respect to whom the credit will be amended accordingly. With respect to the second beneficiary(ies) who rejected the amendment, the credit will remain unamended.

(f) Transferring bank charges in respect of transfers including commissions, fees, costs or expenses are payable by the first beneficiary, unless otherwise agreed. If the transferring bank agrees to transfer the credit it shall be under no obligation to effect the transfer until such charges are paid.

(g) Unless otherwise stated in the credit, a transferable credit can be transferred once only. Consequently, the credit cannot be transferred at the request of the second beneficiary to any subsequent third beneficiary. For the purpose of this article, a re-transfer to the first beneficiary does not constitute a prohibited transfer.

Fractions of a transferable credit (not exceeding in the aggregate the amount of the credit) can be transferred separately, provided partial shipments/drawings are not prohibited, and the aggregate of such transfers will be considered as constituting only one transfer of the credit.

(h) The credit can be transferred only on the terms and conditions specified in the original credit, with the exception of:

- the amount of the credit;
- any unit price stated therein;
- the expiry date;
- the last date for presentation of documents in accordance with Article 43;
- the period for shipment.

any or all of which may be reduced or curtailed.

The percentage for which insurance cover must be effected may be increased in such a way as to provide the amount of cover stipulated in the original credit, or these articles.

In addition, the name of the first beneficiary can be substituted for that of the applicant, but if the name of the applicant is specifically required by the original credit to appear in any document(s) other than the invoice, such requirement must be fulfilled.

(i) The first beneficiary has the right to substitute his own invoice(s) (and draft(s)) for those of the second beneficiary(ies), for amounts not in excess of the original amount stipulated in the credit and for the original unit prices if stipulated in the credit, and upon such substitution of invoice(s) (and draft(s)) the first beneficiary can draw under the credit for the difference, if any, between his invoice(s) and the second beneficiary's(ies') invoice(s).

When a credit has been transferred and the first beneficiary is to supply his own invoice(s) (and draft(s)) in exchange for the second beneficiary's(ies') invoice(s) (and draft(s)) but fails to do so on first demand, the transferring bank has the right to deliver to the issuing bank the documents received under the transferred credit, including the second beneficiary's(ies') invoice(s) (and draft(s)) without further responsibility to the first beneficiary.

(j) The first beneficiary may request that payment or negotiation be effected to the second beneficiary(ies) at the place to which the credit has been transferred up to and including the expiry date of the credit, unless the original credit expressly states that it may not be made available for payment or negotiation at a place other than that stipulated in the credit. This is without prejudice to the first beneficiary's right to substitute subsequently his own invoice(s) (and draft(s)) for those of the second beneficiary(ies) and to claim any difference due to him.

G Assignment of proceeds

Article 49 – Assignment of proceeds

The fact that a credit is not stated to be transferable shall not affect the beneficiary's right to assign any proceeds to which he may be, or may become, entitled under such credit, in accordance with the provisions of the applicable law. This article relates only to the assignment of proceeds and not to the assignment of the right to perform under the credit itself.

ICC arbitration

Contracting parties that wish to have the possibility of resorting to ICC arbitration in the event of a dispute with their contracting partner should specifically and clearly agree upon ICC arbitration in their contract or, in the event no single contractual document exists, in the exchange of correspondence which constitutes the agreement between them. The fact of issuing a letter of credit subject to the UCP 500 does *not* by itself constitute an agreement to have resort to ICC arbitration. The following standard arbitration clause is recommended by the ICC:

All disputes arising in connection with the present contract shall be finally settled under the Rules of Conciliation and Arbitration of the International Chamber of Commerce by one or more arbitrators appointed in accordance with the said rules.

CHAPTER 7

THE WORLD TRADE ORGANISATION (WTO)

A HISTORICAL PERSPECTIVE

Even before the end of the Second World War, trade leaders in the Allied countries realised that trade tensions had contributed to the outbreak of the War. There was a critical need for international co-operation to establish a framework that would prevent the recurrence of a World War.[1] In February 1946 at the meeting of the United Nations Economic and Social Council (ECOSOC) a resolution was passed to draft a convention to establish a world organisation dealing with the rules of trade between nations. This effort was to be embodied in the International Trade Organisation (ITO). This resolution led to the Havana Conference which was held between November 1947 and March 1948. The Conference prepared the ITO Charter, also known as The Havana Charter. The Charter establishing the ITO provided for a governing body consisting of representation from all member countries. This was the first attempt by an international body to set out fair and uniform guidelines for international trade. However, the ITO did not become a reality because many countries disagreed with the terms of the Charter. In the USA, the ITO was submitted to Congress, but in December 1950 the President withdrew the Charter from further consideration.

At earlier meetings of the Havana Conference held in Geneva from April to October 1947, multilateral tariff negotiations had been conducted to draft the General Agreement on Tariffs and Trade (GATT). The GATT incorporated the agreed tariff reductions along with a code of conduct aimed at preserving the trade benefits flowing from tariff reductions. This code aimed to restrict certain government practices that operated to circumvent the tariff commitments. As the code of conduct was itself a part of the anticipated ITO Charter, it was never formally implemented. It was, however, brought into force by means of a Provisional Protocol, signed on 30 October 1947 and effective from 1 January 1948, under which the signatory countries[2] agreed to apply the provisions of the GATT until the ITO could take over supervision of its operation following ratification by each of the signatory countries. With the collapse of the ITO,

---

1   The editors thank Dr Alex Low for his contribution entitled 'The General Agreement on Tariffs and Trade (GATT) and the World Trade Organisation (WTO)' which appeared as Chapter 7 in the first edition of this book. Some parts of the first edition have been relied upon in the preparation of this chapter on the World Trade Organisation.
    For detailed discussions of the history of GATT, see Jackson, JH, *World Trade and the Law of GATT*, 1969, Virginia, USA: The Bobbs-Merrill Co Inc, Chapters 3 and 4. For a discussion of the various issues, see Wang, G, *International Trade Order*, 1988, Beijing: Publishing House of Law, Chapters 1 and 3; Wang, G, *International Monetary and Financial Law*, 1993, Hong Kong: Wide Angle Press, Chapter 1.

2   In 1934, Congress empowered the US President to negotiate and implement reciprocal tariff reduction agreements. It was under this power that the USA participated in the negotiations resulting in the GATT. This authority has been renewed periodically, usually for three-year periods, and during the Tokyo and Uruguay Rounds became associated with 'fast track' authority. The fact that this authority was scheduled to expire in mid-1948, prior to the expected ratification of the ITO Charter, gave extra incentive for a timely signing of the protocol. The eight original signatories were Australia, Belgium, Canada, France, Luxemburg, The Netherlands, the UK and the USA. Twenty three countries signed what was called a Final Act authenticating the text of the GATT (55 UNTS 194; TIAS 1700. See Jackson, *op cit*, Chapter 2).

the GATT became the centrepiece for the ordering of the international trade relationships of its signatories.

There has been a series of eight periods of negotiations, called multilateral trade negotiations or rounds since the GATT was established, the most recent being the Uruguay Round, ending in 1994. The first five of these rounds focused on the reduction of tariffs. The sixth, the Kennedy Round, saw the inclusion of some negotiation on non-tariff barriers and anti-dumping. The elimination of non-tariff barriers to trrade became the primary focus of the Tokyo and Uruguay Rounds. The last round, the 1986–94 Uruguay Round, led to the establishment of the new World Trade Organisation (WTO), similar to the original ITO, which has become an umbrella organisation with responsibility for the GATT and its associated agreements. The WTO has a greatly expanded scope of coverage, including services, under the General Agreement on Trade in Services (GATS), and intellectual property, under the Agreement on Trade-Related Aspects of Intellectual Property Rights (TRIPS). The GATT 1947 was revised in 1994 during the Urugay Round. The GATT 1994 now consists of GATT 1947 as rectified, amended or modified by the terms of legal instruments which have entered into force before the date of entry into force of the WTO Agreement. In 2000 talks were commenced on services and agriculture; these were incorporated into the agenda discussed by the international community in Doha, Qatar in November 2001.

THE WTO AGREEMENT

Introduction

In 1991, the then Director General of GATT, Arthur Dunkle, assumed responsibility for the preparation of what became known as the 'Dunkle Text' dealing with the anticipated achievements of the Uruguay Round. The Text contained a charter for a Multilateral Trade Organisation (MTO) with the aim of providing an institutional framework within which the results of the Uruguay Round could operate. Within the MTO was set up a new dispute settlement mechanism and a Trade Policy Review Mechanism (TPRM). In addition, the framework provided annexes of the more important areas such as the General Agreement on Trade in Services (GATS) and the Agreement on Trade-Related Aspects of Intellectual Property Rights (TRIPS). Virtually all contracting parties to GATT favoured the new MTO, although at the insistence of the USA it was renamed the World Trade Organisation (WTO). The contracting parties to GATT 1947 were invited by virtue of Article XI of the Agreement Establishing the World Trade Organisation to become original members of the WTO. There are about 60 agreements and decisions totalling 550 pages. These agreements have resulted from the 1986–94 Uruguay Round negotiations, and were signed at the Marrakesh Ministerial Meeting on 15 April 1994. At present, the WTO has 148 member states. In addition, some 30 countries are negotiating membership of the WTO.

The WTO's framework

1   There is a Ministerial Conference composed of representatives of all the members, which meets at least once every two years (Art IV(1)). This Conference has the authority to take decisions on all matters under any of the Multilateral

Trade Agreements. Ministerial Conferences have been held in Singapore (1996), Geneva (1998), Seattle (1999), Doha (2001) and Cancun (2003). The sixth WTO Ministerial Conference will be held in Hong Kong in December 2005.

2   Below the Ministerial Conference is the General Council which consists of officials from member states. This Council meets several times a year in the headquarters of the WTO in Geneva.

3   Councils are established to supervise the implementation of WTO's obligations with regard to trade in goods, services and intellectual property. There are also numerous specialised committees, working groups and working parties.

4   A series of annexes set out treaty rights and obligations of members. For example, Annex 2 to the WTO Agreement is the Understanding on Rules and Procedures Governing the Settlement of Disputes and Annex 3 deals with the Trade Policy Review Mechanism.

5   Unlike GATT 1947, the WTO agreements do not contain provisional applications.

6   The WTO recognises that depending on a country's level of development, its reaction to environment matters may differ. Hence, the WTO recognises the special position of less-developed countries.

7   The dispute resolution procedures available to contracting parties aim at ensuring that any decision is made by 'consensus'. Consensus is arrived at if no member present at the meeting when the decision is taken, formally objects to the proposed decision. In such a case, no voting is necessary. If a solution cannot be found in a mediation, consultation or conciliation, a complaints panel comprising trade experts, who report in accordance with a time line to a committee of the contracting parties, is formed. Appeals are allowed only on legal issues to a body of legal experts. If the defending party does not conform, then the Dispute Settlement Body (DSB) comprising WTO members, can sanction the complainant by withdrawing benefits.

Significance of the WTO

The WTO is a high-profile and prestigious organisation properly accredited by national governments. In its 2005 Annual Report, the present Director General Dr Supachai Panitchpakdi, reviewed the first 10 years of the WTO and identified some of the challenges looming ahead.

One of the key developments is the adoption of the WTO dispute settlement mechanism. The dispute mechanism provides for a regime that is capable of solving disputes, thereby producing a credible system that effectively implements a contracting party's treaty obligations. Another important feature of the institutional framework is the Trade Policy Review Mechanism (TPRM). The TPRM examines a contracting party's trading policies, whilst the dispute mechanism, as mentioned earlier, concentrates on specific obligations under the WTO Charter. The TPRM looks at general trade policies of contracting parties to ascertain whether they have or potentially will have any adverse effects on member countries. Over time the TPRM is expected to play a very important role in raising potential problems before they actually affect the trading order.

THE PRINCIPLES OF THE GENERAL AGREEMENT ON TARIFFS AND TRADE (GATT) 1994

The GATT 1994 consists principally of the provisions of GATT 1947, as 'rectified, amended or modified by the terms of legal instruments which have entered into force before the date of entry into force of the WTO Agreement'. The Preamble to GATT 1947 reveals that the main objective of GATT is the conduct of relations in the field of trade and economic endeavour 'with a view to raising standards of living, ensuring full employment and a large and steadily growing volume of real income and effective demand, developing the full use of the resources of the world and expanding the production and exchange of goods'. In attaining this objective, the contracting parties are described as:

> Being desirous of contributing to these objectives by entering into reciprocal and mutually advantageous arrangements directed to the substantial reduction of tariffs and other barriers to trade and to the elimination of discriminatory treatment in international commerce.

The basic principle of GATT 1947 is the principle of non-discrimination from which the following three other principles are derived:

1   The most-favoured-nation principle.
2   The national treatment principle.
3   The reciprocity principle.

The most-favoured-nation (MFN) principle

The most-favoured-nation (MFN) principle is found in Art I of the GATT. Article I(1) provides:

> With respect to customs duties and charges of any kind imposed on or in connection with importation or exportation or imposed on the international transfer of payments for imports or exports, and with respect to the method of levying such duties and charges, and with respect to all rules and formalities in connection with importation and exportation and with respect to all matters referred to in paras 2 and 4 of Article III, any advantage, favour, privilege or immunity granted by any contracting party to any product originating in or destined for any other country shall be accorded immediately and unconditionally to the like product originating in or destined for the territories of all other contracting parties.

This Article specifies four categories of exchange concession agreements:

1   Those relating to an obligation to pay customs duties and charges of any kind imposed on the export and import of goods or imposed on the international transfer of payments for import and export purposes.
2   Those relating to the methods of levying such duties and charges.
3   Those relating to the rules and formalities in connection with import and export.
4   Those relating to all matters referred to in paras 2 and 4 of Art III regarding internal taxation.

Trade negotiations involve the exchange of concessions among the principal supplying States and result in the grant of advantages, favours, privileges and immunities. These concessions may be given to a product originating in or destined for a particular country. According to the MFN principle all other contracting parties (which are known under the WTO Agreement as 'members' may automatically take advantage of any concession exchange. The MFN principle set out in the GATT is unconditional. It applies automatically and immediately to third States without any need for the grant of any compensation to the member states involved in the granting of these concessions. Tariffs which have been negotiated based on the MFN principle are included in the Tariffs Schedules of the GATT. As a result all contracting parties may benefit from any such negotiations. Even developing countries not involved in the tariff negotiations may benefit from these, although the GATT rounds seem to have been more beneficial to the developed countries than to developing countries.

The national treatment principle

The national treatment principle is contained in Art III of the GATT. Article III(2) reads as follows:

> The products of the territory of any conctracting party imported into the territory of any other contracting party shall not be subject, directly or indirectly, to internal taxes or other internal charges of any kind in excess of those applied, directly or indirectly, to like domestic products. Moreover, no contracting party shall otherwise apply internal taxes or other internal charges to imported or domestic products in a manner contrary to the principles set forth in para 1.

'National treatment' is a liberal economic concept, which is difficult to implement because it potentially impedes the fulfilment of national development policy. The national treatment principle prohibits discrimination between imported and like domestic products. GATT does not define 'like products' and it is left to the GATT panels to decide what constitutes a 'like' product. The overall purpose of Art III is to ensure that the determination of 'like' product is not made in such a way that it infringes the regulatory authority and domestic policy options of contracting parties. In so doing, the WTO panels usually consider tariff classifications, nature of the product, intended use, commercial value, and price and substitutability.

In the legal framework of the GATT, the national treatment principle supplements the MFN principle which gives third parties the opportunity to benefit from concessions already negotiated. But there are certain exceptions. Thus, Art XX(g) of the GATT, among others, exempts measures 'relating to the conservation of exhaustible natural resources if such measures are made effective in conjunction with restrictions on domestic production or consumption'. And Art XX(i) excludes measures:

> involving restrictions on exports of domestic materials necessary to ensure essential quantities of such materials to a domestic processing industry during periods when the domestic price of such materials is held below the world price as part of a governmental stabilisation plan; provided that such restrictions shall not operate to increase the exports of or the protection afforded to such domestic industry, and shall not depart from the provisions of this agreement relating to non-discrimination.

The reciprocity principle

One of the objectives of the GATT is to give a mutual advantage to all contracting parties. The preamble of the GATT describes the contracting parties as:

Being desirous of contributing to these objectives by entering into reciprocal and mutually advantageous arrangements directed to the substantial reduction of tariffs and other barriers to trade and to the elimination of discriminatory treatment in international commerce.

GATT encourages negotiations based on the reciprocity principle. Article XXVIII *bis*(1) provides:

The contracting parties recognise that customs duties often constitute serious obstacles to trade; thus negotiations on a reciprocal and mutually advantageous basis, directed to the substantial reduction of the general level of tariffs and other charges on imports and exports and in particular to the reduction of such high tariffs as discourage the importation even of minimum quantities, and conducted with due regard to the objectives of this agreement and the varying needs of individual contracting parties, are of great importance to the expansion of international trade. The contracting parties may therefore sponsor such negotiations from time to time.

The reciprocity principle and its implementation may be found in the following Articles:

1   Article III(1) which prohibits the use of internal tax for the purpose of affording protection to domestic production.

2   Article VI which condemns dumping if it causes or threatens material injury. This Article permits the levying of anti-dumping duties to offset dumping.

3   Article VII which establishes general principles of valuation and Art VIII which provides that fees and charges must not constitute an indirect protection.

The reciprocity principle has these consequences:

1   A concession which is given to another country must be carried out on an equitable basis.

2   All contracting parties will gain an advantage from every negotiated concession by the negotiator and that advantage would be given reciprocally through the application of the MFN principle.

3   All imported goods must be treated equally to, and as promptly and adequately as, domestic products.

The strict application of the reciprocity principle in relations between developed and developing countries could be to the latter's disadvantage because developing countries may want to develop 'infant industries'. Developing countries frequently promote their infant industries with the purpose of raising the general standard of living of their people. Hence, the protection of infant industries may make it difficult for some developing countries to implement direct reciprocity between developed countries and developing countries.

Breach of GATT obligations violates the legitimate expectations that a member country has in regard to the reciprocal performance of obligations by other member countries. If a member country acts in a manner inconsistent with its obligations, it will be potentially subject to retaliatory action by other member countries, provided the relevant dispute resolution procedures have been followed. The GATT imposes an obligation on member countries seeking to impose trade sanctions in response to an alleged breach of GATT obligations, to use the WTO dispute resolution process. There are, however, many exceptions within the GATT that may provide a defence to a claim of breach of a country's obligations.

The obligations of GATT members (which result in corresponding rights of other members) include MFN treatment, national treatment and the granting of tariff concessions. GATT members must also seek to eliminate or reduce non-tariff barriers such as subsidies, dumping and quantitative restrictions. In particular, GATT members must grant other contracting parties equal tariff treatment or MFN trading status automatically; and domestic policy must also be non-discriminatory. This requires that internal taxes and other charges, laws, regulations and other requirements affecting business transactions be applied to domestic entities and foreign concerns on an equal basis.

Transparency of the laws and regulations in respect of trade is also required by the GATT. Under Art X, the contracting parties must publish, among other things, their trade policies and laws, import and export systems and domestic regulations in respect of trade. In addition, on becoming a member, a country may not raise its tariffs for a period of three years. After this period, any move to modify or raise tariffs must be discussed with the other contracting parties. Should a country increase its tariff rates in one category of products, it may be required to reduce the rates in another category or categories.

The escape clause: Article XIX

Article XIX(1)(a) of GATT provides that, where 'as a result of unforeseen developments and of the effect of the obligations incurred by a contracting party under this Agreement ... any product is being imported into the territory of that contracting party in such increased quantities and under such conditions as to cause or threaten serious injury to domestic producers in that territory of like or directly competitive products', members may impose increased tariffs on imported products or suspend its obligations or withdraw or modify any concessions granted. This Article justifies the taking of temporary action to adjust imports. Article XIX is implemented by the WTO's Agreement on Safeguards. The escape clause has been implemented in the United States in Section 201 of the Trade Act 1974 (as amended): import relief may be granted if increased imports are a substantial cause of serious injury or threat to the domestic industry producing a like or competitive product. Hence, the 'unforeseen developments' part of Art XIX(1)(a) is not part of American law.

The legal framework of dispute settlement

The procedure for dispute settlement under GATT is found in:

1 Articles XXII and XXIII; and
2 Annex 2 to the Agreement Establishing the World Trade Organisation, namely the Understanding on Rules and Procedures Governing the Settlement of Disputes.

Article XXII(I) states:

> Each contracting party shall accord sympathetic consideration to, and shall afford adequate opportunity for consultation regarding, such representations as may be made by another contracting party with respect to any matter affecting the operation of this agreement.

If consultation fails, a Member may seek multilateral consultation with the contracting parties as a whole under Art XXII(2) which provides that: 'The contracting parties may, at the request of a contracting party consult with any contracting party or parties in respect of any matter for which it has not been possible to find a satisfactory solution through consultation under para 1.' This consultative process outlined in Art XXII becomes a more formal process of dispute settlement in Art XXIII(1) which provides for consultation in specific instances. If agreement cannot be reached, Art XXIII(2) provides a procedure for investigation, possibly resulting in the authorisation of suspension of concessions or other obligations by the complaining member. A dispute is normally settled by a panel of 3–5 experts. A dispute can be settled by adopting the panel report or a negotiated settlement resulting from the report.

The Understanding on Rules and Procedures Governing the Settlement of Disputes constitutes an attempt to codify the WTO dispute settlement procedures. The Understanding creates in its Art 2(1) a new Dispute Settlement Body (DSB) 'to administer these rules and procedures and . . . the consultation and dispute settlement provisions of the covered agreements'. To this end, Art 2(1) further provides that the DSB 'shall have the authority to establish panels, adopt panel and Appellate Body reports, maintain surveillance of implementation of rulings and recommendations, and authorize suspension of concessions and other obligations under a covered agreement.' More importantly, the Understanding also provides for the establishment of an appellate body of seven members, elected for a four-year term, serving in rotation at three-year intervals; these members are 'broadly representative of membership in the WTO' (Art 17(3)). The Understanding also provides for limited arbitration relating to specific matters like damages and compensation amounts (Art 25). Thus, the features of the system are the DSB, the panels including the appellate body, with an arbitration arm. Following an appeal to the appellate body, the adoption of its report is automatic and final (Art 14).

The Understanding also redefined a number of general principles, namely:

1 Dispute settlement is central to the provision of security and predictability in the multilateral trading system.
2 Dispute settlement cannot add to or diminish the rights and obligations provided in the GATT.
3 Dispute settlement, which involves the conciliation of disputes, aims at maintaining a proper balance between the rights and obligations of members.
4 A positive approach should be adopted by the panels to any dispute.
5 A solution mutually acceptable to the parties is preferred.
6 Dispute settlement procedures seek to result in the withdrawal of the impugned measure concerned. Compensation should be resorted to only if immediate withdrawal of the measure is impracticable.

Panel members are selected 'with a view to ensuring the independence of the members, a sufficiently diverse background and a wide spectrum of experience' (Art 8(2)). Panels are usually made up of three members, but the parties are entitled to seek the appointment of five panelists (Art 8(5)). The WTO's Secretariat proposes nominations for the panel to the parties to the dispute. These nominations may only be opposed by the parties for the most compelling reasons (Art 8(6)). Article 11 describes the function of panels as follows:

The function of panels is to assist the DSB in discharging its responsibilities under this Understanding and the covered agreements. Accordingly, a panel should make an objective assessment of the matter before it, including an objective assessment of the facts of the case and the applicability of and conformity with the relevant covered agreements, and make such other findings as will assist the DSB in making the recommendations or in giving the rulings provided for in the covered agreements. Panels should consult regularly with the parties to the dispute and give them adequate opportunity to develop a mutually satisfactory solution.

There is a rule that citizens of members involved in the dispute are debarred from having a panel member (Art 8(3)). Third parties that have a substantial interest in a dispute heard by a panel shall, provided it has notified its interest to the DSB, have an opportunity to be heard by the panel and to make written submissions to it (Art 10(2)). The panel procedures are set out in Arts 12 and 13. In accordance with Art 14, panel deliberations are confidential and panel reports are drafted without the presence of the parties to the dispute. The opinions expressed by individual panelists remain anonymous.

PREFERENTIAL TREATMENT

Preferential treatment is provided for under Art XVIII and Part IV of the GATT, but other Articles are also relevant. The prohibition on quantitative restrictions contained in Art XI of the GATT is subject to an exception regarding measures imposed for balance-of-payments purposes. This exception is found in Art XII with special provision for developing countries being made in Art XVIII s B of the GATT. Under these provisions, any country may restrict the quantity or value of imports in order to safeguard its external financial position to protect its balance-of-payments or to ensure a level of reserves adequate for the implementation of its programme of economic development.

Restrictions must not exceed those necessary to forestall the imminent threat of, or to stop, a serious decline in monetary reserves; or if such reserves are very low, to achieve a reasonable rate of increase (Art XVIII does not use the word 'imminent', and refers to reserves which are 'inadequate' rather than very low). Due regard must be paid to special factors which may affect reserves or the need for reserves. As conditions improve the restrictions must be progressively relaxed.

Article XVIII(2) gives developing countries special rights in regards to balance-of-payments measures and safeguards action for development. Under this Article, a developing country is permitted to apply a discriminatory quantitative restriction to assist in its development and the improvement of its economy. In particular, Art XVIII(2) allows a developing country 'to maintain sufficient flexibility in their tariff structure to be able to grant the tariff protection required for the establishment of a particular industry, and to apply quantitative restrictions for balance of payments purposes in a manner which takes full account of the continued high level of demand for imports likely to be generated by their programmes of economic development.'

However, before a country adopts quantitative restrictions, a number of requirements must be satisfied. First, the contracting party must be one which can only support a low standard of living and is in the early stage of development. Further, it must be undergoing a process of industrialisation to correct an excessive dependence on primary production. Secondly, the measures must be intended to protect an infant industry. An infant industry involves not only the establishment of a new industry, but also the establishment of a new branch of production in an existing industry, the substantial transformation of an existing industry and the substantial expansion of an existing industry, supplying a relatively small proportion of domestic demand. It may also cover the reconstruction of an industry destroyed or substantially damaged as a result of hostilities or natural disasters.

Article XVIII(4) provides that a contracting party the economy of which can only support low standards of living is allowed to deviate temporarily from the GATT as set out in ss A to D; ss A to C apply to a country which has a low standard of living and is in the early stages of development. The terms 'low standards of living' and 'early stages of development' under this Article are obscure. Sections A to C may be applied by countries which fulfil the following criteria:

- the country should be underdeveloped in the sense that there are resources which have not yet been tapped; and
- it should have a low standard of living.

Thus, a country which has a low standard of living, but does not have resources which can be exploited, may not use the facility provided by ss A to C. Similarly, a country which has resources which have been exploited may also not use these facilities. The GATT does not set out the level of per capita income below which a country can only support low standards of living nor does it provide criteria for determining when a country is in the early stages of development.

A member whose economic development does not come within the scope of Art XVIII(4)(a) may submit an application to the contracting parties under s D. Both ss C and D make provision for government assistance to promote the establishment of a particular industry.

Quantitative restriction: a protection for developing countries

Developing countries which 'can only support a low standard of living' and 'are at an early stage of development' typically face balance-of-payments difficulties and instability in their trade performance. Frequently they will attempt to protect their markets from foreign exporters. The purpose of this is to safeguard the country's external position and to protect its economic programme.

To prevent misuse of the facilities offered by Art XVIII(4), s B(9) of this Article provides that the import restrictions instituted, maintained or intensified shall not exceed those necessary:

(a) to forestall the threat of, or to stop, a serious decline in its monetary reserves; or

(b) in the case of a contracting party with inadequate monetary reserves, to achieve a reasonable rate of increase in its reserves.

In applying these restrictions, the contracting party may determine their incidence on imports of different products or classes of products in such a way as to give priority to the importation of those products which are more essential in the light of its policy of economic development provided that:

(a) the restrictions avoid unnecessary damage to the commercial or economic interests of any other contracting party and do not prevent unreasonably the importation of any description of goods in minimum commercial quantities the exclusion of which would impair regular channels of trade; and

(b)   provided further that the restrictions are not so applied as to prevent the importation of commercial samples or to prevent compliance with patent, trade mark, copyright or similar procedures.

Furthermore, Art XVIII s B(11) of the GATT provides, among other things:

In carrying out its domestic policies, the contracting party concerned shall pay due regard to the need for restoring equilibrium in its balance of payments on a sound and lasting basis and to the desirability of assuring an economic employment of productive resources.

Three safeguard measures were adopted during the Tokyo Round:

1 Declaration on trade measures for balance-of-payments purposes

The contracting parties decided in 1979 that all restrictive import measures taken for balance-of-payments purposes should be subject to the same rules and procedures. Three additional conditions were adopted: (a) parties must abide by GATT disciplines and give preference to those measures which have the least disruptive effect on trade; (b) they should avoid the simultaneous application of more than one type of trade measures; and (c) whenever practicable they should publicly announce a time schedule for the removal of the measures. The contracting parties also decided that all import restriction measures undertaken by developed countries based on Art XII and developing countries based on Art XVIII s B should be carried out in consultation with 'Balance of Payments Restriction Committees'. In this declaration, GATT's members expressed their conviction that restrictive trade measures are in general an inefficient means to maintain or to restore the balance-of-payments equilibrium and they recognised that developed contracting parties should avoid the imposition of restrictive trade measures for balance-of-payments purposes to the maximum extent possible.

2 Decision on safeguard action for development purposes

A decision of the contracting parties in 1979 brought within the scope of Art XVIII the development of new or the modification or extension of existing production structures in order to achieve a more efficient use of resources. Furthermore, the contracting parties recognised that there may be unusual circumstances where delay in the application of the measures may give rise to difficulties and they agreed that in such circumstances developing countries may temporarily deviate from GATT rules by introducing the measures on a provisional basis immediately after their notification. Thus, this decision permits emergency action to be taken pending consultation.

3 Understanding regarding notification, consultation, dispute settlement and surveillance

This concerns the notification requirements found both in GATT and in decisions made under it, linking them with the notion of surveillance of national measures adopted by GATT members. These requirements are related to dispute settlement because notifications provide opportunities for aggrieved parties to raise issues when they would be reluctant to invoke the more formal procedures of Art XXIII.

The conditions to be observed by an applicant country

Article XVIII(12)(a) provides that:

Any contracting party applying new restrictions or raising the general level of its existing restrictions by a substantial intensification of the measures applied under this Section, shall immediately after instituting or intensifying such restrictions (or, in circumstances in which prior consultation is practicable, before doing so) consult with the contracting parties as to the nature of its balance of payments difficulties, alternative corrective measures which may be available, and the possible effect of the restrictions on the economies of other contracting parties.

Hence, full consultation with GATT members is required immediately after or prior to the application of quantitative restrictions. Article XVIII s B(12)(b) stipulates that:

On a date to be determined by them the contracting parties shall review all restrictions still applied under this Section on that date. Beginning two years after that date, contracting parties applying restrictions under this Section shall enter into consultations of the type provided for in subparagraph (a) above with the contracting parties at intervals of approximately, but not less than, two years according to a programme to be drawn up each year by the contracting parties; *Provided* that no consultation under this subparagraph shall take place within two years after the conclusion of a consultation of a general nature under any other provision of this paragraph.

Since 1972, a more simplified procedure than full consultation is permitted under Art XVIII s B. This procedure minimises the burden of the administrative procedures and encourages transparency in quantitative restrictions imposed by developing countries. If full consultation before the imposition of quantitative restrictions is impracticable, such consultation may be delayed until after the imposition of these restrictions.

If the contracting parties conclude that the quantitative restrictions applied by a relevant member are inconsistent with Art XIII (subject to the exception in Art XIV), they shall indicate the nature of the inconsistency and may recommend the appropriate modification of the restrictions. If the consultation results in a declaration that the quantitative restrictions are inconsistent with Art XIII and have impeded international trade, the relevant contracting parties will be informed and appropriate recommendations made for securing conformity with GATT provisions within a specified period. In particular, the contracting parties may decide on the following actions. First, if in the course of consultation it is found that the restrictions are inconsistent with Art XVIII s B or with Art XIII (subject to the provisions of Art XIV), they shall indicate the nature of the inconsistency and may advise that the restrictions be suitably modified. Secondly, if the consultations do not result in an agreement, they may recommend the withdrawal or modification of the restrictions. If the restrictions are not withdrawn or modified within a specified time, they may release the complaining member from its obligations to the contracting party that adopted the restrictions.

Protection for an infant industry

The GATT provides protection for infant industries under Art XVIII. Developing countries whose economy can only support low standards of living and are in the early stages of development enjoy additional facilities allowing them to grant tariff protection required for the establishment of a particular industry. A country which can only support a low standard of living and is in the early stages of development may require government assistance to promote the establishment of a particular industry. A developing country may have recourse to the procedures under Art XVIII s C(13):

If a contracting party . . . finds that governmental assistance is required to promote the establishment of a particular industry with a view to raising the general standard of living of its people, but that no measure consistent with the other provisions of this Agreement is practicable to achieve that objective, it may have recourse to the provisions and procedures set out in this Section.

Article XVIII is an important article for developing countries because it allows these countries to apply non-discriminatory quantitative restrictions to assist in the development and restructuring of its economy. But where protection measures are proposed by a developing country for an infant industry, the contracting parties must be notified about the proposed adoption of these measures. The notification process must comply with the appropriate time limit determined by Art XVIII(14). Gilbert P Verbit observes in his book *Trade Agreements for Developing Countries* (1969, New York: Columbia University Press at 57) that: 'Article XVIII has been interpreted liberally, too liberally for some commentators have characterised it as a "rubber clause" and many developing countries have taken advantage of it to impose quantitative import restrictions.'

Part IV of the GATT

Part IV, consisting of Arts XXXVI, XXXVII, XXXVIII commits developed countries to assist developing countries in their development programmes.

The developed countries agreed that 'There is need for a rapid and sustained expansion of the export earnings of the less-developed contracting parties' (Art XXXVI(2)) and 'for positive efforts designed to ensure that less-developed contracting parties secure a share in the growth in international trade commensurate with the needs of their economic development' (Art XXXVI(3)). Article XXXVI which sets out the general principles and objectives, recognises the development needs of less-developed contracting parties; it emphasises the importance to these countries of improved market access, commodity price stability, and the diversification of economic structures. The commitments of the developed contracting parties are contained in Art XXXVII(1)(a). They undertake, among other things, to 'accord high priority to the reduction and elimination of barriers to products currently or potentially of particular export interest to less-developed contracting parties, including customs duties and other restrictions which differentiate unreasonably between such products in their primary and in their processed forms'. Importantly, Art XXXVI(8) of the GATT provides that: 'The developed contracting parties do not expect reciprocity for commitments made by them in trade negotiations to reduce or remove tariffs and other barriers to the trade of less-developed contracting parties.'

Contracting parties, without prejudice to any bilateral consultations that may be undertaken, are obliged to consult with other concerned countries to reach solutions satisfactory to all contracting parties to further the objectives set out in Art XXXVI. In the course of these consultations, the reasons for not complying with the provisions of Art XXXVII(1–3) are examined. In accordance with Art XXXVIII(2)(c), the consultations by the contracting parties may result in joint action designed to further the objectives of GATT. In particular, Art XXXVIII provides for joint action, where appropriate, to take action:

1   to provide improved and acceptable conditions of access to world markets for primary products of particular interest to developing countries;
2   to devise measures designed to attain stable, equitable and remunerative prices for exports of such products;

3   to seek appropriate collaboration in matters of trade and development policy
     with the United Nations and its organs and agencies, including any institutions
     that may be created on the basis of recommendations by the United Nations
     Conference on Trade and Development;

4   to analyse the export potential of developing countries to facilitate access to
     export markets for the products of the industries thus developed; and

5   to seek appropriate collaboration with governments and international
     organisations.

DUMPING AND SUBSIDIES

Anti-dumping and countervailing measures are dealt with in Art VI of the GATT. This
Article, to the extent that it deals with anti-dumping, is discussed in detail in Chapter 8
of this book.

Article XVI of the GATT has two sections dealing with subsidies. Section A of
this Article deals with subsidies that operate 'directly or indirectly to increase
exports of any product from, or to reduce imports of any product into, its territory'.
If a state grants this type of subsidy, that state is obligated to notify the other
contracting parties. Furthermore, if it is determined that this subsidy may prejudice
the interest of another contracting party, then the subsidising state is obliged to enter
into negotiations to limit this subsidy at the request of an affected party. Section B of
this Article sets out additional provisions which recognise that the granting of a
subsidy can cause harm to another contracting party. Therefore, the use of subsidies
should be avoided as far as possible. If a subsidy must be applied, then it should not
result in the imposing member gaining more than an equitable share of world
exports in that product, taking into account the contracting parties' share of that
trade in a prior representative period.

Article XVI s B(4) stipulates that:

> as from 1 January 1958 or the earliest practicable date thereafter, contracting parties
> shall cease to grant either directly or indirectly any form of subsidy on the export of
> any product other than a primary product which subsidy results in the sale of such
> product for export at a price lower than the comparable price charged for the like
> product to buyers in the domestic market.

Primary products include farm, forest or fishery products, or any mineral, in its
natural form or which has undergone such processing as is customarily required to
prepare it for marketing in a substantial volume in international trade.

When members subsidise goods for export, the importing state may impose
countervailing duties under Art VI of the GATT. Whilst the GATT only contains
general principles on subsidies, a Subsidies Code introduced in the Tokyo Round of
1979 attempted to give meaning to the term 'subsidy' without defining it. Specifically
the Code forbids the subsidisation of non-primary products. Minerals are not
included, but export subsidies on minerals that cause adverse effects are prohibited
(Art 9). The Code permits the use of domestic subsidies and acknowledges the role
they play in the development of a country's economy. Domestic subsidies provide for
preferential treatment for all companies, for example, the provision by the contracting
party of retraining schemes.

An Agreement on Subsidies and Countervailing Measures is annexed to the WTO Agreement. In Art 1.1 it states that a subsidy exists if 'there is a financial contribution by a government or any public body within the territory of a Member ... where a government practice involves a direct transfer of funds'. Article 2 contains a 'specificity' requirement: a subsidy will only be involved in circumstances where it is given by the granting authority to certain enterprises. Subsidies benefiting domestic industries, such as public investment in infrastructure, roads, electricity grids, and the like, are non-specific and therefore outside the reach of the Agreement. If 'objective criteria or conditions governing the eligibility' for the subsidy exist, it is considered non-specific (Art 2(b)). However, 'notwithstanding any appearance of non-specificity ... other factors may be considered', such as provision of a subsidy to a limited number of enterprises, predominant use of the subsidy by a limited number of enterprises the granting of disproportionately large amounts to certain enterprises or the discretion exercised by the granting authority in providing the subsidy (Art 2(c)).

THE GENERAL AGREEMENT ON TRADE IN SERVICES (GATS)

Services are of great importance to the international trading order because the world has become service-oriented. Banking, management consultancy, law, engineering, advertising, telecommunications and many other professions and trades are all based on service. The installation of computers and the accompanying software provides a good example of the interconnectedness of trade in services and trade in goods. Annex 1B of the WTO Agreement deals with the General Agreement on Trade in Services (GATS). GATS deals with the obligations of its member states in Part I; specific commitments with regard to market access and national treatment are found in Part II. There are also a number of Annexes, dealing with such matters as movement of personnel, the service provided and the industry involved.

Article I(1) stipulates that: 'This Agreement applies to measures by Members affecting trade in services.' Article I(2) defines the meaning of 'supply of a service':

> For the purposes of this Agreement, trade in services is defined as the supply of a service:
>
> (a) from the territory of one Member into the territory of any other Member;
>
> (b) in the territory of one Member to the service consumer of any other Member;
>
> (c) by a service supplier of one Member, through commercial presence in the territory of any other Member;
>
> (d) by a service supplier of one Member, through presence of natural persons of a Member in the territory of any other Member.

Article I(3) describes any 'measures by Members' as measures taken by central, regional or a local governments or authorities and includes measures delegated by them to non-governmental bodies.

The most-favoured-nation (MFN) principle

Article II identifies the 'most-favoured-nation treatment' principle as the core obligation of member states. Member states: 'shall accord immediately and unconditionally to services and service suppliers of any other Member treatment no less favourable than that it accords to like services and service suppliers of any other country.' However, 'a Member may maintain a measure inconsistent' with this principle 'provided that such a measure is listed in, and meets the conditions of, the Annex on Article II Exemptions'. This list allows for specific or temporary exemptions. In particular, the Annex provides that (i) an exemption is only granted if it refers to an existing measure that was in existence at the completion of the Uruguay Round in December 1993, (ii) an exemption must not be given for more than 10 years and (iii) the Council for Trade in Services must review all exemptions granted for more than five years. The review considers whether the enabling condition for the exemption still exists and if so, it sets a date for the next review.

When dealing with the MFN principle, it is also necessary to consider Arts XVI and XXII. Article XVI(1) deals with market access commitments under which 'each member shall accord services and service suppliers of any other Member treatment no less favourable than that provided for under the terms, limitations and conditions agreed and specified in its Schedule'. Article XVI(2)(e)–(f) requires that member states do not maintain or adopt 'measures which restrict or require specific types of legal entity or joint venture through which a service supplier may supply a service' and place 'limitations on the participation of foreign capital in terms of maximum percentage limit on foreign shareholding or the total value of individual or aggregate foreign investment'.

The national treatment principle

The national treatment principle is found in Art XVII(1) which states that 'each member shall accord to services and service suppliers of any other Member, in respect of all measures affecting the supply of services, treatment no less favourable than that it accords to its own like services and service suppliers'. It further states in para (2) that: 'Formally identical or formally different treatment shall be considered to be less favourable if it modifies the conditions of competition in favour of services or service suppliers of the Member compared to like services or services suppliers of any other Member.' Article XVII in effect protects foreign suppliers from being discriminated against by a member's taxation laws. The Article is important in situations where foreign suppliers enjoy *de jure* equality with domestic competitors, but suffer from *de facto* inequality.

Other core Articles

Article III(1) requires each member to publish promptly 'all relevant meassures of general application which pertain to or affect the operation of this Agreement'. In addition, there is an obligation also to publish 'international agreements pertaining to or affecting trade in services to which a Member is a signatory'. In accordance with para (3), there is further duty to inform the Council for Trade in Services of 'the introduction of any new, or any changes to existing, laws, regulations or administrative guidelines which significantly affect trade in services covered by its specific commitments under this Agreement'.

Article IV facilitates the participation of developing countries in GATS. Article VII(1) provides that a member, in order to fulfil its standards or criteria for the authorisation, licensing or certification of services suppliers 'may recognise the education or experience obrtained, requirements met, or licenses or certifications granted in a particular county'. This Article presumably facilitates the development of recognisable and attainable standards among GATS Members.

Articles VIII and IX can be looked at together. Article VIII ensures that monopolies and exclusive service suppliers in any Member state do not act in a manner inconsistent with that member's GATS obligation. Article IX imposes an obligation on Members to consult with the aim of eliminating restrictive business practices if such practices restrict competition. Articles X to XV provide for emergency safeguard measures based on the non-discrimination principle (Art X); for non-discriminatory, temporary restrictions to safeguard the balance of payment (Art XII); for government procurement (Art XIII); and for certain public policy and security measures (Arts XIV, XIV *bis*). Similar to the commitments to negotiate emergency measures (cf Arts X(1) and XIII(2)) for government procurement in services, Art XV, which deals with subsidies, provides for 'negotiations with a view to developing the necessary multilateral disciplines' to avoid the trade-distortive effects of subsidies and to address 'the appropriateness of countervailing procedures'. Article XV(2) stipulates that 'any Member which considers that it is adversely affected by a subsidy of another Member may request consultations with that Member on such matters'.

Part III of GATS deals with specific commitments with regard to market access (Art XVI), national treatment (Art XVII) and additional commitments (Art XVIII). Article XVI provides that members give market access to services suppliers subject to 'the terms, limitations and conditions agreed and specified' by each member in its national schedule. The obligation does not apply to services for which a member did not make a market access commitment in its national schedule. Article XVI lists six limitations which a member is not allowed to maintain in sectors where market access commitments are undertaken. They are limitations on the:

1   number of service suppliers allowed;
2   total value of transactions or assets;
3   total number of service operations or on the total quantity of service output;
4   total numbers of natural persons employed in a particular service;
5   type of legal entity used by a service supplier; and
6   maximum amount of foreign participation allowed.

Part IV, dealing with progressive liberalisation of GATS, provides in Art XIX(4) that future rounds be directed 'towards increasing the general level of specific commitments undertaken by Members under this Agreement'.

The Annexes provide for exemptions to the general principles enshrined in GATS.

1   The Annex on Movement of Natural Persons Supplying Services under the Agreement enables members to agree on criteria to allow temporary entry of all categories of natural persons on their territory. However, it does not apply to persons seeking employment, citizenship, residence or employment on a permanent basis. It merely allows natural persons who supply services or are employees of services suppliers to provide services according to the terms of specific commitments entered into by members.

2   The Annex on Air Transport Services states that the Agreement does not apply to measures affecting traffic rights, however granted; or services directly related to the exercise of traffic rights. The Annex does not apply to aircraft repair, maintenance, reservations or marketing. The Annex provides for a review of this sector every five years by the Council for Trade in Services.

3   The Annex on financial services lists activities which are deemed to be financial services. In accordance with this Annex 'a Member shall not be prevented from taking measures for prudential reasons, including for the protection of investors, depositors, policy holders or persons to whom a fiduciary duty is owed by a financial service supplier, or to ensure the intgegrity and stability of the financial sytem'.

4   The Annex on telecommunications aims at ensuring that 'any service supplier of any other Member is accorded access to and use of public telecommunications transport networks and services on reasonable and non-discriminatory terms and conditions, for the supply of a service included in its Schedule'. The Annex on negotiations on basic telecommunications deals with market accessibility and commitment at a national level of this service.

GATS is a set of legally binding and transparent rules which allow and encourage trade and investment liberalisation of services. There is an expectation that GATS will lead to a more efficient allocation of domestic resources and access to technology available in member countries. However, GATS obligations are often non-specific, and allow for many exemptions.

TUTORIAL QUESTIONS

1   Dumping is widely deemed to be unfair and injurious to Australia's domestic industries. But an increasing number of trade commentators argue that dumping is generally beneficial to the importing country and that anti-dumping laws harm the prospects for world trade liberalisation and 'should be dumped'.

Answer the following questions:

   (i)   What constitutes 'dumping' in GATT/WTO law?

   (ii)   Should contracting parties to GATT/WTO dump its anti-dumping laws? Give reasons for your view.

   (iii) What advice would you give your client – a respected Australian importer of American goods – who claims that anti-dumping duties have been unfairly levied on the goods imported?

2   Describe the most-favoured-nation (MFN) principle of the GATT and explain its importance for international trade.

3   Discuss the importance for international trade of the implementation of the non-discrimination principle.

4   Discuss the escape clause of Article XIX of the GATT and research its implementation in your own national system.

5   Undertake a SWOT analysis of GATT's and WTO's dispute settlement mechanisms.

6   Discuss the importance of the General Agreement on Trade in Services (GATS) for the development of international trade.

FURTHER READING

Books

Burnett, R, *The Law of International Business Transactions*, 1994, Sydney: Federation Press.

Cheng, CJ (ed), *Basic Documents on International Trade Law*, 1986, Dordrecht: Martinus Nijhoff.

Das, DK, *International Trade Policy: a Developing Country Perspective*, 1990, London: Macmillan.

Department of Foreign Affairs and Trade, *Uruguay Round Outcomes: Agriculture*, July 1994; *Services*, September 1994; *Industrials*, September 1994; *Intellectual Property*, September 1994, Canberra, Australia.

Department of International Liaison of the Ministry of Foreign Economic Relations and Trade of China (eds), *GATT: a Handbook*, 1992, Beijing: Economic Administration Press.

Gupta, KR, *A Study of the General Agreement on Tariffs and Trade*, 1967, Delhi: S Chand and Co, p 149.

Henkin, L, Pugh, RC, Schachter, O and Smit, H, *International Law: Cases and Materials*, 3rd edn, 1992, St Paul, Minnesota: West Publishing.

Hudec, R, *Developing Countries in the GATT Legal System*, 1987, Aldershot: Gower.

Jackson, JH, *World Trade and the Law of GATT*, 1969, Indianapolis, Bobbs Merrill.

Jackson, JH, *Legal Problems of International Economic Relations*, 1977, St Paul, Minnesota: West Publishing.

Kirdar, U, *The Structure of United Nations Economic Aid to Underdeveloped Countries*, 1966, The Hague: Martinus Nijhoff.

Long, O, *Law and its Limitations in the GATT Multilateral Trade System*, 1985, The Hague: Martinus Nijhoff.

McGovern, E, *International Trade Regulations*, 2nd edn, 1986, Exeter: Globefield Press.

Mosler, H, *The International Society as a Legal Community*, 1980, German town, Md: Sijtihoff & Nordhoff, p 255.

Raworth, P and Reif, LC, *The Law of the WTO*, 1995, New York: Oceana Publications.

Sampson, G, *Trade, Environment and the WTO*, 1999, Bertrams Print on Demand.

Schmitthoff, CM, *The Law and Practice of International Trade*, 9th edn, 1990, London: Stevens.

Schwarzenberger, G, *The Frontiers of International Law*, 1962, London: Stevens, p 220.

Simmonds, KR and Hill, BHW, *Law Practice Under the GATT*, 1994, New York: Oceana Publications.

Synder, F and Slinn, P (eds) *International Law of Development: Corporate Perspectives*, 1987, Abingdon: Professional Books.

US International Trade Commission Review of the Effectiveness of Trade Dispute Settlement under the GATT, 1985, US International Trade Commission (USITC) Publication 1793, December.

Verbit, PG, *Trade Agreements for Developing Countries*, 1969, New York and London: Columbia University Press, p 57.

Weiss, F (ed), *Improving WTO Dispute Settlement Procedures: Issues and Lessons from the Practice of Other International Courts and Tribunals*, 2001, London: Cameron May.

Whalley, J, *The Uruguay Round and Beyond*, 1989, London: Macmillan.

Wilde, KCDM and Islam, MR (eds), *International Transactions, Trade and Investment, Law and Finance*, 1993, Sydney: The Law Book Co.

Articles

Arup, CJ, 'The prospective GATT agreement for intellectual property protection' (1993) 4 *Australian Intellectual Property Journal* 181–208.

Bagchi, S, 'The integration of the textile trade into GATT' (1994) 28 *Journal of World Trade* 31–42.

Castel, JG, 'The Uruguay Round and the improvements to the GATT Dispute Settlement Rules and Procedures' (1989) 38 *International and Comparative Law Quarterly* 835–49.

Ching, MM, 'Evaluating the effectiveness of the GATT Dispute Settlement System for Developing Countries' (1992–93) 16 *World Competition* 81–112.

Dharjee, R and Boisson de Chazournes, L, 'Trade-Related Aspects of Intellectual Property Rights (TRIPS): objectives, approaches and basic principles of the GATT and of intellectual property conventions' (1990) 24 *Journal of World Trade* 5–15.

Evans, GE, 'Intellectual property as a trade issue' (1994–95) 18 *World Competition* 137–180.

Feaver, D and Wilson, K, 'An evaluation of Australia's anti-dumping and countervailing law and policy' (1995) 29 *Journal of World Trade* 207–37.

Finger, JM, 'That old GATT magic no more casts its spell' (1991) 25 *Journal of World Trade* 19–22.

Gibbs, JM, 'The Uruguay Round and the international trade system' (1987) 21 *Journal of World Trade* 5–12.

Horlick, GN and Shea, EC, 'The World Trade Organisation Anti-Dumping Agreement' (1994) 29 *Journal of World Trade* 5–31.

Knobl, PF, 'GATT application: the grandfather is still alive' (1991) 25 *Journal of World Trade* 101–18.

Kohona, PTB, 'Dispute resolution under the World Trade Organisation' (1994) 28 *Journal of World Trade* 23–47.

Komuro, N, 'The WTO Dispute Settlement Mechanism' (1995) 29 *Journal of World Trade* 5–95.

Lukas, M, 'The role of private parties in the enforcement of the Uruguay Round agreements' (1995) 29 *Journal of World Trade* 181–205.

Lutz, JM, 'GATT reform or regime maintenance: differing solutions to world trade problems' (1991) 25 *Journal of World Trade* 107–22.

Marceau, G, 'Transition from GATT to WTO' (1995) 29 *Journal of World Trade* 147–63.

Nordgren, I, 'The GATT panels during the Uruguay Round' (1991) 25 *Journal of World Trade* 57–72.

Pangratis, A and Vermulst, E, 'Injury in anti-dumping proceedings' (1994) 28 *Journal of World Trade* 61–96.

Qureski, AH, 'The New GATT Trade Policy Review Mechanism: an exercise in transparency or enforcement?' (1990) 24 *Journal of World Trade* 147–60.

Roessler, F, 'The competence of GATT' (1987) 21 *Journal of World Trade* 73–83.

Rom, M, 'Some early reflections on the Uruguay Round Agreement as seen from the viewpoint of a developing country' (1994) 28 *Journal of World Trade* 5–30.

Sauve, P, 'Assessing the General Agreement on Trade in Services' (1995) 29 *Journal of World Trade* 125–45.

Smeets, M, 'Main features of the Uruguay Round Agreement on Textiles and Clothing, and implications for the grading system' (1995) 29 *Journal of World Trade* 97–109.

Smeets, M, 'Tariff issues in the Uruguay Round' (1995) 29 *Journal of World Trade* 91–105.

'Various issues of focus', *GATT Newsletter* and *Inside US Trade*.

Vernon, R, 'The World Trade Organisation: a new stage in international trade and development' (1995) 36 *Harvard International Law Journal* 329–40.

Waincymer, JM, 'Revitalising GATT Article XXIII issues in the context of the Uruguay Round' (1988–89) 12 *World Competition* 5–47.

APPENDIX

AGREEMENT ESTABLISHING THE WORLD TRADE ORGANISATION

The *Parties* to this agreement,

Recognising that their relations in the field of trade and economic endeavour should be conducted with a view to raising standards of living, ensuring full employment and a large and steadily growing volume of real income and effective demand, and expanding the production of and trade in goods and services, while allowing for the optimal use of the world's resources in accordance with the objective of sustainable development, seeking both to protect and preserve the environment and to enhance the means for doing so in a manner consistent with their respective needs and concerns at different levels of economic development,

Recognising further that there is need for positive efforts designed to ensure that developing countries, and especially the least developed among them, secure a share in the growth in international trade commensurate with the needs of their economic development,

Being desirous of contributing to these objectives by entering into reciprocal and mutually advantageous arrangements directed to the substantial reduction of tariffs and other barriers to trade and to the elimination of discriminatory treatment in international trade relations,

Resolved, therefore, to develop an integrated, more viable and durable multilateral trading system encompassing the General Agreement on Tariffs and Trade, the results of past trade liberalisation efforts, and all of the results of the Uruguay Round of Multilateral Trade Negotiations,

Determined to preserve the basic principles and to further the objectives underlying this multilateral trading system,

Agree as follows:

Article I – Establishment of the organisation

The World Trade Organisation (hereinafter referred to as 'the WTO') is hereby established.

Article II – Scope of the WTO

1   The WTO shall provide the common institutional framework for the conduct of trade relations among its Members in matters related to the agreements and associated legal instruments included in the Annexes to this agreement.

2   The agreements and associated legal instruments included in Annexes 1, 2 and 3 (hereinafter referred to as 'Multilateral Trade Agreements') are integral parts of this agreement, binding on all Members.

3   The agreements and associated legal instruments included in Annex 4 (hereinafter referred to as 'Plurilateral Trade Agreements') are also part of this agreement for those Members that have accepted them, and are binding on those Members. The Plurilateral Trade Agreements do not create either obligations or rights for Members that have not accepted them.

4   The General Agreement on Tariffs and Trade 1994 as specified in Annex 1A (hereinafter referred to as 'GATT 1994') is legally distinct from the General Agreement on Tariffs and Trade, dated 30 October 1947, annexed to the Final Act Adopted at the Conclusion of the Second Session of the Preparatory Committee of the United Nations Conference on Trade and Employment, as subsequently rectified, amended or modified (hereinafter referred to as 'GATT 1947').

Article III – Functions of the WTO

1   The WTO shall facilitate the implementation, administration and operation and further the objectives, of this agreement and of the Multilateral Trade Agreements, and shall also provide the framework for the implementation administration and operation of the Plurilateral Trade Agreements.

2   The WTO shall provide the forum for negotiations among its Members concerning their multilateral trade relations in matters dealt with under the agreements in the Annexes to this agreement. The WTO may also provide a forum for further negotiations among its Members concerning their multilateral trade relations, and a framework for the implementation of the results of such negotiations, as may be decided by the Ministerial Conference.

3   The WTO shall administer the Understanding on Rules and Procedures Governing the Settlement of Disputes (hereinafter referred to as the 'Dispute Settlement Understanding' or 'DSU') in Annex 2 to this agreement.

4   The WTO shall administer the Trade Policy Review Mechanism (hereinafter referred to as the 'TPRM') provided for in Annex 3 to this agreement.

5   With a view to achieving greater coherence in global economic policy making the WTO shall cooperate, as appropriate, with the International Monetary Fund and with the International Bank for Reconstruction and Development and its affiliated agencies.

Article IV – Structure of the WTO

1   There shall be a Ministerial Conference composed of representatives of all the Members, which shall meet at least once every two years. The Ministerial Conference shall carry out the functions of the WTO and take actions necessary to this effect. The Ministerial Conference shall have the authority to take decisions on all matters under any of the Multilateral Trade Agreements, if so requested by a Member, in accordance with the specific requirements for decision-making in this agreement and in the relevant Multilateral Trade Agreement.

2   There shall be a General Council composed of representatives of all the Members, which shall meet as appropriate. In the intervals between meetings of the Ministerial Conference, its functions shall be conducted by the General Council. The General Council shall also carry out the functions assigned to it by this Agreement. The General Council shall establish its rules of procedure and approve the rules of procedure for the Committees provided for in para 7.

3   The General Council shall convene as appropriate to discharge the responsibilities of the Dispute Settlement Body provided for in the Dispute Settlement Understanding. The Dispute Settlement Body may have its own chairman and shall establish such rules of procedure as it deems necessary for the fulfillment of those responsibilities.

4   The General Council shall convene as appropriate to discharge the responsibilities of the Trade Policy Review Body provided for in the TPRM. The Trade Policy Review Body may have its own chairman and shall establish such rules of procedure as it deems necessary for the fulfillment of those responsibilities.

5   There shall be a Council for Trade in Goods, a Council for Trade in Services and a Council for Trade-Related Aspects of Intellectual Property Rights (hereinafter referred to as the 'Council for TRIPS'), which shall operate under the general guidance of the General Council. The Council for Trade in Goods shall oversee the functioning of the Multilateral Trade Agreements in Annex 1A. The Council for Trade in Services shall oversee the functioning of the General Agreement on Trade in Services (hereinafter referred to as 'GATS'). The Council for TRIPS shall oversee the functioning of the Agreement on Trade-Related Aspects of Intellectual Property Rights (hereinafter referred to as the 'Agreement on TRIPS'). These Councils shall carry out the functions assigned to them by their respective agreements and by the General Council. They shall establish their respective rules of procedure subject to the approval of the General Council. Membership in these Councils shall be open to representatives of all Members. These Councils shall meet as necessary to carry out their functions.

6   The Council for Trade in Goods, the Council for Trade in Services and the Council for TRIPS shall establish subsidiary bodies as required. These subsidiary bodies shall establish their respective rules of procedure subject to the approval of their respective Councils.

7   The Ministerial Conference shall establish a Committee on Trade and Development, a Committee on Balance-of-Payments Restrictions and a Committee on Budget, Finance and Administration, which shall carry out the functions assigned to them by this agreement and by the Multilateral Trade Agreements, and any additional functions assigned to them by the General Council, and may establish such additional Committees with such functions as it may deem appropriate. As part of its functions, the Committee on Trade and Development shall periodically review the special provisions in the Multilateral Trade Agreements in favour of the least-developed country Members and report to the General Council for appropriate action. Membership in these Committees shall be open to representatives of all Members.

8   The bodies provided for under the Plurilateral Trade Agreements shall carry out the functions assigned to them under those agreements and shall operate within the institutional framework of the WTO. These bodies shall keep the General Council informed of their activities on a regular basis.

Article V – Relations with other organisations

1   The General Council shall make appropriate arrangements for effective cooperation with other intergovernmental organisations that have responsibilities related to those of the WTO.

2   The General Council may make appropriate arrangements for consultation and cooperation with non-governmental organisations concerned with matters related to those of the WTO.

Article VI – The Secretariat

1   There shall be a Secretariat of the WTO (hereinafter referred to as 'the Secretariat') headed by a Director General.

2   The Ministerial Conference shall appoint the Director General and adopt regulations setting out the powers, duties, and conditions of service and term of office of the Director General.

3   The Director General shall appoint the members of the staff of the Secretariat and determine their duties and conditions of service in accordance with regulations adopted by the Ministerial Conference.

4   The responsibilities of the Director General and of the staff of the Secretariat shall be exclusively international in character. In the discharge of their duties, the Director General and the staff of the Secretariat shall not seek or accept instructions from any government or any other authority external to the WTO. They shall refrain from any action which might adversely reflect on their position as international officials. The Members of the WTO shall respect the international character of the responsibilities of the Director General and of the staff of the Secretariat and shall not seek to influence them in the discharge of their duties.

Article VII – Budget and contributions

1   The Director General shall present to the Committee on Budget, Finance and Administration the annual budget estimate and financial statement of the WTO. The Committee on Budget, Finance and Administration shall review the annual budget estimate and the financial statement presented by the Director General and make recommendations thereon to the General Council. The annual budget estimate shall be subject to approval by the General Council.

2   The Committee on Budget, Finance and Administration shall propose to the General Council financial regulations which shall include provisions setting out:

(a)   the scale of contributions apportioning the expenses of the WTO among its Members; and

(b)   the measures to be taken in respect of Members in arrears.

The financial regulations shall be based, as far as practicable, on the regulations and practices of GATT 1947.

3   The General Council shall adopt the financial regulations and the annual budget estimate by a two thirds majority comprising more than half of the Members of the WTO.

4   Each Member shall promptly contribute to the WTO its share in the expenses of the WTO in accordance with the financial regulations adopted by the General Council.

Article VIII – Status of the WTO

1   The WTO shall have legal personality, and shall be accorded by each of its Members such legal capacity as may be necessary for the exercise of its functions.

2   The WTO shall be accorded by each of its Members such privileges and immunities as are necessary for the exercise of its functions.

3   The officials of the WTO and the representatives of the Members shall similarly be accorded by each of its Members such privileges and immunities as are necessary for the independent exercise of their functions in connection with the WTO.

4   The privileges and immunities to be accorded by a Member to the WTO, its officials, and the representatives of its Members shall be similar to the privileges and immunities stipulated in the Convention on the Privileges and Immunities of the Specialised Agencies, approved by the General Assembly of the United Nations on 21 November 1947.

5   The WTO may conclude a headquarters agreement.

Article IX – Decision making

1   The WTO shall continue the practice of decision-making by consensus followed under GATT 1947. Except as otherwise provided, where a decision cannot be arrived at by consensus, the matter at issue shall be decided by voting. At meetings of the Ministerial Conference and the General Council, each Member of the WTO shall have one vote. Where the European Communities exercise their right to vote, they shall have a number of votes equal to the number of their Member States which are Members of the WTO. Decisions of the Ministerial Conference and the General Council shall be taken by a majority of the votes cast, unless otherwise provided in this agreement or in the relevant Multilateral Trade Agreement.

2   The Ministerial Conference and the General Council shall have the exclusive authority to adopt interpretations of this agreement and of the Multilateral Trade Agreements. In the case of an interpretation of a Multilateral Trade Agreement in Annex 1, they shall exercise their authority on the basis of a recommendation by the Council overseeing the functioning of that agreement. The decision to adopt an interpretation shall be taken by a three fourths majority of the Members. This paragraph shall not be used in a manner that would undermine the amendment provisions in Article X.

3   In exceptional circumstances, the Ministerial Conference may decide to waive an obligation imposed on a Member by this agreement or any of the Multilateral Trade Agreements, provided that any such decision shall be taken by three fourths of the Members unless otherwise provided for in this paragraph.

     (a) A request for a waiver concerning this agreement shall be submitted to the Ministerial Conference for consideration pursuant to the practice of decision making by consensus. The Ministerial Conference shall establish a time period, which shall not exceed 90 days, to consider the request. If consensus is not reached during the time period, any decision to grant a waiver shall be taken by three fourths of the Members.

     (b) A request for a waiver concerning the Multilateral Trade Agreements in Annexes 1A or 1B or 1C and their annexes shall be submitted initially to the Council for Trade in Goods, the Council for Trade in Services or the Council for TRIPS, respectively, for consideration during a time period which shall not exceed 90 days. At the end of the time period, the relevant Council shall submit a report to the Ministerial Conference.

4   A decision by the Ministerial Conference granting a waiver shall state the exceptional circumstances justifying the decision, the terms and conditions governing the application of the waiver, and the date on which the waiver shall terminate. Any waiver granted for a period of more than one year shall be reviewed by the Ministerial Conference not later than one year after it is granted, and thereafter annually until the waiver terminates. In each review, the Ministerial Conference shall examine whether the exceptional circumstances justifying the waiver still exist and whether the terms and conditions attached to the waiver have been met. The Ministerial Conference, on the basis of the annual review, may extend, modify or terminate the waiver.

5   Decisions under a Plurilateral Trade Agreement, including any decisions on interpretations and waivers, shall be governed by the provisions of that agreement.

Article X – Amendments

1   Any Member of the WTO may initiate a proposal to amend the provisions of this agreement or the Multilateral Trade Agreements in Annex 1 by submitting such proposal to the Ministerial Conference. The Councils listed in para 5 of Article IV may also submit to the Ministerial Conference proposals to amend the provisions of the corresponding Multilateral Trade Agreements in Annex 1 the functioning of which they oversee. Unless the Ministerial Conference decides on a longer period, for a period of 90 days after the proposal has been tabled formally at the Ministerial Conference any decision by the Ministerial Conference to submit the proposed amendment to the Members for acceptance

shall be taken by consensus. Unless the provisions of paras 2, 5 or 6 apply, that decision shall specify whether the provisions of paras 3 or 4 shall apply. If consensus is reached, the Ministerial Conference shall forthwith submit the proposed amendment to the Members for acceptance. If consensus is not reached at a meeting of the Ministerial Conference within the established period, the Ministerial Conference shall decide by a two thirds majority of the Members whether to submit the proposed amendment to the Members for acceptance. Except as provided in paras 2, 5 and 6, the provisions of para 3 shall apply to the proposed amendment, unless the Ministerial Conference decides by a three fourths majority of the Members that the provisions of para 4 shall apply.

2   Amendments to the provisions of this article and to the provisions of the following articles shall take effect only upon acceptance by all Members:

Article IX of this agreement;

Articles I and II of GATT 1994;

Article II(1) of GATTS;

Article 4 of the Agreement on TRIPS.

3   Amendments to provisions of this agreement, or of the Multilateral Trade Agreements in Annexes 1A and 1C, other than those listed in paras 2 and 6 of a nature that would alter the rights and obligations of the Members, shall take effect for the Members that have accepted them upon acceptance by two thirds of the Members and thereafter for each other Member upon acceptance by it. The Ministerial Conference may decide by a three fourths majority of the Members that any amendment made effective under this paragraph is of such a nature that any Member which has not accepted it within a period specified by the Ministerial Conference in each case shall be free to withdraw from the WTO or to remain a Member with the consent of the Ministerial Conference.

4   Amendments to provisions of this agreement or of the Multilateral Trade Agreements in Annexes 1A and 1C, other than those listed in paras 2 and 6, of a nature that would not alter the rights and obligations of the Members, shall take effect for all Members upon acceptance by two thirds of the Members.

5   Except as provided in para 2 above, amendments to Parts I, II and III of GATS and the respective annexes shall take effect for the Members that have accepted them upon acceptance by two thirds of the Members and thereafter for each Member upon acceptance by it. The Ministerial Conference may decide by a three fourths majority of the Members that any amendment made effective under the preceding provision is of such a nature that any Member which has not accepted it within a period specified by the Ministerial Conference in each case shall be free to withdraw from the WTO or to remain a Member with the consent of the Ministerial Conference. Amendments to Parts IV, V and VI of GATS and the respective annexes shall take effect for all Members upon acceptance by two thirds of the Members.

6   Notwithstanding the other provisions of this Article, amendments to the Agreement on TRIPS meeting the requirements of para 2 of Article 71 thereof may be adopted by the Ministerial Conference without further formal acceptance process.

7   Any Member accepting an amendment to this agreement or to a Multilateral Trade Agreement in Annex 1 shall deposit an instrument of acceptance with the Director General of the WTO within the period of acceptance specified by the Ministerial Conference.

8   Any Member of the WTO may initiate a proposal to amend the provisions of the Multilateral Trade Agreements in Annexes 2 and 3 by submitting such proposal to the Ministerial Conference. The decision to approve amendments to the Multilateral Trade Agreement in Annex 2 shall be made by consensus and these amendments shall take effect for all Members upon approval by the Ministerial Conference. Decisions to approve amendments to the Multilateral Trade Agreement in Annex 3 shall take effect for all Members upon approval by the Ministerial Conference.

9   The Ministerial Conference, upon the request of the Members parties to a trade agreement, may decide exclusively by consensus to add that agreement to Annex 4. The Ministerial Conference, upon the request of the Members parties to a Plurilateral Trade Agreement, may decide to delete that agreement from Annex 4.

10   Amendments to a Plurilateral Trade Agreement shall be governed by the provisions of that agreement.

Article XI – Original membership

1   The contracting parties to GATT 1947 as of the date of entry into force of this agreement, and the European Communities, which accept this agreement and the Multilateral Trade Agreements and for which Schedules of Concessions and Commitments are annexed to GATT 1994 and for which Schedules of Specific Commitments are annexed to GATS shall become original Members of the WTO.

2   The least-developed countries recognised as such by the United Nations will only be required to undertake commitments and concessions to the extent consistent with their individual development, financial and trade needs or their administrative and institutional capabilities.

Article XII – Accession

1   Any State or separate customs territory possessing full autonomy in the conduct of its external commercial relations and of the other matters provided for in this agreement and the Multilateral Trade Agreements may accede to this agreement, on terms to be agreed between it and the WTO. Such accession shall apply to this agreement and the Multilateral Trade Agreements annexed thereto.

2   Decisions on accession shall be taken by the Ministerial Conference. The Ministerial Conference shall approve the agreement on the terms of accession by a two thirds majority of the Members of the WTO.

3   Accession to a Plurilateral Trade Agreement shall be governed by the provisions of that agreement.

Article XIII – Non-application of Multilateral Trade Agreements between particular Members

1   This agreement and the Multilateral Trade Agreements in Annexes 1 and 2 shall not apply as between any Member and any other Member if either of the Members, at the time either becomes a Member, does not consent to such application.

2   Paragraph 1 may be invoked between original Members of the WTO which were contracting parties to GATT 1947 only where Article XXXV of that agreement had been invoked earlier and was effective as between those contracting parties at the time of entry into force for them of this agreement.

3   Paragraph 1 shall apply between a Member and another Member which has acceded under Article XII only if the Member not consenting to the application has so notified the Ministerial Conference before the approval of the agreement on the terms of accession by the Ministerial Conference.

4   The Ministerial Conference may review the operation of this Article in particular cases at the request of any Member and make appropriate recommendations.

5   Non-application of a Plurilateral Trade Agreement between parties to that agreement shall be governed by the provisions of that agreement.

Article XIV – Acceptance, entry into force and deposit

1   This Agreement shall be open for acceptance, by signature or otherwise, by contracting parties to GATT 1947, and the European Communities, which are eligible to become original Members of the WTO in accordance with Article XI of this agreement. Such acceptance shall apply to this agreement and the Multilateral Trade agreements annexed hereto. This agreement and the Multilateral Trade Agreements annexed hereto shall enter into force on the date determined by Ministers in accordance with para 3 of the Final Act Embodying the Results of the Uruguay Round of Multilateral Trade Negotiations and shall remain open for acceptance for a period of two years following that date unless the Ministers decide otherwise. An acceptance following the entry into force of this agreement shall enter into force on the 30th day following the date of such acceptance.

2   A Member which accepts this agreement after its entry into force shall implement those concessions and obligations in the Multilateral Trade Agreements that are to be implemented over a period of time starting with the entry into force of this agreement as if it had accepted this agreement on the date of its entry into force.

3   Until the entry into force of this agreement, the text of this agreement and the Multilateral Trade Agreements shall be deposited with the Director General to the contracting parties to GATT 1947. The Director General shall promptly furnish a certified true copy of this

agreement and the Multilateral Trade Agreements, and a notification of each acceptance thereof, to each government and the European Communities having accepted this agreement. This agreement and the Multilateral Trade Agreements, and any amendments thereto, shall, upon the entry into force of this agreement, be deposited with the Director General of the WTO.

4   The acceptance and entry into force of a Plurilateral Trade Agreement shall be governed by the provisions of that agreement. Such agreements shall be deposited with the Director General to the contracting parties to GATT 1947. Upon the entry into force of this agreement, such agreements shall be deposited with the Director General of the WTO.

Article XV – Withdrawal

1   Any Member may withdraw from this agreement. Such withdrawal shall apply both to this agreement and the Multilateral Trade Agreements and shall take effect upon the expiration of six months from the date on which written notice of withdrawal is received by the Director General of the WTO.

2   Withdrawal from a Plurilateral Trade Agreement shall be governed by the provisions of that agreement.

Article XVI – Miscellaneous provisions

1   Except as otherwise provided under this agreement or the Multilateral Trade Agreements, the WTO shall be guided by the decisions, procedures and customary practices followed by the contracting parties to GATT 1947 and the bodies established in the framework of GATT 1947.

2   To the extent practicable, the Secretariat of GATT 1947 shall become the Secretariat of the WTO, and the Director General to the contracting parties to GATT 1947, until such time as the Ministerial Conference has appointed a Director General in accordance with para 2 of Article VI of this agreement, shall serve as Director General of the WTO.

3   In the event of a conflict between the provision of this agreement and a provision of any of the Multilateral Trade Agreements, the provision of this agreement shall prevail to the extent of the conflict.

4   Each Member shall ensure the conformity of its laws, regulations and administrative procedures with its obligations as provided in the annexed agreements.

5   No reservations may be made in respect of any provision of this agreement. Reservations in respect of any of the provisions of the Multilateral Trade Agreements may only be made to the extent provided for in those agreements. Reservations in respect of a provision of a Plurilateral Trade Agreement shall be governed by the provisions of that agreement.

6   This agreement shall be registered in accordance with the provisions of Article 102 of the Charter of the United Nations.

Done at Marrakesh this fifteenth day of April one thousand nine hundred and ninety-four, in a single copy, in the English, French and Spanish languages, each text being authentic.

Explanatory notes

The terms 'country' or 'countries' as used in this agreement and the Multilateral Trade Agreements are to be understood to include any separate customs territory Member of the WTO.

In the case of a separate customs territory Member of the WTO, where an expression in this agreement and the Multilateral Trade Agreements is qualified by the term 'national', such expression shall be read as pertaining to that customs territory, unless otherwise specified.

LIST OF ANNEXES

Annex 1

Annex 1A: Multilateral Agreements on Trade in Goods

General Agreement on Tariffs and Trade 1994

Agreement on Agriculture

Agreement on the Application of Sanitary and Phytosanitary Measures

Agreement on Textiles and Clothing

Agreement on Technical Barriers to Trade

Agreement on Trade-Related Investment Measures

Agreement on Implementation of Article VI of the General Agreement on Tariffs and Trade 1994

Agreement on Implementation of Article VII of the General Agreement on Tariffs and Trade 1994

Agreement on Preshipment Inspection

Agreement on Rules of Origin

Agreement on Import Licensing Procedures

Agreement on Subsidies and Countervailing Measures

Agreement on Safeguards.

Annex 1B: General Agreement on Trade in Services and Annexes

Annex 1C: Agreement on Trade-Related Aspects of Intellectual Property Rights.

Annex 2

Understanding on Rules and Procedures Governing the Settlement of Disputes

Annex 3

Trade Policy Review Mechanism

Annex 4

Plurilateral Trade Agreements

Agreement on Trade in Civil Aircraft

Agreement on Government Procurement

International Dairy Agreement

International Bovine Meat Agreement

THE GENERAL AGREEMENT ON TARIFFS AND TRADE

The governments of the Commonwealth of Australia, the Kingdom of Belgium, the United States of Brazil, Burma, Canada, Ceylon, the Republic of Chile, the Republic of China, the Republic of Cuba, the Czechoslovak Republic, the French Republic, India, Lebanon, the Grand-Duchy of Luxemburg, the Kingdom of The Netherlands, New Zealand, the Kingdom of Norway, Pakistan, Southern Rhodesia, Syria, the Union of South Africa, the United Kingdom of Great Britain and Northern Ireland, and the United States of America:

Recognising that their relations in the field of trade and economic endeavour should be conducted with a view to raising standards of living, ensuring full employment and a large and steadily growing volume of real income and effective demand, developing the full use of the resources of the world and expanding the production and exchange of goods,

Being desirous of contributing to these objectives by entering into reciprocal and mutually advantageous arrangements directed to the substantial reduction of tariffs and other barriers to trade and to the elimination of discriminatory treatment in international commerce,

Have through their Representatives agreed as follows:

PART I

Article I – General most-favoured-nation treatment

1   With respect to customs duties and charges of any kind imposed on or in connection with importation or exportation or imposed on the international transfer of payments for imports or exports, and with respect to the method of levying such duties and charges, and with respect to all rules and formalities in connection with importation and exportation, and with respect to all matters referred to in paras 2 and 4 of Article III, any advantage, favour, privilege or immunity granted by any contracting party to any product originating in or destined for any other country shall be accorded immediately and unconditionally to the like product originating in or destined for the territories of all other contracting parties.

2   The provisions of para 1 of this article shall not require the elimination of any preferences in respect of import duties or charges which do not exceed the levels provided for in para 4 of this article and which fall within the following descriptions:

(a)   preferences in force exclusively between two or more of the territories listed in Annex A, subject to the conditions set forth therein:

(b)   preferences in force exclusively between two or more territories which on 1 July 1939, were connected by common sovereignty or relations of protection or suzerainty and which are listed in Annexes B, C and D, subject to the conditions set forth therein;

(c)   preferences in force exclusively between the USA and the Republic of Cuba;

(d)   preferences in force exclusively between neighbouring countries listed in Annexes E and F.

3   The provisions of para 1 shall not apply to preferences between the countries formerly a part of the Ottoman Empire and detached from it on 24 July 1923, provided such preferences are approved under para 5 of Article XXV, which shall be applied in this respect in the light of para 1 of Article XXIX.

4   The margin of preference on any product in respect of which a preference is permitted under para 2 of this article but is not specifically set forth as a maximum margin of preference in the appropriate Schedule annexed to this agreement shall not exceed:

(a)   in respect of duties or charges on any product described in such Schedule, the difference between the most-favoured-nation and preferential rates provided for therein; if no preferential rate is provided for, the preferential rate shall for the purposes of this paragraph be taken to be that in force on 10 April 1947, and, if no most-favoured-nation rate is provided for, the margin shall not exceed the difference between the most-favoured-nation and preferential rates existing on 10 April 1947;

(b)   in respect of duties or charges on any product not described in the appropriate Schedule, the difference between the most-favoured-nation and preferential rates existing on 10 April 1947.

In the case of the contracting parties named in Annex G. the date of 10 April 1947, referred to in sub-paras (a) and (b) of this para shall be replaced by the respective dates set forth in that Annex.

Article II – Schedules of concessions

1   (a)   Each contracting party shall accord to the commerce of the other contracting parties treatment no less favourable than that provided for in the appropriate Part of the appropriate Schedule annexed to this agreement.

(b)   The products described in Part I of the Schedule relating to any contracting party, which are the products of territories of other contracting parties, shall on their importation into the territory to which the Schedule relates, and subject to the terms, conditions or qualifications set forth in that Schedule, be exempt from ordinary customs duties in excess of those set forth and provided for therein. Such products shall also be exempt from all other duties or charges of any kind imposed on or in connection with importation in excess of those imposed on the date of this agreement or those directly and mandatorily required to be imposed thereafter by legislation in force in the importing territory on that date.

(c)   The products, described in Part II of the Schedule relating to any contracting party which are the products of territories entitled under Article I to receive preferential treatment upon importation into the territory to which the Schedule relates shall, on their importation into such territory, and subject to the terms, conditions or qualifications set forth in that Schedule, be exempt from ordinary customs duties in excess of those set forth and provided for in Part II of that Schedule. Such products shall also be exempt from all other duties or charges of any kind imposed on or in connection with importation in excess of those imposed on the date of this agreement or those directly and mandatorily required to be imposed thereafter by legislation in force in the importing territory on that date. Nothing in this article shall prevent any contracting party from maintaining its requirements existing on the date of this agreement as to the eligibility of goods for entry at preferential rates of duty.

2   Nothing in this article shall prevent any contracting party from imposing at any time on the importation of any product:

(a) a charge equivalent to an internal tax imposed consistently with the provisions of para 2 of Article III in respect of the like domestic product or in respect of an article from which the imported product has been manufactured or produced in whole or in part;

(b) any anti-dumping or countervailing duty applied consistently with the provisions of Article VI;

(c) fees or other charges commensurate with the cost of services rendered.

3   No contracting party shall alter its method of determining dutiable value or of converting currencies so as to impair the value of any of the concessions provided for in the appropriate Schedule annexed to this agreement.

4   If any contracting party establishes, maintains or authorises, formally or in effect, a monopoly of the importation of any product described in the appropriate Schedule annexed to this agreement, such monopoly shall not, except as provided for in that Schedule or as otherwise agreed between the parties which initially negotiated the concession, operate so as to afford protection on the average in excess of the amount of protection provided for in that Schedule. The provisions of this paragraph shall not limit the use by contracting parties of any form of assistance to domestic producers permitted by other provisions of this agreement.

5   If any contracting party considers that a product is not receiving from another contracting party the treatment which the first contracting party believes to have been contemplated by a concession provided for in the appropriate Schedule annexed to this agreement, it shall bring the matter directly to the attention of the other contracting party. If the latter agrees that the treatment contemplated was that claimed by the first contracting party, but declares that such treatment cannot be accorded because a court or other proper authority has ruled to the effect that the product involved cannot be classified under the tariff laws of such contracting party so as to permit the treatment contemplated in this agreement, the two contracting parties, together with any other contracting parties substantially interested, shall enter promptly into further negotiations with a view to a compensatory adjustment of the matter.

6   (a) The specific duties and charges included in the Schedules relating to contracting parties members of the International Monetary Fund, and margins of preference in specific duties and charges maintained by such contracting parties, are expressed in the appropriate currency at the par value accepted or provisionally recognised by the Fund at the date of this agreement. Accordingly, in case this par value is reduced consistently with the Articles of Agreement of the International Monetary Fund by more than 20%, such specific duties and charges and margins of preference may be adjusted to take account of such reduction; provided that the contracting, parties (ie the contracting parties acting jointly as provided for in Article XXV) concur that such adjustments will not impair the value of the concessions provided for in the appropriate Schedule or elsewhere in this agreement, due account being taken of all factors which may influence the need for, or urgency of such adjustments.

(b) Similar provisions shall apply to any contracting party not a member of the Fund, as from the date on which such contracting party becomes a member of the Fund or enters into a special exchange agreement in pursuance of Article XV.

7   The Schedules annexed to this agreement are hereby made an integral part of Part I of this agreement.

PART II

Article III – National treatment on internal taxation and regulation

1   The contracting parties recognise that internal taxes and other internal charges, and laws, regulations and requirements affecting the internal sale, offering for sale, purchase, transportation, distribution or use of products, and internal quantitative regulations requiring the mixture, processing or use of products in specified amounts or proportions, should not be applied to imported or domestic products so as to afford protection to domestic production.

2   The products of the territory of any contracting party imported into the territory of any other contracting party shall not be subject, directly or indirectly, to internal taxes or other internal charges of any kind in excess of those applied, directly or indirectly, to like domestic products. Moreover, no contracting party shall otherwise apply internal taxes or other internal charges to imported or domestic products in a manner contrary to the principles set forth in para 1.

3   With respect to any existing internal tax which is inconsistent with the provisions of para 2, but which is specifically authorised under a trade agreement, in force on 10 April 1947, in which the import duty on the taxed product is bound against increase, the contracting party imposing the tax shall be free to postpone the application of the provisions of para 2 try such tax until such time as it can obtain release from the obligations of such trade agreement in order to permit the increase of such duty to the extent necessary to compensate for the elimination of the protective element of the tax.

4   The products of the territory of any contracting party imported into the territory of any other contracting party shall be accorded treatment no less favourable than that accorded to like products of national origin in respect of all laws, regulations and requirements affecting their internal sale, offering for sale, purchase, transportation, distribution or use. The provisions of this paragraph shall not prevent the application of differential internal transportation charges which are based exclusively on the economic operation of the means of transport and not on the nationality of the product.

5   No contracting party shall establish or maintain any internal quantitative regulation relating to the mixture, processing or use of products in specified amounts or proportions which requires, directly or indirectly, that any specified amount or proportion of any product which is the subject of the regulation must be supplied from domestic sources. Moreover, no contracting party shall otherwise apply internal quantitative regulations in a manner contrary to the principles set forth in para 1.

6   The provisions of para 5 shall not apply to any internal quantitative regulation in force in the territory of any contracting party on 1 July 1939, 10 April 1947 or 24 March 1948, at the option of that contracting party; Provided that any such regulation which is contrary to the provisions of para 5 shall not be modified to the detriment of imports and shall be treated as a customs duty for the purpose of negotiation.

7   No internal quantitative regulation relating to the mixture, processing or use of products in specified amounts or proportions shall be applied in such a manner as to allocate any such amount or proportion among external sources of supply.

8   (a)   The provisions of this article shall not apply to laws, regulations or requirements governing the procurement by governmental agencies of products purchased for governmental purposes and not with a view to commercial resale or with a view to use in the production of goods for commercial sale.

     (b)   The provisions of this article shall not prevent the payment of subsidies exclusively to domestic producers, including payments to domestic producers derived from the proceeds of internal taxes or charges applied consistently with the provisions of this article and subsidies effected through governmental purchases of domestic products.

9   The contracting parties recognise that internal maximum price control measures, even though conforming to the other provisions of this article, can have effects prejudicial to the interests of contracting parties supplying imported products. Accordingly, contracting parties applying such measures shall take account of the interests of exporting contracting parties with a view to avoiding to the fullest practicable extent such prejudicial effects.

10 The provisions of this article shall not prevent any contracting party from establishing or maintaining internal quantitative regulations relating to exposed cinematograph films and meeting the requirements of Article IV.

Article IV – Special provisions relating to cinematograph films

If any contracting party establishes or maintains internal quantitative regulations relating to exposed cinematograph films, such regulations shall take the form of screen quotas which shall conform to the following requirements:

(a) screen quotas may require the exhibition of cinematograph films of national origin during a specified minimum proportion of the total screen time actually utilised, over a specified period of not less than one year, in the commercial exhibition of all films of whatever origin, and shall be computed on the basis of screen time per theatre per year or the equivalent thereof;

(b) with the exception of screen time reserved for films of national origin under a screen quota, screen time including that released by administrative action from screen time reserved for films of national origin, shall not be allocated formally or in effect among sources of supply;

(c) notwithstanding the provisions of sub-para (b) of this article, any contracting party may maintain screen quotas conforming to the requirements of sub-para (a) of this article which reserve a minimum proportion of screen time for films of a specified origin other than that of the contracting party imposing such screen quotas; provided that no such minimum proportion of screen time shall be increased above the level in effect on 10 April 1947;

(d) screen quotas shall be subject to negotiation for their limitation, liberalisation or elimination.

Article V – Freedom of transit

1 Goods (including baggage), and also vessels and other means of transport, shall be deemed to be in transit across the territory of a contracting party when the passage across such territory, with or without trans-shipment,. warehousing, breaking bulk, or change in the mode of transport, is only a portion of a complete journey beginning and terminating beyond the frontier of the contracting party across whose territory the traffic passes. Traffic of this nature is termed in this article 'traffic in transit'.

2 There shall be freedom of transit through the territory of each contracting party, via the routes most convenient for international transit, for traffic in transit to or from the territory of other contracting parties. No distinction shall be made which is based on the flag of vessels, the place of origin, departure, entry, exit or destination. or on any circumstances relating to the ownership of goods, of vessels or of other means of transport.

3 Any contracting party may require that traffic in transit through its territory be entered at the proper custom house, but, except in cases of failure to comply with applicable customs laws and regulations, such traffic coming from or going to the territory of other contracting parties shall not be subject to any unnecessary delays or restrictions and shall be exempt from customs duties and from all transit duties or other charges imposed in respect of transit, except charges for transportation or those commensurate with administrative expenses entailed by transit or with the cost of services rendered.

4 All charges and regulations imposed by contracting parties on traffic in transit to or from the territories of other contracting parties shall be reasonable, having regard to the conditions of the traffic.

5 With respect to all charges, regulations and formalities in connection with transit, each contracting party shall accord to traffic in transit to or from the territory of any other contracting party treatment no less favourable than the treatment accorded to traffic in transit to or from any third country.

6 Each contracting party shall accord to products which have been in transit through the territory of any other contracting party treatment no less favourable than that which would have been accorded to such products had they been transported from their place of origin to their destination without going through the territory of such other contracting party. Any contracting party shall, however, be free to maintain its requirements of direct consignment existing on the date of this agreement, in respect of any goods in regard to which such direct consignment is a requisite condition of eligibility for entry of the goods

at preferential rates of duty or has relation to the contracting party's prescribed method of valuation for duty purposes.

7   The provisions of this article shall not apply to the operation of aircraft in transit, but shall apply to air transit of goods (including baggage).

Article VI – anti-dumping and countervailing duties

1   The contracting parties recognise that dumping, by which products of one country are introduced into the commerce of another country at less than the normal value of the products, is to be condemned if it causes or threatens material injury to an established industry in the territory of a contracting party or materially retards the establishment of a domestic industry. For the purposes of this article, a product is to be considered as being introduced into the commerce of an importing country at less than its normal value, if the price of the product exported from one country to another:

(a)   is less than the comparable price, in the ordinary course of trade, for the like product when destined for consumption in the exporting country; or

(b)   in the absence of such domestic price, is less than either:

(i)   the highest comparable price for the like product for export to any third country in the ordinary course of trade; or

(ii)   the cost of production of the product in the country of origin plus a reasonable addition for selling cost and profit.

Due allowance shall be made in each case for differences in conditions and terms of sale, for differences in taxation, and for other differences affecting price comparability.

2   In order to offset or prevent dumping, a contracting party may levy on any dumped product an anti-dumping duty not greater in amount than the margin of dumping in respect of such product. For the purposes of this article, the margin of dumping is the price difference determined in accordance with the provisions of para 1.

3   No countervailing duty shall be levied on any product of the territory of any contracting party imported into the territory of another contracting party in excess of an amount equal to the estimated bounty or subsidy determined to have been granted, directly or indirectly, on the manufacture, production or export of such product in the country of origin or exportation, including any special subsidy to the transportation of a particular product. The term 'countervailing duty' shall be understood to mean a special duty levied for the purpose of offsetting any bounty or subsidy bestowed, directly or indirectly, upon the manufacture, production or export of any merchandise.

4   No product of the territory of any contracting party imported into the territory of any other contracting party shall he subject to anti-dumping or countervailing duty by reason of the exemption of such product from duties or taxes borne by the like product when destined for consumption in the country of origin or exportation, or by reason of the refund of such duties or taxes.

5   No product of the territory of any contracting party imported into the territory of any other contracting party shall be subject to both anti-dumping and countervailing duties to compensate for the same situation of dumping or export subsidisation.

6   (a)   No contracting party shall levy any anti-dumping or countervailing duty on the importation of any product of the territory of another contracting party unless it determines that the effect of the dumping or subsidisation, as the case may be, is such as to cause or threaten material injury to an established domestic industry, or is such as to retard materially the establishment of a domestic industry.

(b)   The contracting parties may waive the requirement of sub-para (a) of this paragraph so as to permit a contracting party to levy an anti-dumping or countervailing duty on the importation of any product for the purpose of offsetting dumping or subsidisation which causes or threatens material injury to an industry in the territory of another contracting party exporting the product concerned to the territory of the importing contracting party. The contracting parties shall waive the requirements of sub-para (a) of this paragraph, so as to permit the levying of a countervailing duty, in cases in which they find that a subsidy is causing or threatening material injury to an industry in the territory of another contracting party exporting the product concerned to the territory of the importing contracting party.

(c) In exceptional circumstances, however, where delay might cause damage which would be difficult to repair, a contracting party may levy a countervailing duty for the purpose referred to in sub-para (b) of this paragraph without the prior approval of the contracting parties; provided that such action shall be reported immediately to the contracting parties and that the countervailing duty shall be withdrawn promptly if the contracting parties disapprove.

7   A system for the stabilisation of the domestic price or of the return to domestic producers of a primary commodity, independently of the movements of export prices, which results at times in the sale of the commodity for export at a price lower than the comparable price charged for the like commodity to buyers in the domestic market, shall be presumed not to result in material injury within the meaning of para 6 if it is determined by consultation among the contracting parties substantially interested in the commodity concerned that:

(a) the system has also resulted in the sale of the commodity for export at a price higher than the comparable price charged for the like commodity to buyers in the domestic market, and

(b) the system is so operated, either because of the effective regulation of production, or otherwise, as not to stimulate exports unduly or otherwise seriously prejudice the interests of other contracting parties.

Article VII – Valuation for customs purposes

1   The contracting parties recognise the validity of the general principles of valuation set forth in the following paragraphs of this article, and they undertake to give effect to such principles, in respect of all products subject to duties or other charges or restrictions on importation and exportation based upon or regulated in any manner by value. Moreover, they shall, upon a request by another contracting party, review the operation of any of their laws or regulations relating to value for customs purposes in the light of these principles. The contracting parties may request from contracting parties reports on steps taken by them in pursuance of the provisions of this article.

2   (a) The value for customs purposes of imported merchandise should be based on the actual value of the imported merchandise on which duty is assessed, or of like merchandise, and should not be based on the value of merchandise of national origin or on arbitrary or fictitious values.

(b) 'Actual value' should be the price at which, at a time and place determined by the legislation of the country of importation such or like merchandise is sold or offered for sale in the ordinary course of trade under fully competitive conditions. To the extent to which the price of such or like merchandise is governed by the quantity in a particular transaction, the price to be considered should uniformly be related to either (i) comparable quantities, or (ii) quantities, not less favourable to importers than those in which the greater volume of the merchandise is sold in the trade between the countries of exportation and importation.

(c) When the actual value is not ascertainable in accordance with sub-para (b) of this paragraph, the value for customs purposes should be based on the nearest ascertainable equivalent of such value.

3   The value for customs purposes of any imported product should not include the amount of any internal tax, applicable within the country of origin or export, from which the imported product has been exempted or has been or will be relieved by means of refund.

4   (a) Except as otherwise provided for in this paragraph, where it is necessary for the purposes of para 2 of this article for a contracting party to convert into its own currency a price expressed in the currency of another country, the conversion rate of exchange to be used shall be based, for each currency involved, on the par value as established pursuant to the Articles of Agreement of the International Monetary Fund or on the rate of exchange recognised by the Fund. or on the par value established in accordance with a special exchange agreement entered into pursuant to Article XV of this agreement.

(b) Where no such established par value and no such recognised rate of exchange exist, the conversion rate shall reflect effectively the current value of such currency in commercial transactions.

(c) The contracting parties, in agreement with the International Monetary Fund, shall formulate rules governing the conversion by contracting parties of any foreign currency in respect of which multiple rates of exchange are maintained consistently with the Articles of Agreement of the International Monetary Fund. Any contracting party may apply such rules in respect of such foreign currencies for the purposes of para 2 of this article as an alternative to the use of par values. Until such rules are adopted by the contracting parties, any contracting party may employ, in respect of any such foreign currency, rules of conversion for the purposes of para 2 of this article which are designed to reflect effectively the value of such foreign currency in commercial transactions.

(d) Nothing in this paragraph shall be construed to require any contracting party to alter the method of converting currencies for customs purposes which is applicable in its territory on the date of this agreement, if such alteration would have the effect of increasing generally the amounts of duty payable.

5   The bases and methods for determining the value of products subject to duties or other charges or restrictions based upon or regulated in any manner by value should be stable and should be given sufficient publicity to enable traders to estimate, with a reasonable degree of certainty, the value for customs purposes.

Article VIII – Fees and formalities connected with importation and exportation

1   (a) All fees and charges of whatever character (other than import and export duties and other than taxes within the purview of Article III) imposed by contracting parties on or in connection with importation or exportation shall be limited in amount to the approximate cost of services rendered and shall not represent an indirect protection to domestic products or a taxation of imports or exports for fiscal purposes.

(b) The contracting parties recognise the need for reducing the number and diversity of fees and charges referred to in sub-para (a).

(c) The contracting parties also recognise the need for minimising the incidence and complexity of import and export formalities and for decreasing and simplifying import and export documentation requirements.

2   A contracting party shall, upon request by another contracting party or by the contracting parties, review the operation of its laws and regulations in the light of the provisions of this article.

3   No contracting party shall impose substantial penalties for minor breaches of customs regulations or procedural requirements. In particular, no penalty in respect of any omission or mistake in customs documentation which is easily rectifiable and obviously made without fraudulent intent or gross negligence shall be greater than necessary to serve merely as a warning.

4   The provisions of this article shall extend to fees, charges, formalities and requirements imposed by governmental authorities in connection with importation and exportation, including those relating to: (a) consular transactions, such as consular invoices and certificates; (b) quantitative restrictions; (c) licensing; (d) exchange control; (e) statistical services; (f) documents, documentation and certification; (g) analysis and inspection; and (h) quarantine, sanitation and fumigation.

Article IX – Marks of origin

1   Each contracting party shall accord to the products of the territories of other contracting parties treatment with regard to marking requirements no less favourable than the treatment accorded to like products of any third country.

2   The contracting parties recognise that, in adopting and enforcing laws and regulations relating to marks of origin, the difficulties and inconveniences which such measures may cause to the commerce and industry of exporting countries should be reduced to a minimum, due regard being had to the necessity of protecting consumers against fraudulent or misleading indications.

3   Whenever it is administratively practicable to do so, contracting parties should permit required marks of origin to be affixed at the time of importation.

4   The laws and regulations of contracting parties relating to the marking of imported products shall be such as to permit compliance without seriously damaging the products, or materially reducing their value, or unreasonably increasing their cost.

5   As a general rule, no special duty or penalty should be imposed by any contracting party for failure to comply with marking requirements prior to importation unless corrective marking is unreasonably delayed or deceptive marks have been affixed or the required marking has been intentionally omitted.

6   The contracting parties shall cooperate with each other with a view to preventing the use of trade names in such manner as to misrepresent the true origin of a product, to the detriment of such distinctive regional or geographical names of products of the territory of a contracting party as are protected by its legislation. Each contracting party shall accord full and sympathetic consideration to such requests or representations as may be made by any other contracting party regarding the application of the undertaking set forth in the preceding sentence to names of products which have been communicated to it by the other contracting party.

Article X – Publication and administration of trade regulations

1   Laws, regulations, judicial decisions and administrative rulings of general application, made effective by any contracting party, pertaining to the classification or the valuation of products for customs purposes, or to rates of duty, taxes or other charges, or to requirements, restrictions or prohibitions on imports or exports or on the transfer of payments therefore, or affecting their sale, distribution, transportation, insurance, warehousing, inspection, exhibition, processing, mixing or other use, shall be published promptly in such a manner as to enable governments and traders to become acquainted with them. Agreements affecting international trade policy which are in force between the government or a governmental agency of any contracting party and the government or governmental agency of any other contracting party shall also be published. The provisions of this paragraph shall not require any contracting party to disclose confidential information which would impede law enforcement or otherwise be contrary to the public interest or would prejudice the legitimate commercial interests of particular enterprises, public or private.

2   No measure of general application taken by any contracting party effecting an advance in a rate of duty or other charge on imports under an established and uniform practice, or imposing a new or more burdensome requirement, restriction or prohibition on imports, or on the transfer of payments, therefore, shall be enforced before such measure has been officially published.

3   (a)   Each contracting party shall administer in a uniform, impartial and reasonable manner all its laws, regulations, decisions and rulings of the kind described in para 1 of this article.

    (b)   Each contracting party shall maintain, or institute as soon as practicable, judicial, arbitral or administrative tribunals or procedures for the purpose, *inter alia*, of the prompt review and correction of administrative action relating to customs matters. Such tribunals or procedures shall be independent of the agencies entrusted with administrative enforcement and their decisions shall be implemented by, and shall govern the practice of, such agencies unless an appeal is lodged with a court or tribunal of superior jurisdiction within the time prescribed for appeals to be lodged by importers; provided that the central administration of such agency may take steps to obtain a review of the matter in another proceeding if there is good cause to believe that the decision is inconsistent with established principles of law or the actual facts.

    (c)   The provisions of sub-para (b) of this paragraph shall not require the elimination or substitution of procedures in force in the territory of a contracting party on the date of this agreement which in fact provide for an objective and impartial review of administrative action even though such procedures are not fully or formally independent of the agencies entrusted with administrative enforcement. Any contracting party employing such procedures shall, upon request, furnish the contracting parties with full information thereon in order that they may determine whether such procedures conform to the requirements of this sub-paragraph.

Article XI – General elimination of quantitative restrictions

1   No prohibitions or restrictions other than duties, taxes or other charges whether made effective through quotas, import or export licences or other measures, shall be instituted or maintained by any contracting party on the importation of any product of the territory of any other contracting party or on the exportation or sale for export of any product destined for the territory of any other contracting party.

2   The provisions of para 1 of this article shall not extend to the following:

(a)   export prohibitions or restrictions temporarily applied to prevent or relieve critical shortages of foodstuffs or other products essential to the exporting contracting party;

(b)   import and export prohibitions or restrictions necessary to the application of standards or regulations for the classification, grading or marketing of commodities in international trade;

(c)   Import restrictions on any agricultural or fisheries product. imported in any form, necessary to the enforcement of governmental measures which operate:

(i)   to restrict the quantities of the like domestic product permitted to be marketed or produced, or, if there is no substantial domestic production of the like product, of a domestic product for which the imported product can be directly substituted; or

(ii)   to remove a temporary surplus of the like domestic product, or, if there is no substantial domestic production of the like product, of a domestic product for which the imported product can be directly substituted, by making the surplus available to certain groups of domestic consumers free of charge or at prices below the current market level; or

(iii)   to restrict the quantities permitted to be produced of any animal product the production of which is directly dependent, wholly or mainly, on the imported commodity, if the domestic production of that commodity is relatively negligible.

Any contracting party applying restrictions on the importation of any product pursuant to sub-para (c) of this paragraph shall give public notice of the total quantity or value of the product permitted to be imported during a specified future period and of any change in such quantity or value. Moreover, any restrictions applied under (i) above shall not be such as will reduce the total of imports relative to the total of domestic production, as compared with the proportion which might reasonably be expected to rule between the two in the absence of restrictions. In determining this proportion, the contracting party shall pay due regard to the proportion prevailing during a previous representative period and to any special factors. which may have affected or may be affecting the trade in the product concerned.

Article XII – Restrictions to safeguard the balance of payments

1   Notwithstanding the provisions of para 1 of Article XI, any contracting party, in order to safeguard its external financial position and its balance of payments, may restrict the quantity or value of merchandise permitted to be imported, subject to the provisions of the following paragraphs of this article.

2   (a)   Import restrictions instituted, maintained or intensified by a contracting party under this article shall not exceed those necessary:

(i)   to forestall the imminent threat of, or to stop, a serious decline in its monetary reserves; or

(ii)   in the case of a contracting party with very low monetary reserves, to achieve a reasonable rate of increase in its reserves.

Due regard shall be paid in either case to any special factors which may be affecting the reserves of such contracting party or its need for reserves, including, where special external credits or other resources are available to it, the need to provide for the appropriate use of such credits or resources.

(b)   contracting parties applying restrictions under sub-para (a) of this paragraph shall progressively relax them as such conditions improve, maintaining them only to the extent that the conditions specified in that sub-paragraph still justify their application. They shall eliminate the restrictions when conditions would no longer justify their institution or maintenance under that sub-paragraph.

3   (a) Contracting parties undertake, in carrying out their domestic policies, to pay due regard to the need for maintaining or restoring equilibrium in their balance of payments on a sound and lasting basis and to the desirability of avoiding an uneconomic employment of productive resources. They recognise that, in order to achieve these ends, it is desirable so far as possible to adopt measures which expand rather than contract international trade.

    (b) contracting parties applying restrictions under this article may determine the incidence of the restrictions on imports of different products or classes of products in such a way as to give priority to the importation of those products which are more essential.

    (c) contracting parties applying restrictions under this article undertake:

        (i)   to avoid unnecessary damage to the commercial or economic interests of any other contracting party;

        (ii) not to apply restrictions so as to prevent unreasonably the importation of any description of goods in minimum commercial quantities the exclusion of which would impair regular channels of trade; and

        (iii) not to apply restrictions which would prevent the importation of commercial samples or prevent compliance with patent, trade mark, copyright, or similar procedures.

    (d) The contracting parties recognise that, as a result of domestic policies directed towards the achievement and maintenance of full and productive employment or towards the development of economic resources, a contracting party may experience a high level of demand for imports involving a threat to its monetary reserves of the sort referred to in para 2(a) of this article. Accordingly, a contracting party otherwise complying with the provisions of this article shall not be required to withdraw or modify restrictions on the ground that a change in those policies would render unnecessary restrictions which it is applying under this article.

4   (a) Any contracting party applying new restrictions or raising the general level of its existing restrictions by a substantial intensification of the measures applied under this article shall immediately, after instituting or intensifying such restrictions (or, in circumstances in which prior consultation is practicable, before doing so) consult with the contracting parties as to the nature of its balance of payments difficulties, alternative corrective measures which may be available, and the possible effect of the restrictions on the economies of other contracting parties.

    (b) On a date to be determined by them, the contracting parties shall review all restrictions still applied under this article on that date. Beginning one year after that date, contracting parties applying import restrictions under this article shall enter into consultations of the type provided for in sub-para (a) of this paragraph with the contracting parties annually.

    (c) (i) If, in the course of consultations with a contracting party under sub-para (a) or (b) above, the contracting parties find that the restrictions are not consistent with the provisions of this article or with those of Article XIII (subject to the provisions of Article XIV), they shall indicate the nature of the inconsistency and may advise that the restrictions be suitably modified.

        (ii) If, however, as a result of the consultations, the contracting parties determine that the restrictions are being applied in a manner involving an inconsistency of a serious nature with the provisions of this article or with those of Article XIII (subject to the provisions of Article XIV) and that damage to the trade of any contracting party is caused or threatened thereby, they shall so inform the contracting party applying the restrictions and shall make appropriate recommendations for securing conformity with such provisions within a specified period of time. If such contracting party does not comply with these recommendations within the specified period, the contracting parties may release any contracting party the trade of which is adversely affected by the restrictions from such obligations under this agreement towards the contracting party applying the restrictions as they determine to be appropriate in the circumstances.

(d) The contracting parties shall invite any contracting party which is applying restrictions under this article to enter into consultations with them at the request of any contracting party which can establish a *prima facie* case that the restrictions are inconsistent with the provisions of this article or with those of Article XIII (subject to the provisions of Article XIV) and that its trade is adversely affected thereby. However, no such invitation shall be issued unless the contracting parties have ascertained that direct discussions between the contracting parties concerned have not been successful. If, as a result of the consultations with the contracting parties, no agreement is reached and they determine that the restrictions are being applied inconsistently with such provisions, and that damage to the trade of the contracting party initiating the procedure is caused or threatened thereby, they shall recommend the withdrawal or modification of the restrictions. If the restrictions are not withdrawn or modified within such time as the contracting parties may prescribe, they may release the contracting party initiating the procedure from such obligations under this agreement towards the contracting party applying the restrictions as they determine to be appropriate in the circumstances.

(e) In proceeding under this paragraph, the contracting parties shall have due regard to any special external factors adversely affecting the export trade of the contracting party applying restrictions.

(f) Determinations under this paragraph shall be rendered expeditiously and, if possible, within 60 days of the initiation of the consultations.

5   If there is a persistent and widespread application of import restrictions under this article, indicating the existence of a general disequilibrium which is restricting international trade, the contracting parties shall initiate discussions to consider whether other measures might be taken, either by those contracting parties the balances of payments of which are under pressure or by those the balances of payments of which are tending to be exceptionally favourable, or by any appropriate intergovernmental organisation, to remove the underlying causes of the disequilibrium. On the invitation of the contracting parties, contracting parties shall participate in such discussions.

Article XIII – Non-discriminatory administration of quantitative restrictions

1   No prohibition or restriction shall be applied by any contracting party on the importation of any product of the territory of any other contracting party or on the exportation of any product destined for the territory of any other contracting party, unless the importation of the like product of all third countries or the exportation of the like product of all third countries is similarly prohibited or restricted.

2   In applying import restrictions to any product, contracting parties shall aim at a distribution of trade in such product approaching as closely as possible the shares which the various contracting parties might be expected to obtain in the absence of such restrictions, and to this end shall observe the following provisions:

(a) Wherever practicable, quotas representing the total amount of permitted imports (whether allocated among supplying countries or not) shall be fixed, and notice given of their amount in accordance with para 3(b) of this article.

(b) In cases in which quotas are not practicable, the restrictions may be applied by means of import licences or permits without a quota.

(c) Contracting parties shall not, except for purposes of operating quotas allocated in accordance with sub-para (d) of this paragraph, require that import licences or permits be utilised for the importation of the product concerned from a particular country or source.

(d) In cases in which a quota is allocated among supplying countries, the contracting party applying the restrictions may seek agreement with respect to the allocation of shares in the quota with all other contracting parties having a substantial interest in supplying the product concerned. In cases in which this method is not reasonably practicable, the contracting party concerned shall allot to contracting parties having a substantial interest in supplying the product shares based upon the proportions, supplied by such contracting parties during a previous representative period, of the total quantity or value of imports of the product, due account being taken of any special factors which may have affected or may be affecting the trade in the product.

No conditions or formalities shall be imposed which would prevent any contracting party from utilising fully the share of any such total quantity or value which has been allotted to it, subject to importation being made within any prescribed period to which the quota may relate.

3   (a) In cases in which import licences are issued in connection with import restrictions, the contracting party applying the restrictions shall provide, upon the request of any contracting party having an interest in the trade in the product concerned, all relevant information concerning the administration of the restrictions, the import licences granted over a recent period and the distribution of such licences among supplying countries; provided that there shall be no obligation to supply information as to the names of importing or supplying enterprises.

(b) In the case of import restrictions involving the fixing of quotas, the contracting party applying the restrictions shall give public notice of the total quantity or value of the product or products which will be permitted to be imported during a specified future period and of any change in such quantity or value. Any supplies of the product in question which were *en route* at the time at which public notice was given shall not be excluded from entry: provided that they may be counted so far as practicable, against the quantity permitted to be imported in the period in question, and also, where necessary, against the quantities permitted to be imported in the next following period or periods; and provided further that if any contracting party customarily exempts from such restrictions products entered for consumption or withdrawn from warehouse for consumption during a period of 30 days after the day of such public notice, such practice shall be considered full compliance with this sub-paragraph.

(c) In the case of quotas allocated among supplying countries, the contracting party applying the restrictions shall promptly inform all other contracting parties having an interest in supplying the product concerned of the shares in the quota currently allocated, by quantity or value, to the various supplying countries and shall give public notice thereof.

With regard to restrictions applied in accordance with para 2(d) of this article or under para 2(c) of Article XI, the selection of a representative period for any product and the appraisal of any special factors affecting the trade in the product shall be made initially by the contracting party applying the restriction; provided that such contracting party shall, upon the request of any other contracting party having a substantial interest in supplying that product or upon the request of the contracting parties, consult promptly with the other contracting party or the contracting parties regarding the need for an adjustment of the proportion determined or of the base period selected. or for the reappraisal of the special factors involved, or for the elimination of conditions, formalities or any other provisions established unilaterally relating to the allocation of an adequate quota or its unrestricted utilisation.

5   The provisions of this article shall apply to any tariff quota instituted or maintained by any contracting party, and, in so far as applicable, the principles of this article shall also extend to export restrictions.

Article XIV – exceptions to the rule of non-discrimination

1   A contracting party which applies restrictions under Article XII or under section B of Article XVIII may, in the application of such restrictions, deviate from the provisions of Article XIII in a manner having equivalent effect to restrictions on payments and transfers for current international transactions which that contracting party may at that time apply under Article VIII or XIV of the Articles of Agreement of the International Monetary Fund, or under analogous provisions of a special exchange agreement entered into pursuant to para 6 of Article XV.

2   A contracting party which is applying import restrictions under Article XII or under section B of Article XVIII may, with the consent of the contracting parties, temporarily deviate from the provisions of Article XIII in respect of a small part of its external trade where the benefits to the contracting party or contracting parties concerned substantially outweigh any injury which may result to the trade of other contracting parties.

3   The provisions of Article XIII shall not preclude a group of territories having a common quota in the International Monetary Fund from applying against imports from other

countries, but not among themselves, restrictions in accordance with the provisions of Article XII or of section B of Article XVIII on condition that such restrictions are in all other respects consistent with the provisions of Article XIII.

4   A contracting party applying import restrictions under Article XII or under section B of Article XVIII shall not be precluded by Articles XI to XV or section B of Article XVIII of this agreement from applying measures to direct its exports in such a manner as to increase its earnings of currencies which it can use without deviation from the provisions of Article XIII.

5   A contracting party shall not be precluded by Articles XI to XV, inclusive, or by section B of Article XVIII, of this agreement from applying quantitative restrictions:

   (a) having equivalent effect or exchange restrictions authorised under section 3 (b) of Article VII of the Articles of Agreement of the International Monetary Fund; or

   (b) under the preferential arrangements provided for in Annex A of this Agreement, pending the outcome of the negotiations referred to therein.

Article XV – Exchange arrangements

1   The contracting parties shall seek co-operation with the International Monetary Fund to the end that the contracting parties and the Fund may pursue a co-ordinated policy with regard to exchange questions within the jurisdiction of the Fund and questions of quantitative restrictions and other trade measures within the jurisdiction of the contracting parties.

2   In all cases in which the contracting parties are called upon to consider or deal with problems concerning monetary reserves, balances of payments or foreign exchange arrangements, they shall consult fully with the International Monetary Fund. In such consultations, the contracting parties shall accept all findings of statistical and other facts presented by the Fund relating to foreign exchange, monetary reserves and balances of payments, and shall accept the determination of the Fund as to whether action by a contracting party in exchange matters is in accordance with the Articles of Agreement of the International Monetary Fund, or with the terms of a special exchange agreement between that contracting party and the contracting parties. The contracting parties, in reaching their final decision in cases involving the criteria set forth in para 2(a) of Article XII or in para 9 of Article XVIII, shall accept the determination of the Fund as to what constitutes a serious decline in the contracting party's monetary reserves, a very low level of its monetary reserves or a reasonable rate of increase in its monetary reserves, and as to the financial aspects of other matters covered in consultation in such cases.

3   The contracting parties shall seek agreement with the Fund regarding procedures for consultation under para 2 of this article.

4   Contracting parties shall not, by exchange action frustrate the intent of the provisions of this agreement, nor, by trade action, the intent of the provisions of the Articles of Agreement of the International Monetary Fund.

5   If the contracting parties consider, at any time, that exchange restrictions on payments and transfers in connection with imports are being applied by a contracting party in a manner inconsistent with the exceptions provided for in this agreement for quantitative restrictions, they shall report thereon to the Fund.

6   Any contracting party which is not a member of the Fund shall. within a time to be determined by the contracting parties after consultation with the Fund, become a member of the Fund, or, failing that, enter into a special exchange agreement with the contracting parties. A contracting party which ceases to be a member of the Fund shall forthwith enter into a special exchange agreement with the contracting parties. Any special exchange agreement entered into by a contracting party under this paragraph shall thereupon become part of its obligations under this agreement.

7   (a) A special exchange agreement between a contracting party and the contracting parties under para 6 of this article shall provide to the satisfaction of the contracting parties that the objectives of this agreement will not be frustrated as a result of action in exchange matters by the contracting party in question.

   (b) The terms of any such agreement shall not impose obligations on the contracting party in exchange matters generally more restrictive than those imposed by the Articles of Agreement of the International Monetary Fund on members of the Fund.

8   A contracting party which is not a member of the Fund shall furnish such information within the general scope of section 5 of Article VIII of the Articles of Agreement of the International Monetary Fund as the contracting parties may require in order to carry out their functions under this agreement.

9   Nothing in this agreement shall preclude:

(a) the use by a contracting party of exchange controls or exchange restrictions in accordance with the Articles of Agreement of the International Monetary Fund or with that contracting party's special exchange agreement with the contracting parties; or

(b) the use by a contracting party of restrictions or controls on imports or exports the sole effect of which, additional to the effects permitted under Articles XI XII, XIII and XIV, is to make effective such exchange controls or exchange restrictions.

Article XVI – Subsidies

Section A – Subsidies in general

1   If any contracting party grants or maintains any subsidy, including any form of income or price support, which operates directly or indirectly to increase exports of any product from, or to reduce imports of any product into, its territory, it shall notify the contracting parties in writing of the extent and nature of the subsidisation, of the estimated effect of the subsidisation on the quantity of the affected product or products imported into or exported from its territory and of the circumstances making the subsidisation necessary. In any case in which it is determined that serious prejudice to the interests of any other contracting party is caused or threatened by any such subsidisation, the contracting party granting the subsidy shall, upon request, discuss with the other contracting party or parties concerned, or with the contracting parties, the possibility of limiting the subsidisation.

Section B – Additional provisions on export subsidies

2   The contracting parties recognise that the granting by a contracting party of a subsidy on the export of any product may have harmful effects for other contracting parties, both importing and exporting, may cause undue disturbance to their normal commercial interests, and may hinder the achievement of the objectives of this Agreement.

3   Accordingly, contracting parties should seek to avoid the use of subsidies on the export of primary products. If, however, a contracting party grants directly or indirectly any form of subsidy which operates to increase the export of any primary product from its territory, such subsidy shall not be applied in a manner which results in that contracting party having more than an equitable share of world export trade in that product, account being taken of the shares of the contracting parties in such trade in the product during a previous representative period, and any special factors which may have affected or may be affecting such trade in the product.

4   Further, as from 1 January 1958 or the earliest practicable date thereafter, contracting parties shall cease to grant either directly or indirectly any form of subsidy on the export of any product other than a primary product which subsidy results in the sale of such product for export at a price lower than the comparable price charged for the like product to buyers in the domestic market. Until 31 December 1957, no contracting party shall extend the scope of any such subsidisation beyond that existing on 1 January 1955 by the introduction of new, or the extension of existing, subsidies.

5   The contracting parties shall review the operation of the provisions of this article from time to time with a view to examining its effectiveness, in the light of actual experience, in promoting the objectives of this Agreement and avoiding subsidisation seriously prejudicial to the trade or interests of contracting parties.

Article XVII – State trading enterprises

1   (a) Each contracting party undertakes that if it establishes or maintains a State enterprise, wherever located, or grants to any enterprise, formally or in effect, exclusive or special privileges, such enterprise shall, in its purchases or sales involving either imports or exports, act in a manner consistent with the general principles of non-discriminatory treatment prescribed in this Agreement for governmental measures affecting imports or exports by private traders.

(b)   The provisions of sub-para (a) of this paragraph shall be understood to require that such enterprises shall, having due regard to the other provisions of this agreement, make any such purchases or sales solely in accordance with commercial considerations, including price, quality, availability, marketability transportation and other conditions of purchase or sale, and shall afford the enterprises of the other contracting parties adequate opportunity, in accordance with customary business practice, to compete for participation in such purchases or sales.

(c)   No contracting party shall prevent any enterprise (whether or not an enterprise described in sub-para (a) of this paragraph) under its jurisdiction from acting in accordance with the principles of sub-paras (a) and (b) of this paragraph.

2   The provisions of para 1 of this article shall not apply to imports of products for immediate or ultimate consumption in governmental use and not otherwise for resale or use in the production of goods for sale. With respect to such imports, each contracting party shall accord to the trade of the other contracting parties fair and equitable treatment.

3   The contracting parties recognise that enterprises of the kind described in para 1(a) of this article might be operated so as to create serious obstacles to trade; thus negotiations on a reciprocal and mutually advantageous basis designed to limit or reduce such obstacles are of importance to the expansion of international trade.

4   (a)   Contracting parties shall notify the contracting parties of the products which are imported into or exported from their territories by enterprises of the kind described in para 1(a) of this article.

(b)   A contracting party establishing, maintaining or authorising an import monopoly of a product, which is not the subject of a concession under Article II shall, on the request of another contracting party having a substantial trade in the product concerned, inform the contracting parties of the import mark-up on the product during a recent representative period, or, when it is not possible to do so, of the price charged on the resale of the product.

(c)   The contracting parties may, at the request of a contracting party which has reason to believe that its interests under this agreement are being adversely affected by the operations of an enterprise of the kind described in para 1(a), request the contracting party establishing, maintaining or authorising such enterprise to supply information about its operations related to the carrying out of the provisions of this agreement.

(d)   The provisions of this paragraph shall not require any contracting party to disclose confidential information which would impede law enforcement or otherwise be contrary to the public interest or would prejudice the legitimate commercial interests of particular enterprises.

Article XVIII – Governmental assistance to economic development

1   The contracting parties recognise that the attainment of the objectives of this agreement will be facilitated by the progressive development of their economies, particularly of those contracting parties the economies of which can only support low standards of living and are in the early stages of development.

2   The contracting parties recognise further that it may be necessary for those contracting parties, in order to implement programmes and policies of economic development designed to raise the general standard of living of their people, to take protective or other measures affecting imports, and that such measures are justified in so far as they facilitate the attainment of the objectives of this agreement. They agree, therefore, that those contracting parties should enjoy additional facilities to enable them:

(a)   to maintain sufficient flexibility in their tariff structure to be able to grant the tariff protection required for the establishment of a particular industry; and

(b)   to apply quantitative restrictions for balance of payments purposes in a manner which takes full account of the continued high level of demand for imports likely to be generated by their programmes of economic development.

3   The contracting parties recognise finally that, with those additional facilities which are provided for in sections A and B of this article, the provisions of this agreement would normally be sufficient to enable contracting parties to meet the requirements of their economic development. They agree, however, that there may be circumstances where no

measure consistent with those provisions is practicable to permit a contracting party in the process of economic development to grant the governmental assistance required to promote the establishment of particular industries with a view to raising the general standard of living of its people. Special procedures are laid down in sections C and D of this article to deal with those cases.

4   (a) Consequently, a contracting party the economy of which can only support low standards of living and is in the early stages of development shall be free to deviate temporarily from the provisions of the other articles of this agreement, as provided in sections A, B and C of this article.

(b) A contracting party the economy of which is in the process of development but which does not come within the scope of sub-para (a) above, may submit applications to the contracting parties under section D of this article.

5   The contracting parties recognise that the export earnings of contracting parties, the economies of which are of the type described in para 4(a) and (b) above and which depend on exports of a small number of primary commodities, may be seriously reduced by a decline in the sale of such commodities. Accordingly, when the exports of primary commodities by such a contracting party are seriously affected by measures taken by another contracting party, it may have resort to the consultation provisions of Article XXII of this agreement.

6   The contracting parties shall review annually all measures applied pursuant to the provisions of sections C and D of this article.

Section A

7   (a) If a contracting party coming within the scope of para 4(a) of this article considers it desirable, in order to promote the establishment of a particular industry with a view to raising the general standard of living of its people, to modify or withdraw a concession included in the appropriate Schedule annexed to this agreement, it shall notify the contracting parties to this effect and enter into negotiations with any contracting party with which such concession was initially negotiated, and with any other contracting party determined by the contracting parties to have a substantial interest therein. If agreement is reached between such contracting parties concerned, they shall be free to modify or withdraw concessions under the appropriate Schedules to this agreement in order to give effect to such agreement, including any compensatory adjustments involved.

(b) If agreement is not reached within 60 days after the notification provided for in sub-para (a) above, the contracting party which proposes to modify or withdraw the concession may refer the matter to the contracting parties, which shall promptly examine it. If they find that the contracting party which proposes to modify or withdraw the concession has made every effort to reach an agreement and that the compensatory adjustment offered by it is adequate, that contracting party shall be free to modify or withdraw the concession if, at the same time, it gives effect to the compensatory adjustment. If the contracting parties do not find that the compensation offered by a contracting party proposing to modify or withdraw the concession is adequate, but find that it has made every reasonable effort to offer adequate compensation, that contracting party shall be free to proceed with such modification or withdrawal. If such action is taken, any other contracting party referred to in sub-para (a) above shall be free to modify or withdraw substantially equivalent concessions initially negotiated with the contracting party which has taken the action.

Section B

8   The contracting parties recognise that contracting parties coming within the scope of para 4(a) of this article tend, when they are in rapid process of development, to experience balance of payments difficulties arising mainly from efforts to expand their internal markets as well as from the instability in their terms of trade.

9   In order to safeguard its external financial position and to ensure a level of reserves adequate for the implementation of its programme of economic development, a contracting party coming within the scope of para 4(a) of this article may, subject to the provisions of paras 10–12, control the general level of its imports by restricting the

quantity or value of merchandise permitted to be imported; provided that the import restrictions instituted, maintained or intensified shall not exceed those necessary:

(a) to forestall the threat of, or to stop, a serious decline in its monetary reserves; or

(b) in the case of a contracting party with inadequate monetary reserves, to achieve a reasonable rate of increase in its reserves.

Due regard shall he paid in either case to any special factors which may be affecting the reserves of the contracting party or its need for reserves, including, where special external credits or other resources are available to it, the need to provide for the appropriate use of such credits or resources.

10 In applying these restrictions, the contracting party may determine their incidence on imports of different products or classes of products in such a way as to give priority to the importation of those products which are more essential in the light of its policy of economic development; provided that the restrictions are so applied as to avoid unnecessary damage to the commercial or economic interests of any other contracting party and not to prevent unreasonably the importation of any description of goods in minimum commercial quantities the exclusion of which would impair regular channels of trade; and provided further that the restrictions are not so applied as to prevent the importation of commercial samples or to prevent compliance with patent, trade mark, copyright or similar procedures.

11 In carrying out its domestic policies, the contracting party concerned shall pay due regard to the need for restoring equilibrium in its balance of payments on a sound and lasting basis and to the desirability of assuring an economic employment of productive resources. It shall progressively relax any restrictions applied under this section as conditions improve maintaining them only to the extent necessary under the terms of para 9 of this article and shall eliminate them when conditions no longer justify such maintenance; provided that no contracting party shall be required to withdraw or modify restrictions on the ground that a change in its development policy would render unnecessary the restrictions which it is applying under this section.

12 (a) Any contracting party applying new restrictions or raising the general level of its existing restrictions by a substantial intensification of the measures applied under this section, shall immediately after instituting or intensifying such restrictions (or, in circumstances in which prior consultation is practicable, before doing so) consult with the contracting parties as to the nature of its balance of payments difficulties, alternative corrective measures which may be available, and the possible effect of the restrictions on the economies of other contracting parties.

(b) On a date to be determined by them, the contracting parties shall review all restrictions still applied under this section on that date. Beginning two years after that date, contracting parties applying restrictions under this section shall enter into consultations of the type provided for in sub-para (a) above with the contracting parties at intervals of approximately, but not less than, two years according to a programme to be drawn up each year by the contracting parties; provided that no consultation under this sub-paragraph shall take place within two years after the conclusion of a consultation of a general nature under any other provision of this paragraph.

(c) (i) If, in the course of consultations with a contracting party under sub-para (a) or (b) of this paragraph, the contracting parties find that the restrictions are not consistent with the provisions of this section or with those of Article XIII (subject to the provisions of Article XIV), they shall indicate the nature of the inconsistency and may advise that the restrictions be suitably modified.

(ii) If, however, as a result of the consultations, the contracting parties determine that the restrictions are being applied in a manner involving an inconsistency of a serious nature with the provisions of this section or with those of Article XIII (subject to the provisions of Article XIV) and that damage to the trade of any contracting party is caused or threatened thereby, they shall so inform the contracting party applying the restrictions anti shall make appropriate recommendations for securing conformity with such provisions within a specified period. If such contracting party does not comply with these recommendations within the specified period, the contracting parties may release any contracting party the trade of which is adversely affected by the restrictions from such obligations under this agreement towards the contracting party applying the restrictions as they determine to be appropriate in the circumstances.

(d) The contracting parties shall invite any contracting party which is applying restrictions under this section to enter into consultations with them at the request of any contracting party which can establish a *prima facie* case that the restrictions are inconsistent with the provisions of this section or with those of Article XIII (subject to the provisions of Article XIV) and that its trade is adversely affected thereby. However, no such invitation shall be issued unless the contracting parties have ascertained that direct discussions between the contracting parties concerned have not been successful. If, as a result of the consultations with the contracting parties no agreement is reached and they determine that the restrictions are being applied inconsistently with such provisions, and that damage to the trade of the contracting party initiating the procedure is caused or threatened thereby, they shall recommend the withdrawal or modification of the restrictions. If the restrictions are not withdrawn or modified within such time as the contracting parties may prescribe, they may release the contracting party initiating the procedure from such obligations under this agreement towards the contracting party applying the restrictions as they determine to be appropriate in the circumstances.

(e) If a contracting party against which action has been taken in accordance with the last sentence of sub-para (c)(ii) or (d) of this paragraph, finds that the release of obligations authorised by the contracting parties adversely affects the operation of its programme and policy of economic development, it shall be free, not later than 60 days after such action is taken, to give written notice to the Executive Secretary to the contracting parties of its intention to withdraw from this agreement and such withdrawal shall take effect on the 60th day following the day on which the notice is received by him.

(f) In proceeding under this paragraph the contracting parties shall have due regard to the factors referred to in para 2 of this article. Determinations under this paragraph shall be rendered expeditiously and, if possible within 60 days of the initiation of the consultations.

Section C

13 If a contracting party coming within the scope of para 4(a) of this article finds that governmental assistance is required to promote the establishment of a particular industry with a view to raising the general standard of living of its people, but that no measure consistent with the other provisions of this agreement is practicable to achieve that objective, it may have recourse to the provisions and procedures set out in this section.

14 The contracting party concerned shall notify the contracting parties of the special difficulties which it meets in the achievement of the objective outlined in para 13 of this article and shall indicate the specific measure affecting imports which it proposes to introduce in order to remedy these difficulties. It shall not introduce that measure before the expiration of the time limit laid down in para 15 or 17, as the case may be, or if the measure affects imports of a product which is the subject of a concession included in the appropriate Schedule annexed to this agreement, unless it has secured the concurrence of the contracting parties in accordance with the provisions of paragraph; provided that, if the industry receiving assistance has already started production, the contracting party may, after informing the contracting parties, take such measures as may be necessary to prevent, during that period, imports of the product or products concerned from increasing substantially above a normal level.

15 If, within 30 days of the notification of the measure, the contracting parties do not request the contracting party concerned to consult with them, that contracting party shall be free to deviate from the relevant provisions of the other articles of this agreement to the extent necessary to apply the proposed measure.

16 If it is requested by the contracting parties to so, the contracting party shall consult with them as to the purpose of the proposed measure, as to alternative measures which may be available under this agreement, and as to the possible effect of the measure proposed on the commercial and economic interests of other contracting parties. If, as a result of such

consultation, the contracting parties agree that there is no measure consistent with the other provisions of this agreement which is practicable in order to achieve the objective outlined in para 13 of this article, and concur in the proposed measure, the contracting party concerned shall be released from its obligations under the relevant provisions of the other articles of this agreement to the extent necessary to apply that measure.

17 If, within 90 days after the date of the notification of the proposed measure under para 14 of this article, the contracting parties have not concurred in such measure. the contracting party concerned may introduce the measure proposed after informing the contracting parties.

18 If the proposed measure affects a product which is the subject of a concession included in the appropriate Schedule annexed to this agreement, the contracting party concerned shall enter into consultations with any other contracting party with which the concession was initially negotiated, and with any other contracting party determined by the contracting parties to have a substantial interest therein. The contracting parties shall concur in the measure if they agree that there is no measure consistent with the other provisions of this agreement which is practicable in order to achieve the objective set forth in para 13 of this article, and if they are satisfied:

(a) that agreement has been reached with such other contracting parties as a result of the consultations referred to above; or

(b) if no such agreement has been reached within 60 days after the notification provided for in para 14 has been received by the contracting parties that the contracting party having recourse to this section has made all reasonable efforts to reach an agreement and that the interests of other contracting parties are adequately safeguarded.

The contracting party having recourse to this section shall thereupon be released from its obligations under the relevant provisions of the other articles of this agreement to the extent necessary to permit it to apply the measure.

19 If a proposed measure of the type described in para 13 of this article concerns an industry the establishment of which has in the initial period been facilitated by incidental protection afforded by restrictions imposed by the contracting party concerned for balance of payments purposes under the relevant provisions of this agreement, that contracting party may resort to the provisions and procedures of this section; provided that it shall not apply the proposed measure without the concurrence of the contracting parties.

20 Nothing in the preceding paragraphs of this section shall authorise any deviation from the provisions of Articles I, II and XIII of this agreement. The provisos to para 10 of this article shall also be applicable to any restriction under this section.

21 At any time while a measure is being applied under para 17 of this article any contracting party substantially affected by it may suspend the application to the trade of the contracting party having recourse to this section of such substantially equivalent concessions or other obligations under this agreement the suspension of which the contracting parties do not disapprove, provided that 60 days notice of such suspension is given to the contracting parties not later than six months after the measure has been introduced or changed substantially to the detriment of the contracting party affected. Any such contracting party shall afford adequate opportunity for consultation in accordance with the provisions of Article XXII of this agreement.

Section D

22 A contracting party coming within the scope of sub-para 4(b) of this article desiring, in the interest of the development of its economy, to introduce a measure of the type described in para 13 of this article in respect of the establishment of a particular industry may apply to the contracting parties for approval of such measure. The contracting parties shall promptly consult with such contracting party and shall, in making their decision, be guided by the considerations set out in para 16. If the contracting parties concur in the proposed measure the contracting party concerned shall be released from its obligations under the relevant provisions of the other articles of this agreement to the extent necessary to permit it to apply the measure. If the proposed measure affects a product which is the subject of a concession included in the appropriate Schedule annexed to this agreement, the provisions of para 18 shall apply.

23   Any measure applied under this section shall comply with the provisions of para 20 of this article.

Article XIX – Emergency action on imports of particular products

1   (a) If, as a result of unforeseen developments and of the effect of the obligations incurred by a contracting party under this agreement, including tariff concessions, any product is being imported into the territory of that contracting party in such increased quantities and under such conditions as to cause or threaten serious injury to domestic producers in that territory of like or directly competitive products, the contracting party shall be free, in respect of such product, and to the extent and for such time as may be necessary to prevent or remedy such injury, to suspend the obligation in whole or in part or to withdraw or modify the concession.

     (b) If any product, which is the subject of a concession with respect to a preference, is being imported into the territory of a contracting party in the circumstances set forth in sub-para (a) of this paragraph, so as to cause or threaten serious injury to domestic producers of like or directly competitive products in the territory of a contracting party which receives or received such preference, the importing contracting party shall be free, if that other contracting party so requests, to suspend the relevant obligation in whole or in part or to withdraw or modify the concession in respect of the product, to the extent and for such time as may be necessary to prevent or remedy such injury.

2   Before any contracting party shall take action pursuant to the provisions of para 1 of this article, it shall give notice in writing to the contracting parties as far in advance as may be practicable and shall afford the contracting parties and those contracting parties having a substantial interest as exporters of the product concerned an opportunity to consult with it in respect of the proposed action. When such notice is given in relation to a concession with respect to a preference, the notice shall name the contracting party which has requested the action. In critical circumstances, where delay would cause damage which it would be difficult to repair, action under para 1 of this article may be taken provisionally without prior consultation, on the condition that consultation shall be effected immediately after taking such action.

3   (a) If agreement among the interested contracting parties with respect to the action is not reached, the contracting party which proposes to take or continue the action shall, nevertheless, be free to do so, and if such action is taken or continued, the affected contracting parties shall then be free, not later than 90 days after such action is taken, to suspend, upon the expiration of 30 days from the day on which written notice of such suspension is received by the contracting parties, the application to the trade of the contracting party taking such action, or, in the case envisaged in para 1(b) of this article, to the trade of the contracting party requesting such action, of such substantially equivalent concessions or other obligations under this agreement the suspension of which the contracting parties do not disapprove.

     (b) Notwithstanding the provisions of sub-para (a) of this paragraph, where action is taken under para 2 of this article without prior consultation and causes or threatens serious injury in the territory of a contracting party to the domestic producers of products affected by the action, that contracting party shall, where delay would cause damage difficult to repair, be free to suspend, upon the taking of the action and throughout the period of consultation, such concessions or other obligations as may be necessary to prevent or remedy the injury.

Article XX – General exceptions

Subject to the requirement that such measures are not applied in a manner which would constitute a means of arbitrary or unjustifiable discrimination between countries where the same conditions prevail, or a disguised restriction on international trade, nothing in this agreement shall be construed to prevent the adoption or enforcement by any contracting party of measures:

(a) necessary to protect public morals;

(b) necessary to protect human, animal or plant life or health;

(c) relating to the importation or exportation of gold or silver;

(d) necessary to secure compliance with laws or regulations which are not inconsistent with the provisions of this agreement, including those relating to customs enforcement, the enforcement of monopolies operated under para 4 of Article II and Article XVII, the protection of patents, trade marks and copyrights, and the prevention of deceptive practices;

(e) relating to the products of prison labour;

(f) imposed for the protection of national treasures of artistic, historic or archeological value;

(g) relating to the conservation of exhaustible natural resources if such measures arc made effective in conjunction with restrictions on domestic production or consumption;

(h) undertaken in pursuance of obligations under any intergovernmental commodity agreement which conforms to criteria submitted to the contracting parties and not disapproved by them or which is itself so submitted and not so disapproved;

(i) involving restrictions on exports of domestic materials necessary to ensure essential quantities of such materials to a domestic processing industry during periods when the domestic price of such materials is held below the world price as part of a governmental stabilisation plan; provided that such restrictions shall not operate to increase the exports of or the protection afforded to such domestic industry, and shall not depart from the provisions of this agreement relating to non-discrimination;

(j) essential to the acquisition or distribution of products in general or local short supply; provided that any such measures shall be consistent with the principle that all contracting parties are entitled to an equitable share of the international supply of such products, and that any such measures, which are inconsistent with the other provisions of this agreement, shall be discontinued as soon as the conditions giving rise to them have ceased to exist. The contracting parties shall review the need for this sub-paragraph not later than 30 June 1960.

Article XXI – Security exceptions

Nothing in this agreement shall be construed:

(a) to require any contracting party to furnish any information the disclosure of which it considers contrary to its essential security interests; or

(b) to prevent any contracting party from taking any action which it considers necessary for the protection of its essential security interests:

   (i) relating to fissionable materials or the materials from which they are derived;

   (ii) relating to the traffic in arms, ammunition and implements of war and to such traffic in other goods and materials as is carried on directly or indirectly for the purpose of supplying a military establishment;

   (iii) taken in time of war or other emergency in international relations; or

(c) to prevent any contracting party from taking any action in pursuance of its obligations under the United Nations Charter for the maintenance of international peace and security.

Article XXII – Consultation

1   Each contracting party shall accord sympathetic consideration to, and shall afford adequate opportunity for consultation regarding, such representations as may be made by another contracting party with respect to any matter affecting the operation of this agreement.

2   The contracting parties may, at the request of a contracting party consult with any contracting party or parties in respect of any matter for which it has not been possible to find a satisfactory solution through consultation under para 1.

Article XXIII – Nullification or impairment

1   If any contracting party should consider that any benefit accruing to it directly or indirectly under this agreement is being nullified or impaired or that the attainment of any objective of the agreement is being impeded as the result of:

(a) the failure of another contracting party to carry out its obligations under this agreement; or

(b) the application by another contracting party of any measure, whether or not it conflicts with the provisions of this agreement; or

(c) the existence of any other situation,

the contracting party may, with a view to the satisfactory adjustment of the matter, make written representations or proposals to the other contracting party or parties which it considers to be concerned. Any contracting party thus approached shall give sympathetic consideration to the representations or proposals made to it.

2   If no satisfactory adjustment is effected between the contracting parties concerned within a reasonable time, or if the difficulty is of the type described in para 1(c) of this article, the matter may be referred to the contracting parties. The contracting parties shall promptly investigate any matter so referred to them and shall make appropriate recommendations to the contracting parties which they consider to be concerned, or give a ruling on the matter, as appropriate. The contracting parties may consult with contracting parties, with the Economic and Social Council of the United Nations and with any appropriate intergovernmental organisation in cases where they consider such consultation necessary. If the contracting parties consider that the circumstances are serious enough to justify such action, they may authorise a contracting party or parties to suspend the application to any other contracting party or parties of such concessions or other obligations under this agreement as they determine to be appropriate in the circumstances. If the application to any contracting party of any concession or other obligation is in fact suspended, that contracting party shall then be free, not later than 60 days after such action is taken, to give written notice to the Executive Secretary to the contracting parties of its intention to withdraw from this agreement and such withdrawal shall take effect upon the 60th day following the day on which such notice is received by him.

PART III

Article XXIV – Territorial application, frontier traffic, customs unions and free-trade areas

1   The provisions of this agreement shall apply to the metropolitan customs territories of the contracting parties and to any other customs territories in respect of which this agreement has been accepted under Article XXVI or is being applied under Article XXXIII or pursuant to the Protocol of Provisional Application. Each such customs territory shall, exclusively for the purposes of the territorial application of this agreement, be treated as though it were a contracting party; provided that the provisions of this paragraph shall not be construed to create any rights or obligations as between two or more customs territories in respect of which this agreement has been accepted under Article XXVI or is being applied under Article XXXIII or pursuant to the Protocol of Provisional Application by a single contracting party.

2   For the purposes of this agreement a customs territory shall be understood to mean any territory with respect to which separate tariffs or other regulations of commerce are maintained for a substantial part of the trade of such territory with other territories.

3   The provisions of this agreement shall not be construed to prevent:

   (a) advantages accorded by any contracting party to adjacent countries in order to facilitate frontier traffic;

   (b) advantages accorded to the trade with the Free Territory of Trieste by countries contiguous to that territory, provided that such advantages are not in conflict with the Treaties of Peace arising out of the Second World War.

4   The contracting parties recognise the desirability of increasing freedom of trade by the development, through voluntary agreements, of closer integration between the economies of the countries parties to such agreements. They also recognise that the purpose of a customs union or of a free-trade area should be to facilitate trade between the constituent territories and not to raise barriers to the trade of other contracting parties with such territories.

5   Accordingly, the provisions of this agreement shall not prevent, as between the territories of contracting parties, the formation of a customs union or of a free-trade area or the adoption of an interim agreement necessary for the formation of a customs union or of a free-trade area; provided that:

   (a) with respect to a customs union, or an interim agreement leading to the formation of a customs union, the duties and other regulations of commerce imposed at the institution of any such union or inter-union agreement in respect of trade with contracting parties not parties to such union or agreement shall not on the whole be higher or more restrictive than the general incidence of the duties and regulations of commerce applicable in the constituent territories prior to the formation of such union or the adoption of such interim agreement, as the case may be;

(b) with respect to a free-trade area, or an interim agreement leading to the formation of a free-trade area, the duties and other regulations of commerce maintained in each of the constituent territories and applicable at the formation of such free-trade area or the adoption of such interim agreement to the trade of contracting parties not included in such area or not parties to such agreement shall not be higher or more restrictive than the corresponding duties and other regulations of commerce existing in the same constituent territories prior to the formation of the free-trade area, or interim agreement, as the case may be; and

(c) any interim agreement referred to in sub-paras (a) and (b) shall include a plan and schedule for the formation of such a customs union or of such a free-trade area within a reasonable length of time.

6   If, in fulfilling the requirements of sub-para 5(a), a contracting party proposes to increase any rate of duty inconsistently with the provisions of Article II, the procedure set forth in Article XXVIII shall apply. In providing for compensatory adjustment, due account shall be taken of the compensation already afforded by the reductions brought about in the corresponding duty of the other constituents of the union.

7   (a) Any contracting party deciding to enter into a customs union or free-trade area, or an interim agreement leading to the formation of such a union or area, shall promptly notify the contracting parties and shall make available to them such information regarding the proposed union or area as will enable them to make such reports and recommendations to contracting parties as they may deem appropriate.

(b) If, after having studied the plan and schedule included in an interim agreement referred to in para 5 in consultation with the parties to that agreement and taking due account of the information made available in accordance with the provisions of sub-para (a), the contracting parties find that such agreement is not likely to result in the formation of a customs union or of a free-trade area within the period contemplated by the parties to the agreement or that such period is not a reasonable one, the contracting parties shall make recommendations to the parties to the agreement. The parties shall not maintain or put into force, as the case may be, such agreement if they are not prepared to modify it in accordance with these recommendations.

(c) Any substantial change in the plan or schedule referred to in para 5(c) shall be communicated to the contracting parties, which may request the contracting parties concerned to consult with them if the change seems likely to jeopardise or delay untruly the formation of the customs union or of the free-trade area.

8   For the purposes of this agreement:

(a) A customs union shall be understood to mean the substitution of a single customs territory for two or more customs territories, so that:

(i) duties and other restrictive regulations of commerce (except, where necessary, those permitted under Articles XI, XII, XIII, XIV, XV and XX) are eliminated with respect to substantially all the trade between the constituent territories of the union or at least with respect to substantially all the trade in products originating in such territories; and

(ii) subject to the provisions of para 9, substantially the same duties and other regulations of commerce are applied by each of the members of the union to the trade of territories not included in the union.

(b) A free-trade area shall be understood to mean a group of two or more customs territories in which the duties and other restrictive regulations of commerce (except, where necessary, those permitted under Articles XI, XII, XIII XIV, XV and XX) are eliminated on substantially all the trade between the constituent territories in products originating in such territories.

9   The preferences referred to in para 2 of Article I shall not be affected by the formation of a customs union or of a free-trade area but may be eliminated or adjusted by means of negotiations with contracting parties affected. This procedure of negotiations with affected contracting parties shall, in particular, apply to the elimination of preferences required to conform with the provisions of para 8(a)(i) and para 8(b).

10   The contracting may, by a two thirds majority, approve proposals which do not fully comply with the requirements of paras 5–9 inclusive, provided that such proposals lead to the formation of a customs union or a free-trade area in the sense of this article.

11   Taking into account the exceptional circumstances arising out of the establishment of India and Pakistan as independent States and recognising the fact that they have long constituted an economic unit, the contracting parties agree that the provisions of this agreement shall not prevent the two countries from entering into special arrangements with respect to the trade between them, pending the establishment of their mutual trade relations on a definitive basis.

12   Each contracting party shall take such reasonable measures as may be available to it to ensure observance of the provisions of this agreement by the regional and local governments and authorities within its territory.

Article XXV – Joint action by the contracting parties

1   Representatives of the contracting parties shall meet from time to time for the purpose of giving effect to those provisions of this agreement which involve joint action and generally, with a view to facilitating the operation and furthering the objectives of this agreement. Wherever reference is made in this agreement to the contracting parties acting jointly they are designated as the contracting parties.

2   The Secretary General of the UN is requested to convene the first meeting of the contracting parties, which shall take place not later than 1 March 1948.

3   Each contracting party shall be entitled to have one vote at all meetings of the contracting parties.

4   Except as otherwise provided for in this agreement, decisions of the contracting parties shall be taken by a majority of the votes cast.

5   In exceptional circumstances not elsewhere provided for in this agreement, the contracting parties may waive an obligation imposed upon a contracting party by this agreement; provided that any such decision shall be approved by a two thirds majority of the votes cast and that such majority shall comprise more than half of the contracting parties. The contracting parties may also by such a vote:

   (i)   define certain categories of exceptional circumstances to which other voting requirements shall apply for the waiver of obligations; and

   (ii) prescribe such criteria as may be necessary for the application of this paragraph.

Article XXVI – Acceptance, entry into force and registration

1   The date of this agreement shall be 30 October 1947.

2   This agreement shall be open for acceptance by any contracting party which, on 1 March 1955, was a contracting party or was negotiating with a view to accession to this agreement.

3   This agreement, done in a single English original and in a single French original, both texts authentic, shall be deposited with the Secretary General of the United Nations, who shall furnish certified copies thereof to all interested governments.

4   Each government accepting this agreement shall deposit an instrument of acceptance with the Executive Secretary to the contracting parties, who will inform all interested governments of the date of deposit of each instrument of acceptance and of the day on which this agreement enters into force under para 6 of this article.

5   (a) Each government accepting this agreement does so in respect of its metropolitan territory and of the other territories for which it has international responsibility, except such separate customs territories as it shall notify to the Executive Secretary to the contracting parties at the time of its own acceptance.

   (b) Any government, which has so notified the Executive Secretary under the exceptions in sub-para (a) of this paragraph, may at any time give notice to the Executive Secretary' that its acceptance shall be effective in respect of any separate customs territory or territories so excepted and such notice shall take effect on the 30th day following the day on which it is received by the Executive Secretary.

   (c) If any of the customs territories, in respect of which a contracting party has accepted this agreement, possesses or acquires full autonomy in the conduct of its external commercial relations and of the other matters provided for in this agreement, such territory shall, upon sponsorship through a declaration by the responsible contracting party establishing the above-mentioned fact, be deemed to be a contracting party.

6   This agreement shall enter into force, as among the governments which have accepted it, on the 30th day following the day on which instruments of acceptance have been deposited with the Executive Secretary to the contracting parties on behalf of governments named in Annex H the territories of which account for 85% of the total external trade of the territories of such governments, computed in accordance with the applicable column of percentages set forth therein. The instrument of acceptance of each other government shall take effect on the 30th day following the day on which such instrument has been deposited.

7   The United Nations is authorised to effect registration of this agreement as soon as it enters into force.

Article XXVII – Withholding or withdrawal of concessions

Any contracting party shall at any time be free to withhold or to withdraw in whole or in part any concession, provided for in the appropriate Schedule annexed to this agreement, in respect of which such contracting party determines that it was initially negotiated with a government which has not become, or has ceased to be, a contracting party. A contracting party taking such action shall notify the contracting parties and, upon request, consult with contracting parties which have a substantial interest in the product concerned.

Article XXVIII – Modification of schedules

1   On the first day of each three year period, the first period beginning on 1 January 1958 (or on the first day of any other period that may be specified by the contracting parties by two thirds of the votes cast) a contracting party (hereafter in this article referred to as the 'applicant contracting party') may, by negotiation and agreement with any contracting party with which such concession was initially negotiated and with any other contracting party determined by the contracting parties to have a principal supplying interest (which two preceding categories of contracting parties, together with the applicant contracting party, are in this article hereinafter referred to as the 'contracting parties primarily concerned'), and subject to consultation with any other contracting party determined by the contracting parties to have a substantial interest in such concession, modify or withdraw a concession' included in the appropriate Schedule annexed to this agreement.

2   In such negotiations and agreement, which may include provision for compensatory adjustment with respect to other products, the contracting parties concerned shall endeavour to maintain a general level of reciprocal and mutually advantageous concessions not less favourable to trade than that provided for in this agreement prior to such negotiations.

3   (a) If agreement between the contracting parties primarily concerned cannot be reached before I January 1958 or before the expiration of a period envisaged in para 1 of this article, the contracting party which proposes to modify or withdraw the concession shall, nevertheless, be free to do so and if such action is taken any contracting party with which such concession was initially negotiated, any contracting party determined under para 1 to have a principal supplying interest and any contracting party determined under para 1 to have a substantial interest shall then be free not later than six months after such action is taken, to withdraw, upon the expiration of 30 days from the day on which written notice of such withdrawal is received by the contracting parties, substantially equivalent concessions initially negotiated with the applicant contracting party.

     (b) If agreement between the contracting parties primarily concerned is reached but any other contracting party determined under para 1 of this article to have a substantial interest is not satisfied, such other contracting party shall be free, not later than six months after action under such agreement is taken, to withdraw, upon the expiration of 30 days from the day on which written notice of such withdrawal is received by the contracting parties, substantially equivalent concessions initially negotiated with the applicant contracting party.

4   The contracting parties may, at any time, in special circumstances, authorise a contracting party to enter into negotiations for modification or withdrawal of a concession included in the appropriate Schedule annexed to this agreement subject to the following procedures and conditions:

(a) Such negotiations and any related consultations shall be conducted in accordance with the provisions of paras 1 and 2 of this article.

(b) If agreement between the contracting parties primarily concerned is reached in the negotiations, the provisions of para 3(b) of this article shall apply.

(c) If agreement between the contracting parties primarily concerned is not reached within a period of 60 days after negotiations have been authorised, or within such longer period as the contracting parties may have prescribed, the applicant contracting party may refer the matter to the contracting parties.

(d) Upon such reference, the contracting parties shall promptly examine the matter and submit their views to the contracting parties primarily concerned with the aim of achieving a settlement. If a settlement is reached the provisions of para 3(b) shall apply as if agreement between the contracting parties primarily concerned had been reached. If no settlement is reached between the contracting parties primarily concerned, the applicant contracting party shall be free to modify or withdraw the concession, unless the contracting parties determine that the applicant contracting party has unreasonably failed to offer adequate compensation. If such action is taken, any contracting party with which the concession was initially negotiated, any contracting party determined under para 4(a) to have a principal supplying interest and any contracting party determined under para 4(a) to have a substantial interest, shall be free. not later than six months after such action is taken, to modify or withdraw, upon the expiration of 30 days from the day on which written notice of such withdrawal is received by the contracting parties substantially equivalent concessions initially negotiated with the applicant contracting party.

5   Before I January 1958 and before the end of any period envisaged in para 1 a contracting party may elect by notifying the contracting parties to reserve the right, for the duration of the next period, to modify the appropriate Schedule in accordance with the procedures of paras 1–3. If a contracting party so elects, other contracting parties shall have the right, during the same period, to modify or withdraw, in accordance with the same procedures, concessions initially negotiated with that contracting party.

Article XXVIII bis – Tariff negotiations

1   The contracting parties recognise that customs duties often constitute serious obstacles to trade; thus negotiations on a reciprocal and mutually advantageous basis, directed to the substantial reduction of the general level of tariffs and other charges on imports and exports and in particular to the reduction of such high tariffs as discourage the importation even of minimum quantities, and conducted with due regard to the objectives of this agreement and the varying needs of individual contracting parties, are of great importance to the expansion of international trade. The contracting parties may therefore sponsor such negotiations from time to time.

2   (a) Negotiations under this article may be carried out on a selective product-by-product basis or by the application of such multilateral procedures as may be accepted by the contracting parties concerned. Such negotiations may be directed towards the reduction of duties, the binding of duties at then existing levels or undertakings that individual duties or the average duties on specified categories of products shall not exceed specified levels. The binding against increase of low duties or of duty free treatment shall, in principle, be recognised as a concession equivalent in value to the reduction of high duties.

(b) The contracting parties recognise that in general the success of multilateral negotiations would depend on the participation of all contracting parties which conduct a substantial proportion of their external trade with one another.

3   Negotiations shall be conducted on a basis which affords adequate opportunity to take into account:

(a) the needs of individual contracting parties and individual industries

(b) the needs of less developed countries for a more flexible use of tariff protection to assist their economic development and the special needs of these countries to maintain tariffs for revenue purposes; and

(c) all other relevant circumstances, including the fiscal, developmental, strategic and other needs of the contracting parties concerned.

Article XXIX – The relation of this agreement to the Havana Charter

1 The contracting parties undertake to observe to the fullest extent of their executive authority the general principles of Chapters I to VI inclusive and of Chapter IX of the Havana Charter pending their acceptance of it in accordance with their constitutional procedures.

2 Part II of this agreement shall be suspended on the day on which the Havana Charter enters into force.

3 If by 30 September 1949, the Havana Charter has not entered into force, the contracting parties shall meet before 31 December 1949 to agree whether this agreement shall be amended, supplemented or maintained.

4 If at any time the Havana Charter should cease to be in force, the contracting parties shall meet as soon as practicable thereafter to agree whether this agreement shall be supplemented, amended or maintained. Pending such agreement, Part II of this agreement shall again enter into force; provided that the provisions of Part II other than Article XXIII shall be replaced, *mutatis mutandis*, in the form in which they then appeared in the Havana Charter; and provided further that no contracting party shall be bound by any provisions which did not bind it at the time when the Havana Charter ceased to be in force.

5 If any contracting party has not accepted the Havana Charter by the date upon which it enters into force, the contracting parties shall confer to agree whether, and if so in what way, this agreement in so far as it affects relations between such contracting party and other contracting parties, shall be supplemented or amended. Pending such agreement the provisions of Part II of this agreement shall, notwithstanding the provisions of para 2 of this article, continue to apply as between such contracting party and other contracting parties.

6 Contracting parties which are members of the International Trade Organisation shall not invoke the provisions of this agreement so as to prevent the operation of any provision of the Havana Charter. The application of the principle underlying this paragraph to any contracting party which is not a member of the International Trade Organisation shall be the subject of an agreement pursuant to para 5 of this article.

Article XXX – Amendments

1 Except where provision for modification is made elsewhere in this agreement, amendments to the provisions of Part I of this agreement or to the provisions of Article XXIX or of this agreement shall become effective upon acceptance by all the contracting parties, and other amendments to this agreement shall become effective, in respect of those contracting parties which accept them, upon acceptance by two thirds of the contracting parties and thereafter for each other contracting party upon acceptance by it.

2 Any contracting party accepting an amendment to this agreement shall deposit an instrument of acceptance with the Secretary General of the United Nations within such period as the contracting parties may specify. The contracting parties may decide that any amendment made effective under this article is of such a nature that any contracting party which has not accepted it within a period specified by the contracting parties shall be free to withdraw from this agreement, or to remain a contracting party with the consent of the contracting parties.

Article XXXI – Withdrawal

Without prejudice to the provisions of para 12 of Article XVIII, of Article XXIII or of para 2 of Article XXX, any contracting party may withdraw from this agreement, or may separately withdraw on behalf of any of the separate customs territories for which it has international responsibility and which at the time possesses full autonomy in the conduct of its external commercial relations and of the other matters provided for in this agreement. The withdrawal shall take effect upon the expiration of six months from the day on which written notice of withdrawal is received by the Secretary General of the United Nations.

Article XXXII – Contracting parties

1   The contracting parties to this agreement shall be understood to mean those governments which are applying the provisions of this agreement under Articles XXVI or XXXIII or pursuant to the Protocol of Provisional Application.

2   At any time after the entry into force of this agreement pursuant to para 6 of Article XXVI those contracting parties which have accepted this agreement pursuant to para 4 of Article XXVI may decide that any contracting party which has not so accepted it shall cease to be a contracting party.

Article XXXIII – Accession

A government not party to this agreement. or a government acting on behalf of a separate customs territory possessing full autonomy in the conduct of its external commercial relations and of the other matters provided for in this agreement, may accede to this agreement, on its own behalf or on behalf of that territory, on terms to be agreed between such government and the contracting parties. Decisions of the contracting parties under this paragraph shall be taken by a two thirds majority.

Article XXXIV – Annexes

The annexes to this agreement are hereby made an integral part of this agreement.

Article XXXV – Non-application of the agreement between particular contracting parties

1   This agreement, or alternatively Article II of this agreement, shall not apply as between any contracting party and any other contracting party if:
   (a) the two contracting parties have not entered into tariff negotiations with each other, and
   (b) either of the contracting parties, at the time either becomes a contracting party, does not consent to such application.

2   The contracting parties may review the operation of this article in particular cases at the request of any contracting party and make appropriate recommendations.

PART IV – TRADE AND DEVELOPMENT

Article XXXVI – Principles and objectives

1   The contracting parties:
   (a) recalling that the basic objectives of this agreement include the raising of standards of living and the progressive development of the economies of all contracting parties, and considering that the attainment of these objectives is particularly urgent for less developed contracting parties;
   (b) considering that export earnings of the less developed contracting parties can play a vital part in their economic development and that the extent of this contribution depends on the prices paid by the less developed contracting parties for essential imports, the volume of their exports, and the prices received for these exports;
   (c) noting, that there is a wide gap between standards of living in less developed countries and in other countries;
   (d) recognising that individual and joint action is essential to further the development of the economies of less developed contracting parties and to bring about a rapid advance in the standards of living in these countries;
   (e) recognising that international trade as a means of achieving economic and social advancement should be governed by such rules and procedures – and measures in conformity with such rules and procedures – as are consistent with the objectives set forth in this article;
   (f) noting that the contracting parties may enable less developed contracting parties to use special measures to promote their trade and development;
       agree as follows.

2   There is need for a rapid and sustained expansion of the export earnings of the less developed contracting parties.

3   There is need for positive efforts designed to ensure that less developed contracting parties secure a share in the growth in international trade commensurate with the needs of their economic development.

4   Given the continued dependence of many less developed contracting parties on the exportation of a limited range of primary products, there is need to provide in the largest possible measure more favourable and acceptable conditions of access to world markets for these products, and wherever appropriate to devise measures designed to stabilise and improve conditions of world markets in these products, including in particular measures designed to attain stable, equitable and remunerative prices, thus permitting an expansion of world trade and demand and a dynamic and steady growth of the real export earnings of these countries so as to provide them with expanding resources for their economic development.

5   The rapid expansion of the economies of the less developed contracting parties will be facilitated by a diversification of the structure of their economies and the avoidance of an excessive dependence on the export of primary products. There is, therefore, need for increased access in the largest possible measure to markets under favourable conditions for processed and manufactured products currently or potentially of particular export interest to less developed contracting parties.

6   Because of the chronic deficiency in the export proceeds and other foreign exchange earnings of less developed contracting parties, there are important inter-relationships between trade and financial assistance to development. There is, therefore, need for close and continuing collaboration between the contracting parties and the international lending agencies so that they can contribute most effectively to alleviating the burdens these less developed contracting parties assume in the interest of their economic development.

7   There is need for appropriate collaboration between the contracting parties, other intergovernmental bodies and the organs and agencies of the United Nations system, whose activities relate to the trade and economic development of less developed countries.

8   The developed contracting parties do not expect reciprocity for commitments made by them in trade negotiations to reduce or remove tariffs and other barriers to the trade of less developed contracting parties.

9   The adoption of measures to give effect to these principles and objectives shall be a matter of conscious and purposeful effort on the part of the contracting parties both individually and jointly.

Article XXXVII – Commitments

1   The developed contracting parties shall to the fullest extent possible – ie except when compelling reasons, which may include legal reasons, make it impossible – give effect to the following provisions:
   (a) accord high priority to the reduction and elimination of barriers to products currently or potentially of particular export interest to less developed contracting parties, including customs duties and other restrictions which differentiate unreasonably between such products in their primary and in their processed forms;
   (b) refrain from introducing, or increasing the incidence of, customs duties or non-tariff import barriers on products currently or potentially of particular export interest to less developed contracting parties; and
   (c) (i) refrain from imposing new fiscal measures, and
       (ii) in any adjustments of fiscal policy accord high priority to the reduction and elimination of fiscal measures,
   which would hamper, or which hamper, significantly the growth of consumption of primary products, in raw or processed form, wholly or mainly produced in the territories of less developed contracting parties, and which are applied specifically to those products.

2   (a) Whenever it is considered that effect is not being given to any of the provisions of sub-para (a), (b) or (c) of para 1, the matter shall be reported to the contracting parties either by the contracting party not so giving effect to the relevant provisions or by any other interested contracting party.
   (b) (i) The contracting parties shall, if requested so to do by any interested contracting party, and without prejudice to any bilateral consultations that may be

undertaken, consult with the contracting party concerned and all interested contracting parties with respect to the matter with a view to reaching solutions satisfactory to all contracting parties concerned in order to further the objectives set forth in Article XXXVI. In the course of these consultations, the reasons given in cases where effect was not being given to the provisions of sub-para (a), (b) or (c) of para 1 shall be examined.

(ii) As the implementation of the provisions of sub-para (a), (b) or (c) of para 1 by individual contracting parties may in some cases be more readily achieved where action is taken jointly with other developed contracting parties, such consultation might, where appropriate, be directed towards this end.

(iii) The consultations by the contracting parties might also, in appropriate cases, be directed towards agreement on joint action designed to further the objectives of this agreement as envisaged in para 1 of Article XXV.

3   The developed contracting parties shall:

(a) make every effort, in cases where a government directly or indirectly determines the resale price of products wholly or mainly produced in the territories of less developed contracting parties, to maintain trade margins at equitable levels;

(b) give active consideration to the adoption of other measures designed to provide greater scope for the development of imports from less developed contracting parties and collaborate in appropriate international action to this end;

(c) have special regard to the trade interests of less developed contracting parties when considering the application of other measures permitted under this agreement to meet particular problems and explore all possibilities of constructive remedies before applying such measures where they would affect essential interests of those contracting parties.

4   Less developed contracting parties agree to take appropriate action in implementation of the provisions of Part IV for the benefit of the trade of other less developed contracting parties, in so far as such action is consistent with their individual present and future development, financial and trade needs taking into account past trade developments as well as the trade interests of less developed contracting parties as a whole.

5   In the implementation of the commitments set forth in paras 1–4 each contracting party shall afford to any other interested contracting party or contracting parties full and prompt opportunity for consultations under the normal procedures of this agreement with respect to any matter or difficulty which may arise.

Article XXXVIII – Joint action

1   The contracting parties shall collaborate jointly, within the framework of this agreement and elsewhere, as appropriate, to further the objectives set forth in Article XXXVI.

2   In particular, the contracting parties shall:

(a) where appropriate, take action, including action through international arrangements, to provide improved and acceptable conditions of access to world markets for primary products of particular interest to less developed contracting parties and to devise measures designed to stabilise and improve conditions of world markets in these products including measures designed to attain stable, equitable and remunerative prices for exports of such products;

(b) seek appropriate collaboration in matters of trade and development policy with the United Nations and its organs and agencies, including any institutions that may be created on the basis of recommendations by the United Nations Conference on Trade and Development;

(c) collaborate in analysing the development plans and policies of individual less developed contracting parties and in examining trade and aid relationships with a view to devising concrete measures to promote the development of export potential and to facilitate access to export markets for the products of the industries thus developed and, in this connection, seek appropriate collaboration with governments and international organisations, and in particular with organisations having competence in relation to financial assistance for economic development, in systematic studies of trade and aid relationships in individual less developed contracting parties aimed at obtaining a clear analysis of export potential, market prospects and any further action that may be required;

(d) keep under continuous review the development of world trade with special reference to the rate of growth of the trade of less developed contracting parties and make such recommendations to contracting parties as may, in the circumstances, be deemed appropriate;

(e) collaborate in seeking feasible methods to expand trade for the purpose of economic development, through international harmonisation and adjustment of national policies and regulations, through technical and commercial standards affecting production, transportation and marketing, and through export promotion by the establishment of facilities for the increased flow of trade information and the development of market research; and

(f) establish such institutional arrangements as may be necessary to further the objectives set forth in Article XXXVI and to give effect to the provisions of this Part.

Annex A – List of territories referred to in para 2(a) of Article I

United Kingdom of Great Britain and Northern Ireland; Dependent territories of the United Kingdom of Great Britain and Northern; Ireland; Canada; Commonwealth of Australia; Dependent territories of the Commonwealth of Australia; New Zealand; Dependent territories of New Zealand; Union of South Africa including South West Africa; India (as on 10 April 1947); Newfoundland; Southern Rhodesia; Burma; Ceylon.

Certain of the territories listed above have two or more preferential rates in force for certain products. Any such territory may, by agreement with the other contracting parties which are principal suppliers of such products at the most-favoured-nation rate, substitute for such preferential rates a single preferential rate which shall not on the whole be less favourable to suppliers at the most-favoured-nation rate than the preferences in force prior to such substitution.

The imposition of an equivalent margin of tariff preference to replace a margin of preference in an internal tax existing on 10 April 1947 exclusively between two or more of the territories listed in this Annex or to replace the preferential quantitative arrangements described in the following paragraph, shall not be deemed to constitute an increase in a margin of tariff preference.

The preferential arrangements referred to in para 5(h) of Article XIV are those existing in the UK on 10 April 1947, under contractual agreements with the governments of Canada, Australia and New Zealand, in respect of chilled and frozen beef and veal, frozen mutton and lamb, chilled and frozen pork, and bacon. It is the intention, without prejudice to any action taken under sub-para (h) of Article XX, that these arrangements shall be eliminated or replaced by tariff preferences, and that negotiations to this end shall take place as soon as practicable among the countries substantially concerned or involved.

The film hire tax in force in New Zealand on 10 April 1947, shall, for the purposes of this agreement, be treated as a customs duty under Article I. The renters film quota in force in New Zealand on 10 April 1947, shall, for the purposes of this agreement, be treated as a screen quota under Article IV.

The Dominions of India and Pakistan have not been mentioned separately in the above list since they had not come into existence as such on the base date of 10 April 1947.

Annex B

List of territories of the French union referred to in para 2(b) of Article I

France; French Equatorial Africa (Treaty Basin of the Congo and other territories); French West Africa; Cameroons under French Trusteeship; French Somali Coast and Dependencies; French Establishments in Oceania; French Establishments in the Condominium of the New Hebrides; Indo-China; Madagascar and Dependencies; Morocco (French zone); New Caledonia and Dependencies; Saint-Pierre and Miquelon; Togo under French Trusteeship; Tunisia.

Annex C

List of territories referred to in para 2(h) of Article I as respects the customs union of Belgium, Luxemburg and The Netherlands

The Economic Union of Belgium and Luxemburg; Belgian Congo; Ruanda Urundi; The Netherlands; New Guinea; Surinam; Netherlands Antilles; Republic of Indonesia.

For imports into the territories constituting the Customs Union only.

Annex D

List of territories referred to in para 2(h) of Article I as respects the USA

USA (customs territory); Dependent territories of the USA; Republic of the Philippines.

The imposition of an equivalent margin of tariff preference to replace a margin of preference in an internal tax existing on 10 April 1947, exclusively between two or more of the territories listed in this Annex shall not be deemed to constitute an increase in a margin of tariff preference.

Annex E

List of territories covered by preferential arrangements between Chile and neighbouring countries referred to in para 2(d) of Article I

Preferences in force exclusively between Chile on the one hand and (i) Argentina, (ii) Bolivia and (iii) Peru, on the other hand.

Annex F

List of territories covered by preferential arrangements between Lebanon and Syria and neighbouring countries referred to in para 2(d) of Article I

Preferences in force exclusively between the Lebanon-Syrian Customs Union, on the one hand, and (i) Palestine, (ii) Transjordan, on the other hand.

Annex G

Dates establishing maximum margins of preference referred to para 4 of Article I

Australia	15 October 1946
Canada	1 July 1939
France	1 January 1939
Lebanon-Syrian Customs Union	30 November 1938
Union of South Africa	1 July 1938
Southern Rhodesia	1 May 1941

Annex H

Percentage shares of total external trade to be used for the purpose of making the determination referred to in Article XXVI (based on the average of 1949–53)

If, prior to the accession of the government of Japan to the General Agreement, the present agreement has been accepted by contracting parties the external trade of which under column I accounts for the percentage of such trade specified in para 6 of Article XXVI, column I shall be applicable for the purposes of that paragraph. If the present agreement has not been so accepted prior to the accession of the government of Japan. column II shall be applicable for the purposes of that paragraph.

	Column I (contracting parties on 1/3/55)	Column II (contracting parties on 1/3/55 and Japan)
Australia	3.1	3.0
Austria	0.9	0.8
Belgium-Luxemburg	4.3	4.2

	Column I (contracting parties on 1/3/55)	Column II (contracting parties on 1/3/55 and Japan)
Brazil	2.5	2.4
Burma	0.3	0.3
Canada	6.7	6.5
Ceylon	0.5	0.5
Chile	0.6	0.6
Cuba	1.1	1.1
Czechoslovakia	1.4	1.4
Denmark	1.4	1.4
Dominican Republic	0.1	0.1
Finland	1.0	1.0
France	8.7	8.5
Germany, Federal Republic of	5.3	5.2
Greece	0.4	0.4
Haiti	0.1	0.1
India	2.4	2.4
Indonesia	1.3	1.3
Italy	2.9	2.8
Netherlands, Kingdom of the	4.7	4.6
New Zealand	1.0	1.0
Nicaragua	0.1	0.1
Norway	1.1	1.1
Pakistan	0.9	0.8
Peru	0.4	0.4
Rhodesia and Nyasaland	0.6	0.6
Sweden	2.5	2.4
Turkey	0.6	0.6
Union of South Africa	1.8	1.8
UK	20.3	19.8
USA	20.6	20.1
Uruguay	0.4	0.4
Japan	−	2.3
	100.0	100.0

Note: These percentages have been computed taking into account the trade of all territories in respect of which the General Agreement on Tariffs and Trade is applied.

Annex I

Notes and supplementary provisions

Ad *Article I*

Paragraph 1

The obligations incorporated in para 1 of Article I by reference to paras 2 and 4 of Article III and those incorporated in para 2(b) of Article II by reference to Article VI shall be considered as falling within Part II for the purposes of the Protocol of Provisional Application.

The cross-references, in the paragraph immediately above and in para 1 of Article I, to paras 2 and 4 of Article III shall only apply after Article III has been modified by the entry into force of the amendment provided for in the protocol modifying Part II and Article XXVI of the General Agreement on Tariffs and Trade, dated 14 September 1948.

Paragraph 4

The term 'margin of preference' means the absolute difference between the most-favoured-nation rate of duty and the preferential rate of duty for the like product, and not the proportionate relation between those rates. As examples:

(1) If the most-favoured-nation rate were 36% *ad valorem* and the preferential rate were 24% *ad valorem*, the margin of preference would be 12% *ad valorem*, and not one third of the most-favoured-nation rate;

(2) If the most-favoured-nation rate were 36% *ad valorem* and the preferential rate were expressed as two thirds of the most-favoured-nation rate, the margin of preference would be 12% *ad valorem*;

(3) If the most-favoured-nation rate were 2 francs per kilogramme and the preferential rate were 1.50 francs per kg, the margin of preference would be 0.50 franc per kg.

The following kinds of customs action, taken in accordance with established uniform procedures, would not be contrary to a general binding of margins of preference:

(i) The re-application to an imported product of a tariff classification or rate of duty, properly applicable to such product, in cases in which the application of such classification or rate to such product was temporarily suspended or inoperative on 10 April 1947; and

(ii) The classification of a particular product under a tariff item other than that under which importations of that product were classified on 10 April 1947, in cases in which the tariff law clearly contemplates that such product may be classified under more than one tariff item.

This protocol entered into force on 14 December 1948.

Ad *Article II*

Paragraph 2(a)

The cross-reference, in para 2(a) of Article II, to para 2 of Article III shall only apply after Article III has been modified by the entry into force of the amendment provided for in the Protocol Modifying Part II and Article XXVI of the General Agreement on Tariffs and Trade, dated 14 September 1948.

Paragraph 2(b)

See the note relating to para 1 of Article I.

Paragraph 4

Except where otherwise specifically agreed between the contracting parties which initially negotiated the concession, the provisions of this paragraph will be applied in the light of the provisions of Article 31 of the Havana Charter.

Ad *Article III*

Any internal tax or other internal charge, or any law, regulation or requirement of the kind referred to in para 1 which applies to an imported product and to the like domestic product and is collected or enforced in the case of the imported product at the time or point of importation, is nevertheless to be regarded as an internal tax or other internal charge, or a law, regulation or requirement of the kind referred to in para 1, and is accordingly subject to the provisions of Article III.

Paragraph 1

The application of para 1 to internal taxes imposed by local governments and authorities within the territory of a contracting party is subject to the provisions of the final paragraph of Article XXIV. The term 'reasonable measures' in the last-mentioned paragraph would not require, for example, the repeal of existing national legislation authorising local governments to impose internal taxes which, although technically inconsistent with the letter of Article III, are not in fact inconsistent with its spirit, if such repeal would result in a serious financial hardship for the local governments or authorities concerned. With regard to taxation by local governments or authorities which is inconsistent with both the letter and spirit of Article III, the term 'reasonable measures' would permit a contracting party to eliminate the inconsistent taxation gradually over a transition period, if abrupt action would create serious administrative and financial difficulties.

Paragraph 2

A tax conforming to the requirements of the first sentence of para 2 would be considered to be inconsistent with the provisions of the second sentence only in cases where competition was involved between, on the one hand, the taxed product and, on the other hand, a directly competitive or substitutable product which was not similarly taxed.

Paragraph 5

Regulations consistent with the provisions of the first sentence of para 5 shall not be considered to be contrary to the provisions of the second sentence in any case in which all of the products subject to the regulations are produced domestically in substantial quantities. A regulation cannot be justified as being consistent with the provisions of the second sentence on the ground that the proportion or amount allocated to each of the products which are the subject of the regulation constitutes an equitable relationship between imported and domestic products.

Ad *Article V*

Paragraph 5

With regard to transportation charges, the principle laid down in para 5 refers to like products being transported on the same route under like conditions.

Ad *Article VI*

Paragraph 1

1   Hidden dumping by associated houses (ie the sale by an importer at a price below that corresponding to the price invoiced by an exporter with whom the importer is associated, and also below the price in the exporting country) constitutes a form of price dumping with respect to which the margin of dumping may be calculated on the basis of the price at which the goods are resold by the importer.

2   It is recognised that, in the case of imports from a country which has a complete or substantially complete monopoly of its trade and where all domestic prices are fixed by the State, special difficulties may exist in determining price comparability for the purposes of para 1, and in such cases importing contracting parties may find it necessary to take into account the possibility that a strict comparison with domestic prices in such a country may not always be appropriate.

Paragraphs 2 and 3

1   As in many other cases in customs administration, a contracting party may require reasonable security (bond or cash deposit) for the payment of anti-dumping or countervailing duty pending final determination on the facts in any case of suspected dumping or subsidisation.

2   Multiple currency practices can in certain circumstances constitute a subsidy to exports which may be met by countervailing duties under para 3 or can constitute a form of dumping by means of a partial depreciation of a country's currency which may be met by action under para 2. By 'multiple currency practices' is meant practices by governments or sanctioned by governments.

Paragraph 6(b)

Waivers under the provisions of this sub-paragraph shall be granted only on application by the contracting party proposing to levy an anti-dumping or countervailing duty, as the case may be.

Ad *Article VII*

Paragraph 1

The expression 'or other charges' is not to be regarded as including internal taxes or equivalent charges imposed on or in connection with imported products.

Paragraph 2

1   It would be in conformity with Article VII to presume that 'actual value' may be represented by the invoice price, plus any non-included charges for legitimate costs which

are proper elements of 'actual value' and plus any abnormal discount or other reduction from the ordinary competitive price.

2   It would be in conformity with Article VII, para 2(b), for a contracting party to construe the phrase 'in the ordinary course of trade ... under fully competitive conditions', as excluding any transaction wherein the buyer and seller are not independent of each other and price is not the sole consideration.

3   The standard of 'fully competitive conditions' permits a contracting party to exclude from consideration prices involving special discounts limited to exclusive agents.

4   The wording of sub-paras (a) and (b) permits a contracting party to determine the value for customs purposes uniformly either (1) on the basis of a particular exporter's prices of the imported merchandise, or (2) on the basis of the general price level of like merchandise.

Ad *Article VIII*

1   While Article VIII does not cover the use of multiple rates of exchange as such, paras 1 and 4 condemn the use of exchange taxes or fees as a device for implementing multiple currency practices; if, however, a contracting party is using multiple currency exchange fees for balance of payments reasons with the approval of the International Monetary Fund, the provisions of para 9(a) of Article XV fully safeguard its position.

2   It would be consistent with para 1 if, on the importation of products from the territory of a contracting party into the territory of another contracting party, the production of certificates of origin should only be required to the extent that is strictly indispensable.

Ad *Articles XI, XII, XIII, XIV and XVIII*

Throughout Articles XI, XII, XIII, XIV and XVIII, the terms 'import restrictions' or 'export restrictions' include restrictions made effective through State-trading operations.

Ad *Article XI*

Paragraph 2(c)

The term 'in any form' in this paragraph covers the same products when in an early stage of processing and still perishable, which compete directly with the fresh product and if freely imported would tend to make the restriction on the fresh product ineffective.

Paragraph 2, last sub-paragraph

The term 'special factors' includes changes in relative productive efficiency as between domestic and foreign producers, or as between different foreign producers, but not changes artificially brought about by means not permitted under the agreement.

Ad *Article XII*

The contracting parties shall make provision for the utmost secrecy in the conduct of any consultation under the provisions of this article.

Paragraph 3(c)(i)

Contracting parties applying restrictions shall endeavour to avoid causing serious prejudice to exports of a commodity on which the economy of a contracting party is largely dependent.

Paragraph 4(b)

It is agreed that the date shall be within 90 days after the entry into force of the amendments of this article effected by the Protocol Amending the Preamble and Parts II and III of this agreement. However, should the contracting parties find that conditions were not suitable for the application of the provisions of this sub-paragraph at the time envisaged, they may determine a later date; provided that such date is not more than thirty days after such time as the obligations of Article VIII, sections 2, 3 and 4, of the Articles of Agreement of the International Monetary Fund become applicable to contracting parties, members of the Fund, the combined foreign trade of which constitutes at least 50% of the aggregate foreign trade of all contracting parties.

Paragraph 4(e)

It is agreed that para 4(e) does not add any new criteria for the imposition or maintenance of quantitative restrictions for balance of payments reasons. It is solely intended to ensure that all external factors such as changes in the terms of trade, quantitative restrictions, excessive tariffs and subsidies, which may be contributing to the balance of payments difficulties of the contracting party applying restrictions, will be fully taken into account.

Ad *Article XIII*

Paragraph 2(d)

No mention was made of 'commercial considerations' as a rule for the allocation of quotas because it was considered that its application by governmental authorities might not always be practicable. Moreover, in cases where it is practicable, a contracting party could apply these considerations in the process of seeking agreement, consistently with the general rule laid down in the opening sentence of para 2.

Paragraph 4

See note relating to 'special factors' in connection with the last sub-paragraph of para 2 of Article XI.

Ad *Article XIV*

Paragraph 1

The provisions of this paragraph shall not be so construed as to preclude full consideration by the contracting parties, in the consultations provided for in para 4 of Article XII and in para 12 of Article XVIII, of the nature, effects and reasons for discrimination in the field of import restrictions.

Paragraph 2

One of the situations contemplated in para 2 is that of a contracting party holding balances acquired as a result of current transactions which it finds itself unable to use without a measure of discrimination.

Ad *Article XV*

Paragraph 4

The word 'frustrate' is intended to indicate, for example, that infringements of the letter of any article of this agreement by exchange action shall not be regarded as a violation of that article if, in practice, there is no appreciable departure from the intent of the article. Thus, a contracting party which, as part of its exchange control operated in accordance with the Articles of Agreement of the International Monetary Fund, requires payment to be received for its exports in its own currency or in the currency of one or more members of the International Monetary Fund will not thereby be deemed to contravene Article XI or Article XIII. Another example would be that of a contracting party which specifies on an import licence the country from which the goods may be imported, for the purpose not of introducing any additional element of discrimination in its import licensing system of enforcing permissible exchange controls.

Ad *Article XVI*

The exemption of an exported product from duties or taxes borne by the like product when destined for domestic consumption, or the remission of such duties or taxes in amounts not in excess of those which have accrued, shall not be deemed to be a subsidy.

Section B

1   Nothing in section B shall preclude the use by a contracting party of multiple rates of exchange in accordance with the Articles of Agreement of the International Monetary Fund.

2   For the purposes of section B, a 'primary product' is understood to be any product of farm, forest or fishery, or any mineral, in its natural form or which has undergone such

processing as is customarily required to prepare it for marketing in substantial volume in international trade.

Paragraph 3

1   The fact that a contracting party has not exported the product in question during the previous representative period would not in itself preclude that contracting party from establishing its right to obtain a share of the trade in the product concerned.

2   A system for the stabilisation of the domestic price or of the return to domestic producers of a primary product independently of the movements of export prices, which results at times in the sale of the product for export at a price lower than the comparable price charged for the like product to buyers in the domestic market, shall be considered not to involve a subsidy on exports within the meaning of para 3 if the contracting parties determine that:

   (a) the system has also resulted, or is so designed as to result, in the sale of the product for export at a price higher than the comparable price charged for the like product to buyers in the domestic market, and

   (b) the system is so operated, or is designed so to operate, either because of the effective regulation of production or otherwise, as not to stimulate exports unduly or otherwise seriously to prejudice the interests of other contracting parties.

Notwithstanding such determination by the contracting parties, operations under such a system shall be subject to the provisions of para 3 where they are wholly or partly financed out of government funds in addition to the funds collected from producers in respect of the product concerned.

Paragraph 4

The intention of para 4 is that the contracting parties should seek before the end of 1957 to reach agreement to abolish all remaining subsidies as from 1 January 1958; or, failing this, to reach agreement to extend the application of the standstill until the earliest date thereafter by which they can expect to reach such agreement.

Ad *Article XVII*

Paragraph 1

The operations of Marketing Boards, which are established by contracting parties and are engaged in purchasing or selling, are subject to the provisions of sub-paras (a) and (b).

The activities of Marketing Boards which are established by contracting parties and which do not purchase or sell but lay down regulations covering private trade are governed by the relevant articles of this agreement.

The charging by a state enterprise of different prices for its sales of a product in different markets is not precluded by the provisions of this article, provided that such different prices are charged for commercial reasons, to meet conditions of supply and demand in export markets.

Paragraph 1(a)

Governmental measures imposed to ensure standards of quality and efficiency in the operation of external trade, or privileges granted for the exploitation of national natural resources but which do not empower the government to exercise control over the trading activities of the enterprise in question, do not constitute 'exclusive or special privileges'.

Paragraph 1(b)

A country receiving a 'tied loan' is free to take this loan into account as a 'commercial consideration' when purchasing requirements abroad.

Paragraph 2

The term 'goods' is limited to products as understood in commercial practice, and is not intended to include the purchase or sale of services.

Paragraph 3

Negotiations which contracting parties agree to conduct under this paragraph may be directed towards the reduction of duties and other charges on imports and exports or towards the conclusion of any other mutually satisfactory arrangement consistent with the provisions of this agreement. (See para 4 of Article II and the note to that paragraph.)

Paragraph 4(b)

The term 'import mark-up' in this paragraph shall represent the margin by which the price charged by the import monopoly for the imported product (exclusive of internal taxes within the purview of Article III, transportation, distribution, and other expenses incident to the purchase, sale or further processing, and a reasonable margin of profit) exceeds the landed cost.

Ad *Article XVIII*

The contracting parties and the contracting parties concerned shall preserve the utmost secrecy in respect of matters arising under this article.

Paragraphs 1 and 4

1   When they consider whether the economy of a contracting party 'can only support low standards of living', the contracting parties shall take into consideration the normal position of that economy and shall not base their determination on exceptional circumstances such as those which may result from the temporary existence of exceptionally favourable conditions for the staple export product or products of such contracting party.

2   The phrase 'in the early stages of development' is not meant to apply only to contracting parties which have just started their economic development, but also to contracting parties the economies of which are undergoing a process of industrialisation to correct an excessive dependence on primary production.

Paragraphs 2, 3, 7, 13 and 22

The reference to the establishment of particular industries shall apply not only to the establishment of a new industry, but also to the establishment of a new branch of production in an existing industry and to the substantial transformation of an existing industry, and to the substantial expansion of an existing industry supplying a relatively small proportion of the domestic demand. It shall also cover the reconstruction of an industry destroyed or substantially damaged as a result of hostilities or natural disasters.

Paragraph 7(b)

A modification or withdrawal, pursuant to para 7(b), by a contracting party, other than the applicant contracting party, referred to in para 7(a), shall be made within six months of the day on which the action is taken by the applicant contracting party, and shall become effective on the 30th day following the day on which such modification or withdrawal has been notified to the contracting parties.

Paragraph 11

The second sentence in para 11 shall not be interpreted to mean that a contracting party is required to relax or remove restrictions if such relaxation or removal would thereupon produce conditions justifying the intensification or institution, respectively, of restrictions under para 9 of Article XVIII.

Paragraph 12(b)

The date referred to in para 12(b) shall be the date determined by the contracting parties in accordance with the provisions of para 4(b) of Article XII of this agreement.

Paragraphs 13 and 14

It is recognised that, before deciding on the introduction of a measure and notifying the contracting parties in accordance with para 14, a contracting party may need a reasonable period of time to assess the competitive position of the industry concerned.

Paragraphs 15 and 16

It is understood that the contracting parties shall invite a contracting party proposing to apply a measure under section C to consult with them pursuant to para 16 if they are requested to do so by a contracting party the trade of which would be appreciably affected by the measure in question.

Paragraphs 16, 18, 19 and 22

1   It is understood that the contracting parties may concur in a proposed measure subject to specific conditions or limitations. If the measure as applied does not conform to the terms of the concurrence, it will to that extent be deemed a measure in which the contracting parties have not concurred. In cases in which the contracting parties have concurred in a measure for a specified period, the contracting party concerned, if it finds that the maintenance of the measure for a further period of time is required to achieve the objective for which the measure was originally taken, may apply to the contracting parties for an extension of that period in accordance with the provisions and procedures of section C or D, as the case may be.

2   It is expected that the contracting parties will, as a rule, refrain from concurring in a measure which is likely to cause serious prejudice to exports of a commodity on which the economy of a contracting party is largely dependent.

Paragraphs 18 and 22

The phrase 'that the interests of other contracting parties are adequately safeguarded' is meant to provide latitude sufficient to permit consideration in each case of the most appropriate method of safeguarding those interests. The appropriate method may, for instance, take the form of an additional concession to be applied by the contracting party having recourse to section C or D during such time as the deviation from the other articles of the agreement would remain in force or of the temporary suspension by any other contracting party referred to in para 18 of a concession substantially equivalent to the impairment due to the introduction of the measure in question. Such contracting party would have the right to safeguard its interests through such a temporary suspension of a concession; provided that this right will not be exercised when, in the case of a measure imposed by a contracting party coming within the scope of para 4(a), the contracting parties have determined that the extent of the compensatory concession proposed was adequate.

Paragraph 19

The provisions of para 19 are intended to cover the cases where an industry has been in existence beyond the 'reasonable period of time' referred to in the note to paras 13 and 14, and should not be so construed as to deprive a contracting party coming within the scope of para 4(a) of Article XVIII, of its right to resort to the other provisions of section C, including para 17, with regard to a newly established industry even though it has benefited from incidental protection afforded by balance of payments import restrictions.

Paragraph 21

Any measure taken pursuant to the provisions of para 21 shall be withdrawn forthwith if the action taken in accordance with para 17 is withdrawn or if the contracting parties concur in the measure proposed after the expiration of the 90 day time limit specified in para 17.

Ad *Article XX*

Sub-paragraph (h)

The exception provided for in this sub-paragraph extends to any commodity agreement which conforms to the principles approved by the Economic and Social Council in its resolution (IV) of 28 March 1947.

Ad Article XXIV

Paragraph 9

It is understood that the provisions of Article I would require that, when a product which has been imported into the territory of a member of a customs union or free-trade area at a preferential rate of duty is re-exported to the territory of another member of such union or area, the latter member should collect a duty equal to the difference between the duty already paid and any higher duty that would be payable if the product were being imported directly into its territory.

Paragraph 11

Measures adopted by India and Pakistan in order to carry out definitive trade arrangements between them, once they have been agreed upon, might depart from particular provisions of this agreement, but these measures would general be consistent with the objectives of the agreement.

Ad Article XXVIII

The contracting parties and each contracting party concerned should arrange to conduct the negotiations and consultations with the greatest possible secrecy in order to avoid premature disclosure of details of prospective tariff changes. The contracting parties shall be informed immediately of all changes in national tariffs resulting from recourse to this article.

Paragraph 1

1   If the contracting parties specify a period other than a three year period a contracting party may act pursuant to para 1 or para 3 of Article XXVIII on the first day following the expiration of such other period and, unless the contracting parties have again specified another period, subsequent periods will be three-year periods following the expiration of such specified period.

2   The provision that on 1 January 1958, and on other days determined pursuant to para 1, a contracting party 'may … modify or withdraw a concession means that on such day, and on the first day after the end of each period, the legal obligation of such contracting party under Article II is altered; it does not mean that the changes in its customs tariff should necessarily be made effective on that day. If a tariff change resulting from negotiations undertaken pursuant to this article is delayed, the entry into force of any compensatory concessions may be similarly delayed.

3   Not earlier than six months, nor later than three months, prior to 1 January 1958, or to the termination date of any subsequent period, a contracting party wishing to modify or withdraw any concession embodied in the appropriate Schedule, should notify the contracting parties to this effect. The contracting parties shall then determine, the contracting party or contracting parties with which the negotiations or consultations referred to in para 1 shall take place. Any contracting party so determined shall participate in such negotiations or consultations with the applicant contracting party with the aim of reaching agreement before the end of the period. Any extension of the assured life of the Schedules shall relate to the Schedules as modified after such negotiations, in accordance with paras 1, 2 and 3 of Article XXVIII. If the contracting parties are arranging for multilateral tariff negotiations to take place within the period of six months before 1 January 1958, or before any other day determined pursuant to para 1, they shall include in the arrangements for such negotiations suitable procedures for carrying out the negotiations referred to in this para.

4   The object of providing for the participation in the negotiations of any contracting party with a principal supplying interest, in addition to any contracting party with which the concession was initially negotiated, is to ensure that a contracting party with a larger share in the trade affected by the concession than a contracting party with which the concession was initially negotiated shall have an effective opportunity to protect the contractual right which it enjoys under this agreement. On the other hand, it is not intended that the scope of the negotiations should be such as to make negotiations and agreement under Article XXVIII unduly difficult nor to create complications in the application of this article in the future to concessions which result from negotiations thereunder. Accordingly, the contracting parties should only determine that a contracting party has a principal supplying interest if that contracting party has had, over a reasonable period of time prior to the negotiations, a larger share in the market of the applicant contracting party than a contracting party with which the concession was initially negotiated or would, in the judgment of the contracting parties, have had such a share in the absence of discriminatory quantitative restrictions maintained by the applicant contracting party. It would therefore not be appropriate for the contracting parties to determine that more than one contracting party, or in those exceptional cases where there is near equality more than two contracting parties, had a principal supplying interest.

5   Notwithstanding the definition of a principal supplying interest in note 4 to para 1, the contracting parties may exceptionally determine that a contracting party has a principal supplying interest if the concession in question affects trade which constitutes a major part of the total exports of such contracting party.

6   It is not intended that provision for participation in the negotiations of any contracting party with a principal supplying interest, and for consultation with any contracting party having a substantial interest in the concession which the applicant contracting party is seeking to modify or withdraw, should have the effect that it should have to pay compensation or suffer retaliation greater than the withdrawal or modification sought, judged in the light of the conditions of trade at the time of the proposed withdrawal or modification. making allowance for any discriminatory quantitative restrictions maintained by the applicant contracting party.

7   The expression 'substantial interest' is not capable of a precise definition and accordingly may present difficulties for the contracting parties. It is, however, intended to be construed to cover only those contracting parties which have, or in the absence of discriminatory quantitative restrictions affecting their exports could reasonably be expected to have, a significant share in the market of the contracting party seeking to modify or withdraw the concession.

Paragraph 4

1   Any request for authorisation to enter into negotiations shall be accompanied by all relevant statistical and other data. A decision on such request shall be made within 30 days of its submission.

2   It is recognised that to permit certain contracting parties, depending in large measure on a relatively small number of primary commodities and relying on the tariff as an important aid for furthering diversification of their economies or as an important source of revenue, normally to negotiate for the modification or withdrawal of concessions only under para 1 of Article XXVIII, might cause them at such a time to make modifications or withdrawals which in the long run would prove unnecessary. To avoid such a situation the contracting parties shall authorise any such contracting party, under para 4, to enter into negotiations unless they consider this would result in, or contribute substantially towards, such an increase in tariff levels as to threaten the stability of the Schedules to this agreement or lead to undue disturbance of international trade.

3   It is expected that negotiations authorised under para 4 for modification or withdrawal of a single item, or a very small group of items, could normally be brought to a conclusion in 60 days. It is recognised, however, that such a period will be inadequate for cases involving negotiations for the modification or withdrawal of a larger number of items and in such cases, therefore, it would be appropriate for the contracting parties to prescribe a longer period.

4   The determination referred to in para 4(d) shall be made by the contracting parties within 30 days of the submission of the matter to them unless the applicant contracting party agrees to a longer period.

5   In determining under para 4(d) whether an applicant contracting party has unreasonably failed to offer adequate compensation, it is understood that the contracting parties will take due account of the special position of a contracting party which has bound a high proportion of its tariffs at very low rates of duty and to this extent has less scope than other contracting parties to make compensatory adjustment.

Ad *Article XXVIII bis*

Paragraph 3

It is understood that the reference to fiscal needs would include the revenue aspect of duties and particularly duties imposed primarily for revenue purpose, or duties imposed on products which can be substituted for products subject to revenue duties to prevent the avoidance of such duties.

Ad *Article XXIX*

Paragraph 1

Chapters VII and VIII of the Havana Charter have been excluded from para 1 because they generally deal with the organisation, functions and procedures of the International Trade Organisation.

Ad *Part IV*

The words 'developed contracting parties' and the words 'less developed contracting parties' as used in Part IV are to be understood to refer to developed and less developed countries which are parties to the General Agreement on Tariffs and Trade.

Ad *Article XXXVI*

Paragraph 1

This article is based upon the objectives set forth in Article I as it will be amended by section A of para 1 of the protocol amending Part I and Articles XXIX and XXX when that protocol enters into force.

Paragraph 4

The term 'primary products' includes agricultural products, *vide* para 2 of the note ad Article XVI, section B.

Paragraph 5

A diversification programme would generally include the intensification of activities for the processing of primary products and the development of manufacturing industries, taking into account the situation of the particular contracting party and the world outlook for production and consumption of different commodities.

Paragraph 8

It is understood that the phrase 'do not expect reciprocity' means, in accordance with the objectives set forth in this article, that the less developed contracting parties should not be expected, in the course of trade negotiations, to make contributions which are inconsistent with their individual development, financial and trade needs, taking into consideration past trade developments.

This paragraph would apply in the event of action under section A of Article XVIII, Article XXVIII, Article XXVIII *bis* (Article XXIX after the amendment set forth in section A of para 1 of the protocol amending Part I and Articles XXIX and XXX shall have become effective), Article XXXIII, or any other procedure under this agreement.

Ad *Article XXXVII*

Paragraph 1(a)

This paragraph would apply in the event of negotiations for reduction or elimination of tariffs or other restrictive regulations of commerce under Articles XXVIII, XXVIII *bis* (XXIX after the amendment set forth in section A of para 1 of the protocol amending Part I and Articles XXIX and XXX shall have become effective), and Article XXXIII, as well as in connection with other action to effect such reduction or elimination which contracting parties may be able to undertake.

Paragraph 3(b)

The other measures referred to in this paragraph might include steps to promote domestic structural changes, to encourage the consumption of particular products, or to introduce measures of trade promotion.

UNDERSTANDING ON RULES AND PROCEDURES GOVERNING THE SETTLEMENT OF DISPUTES

Annex 2 to the WTO Agreement

Members hereby agree as follows:

Article 1 – Coverage and application

1   The rules and procedures of this understanding shall apply to disputes brought pursuant to the consultation and dispute settlement provisions of the agreements listed m Appendix 1 to this understanding (referred to in this understanding as the 'covered agreements').

The rules and procedures of this understanding shall also apply to consultations and the settlement of disputes between Members concerning their rights and obligations under the provisions of the Agreement Establishing the World Trade Organisation (referred to in this understanding as the 'WTO Agreement') and of this understanding taken in isolation or in combination with any other covered agreement.

2   The rules and procedures of this understanding shall apply subject to such special or additional rules and procedures on dispute settlement contained in the covered agreements as are identified in Appendix 2 to this understanding. To the extent that there is a difference between the rules and procedures of this understanding and the special or additional rules and procedures set forth in Appendix 2, the special or additional rules and procedures in Appendix 2 shall prevail. In disputes involving rules and procedures under more than one covered agreement, If there is a conflict between special or additional rules and procedures or such agreements under review, and where the parties to the dispute cannot agree on rules and procedures within 20 days of the establishment of the panel, the Chairman of the Dispute Settlement Body provided for in para 1 of Article 2 (referred to in this understanding as the 'DSB'), in consultation with the parties to the dispute, shall determine the rules and procedures to be followed within 10 days after a request by either Member. The Chairman shall be guided by the principle that special or additional rules and procedures should be used where possible, and the rules and procedures set out in this understanding should be used to the extent necessary to avoid conflict.

Article 2 – Administration

1   The Dispute Settlement Body is hereby established to administer these rules and procedures and, except as otherwise provided in a covered agreement, the consultation and dispute settlement provisions of the covered agreements. Accordingly, the DSB shall have the authority to establish panels, adopt panel and Appellate Body reports, maintain surveillance of implementation of rulings and recommendations, and authorise suspension of concessions and other obligations under the covered agreements. With respect to disputes arising under a covered agreement which is a Plurilateral Trade Agreement, the term 'Member' as used herein shall refer only to those Members that are parties to the relevant Plurilateral Trade Agreement. Where the DSB administers the dispute settlement provisions of a Plurilateral Trade Agreement, only those Members that are parties to that agreement may participate in decisions or actions taken by the DSB with respect to that dispute.

2   The DSB shall inform the relevant WTO Councils and Committees of any developments in disputes related to provisions of the respective covered agreements.

3   The DSB shall meet as often as necessary to carry out its functions within the time frames provided in this understanding.

4   Where the rules and procedures of this understanding provide for the DSB to take a decision, it shall do so by consensus.

Article 3 – General provisions

1   Members affirm their adherence to the principles for the management of disputes heretofore applied under Articles XXII and XXIII of GATT 1947, and the rules and procedures as further elaborated and modified herein.

2   The dispute settlement system of the WTO is a central element in providing security and predictability to the multilateral trading system. The Members recognise that it serves to preserve the rights and obligations of Members under the covered agreements, and to clarify the existing provisions of those agreements in accordance with customary rules of interpretation of public international law. Recommendations and rulings of the DSB cannot add to or diminish the rights and obligations provided in the covered agreements.

3   The prompt settlement of situations in which a Member considers that any benefits accruing to it directly or indirectly under the covered agreements are being impaired by measures taken by another is essential to the effective functioning of the WTO and the maintenance of a proper balance between the rights and obligations of Members.

4   Recommendations or rulings made by the DSB shall be aimed at achieving a satisfactory settlement of the matter in accordance with the rights and obligations under this understanding and under the covered agreements.

5   All solutions to matters formally raised under the consultation and dispute settlement provisions of the covered agreements, including arbitration awards, shall be consistent with those agreements and shall not nullify or impair benefits accruing to any Member under those agreements, nor impede the attainment of any objective of those agreements.

6   Mutually agreed solutions to matters formally raised under the consultation and dispute settlement provisions of the covered agreements shall be notified to the DSB and the relevant Councils and Committees, where any Member may raise any point relating thereto.

7   Before bringing a case, a Member shall exercise its judgment as to whether action under these procedures would be fruitful. The aim of the dispute settlement mechanism is to secure a positive solution to a dispute. A solution mutually acceptable to the parties to a dispute and consistent with the covered agreements is clearly to be preferred. In the absence of a mutually agreed solution, the first objective of the dispute settlement mechanism is usually to secure the withdrawal of the measures concerned if these are found to be inconsistent with the provisions of any of the covered agreements. The provision of compensation should be resorted to only if the immediate withdrawal of the measure is impracticable and as a temporary measure pending the withdrawal of the measure which is inconsistent with a covered agreement. The last resort which this understanding provides to the Member invoking the dispute settlement procedures is the possibility of suspending the application of concessions or other obligations under the covered agreements on a discriminatory basis vis à vis the other Member, subject to authorisation by the DSB of such measures.

8   In cases where there is an infringement of the obligations assumed under a covered agreement, the action is considered *prima facie* to constitute a case of nullification or impairment. This means that there is normally a presumption that a breach of the rules has an adverse impact on other Members parties to that covered agreement, and in such cases, it shall be up to the Member against whom the complaint has been brought to rebut the charge.

9   The provisions of this understanding are without prejudice to the rights of Members to seek authoritative interpretation of provisions of a covered agreement through decision-making under the WTO Agreement or a covered agreement which is a Plurilateral Trade Agreement.

10   It is understood that requests for conciliation and the use of the dispute settlement procedures should not be intended or considered as contentious acts and that, if a dispute arises, all Members will engage in these procedures in good faith in an effort to resolve the dispute. It is also understood that complaints and counter-complaints in regard to distinct matters should not be linked.

11   This understanding shall be applied only with respect to new requests for consultations under the consultation provisions of the covered agreements made on or after the date of entry into force of the WTO Agreement. With respect to disputes for which the request for consultations was made under GATT 1947 or under any other predecessor agreement to the covered agreements before the date of entry into force of the WTO Agreement, the relevant dispute settlement rules and procedures in effect immediately prior to the date of entry into force of the WTO Agreement shall continue to apply.

12   Notwithstanding para 11, if a complaint based on any of the covered agreements is brought by a developing country Member against a developed country Member, the complaining party shall have the right to invoke, as an alternative to the provisions contained in Articles 4, 5, 6 and 12 of this understanding, the corresponding provisions of the decision of 5 April 1966 (BISD 14S/18), except that where the panel considers that the time frame provided for in para 7 of that decision is insufficient to provide its report and with the agreement of the complaining party, that time frame may be extended. To the extent that there is a difference between the rules and procedures of Articles 4, 5, 6 and 12 and the corresponding rules and procedures of the decision, the latter shall prevail.

Article 4 – Consultations

1   Members affirm their resolve to strengthen and improve the effectiveness of the consultation procedures employed by Members.

2   Each Member undertakes to accord sympathetic consideration to and afford adequate opportunity for consultation regarding any representations made by another Member concerning measures affecting the operation of any covered agreement taken within the territory of the former.

3   If a request for consultations is made pursuant to a covered agreement, the Member to which the request is made shall, unless otherwise mutually agreed, reply to the request within 10 days after the date of its receipt and shall enter into consultations in good faith within a period of no more than 30 days after the date of receipt of the request, with a view to reaching a mutually satisfactory solution. If the Member does not respond within 10 days after the date of receipt of the request, or does not enter into consultations within a period of no more than 30 days, or a period otherwise mutually agreed, after the date of receipt of the request, then the Member that requested the holding of consultations may proceed directly to request the establishment of a panel.

4   All such requests for consultations shall be notified to the DSB and the relevant Councils and Committees by the Member which requests consultations. Any request for consultations shall be submitted in writing and shall give the reasons for the request, including identification of the measures at issue and an indication of the legal basis for the complaint.

5   In the course of consultations in accordance with the provisions of a covered agreement, before resorting to further action under this understanding, Members should attempt to obtain satisfactory adjustment of the matter.

6   Consultations shall be confidential, and without prejudice to the rights of any Member in any further proceedings.

7   If the consultations fail to settle a dispute within 60 days after the date of receipt of the request for consultations, the complaining party may request the establishment of a panel. The complaining party may request a panel during the 60 day period if the consulting parties jointly consider that consultations have failed to settle the dispute.

8   In cases or urgency, including those watch concern perishable goods, Members shall enter into consultations within a period of no more than 10 days after the date of receipt of the request. If the consultations have failed to settle the dispute within a period of 20 days after the date of receipt of the request, the complaining party may request the establishment of a panel.

9   In cases of urgency, including those which concern perishable goods, the parties to the dispute, panels and the Appellate Body shall make every effort to accelerate the proceedings to the greatest extent possible.

10 During consultations Members should give special attention to the particular problems and interests of developing country Members.

11 Whenever a Member other than the consulting Members considers that it has a substantial trade interest in consultations being held pursuant to para 1 of Article XXII of GATT 1994, para 1 of Article XXII of GATS, or the corresponding provisions in other covered agreements, such Member may notify the consulting Members and the DSB, within 10 days after the date of the circulation of the request for consultations under said article, of its desire to be joined in the consultations. Such Member shall be joined in the consultations, provided that the Member to which the request for consultations was addressed agrees that the claim of substantial interest is well founded. In that event they shall so inform the DSB. If the request to be joined in the consultations is not accepted, the applicant Member shall be free to request consultations under para 1 of Article XXII or para 1 of Article XXIII of GATT 1994, para 1 of Article XXII or para 1 of Article XXIII of GATS, or the corresponding provisions in other covered agreements.

Article 5 – Good offices, conciliation and mediation

1   Good offices, conciliation and mediation are procedures that are undertaken voluntarily if the parties to the dispute so agree.

2   Proceedings involving good offices, conciliation and mediation, and in particular positions taken by the parties to the dispute during these proceedings shall be confidential, and without prejudice to the rights of either party in any further proceedings under these procedures.

3   Good offices, conciliation or mediation may be requested at any time by any party to a dispute. They may begin at any time and be terminated at any time. Once procedures for good offices, conciliation or mediation are terminated, a complaining party may then proceed with a request for the establishment of a panel.

4   When good of offices, conciliation or mediation are entered into within 60 days after the date of receipt of a request for consultations, the complaining party must allow a period of 60 days after the date of receipt of the request for consultations before requesting the establishment of a panel. The complaining party may request the establishment of a panel during the 60 day period if the parties to the dispute jointly consider that the good offices, conciliation or mediation process has failed to settle the dispute.

5   If the parties to a dispute agree, procedures for good offices, conciliation or mediation may continue while the panel process proceeds.

6   The Director General may, acting in an *ex officio* capacity, offer good offices, conciliation or mediation with the view to assisting Members to settle a dispute.

Article 6 – Establishment of panels

1   If the complaining party so requests, a panel shall be established at the latest at the DSB meeting following that at which the request first appears as an item on the DSB's agenda, unless at that meeting the DSB decides by consensus not to establish a panel.

2   The request for the establishment of a panel shall be made in writing. It shall indicate whether consultations were held, identify the specific measures at issue and provide a brief summary of the legal basis of the complaint sufficient to present the problem clearly. In case the applicant requests the establishment of a panel with other than standard terms of reference, the written request shall include the proposed text of special terms of reference.

Article 7 – Terms of reference of panels

1   Panels shall have the following terms of reference unless the parties to the dispute agree otherwise within 20 days from the establishment of the panel:

To examine, in the light of the relevant provisions in (name of the covered agreement(s) cited by the parties to the dispute), the matter referred to the DSB by (name of party) in document … and to make such findings as will assist the DSB in making the recommendations or in giving the rulings provided for in that/those agreement(s).

2   Panels shall address the relevant provisions in any covered agreement or agreements cited by the parties to the dispute.

3   In establishing a panel, the DSB may authorise its Chairman to draw up the terms of reference of the panel in consultation with the parties to the dispute, subject to the provisions of para 1. The terms of reference thus drawn up shall be circulated to all Members. If other than standard terms of reference are agreed upon, any Member may raise any point relating thereto in the DSB.

Article 8 – Composition of panels

1   Panels shall be composed of well qualified governmental and/or non-governmental individuals, including persons who have served on or presented a case to a panel, served as a representative of a Member or of a contracting party to GATT 1947 or as a representative to the Council or Committee of any covered agreement or its predecessor agreement, or in the Secretariat, taught or published on international trade law or policy, or served as a senior trade policy official of a Member.

2   Panel members should be selected with a view to ensuring the independence of the members, a sufficiently diverse background and a wide spectrum of experience.

3   Citizens of Members whose governments are parties to the dispute or third parties as defined in para 2 of Article 10 shall not serve on a panel concerned with that dispute, unless the parties to the dispute agree otherwise.

4   To assist in the selection of panelists, the Secretariat shall maintain an indicative list of governmental and non-governmental individuals possessing the qualifications outlined in para 1, from which panelists may be drawn as appropriate. That list shall include the roster of non-governmental panelists established on 30 November 1984 (BISD 31S/9), and

other rosters and indicative lists established under any of the covered agreements, and shall retain the names of persons on those rosters and indicative lists at the time of entry into force of the WTO Agreement. Members may periodically suggest names of governmental and non-governmental individuals for inclusion on the indicative list, providing relevant information on their knowledge of international trade and of the sectors or subject matter of the covered agreements, and those names shall be added to the list upon approval by the DSB. For each of the individuals on the list, the list shall indicate specific areas of experience or expertise of the individuals in the sectors or subject matter of the covered agreements.

5   Panels shall be composed of three panelists unless the parties to the dispute agree, within 10 days from the establishment of the panel, to a panel composed of five panelists. Members shall be informed promptly of the composition of the panel.

6   The Secretariat shall propose nominations for the panel to the parties to the dispute. The parties to the dispute shall not oppose nominations except for compelling reasons.

7   If there is no agreement on the panelists within 20 days after the date of the establishment of a panel, at the request of either party, the Director General, in consultation with the Chairman of the DSB and the Chairman of the relevant Council or Committee, shall determine the composition of the panel by appointing the panelists whom the Director General considers most appropriate in accordance with any relevant special or additional rules or procedures of the covered agreement or covered agreements which are at issue in the dispute, after consulting with the parties to the dispute. The Chairman of the DSB shall inform the Members of the composition of the panel thus formed no later than 10 days after the date the Chairman receives such a request.

8   Members shall undertake, as a general rule, to permit their officials to serve as panelists.

9   Panelists shall serve in their individual capacities and not as government representatives, nor as representatives of any organisation. Members shall therefore not give them instructions nor seek to influence them as individuals with regard to matters before a panel.

10   When a dispute is between a developing country Member and a developed country Member the panel shall, if the developing country Member so requests, include at least one panelist from a developing country Member.

11   Panelists' expenses, including travel and subsistence allowance, shall be met from the WTO budget in accordance with criteria to be adopted by the General Council, based on recommendations of the Committee on Budget, Finance and Administration.

Article 9 – Procedures for multiple complainants

1   Where more than one Member requests the establishment of a panel related to the same matter, a single panel may be established to examine these complaints taking into account the rights of all Members concerned. A single panel should be established to examine such complaints whenever feasible.

2   The single panel shall organise its examination and present its findings to the DSB in such a manner that the rights which the parties to the dispute would have enjoyed had separate panels examined the complaints are in no way impaired. If one of the parties to the dispute so requests, the panel shall submit separate reports on the dispute concerned. The written submissions by each of the complainants shall be made available to the other complainants, and each complainant shall have the right to be present when any one of the other complainants presents its views to the panel.

3   If more than one panel is established to examine the complaints related to the same matter, to the greatest extent possible the same persons shall serve as panelists on each of the separate panels and the timetable for the panel process in such disputes shall be harmonised.

Article 10 – Third parties

1   The interests of the parties to a dispute and those of other Members under a covered agreement at issue in the dispute shall be fully taken into account during the panel process.

2   Any Member having a substantial interest in a matter before a panel and having notified its interest to the DSB (referred to in this understanding as a 'third party') shall have an opportunity to be heard by the panel and to make written submissions to the panel. These submissions shall also be given to the parties to the dispute and shall be reflected in the panel report.

3   Third parties shall receive the submissions of the parties to the dispute to the first meeting of the panel.

4   If a third party considers that a measure already the subject of a panel proceeding nullifies or impairs benefits accruing to it under any covered agreement, that Member may have recourse to normal dispute settlement procedures under this understanding. Such a dispute shall be referred to the original panel wherever possible.

Article 11 – Function of panels

The function of panels is to assist the DSB in discharging its responsibilities under this understanding and the covered agreements. Accordingly, a panel should make an objective assessment of the matter before it, including an objective assessment of the facts of the case and the applicability of and conformity with the relevant covered agreements, and make such other findings as will assist the DSB in making the recommendations or in giving the rulings provided for in the covered agreements. Panels should consult regularly with the parties to the dispute and give them adequate opportunity to develop a mutually satisfactory solution.

Article 12 – Panel procedures

1   Panels shall follow the working procedures in Appendix 3 unless the panel decides otherwise after consulting the parties to the dispute.

2   Panel procedures should provide sufficient flexibility so as to ensure high quality panel reports, while not unduly delaying the panel process.

3   After consulting the parties to the dispute, the panelists shall, as soon as practicable and whenever possible within one week after the composition and terms of reference of the panel have been agreed upon, fix the timetable for the panel process, taking into account the provisions of para 9 of Article 4, if relevant.

4   In determining the timetable for the panel process, the panel shall provide sufficient time for the parties to the dispute to prepare their submissions.

5   Panels should set precise deadlines for written submissions by the parties and the parties should respect those deadlines.

6   Each party to the dispute shall deposit its written submissions with the Secretariat for immediate transmission to the panel and to the other party or parties to the dispute. The complaining party shall submit its first submission in advance of the responding party's first submission unless the panel decides, in fixing the timetable referred to in para 3 and after consultations with the parties to the dispute, that the parties should submit their first submissions simultaneously. When there are sequential arrangements for the deposit of first submissions, the panel shall establish a firm time period for receipt of the responding party's submission. Any subsequent written submissions shall be submitted simultaneously.

7   Where the parties to the dispute have failed to develop a mutually satisfactory solution, the panel shall submit its findings in the form of a written report to the DSB. In such cases, the report of a panel shall set out the findings of fact, the applicability of relevant provisions and the basic rationale behind any findings and recommendations that it makes. Where a settlement of the matter among the parties to the dispute has been found, the report of the panel shall be confined to a brief description of the case and to reporting that a solution has been reached.

8   In order to make the procedures more efficient, the period in which the panel shall conduct its examination, from the date that the composition and terms of reference of the panel have been agreed upon until the date the final report is issued to the parties to the dispute, shall, as a general rule, not exceed six months. In cases of urgency, including those relating to perishable goods, the panel shall aim to issue report to the parties to the dispute within three months.

9   When the panel considers that it cannot issue its report within six months, or within three months in cases of urgency, it shall inform the DSB in writing of the reasons for the delay together with an estimate of the period within which it will issue its report. In no case should the period from the establishment of the panel to the circulation of the report to the Members exceed nine months.

10   In the context of consultations involving a measure taken by a developing country Member, the parties may agree to extend the periods established in paras 7 and 8 of Article 4. If, after the relevant period has elapsed, the consulting parties cannot agree that the consultations have concluded, the Chairman of the DSB shall decide, after consultation with the parties, whether to extend the relevant period and, If so, for how long. In addition, in examining a complaint against a developing country Member, the pane! shall accord sufficient time for the developing country Member to prepare and present its argumentation. The provisions of para 1 of Article 20 and para 4 of Article 21 are not affected by any action pursuant to this paragraph.

11   Where one or more of the parties is a developing country Member, the panel's report shall explicitly indicate the form in which account has been taken of relevant provisions on differential and more-favourable treatment for developing country Members that form part of the covered agreements which have been raised by the developing country Member in the course of the dispute settlement procedures.

12   The panel may suspend its work at any time at the request of the complaining party for a period not to exceed 12 months. In the event of such a suspension, the time frames set out in paras 8 and 9 of this Article, para 1 of Article 20, and para 4 of Article 21 shall be extended by the amount of time that the work was suspended. If the work of the panel has been suspended for more than 12 months, the authority for establishment of the panel shall lapse.

Article 13 – Right to seek information

1   Each panel shall have the right to seek information and technical advice from any individual or body which it deems appropriate. However, before a panel seeks such information or advice from any individual or body within the jurisdiction of a Member it shall inform the authorities of that Member. A Member should respond promptly and fully to any request by a panel for such information as the panel considers necessary and appropriate. Confidential information which is provided shall not be revealed without formal authorisation from the individual, body, or authorities of the Member providing the information.

2   Panels may seek information from any relevant source and may consult experts to obtain their opinion on certain aspects of the matter. With respect to a factual issue concerning a scientific or other technical matter raised by a party to a dispute, a panel may request an advisory report in writing from an expert review group. Rules for the establishment of such a group and its procedures are set forth in Appendix 4.

Article 14 – Confidentiality

1   Panel deliberations shall be confidential.

2   The reports of panels shall be drafted without the presence of the parties to the dispute in the light of the information provided and the statements made.

3   Opinions expressed in the panel report by individual panelists shall be anonymous.

Article 15 – Interim review stage

1   Following the consideration of rebuttal submissions and oral arguments, the panel shall issue the descriptive (factual and argument) sections of its draft report to the parties to the dispute. Within a period of time set by the panel, the parties shall submit their comments in writing.

2   Following the expiration of the set period of time for receipt of comments from the parties to the dispute, the panel shall issue an interim report to the parties, including both the descriptive sections and the panel's findings and conclusions. Within a period of time set by the panel, a party may submit a written request for the panel to review precise aspects of the interim report prior to circulation of the final report to the Members. At the request of a party, the panel shall hold a further meeting with the parties on the issues identified in

the written comments. If no comments are received from any party within the comment period, the interim report shall be considered the final panel report and circulated promptly to the Members.

3   The findings of the final panel report shall include a discussion of the arguments made at the interim review stage. The interim review stage shall be conducted within the time period set out in para 8 of Article 12.

Article 16 – Adoption of panel reports

1   In order to provide sufficient time for the Members to consider panel reports the reports shall not be considered for adoption by the DSB until 20 days after the date they have been circulated to the Members.

2   Members having objections to a panel report shall give written reasons to explain their objections for circulation at least 10 days prior to the DSB meeting at which the panel report will be considered.

3   The parties to a dispute shall have the right to participate fully in the consideration of the panel report by the DSB, and their views shall be fully recorded.

4   Within 60 days after the date of circulation of a panel report to the Members the report shall be adopted at a DSB meetings unless a party to the dispute formally notifies the DSB of its decision to appeal or the DSB decides by consensus not to adopt the report. If a party has notified its decision to appeal, the report by the panel shall not be considered for adoption by the DSB until after completion of the appeal. This adoption procedure is without prejudice to the right of Members to express their views on a panel report.

7   If a meeting of the DSB is not scheduled within this period at a time that enables the requirements of paras 1 and 4 of Article 16 to be met, a meeting of the DSB shall be held for this purpose.

Article 17 – Appellate review

Standing Appellate Body

1   A Standing Appellate Body shall be established by the DSB. The Appellate Body shall hear appeals from panel cases. It shall be composed of seven persons three of whom shall serve on any one case. Persons serving on the Appellate Body shall serve in rotation. Such rotation shall be determined in the working procedures of the Appellate Body.

2   The DSB shall appoint persons to serve on the Appellate Body for a four year term, and each person may be reappointed once. However, the terms of three of the seven persons appointed immediately after the entry into force of the WTO Agreement shall expire at the end of two years, to be determined by lot. Vacancies shall be filled as they arise. A person appointed to replace a person whose term of office has not expired shall hold office for the remainder of the predecessor's term.

3   The Appellate Body shall comprise persons of recognised authority, with demonstrated expertise in law, international trade and the subject matter of the covered agreements generally. They shall be unaffiliated with any government. The Appellate Body membership shall be broadly representative of membership in the WTO. All persons serving on the Appellate Body shall be available at all times and on short notice, and shall stay abreast of dispute settlement activities and other relevant activities of the WTO. They shall not participate in the consideration of any disputes that would create a direct or indirect conflict of interest.

4   Only parties to the dispute, not third parties, may appeal a panel report. Third parties which have notified the DSB of a substantial interest in the matter pursuant to para 2 of Article 10 may make written submissions to, and be given an opportunity to be heard by the Appellate Body.

5   As a general rule, the proceedings shall not exceed 60 days from the date a party to the dispute formally notifies its decision to appeal to the date the Appellate Body circulates its report. In fixing its timetable the Appellate Body shall take into account the provisions of para 9 of Article 4, if relevant. When the Appellate Body considers that it cannot provide its report within 60 days, it shall inform the DSB in writing of the reasons for the delay together with an estimate of the period within which it will submit its report. In no case shall the proceedings exceed 90 days.

6   An appeal shall be limited to issues of law covered in the panel report and legal interpretations developed by the panel.

7   The Appellate Body shall be provided with appropriate administrative and legal support as it requires.

8   The expenses of persons serving on the Appellate Body, including travel and subsistence allowance, shall be met from the WTO budget in accordance with criteria to be adopted by the General Council, based on recommendations of the Committee on Budget, Finance and Administration.

Procedures for appellate review

9   Working procedures shall be drawn up by the Appellate Body in consultation with the Chairman of the DSB and the Director General, and communicated to the Members for their information.

10   The proceedings of the Appellate Body shall be confidential. The reports of the Appellate Body shall be drafted without the presence of the parties to the dispute and in the light of the information provided and the statements made.

11   Opinions expressed in the Appellate Body report by individuals serving on the Appellate Body shall be anonymous.

12   The Appellate Body shall address each of the issues raised in accordance with para 6 during the appellate proceeding.

13   The Appellate Body may uphold, modify or reverse the legal findings and conclusions of the panel.

Adoption of appellate body reports

14   An Appellate Body report shall be adopted by the DSB and unconditionally accepted by the parties to the dispute unless the DSB decides by consensus not to adopt the Appellate Body report within 30 days following its circulation to the Members. This adoption procedure is without prejudice to the right of Members to express their views on an Appellate Body report.

Article 18 – Communications with the panel or Appellate Body

1   There shall be no *ex parte* communications with the panel or Appellate Body concerning matters under consideration by the panel or Appellate Body.

2   Written submissions to the panel or the Appellate Body shall be treated as confidential, but shall be made available to the parties to the dispute. Nothing in this understanding shall preclude a party to a dispute from disclosing statements of its own positions to the public. Members shall treat as confidential information submitted by another Member to the panel or the Appellate Body which that Member has designated as confidential. A party to a dispute shall also, upon request of a Member, provide a non-confidential summary of the information contained in its written submissions that could be disclosed to the public.

Article 19 – Panel and appellate body recommendations

1   Where a panel or the Appellate Body concludes that a measure is inconsistent with a covered agreement, it shall recommend that the Member concerned bring the measure into conformity with that agreement. In addition to its recommendations, the panel or Appellate Body may suggest ways in which the Member concerned could implement the recommendations.

2   In accordance with para 2 of Article 3, in their findings and recommendations, the panel and Appellate Body cannot add to or diminish the rights and obligations provided in the covered agreements.

Article 20 – Time frame for DSB decisions

Unless otherwise agreed to by the parties to the dispute, the period from the date of establishment of the panel by the DSB until the date the DSB considers the panel or appellate report for adoption shall as a general rule not exceed nine months where the panel report is not appealed or 12 months where the report is appealed. Where either the panel or the Appellate Body has acted, pursuant to para 9 of Article 12 or para 5 of Article 17, to extend the time for providing its report, the additional time taken shall be added to the above periods.

Article 21 – Surveillance of implementation of recommendations and rulings

1   Prompt compliance with recommendations or rulings of the DSB is essential at order to ensure effective resolution of disputes to the benefit of all Members.

2   Particular attention should be paid to matters affecting the interest of developing country Members with respect to measures which have been subject to dispute settlement.

3   At a DSB meeting held within 30 days after the date of adoption of the panel or Appellate Body report, the Member concerned shall inform the DSB of its intentions in respect of implementation of the recommendations and rulings of the DSB. If it is impracticable to comply immediately with the recommendations and rulings the Member concerned shall have a reasonable period of time in which to do so. The reasonable period of time shall be:

   (a) the period of time proposed by the Member concerned, provided that such period is approved by the DSB; or, in the absence of such approval;

   (b) a period of time mutually agreed by the parties to the dispute within 45 days after the date of adoption of the recommendations and rulings; or, in the absence of such agreement;

   (c) a period of time determined through binding arbitration within 90 days after the date of adoption of the recommendations and rulings. In such arbitration, a guideline for the arbitrator should be that the reasonable period of time to implement panel or Appellate Body recommendations should not exceed 15 months from the date of adoption of a panel or Appellate Body report. However, that time may be shorter or longer, depending upon the particular circumstances.

4   Except where the panel or the Appellate Body has extended, pursuant to para 9 of Article 12 or para 5 of Article 17, the time of providing its report, the period from the date of establishment of the panel by the DSB until the date of determination of the reasonable period of time shall not exceed 15 months unless the parties to the dispute agree otherwise. Where either the panel or the Appellate Body has acted to extend the time of providing its report, the additional time taken shall be added to the 15-month period; provided that unless the parties to the dispute agree that there are exceptional circumstances, the total time shall not exceed 18 months.

5   Where there is disagreement as to the existence or consistency with a covered agreement of measures taken to comply with the recommendations and rulings such dispute shall be decided through recourse to these dispute settlement procedures, including wherever possible resort to the original panel. The panel shall circulate its report within 90 days after the date of referral of the matter to it. When the panel considers that it cannot provide its report within this time frame, it shall inform the DSB in writing of the reasons for the delay together with an estimate of the period within which it will submit its report.

6   The DSB shall keep under surveillance the implementation of adopted recommendations or rulings. The issue of implementation of the recommendations or rulings may be raised at the DSB by any Member at any time following their adoption. Unless the DSB decides otherwise, the issue of implementation of the recommendations or rulings shall be placed on the agenda of the DSB meeting after six months following the date of establishment of the reasonable period of time pursuant to para 3 and shall remain on the DSB's agenda until the issue is resolved. At least 10 days prior to each such DSB meeting, the Member concerned shall provide the DSB with a status report in writing of its progress in the implementation of the recommendations or rulings.

7   If the matter is one which has been raised by a developing country Member, the DSB shall consider what further action it might take which would be appropriate to the circumstances.

8   If the case is one brought by a developing country Member, in considering what appropriate action might be taken, the DSB shall take into account not only the trade coverage of measures complained of, but also their impact on the economy of developing country Members concerned.

Article 22 – Compensation and the suspension of concessions

1   Compensation and the suspension of concessions or other obligations are temporary measures available in the event that the recommendations and rulings are not Implemented within a reasonable period of time. However, neither compensation nor the

suspension of concessions or other obligations is preferred to full implementation of a recommendation to bring a measure into conformity with the covered agreements. Compensation is voluntary and, if granted, shall be consistent with the covered agreements.

2   If the Member concerned fails to bring the measure found to be inconsistent with a covered agreement into compliance therewith or otherwise comply with the recommendations and rulings within the reasonable period of time determined pursuant to para 3 of Article 21, such Member shall, if so requested, and no later than the expiry of the reasonable period of time, enter into negotiations with any party having invoked the dispute settlement procedures, with a view to developing mutually acceptable compensation. If no satisfactory compensation has been agreed within 20 days after the date of expiry of the reasonable period of time any party having invoked the dispute settlement procedures may request authorisation from the DSB to suspend the application to the Member concerned of concessions or other obligations under the covered agreements.

3   In considering what concessions or other obligations to suspend, the complaining party shall apply the following principles and procedures:

   (a) the general principle is that the complaining party should first seek to suspend concessions or other obligations with respect to the same sector(s) as that in which the panel or Appellate Body has found a violation or other nullification or impairment;

   (b) if that party considers that it is not practicable or effective to suspend concessions or other obligations with respect to the same sector(s), it may seek to suspend concessions or other obligations in other sectors under the same agreement;

   (c) if that party considers that it is not practicable or effective to suspend concessions or other obligations with respect to other sectors under the same agreement, and that the circumstances are serious enough, it may seek to suspend concessions or other obligations under another covered agreement;

   (d) in applying the above principles, that party shall take into account:

      (i) the trade in the sector or under the agreement under which the panel or Appellate Body has found a violation or other nullification or impairment, and the importance of such trade to that party;

      (ii) the broader economic elements related to the nullification or impairment and the broader economic consequences of the suspension of concessions or other obligations;

   (c) if that party decides to request authorisation to suspend concessions or other obligations pursuant to sub-paras (b) or (c), it shall state the reasons therefore In its request. At the same time as the request is forwarded to the DSB, it also shall be forwarded to the relevant Councils and also, in the case of a request pursuant to sub-para (b), the relevant sectoral bodies;

   (f) for purposes of this paragraph, 'sector' means:

      (i) with respect to goods, all goods;

      (ii) with respect to services, a principal sector as identified in the current 'Services Sectoral Classification List' which identifies such sectors;

      (iii) with respect to trade-related intellectual property rights, each of the categories of intellectual property rights covered in sections 1–7 of Part II, or the obligations under Part III, or Part IV of the Agreement on TRIPS;

   (g) for purposes of this para, 'agreement' means:

      (i) with respect to goods, the agreements listed in Annex IA of the WTO Agreement, taken as a whole as well as the Plurilateral Trade Agreements in so far as the relevant parties to the dispute are parries to these agreements;

      (ii) with respect to services, the GATS;

      (iii) with respect to intellectual property rights, the Agreement on TRIPS.

4   The level of the suspension of concessions or other obligations authorised by the DSB shall be equivalent to the level of the nullification or impairment.

5   The DSB shall not authorise suspension of concessions or other obligations if a covered agreement prohibits such suspension.

6   When the situation described in para 2 occurs, the DSB, upon request, shall grant authorisation to suspend concessions or other obligations within 30 days of the expiry of the reasonable period of time unless the DSB decides by consensus to reject the request. However, if the Member concerned objects to the level of suspension proposed, or claims that the principles and procedures set forth in para 3 have not been followed where a complaining party has requested authorisation to suspend concessions or other obligations pursuant to para 3(b) or (c), the matter shall be referred to arbitration. Such arbitration shall be carried out by the original panel, if members are available, or by an arbitrators appointed by the Director General and shall be completed within 60 days after the date of expiry of the reasonable period of time. Concessions or other obligations shall not be suspended during the course of the arbitration.

7   The arbitrators acting pursuant to para 6 shall not examine the nature of the concessions or other obligations to be suspended but shall determine whether the level of such suspension is equivalent to the level of nullification or impairment. The arbitrator may also determine if the proposed suspension of concessions or other obligations is allowed under the covered agreement. However, if the matter referred to arbitration includes a claim that the principles and procedures set forth in para 3 have not been followed, the arbitrator shall examine that claim. In the event the arbitrator determines that those principles and procedures have not been followed, the complaining party shall apply them consistent with para 3. The parties shall accept the arbitrator's decision as final and the parties concerned shall not seek a second arbitration. The DSB shall be informed promptly of the decision of the arbitrator and shall upon request, grant authorisation to suspend concessions or other obligations where the request is consistent with the decision of the arbitrator, unless the DSB decides by consensus, to reject the request.

8   The suspension of concessions or other obligations shall be temporary and shall only be applied until such time as the measure found to be inconsistent with a covered agreement has been removed, or the Member that must implement recommendations or rulings provides a solution to the nullification or impairment of benefits, or a mutually satisfactory solution is reached. In accordance with para 6 of Article 21, the DSB shall continue to keep under surveillance the implementation adopted recommendations or rulings including those cases where compensation has been provided or concessions or other obligations have been suspended but the recommendations to bring a measure into conformity with the covered agreements have not been implemented.

9   The dispute settlement provisions of the covered agreements may be invoked m respect of measures affecting their observance taken by regional or local governments or authorities within the territory of a Member. When the DSB has ruled that a provision of a covered agreement has not been observed, the responsible Member shall take such reasonable measures as may be available to it to ensure its observance. The provisions of the covered agreements and this understanding relating to compensation and suspension of concessions or other obligations apply in cases where it has not been possible to secure such observance.

Article 23 – Strengthening of the multilateral system

1   When Members seek the redress of a violation of obligations or other nullification or impairment of benefits under the covered agreements or an impediment to the attainment of any objective of the covered agreements, they shall have recourse to, and abide by, the rules and procedures of this understanding.

2   In such cases, Members shall:

(a) not make a determination to the effect that a violation has occurred, that benefits have been nullified or impaired or that the attainment of any objective of the covered agreements has been impeded, except through recourse to dispute settlement in accordance with the rules and procedures of this understanding, and shall make any such determination consistent with the findings contained in the panel or Appellate Body report adopted by the DSB or an arbitration award rendered under this understanding;

(b) follow the procedures set forth in Article 21 to determine the reasonable period of time for the Member concerned to implement the recommendations and rulings; and

(c) follow the procedures set forth in Article 22 to determine the level of suspension of concessions or other obligations and obtain DSB authorisation in accordance with those procedures before suspending concessions or other obligations under the covered agreements in response to the failure of the Member concerned to implement the recommendations and rulings within that reasonable period of time.

Article 24 – Special procedures involving least-developed country members

1 At all stages of the determination of the causes of a dispute and of dispute settlement procedures involving a least-developed country Member, particular consideration shall he given to the special situation of least-developed country Members. In this regard, Members shall exercise due restraint in raising matters under these procedures involving a least-developed country Member. If nullification or impairment is found to result from a measure taken by a least-developed country Member, complaining parties shall exercise due restraint in asking for compensation or seeking authorisation to suspend the application of concessions or other obligations pursuant to these procedures.

2 In dispute settlement cases involving a less developed country Member, where a satisfactory solution has not been found in the course of consultations the Director General or the Chairman of the DSB shall, upon request by a least-developed country Member, offer their good of offices, conciliation and mediation with a view to assisting the parties to settle the dispute, before a request for a panel is made. The Director General or the Chairman of the DSB, in providing the above assistance, may consult any source which either deems appropriate.

Article 25 – Arbitration

1 Expeditious arbitration within the WTO as an alternative means of dispute settlement can facilitate the solution of certain disputes that concern issues that are clearly defined by both parties.

2 Except as otherwise provided in this understanding, resort to arbitration shall be subject to mutual agreement of the parties which shall agree on the procedures to be followed. Agreements to resort to arbitration shall be notified to all Members sufficiently in advance of the actual commencement of the arbitration process.

3 Other Members may become party to an arbitration proceeding only upon the agreement of the parties which have agreed to have recourse to arbitration. The parties to the proceeding shall agree to abide by the arbitration award. Arbitration awards shall be notified to the DSB and the Council or Committee of any relevant agreement where any Member may raise any point relating thereto.

4 Articles 21 and 22 of this understanding shall apply *mutatis mutandis* to arbitration awards.

Article 26

1 Non-violation complaints of the type described in para l(b) of Article XXIII of GATT 1994

Where the provisions of para l(b) of Article XXIII of GATT 1994 are applicable to a covered agreement, a panel or the Appellate Body may only make rulings and recommendations where a party to the dispute considers that any benefit accruing to it directly or indirectly under the relevant covered agreement is being nullified or impaired or the attainment of any objective of that agreement is being impeded as a result of the application by a Member of any measure, whether or not it conflicts with the provisions of that agreement. Where and to the extent that such party considers and a panel or the Appellate Body determines that a case concerns a measure that does not conflict with the provisions of a covered agreement to which the provisions of para l(b) of Article XXIII of GATT 1994 are applicable, the procedures in this understanding shall apply, subject to the following:

(a) the complaining party shall present a derailed justification in support of any complaint relating to a measure which does not conflict with the relevant covered agreement;

(b) where a measure has been found to nullify or impair benefits under, or impede the attainment of objectives of, the relevant covered agreement without violation thereof, there is no obligation to withdraw the measure. However, in such cases, the panel or the Appellate Body shall recommend that the Member concerned make a mutually satisfactory adjustment;

(c) notwithstanding the provisions of Article 21, the arbitration provided for in para 3 of Article 21, upon request of either party, may include a determination of the level of benefits which have been nullified or impaired, and may also suggest ways and means of reaching a mutually satisfactory adjustment; such suggestions shall not be binding upon the parties to the dispute;

(d) notwithstanding the provisions of para 1 of Article 22, compensation may be part of a mutually satisfactory adjustment as final settlement of the dispute.

2   Complaints of the type described in para 1(c) of Article XXIII of GATT 1994

Where the provisions of para 1(c) of Article XXIII of GATT 1994 are applicable to a covered agreement, a panel may only make rulings and recommendations where a party considers that any benefit accruing to it directly or indirectly under the relevant covered agreement is being nullified or impaired or the attainment of any objective of that agreement is being impeded as a result of the existence of any situation other than those to which the provisions of paras 1(a) and 1(b) of Article XXIII of GATT 1994 are applicable. Where and to the extent that such party considers and a panel determines that the matter is covered by this paragraph, the procedures of this understanding shall apply only up to and including the point in the proceedings where the panel report has been circulated to the Members. The dispute settlement rules and procedures contained in the decision of 12 April 1989 (BISD 36S/61–67) shall apply to consideration for adoption, and surveillance and implementation of recommendations and rulings. The following shall also apply:

(a) the complaining party shall present a detailed justification in support of any argument made with respect to issues covered under this paragraph;

(b) in cases involving matters covered by this paragraph, if a panel finds that cases also involve dispute settlement matters other than those covered by this paragraph, the panel shall circulate a report to the DSB addressing any such matters and a separate report on matters falling under this paragraph.

Article 27 – Responsibilities of the secretariat

1   The Secretariat shall have the responsibility of assisting panels, especially on the legal, historical and procedural aspects of the matters dealt with, and of providing secretarial and technical support.

2   While the Secretariat assists Members in respect of dispute settlement at their request, there may also be a need to provide additional legal advice and assistance in respect of dispute settlement to developing country Members. To this end, the Secretariat shall make available a qualified legal expert from the WTO technical cooperation services to any developing country Member which so requests. This expert shall assist the developing country Member in a manner ensuring the continued impartiality of the Secretariat.

3   The Secretariat shall conduct special training courses for interested Members concerning these dispute settlement procedures and practices so as to enable Members' experts to be better informed in this regard.

Appendix 1

Agreements covered by the understanding

(A) Agreement Establishing the World Trade Organisation

(B) Multilateral Trade Agreements

Annex 1A

Multilateral Agreements on Trade in Goods

Annex 1B

General Agreement on Trade in Services

Annex 1C

Agreement on Trade-Related Aspects of Intellectual Property Rights

Annex 2

Understanding on Rules and Procedures Governing the Settlement of Disputes

(C)   Plurilateral Trade Agreements

Annex 4

Agreement on Trade in Civil Aircraft Agreement on Government Procurement International Dairy Agreement International Bovine Meat Agreement

The applicability of this Understanding to the Plurilateral Trade Agreements shall be subject to the adoption of a decision by the parties to each agreement setting out the terms for the application of the understanding to the individual agreement, including any special or additional rules or procedures for inclusion in Appendix 2, as notified to the DSB.

Appendix 2

Special or additional rules and procedures contained in the covered agreements

Agreement	*Rules and Procedures*
Agreement on the Application of Sanitary and Phytosanitary Measures	11.2
Agreement on Textiles and Clothing	2.14, 2.21, 4.4, 5.2, 5.4, 5.6, 6.9, 6.10, 6.11, 8.1 through 8.12
Agreement on Technical Barriers to Trade	14.2 through 14.4, Annex 2
Agreement on Implementation of Article VI of GATT 1994	17.4 through 17.7
Agreement on Implementation of Article VII of GATT 1994	19.3 through 19.5, Annex 11.2(f), 3, 9, 21
Agreement on Subsidies and Countervailing Measures	4.2 through 4.12, 6.6. 7.2 through 7.10, 8.5, footnote 35, 24.4, 27.7, Annex V
General Agreement on Trade in Services	XXII:3, XXIII:3
Annex on Financial Services	4
Annex on Air Transport Services	4
Decision on Certain Dispute Settlement procedures for the GATS	1 through 5

The list of rules and procedures in this Appendix includes provisions where only a part of the provision may be relevant in this context.

Any special or additional rules or procedures in the Plurilateral Trade Agreements as determined by the competent bodies of each agreement and as notified to the DSB.

Appendix 3

Working procedures

1   In its proceedings the panel shall follow the relevant provisions of this understanding. In addition, the following working procedures shall apply.

2   The panel shall meet in closed session. The parties to the dispute, and interested parties, shall be present at the meetings only when invited by the panel to appear before it.

3   The deliberations of the panel and the documents submitted to it shall be kept confidential. Nothing in this understanding shall preclude a party to a dispute from disclosing statements of its own positions to the public. Members shall treat as confidential information submitted by another Member to the panel which that Member has designated as confidential. Where a party to a dispute submits a confidential version of its written submissions to the panel, it shall also, upon request of a Member, provide a non-confidential summary of the information contained in its submissions that could be disclosed to the public.

4   Before the first substantive meeting of the panel with the parties, the parties to the dispute shall transmit to the panel written submissions in which they present the facts of the case and their arguments.

5   At its first substantive meeting with the parties, the panel shall ask the party which has brought the complaint to present its case. Subsequently, and still at the same meeting, the party against which the complaint has been brought shall be asked to present its point of view.

6   All third parties which have notified their interest in the dispute to the DSB shall be invited in writing to present their views during a session of the first substantive meeting of the panel set aside for that purpose. All such third parties may be present during the entirety of this session.

7   Formal rebuttals shall be made at a second substantive meeting of the panel. The party complained against shall have the right to take the floor first to be followed by the complaining party. The parties shall submit, prior to that meeting, written rebuttals to the panel.

8   The panel may at any time put questions to the parties and ask them for explanations either in the course of a meeting with the parties or in writing.

9   The parties to the dispute and any third party invited to present its views in accordance with Article 10 shall make available to the panel a written version of their oral statements.

10   In the interest of full transparency, the presentations, rebuttals and statements referred to in paras 5–9 shall be made in the presence of the parties. Moreover, each party's written submissions, including any comments on the descriptive part of the report and responses to questions put by the panel, shall be made available to the other party or parties.

11   Any additional procedures specific to the panel.

12   Proposed timetable for panel work:
     (a) Receipt of first written submissions of the parties:
          (i)   complaining party: 3–6 weeks;
          (ii) party complained against: 2–3 weeks.
     (b) Date, time and place of first substantive meeting with the parties; third party session: 1-2 weeks.
     (c) Receipt of written rebuttals of the parties: 2–3 weeks.
     (d) Date, time and place of second substantive meeting with the parties: 1–2 weeks.
     (e) Issuance of descriptive part of the report to the parties: 2–4 weeks.
     (f) Receipt of comments by the parties on the descriptive part of the report: 2 weeks.
     (g) Issuance of the interim report, including the findings and conclusions, to the parties: 2–4 weeks.
     (h) Deadline for party to request review of part(s) of report: 1 week.
     (i) Period of review by panel, including possible additional meeting with parties: 2 weeks.
     (j) Issuance of final report to parties to dispute: 2 weeks.
     (k) Circulation of the final report to the Members: 3 weeks.

The above calendar may be changed in the light of unforeseen developments. Additional meetings with the parties shall be scheduled if required.

Appendix 4

Expert review groups

The following rules and procedures shall apply to expert review groups established in accordance with the provisions of para 2 of Article 13.

1   Expert review groups are under the panel's authority. Their terms of reference and detailed working procedures shall be decided by the panel, and they shall report to the panel.

2   Participation in expert review groups shall be restricted to persons of professional standing and experience in the field in question.

3   Citizens of parties to the dispute shall not serve on an expert review group without the joint agreement of the parties to the dispute, except in exceptional circumstances when the panel considers that the need for specialised scientific expertise cannot be fulfilled otherwise. government of officials of parties to the dispute shall not serve on an expert review group. Members of expert review groups shall serve in their individual capacities and not as government representatives, nor as representatives or any organisation. governments or organisations shall therefore not give them instructions with regard to matters before an expert review group.

4   Expert review groups may consult and seek information and technical advice from any source they deem appropriate. Before an expert review group seeks such information or advice from a source within the jurisdiction of a Member, it shall inform the government of that Member. Any Member shall respond promptly and fully to any request by an expert review group for such information as the expert review group considers necessary and appropriate.

5   The parties to a dispute shall have access to all relevant information provided to an expert review group, unless it is of a confidential nature. Confidential information provided to the expert review group shall not be released without formal authorisation from the government, organisation or person providing the information. Where such information is requested from the expert review group but release of such information by the expert review group is not authorised, a non-confidential summary of the information will be provided by the government organisation or person supplying the information.

6   The expert review group shall submit a draft report to the parties to the dispute with a view to obtaining their comments, and taking them into account, as appropriate, in the final report, which shall also be issued to the parties to the dispute when it is submitted to the panel. The final report of the expert review group shall be advisory only.

THE GENERAL AGREEMENT ON TRADE IN SERVICES

PART I – SCOPE AND DEFINITION

Article I – Scope and definition

1   This agreement applies to measures by Members affecting trade in services.

2   For the purposes of this agreement, trade in services is defined as the supply of:

(a) from the territory of one Member into the territory of any other Member;

(b) in the territory of one Member to the service consumer of any other Member;

(c) by a service supplier of one Member, through commercial presence in the territory of any other Member;

(d) by a service supplier of one Member, through presence of natural persons of a Member in the territory of any other Member.

3   For the purposes of this agreement:

(a) 'measures by Members' means measures taken by:

   (i)   central, regional or local governments and authorities; and

   (ii) non-governmental bodies in the exercise of powers delegated by central regional or local governments or authorities;

   in fulfilling its obligations and commitments under the agreement, each member shall take such reasonable measures as may be available to it to ensure their observance by regional and local governments and authorities and non-governmental bodies within its territory;

(b) 'services' includes any service in any sector except services supplied in the exercise of governmental authority;

(c) 'a service supplied in the exercise of governmental authority' means any service which is supplied neither on a commercial basis nor in competition with one or more service suppliers.

PART II – GENERAL OBLIGATIONS AND DISCIPLINES

Article II – Most-favoured-nation treatment

1 With respect to any measure covered by this agreement, each Member shall accord immediately and unconditionally to services and service suppliers of any other Member treatment no less favourable than that it accords to like services and service suppliers of any other country.

2 A Member may maintain a measure inconsistent with para 1 provided that such a measure is listed in, and meets the conditions of, the Annex on Article II Exemptions.

3 The provisions of this agreement shall not be so construed as to prevent any Member from conferring or according advantages to adjacent countries in order to facilitate exchanges limited to contiguous frontier zones of services that are both locally produced and consumed.

Article III – Transparency

1 Each Member shall publish promptly and, except in emergency situations, at the latest by the time of their entry into force, all relevant measures of general application which pertain to or affect the operation of this agreement. International agreements pertaining to or affecting trade in services to which a Member is a signatory shall also be published.

2 Where publication as referred to in para 1 is not practicable, such information shall be made otherwise publicly available.

3 Each Member shall promptly and at least annually inform the Council for Trade in Services of the introduction of any new, or any changes to existing, laws, regulations or administrative guidelines which significantly affect trade in services covered by its specific commitments under this agreement.

4 Each Member shall respond promptly to all requests by any other member for specific information on any of its measures of general application or international agreements within the meaning of para 1. Each Member shall also establish one or more enquiry points to provide specific information to other Members, upon request, on all such matters as well as those subject to the notification requirement in para 3. Such enquiry points shall be established within two years from the date of entry into force of the Agreement Establishing the WTO (referred to in this agreement as the 'WTO Agreement'). Appropriate flexibility with respect to the time limit within which such enquiry points are to be established may be agreed upon for individual developing country Members. Enquiry points need not be depositories of laws and regulations.

5 Any Member may notify to the Council for Trade in Services any measure, taken by any other Member, which it considers affects the operation of this agreement.

Article III bis – Disclosure of confidential information

Nothing in this agreement shall require any Member to provide confidential information, the disclosure of which would impede law enforcement, or otherwise be contrary to the public interest, or which would prejudice legitimate commercial interests of particular enterprises, public or private.

Article V – Economic integration

1 This agreement shall not prevent any of its Members from being a party to or entering into an agreement liberalising trade in services between or among the parties to such an agreement, provided that such an agreement:

(a) has substantial sectoral coverage; and

(b) provides for the absence or elimination of substantially all discrimination, in the sense of Article XVII, between or among the parties, in the sectors covered under sub-para (a), through:

(i) elimination of existing discriminatory measures; and/or

(ii) prohibition of new or more discriminatory measures, either at the entry into force of that agreement or on the basis of a reasonable time frame, except for measures permitted under Articles XI, XII, XIV and XIV *bis*.

2   In evaluating whether the conditions under para 1(b) are met, consideration may be given to the relationship of the agreement to a wider process of economic integration or trade liberalisation among the countries concerned.

3   (a) Where developing countries are parties to an agreement of the type referred to in para 1, flexibility shall be provided for regarding the conditions set out in para 1, particularly with reference to sub-para (b) thereof, in accordance with the level of development of the countries concerned, both overall and in individual sectors and sub-sectors.

   (b) Notwithstanding para 6, in the case of an agreement of the type referred to in para 1 involving only developing countries, more favourable treatment may be granted to juridical persons owned or controlled by natural persons of the parties to such an agreement.

4   Any agreement referred to in para 1 shall be designed to facilitate trade between the parties to the agreement and shall not in respect of any Member outside the agreement raise the overall level of barriers to trade in services within the respective sectors or sub-sectors compared to the level applicable prior to such an agreement.

5   If, in the conclusion, enlargement or any significant modification of any agreement under para 1, a Member intends to withdraw or modify a specific commitment inconsistently with the terms and conditions set out in its Schedule, it shall provide at least 90 days advance notice of such modification or withdrawal and the procedure set forth in paras 2, 3 and 4 of Article XXI shall apply.

6   A service supplier of any other Member that is a juridical person constituted under the laws of a party to an agreement referred to in para 1 shall be entitled to treatment granted under such agreement, provided that it engages in substantive business operations in the territory of the parties to such agreement.

7   (a) Members which are parties to any agreement referred to in para 1 shall promptly notify any such agreement and any enlargement or any significant modification of that agreement to the Council for Trade in Services. They shall also make available to the Council such relevant information as may be requested by it. The Council may establish a working party to examine such an agreement or enlargement or modification of that agreement and to report to the Council on its consistency with this article.

   (b) Members which are parties to any agreement referred to in para 1 which is implemented on the basis of a time frame shall report periodically to the Council for Trade in Services on its implementation. The Council may establish a working party to examine such reports if it deems such a working party necessary.

   (c) Based on the reports of the working parties referred to in sub-paras (a) and (b), the Council may make recommendations to the parties as it deems appropriate.

8   A Member which is a party to any agreement referred to in para 1 may not seek compensation for trade benefits that may accrue to any other Member from such agreement.

Article VI – Domestic regulation

1   In sectors where specific commitments are undertaken, each Member shall ensure that all measures of general application affecting trade in services are administered in a reasonable, objective and impartial manner.

2   (a) Each Member shall maintain or institute as soon as practicable judicial, arbitral or administrative tribunals or procedures which provide, at the request of an affected service supplier, for the prompt review of, and where justified, appropriate remedies for, administrative decisions affecting trade in services. Where such procedures are not independent of the agency entrusted with the administrative decision concerned, the Member shall ensure that the procedures in fact provide for an objective and impartial review.

   (b) The provisions of sub-para (a) shall not be construed to require a Member to institute such tribunals or procedures where this would be inconsistent with its constitutional structure or the nature of its legal system.

3   Where authorisation is required for the supply of a service on which a specific commitment has been made, the competent authorities of a Member shall, within a reasonable period of time after the submission of an application considered complete under domestic laws and regulations, inform the applicant of the decision concerning the application. At the request of the applicant, the competent authorities of the Member shall provide, without undue delay, information concerning the status of the application.

4   With a view to ensuring that measures relating to qualification requirements and procedures, technical standards and licensing requirements do not constitute unnecessary barriers to trade in services, the Council for Trade in Services shall, through appropriate bodies it may establish, develop any necessary disciplines. Such disciplines shall aim to ensure that such requirements are, *inter alia*:

(a)   based on objective and transparent criteria, such as competence and the ability to supply the service;

(b)   not more burdensome than necessary to ensure the quality at the service;

(c)   in the case of licensing procedures, not in themselves a restriction on the supply of the service.

5   (a)   In sectors in which a Member has undertaken specific commitments pending the entry into force of disciplines developed in these sectors pursuant to para 4, the Member shall not apply licensing and qualification requirements and technical standards that nullify or impair such specific commitments in a manner which:

(i)   does not comply with the criteria outlined in sub-paras 4(a), (b) or (c); and

(ii)   could not reasonably have been expected of that Member at the time the specific commitments in those sectors were made.

(b)   In determining whether a Member is in conformity with the obligation under para 5(a), account shall be taken of international standards of relevant international organisations applied by that Member.

6   In sectors where' specific commitments regarding professional services are undertaken, each Member shall provide for adequate procedures to verify the competence of professionals of any other Member.

Article VII – Recognition

1   For the purposes of the fulfilment, in whole or in part, of its standards or criteria for the authorisation, licensing or certification of services suppliers, and subject to the requirements of para 3, a Member may recognise the education or experience obtained, requirements met, or licenses or certifications granted in a particular country. Such recognition, which may be achieved through harmonisation or otherwise, may be based upon an agreement or arrangement with the country concerned or may be accorded autonomously.

2   A Member that is a party to an agreement or arrangement of the type referred to in para 1, whether existing or future, shall afford adequate opportunity for other interested Members to negotiate their accession to such an agreement or arrangement or to negotiate comparable ones with it. Where a Member accords recognition autonomously, it shall afford adequate opportunity for any other Member to demonstrate that education, experience, licenses, or certifications obtained or requirements met in that other Member's territory should be recognised.

3   A Member shall not accord recognition in a manner which would constitute a means of discrimination between countries in the application of its standards or criteria for the authorisation, licensing or certification of services suppliers, or a disguised restriction on trade in services.

4   Each member shall:

(a)   within 12 months from the date on which the WTO Agreement takes effect for it, inform the Council for Trade in Services of its existing recognition measures and state whether such measures are based on agreements or arrangements of the type referred to in para 1;

(b)   promptly inform the Council for Trade in Services as far in advance as possible of the opening of negotiations on an agreement or arrangement of the type referred to in para 1 in order to provide adequate opportunity to any other Member to indicate their interest in participating in the negotiations before they enter a substantive phase;

(c) promptly inform the Council for Trade in Services when it adopts new recognition measures or significantly modifies existing ones and state whether the measures are based on an agreement or arrangement of the type referred to in para 1.

5 Wherever appropriate, recognition should be based on multilaterally agreed criteria. In appropriate cases, Members shall work in cooperation with relevant intergovernmental and non-governmental organisations towards the establishment and adoption of common international standards and criteria for recognition and common international standards for the practice of relevant services trades and professions.

Article VIII – Monopolies and exclusive service suppliers

1 Each Member shall ensure that any monopoly supplier of a service in its territory does not, in the supply of the monopoly service in the relevant market, act in a manner inconsistent with that Member's obligations under Article II and specific commitments.

2 Where a Member's monopoly supplier competes, either directly or through an affiliated company, in the supply of a service outside the scope of its monopoly rights and which is subject to that Member's specific commitments, the Member shall ensure that such a supplier does not abuse its monopoly position to act in its territory in a manner inconsistent with such commitments.

3 The Council for Trade in Services may, at the request of a Member which has a reason to believe that a monopoly supplier of a service of any other Member is acting in a manner inconsistent with para 1 or 2, request the Member establishing, maintaining or authorising such supplier to provide specific information concerning the relevant operations.

4 If, after the date of entry into force of the WTO Agreement, a Member grants monopoly rights regarding the supply of a service covered by its specific commitments, that Member shall notify the Council for Trade in Services no later than three months before the intended implementation of the grant of monopoly rights and the provisions of paras 2, 3 and 4 of Article XXI shall apply.

5 The provisions of this article shall also apply to cases of exclusive service suppliers, where a Member, formally or in effect, (a) authorises or establishes a small number of service suppliers and (b) substantially prevents competition among those suppliers in its territory.

Article IX – Business practices

1 Members recognise that certain business practices of service suppliers, other than those falling under Article VIII, may restrain competition and thereby restrict trade in services.

2 Each Member shall, at the request of any other Member, enter into consultations with a view to eliminating practices referred to in para 1. The Member addressed shall accord full and sympathetic consideration to such a request and shall cooperate through the supply of publicly available non-confidential information of relevance to the matter in question. The Member addressed shall also provide other information available to the requesting Member, subject to its domestic law and to the conclusion of satisfactory agreement concerning the safeguarding of its confidentiality by the requesting Member.

Article X – Emergency safeguard measures

1 There shall be multilateral negotiations on the question of emergency safeguard measures based on the principle of non-discrimination. The results of such negotiations shall enter into effect on a date not later than three years from the date of entry into force of the WTO Agreement.

2 In the period before the entry into effect of the results of the negotiations referred to in para 1, any Member may, notwithstanding the provisions of para 1 of Article XXI, notify the Council on Trade in Services of its intention to modify or withdraw a specific commitment after a period of one year from the date on which the commitment enters into force; provided that the Member shows cause to the Council that the modification or withdrawal cannot await the lapse of the three year period provided for in para 1 of Article XXI.

3 The provisions of para 2 shall cease to apply three years after the date of entry into force of the WTO Agreement.

Article XI – Payments and transfers

1   Except under the circumstances envisaged in Article XII, a Member shall not apply restrictions on international transfers and payments for current transactions relating to its specific commitments.

2   Nothing in this agreement shall affect the rights and obligations of the members of the International Monetary Fund under the Articles of Agreement of the Fund, including the use of exchange actions which are in conformity with the articles of agreement, provided that a Member shall not impose restrictions on any capital transactions inconsistently with its specific commitments regarding such transactions, except under Article XII or at the request of the Fund.

Article XII – Restrictions to safeguard the balance-of-payments

1   In the event of serious balance-of-payments and external financial difficulties or threat thereof, a Member may adopt or maintain restrictions on trade in services on which it has undertaken specific commitments, including on payments or transfers for transactions related to such commitments. It is recognised that particular pressures on the balance of payments of a Member in the process of economic development or economic transition may necessitate the use of restrictions to ensure, *inter alia*, the maintenance of a level of financial reserves adequate for the implementation of its programme of economic development or economic transition.

2   The restrictions referred to in para 1:

(a) shall not discriminate among Members;

(b) shall be consistent with the Articles of Agreement of the International Monetary Fund;

(c) shall avoid unnecessary damage to the commercial, economic and financial interests of any other Member;

(d) shall not exceed those necessary to deal with the circumstances described in para 1;

(e) shall be temporary and be phased out progressively as the situation specified in para 1 improves.

3   In determining the incidence of such restrictions, Members may give priority to the supply of services which are more essential to their economic or development programmes. However, such restrictions shall not be adopted or maintained for the purpose of protecting a particular service sector.

4   Any restrictions adopted or maintained under para 1, or any changes therein, shall be promptly notified to the General Council.

5   (a) Members applying the provisions pf this article shall consult promptly with the Committee on Balance of Payments Restrictions on restrictions adopted under this article.

(b) The Ministerial Conference shall establish procedures for periodic consultations with the objective of enabling such recommendations to be made to the Member concerned as it may deem appropriate.

(c) Such consultations shall assess the balance of payments situation of the Member concerned and the restrictions adopted or maintained under this article, taking into account, *inter alia*, such factors as:

(i)   the nature and extent of the balance of payments and the external financial difficulties;

(ii) the external economic and trading environment of the consulting Member;

(iii) alternative corrective measures which may be available.

(d) The consultations shall address the compliance of any restrictions with para 2, in particular the progressive phaseout of restrictions in accordance with para 2(e).

(e) In such consultations, all findings of statistical and other facts presented by the International Monetary Fund relating to foreign exchange, monetary reserves and balance of payments, shall be accepted and conclusions shall be based on the assessment by the Fund of the balance of payments and the external financial situation of the consulting Member.

6   If a Member which is not a member of the International Monetary Fund wishes to apply the provisions of this article, the Ministerial Conference shall establish a review procedure and any other procedures necessary.

Article XIII – Government procurement

1   Articles II, XVI and XVII shall not apply to laws, regulations or requirements governing the procurement by governmental agencies of services purchased for governmental purposes and not with a view to commercial resale or with a view to use in the supply of services for commercial sale.

2   There shall be multilateral negotiations on government procurement in services under this agreement within two years from the date of entry into force of the WTO Agreement.

Article XIV – General exceptions

Subject to the requirement that such measures are not applied in a manner which would constitute a means of arbitrary or unjustifiable discrimination between countries where like conditions prevail, or a disguised restriction on trade in services, nothing in this agreement shall be construed to prevent the adoption or enforcement by any Member of measures:

(a) necessary to protect public morals or to maintain public order;

(b) necessary to protect human, animal or plant life or health;

(c) necessary to secure compliance with laws or regulations which are not inconsistent with the provisions of this agreement including those relating to:

    (i) the prevention of deceptive and fraudulent practices or to deal with the effects or a default on services contracts;

    (ii) the protection of the privacy of individuals in relation to the processing and dissemination of personal data and the protection of confidentiality of individual records and accounts;

    (iii) safety;

(d) inconsistent with Article XVII, provided that the difference in treatment is aimed at ensuring the equitable or effective imposition or collection of direct taxes in respect of services or service suppliers of other Members;

(e) inconsistent with Article II, provided that the difference in treatment is the result of an agreement on the avoidance of double taxation or provisions on the avoidance of double taxation in any other international agreement or arrangement by which the Member is bound.

Article XIV bis – Security exceptions

1   Nothing in this agreement shall be construed:

(a) to require any Member to furnish any information, the disclosure of which it considers contrary to its essential security interests; or

(b) to prevent any Member from taking any action which it considers necessary for the protection of its essential security interests:

    (i) relating to the supply of services as carried our directly or indirectly for the purpose of provisioning a military establishment;

    (ii) relating to fissionable and fusionable materials or the materials from which they are derived;

    (iii) taken in time of war or other emergency in international relations; or

(c) to prevent any Member from taking any action in pursuance of its obligations under the United Nations Charter for the maintenance of international peace and security.

2   The Council for Trade in Services shall be informed to the fullest extent possible of measures taken under paras 1(b) and (c) and of their termination.

Article XV – Subsidies

1   Members recognise that, in certain circumstances, subsidies may have distortive effects on trade in services. Members shall enter into negotiations with a view to developing the necessary multilateral disciplines to avoid such trade-distortive effects. The negotiations shall also address the appropriateness of countervailing procedures. Such negotiations

shall recognise the role of subsidies in relation to the development programmes of developing countries and take into account the needs of Members, particularly developing country Members, for flexibility in this area. For the purpose of such negotiations, Members shall exchange information concerning all subsidies related to trade in services that they provide to their domestic service suppliers.

2   Any Member which considers that it is adversely affected by a subsidy of another Member may request consultations with that Member on such matters. Such requests shall be accorded sympathetic consideration.

PART III – SPECIFIC COMMITMENTS

Article XVI – Market access

1   With respect to market access through the modes of supply identified in Article 1, each member shall accord services and service suppliers of any other Member treatment no less favourable than that provided for under the terms, limitations and conditions agreed and specified in its Schedule.

2   In sectors where market access commitments are undertaken, the measures which a member shall not maintain or adopt either on the basis of a regional subdivision or on the basis of its entire territory, unless otherwise specified in its Schedule, are defined as:

(a) limitations on the number of service suppliers whether in the form of numerical quotas, monopolies, exclusive service suppliers or the requirements of an economic needs test;

(b) limitations on the total value of service transactions or assets in the form of numerical quotas or the requirement of an economic needs test;

(c) limitations on the total number of service operations or on the total quantity of service output expressed in terms at designated numerical units in the form of quotas or the requirement of an economic needs test;

(d) limitations on the total number of natural persons that may be employed m a particular service sector or that a service supplier may employ and who are necessary for, and directly related to, the supply of a specific service in the form of numerical quotas or the requirement of an economic needs test;

(e) measures which restrict or require specific types of legal entity or joint venture through which a service supplier may supply a service; and

(f) limitations on the participation of foreign capital in terms of maximum percentage limit on foreign shareholding or the total value of individual or aggregate foreign investment.

Article XVII – National treatment

1   In the sectors inscribed in its Schedule, and subject to any conditions and qualifications set out therein, each Member shall accord to services and service suppliers of any other Member, in respect of all measures affecting the supply of services, treatment no less favourable than that it accords to its own like services and service suppliers.

2   A Member may meet the requirement of para 1 by according to services and service suppliers of any other Member, either formally identical treatment or formally different treatment to that it accords to its own like services and service suppliers.

3   Formally identical or formally different treatment shall be considered to be less favourable if it modifies the conditions of competition in favour of services or service suppliers of the Member compared to like services or service suppliers of any other Member.

Article XVIII – Additional commitments

Members may negotiate commitments with respect to measures affecting trade in services not subject to scheduling under Articles XVI or XVII, including those regarding qualifications, standards or licensing matters. Such commitments shall be inscribed in a Member's Schedule.

PART IV – PROGRESSIVE LIBERALISATION

Article XIX – Negotiation of specific commitments

1   In pursuance of the objectives of this agreement, Members shall enter into successive rounds of negotiations, beginning not later than five years from the date of entry into force

of the WTO Agreement and periodically thereafter, with a view to achieving a progressively higher level of liberalisation. Such negotiations shall be directed to the reduction or elimination of the adverse effects on trade in services of measures as a means of providing effective market access. This process shall take place with a view to promoting the interests of all participants on a mutually advantageous basis and to securing an overall balance of rights and obligations.

2   The process of liberalisation shall take place with due respect for national policy objectives and the level of development of individual Members, both overall and in individual sectors. There shall be appropriate flexibility for individual developing country Members for opening fewer sectors, liberalising fewer types of transactions, progressively extending market access in line with their development situation and, when making access to their markets available to foreign service suppliers, attaching to such access conditions aimed at achieving the objectives referred to in Article IV.

3   For each round, negotiating guidelines and procedures shall be established. For the purposes of establishing such guidelines, the Council for Trade in Services shall carry out an assessment of trade in services in overall terms and on a sectoral basis with reference to the objectives of this agreement, including those set out in para 1 of Article IV. Negotiating guidelines shall establish modalities for the treatment of liberalisation undertaken autonomously by Members since previous negotiations, as well as for the special treatment for least developed country Members under the provisions of para 3 of Article IV.

4   The process of progressive liberalisation shall be advanced in each such round through bilateral, plurilateral or multilateral negotiations directed towards increasing the general level of specific commitments undertaken by Members under this agreement.

Article XX – Schedules of specific c commitments

1   Each Member shall set out in a schedule the specific commitments it undertakes under Part III of this agreement. With respect to sectors where such commitments are undertaken, each Schedule shall specify:

(a) terms, limitations and conditions on market access;

(b) conditions and qualifications on national treatment;

(c) undertakings relating to additional commitments;

(d) where appropriate the time frame for implementation of such commitments; and

(e) the date of entry into force of such commitments.

2   Measures inconsistent with both Articles XVI and XVII shall be inscribed in the column relating to Article XVI. In this case the inscription will be considered to provide a condition or qualification to Article XVII as well.

3   Schedules of specific commitments shall be annexed to this agreement and shall form an integral part thereof.

Article XXI – Modification of Schedules

1   (a) A Member (referred to in this article as the 'modifying Member') may modify or withdraw any commitment in its Schedule, at any time after three years have elapsed from the date on which that commitment entered into force, in accordance with the provisions of this article.

(b) A modifying Member shall notify its intent to modify or withdraw a commitment pursuant to this article to the Council for Trade in Services no later than three months before the intended date of implementation of the modification or withdrawal.

2   (a) At the request of any Member the benefits of which under this agreement may be affected (referred to in this article as an 'affected Member') by a proposed modification or withdrawal notified under sub-para 1(b) the modifying Member shall enter into negotiations with a view to reaching agreement on any necessary compensatory adjustment. In such negotiations and agreement, the Members concerned shall endeavour to maintain a general level of mutually advantageous commitments not less favourable to trade than that provided for in Schedules of specific commitments prior to such negotiations.

(b) Compensatory adjustments shall be made on a most-favoured-nation basis.

3   (a) If agreement is not reached between the modifying Member and any affected Member before the end of the period provided for negotiations such affected Member may refer the matter to arbitration. Any affected Member that wishes to enforce a right that it may have to compensation must participate in the arbitration.

    (b) If no affected Member has requested arbitration, the modifying Member shall be free to implement the proposed modification or withdrawal.

4   (a) The modifying Member may not modify or withdraw its commitment until it has made compensatory adjustments in conformity with the findings of the arbitration.

    (b) If the modifying Member implements its proposed modification or withdrawal and does not comply with the findings of the arbitration, any affected Member that participated in the arbitration may modify or withdraw substantially equivalent benefits in conformity with those findings. Notwithstanding Article II, such a modification or withdrawal may be implemented solely with respect to the modifying Member.

5   The Council for Trade in Services shall establish procedures for rectification or modification of Schedules. Any Member which has modified or withdrawn scheduled commitments under this article shall modify its Schedule according to such procedures.

PART V – INSTITUTIONAL PROVISIONS

Article XXII – Consultation

1   Each Member shall accord sympathetic consideration to, and shall afford adequate opportunity for, consultation regarding such representations as may be made by any other Member with respect to any matter affecting the operation of this agreement. The Dispute Settlement Understanding (DSU) shall apply to such consultations.

2   The Council for Trade in Services or the Dispute Settlement Body (DSB) may, at the request of a Member, consult with any Member or Members in respect of any matter for which it has not been possible to find a satisfactory solution through consultation under para 1.

3   A Member may not invoke Article XVII, either under this article or Article XXIII, with respect to a measure of another Member that falls within the scope of an international agreement between them relating to the avoidance of double taxation. In case of disagreement between Members as to whether a measure falls within the scope of such an agreement between them, it shall be open to either Member to bring this matter before the council for Trade in Services. The Council shall refer the matter to arbitration. The decision of the arbitrator shall be final and binding on the Members.

With respect to agreements on the avoidance of double taxation which exist on the date of entry into force of the WTO Agreement, such a matter may be brought before the Council for Trade in services only with the consent of both parties to such an agreement.

Article XXIII – Dispute settlement and enforcement

1   If any Member should consider that any other Member fails to carry out its obligations or specific commitments under this agreement, it may with a view to reaching a mutually satisfactory resolution of the matter have recourse to the DSU.

2   If the DSB considers that the circumstances are serious enough to justify such action, it may authorise a Member or Members to suspend the application to any other Member or Members of obligations and specific commitments in accordance with Article 22 of the DSU.

3   If any Member considers that any benefit it could reasonably have expected to accrue to it under a specific commitment of another Member under Part III of this agreement is being nullified or impaired as a result of the application of any measure which does not conflict with the provisions of this agreement, it may have recourse to the DSU. If the measure is determined by the DSB to have nullified or impaired such a benefit, the Member affected shall be entitled to a mutually satisfactory adjustment on the basis of para 2 of Article XXI, which may include the modification or withdrawal of the measure. In the event an agreement cannot be reached between the Members concerned, Article 22 of the DSU shall apply.

Article XXIV – Council for trade in services

1   The Council for Trade in Services shall carry out such functions as may be assigned to it to facilitate the operation of this agreement and further its objectives. The Council may establish such subsidiary bodies as it considers appropriate for the effective discharge of its functions.

2   The Council and, unless the Council decides otherwise, its subsidiary bodies shall be open to participation by representatives of all Members.

3   The Chairman of the Council shall be elected by the Members.

PART VI – FINAL PROVISIONS

Article XXVII – Denial of benefits

A Member may deny the benefits of this agreement:

(a) to the supply of a service, if it establishes that the service is supplied from or in the territory of a non-Member or of a Member to which the denying Member does not apply the WTO Agreement;

(b) in the case of the supply of a maritime transport service, if it establishes that the service is supplied:

    (i)   by a vessel registered under the laws of a non-Member or of a Member to which the denying Member does not apply the WTO Agreement; and

    (ii) by a person which operates and/or uses the vessel in whole or in part but which is of a non-Member or of a Member to which the denying Member does not apply the WTO Agreement;

(c) to a service supplier that is a juridical person, if it establishes that it is not a service supplier of another Member, or that it is a service supplier of a Member to which the denying Member does not apply the WTO Agreement.

Article XXVIII – Definitions

For the purpose of this agreement:

(a) 'measure' means any measure by a Member, whether in the form of a law regulation, rule, procedure, decision, administrative action, or any other form;

(b) 'supply of a service' includes the production, distribution, marketing, sale and delivery of a service;

(c) 'measures by Members affecting trade in services' include measures in respect of:

    (i)   the purchase, payment or use of a service;

    (ii) the access to and use of, in connection with the supply of a service, services which are required by those Members to be offered to the public generally;

    (iii) the presence, including commercial presence, of persons of a Member for the supply of a service in the territory of another Member;

(d) 'commercial presence' means any type of business or professional establishment, including through:

    (i)   the constitution, acquisition or maintenance of a juridical person; or

    (ii) the creation or maintenance of a branch or a representative office, within the territory of a Member for the purpose of supplying a service;

(e) 'sector' of a service means:

    (i)   with reference to a specific commitment, one or more, or all, sub-sectors of that service, as specified in a Member's Schedule;

    (ii) otherwise, the whole of that service sector, including all of its sub-sectors;

(f) 'service of another Member' means a service which is supplied:

    (i)   from or in the territory of that other Member, or in the case of maritime transport, by a vessel registered under the laws of that other Member, or by a person of that other Member which supplies the service through the operation of a vessel and/or its use in whole or in part; or

    (ii) in the case of the supply of a service through commercial presence or through the presence of natural persons, by a service supplier of that other Member;

(g) 'service supplier' means any person that supplies a service;

(h) 'monopoly supplier of a service' means any person, public or private, which in the relevant market of the territory of a Member is authorised or established formally or in effect by that Member as the sole supplier of that service;

(i) 'service consumer' means any person that receives or uses a service;

(j) 'person' means either a natural person or a juridical person;

(k) 'natural person of another Member' means a natural person who resides in the territory of that other Member or any other Member, and who under the law of that other Member:

    (i) is a national of that other Member; or

    (ii) has the right of permanent residence in that other Member, in the case of a Member which:

        1 does not have nationals; or

        2 accords substantially the same treatment to its permanent residents as it does to its nationals in respect of measures affecting trade in services, as notified in its acceptance of or accession to the WTO Agreement, provided that no Member is obligated to accord to such permanent residents treatment more favourable than would be accorded by that other member to such permanent residents. Such notification shall include the assurance to assume, with respect to those permanent residents, in accordance with its laws and regulations, the same responsibilities that other Member bears with respect to its nationals;

(l) 'juridical person' means any legal entity duly constituted or otherwise organised under applicable law, whether for profit or otherwise, and whether privately-owned or governmentally-owned, including any corporation, trust, partnership, joint venture, sole proprietorship or association;

(m) 'juridical person of another Member' means a juridical person which is either:

    (i) constituted or otherwise organised under the law of that other Member, and is engaged in substantive business operations in the territory of that Member or any other Member; or

    (ii) in the case of the supply of a service through commercial presence, owned or controlled by:

        1 natural persons of that Member; or

        2 juridical persons of that other Member identified under sub-para (i);

(n) a juridical person is:

(i) 'owned' by persons of a Member if more than 50% of the equity interest in its beneficially owned by persons of that Member;

    (ii) 'controlled' by persons of a Member if such persons have the power to name a majority of its directors or otherwise to legally direct its actions;

    (iii) 'affiliated' with another person when it controls or is controlled by that other person; or when it and the other person are both controlled by the same person;

(o) 'direct taxes' comprise all taxes on total income, on total capital or on elements of income or of capital, including taxes on gains from the alienation of property, taxes on estates, inheritances and gifts, and taxes on the total amounts of wages or salaries paid by enterprises, as well as taxes on capital appreciation.

Article XXIX – Annexes

The Annexes to this agreement are an integral part of this agreement.

Annex on Article II exemptions

Scope

1 This Annex specifies the conditions under which a Member, at the entry into force of this agreement, is exempted from its obligations under para 1 of Article II.

2 Any new exemptions applied for after the date of entry into force of the WTO Agreement shall be dealt with under para 3 of Article IX of that agreement.

Review

3   The Council for Trade in Services shall review all exemptions granted for a period of more than five years. The first such review shall take place no more than five years after the entry into force of the WTO Agreement.

4   The Council for Trade in Services in a review shall:

   (a) examine whether the conditions which created the need for the exemption still prevail; and

   (b) determine the date of any further review.

Termination

5   The exemption of a Member from its obligations under para 1 of Article II of the agreement with respect to a particular measure terminates on the date provided for in the exemption.

6   In principle, such exemptions should not exceed a period of 10 years. In any event, they shall be subject to negotiation in subsequent trade liberalising rounds.

7   A Member shall notify the Council for Trade in Services at the termination of the exemption period that the inconsistent measure has been brought into conformity with para 1 of Article II of the agreement.

Lists of Article II exemptions

[The agreed lists of exemptions under para 2 of Article II will be annexed here in the treaty copy of the WTO Agreement.]

Annex on movement of natural persons supplying services under the agreement

1   This Annex applies to measures affecting natural persons who are service suppliers of a Member, and natural person of a Member who are employed by a service supplier of a Member, in respect of the supply of a service.

2   The agreement shall not apply to measures affecting natural persons seeking access to the employment market of a Member, nor shall it apply to measures regarding citizenship, residence or employment on a permanent basis.

3   In accordance with Parts III and IV of the agreement, Members may negotiate specific commitments applying to the movement of all categories of natural persons supplying services under the agreement. Natural persons covered by a specific commitment shall be allowed to supply the service in accordance with the terms of that commitment.

4   The agreement shall not prevent a Member from applying measures to regulate the entry of natural persons into, or their temporary stay in, its territory, including those measures necessary to protect the integrity of, and to ensure the orderly movement of natural persons across its borders, provided that such measures are not applied in such a manner as to nullify or impair the benefits accruing to any Member under the terms of a specific commitment.

CHAPTER 8

ANTI-DUMPING AND COUNTERVAILING MEASURES REGIMES

INTRODUCTION

Material injury can be done to the domestic industry of a country by exporters that send to the market of this country like competing goods that are priced at artificially low levels. This category of trading practices is regulated by the General Agreement on Tariffs and Trade (GATT) and certain supplementary agreements. These instruments target two types of trading strategy – (1) the so called dumping of product in an importing economy's market at prices below which these goods are sold in the exporter's home market; and (2) the exporting of goods to another economy which goods have been subsidised by the government or other state authority in the exporter's home economy. These provisions provide for the setting up of regimes in member countries (implemented by domestic legislation mirroring the provisions) for countering these trading strategies. These regimes operate by way of exception to the overall philosophy of the World Trade Organisation (WTO) and GATT, which is to promote free trade.

THE ANTI-DUMPING REGIME

Introduction

It has long been recognised that material damage can be done to a given industry of a country (the importing country) if another country (the exporting country) exports competing products to the importing country at a cost below that of the market price in the exporting country. Broadly, this practice is known as dumping. It is one of the unfair trade practices targeted by the GATT. The GATT does not, however, condemn all acts of dumping. It is also recognised that anti-dumping measures can be used by an importing country as an anti-competitive protectionist device.

The current anti-dumping regime provided for by the GATT pivots on Art VI of the GATT 1994.[1] Article VI(1) provides that:

> The contracting parties recognise that dumping, by which products of one country are introduced into the commerce of another country at less than the normal value of the products, is to be condemned if it causes or threatens material injury to an established industry in the territory of a contracting party or materially retards the establishment of a domestic industry.

---

1   Anti-dumping measures have long been employed by individual countries. Article VI was inserted into the GATT in 1947. It was amplified and modified by the GATT Anti-dumping Agreement of 1967 pursuant to the Kennedy Round of trade talks, which agreement was displaced by the Tokyo Round Code 1979. For a history of the GATT anti-dumping provisions see: Stewart (ed), *The GATT Uruguay Round: A Negotiating History*, 1993, Deventer: Kluwer Law and Taxation Publishers; Horlick and Shea, 'The World Trade Organisation Anti-dumping Agreement' (1995) 29:1 *J World Trade* 5; Collins-Williams and Salembier, 'International disciplines on subsidies – the GATT, the WTO and the future agenda', (1996) 30:1 *J World Trade* 5.

The Agreement on Implementation of Art VI of the General Agreement on Tariffs and Trade 1994 was agreed upon in the Uruguay Round of trade talks. Known as 'The Dumping Agreement', it provides for a detailed set of rules which amplify the terms of the Art VI provisions, covering a range of matters including the definition of dumping and associated concepts such as material injury, the procedures to be employed in determining whether an export amounts to actionable dumping, and the remedies which are available to a successful complainant. For the regime to be effective, members of the GATT need to implement the GATT anti-dumping rules through the enactment of conforming legislation. As anti-dumping measures have to be enforced in the importing country, the GATT anti-dumping regime can only operate when it has been underwritten by domestic legislation.

No specific action against dumping of exports from another member can be taken except in accordance with the provisions of the GATT 1994, as interpreted by the Anti-Dumping Agreement 1994 (Art 18 of the latter agreement). It follows that members have an incentive to implement the GATT anti-dumping regime, if they are minded to take anti-dumping measures. The main users of the anti-dumping regime it has been said, are Australia, the European Union and the USA.[2]

Dumping and measures to counter it, have a long history.[3] Anti-dumping measures for a very long time were the product of unilateral action by the importing country. Only in relatively recent times have anti-dumping regimes been underwritten by multilateral trade agreements. The traditional remedy, in earlier times as now, was the imposition of anti-dumping duties, normally the difference between the price at which the goods were sold in the exporter's own domestic market, and the price at which they were sold in the import market.

The motivations for dumping may be broadly classified. An exporter may be able to sell cheaply in the foreign market because the exporter enjoys a subsidy, direct or indirect, from its own government. Where the government of the exporter's country subsidises the exporter, the regime provided for in the 1994 GATT Agreement on Subsidies and Countervailing Measures applies (assuming implementation by the importing country) – see 'Subsidies and countervailing measures' below. The 1994 GATT Anti-Dumping Agreement is applicable in all other cases of dumping, assuming implementation by the importing nation.

This latter category of dumping then, is concerned with situations where the dumping is essentially the initiative of the exporting producer, independently of government subsidisation.[4] An export producer may be content to sell the product at a loss in the export market because of transient overproduction. This would not normally cause problems in the importing country. The export producer may seek economies of scale by producing more than the domestic market can absorb, with the

2   Moore, 'Department of Commerce administration of anti-dumping sunset reviews: a first assessment' (2002) 36:4 *J of World Trade* 675.

3   *Ibid.*

4   The motivations for dumping, which correspond to categories of dumping, are explored by BS Fisher in 'The anti-dumping law of the United States: a legal and economic analysis' (1973) 5 *Law and Policy in International Business* 85.

balance of production being exported. This by itself would not *per se* lead to dumping. The producer may be able to produce goods more cheaply than the industry in the importing country, because of lower costs, the exchange rate, etc – again, this *per se* would not lead to dumping. But again, if other circumstances intervene, the producer might be promoted to dump. Most obviously this would happen because the producer is in a position to engage in differential pricing. The competitive forces in the domestic market may constrain the price that the producer can charge for the product; conversely, these same forces may mean that the producer can sell reasonable volumes of product in the importing country at a higher price. This would typically be true where the producer is operating in a less developed, lower cost national economy with a soft currency, as compared to the importing economy. Or a producer may for a period be prepared to dump product at a loss, or without making a profit, in order to establish a market presence in the importing country.

The anti-dumping regime protects domestic producers and those dependent upon them, such as staff and suppliers, as distinct from consumers. It is unconcerned with the welfare of consumers, who may of course benefit from the cheaper prices resulting from dumping (provided of course that the domestic industry is not eradicated, leading to higher prices than obtained prior to the dumping).[5] As such, the dumping regime is on one view somewhat counter to the overall thrust of the WTO-GATT, which is to break down trade barriers, with a view to benefiting producers and consumers. The anti-dumping rules are one of the declining range of protectionist devices sanctioned by the international trading regime.

Defining dumping

Article VI, it has been seen, defines dumping as 'involving (1) the introduction of products of one country into the commerce of another (that is, their export), at (2) less than their normal value, which export (3) causes or threatens material injury to an established territory in the importing country, or which materially retards the establishment of a domestic industry'. Both exporting and importing nations must be contracting parties for the regime to be applicable.

The 1994 Agreement amplifies these concepts.

Determination of dumping

Pursuant to Art 2.1 of the 1994 Agreement, a product is introduced into the commerce of the importing country at less than normal value if the export price of the product is less than the comparable price, in the ordinary course of trade, for the like product when destined for consumption in the exporting country.

---

5   See the US case of *Brother Industries (USA) Inc v United States* (1982) 801 F Supp 751, United States Court of International Trade, where the Japanese owned US subsidiary of Brother Industries succeeded in its application to have anti-dumping duties placed on typewriters exported to the US by the Singapore subsidiary of a British-owned company, Smith-Corona. It is commented in Schaffer *et al, International Business Law and its Environment*, 4th edn, 1999, Cincinnati, Ohio: West Educational Publishers, at p 362, that the real losers in this and related typewriter company battles were the consumers, who ended up paying the cost of anti-dumping duties on these machines for 14 years.

What is pivotal, then, is comparison of the like price in the importing country as compared to the exporting country. The rules are not concerned with the situation where the products are sold in the importing country at less than the prevailing market price in that country. This circumstance may, but need not be, indicative of dumping. The critical issue is – is the like price in the importing country below that of the market price in the exporting country? So, for example, if the exporter sells wholesale to the importing country, the question is one of whether the wholesale price in the exporting country is more than that for which the goods are supplied wholesale in the importing country.

Articles 2.2ff provide assistance in testing whether the product has been 'introduced at less than normal value'. Article 2.2 deals with the case where there are no sales of the like product in the ordinary course of trade in the domestic market of the exporting country, or the volume of sales in this context is too small to permit a proper comparison. In such a case, the margin of dumping is to be determined by comparing the comparable price of the like product when exported to an appropriate third country with the cost of production in the exporting country plus a reasonable margin for selling and other costs and profits.

Sales may be treated as 'not being in the ordinary course of trade', for the purposes of Art 2.2, where sales are made within an extended period of time and in substantial quantities and at prices that do not provide for the recovery of all costs within a reasonable period of time. In this event, an appropriate adjustment will need to be made (Art 2.2.1).

Article 2.4 requires that a fair comparison be made between the export price and the normal value. *Inter alia*, it requires that the comparison be made between prices at the same level of trade (such as wholesale to wholesale). If the anti-dumping provisions are to operate in a fair and consistent manner, it is of course critical that the normal and export sale price be derived using like methodology. However, the provisions are not free of ambiguity.

The key provision in this regard is Art 2.4.2. Article 2.4.2 provides that the existence of margins of dumping during the investigative phase shall normally be established on the basis of a comparison of a weighted average normal value with a weighted average of prices of all comparable export transactions, or by a comparison of normal value and export prices on a transaction-by-transaction basis. If the provision ended there it would be uncontroversial – like must be compared to like on a comprehensive basis. Prices in a market will fluctuate over time – but if the weighted average of each side of the equation is derived and the two compared, a fair comparison between normal price in the exporter's market, and the export price of the product, could be made. But exceptionally, Art 2.4.2 goes on to provide that:

> A normal value established on a weighted average basis may be compared to prices of individual export transactions if the authorities find a pattern of export prices which differ significantly among different purchasers, regions or time periods, and if explanation is provided as to why such differences cannot be taken into account appropriately by the use of weighted average-to-weighted-average or a transaction-to-transaction.

The exception is potentially problematic – it provides for the normal value (the price in the domestic market of the exporter) to be established on a weighted average basis, but for the existence if any, and extent of any dumping margin to be determined by a comparison of individual transaction prices of the like product in the importing market. Thus, for the sake of argument, the normal price might be X, but a dumping margin will be found to exist if individual sale prices in the importing market are above X, even though the weighted average of the later sale prices may be X (or even below X).

The provision, termed the 'target dumping' provision, is aimed at targeted, or opportunistic dumping.[6] It has been commented that the anti-dumping authorities in some countries, including the USA, have exploited this exception in such a manner as to more readily determine that an exporter has dumped product in their markets. The US in particular, has in reliance upon the provision contended 'that it is free to use its standard methodology of comparing individual export sales to average normal value in the review phase of an anti-dumping proceeding'.[7]

The determination of normal value in anti-dumping cases has generated considerable litigation. The normal value of the price at which the goods sold is their sale price in the ordinary course of trade in the exporter's market, so it has been noted (Art 2.1). Critical to this concept of ordinary course of trade is of course that the transaction was an arms length transaction with an unrelated buyer. This is typically written into implementing legislation. The relevant provision in the Australian anti-dumping legislation, for instance, provides that (subject to other provisions in the section):

> the normal value of any goods exported to Australia is the price paid for like goods sold in the ordinary course of trade for home consumption in the country of export in sales that are arms length transactions by the exporter or, if the goods are not so sold by the exporter, by like sellers of like goods.[8]

Where there relationship is not arms length, the anti-dumping authority will need to construct a normal value based on the available data.

In comparing the export price (in the export market) and the normal value (in the exporter's home market) due allowance is to be made on the merits of each case for such factors as differential taxation levels, levels of trade, quantities, physical characteristics and other differences which are demonstrated to affect price

---

6   Palmeter, 'A commentary on the WTO Anti-dumping Code' (1996) 30:4 *J World Trade* 43 at 46.

7   *Ibid* at 47. The methodology has been considered in the GATT panel cases, such as *United States – Imposition of Anti-dumping Duties on Imports of Fresh and Chilled Atlantic Salmon from Norway* (Report of the Panel adopted by the Committee on Anti-Dumping Practices on 27 April 1994, GATT Document ADP87, 30 November 1992), discussed in Kim, 'Fair price comparison in the WTO Anti-dumping Agreement' (2002) 36:1 *J World Trade* 39 at 46. The Panel determined that Art 2.6 (dealing with the interpretation of the term 'like product') did not address the issue of whether the methodology could be employed, but that it was consistent with a requirement of 'fair comparison'. It found that in the particular circumstances, Norway had not discharged its burden of proving that the US had breached any fair comparison requirement in Art 2. Kim also deals with the methodology known as zeroing, pursuant to which some anti-dumping authorities assign a value of zero to where the export price exceeds the normal value. The effect of this is to drag down the weighted average export sale price. Only prices equal to or below the normal price are used in working out the average export price. In the panel decision in *European Communities – Anti-dumping Duties on Imports of Cotton-type Bed Linen from India* ('*Bed Linen*') (WTO document WT/DS141/R) it was determined that the procedure that was employed by the EU was inconsistent with the anti-dumping agreement – Kim at 40, 56. See also Moore, 'Department of Commerce administration of anti-dumping sunset reviews: a first assessment' (2002) 36:4 *J of World Trade* 675 at 676, referring to US bias in calculating dumping margins, and the references at fn 1.

8   Customs Act 1901 (Cth), s 269 TAC(1).

comparability (Art 2.4). So, for example, if goods are sold at normal value in the exporter's country at $120, but sold at $100 in the importing market, the *prima facie* dumping margin will be $20. If, however, investigation shows that $20 of the exporting country's price is due to the imposition of a 20% wholesale tax, and that the goods are sold tax free in the importing country, the apparent dumping margin disappears. This is because allowance must be made for the tax to effect a fair price comparison. Likewise, such factors as freight costs need to be factored in to effect a fair price comparison.

What of rebates granted to volume purchasers? Suppose that the normal price of goods in the exporting country would be $100, but in practice it is $90 in most cases because buyers purchase large volumes and get a 10% volume rebate. The goods are sold in the importing country for $90. Is the normal value $90, or is the rebate to be disregarded, with the result that the true (albeit constructed) normal value is $100, with the result that there is a dumping margin of $10?

This issue arose in the Australian case of *Nordland Papier AG v Anti-Dumping Authority*,[9] where it was contended that the practice of the exporter in giving a volume rebate to customers of its paper in its home market of Germany meant that these sales were not arms length transactions as required by the legislation and therefore were not in the ordinary course of trade (a precondition for relying upon them to determine normal value). If the volume rebate was disregarded, and a price constructed, then necessarily the normal value would be higher than otherwise, which would more readily permit a determination of dumping. The anti-dumping authority had ignored the rebate and had constructed a higher normal value.

The court held upon review that the volume rebate had to be considered, in order to determine the normal value and permit a fair price comparison. Having regard to the terms of the anti-dumping treaty, and to the terms of the legislative provisions, which were broadly drawn and directed to, in substance implementing Art 2.3 of the Agreement, this was an appropriate interpretation of the objectives of the legislation.[10] This conclusion was fortified, the court considered, by amendments to the legislation that came into effect a few days after the case was heard. In the terms of the explanatory memorandum which had dealt with the meaning and effect of these draft provisions when introduced into Parliament, the intent of the provisions was (quoting the memorandum), '... to allow transactions affected by reimbursements between non-related parties that are normal business practice in many industries and markets to be treated as being at arms length'.[11] The rebate, even if paid in cash, was 'simply part of the process by which the price is established and settled between buyer and seller'.[12]

In a US case, the normal value was determined by subtracting from it the value of accessories supplied with the product, in a case where accessories were not supplied (and therefore not factored into the price) in the importing country.[13] This is consistent with Art 2.4.

9   [1999] FCA 10 (14 January 1999, at www.austlii.edu.au), a decision of the Federal Court.
10 *Ibid* at para 29, *per* Lehane J.
11 *Ibid* at paras 31ff.
12 *Ibid* at para 30. For a decision to like effect in the United States, see *Smith-Corona Group v United States* (1983) 713 F 2d 1568 United States Court of Appeals (Federal Cir).
13 *Ibid*.

Does the fact that the exporter enjoys a monopoly or share of an oligopoly in its home market (a factor which would normally be expected to make the normal value higher than it would otherwise be), have to be factored into assessment of the normal value? This would work to the exporter's advantage in a case where it was accused of dumping, because it would enable construction of a normal value lower than otherwise.

In an Australian case, it was noted that the mere existence of a natural monopoly in production of the product in its home product did not mean that an exporter had used its monopoly to charge higher prices than otherwise. As the exporter had not adduced evidence to this effect, the submission that monopoly had to be factored into assessment of the normal value did not have to be considered.[14] Another Australian decision soon afterwards expressed scepticism that the existence of an oligopoly needed to be factored into an assessment of normal value, although the possibility was not entirely precluded. According to the review judge, the Australian legislation treated the cause of dumping as a matter of 'little significance'. Essentially, the legislation will operate in all cases where the goods in question are priced in Australia at a figure lower than they are priced in the country of export.[15] Monopoly *per se* does not make the prices actually charged in the exporting country unsuitable for determining normal value, although it was possible that in some circumstances the existence of a monopoly or oligopoly would need to be taken into account and an alternative price constructed.[16]

Injury

Article 3 deals with the determination of when the requisite injury to a domestic industry in the importing country has occurred. Article 3.1 provides that this determination requires an objective examination of both (a) the *volume* of the dumped imports and the *effects* of dumped imports in the domestic market for like products, and (b) the consequent *impact* of these imports on domestic producers of such products.

Where *volume* is concerned, the investigation is to be directed to whether there has been a significant increase in dumped exports, either absolutely or in relation to production or consumption in the importing country. Where *effect* on prices is concerned, consideration is to be given as to whether there has been significant price undercutting by the dumped imports compared to the price of like products in the importing country, or whether the dumped prices operate to depress domestic prices or prevent price increases that would otherwise have occurred (Art 3.2). It will be noted that while the determination of whether dumping has occurred requires comparison of the dumped price with the price in the exporting country's market, determination of the effect of dumping involves comparison with the domestic prices in the importing country's economy. In this two-stage process, then, comparison is made between all prevailing prices – those in the exporting economy, the dumped price, and those in the importing economy.

---

14   *Enichem Anic v Anti-Dumping Authority* (1992) 39 FCR 458 at 467ff.
15   *Ibid, per* Hill J at 373.
16   *Ibid.*

Examination of the *impact* of the dumped imports on the domestic industry requires consideration of all relevant economic factors bearing upon the state of the industry, such as actual and potential decline in sales, effects on cash flow, employment, wages, and the ability to raise capital or to invest in the domestic industry (Art 3.4).

Article 3.5 provides that proof of *causation of injury* is required for the purposes of Art VI(1) of the GATT, in so far as it condemns dumping which causes *material injury* to a domestic industry. All relevant evidence is to be reviewed in making this determination, including factors independent of the dumping which are concurrently injuring the domestic industry, such as contraction in demand for the like product.

Article VI(1) of the GATT provides, in the alternative, that dumping is to be condemned where it *threatens material injury* to a domestic industry. Such a determination is to be based on facts and not merely on allegation, conjecture or remote possibility. The relevant change in circumstances must be foreseen and imminent. Factors to be considered include those such as a significant increase in dumped imports, an imminent substantial increase in the capacity of the exporter to export, indicating the substantial likelihood of substantially increased dumping, and whether the dumped prices are at such levels as to significantly depress domestic prices and likely to increase demand for further imports (Art 3.7). The threshold for proving relevant material injury is relatively demanding.

Can an injury to the domestic industry be material when the market share of the allegedly dumped product is very small? In a GATT panel report, a Finnish company was found to have dumped power transformers in New Zealand. But its market share in the period in question was small – it had sold two such transformers, which represented 2.4% of the market for this equipment in the relevant period. The panel found that there had been no material injury to the domestic transformer manufacturing industry.[17]

On the other hand, an exporter of sodium cyanide to Australia, which product was found to be dumped, was held to have caused material injury, although its share of the market was small. This was because it was proper, the court held (affirming the anti-dumping authority's determination) to aggregate the exporter's share with those of other concurrent exporters, the products of which were also found to be dumped. Viewed in aggregate, they had caused material damage or threatened this.[18] The court quoted an earlier judgment: the existence of 'material injury' was:

> Essentially a practical exercise designed to achieve the objective of determining whether, when viewed as a whole, the relevant Australian industry is suffering material injury from the dumping of goods.[19]

According to another Australian decision, in assessing whether an injury is material, the detriment caused by the dumping must be separated out from the detriment caused by other factors, such as declining demand due to economic recession,

---

17 *Report on New Zealand Imports of Electrical Transformers from Finland*, BISD 32S/55, Document 1-B-18 (1985), Report of the GATT Dispute Settlement Panel.

18 *Enichem ANIC Srl v Anti-Dumping Authority* (1992) 39 FCR 458 at 470.

19 *Swan Portland Cement Ltd v Minister for Small Business and Customs* (1991) 28 FCR 135 at 144, *per* Lockhart J.

industrial unrest, or insufficiency of raw materials.[20] This factor *per se* must be found to have caused material injury.[21] A material injury was described as one which is 'not immaterial, insubstantial or insignificant an injury which will in most but not all cases be an injury which is greater than that likely to occur in the normal ebb and flow of business uninfluenced by dumping ...'.[22] In this case, a group of exporters was found to have dumped product (low density polyethylene) in Australia. These imports held a small share of the market (under 10%). The court held that it had not been established that a causal link existed between this dumped product and material injury to the industry, especially when in addition to the smallness of the share, regard was had to other concurrent but unrelated factors at work domestically causing material injury to the industry.[23]

Domestic industry

The domestic industry that is the focus of the dumping investigation, is defined by Art 4. This industry may be the whole of the producers of the like product, or a proportion of them, which produces the major proportion of this product, as appropriate. Exceptionally, the territory of the importing country may be divided into two or more competitive markets, if this is appropriate, with any anti-dumping duties to be levied only on the products consigned for final consumption in the appropriate geographic area, as appropriate.

Initiation and subsequent investigation

It is for the importing country to create appropriate dumping investigative entities for the purposes of implementing the GATT anti-dumping regime. Pursuant to Art 5, an investigation is ordinarily to be commenced upon service of a written application by or on behalf of the domestic industry in question. This application must address the relevant tests that identify actionable dumping, that is, dumping, injury, and the necessity for a causal link to exist between the dumped product and the alleged injury. Simple assertion will not suffice – evidence must be adduced. The authorities are to examine the accuracy and adequacy of this evidence. The investigation is not to be initiated unless the investigating entity determines that the application has been made by or on behalf of the domestic industry. If the application is supported by producers who in aggregate produce at least 50% of the domestic production, the application is deemed to be by or on behalf of the domestic industry. In no circumstance will an application be acted upon where it is not expressly supported by those responsible for at least 25% of domestic production.

An application will be rejected and an investigation terminated if the authorities find that there is not sufficient evidence of either dumping or injury to justify proceeding with the case.

---

20   *ICI Aust Operations Pty Ltd v Fraser* (1992) 34 FCR 564 at 572.
21   *Ibid* at 573, 577.
22   *Ibid* at 577.
23   *Ibid* at 573, 578.

Article 6 deals with the evidential aspects of the case. All interested parties are to be given notice of the application so that they can respond with relevant evidence.

When the authorities are satisfied that there is sufficient evidence to justify the initiation of an investigation under Art 5, the exporting country or countries and other interested parties are to be notified and a public notice given (Art 12.1). Public notices are to be given of other relevant determinations, such as preliminary or final determinations, the imposition of provisional measures, or a decision not to conclude or suspend an investigation (Art 12).

Provisional measures; price undertakings

If the investigation has proceeded to a point where interested parties have been given an opportunity to be heard and a preliminary finding has been made that injurious dumping has occurred, and the authorities consider it necessary to prevent further injury during the remainder of the investigation, then they can apply provisional measures pursuant to Art 7. These can take the form of a provisional duty or, preferably, a security by cash deposit bond, equal to the amount of the anti-dumping provisionally estimated, being not greater than the provisionally estimated margin of dumping (that is, the difference between the dumped price, and the price at which the product would have been supplied had it not been below the normal price in the exporting economy).

Proceedings may be suspended or terminated without the imposition of provisional measures or anti-dumping duties where the exporter gives voluntary undertakings to revise its prices or to cease exports in the disputed area, provided that the authorities are confident that the injurious effect will thereby be eliminated (Art 8.1). The authorities can refuse these undertakings if acceptance would be impracticable (Art 8.3).

Anti-dumping duties

If the investigative authority determines that the dumping has caused the requisite prejudice, it may impose an anti-dumping duty. This may not exceed the full margin of dumping, and should be less if a lesser margin would suffice to remove the injury (Art 9.1). Such a duty is to be imposed on a non-discriminatory basis on imports of such products from all sources found to be dumped and causing injury, except in respect of sources whose price undertakings have been accepted (Art 9.2). The anti-dumping duty is not to exceed the margin of dumping (Art 9.3). Where the amount of duty is assessed on a retrospective basis, the determination of the final liability for payment must be done in a timely manner pursuant to Art 9.3.1. When duty is levied on a prospective basis, provision is to be made for a prompt refund of any duty paid in excess of the dumping margin (Art 9.3.2).

Provisional measures and anti-dumping duties are to be applied only to imports entering for consumption after the time that the decision to impose these comes into force, except as provided under Art 10. Where an appropriate determination of injury or threatened injury is made, anti-dumping duties may be levied retroactively for the period, if any, during which provisional measures have been applied (Art 10.2).

Duration and review of anti-dumping duties and price undertakings

Article 11 regulates the duration of anti-dumping duties and price undertakings. The authorities are to review the need for the continued imposition of the duty on their own initiative where warranted, or, after a reasonable period has elapsed since the application of duties, upon the request of an interested party. If after review it is determined that the duty should no longer apply, it is to be removed immediately (Art 11.2). Quite independently of any such review, the anti-dumping duty is to be removed after five years since application, unless the authorities determine after a fresh investigation that expiry of the duty would be likely to lead to a continuation of dumping and relevant injury (Art 11.4). These provisions apply also to price undertakings accepted under Art 8 (Art 11.5).

Member countries are required to provide for the judicial review of anti-dumping measures by the anti-dumping authority (Art 13).

Committee on anti-dumping practices

The 1994 Agreement provides in Art 16 for the establishment of a Committee on Anti-Dumping Practices, to be supported by the WTO Secretariat. The Committee is composed of representatives of members. The Committee carries out responsibilities assigned to it by the Agreement or by the members, and is designed to facilitate consultation by members of matters relating to the Agreement and its operation. Members are to report promptly any anti-dumping determinations. Members are also to file semi-annual reports of anti-dumping actions.

Consultation and dispute settlement

Article 17 provides for dispute settlement between members in cases where a member has concerns regarding any matter affecting the operation of the Agreement, such as where a member believes that a benefit provided to it under the Agreement is being impaired by the action of another member. Members are enjoined to afford sympathetic consideration to any request from another member for consultation.

If the dispute concerns an anti-dumping determination (including provisional measures that have a significant impact) by an importing member, and the parties cannot settle the matter by consultation, the exporting member can refer the matter to the Dispute Settlement Body (DSB). The DSB is empowered to establish a panel to examine the matter. This review is to include examination of whether the importing member's anti-dumping authority proceeded in an unbiased and objective way. If it did, the panel is to allow the determination to stand, even if it would have reached a different view on the merits. The review, that is, is not a *de novo* one. It is directed not towards a merit review, so much as towards ensuring fairness of process.

SUBSIDIES AND COUNTERVAILING MEASURES

Introduction

The WTO-GATT anti-dumping regime, which has been reviewed above, is paralleled by the WTO-GATT regime dealing with government subsidies of producers and countervailing measures. This latter regime targets government subsidies to producers whether their product is bound for the export or domestic markets. These subsidies can take numerous forms, such as grants and bounties. In practice the focus of the subsidies regime is on the problems caused by subsidised exports. In the latter case, the importing country can in certain circumstances impose a special tariff known as a countervailing duty, designed to nullify the effect of the subsidy.

This type of subsidisation (1) has the potential to lead to the export of goods to other countries for sale at a lower price than would otherwise obtain, with the further potential for damage to the competing producers in these importing economies. In this respect, the subsidies regime targets a mischief paralleling dumping. The regime also (2) targets the subsidisation of the production of goods for internal sale, which can lead to lower domestic prices than would otherwise apply. This import protection strategy potentially has the effect of prejudicing members who seek to export goods to the subsidising economy. As it will be seen, the subsidies regime targets producers of non-agricultural goods. The agricultural sectors in member countries enjoy a measure of immunity from the regime.

The two systems differ in a critical respect – the anti-dumping regime targets dumping which is made possible by private initiative (that is, the support for below normal pricing in the importing economy is provided by the producer itself); while the subsidies regime focuses on public initiative (where support for sub-normal pricing is provided by the government of the production country). The subsidies regime, like its anti-dumping twin, runs counter to the overall free trade philosophy of the WTO-GATT.

The first GATT agreement contained a very weak subsidies provision, that is, Art XVI, which provided merely for consultation between members where a member was adversely affected by subsidisation of a producer.[24] This was amended in 1955 to prohibit export subsidies that led to a lower import economy price than that normally obtained in the exporting economy, although an exception was enacted in respect of agricultural produce. The subsidies regime was strengthened in the Tokyo Round (leading to the Tokyo Round Subsidies Code 1979). The current regime was settled in the Uruguay Round.

The Uruguay Round provided for an elaborate subsidies and countervailing duties code. Its achievements include the following.[25] It applied a subsidies regime for the first time to developing countries. It defined the concept of a subsidy in this context, provided for a multilateral mechanism for resolving subsidies disputes (over and beyond domestic responses), and made detailed provision for countervailing duty investigations.

---

24 For the background to the present subsidies regime, see Zampetti, 'The Uruguay Round Agreement on Subsidies' (1995) 29:6 *J World Trade* 5 at 10ff; Collins-Williams and Salembier, 'International discipline on subsidies' (1996) 30:1 *J World Trade* 5ff.
25 See those enumerated in Collins-Williams and Salembier, *ibid* at 9.

Categories of subsidy

The 1994 Subsidies Agreement recognises that not all subsidies damage international trade, or the domestic industry of the non-subsidising economy, or if they do, that other considerations may justify them. For example, a government may be able to justify a measure of *de facto* subsidisation of an export industry, on the basis that the support takes the form of improvements to essential infrastructure. Accordingly, the Agreement does not prohibit all forms of subsidy. It provides for several categories of subsidy – (1) prohibited subsidies, which are *per se* illegal; (2) actionable subsidies, which are not *per se* illegal but are governed by an adverse effects test; and (3) non-actionable subsidies.

Remedies

The remedies provided vary according to the nature of the subsidy. The Agreement provides for consultation among members in dispute regarding both prohibited and actionable subsidies, and if they cannot come to a solution, for reference of the dispute to the DSB of the WTO for a determination.

The Agreement provides additionally for the imposition by the importing country of countervailing measures including duties, in the case of exports that are actionable subsidies. (Logically such countervailing measures can only be imposed upon imports.) It provides for a proper investigative process in the importing country before these measures may be imposed. Like the anti-dumping regime, the countervailing duty regime must be enacted by the importing member before the Agreement can be relied upon. The Agreement provides for special and differential treatment of developing country members.

Defining a subsidy

Articles 1 and 2 define when a subsidy is a *specific* subsidy. Non-specific subsidies do not fall within the ambit of the Agreement. A subsidy must be specific to attract the operation of the Agreement, but as it will be seen, the fact that a subsidy is specific does not necessarily mean that it attracts sanctions under the Agreement. As well as being specific, the subsidy must fall within one of the two categories of subsidy attracting remedies under the Agreement, that is, it must be *prohibited* or *actionable*.

A subsidy can be direct (such as an export subsidy based on the volume or value of exports), or indirect (such as a targeted tax credits or other tax concessions for exporters).

A subsidy is deemed by Art 1 to exist when the government or a public body of the producer country makes a financial contribution to the producer enterprise or industry. These contributions can take a variety of forms including: the direct transfer of funds to the producer (including grants or loans), or the foregoing of revenue (such as where tax credits are conferred), or the provision of goods and services (other than general infrastructure such as a highway or port facilities), or the provision of any form of income or price support amounting to a benefit (such as where an export subsidy is conferred).

This subsidy must be specific to an industry or enterprise or group of these, as defined by Art 2. A subsidy is specific where it is explicitly limited to certain enterprises (such as an exporter or exporters of leather car seats). It is not specific where objective criteria governing eligibility for the subsidy make it clear that eligibility is automatic provided that the criteria are strictly adhered to. These criteria must be spelled out in law or a like instrument. For example, a depreciation allowance (that is, a tax deduction) granted by tax law to all purchasers of capital machinery for use in a business such as manufacturing, will not be a specific subsidy. It may be classifiable as specific where, say, it is granted solely to ship builders, most of the product of which is exported. Likewise, provision for wage support for apprentices in the manufacturing and construction sectors generally will not amount to a specific subsidy. Governments, through the provision of general infrastructure, research and development support, and other developmental initiatives and tax concessions, typically do provide support for industry (measures sometimes referred to as 'industry welfare'), but these will not normally be classifiable as specific subsidies.

However, even if on the face of things the subsidy is not specific, but there are reasons to believe that it is, certain other factors may be considered. These include the *de facto* use of the subsidy program by a limited number of certain enterprises, its predominant use by certain enterprises, the granting of disproportionately large amounts of subsidy to certain enterprises, and the manner in which the granting authority exercised its discretion.[26]

A subsidy that is limited to certain enterprises in a particular geographical region is specific. The setting of generally applicable tax rates is not a specific subsidy.

A recent decision of the WTO Appellate Body illustrates a subsidy found to be both specific and to attract a remedy under the Agreement. Pursuant to the '*Byrd Amendment*' (the Continued Dumping and Subsidy Offset Act of 2000 (US)), anti-dumping and countervailing duties collected by the US were distributed to US manufacturers of the like product, which supported the imposition of these duties. This clearly had the effect of disadvantaging foreign exporters of the like product that had not enjoyed any price support from their own government (or dumped product into the US). The subsidy was specific and fell within the categories of actionable subsidies (see 'Actionable subsidies; remedies' below).[27]

It was determined in an Australian case, *Rocklea Spinning Mills Pty Ltd v Anti-Dumping Authority*,[28] turning on Australian legislation implementing the Agreement, that the Government of Pakistan did not confer a subsidy for the purposes of the Agreement when it set compulsory prices for the export of cotton yarn, even though these, taken with other circumstances, had the effect of making the price paid for raw cotton in the domestic market cheaper. The result was that the exported product could be cheaper than otherwise it might have been. The benefit was not a subsidy, there being no payment to the exporters. There was 'no payment or remission by the

---

26   Thus, for example, a court found that (subject to review of the precise facts) the supply by the government of Mexico of carbon black feedstock and natural gas at below market prices to Mexican manufacturers, although available to all industry in Mexico, could in practice end up being disproportionately utilised by, and being to the benefit of, two Mexican producers that exported carbon black, and as such, could amount to an actionable subsidy under US countervailing legislation implementing the agreement: see *Cabot Corp v US* (1985) 620 F Supp 722, United States Court of International Trade.

27   Jan 2003 – see www.wto.org.

28   (1995) 129 ALR 401 (Full Federal Court).

Pakistan Government, nor [was] there any charge on the public purse of Pakistan either in the sense of a payment from public funds or the remission of duty or tax or in the foregoing of other government revenue'.[29] Further, the arrangement was not a public subsidy, because a subsidy necessarily involved a charge on the public account.[30]

The European Court of Justice decided that a differential tax imposed by the government of Argentina, whereby a 25% tax was imposed upon the export of soya beans, but only a 10% tax was imposed upon the export of products intended to be crushed or processed, such as soya meat, did not give rise to an export subsidy, because there was no charge on the account of a public body.[31]

Per se illegality – prohibited subsidies; remedies

A subsidy is *prohibited* when the subsidy is both specific and (a) wholly or partly dependent upon export performance,[32] or (b) it is wholly or partly dependent upon the use of domestic over imported goods (Art 3.1).

Members are prohibited from granting or maintaining these subsidies (Art 3.2). In conformity with Art 4, an importing member, who has reason to believe that a prohibited subsidy is being granted or maintained by another member, can seek consultations with the other member. Should they not be able to reach an agreement on the issue within 30 days, any member may refer the matter to the DSB. The DSB by consensus can determine to establish a panel. The panel, if it determines that the subsidy is a prohibited subsidy, can recommend to the subsidising member that it withdraw the subsidy without delay. Provision is made for appeal to the Appellate Body.

It will be observed that these so called prohibited subsidies are *per se* illegal – it does not have to be established that they had a relevant adverse effect on the complainant member's industry or otherwise.

The Agreement recognises that subsidies may assist the economic development of developing countries. Accordingly, those developing members referred to in Annex VII of the Agreement are exempted from the Art 3.1(a) prohibition on subsidies contingent upon export performance, until such time as they attain export competitiveness in respect of the particular product (see 'Actionable subsidies; remedies' below).

---

29 *Ibid* at 415.
30 *Ibid* at 414, citing *EEC Seed Crushers and Oil Processors Federation (Fedoil) v Commission of European Communities* (1988) ECR 4155 (Argentina) and 4193 (Brazil).
31 *EEC Seed Crushers and Oil Processors Federation (Fedoil) v Commission of European Communities, ibid* at 4155.
32 Annex I to the agreement contains an illustrative list of export subsidies, such as the provision by governments or direct subsidies to an industry contingent upon export performance; or internal transport and freight charges set by the government which are more favourable than for domestic consumption; or the exemption or remission, in respect of the production and distribution of exported products, of indirect taxes in excess of those levied in respect of the distribution of like products when sold for domestic consumption. (In this latter case, eg, a remission of GST/VAT in excess of that levied on domestic products, would qualify as an export subsidy.)

Actionable subsidies; remedies

A subsidy is *actionable* when it is specific and causes adverse effects to the interests of other members, taking the form of (a) injury to the domestic industry of another member; (b) nullification of benefits accruing under the GATT 1994;[33] or (c) serious prejudice to the interests of another member. Unlike prohibited subsides (see *'Per se illegality* – prohibited subsidies; remedies' above), it must be proven that these subsidies have a prescribed adverse effect.

Article 3 does not apply to subsidies maintained on agricultural products as provided in Art 13 of the Agreement on Agriculture. These sectors may be subsidised by members without repercussion. This provision reflects the protected status of the politically influential farming sector in numerous countries, such as the EU and the US.

What is 'serious prejudice' for the purpose of Art 5(c)? This is defined in Art 6. Serious prejudice is deemed to exist in certain cases, including where the total *ad valorem* subsidisation of a product exceeds 5%; or where subsidies are granted to cover operating losses sustained by an industry or an enterprise (except, in the latter case, where they are granted on a one-off basis to provide time to develop long-term solutions and to avoid acute social problems). The effect of this deeming provision is that no actual proof of prejudice need be shown by the importing member. The deeming provision is not a conclusive one, however – the subsidising member has the option of proving positively that, notwithstanding that the facts ground the deeming provision, there was no serious prejudice in fact. In this case the subsidy will not be a prohibited one. A simple illustration of this type of case is where the exporter proves that, notwithstanding an *ad valorem* subsidy of 10%, the importing member did not suffer injury to its domestic industry, etc.

Quite independently of the deeming provisions, serious prejudice may be found to exist in the situations listed in Art 6(3). These cases include those where: the effect of the subsidy is to displace or impede the imports of a like product of another member into the market of the subsidising member; the effect of the subsidy is to displace or impede the exports of a like product of another member from a third country market; or the effect of the subsidy is a significant price undercutting by the subsidised product in defined circumstances. The absence of a deeming provision, however, means that serious prejudice must be established on the evidence.

Displacement or impediment causing serious prejudice shall not arise in defined circumstances, such as: natural disasters, strikes, transport disruptions or other *force majeure* substantially affecting production, prices, etc, of the product available for export from the complaining member; the existence of arrangements limiting exports from the complaining member; or failure to conform to standards and other regulatory requirements in the importing country (Art 6(7)).

Article 6, dealing with serious prejudice, does not apply to subsidies maintained on export products as provided in Art 13 of the Agreement on Agriculture.

---

33 In particular the benefits or concessions bound under Art II of the GATT 1994.

Remedies

Remedies available where actionable subsidies are deemed or proven to exist are provided for in Art 7. A member that believes that another member has granted or maintained any subsidy (as defined in Art 1) that has resulted in injury to its domestic industry, nullification or impairment or serious prejudice, may request consultation with the other member. If the members cannot agree on a solution within 60 days, any member may refer the issue to the WTO DSB for establishment of a panel, unless the DSB decides by consensus not to establish one. The panel, once established, is to review the matter and issue a report, which report can be appealed to the Appellate Body. Where the panel or Appellate Body reports that a member has suffered adverse effects within the meaning of Art 5 as a result of a subsidy, the member granting or maintaining this subsidy is to take appropriate steps to remove the adverse effects of the subsidy or shall withdraw the subsidy. If the member does not do this, the DSB shall grant authorisation to the complainant to take countermeasures, commensurate with the degree and nature of the effects, unless the DSB decides by consensus not to do this.

Alternatively (and more commonly) the importing member can impose countervailing measures, such as countervailing duties. This topic is examined below.

Non-actionable subsidies

Article 8(1) provides that two types of subsidies are not actionable under the GATT. The first are those subsidies that are non-specific (see 'Defining a subsidy' above).

The second type of subsidy is that which is of scientific of social benefit. In these cases, the non-economic benefit is deemed to outweigh the economic benefit (if there is one). Thus, subsidies taking the form of assistance for research activities conducted by firms or by higher education or research establishments on a contract basis are non-actionable, provided that certain tests are satisfied. A subsidy taking the form of assistance to a disadvantaged region within the territory of a member, given pursuant to a general framework of regional development and non-specific within eligible regions is non-actionable, provided that certain requirements are met.

Proposed subsidies in these categories are to be notified to other members in advance of their implementation. Ongoing details of implementation are to be notified. If a member considers that the program, even though it qualifies as a non-actionable subsidy, has resulted in serious adverse effects to its domestic industry, such as to cause damage that would be difficult to repair, the member can request consultation with the member granting the subsidy. If the parties cannot agree on a solution, the WTO Committee on Subsidies and Countervailing Measures may, after examining the facts, authorise the adversely affected member to take appropriate countermeasures. It follows that the so called non-actionable subsidy may ultimately be determined to be actionable.

Countervailing measures

As it has been noted, in certain cases a member can impose countervailing measures as an alternative to seeking arbitration of the dispute through the WTO DSB.

An importing country that is adversely affected by export subsidies conferred upon a producer or industry by the government of the country from which the goods are imported, may, provided that the subsidy is actionable, take countervailing measures. There are then two key conditions for this remedy: (1) the subsidy must be actionable; and (2) it must have been used to confer price support for exports to the aggrieved member. Logically, such measures cannot be used to overcome the problems created by a member's subsidisation of domestic prices, to the prejudice of a member that exports like products to this member.

Normally, the countervailing measure is in the form of imposing a countervailing duty, or tariff, on the imported goods, no greater than the value of the subsidy. This tariff may be cumulative upon any applicable general tariff. The intent is that the price of the import will be brought up to the level that would have applied in the absence of the subsidy. This price will not necessarily be equal to the price for the like domestically produced good – the GATT does not require any such parity.

Countervailing measures may only be imposed after following procedures spelled out in the Agreement. The Agreement provides for the notification of, and investigation of, a complaint of actionable subsidy by a public authority of the importing country. Necessarily the importing country must implement the GATT provisions in general law.

An application to the authority to determine the existence, degree and effect of any alleged subsidy must be in writing and accompanied by sufficient evidence of the subsidy and if possible its amount, relevant injury to the domestic industry, and a causal link between the imports and the injury (Art 11). The authority is to undertake an investigation of the application. The authority is to terminate the investigation promptly if it is satisfied that there is not sufficient evidence of either subsidisation or injury to justify proceeding with the case, or that the amount of the subsidy is *de minimis* or where the volume of imports, actual or potential, is negligible. Interested parties are to be notified of the investigation and given an opportunity to adduce evidence (Art 12).

The Agreement encourages less formal dispute resolution prior to commencement of a formal investigation. A member, the products of which may be subject to investigation, is to be invited for consultation with a view to arriving at a mutually agreed solution. If this is unavailing, the member in question is to be afforded the opportunity for consultation throughout the investigation (Art 13).

The investigating authority, if it is to make a determination of injury, must base this on positive evidence and an objective evaluation of relevant matters. It must be demonstrated that the subsidised imports are causing injury within the meaning of the Agreement. A determination of threat of immediate injury must be based upon facts and not merely allegation, conjecture or remote possibility. In the case of mere threat, the application of countervailing measures is to be considered and decided with great care (Art 15).

Provisional measures may be authorised by the authority if it judges that such measures are necessary to prevent injury being caused during an investigation. Two preconditions apply: the investigation has been duly convened and conducted; and a preliminary affirmative determination has been made that a subsidy exists and that this has caused injury to a domestic industry. These measures may take the form of provisional countervailing duties guaranteed by cash deposits or bonds (Art 17).

Provision is made for the suspension or termination of proceedings without the imposition of provisional measures or countervailing duties upon the giving of relevant undertakings by the subsidising member, such as one to eliminate or limit the subsidy in question (Art 18).

If the issue cannot be resolved by consultation, and a member, through the relevant authority, makes a final determination that the subsidy is causing the prescribed injury, it may impose a countervailing duty unless the subsidy is withdrawn. The duty may be equal to the full amount of the subsidy, but should be less than this if a lesser duty would be adequate to remove the injury to the domestic industry. Normally, the duty should be non-discriminatory as between products from all sources found to be subsidised and causing injury (Art 19).

Countervailing duties and provisional measures normally are to be applied only after the date when an adverse determination was made (Art 20).[34]

A countervailing duty is only to remain in force for as long as, and to the extent necessary, to counteract the subsidisation that is causing injury. The imposition of the duty is subject to review by the authority at its own initiative or (after a reasonable period) upon application by an interested party. In any event, the duty is to be terminated after five years unless the authority prior to this time has re-examined the issue and determined that the duty needs to be continued in order to prevent the prescribed injury (Art 21).

The Committee on Subsidies and Countervailing Measures; notification of subsidies

The Agreement provides for the establishment of a Committee on Subsidies and Countervailing Measures (Art 24), composed of representatives of the members. The Committee has, pursuant to the Agreement, set up a Permanent Group of Experts. Members may refer current or proposed subsidies to the Group for advice.

Members are required to notify subsidies maintained by them, annually (Art 25).

Developing country members

The Agreement recognises that the subsidies may play an important role in the economic development of developing countries. Accordingly, designated developing country members enjoy certain exceptions from the prohibition on subsidies, pursuant to Art 27. In particular, those members referred to in Annex VII of the Agreement are not bound by para 1(a) of Art 3 (which prohibits subsidies contingent wholly or partly upon export performance). When, however, a member reaches export competitiveness in respect of a given product or products, subsidies are to be phased out gradually over eight years.

---

34 Certain exceptions apply, such as where a final determination of injury would have been made but for the fact that provisional measures were applied. In this case duties may be applied retroactively for the period for which provisional measures, if any, have applied – Art 20(2).

Conclusion

The Subsidies Agreement is very well described by AB Zampetti as follows:

> ... The Uruguay Round Subsidies Agreement may be interpreted as providing rules for the elimination of market distortions arising from the use of one important public policy instrument, subsidies. This would keep the objective of the Agreement in line with the overall aims of the multilateral trading system. The standard which appears to underpin the Agreement is that of 'normal competition' based on market and efficiency principles. The economic behaviour of governments in the international market-place needs to be assessed against this standard. But due account needs to be taken of the various efficiency-enhancing interventions governments carry out. This implies that only a subset of subsidies are deemed to be actually distortive. Except in the case of subsidies contingent upon export performance or local content, which are prohibited *per se*, all other subsidies that cause adverse trade effects, and thus fall under the purview of international regulation, require a rule-of-reason-like analysis before a remedy can be granted.[35]

TUTORIAL QUESTIONS

General: anti-dumping and subsides

Why does the WTO-GATT sanction the anti-dumping and subsidies regimes by way of exception to its philosophical objective of free trade?

Dumping

1   What are the motivations for dumping?

2   Are consumers protected by the anti-dumping regime?

3   When is the dumping of products actionable?

4   How are prices in the exporting and importing economies to be compared? Does the regime require comparison of like with like in all circumstances, or are there exceptions?

5   If a producer can export cars to another economy at cheaper prices than those prevailing in its home economy, because its home economy currency is pegged at an artificially low rate, is it dumping?

6   If this producer can export cars to another economy at cheaper prices than those prevailing in its home economy because wages are kept very low by government regulation in the latter economy, is this dumping?

7   Is it a defence to a dumping action if the export producer establishes that its home economy prices are unduly high because of high tariffs limiting import competition in the home economy?

8   Why are government subsidies dealt with in a different regime? Could they have been dealt with by a more comprehensive anti-dumping regime?

---

35   Zampetti, 'The Uruguay Round Agreement on Subsidies' (1995) 29:6 *J World Trade* 5 at 25.

Subsidies

1   Why is it unfair for a government to subsidise its local industry?

2   Should the definition of subsidy be broadened to include cases where there is effectively a policy of price support by government, but there is no charge on the public account?

3   Should the concept of a subsidy attracting sanctions be limited to specific subsides? If so, why?

4   When are adverse effects required to be proven?

5   Should the concept of prohibited subsidy be revised and limited by an adverse effects test?

6   In what circumstances can a complainant member take unilateral action against subsidies?

7   A manufacturer subsidises its subsidiary to produce goods for export – is there any circumstance in which the operation of the subsidies regime can be invoked?

8   What is the relationship between 'ordinary' tariffs and countervailing duties?

9   The European Union, among other trading entities, subsidises the production of farm produce. Does this contravene the Subsidies Agreement?

10   What requirements must be met before countervailing measures may be imposed?

11   What countervailing measures can be employed apart from duties? Why would other measures be taken in preference?

12   How do the anti-dumping and subsidies regime differ? Do they overlap at any point or points in their operation?

FURTHER READING

Almsted and Norton, 'China's anti-dumping laws and the WTO Anti-dumping Agreement' (2000) 34:6 *J World Trade* 75.

Collins-Williams and Salembier, 'International disciplines on subsidies – the GATT, the WTO and the future agenda' (1996) 30:1 *J World Trade* 5.

Fisher, 'The anti-dumping law of the United States: a legal and economic analysis' (1973) 5 *Law and Policy in International Business* 85.

Horlick and Clark, 'The 1994 WTO Subsidies Agreement' (1994) 17 *W Comp* 4.

Horlick and Shea, 'The World Trade Organisation Anti-dumping Agreement' (1995) 29:1 *J World Trade* 5.

Kim, 'Fair price comparison in the WTO Anti-dumping Agreement' (2002) 36:1 *J World Trade* 39.

Moore, 'Department of Commerce administration of anti-dumping sunset reviews: a first assessment' (2002) 36:4 *J of World Trade* 675.

Palmeter, 'A commentary on the WTO Anti-dumping Code' (1996) 30:4 *J World Trade* 43 at 46.

Prusa, 'On the spread and impact of anti-dumping' (2001) 34:3 *Canadian J Econ* 591.

Quresh, 'Drafting anti-dumping legislation' (2000) 34:6 *J World Trade* 19.

Stewart (ed), *The GATT Uruguay Round: a Negotiating History*, 1993, Deventer: Kluwer Law and Taxation Publishers.

Wood, '"Unfair" trade injury: a competition-based approach' (1989) 41 *Stan LR* 1173.

Zampetti, 'The Uruguay Round Agreement on Subsidies' (1995) 29:6 *J World Trade* 5.

APPENDIX

AGREEMENT ON IMPLEMENTATION OF ARTICLE VI OF THE GENERAL AGREEMENT ON TARIFFS AND TRADE 1994

Members hereby agree as follows:

PART I

Article 1 – Principles

An anti-dumping measure shall be applied only under the circumstances provided for in Article VI of GATT 1994 and pursuant to investigations initiated and conducted in accordance with the provisions of this agreement. The following provisions govern the application of Article VI of GATT 1994 in so far as actions taken under anti-dumping legislation or regulations.

Article 2 – Determination of dumping

2.1   For the purpose of this agreement a product is to be considered as being dumped, ie introduced into the commerce of another country at less than its normal value, if the export price of the product exported from one country to another is less than the comparable price, in the ordinary course of trade, for the like product when destined for consumption in the exporting country.

2.2   When there are no sales of the like product in the ordinary course of trade in the domestic market of the exporting country or when, because of the particular market situation or the low volume of the sales in the domestic market of the exporting country such sales do not permit a proper comparison, the margin of dumping shall be determined by comparison with a comparable price of the like product when exported to an appropriate third country, provided that this price is representative, or with the cost of production in the country of origin plus a reasonable amount for administrative, selling and general costs and for profits.

2.2.1   Sales of the like product in the domestic market of the exporting country or sales to a third country at prices below per unit (fixed and variable) costs of production plus administrative, selling and general costs may be treated as not being in the ordinary course of trade by reason of price and may be disregarded in determining normal value only if the authorities determine that such sales are made within an extended period of time in substantial quantities and are at prices which do not provide for the recovery of all costs within a reasonable period of time. If prices which are below per unit costs at the time of sale are above weighted average per unit costs for the period of investigation, such prices shall be considered to provide for recovery of costs within a reasonable period of time.

2.2.1.1   For the purpose of para 2, costs shall normally be calculated on the basis of records kept by the exporter or producer under investigation, provided that such records are in accordance with the generally accepted accounting principles of the exporting country and reasonably reflect the costs associated with the production and sale of the product under consideration. Authorities shall consider all available evidence on the proper allocation of costs, including that which is made available by the exporter or producer in the course of the investigation provided that such allocations have been historically utilised by the exporter or producer, in particular in relation to establishing appropriate amortisation and depreciation periods and allowances for capital expenditures and other development costs. Unless already reflected in the cost allocations under this sub-paragraph, costs shall be adjusted appropriately for those non-recurring items of cost which benefit future and/or current production, or for circumstances in which costs during the period of investigation are affected by start-up operations.

2.2.2   For the purpose of para 2, the amounts for administrative, selling and general costs and for profits shall be based on actual data pertaining to production and sales in the ordinary course of trade of the like product by the exporter or producer under investigation When such amounts cannot be determined on this basis, the amounts may be determined on the basis of:

(i) the actual amounts incurred and realised by the exporter or producer in question in respect of production and sales in the domestic market of the country of origin of the same general category of products;

(ii) the weighted average of the actual amounts incurred and realised by other exporters or producers subject to investigation in respect of production and sales of the like product in the domestic market of the country of origin;

(iii) any other reasonable method, provided that the amount for profit so established shall not exceed the profit normally realised by other exporters or producers on sales of products of the same general category in the domestic market of the country of origin.

2.3   In cases where there is no export price or where it appears to the authorities concerned that the export price is unreliable because of association or a compensatory arrangement between the exporter and the importer or a third party, the export price may be constructed on the basis of the price at which the imported products are first resold to an independent buyer, or if the products are not resold to an independent buyer, or not resold in the condition as imported, on such reasonable basis as the authorities may determine.

2.4   A fair comparison shall be made between the export price and the normal value. This comparison shall be made at the same level of trade, normally at the ex-factory level, and in respect of sales made at as nearly as possible the same time. Due allowance shall be made in each case, on its merits, for differences which affect price comparability, including differences in conditions and terms of sale, taxation, levels of trade, quantities, physical characteristics, and any other differences which are also demonstrated to affect price comparability. In the cases referred to in para 3, allowances for costs, including duties and taxes, incurred between importation and resale, and for profits accruing, should also be made. If in these cases price comparability has been affected, the authorities shall establish the normal value at a level of trade equivalent to the level of trade of the constructed export price, or shall make due allowance as warranted under this paragraph. The authorities shall indicate to the parties in question what information is necessary to ensure a fair comparison and shall not impose an unreasonable burden of proof on those parties.

2.4.1   When the comparison under para 4 requires a conversion of currencies, such conversion should be made using the rate of exchange on the date of sale provided that when a sale of foreign currency on forward markets is directly linked to the export sale involved, the rate of exchange in the forward sale shall be used. Fluctuations in exchange rates shall be ignored and in an investigation the authorities shall allow exporters at least 60 days to have adjusted their export prices to reflect sustained movements in exchange rates during the period of investigation.

2.4.2   Subject to the provisions governing fair comparison in para 4, the existence of margins of dumping during the investigation phase shall normally be established on the basis of a comparison of a weighted average normal value with a weighted average of prices of all comparable export transactions or by a comparison of normal value and export prices on a transaction-to-transaction basis. A normal value established on a weighted average basis may be compared to prices of individual export transactions if the authorities find a pattern of export prices which differ significantly among different purchasers, regions or time periods, and if an explanation is provided as to why such differences cannot be taken into account appropriately by the use of a weighted average-to-weighted average or transaction-to-transaction comparison.

2.5   In the case where products are not imported directly from the country of origin but are exported to the importing Member from an intermediate country, the price at which the products are sold from the country of export to the importing Member shall normally be compared with the comparable price in the country of export. However, comparison may be made with the price in the country of origin, if, for example, the products are merely trans-shipped through the country of export, or such products are not produced in the country of export, or there is no comparable price for them in the country of export.

2.6   Throughout this agreement, the term 'like product' (*'produit similaire'*) shall be interpreted to mean a product which is identical, ie alike in all respects to the product under consideration, or in the absence of such a product, another product which, although not alike in all respects, has characteristics closely resembling those of the product under consideration.

2.7   This article is without prejudice to the second Supplementary Provision to para 1 of Article VI in Annex I to GATT 1994.

Article 3 – Determination of injury

3.1   A determination of injury for purposes of Article VI of GATT 1994 shall be based on positive evidence and involve an objective examination of both (a) the volume of the dumped imports and the effect of the dumped imports on prices in the domestic market for like products, and (b) the consequent impact of these imports on domestic producers of such products.

3.2   With regard to the volume of the dumped imports, the investigating authorities shall consider whether there has been a significant increase in dumped imports, either in absolute terms or relative to production or consumption in the importing Member. With regard to the effect of the dumped imports on prices, the investigating authorities shall consider whether there has been a significant price undercutting by the dumped imports as compared with the price of a like product of the importing Member, or whether the effect of such imports is otherwise to depress prices to a significant degree or prevent price increases, which otherwise would have occurred, to a significant degree. No one or several of these factors can necessarily give decisive guidance.

3.3   Where imports of a product from more than one country are simultaneously subject to anti-dumping investigations, the investigating authorities may cumulatively assess the effects of such imports only if they determine that (a) the margin of dumping established in relation to the imports from each country is more than *de minimis* as defined in para 8 of Article 5 and the volume of imports from each country is not negligible, and (b) a cumulative assessment of the effects of the imports is appropriate in light of the conditions of competition between the imported products and the conditions of competition between the imported products and the like domestic product.

3.4   The examination of the impact of the dumped imports on the domestic industry concerned shall include an evaluation of all relevant economic factors and indices having a bearing on the state of the industry, including actual and potential decline in sales, profits, output, market share, productivity, return on investments, or utilisation of capacity; factors affecting domestic prices; the magnitude of the margin of dumping; actual and potential negative effects on cash flow, inventories, employment, wages, growth, ability to raise capital or investments. This list is not exhaustive, nor can one or several of these factors necessarily give decisive guidance.

3.5   It must be demonstrated that the dumped imports are, through the effects of dumping, as set forth in paras 2 and 4, causing injury within the meaning of this agreement. The demonstration of a causal relationship between the dumped imports and the injury to the domestic industry shall be based on an examination of all relevant evidence before the authorities. The authorities shall also examine any known factors other than the dumped imports which at the same time are injuring the domestic industry, and the injuries caused by these other factors must not be attributed to the dumped imports. Factors which may be relevant in this respect include, *inter alia*, the volume and prices of imports not sold at dumping prices, contraction in demand or changes in the patterns of consumption, trade restrictive practices of and competition between the foreign and domestic producers, developments in technology and the export performance and productivity of the domestic industry.

3.6   The effect of the dumped imports shall be assessed in relation to the domestic production of the like product when available data permit the separate identification of that production on the basis of such criteria as the production process, producers' sales and profits. If such separate identification of that production is not possible, the effects of the dumped imports shall be assessed by the examination of the production of the narrowest group or range of products, which includes the like product, for which the necessary information can be provided.

3.7   A determination of a threat of material injury shall be based on facts and not merely on allegation, conjecture or remote possibility. The change in circumstances which would create a situation in which the dumping would cause injury must be clearly foreseen and imminent. In making a determination the existence of a threat of material injury, the authorities should consider, *inter alia*, such factors as:

(i)   a significant rate of increase of dumped imports into the domestic market indicating the likelihood of substantially increased importation;

(ii) sufficient freely disposable, or an imminent, substantial increase in, capacity of the exporter indicating the likelihood of substantially increased dumped exports to the importing Member's market, taking into account the availability of other export markets to absorb any additional exports;

(iii) whether imports are entering at prices that will have a significant depressing or suppressing effect on domestic prices, and would likely increase demand for further imports; and

(iv) inventories of the product being investigated.

No one of these factors by itself can necessarily give decisive guidance but the totality of the factors considered must lead to the conclusion that further dumped exports are imminent and that, unless protective action is taken, material injury would occur.

3.8   With respect to cases where injury is threatened by dumped imports, the application of anti-dumping measures shall be considered and decided with special care.

Article 4 – Definition of domestic industry

4.1   For the purposes of this agreement, the term 'domestic industry' shall be interpreted as referring to the domestic producers as a whole of the like products or to those of them whose collective output of the products constitutes a major proportion of the total domestic production of those products, except that:

(i)   when producers are related to the exporters or importers or are themselves importers of the allegedly dumped product, the term 'domestic industry' may be interpreted as referring to the rest of the producers;

(ii) in exceptional circumstances the territory of a Member may, for the production in question, be divided into two or more competitive markets and the producers within each market may be regarded as a separate industry if (a) the producers within such market sell all or almost all of their production of the product in question in that market, and (b) the demand in that market is not to any substantial degree supplied by producers of the product in question located elsewhere in the territory. In such circumstances, injury may be found to exist even where a major portion of the total domestic industry is not injured, provided there is a concentration of dumped imports into such an isolated market and provided further that the dumped imports are causing injury to the producers of all or almost all of the production within such market.

4.2   When the domestic industry has been interpreted as referring to the producers in a certain area, ie a market as defined in para 1(ii), anti-dumping duties shall be levied only on the products in question consigned for final consumption to that area. When the constitutional law of the importing Member does not permit the levying of anti-dumping duties on such a basis, the importing Member may levy the anti-dumping duties without limitation only if (a) the exporters shall have been given an opportunity to cease exporting at dumped prices to the area concerned or otherwise give assurances pursuant to Article 8 and adequate assurances in this regard have not been promptly given, and (b) such duties cannot be levied only on products of specific producers which supply the area in question.

4.3   Where two or more countries have reached under the provisions of para 8(a) of Article XXIV of GATT 1994 such a level of integration that they have the characteristics of a single, unified market, the industry in the entire area of integration shall be taken to be the domestic industry referred to in para 1.

4.4   The provisions of para 6 of Article 3 shall be applicable to this article.

Article 5 – Initiation and subsequent investigation

5.1   Except as provided for in para 6, an investigation to determine the existence, degree and effect of any alleged dumping shall be initiated upon a written application by or on behalf of the domestic industry.

5.2   An application under para 1 shall include evidence of (a) dumping, (b) injury within the meaning of Article VI of GATT 1994 as interpreted by this agreement and (c) a causal link between the dumped imports and the alleged injury. Simple assertion, unsubstantiated by relevant evidence, cannot be considered sufficient to meet the requirements of this paragraph. The application shall contain such information as is reasonably available to the applicant on the following:

  (i)   the identity of the applicant and a description of the volume and value of the domestic production of the like product by the applicant. Where a written application is made on behalf of the domestic industry, the application shall identify the industry on behalf of which the application is made by a list of all known domestic producers of the like product (or associations of domestic producers of the like product) and, to the extent possible, a description of the volume and value of domestic production of the like product accounted for by such producers;

  (ii) a complete description of the allegedly dumped product, the names of the country or countries of origin or export in question, the identity of each known exporter or foreign producer and a list of known persons importing the product in question;

  (iii) information on prices at which the product in question is sold when destined for consumption in the domestic markets of the country or countries of origin or export (or, where appropriate, information on the prices at which the product is sold from the country or countries of origin or export to a third country or countries, or on the constructed value of the product) and information on export prices or, where appropriate, on the prices at which the product is first resold to an independent buyer in the territory of the importing Member;

  (iv) information on the evolution of the volume of the allegedly dumped imports, the effect of these imports on prices of the like product in the domestic market and the consequent impact of the imports on the domestic industry, as demonstrated by relevant factors and indices having a bearing on the state of the domestic industry, such as those listed in paras 2 and 4 of Article 3.

5.3   The authorities shall examine the accuracy and adequacy of the evidence provided in the application to determine whether there is sufficient evidence to justify the initiation of an investigation.

5.4   An investigation shall not be initiated pursuant to para 1 unless the authorities have determined, on the basis of an examination of the degree of support for, or opposition to, the application expressed by domestic producers of the like product, that the application has been made by or on behalf of the domestic industry. The application shall be considered to have been made 'by or on behalf of the domestic industry' if it is supported by those domestic producers whose collective output constitutes more than 50% of the total production of the like product produced by that portion of the domestic industry expressing either support for or opposition to the application. However, no investigation shall be initiated when domestic producers expressly supporting the application account for less than 25% of total production of the like product produced by the domestic industry.

5.5   The authorities shall avoid, unless a decision has been made to initiate an investigation, any publicising of the application for the initiation of an investigation. However, after receipt of a properly documented application and before proceeding to initiate an investigation, the authorities shall notify the government of the exporting Member concerned.

5.6   If, in special circumstances, the authorities concerned decide to initiate an investigation without having received a written application by or on behalf of a domestic industry for the initiation of such investigation, they shall proceed only if they have sufficient evidence of dumping, injury and a causal link, as described in para 2, to justify the initiation of an investigation.

5.7 The evidence of both dumping and injury shall be considered simultaneously (a) in the decision whether or not to initiate an investigation, and (b) thereafter, during the course of the investigation, starting on a date not later than the earliest date on which in accordance with the provisions of this agreement provisional measures may be applied.

5.8 An application under para 1 shall be rejected and an investigation shall be terminated promptly as soon as the authorities concerned are satisfied that there is not sufficient evidence of either dumping or of injury to justify proceeding with the case. There shall be immediate termination in cases where the authorities determine that the margin of dumping is *de minimis,* or that the volume of dumped imports, actual or potential, or the injury, is negligible. The margin of dumping shall he considered to be *de minimis* if this margin is less than 2%, expressed as a percentage of the export price. The volume of dumped imports shall normally be regarded as negligible if the volume of dumped imports from a particular country is found to account for less than 3% of imports of the like product in the importing Member, unless countries which individually account for less than 3% of the imports of the like product in the importing Member collectively account for more than 7% of imports of the like product in the importing Member.

5.9 An anti-dumping proceeding shall not hinder the procedures of customs clearance.

5.10 Investigations shall, except in special circumstances, be concluded within one year, and in no case more than 18 months, after their initiation.

Article 6 – Evidence

6.1 All interested parties in an anti-dumping investigation shall be given notice of the information which the authorities require and ample opportunity to present in writing all evidence which they consider relevant in respect of the investigation in question.

6.1.1 Exporters or foreign producers receiving questionnaires used in an anti-dumping investigation shall be given at least 30 days for reply. Due consideration should be given to any request for an extension of the 30 day period and, upon cause shown, such an extension should be granted whenever practicable.

6.1.2 Subject to the requirement to protect confidential information, evidence presented in writing by one interested party shall be made available promptly to other interested parties participating in the investigation.

6.1.3 As soon as an investigation has been initiated, the authorities shall provide the full text of the written application received under para 1 of Article 5 to the known exporters and to the authorities of the exporting Member and shall make it available, upon request, to other interested parties involved. Due regard shall be paid to the requirement for the protection of confidential information, as provided for in para 5.

6.2 Throughout the anti-dumping investigation all interested parties shall have a full opportunity for the defence of their interests. To this end, the authorities shall, on request, provide opportunities for all interested parties to meet those parties with adverse interests, so that opposing views may be presented and rebuttal arguments offered. Provision of such opportunities must take account of the need to preserve confidentiality and of the convenience to the parties. There shall be no obligation on any party to attend a meeting, and failure to do so shall not be prejudicial to that party's case. Interested parties shall also have the right, on justification, to present other information orally.

6.3 Oral information provided under para 2 shall be taken into account by the authorities only in so far as it is subsequently reproduced in writing and made available to other interested parties, as provided for in sub-para 1.2.

6.4 The authorities shall whenever practicable provide timely opportunities for all interested parties to see all information that is relevant to the presentation of their cases, that is not confidential as defined in para 5, and that is used by the authorities in an anti-dumping investigation, and to prepare presentations on the basis of this information.

6.5 Any information which is by nature confidential (for example, because its disclosure would be of significant competitive advantage to a competitor or because its disclosure would have a significantly adverse effect upon a person supplying the information or upon a person from whom that person acquired the information), or which is provided on a confidential basis by parties to an investigation shall, upon good cause shown, be treated as such by the authorities. Such information shall not be disclosed without specific permission of the party submitting it.

6.5.1 The authorities shall require interested parties providing confidential information to furnish non-confidential summaries thereof. These summaries shall be in sufficient detail to permit a reasonable understanding of the substance of the information submitted in confidence. In exceptional circumstances, such parties may indicate that such information is not susceptible of summary. In such exceptional circumstances, a statement of the reasons why summarisation is not possible must be provided.

6.5.2 If the authorities find that a request for confidentiality is not warranted and if the supplier of the information is either unwilling to make the information public or to authorise its disclosure in generalised or summary form, the authorities may disregard such information unless it can be demonstrated to their satisfaction from appropriate sources that the information is correct.

6.6 Except in circumstances provided for in para 8, the authorities shall during the course of an investigation satisfy themselves as to the accuracy of the information supplied by interested parties upon which their findings are based.

6.7 In order to verify information provided or to obtain further details, the authorities may carry out investigations in the territory of other Members as required, provided they obtain the agreement of the firms concerned and notify the representatives of the government of the Member in question, and unless that Member objects to the investigation. The procedures described in Annex I shall apply to investigations carried out in the territory of other Members. Subject to the requirement to protect confidential information, the authorities shall make the results of any such investigations available, or shall provide disclosure thereof pursuant to para 9, to the firms to which they pertain and may make such results available to the applicants.

6.8 In cases in which any interested party refuses access to, or otherwise does not provide, necessary information within a reasonable period or significantly impedes the investigation, preliminary and final determinations, affirmative or negative, may be made on the basis of the facts available. The provisions of Annex II shall be observed in the application of this paragraph.

6.9 The authorities shall, before a final determination is made, inform all interested parties of the essential facts under consideration which form the basis for the decision whether to apply definitive measures. Such disclosure should take place in sufficient time for the parties to defend their interests.

6.10 The authorities shall, as a rule, determine an individual margin of dumping for each known exporter or producer concerned of the product under investigation. In cases where the number of exporters, producers, importers or types of products involved is so large as to make such a determination impracticable, the authorities may limit their examination either to a reasonable number of interested parties or products by using samples which are statistically valid on the basis of information available to the authorities at the time of the selection, or to the largest percentage of the volume of the exports from the country in question which can reasonably be investigated.

6.10.1 Any selection of exporters, producers, importers or types of products made under this paragraph shall preferably be chosen in consultation with and with the consent of the exporters, producers or importers concerned.

6.10.2 In cases where the authorities have limited their examination, as provided for in this paragraph, they shall nevertheless determine an individual margin of dumping for any exporter or producer not initially selected who submits the necessary information in time for that information to be considered during the course of the investigation, except where the number of exporters or producers is so large that individual examinations would be unduly burdensome to the authorities and prevent the timely completion of the investigation. Voluntary responses shall not be discouraged.

6.11 For the purposes of this agreement, interested parties' shall include:

(i) an exporter or foreign producer or the importer of a product subject to investigation, or a trade or business association a majority of the members of which are producers, exporters or importers of such product;

(ii) the government of the exporting Member; and

(iii) a producer of the like product in the importing Member or a trade and business association a majority of the members of which produce the like product in the territory of the importing Member.

This list shall not preclude Members from allowing domestic or foreign parties other than those mentioned above to be included as interested parties.

6.12   The authorities shall provide opportunities for industrial users of the product under investigation, and for representative consumer organisations in cases where the product is commonly sold at the retail level, to provide information which is relevant to the investigation regarding dumping, injury and causality.

6.13   The authorities shall take due account of any difficulties experienced by interested parties, in particular small companies, in supplying information requested, and shall provide any assistance practicable.

6.14   The procedures set out above are not intended to prevent the authorities of a Member from proceeding expeditiously with regard to initiating an investigation, reaching preliminary or final determinations, whether affirmative or negative, or from applying provisional or final measures, in accordance with relevant provisions of this agreement.

Article 7 – Provisional measures

7.1   Provisional measures may be applied only if:

(i) an investigation has been initiated in accordance with the provisions of Article 5, a public notice has been given to that effect and interested parties have been given adequate opportunities to submit information and make comments;

(ii) a preliminary affirmative determination has been made of dumping and consequent injury to a domestic industry; and

(iii) the authorities concerned judge such measures necessary to prevent injury being caused during the investigation.

7.2   Provisional measures may take the form of a provisional duty or, preferably, a security by cash deposit or bond – equal to the amount of the anti-dumping duty provisionally estimated, being not greater than the provisionally estimated margin of dumping. Withholding appraisement is an appropriate provisional measure, provided that the normal duty and the estimated amount of the anti-dumping duty be indicated and as long as the withholding of appraisement is subject to the same conditions as other provisional measures.

7.3   Provisional measures shall not be applied sooner than 60 days from the date of initiation of the investigation.

7.4   The application of provisional measures shall be limited to as short a period as possible, not exceeding four months or, on decision of the authorities concerned, upon request by exporters representing a significant percentage of the trade involved, to a period not exceeding six months. When authorities, in the course of an investigation, examine whether a duty lower than the margin of dumping would be sufficient to remove injury, these periods may be six and nine months, respectively.

7.5   The relevant provisions of Article 9 shall be followed in the application of provisional measures.

Article 8 – Price undertakings

8.1   Proceedings may suspended or terminated without the imposition of provisional measures or anti-dumping duties upon receipt of satisfactory voluntary undertakings from any exporter to revise its prices or to cease exports to the area in question at dumped prices so that the authorities are satisfied that the injurious effect of the dumping is eliminated. Price increases under such undertakings shall not be higher than necessary to eliminate the margin of dumping. It is desirable that the price increases be less than the margin of dumping if such increases would be adequate to remove the injury to the domestic industry.

8.2   Price undertakings shall not be sought or accepted from exporters unless the authorities of the importing Member have made a preliminary affirmative determination of dumping and injury caused by such dumping.

8.3   Undertakings offered need not be accepted if the authorities consider their acceptance impractical, for example, if the number of actual or potential exporters is too great, or for other reasons, including reasons of general policy. Should the case arise and where practicable, the authorities shall provide to the exporter the reasons which have led them to consider acceptance of an undertaking as inappropriate, and shall, to the extent possible, give the exporter an opportunity to make comments thereon.

8.4   If an undertaking is accepted, the investigation of dumping and injury shall nevertheless be completed if the exporter so desires or the authorities so decide. In such a case, if a negative determination of dumping or injury is made, the undertaking shall automatically lapse, except in cases where such a determination is due in large part to the existence of a price undertaking. In such cases, the authorities may require that an undertaking be maintained for a reasonable period consistent with the provisions of this agreement. In the event that an affirmative determination of dumping and injury is made, the undertaking shall continue consistent with its terms and the provisions of this agreement.

8.5   Price undertakings may be suggested by the authorities of the importing Member: but no exporter shall be forced to enter into such undertakings. The fact that exporters do not offer such undertakings, or do not accept an invitation to do so, shall in no way prejudice the consideration of the case. However, the authorities are free to determine that a threat of injury is more likely to be realised if the dumped imports continue.

8.6   Authorities of an importing Member may require any exporter from whom an undertaking has been accepted to provide periodically information relevant to the fulfilment of such an undertaking and to permit verification of pertinent data. In case of violation of an undertaking, the authorities of the importing Member may take, under this agreement in conformity with its provisions, expeditious actions which may constitute immediate application of provisional measures using the best information available. In such cases, definitive duties may be levied in accordance with this agreement on products entered for consumption not more than 90 days before the application of such provisional measures, except that any such retroactive assessment shall not apply to imports entered before the violation of the undertaking.

Article 9 – Imposition and collection of anti-dumping duties

9.1   The decision whether or not to impose an anti-dumping duty in cases where all requirements for the imposition have been fulfilled, and the decision whether the amount of the anti-dumping duty to be imposed shall be the full margin of dumping or less, are decisions to be made by the authorities of the importing Member. It is desirable that the imposition be permissive in the territory of all Members, and that the duty be less than the margin if such lesser duty would be adequate to remove the injury to the domestic industry.

9.2   When an anti-dumping duty is imposed in respect of any product, such anti-dumping duty shall be collected in the appropriate amounts in each case, on a non-discriminatory basis on imports of such product from all sources found to be dumped and causing injury, except as to imports from those sources from which price undertakings under the terms of this agreement have been accepted. The authorities shall name the supplier or suppliers of the product concerned. If, however, several suppliers from the same country are involved, and it is impracticable to name all these suppliers, the authorities may name the supplying country concerned. If several suppliers from more than one country are involved, the authorities may name either all the suppliers involved, or, if this is impracticable, ail the supplying countries involved.

9.3   The amount of the anti-dumping duty shall not exceed the margin of dumping as established under Article 2.

9.3.1   When the amount of the anti-dumping duty is assessed on a retrospective basis, the determination of the final liability for payment of anti-dumping duties shall take place as soon as possible, normally within 12 months, and in no case more than 18 months, after the date on which a request for a final assessment of the amount of the anti-dumping duty has been made. Any refund shall be made promptly and normally in not more than 90 days following the determination of final liability made pursuant to this sub-paragraph. In any case, where a refund is not made within 90 days, the authorities shall provide an explanation if so requested.

9.3.2	When the amount of the anti-dumping duty is assessed on a prospective basis, provision shall be made for a prompt refund, upon request, of any duty paid in excess of the margin of dumping. A refund of any such duty paid in excess of the actual margin of dumping shall normally take place within 12 months, and in no case more than 18 months, after the date on which a request for a refund, duly supported by evidence, has been made by an importer of the product subject to the anti-dumping duty. The refund authorised should normally be made within 90 days of the above-noted decision.

9.3.3	In determining whether and to what extent a reimbursement should be made when the export price is constructed in accordance with para 3 of Article 2, authorities should take account of any change in normal value, any change in costs incurred between importation and resale, and any movement in the resale price which is duly reflected in subsequent selling prices, and should calculate the export price with no deduction for the amount of anti-dumping duties paid when conclusive evidence of the above is provided.

9.4	When the authorities have limited their examination in accordance with the second sentence of para 10 of Article 6, any anti-dumping duty applied to imports from exporters or producers not included in the examination shall not exceed:

	(i)	the weighted average margin of dumping established with respect to the selected exporters or producers; or

	(ii)	where the liability for payment of anti-dumping duties is calculated on the basis of a prospective normal value, the difference between the weighted average normal value of the selected exporters or producers and the export prices of exporters or producers not individually examined,

	provided that the authorities shall disregard for the purpose of this paragraph any zero and *de minimis* margins and margins established under the circumstances referred to in para 8 of Article 6. The authorities shall apply individual duties or normal values to imports from any exporter or producer not included in the examination who has provided the necessary information during the course of the investigation, as provided for in sub-para 10.2 of Article 6.

9.5	If a product is subject to anti-dumping duties in an importing Member, the authorities shall promptly carry out a review for the purpose of determining individual margins of dumping for any exporters or producers in the exporting country in question who have not exported the product to the importing Member during the period of investigation, provided that these exporters or producers can show that they are not related to any of the exporters or producers in the exporting country who are subject to the anti-dumping duties on the product. Such a review shall be initiated and carried out on an accelerated basis, compared to normal duty assessment and review proceedings in the importing Member. No anti-dumping duties shall be levied on imports from such exporters or producers while the review is being carried out. The authorities may, however, withhold appraisement and/or request guarantees to ensure that, should such a review result in a determination of dumping in respect of such producers or exporters, anti-dumping duties can be levied retroactively to the date of the initiation of the review.

Article 10 – Retroactivity

10.1	Provisional measures and anti-dumping duties shall only be applied to products which enter for consumption after the time when the decision taken under para 1 of Article 7 and para 1 of Article 9, respectively, enters into force, subject to the exceptions set out in this article.

10.2	Where a final determination of injury (but not of a threat thereof or of a material retardation of the establishment of an industry) is made or, in the case of a final determination of a threat of injury, where the effect of the dumped imports would, in the absence of the provisional measures, have led to a determination of injury, anti-dumping duties may be levied retroactively for the period for which provisional measures, if any, have been applied.

10.3   If the definitive anti-dumping duty is higher than the provisional duty paid or payable, or the amount estimated for the purpose of the security, the difference shall not be collected. If the definitive duty is lower than the provisional duty paid or payable, or the amount estimated for the purpose of the security, the difference shall be reimbursed or the duty recalculated, as the case may be.

10.4   Except as provided in para 2, where a determination of threat of injury or material retardation is made (but no injury has yet occurred) a definitive anti-dumping duty may be imposed only from the date of the determination of threat of injury or material retardation, and any cash deposit made during the period of the application of provisional measures shall be refunded and any bonds released in an expeditious manner.

10.5   Where a final determination is negative, any cash deposit made during the period of the application of provisional measures shall be refunded and any bonds released in an expeditious manner.

10.6   A definitive anti-dumping duty may be levied on products which were entered for consumption not more than 90 days prior to the date of application of provisional measures, when the authorities determine for the dumped product in question that:

   (i)   there is a history of dumping which caused injury or that the importer was, or should have been, aware that the exporter practises dumping and that such dumping would cause injury; and

   (ii) the injury is caused by massive dumped imports of a product in a relatively short time which in light of the timing and the volume of the dumped imports and other circumstances (such as a rapid build-up of inventories of the imported product) is likely to seriously undermine the remedial effect of the definitive anti-dumping duty to be applied, provided that the importers concerned have been given an opportunity to comment.

10.7   The authorities may, after initiating an investigation, take such measures as the withholding of appraisement or assessment as may be necessary to collect anti-dumping duties retroactively, as provided for in para 6, once they have sufficient evidence that the conditions set forth in that paragraph are satisfied.

10.8   No duties shall be levied retroactively pursuant to para 6 on products entered for consumption prior to the date of initiation of the investigation.

Article 11 – Duration and review of anti-dumping duties and price undertakings

11.1   An anti-dumping duty shall remain in force only as long as and to the extent necessary to counteract dumping which is causing injury.

11.2   The authorities shall review the need for the continued imposition of the duty, where warranted, on their own initiative or, provided that a reasonable period of time has elapsed since the imposition of the definitive anti-dumping duty, upon request by any interested party which submits positive information substantiating the need for a review. Interested parties shall have the right to request the authorities to examine whether the continued imposition of the duty is necessary to offset dumping, whether the injury would be likely to continue or recur if the duty were removed or varied, or both. If, as a result of the review under this paragraph, the authorities determine that the anti-dumping duty is no longer warranted, it shall be terminated immediately.

11.3   Notwithstanding the provisions of paras 1 and 2, any definitive anti-dumping duty shall be terminated on a date not later than five years from its imposition (or from the date of the most recent review under para 2 if that review has covered both dumping and injury, or under this paragraph), unless the authorities determine, in a review initiated before that date on their own initiative or upon a duly substantiated request made by or on behalf of the domestic industry within a reasonable period of time prior to that date, that the expiry of the duty would be likely to lead to continuation or recurrence of dumping and injury. The duty may remain in force pending the outcome of such a review.

11.4   The provisions of Article 6 regarding evidence and procedure shall apply to any review carried out under this article. Any such review shall be carried out expeditiously and shall normally be concluded within 12 months of the date of initiation of the review.

11.5   The provisions of this article shall apply *mutatis mutandis* to price undertakings accepted under Article 8.

Article 12 – Public notice and explanation of determinations

12.1   When the authorities are satisfied that there is sufficient evidence to justify the initiation of an anti-dumping investigation pursuant to Article 5, the Member or Members the products of which are subject to such investigation and other interested parties known to the investigating authorities to have an interest therein shall be notified and a public notice shall be given.

12.1.1   A public notice of the initiation of an investigation shall contain, or otherwise make available through a separate report, adequate information on the following:

   (i)   the name of the exporting country or countries and the product involved;
   (ii) the date of initiation of the investigation;
   (iii) the basis on which dumping is alleged in the application;
   (iv) a summary of the factors on which the allegation of injury is based;
   (v)   the address to which representations by interested parties should be directed;
   (vi) the time limits allowed to interested parties for making their views known.

12.2   Public notice shall tee given of any preliminary or final determination, whether affirmative or negative, of any decision to accept an undertaking pursuant to Article 8, of the termination of such an undertaking, and of the termination of a definitive anti-dumping duty. Each such notice shall set forth, or otherwise make available through a separate report, in sufficient detail the findings and conclusions reached on all issues of fact and law considered material by the investigating authorities. All such notices and reports shall be forwarded to the Member or Members the products of which are subject to such determination or undertaking and to other interested parties known to have an interest therein.

12.2.1   A public notice of the imposition of provisional measures shall set forth, or otherwise make available through a separate report, sufficiently detailed explanations for the preliminary determinations on dumping and injury and shall refer to the matters of fact and law which have led to arguments being accepted or rejected. Such a notice or report shall, due regard being paid to the requirement for the protection of confidential information, contain in particular:

   (i)   the names of the suppliers, or when this is impracticable, the supplying countries involved;
   (ii) a description of the product which is sufficient for customs purposes;
   (iii) the margins of dumping established and a full explanation of the reasons for the methodology used in the establishment and comparison of the export price and the normal value under Article 2;
   (iv) considerations relevant to the injury determination as set out in Article 3;
   (v)   the main reasons leading to the determination.

12.2.2   A public notice of conclusion or suspension of an investigation in the case of an affirmative determination providing for the imposition of a definitive duty or the acceptance of a price undertaking shall contain, or otherwise make available through a separate report, all relevant information on the matters of fact and law and reasons which have led to the imposition of final measures or the acceptance of a price undertaking, due regard being paid to the requirement for the protection of confidential information. In particular, the notice or report shall contain the information described in sub-para 2.1, as well as the reasons for the acceptance or rejection of relevant arguments or claims made by the exporters and importers, and the basis for any decision made under sub-para 10.2 of Article 6.

12.2.3   A public notice of the termination or suspension of an investigation following the acceptance of an undertaking pursuant to Article 8 shall include, or otherwise make available through a separate report, the non-confidential part of this undertaking.

12.3   The provisions of this article shall apply *mutatis mutandis* to the initiation and completion of reviews pursuant to Article 11 and to decisions under Article 10 to apply duties retroactively.

Article 13 – Judicial review

Each Member whose national legislation contains provisions on anti-dumping measures shall maintain judicial, arbitral or administrative tribunals or procedures for the purpose, *inter alia*, of the prompt review of administrative actions relating to final determinations and reviews of determinations within the meaning of Article 11. Such tribunals or procedures shall be independent of the authorities responsible for the determination or review in question.

Article 14 – Anti-dumping action on behalf of a third country

14.1   An application for anti-dumping action on behalf of a third country shall be made by the authorities of the third country requesting action.

14.2   Such an application shall be supported by price information to show that the imports are being dumped and by detailed information to show that the alleged dumping is causing injury to the domestic industry concerned in the third country. The government of the third country shall afford all assistance to the authorities of the importing country to obtain any further information which the latter may require.

14.3   In considering such an application, the authorities of the importing country shall consider the effects of the alleged dumping on the industry concerned as a whole in the third country; that is to say, the injury shall not be assessed in relation only to the effect of the alleged dumping on the industry's exports to the importing country or even on the industry's total exports.

14.4   The decision whether or not to proceed with a case shall rest with the importing country. If the importing country decides that it is prepared to take action, the initiation of the approach to the Council for Trade in Goods seeking its approval for such action shall rest with the importing country.

Article 15 – Developing country members

It is recognised that special regard must be given by developed country Members to the special situation of developing country Members when considering the application of anti-dumping measures under this agreement. Possibilities of constructive remedies provided for by this agreement shall be explored before applying anti-dumping duties where they would affect the essential interests of developing country Members.

PART II

Article 16 – Committee on anti-dumping practices

16.1   There is hereby established a Committee on Anti-Dumping Practices (referred to in this agreement as the 'committee') composed of representatives from each of the Members. The committee shall elect its own Chairman and shall meet not less than twice a year and otherwise as envisaged by relevant provisions of this agreement at the request of any Member. The committee shall carry out responsibilities as assigned to it under this agreement or by the Members and it shall afford Members the opportunity of consulting on any matters relating to the operation of the agreement or the furtherance of its objectives. The WTO Secretariat shall act as the secretariat to the committee.

16.2   The committee may set up subsidiary bodies as appropriate.

16.3   In carrying out their functions, the committee and any subsidiary bodies may consult with and seek information from any source they deem appropriate. However, before the committee or a subsidiary body seeks such information from a source within the jurisdiction of a Member, it shall inform the Member involved. It shall obtain the consent of the Member and any firm to be consulted.

16.4   Members shall report without delay to the committee all preliminary or final anti-dumping actions taken. Such reports shall be available in the Secretariat for inspection by other Members. Members shall also submit, on a semi-annual basis, reports of any anti-dumping actions taken within the preceding six months. The semi-annual reports shall be submitted on an agreed standard form.

16.5Each Member shall notify the committee (a) which of its authorities are competent to initiate and conduct investigations referred to in Article 5, and (b) its domestic procedures governing the initiation and conduct of such investigations.

Article 17 – Consultation and dispute settlement

17.1Except as otherwise provided herein, the Dispute Settlement Understanding is applicable to consultations and the settlement of disputes under this agreement.

17.2Each Member shall afford sympathetic consideration to, and shall afford adequate opportunity for consultation regarding, representations made by another Member with respect to any matter affecting the operation of this agreement.

17.3If any Member considers that any benefit accruing to it, directly or indirectly, under this agreement is being nullified or impaired, or that the achievement of any objective is being impeded, by another Member or Members, it may, with a view to reaching a mutually satisfactory resolution of the matter, request in writing consultations with the Member or Members in question. Each Member shall afford sympathetic consideration to any request From another Member for consultation.

17.4If the Member that requested consultations considers that the consultations pursuant to para 3 have failed to achieve a mutually agreed solution, and if final action has been taken by the administering authorities of the importing Member to levy definitive anti-dumping duties or to accept price undertakings, it may refer the matter to the Dispute Settlement Body (DSB). When a provisional measure has a significant impact and the Member that requested consultations considers that the measure was taken contrary to the provisions of para 1 of Article 7, that Member may also refer such matter to the DSB.

17.5The DSB shall, at the request of the complaining party, establish a panel to examine the matter based upon:

(i)a written statement of the Member making the request indicating how a benefit accruing to it, directly or indirectly, under this agreement has been nullified or impaired, or that the achieving of the objectives of the agreement is being impeded; and

(ii)the facts made available in conformity with appropriate domestic procedures to the authorities of the importing Member.

17.6In examining the matter referred to in para 5:

(i)in its assessment of the facts of the matter, the panel shall determine whether the authorities' establishment of the facts was proper and whether their evaluation of those facts was unbiased and objective. If the establishment of the facts was proper and the evaluation was unbiased and objective, even though the panel might have reached a different conclusion, the evaluation shall not be overturned;

(ii)the panel shall interpret the relevant provisions of the agreement in accordance with customary rules of interpretation of public international law. Where the panel finds that a relevant provision of the agreement admits of more than one permissible interpretation, the panel shall find the authorities' measure to be in conformity with the agreement if it rests upon one of those permissible interpretations.

17.7Confidential information provided to the panel shall not be disclosed without formal authorisation from the person, body or authority providing such information. Where such information is requested from the panel but release of such information by the panel is not authorised, a non-confidential summary of the information, authorised by the person, body or authority providing the information, shall be provided.

PART III

Article 18 – Final provisions

18.1No specific action against dumping of exports from another Member can be taken except in accordance with the provisions of GATT 1994, as interpreted by this agreement.

18.2   Reservations may not be entered in respect of any of the provisions of this agreement without the consent of the other Members.

18.3   Subject to sub-para 3.1 and 3.2, the provisions of this agreement shall apply to investigations, and reviews of existing measures, initiated pursuant to applications which have been made on or after the date of entry into force for a Member of the WTO Agreement.

18.3.1 With respect to the calculation of margins of dumping in refund procedures under para 3 of Article 9, the rules used in the most recent determination or review of dumping shall apply.

18.3.2 For the purposes of para 3 of Article 11, existing anti-dumping measures shall be deemed to be imposed on a date not later than the date of entry into force for a Member of the WTO Agreement, except in cases in which the domestic legislation of a Member in force on that date already included a clause of the type provided for in that paragraph.

18.4   Each Member shall take all necessary steps, of a general or particular character, to ensure, not later than the date of entry into force of the WTO Agreement for it, the conformity of its laws, regulations and administrative procedures with the provisions of this agreement as they may apply for the Member in question.

18.5   Each Member shall inform the committee of any changes in its laws and regulations relevant to this agreement and in the administration of such laws and regulations.

18.6   The committee shall review annually the implementation and operation of this agreement taking into account the objectives thereof. The committee shall inform annually the Council for Trade in Goods of developments during the period covered by such reviews.

18.7   The Annexes to this agreement constitute an integral part thereof.

Annex I

Procedures on-the-spot investigations pursuant to para 7 of Article 6

1   Upon initiation of an investigation, the authorities of the exporting Member and the firms known to be concerned should be informed of the intention to carry out on-the-spot investigations.

2   If in exceptional circumstances it is intended to include non-governmental experts in the investigating team, the firms and the authorities of the exporting Member should be so informed. Such non-governmental experts should be subject to effective sanctions for breach of confidentiality requirements.

3   It should be standard practice to obtain explicit agreement of the firms concerned in the exporting Member before the visit is finally scheduled.

4   As soon as the agreement of the firms concerned has been obtained, the investigating authorities should notify the authorities of the exporting Member of the names and addresses of the firms to be visited and the dates agreed.

5   Sufficient advance notice should be given to the firms in question before the visit is made.

6   Visits to explain the questionnaire should only be made at the request of an exporting firm. Such a visit may only be made if (a) the authorities of the importing Member notify the representatives of the Member in question, and (b) the latter do not object to the visit.

7   As the main purpose of the on-the-spot investigation is to verify information provided or to obtain further details, it should be carried out after the response to the questionnaire has been received unless the firm agrees to the contrary and the government of the exporting Member is informed by the investigating authorities of the anticipated visit and does not object to it; further, it should be standard practice prior to the visit to advise the firms concerned of the general nature of the information to be verified and of any further information which needs to be provided, though this should not preclude requests to be made on the spot for further details to be provided in the light of information obtained.

8   Enquiries or questions put by the authorities or firms of the exporting Members and essential to a successful on-the-spot investigation should, whenever possible, be answered before the visit is made.

Annex II

Best information available in terms of para 8 of Article 6

1   As soon as possible after the initiation of the investigation, the investigating authorities should specify in detail the information required from any interested party, and the manner in which that information should be structured by the interested party in its response. The authorities should also ensure that the party is aware that if information is not supplied within a reasonable time, the authorities will be free to make determinations on the basis of the facts available, including those contained in the application for the initiation of the investigation by the domestic industry.

2   The authorities may also request that an interested party provide its response in a particular medium (eg computer tape) or computer language. Where such a request is made, the authorities should consider the reasonable ability of the interested party to respond in the preferred medium or computer language, and should not request the party to use for its response a computer system other than that used by the party. The authority should not maintain a request for a computerised response if the interested party does not maintain computerised accounts and if presenting the response as requested would result in an unreasonable extra burden on the interested party, eg it would entail unreasonable additional cost and trouble. The authorities should not maintain a request for a response in a particular medium or computer language if the interested party does not maintain its computerised accounts in such medium or computer language and if presenting the response as requested would result in an unreasonable extra burden on the interested party, eg it would entail unreasonable additional cost and trouble.

3   All information which is verifiable, which is appropriately submitted so that it can be used in the investigation without undue difficulties, which is supplied in a timely fashion, and, where applicable, which is supplied in a medium or computer language requested by the authorities, should be taken into account when determinations are made. If a party does not respond in the preferred medium or computer language but the authorities find that the circumstances set out in para 2 have been satisfied, the failure to respond in the preferred medium or computer language should not be considered to significantly impede the investigation.

4   Where the authorities do not have the ability to process information if provided in a particular medium (eg computer tape), the information should be supplied in the form of written material or any other form acceptable to the authorities.

5   Even though the information provided may not be ideal in all respects, this should not justify the authorities from disregarding it, provided the interested party has acted to the best of its ability.

6   If evidence or information is not accepted, the supplying party should be informed forthwith of the reasons therefore, and should have an opportunity to provide further explanations within a reasonable period, due account being taken of the time limits of the investigation. If the explanations are considered by the authorities as not being satisfactory, the reasons for the rejection of such evidence or information should be given in any published determinations.

7   If the authorities have to base their findings, including those with respect to normal value, on information from a secondary source, including the information supplied in the application for the initiation of the investigation, they should do so with special circumspection. In such cases, the authorities should, where practicable, check the information from other independent sources at their disposal, such as published price lists, official import statistics and customs returns, and from the information obtained from other interested parties during the investigation. It is clear, however, that if an interested party does not cooperate and thus relevant information is being withheld from the authorities, this situation could lead to a result which is less favourable to the party than if the party did cooperate.

AGREEMENT ON SUBSIDIES AND COUNTERVAILING MEASURES

Members hereby agree as follows:

PART I – GENERAL PROVISIONS

Article 1 – Definition of a subsidy

1.1 For the purpose of this agreement, a subsidy shall be deemed to exist if:

(a)(1)   there is a financial contribution by a government or any public body within the territory of a Member (referred to in this agreement as 'government'), ie where:

(i)   a government practice involves a direct transfer of funds (eg grants, loans, and equity infusion), potential direct transfers of funds or liabilities (eg loan guarantees);

(ii)   government revenue that is otherwise due is foregone or not collected (eg fiscal incentives such as tax credits);

(iii) a government provides goods or services other than general infrastructure, or purchases goods;

(iv) a government makes payments to a funding mechanism, or entrusts or directs a private body to carry out one or more of the type of functions illustrated in (i) to (iii) above which would normally be vested in the government and the practice, in no real sense, differs from practices normally followed by governments; or

(a)(2)   there is any form of income or price support in the sense of Article XVI of GATT 1994; and

(b)   a benefit is thereby conferred.

1.2 A subsidy as defined in para 1 shall be subject to the provisions of Part II or shall be subject to the provisions of Part III or V only if such a subsidy is specific in accordance with the provisions of Article 2.

Article 2 – Specificity

2.1 In order to determine whether a subsidy, as defined in para 1 of Article l, is specific to an enterprise or industry or group of enterprises or industries (referred to in this agreement as 'certain enterprises') within the jurisdiction of the granting authority, the following principles shall apply:

(a) Where the granting authority, or the legislation pursuant to which the granting authority operates, explicitly limits access to a subsidy to certain enterprises, such subsidy shall be specific.

(b) Where the granting authority, or the legislation pursuant to which the granting authority operates, establishes objective criteria or conditions governing the eligibility for, and the amount of, a subsidy, specificity shall not exist, provided that the eligibility is automatic and that such criteria and conditions are strictly adhered to. The criteria or conditions must be clearly spelled out in law, regulation, or other official document, so as to be capable of verification.

(c) If, notwithstanding any appearance of non-specificity resulting from the application of the principles laid down in sub-paras (a) and (b), there are reasons to believe that the subsidy may in fact be specific, other factors may be considered. Such factors are: use of a subsidy programme by a limited number of certain enterprises, predominant use by certain enterprises, the granting of disproportionately large amounts of subsidy to certain enterprises, and the manner in which discretion has been exercised by the granting authority in the decision to grant a subsidy. In applying this sub-paragraph, account shall be taken of the extent of diversification of economic activities within the jurisdiction of the granting authority, as well as of the length of time during which the subsidy programme has been in operation.

2.2 A subsidy which is limited to certain enterprises located within a designated geographical region within the jurisdiction of the granting authority shall be specific. It is understood that the setting or change of generally applicable tax rates by all levels of government entitled to do so shall not be deemed to be a specific subsidy for the purposes of this agreement.

2.3   Any subsidy falling under the provisions of Article 3 shall be deemed to be specific.

2.4   Any determination of specificity under the provisions of this article shall be clearly substantiated on the basis of positive evidence.

PART II – PROHIBITED SUBSIDIES

Article 3 – Prohibition

3.1   Except as provided in the Agreement on Agriculture, the following subsidies, within the meaning of Article 1, shall be prohibited:

(a)   subsidies contingent, in law or in fact whether solely or as one of several other conditions, upon export performance, including those illustrated in Annex I:

(b)   subsidies contingent, whether solely or as one of several other conditions, upon the use of domestic over imported goods.

3.2   A Member shall neither grant nor maintain subsidies referred to in para 1.

Article 4 – Remedies

4.1   Whenever a Member has reason to believe that a prohibited subsidy is being granted or maintained by another Member, such Member may request consultations with such other Member.

4.2   A request for consultations under para 1 shall include a statement of available evidence with regard to the existence and nature of the subsidy in question.

4.3   Upon request for consultations under para 1, the Member believed to be granting or maintaining the subsidy in question shall enter into such consultations as quickly as possible. The purpose of the consultations shall be to clarify the facts of the situation and to arrive at a mutually agreed solution.

4.4   If no mutually agreed solution has been reached within 30 days of the request for consultations, any Member party to such consultations may refer the matter to the Dispute Settlement Body ('DSB') for the immediate establishment of a panel, unless the DSB decides by consensus not to establish a panel.

4.5   Upon its establishment, the panel may request the assistance of the Permanent Group of Experts (referred to in this agreement as the 'PGE') with regard to whether the measure in question is a prohibited subsidy. If so requested, the PGE shall immediately review the evidence with regard to the existence and nature of the measure in question and shall provide an opportunity for the Member applying or maintaining the measure to demonstrate that the measure in question is not a prohibited subsidy. The PGE shall report its conclusions to the panel within a time-limit determined by the panel. The PGE's conclusions on the issue of whether or not the measure in question is a prohibited subsidy shall be accepted by the panel without modification.

4.6   The panel shall submit its final report to the parties to the dispute. The report shall be circulated to all Members within 90 days of the date of the composition and the establishment of the panel's terms of reference.

4.7   If the measure in question is found to be a prohibited subsidy, the panel shall recommend that the subsidising Member withdraw the subsidy without delay. In this regard, the panel shall specify in its recommendation the time period within which the measure must be withdrawn.

4.8   Within 30 days of the issuance of the panel's report to all Members, the report shall be adopted by the DSB unless one of the parties to the dispute formally notifies the DSB of its decision to appeal or the DSB decides by consensus not to adopt the report.

4.9   Where a panel report is appealed, the Appellate Body shall issue its decision within 30 days from the date when the party to the dispute formally notifies its intention to appeal. When the Appellate Body considers that it cannot provide its report within 30 days, it shall inform the DSB in writing of the reasons for the delay together with an estimate of the period within which it will submit its report. In no case shall the proceedings exceed 60 days. The appellate report shall be adopted by the DSB and unconditionally accepted by the parties to the dispute unless the DSB decides by consensus not to adopt the appellate report within 20 days following its issuance to the Members.

4.10 In the event the recommendation of the DSB is not followed within the time period specified by the panel, which shall commence from the date of adoption of the panel's report or the Appellate Body's report, the DSB shall grant authorisation to the complaining Member to take appropriate countermeasures, unless the DSB decides by consensus to reject the request.

4.11 In the event a party to the dispute requests arbitration under para 6 of Article 22 of the Dispute Settlement Understanding (DSU), the arbitrator shall determine whether the countermeasures are appropriate.

4.12 For purposes of disputes conducted pursuant to this article, except for time-periods specifically prescribed in this article, time periods applicable under the DSU for the conduct of such disputes shall be half the time prescribed therein.

PART III – ACTIONABLE SUBSIDIES

Article 5 – Adverse effects

No Member should cause, through the use of any subsidy referred to in paras 1 and 2 of Article 1, adverse effects to the interests of other Members, ie:

(a) injury to the domestic industry of another Member;

(b) nullification or impairment of benefits accruing directly or indirectly to other Members under GATT 1994 in particular the benefits of concessions bound under Article II of GATT 1994;

(c) serious prejudice to the interests of another Member.

This article does not apply to subsidies maintained on agricultural products as provided in Article 13 of the Agreement on Agriculture.

Article 6 – Serious prejudice

6.1 Serious prejudice in the sense of para (c) of Article 5 shall be deemed to exist in the case of:

(a) the total *ad valorem* subsidisation of a product exceeding 5%;

(b) subsidies to cover operating losses sustained by an industry;

(c) subsidies to cover operating losses sustained by an enterprise, other than one-time measures which are non-recurrent and cannot be repeated for that enterprise and which are given merely to provide time for the development of long term solutions and to avoid acute social problems;

(d) direct forgiveness of debt, ie forgiveness of government-held debt, and grants to cover debt repayment.

6.2 Notwithstanding the provisions of para 1, serious prejudice shall not be found if the subsidising Member demonstrates that the subsidy in question has not resulted in any of the effects enumerated in para 3.

6.3 Serious prejudice in the sense of para (c) of Article 5 may arise in any case where one or several of the following apply:

(a) the effect of the subsidy is to displace or impede the imports of a like product of another Member into the market of the subsidising Member;

(b) the effect of the subsidy is to displace or impede the exports of a like product of another Member from a third country market;

(c) the effect of the subsidy is a significant price undercutting by the subsidised product as compared with the price of a like product of another Member in the same market or significant price suppression, price depression or lost sales in the same market;

(d) the effect of the subsidy is an increase in the world market share of the subsidising Member in a particular subsidised primary product or commodity as compared to the average share it had during the previous period of three years and this increase follows a consistent trend over a period when subsidies have been granted.

6.4 For the purpose of para 3(b), the displacement or impeding of exports shall include any case in which, subject to the provisions of para 7, it has been demonstrated that there has been a change in relative shares of the market to the disadvantage of the non-subsidised like product (over an appropriately representative period sufficient to demonstrate clear trends in the development of the market for the product concerned, which, in normal circumstances, shall be at least one year). 'Change in relative shares of the market' shall include any of the following situations: (a) there is an increase in the market share of the subsidised product; (b) the market share of the subsidised product remains constant in circumstances in which, in the absence of the subsidy, it would have declined; (c) the market share of the subsidised product declines, but at a slower rate than would have been the case in the absence of the subsidy.

6.5 For the purpose of para 3(c), price undercutting shall include any case in which such price undercutting has been demonstrated through a comparison of prices of the subsidised product with prices of a non-subsidised like product supplied to the same market. The comparison shall be made at the same level of trade and at comparable times, due account being taken of any other factor affecting price comparability. However, if such a direct comparison is not possible, the existence of price undercutting may be demonstrated on the basis of export unit values.

6.6 Each Member in the market of which serious prejudice is alleged to have arisen shall subject to the provisions of para 3 of Annex V, make available to the parties to a dispute arising under Article 7, and to the panel established pursuant to para 4 of Article 7, all relevant information that can be obtained as to the changes in market shares of the parties to the dispute as well as concerning prices of the products involved.

6.7 Displacement or impediment resulting in serious prejudice shall not arise under para 3 where any of the following circumstances exist during the relevant period:

(a) prohibition or restriction on exports of the like product from the complaining Member or on imports from the complaining Member into the third country market concerned;

(b) decision by an importing government operating a monopoly of trade or state trading in the product concerned to shift, for non-commercial reasons, imports from the complaining Member to another country or countries;

(c) natural disasters, strikes, transport disruptions or other *force majeure* substantially affecting production, qualities, quantities or prices of the product available for export from the complaining Member;

(d) existence of arrangements limiting exports from the complaining Member;

(e) voluntary decrease in the availability for export of the product concerned from the complaining Member (including, *inter alia*, a situation where firms in the complaining Member have been autonomously reallocating exports of this product to new markets);

(f) failure to conform to standards and other regulatory requirements in the importing country.

6.8 In the absence of circumstances referred to in para 7, the existence of serious prejudice should be determined on the basis of the information submitted to or obtained by the panel, including information submitted in accordance with the provisions of Annex V.

6.9 This article does not apply to subsidies maintained on agricultural products as provided in Article 13 of the Agreement on Agriculture.

Article 7 – Remedies

7.1 Except as provided in Article 13 of the Agreement on Agriculture, whenever a Member has reason to believe that any subsidy referred to in Article 1, granted or maintained by another Member, results in injury to its domestic industry, nullification or impairment or serious prejudice, such Member may request consultations with such other Member.

7.2 A request for consultations under para 1 shall include a statement of available evidence with regard to (a) the existence and nature of the subsidy in question, and (b) the injury caused to the domestic industry, or the nullification or impairment, or serious prejudice caused to the interests of the Member requesting consultations.

7.3 Upon request for consultations under para 1, the Member believed to be granting or maintaining the subsidy practice in question shall enter into such consultations as quickly as possible. The purpose of the consultations shall be to clarify the facts of the situation and to arrive at a mutually agreed solution.

7.4   If consultations do not result in a mutually acceptable solution within 60 days, any Member party to such consultations may refer the matter to the DSB for the establishment of a panel, unless the DSB decides by consensus not to establish a panel. The composition of the panel and its terms of reference shall be established within 15 days from the date when it is established.

7.5   The panel shall review the matter and shall submit its final report to the parties to the dispute. The report shall be circulated to all Members within 120 days of the date of the composition and establishment of the panel's terms of reference.

7.6   Within 30 days of the issuance of the panel's report to all Members, the report shall be adopted by the DSB unless one of the parties to the dispute formally notifies the DSB of its decision to appeal or the DSB decides by consensus not to adopt the report.

7.7   Where a panel report is appealed, the Appellate Body shall issue its decision within 60 days from the date when the party to the dispute formally notifies its intention to appeal. When the Appellate Body considers that it cannot provide its report within 60 days, it shall inform the DSB in writing of the reasons for the delay together with an estimate of the period within which it will submit its report. In no case shall the proceedings exceed 90 days. The appellate report shall be adopted by the DSB and unconditionally accepted by the parties to the dispute unless the DSB decides by consensus not to adopt the appellate report within 20 days following its issuance to the Members.

7.8   Where a panel report or an Appellate Body report is adopted in which it is determined that any subsidy has resulted in adverse effects to the interests of another Member within the meaning of Article 5, the Member granting or maintaining such subsidy shall take appropriate steps to remove the adverse effects or shall withdraw the subsidy.

7.9   In the event the Member has not taken appropriate steps to remove the adverse effects of the subsidy or withdraw the subsidy within six months from the date when the DSB adopts the panel report or the Appellate Body report, and in the absence of agreement on compensation, the DSB shall grant authorisation to the complaining Member to take countermeasures, commensurate with the degree and nature of the adverse effects determined to exist, unless the DSB decides by consensus to reject the request.

7.10 In the event that a party to the dispute requests arbitration under para 6 of Article 22 of the DSU, the arbitrator shall determine whether the countermeasures are commensurate with the degree and nature of the adverse effects determined to exist.

PART IV – NON-ACTIONABLE SUBSIDIES

Article 8 – Identification of non-actionable subsidies

8.1 The following subsidies shall be considered as non-actionable:

(a) subsidies which are not specific within the meaning of Article 2;

(b) subsidies which are specific within the meaning of Article 2 but which meet all of the conditions provided for in paras 2(a), 2(b) or 2(c) below.

8.2 Notwithstanding the provisions of Parts III and V, the following subsidies shall be non-actionable:

(a) assistance for research activities conducted by firms or by higher education or research establishments on a contract basis with firms if the assistance covers not more than 75% of the costs of industrial research or 50% of the costs of pre-competitive development activity; and provided that such assistance is limited exclusively to:

(i)   costs of personnel (researchers, technicians and other supporting staff employed exclusively in the research activity);

(ii) costs of instruments, equipment, land and buildings used exclusively and permanently (except when disposed of on a commercial basis) for the research activity;

(iii) costs of consultancy and equivalent services used exclusively for the research activity, including bought-in research, technical knowledge, patents, etc;

     (iv) additional overhead costs incurred directly as a result of the research activity;

     (v) other running costs (such as those of materials, supplies and the like), incurred directly as a result of the research activity;

  (b) assistance to disadvantaged regions within the territory of a Member given pursuant to a general framework of regional development and non-specific (within the meaning of Article 2) within eligible regions provided that:

     (i) each disadvantaged region must be a clearly designated contiguous geographical area with a definable economic and administrative identity;

     (ii) the region is considered as disadvantaged on the basis of neutral and objective criteria, indicating that the region's difficulties arise out of more than temporary circumstances; such criteria must be clearly spelled out in law, regulation, or other official document, so as to be capable of verification;

     (iii) the criteria shall include a measurement of economic development which shall be based on at least one of the following factors:

- one of either income per capita or household income per capita, or GDP per capita, which must not be above 85% of the average for the territory concerned;

- unemployment rate, which must be at least 110% of the average for the territory concerned;

- as measured over a three year period; such measurement, however, may be a composite one and may include other factors;

  (c) assistance to promote adaptation of existing facilities to new environmental requirements imposed by law and/or regulations which result in greater constraints and financial burden on firms, provided that the assistance:

     (i) is a one time non-recurring measure; and

     (ii) is limited to 20% of the cost of adaptation; and

     (iii) does not cover the cost of replacing and operating the assisted investment, which must be fully borne by firms; and

     (iv) is directly linked to and proportionate to a firm's planned reduction of nuisances and pollution, and does not cover any manufacturing cost savings which may be achieved; and

     (v) is available to all firms which can adopt the new equipment and/or production processes.

8.3 A subsidy programme for which the provisions of para 2 are invoked shall be notified in advance of its implementation to the committee in accordance with the provisions of Part VII. Any such notification shall be sufficiently precise to enable other Members to evaluate the consistency of the programme with the conditions and criteria provided for in the relevant provisions of para 2. Members shall also provide the committee with yearly updates of such notifications, in particular, by supplying information on global expenditure for each programme, and on any modification of the programme. Other Members shall have the right to request information about individual cases of subsidisation under a notified programme.

8.4 Upon request of a Member, the Secretariat shall review a notification made pursuant to para 3 and, where necessary, may require additional information from the subsidising Member concerning the notified programme under review. The Secretariat shall report its findings to the committee. The committee shall, upon request, promptly review the findings of the Secretariat (or, if a review by the Secretariat has not been requested, the notification itself), with a view to determining whether the conditions and criteria laid down in para 2 have not been met. The procedure provided for in this paragraph shall be completed at the latest at the first regular meeting of the committee following the notification of a subsidy programme, provided that at least two months have elapsed between such notification and the regular meeting of the committee. The review procedure described in this paragraph shall also apply, upon request, to substantial modifications of a programme notified in the yearly updates referred to in para 3.

8.5 Upon the request of a Member, the determination by the committee referred to in para 4, or a failure by the committee to make such a determination, as well as the violation, in individual cases, of the conditions set out in a notified programme, shall be submitted to binding arbitration. The arbitration body shall present its conclusions to the Members within 120 days from the date when the matter was referred to the arbitration body. Except as otherwise provided in this paragraph, the DSU shall apply to arbitrations conducted under this paragraph.

Article 9 – Consultations and authorised remedies

9.1 If, in the course of implementation of a programme referred to in para 2 of Article 8, notwithstanding the fact that the programme is consistent with the criteria laid down in that paragraph, a Member has reasons to believe that this programme has resulted in serious adverse effects to the domestic industry of that Member, such as to cause damage which would be difficult to repair, such Member may request consultations with the Member granting or maintaining the subsidy.

9.2 Upon request for consultations under para 1, the Member granting or maintaining the subsidy programme in question shall enter into such consultations as quickly as possible The purpose of the consultations shall be to clarify the facts of the situation and to arrive at a mutually acceptable solution.

9.3 If no mutually acceptable solution has been reached in consultations under para 2 within 60 days of the request for such consultations, the requesting Member may refer the matter to the committee.

9.4 Where a matter is referred to the committee, the committee shall immediately review the facts involved and the evidence of the effects referred to in para 1. If the committee determines that such effects exist, it may recommend to the subsidising Member to modify this programme in such a way as to remove these effects. The committee shall present its conclusions within 120 days from the date when the matter is referred to it under para 3. In the event the recommendation is not followed within six months, the committee shall authorise the requesting Member to take appropriate countermeasures commensurate with the nature and degree of the effects determined to exist.

PART V – COUNTERVAILING MEASURES

Article 10 – Application of Article VI of GATT 1994

Members shall take all necessary steps to ensure that the imposition of a countervailing duty on any product of the territory of any Member imported into the territory of another Member is in accordance with the provisions of Article VI of GATT 1994 and the terms of this agreement. Countervailing duties may only be imposed pursuant to investigations initiated and conducted in accordance with the provisions of this agreement and the Agreement on Agriculture.

Article 11 – Initiation and subsequent investigation

11.1 Except as provided in para 6, an investigation to determine the existence, degree and effect of any alleged subsidy shall be initiated upon a written application by or on behalf of the domestic industry.

11.2 An application under para 1 shall include sufficient evidence of the existence of (a) a subsidy and, if possible, its amount, (b) injury within the meaning of Article VI of GATT 1994 as interpreted by this agreement, and (c) a causal link between the subsidised imports and the alleged injury. Simple assertion, unsubstantiated by relevant evidence, cannot be considered sufficient to meet the requirements of this paragraph. The application shall contain such information as is reasonably available to the applicant on the following:

(i) the identity of the applicant and a description of the volume and value of the domestic production of the like product by the applicant. Where a written application is made on behalf of the domestic industry, the application shall identify the industry on behalf of which the application is made by a list of all known domestic producers of the like product (or associations of domestic producers of the like product) and, to the extent possible, a description of the volume and value of domestic production of the like product accounted for by such producers;

(ii) a complete description of the allegedly subsidised product, the names of the country or countries of origin or export in question, the identity of each known exporter or foreign producer and a list of known persons importing the product in question;

(iii) evidence with regard to the existence, amount and nature of the subsidy in question;

(iv) evidence that alleged injury to a domestic industry is caused by subsidised imports through the effects of the subsidies, this evidence includes information on the evolution of the volume of the allegedly subsidised imports, the effect of these imports on prices of the like product in the domestic market and the consequent impact of the imports on the domestic industry, as demonstrated by relevant factors and indices having a bearing on the state of the domestic industry, such as those listed in paras 2 and 4 of Article 15.

11.3 The authorities shall review the accuracy and adequacy of the evidence provided in the application to determine whether the evidence is sufficient justify the initiation of an investigation.

11.4 An investigation shall not be initiated pursuant to para 1 unless the authorities have determined, on the basis of an examination of the degree of support for, or opposition to, the application expressed by domestic producers of the like product, that the application has been made by or on behalf of the domestic industry. The application shall be considered to have been made 'by or on behalf of the domestic industry' if it is supported by those domestic producers whose collective output constitutes more than 50% of the total production of the like product produced by that portion of the domestic industry expressing either support for or opposition to the application. However, no investigation shall be initiated when domestic producers expressly supporting the application account for less than 25% of total production of the like product produced by the domestic industry.

11.5 The authorities shall avoid, unless a decision has been made to initiate an investigation, any publicising of the application for the initiation of an investigation.

11.6 If, in special circumstances, the authorities concerned decide to initiate an investigation without having received a written application by or on behalf of a domestic industry for the initiation of such investigation, they shall proceed only if they have sufficient evidence of the existence of a subsidy, injury and causal link, as described in para 2, to justify the initiation of an investigation.

11.7 The evidence of both subsidy and injury shall be considered simultaneously (a) in the decision whether or not to initiate an investigation and (b) thereafter, during the course of the investigation, starting on a date not later than the earliest date on which in accordance with the provisions of this agreement provisional measures may be applied.

11.8 In cases where products are not imported directly from the country of origin but are exported to the importing Member from an intermediate country, the provisions of this agreement shall be fully applicable and the transaction or transactions shall, for the purposes of this agreement, be regarded as having taken place between the country of origin and the importing Member.

11.9 An application under para 1 shall be rejected and an investigation shall be terminated promptly as soon as the authorities concerned are satisfied that there is not sufficient evidence of either subsidisation or of injury to justify proceeding with the case. There shall be immediate termination in cases where the amount of a subsidy is *de minimis*, or where the volume of subsidised imports, actual or potential, or the injury, is negligible. For the purpose of this paragraph, the amount of the subsidy shall be considered to be *de minimis* if the subsidy is less than 1% *ad valorem*.

11.10 An investigation shall not hinder the procedures of customs clearance.

11.11 Investigations shall, except in special circumstances, be concluded within one year, and in no case more than 18 months, after their initiation.

Article 12 – Evidence

12.1 Interested Members and all interested parties in a countervailing duty investigation shall be given notice of the information which the authorities require and ample opportunity to present in writing all evidence which they consider relevant in respect of the investigation in question.

12.1.1 Exporters, foreign producers or interested Members receiving questionnaires used in a countervailing duty investigation shall be given at least 30 days for reply. Due consideration should be given to any request for an extension of the 30 day period and, upon cause shown, such an extension should be granted whenever practicable.

12.1.2 Subject to the requirement to protect confidential information, evidence presented in writing by one interested Member or interested party shall be made available promptly to other interested Members or interested parties participating in the investigation.

12.1.3 As soon as an investigation has been initiated, the authorities shall provide the full text of the written application received under para 1 of Article 11 to the known exporters and to the authorities of the exporting Member and shall make it available, upon request, to other interested parties involved. Due regard shall be paid to the protection of confidential information, as provided for in para 4.

12.2   Interested Members and interested parties also shall have the right, upon justification, to present information orally. Where information is provided orally, the interested Members and interested parties subsequently shall be required to reduce such submissions to writing. Any decision of the investigating authorities can only be based on such information and arguments as were on the written record of this authority and which were available to interested Members and interested parties participating in the investigation, due account having been given to the need to protect confidential information.

12.3   The authorities shall whenever practicable provide timely opportunities for all interested Members and interested parties to see all information that is relevant to the presentation of their cases, that is not confidential as defined in para 4, and that is used by the authorities in a countervailing duty investigation, and to prepare presentations on the basis of this information.

12.4   Any information which is by nature confidential (eg because its disclosure would be of significant competitive advantage to a competitor or because its disclosure would have a significantly adverse effect upon a person supplying the information or upon a person from whom the supplier acquired the information), or which is provided on a confidential basis by parties to an investigation shall, upon good cause shown, be treated as such by the authorities. Such information shall not be disclosed without specific permission of the party submitting it.

12.4.1 The authorities shall require interested Members or interested parties providing confidential information to furnish non-confidential summaries thereof. These summaries shall be in sufficient detail to permit a reasonable understanding of the substance of the information submitted in confidence. In exceptional circumstances, such Members or parties may indicate that such information is not susceptible of summary. In such exceptional circumstances, a statement of the reasons why summarisation is not possible must be provided.

12.4.2 If the authorities find that a request for confidentiality is not warranted and if the supplier of the information is either unwilling to make the information public or to authorise its disclosure in generalised or summary form, the authorities may disregard such information unless it can be demonstrated to their satisfaction from appropriate sources that the information is correct.

12.5   Except in circumstances provided for in para 7, the authorities shall during the course of an investigation satisfy themselves as to the accuracy of the information supplied by interested Members or interested parties upon which their findings are based.

12.6   The investigating authorities may carry out investigations in the territory of other Members as required, provided that they have notified in good time the Member in question and unless that Member objects to the investigation. Further, the investigating authorities may carry out investigations on the premises of a firm and may examine the records of a firm if (a) the firm so agrees, and (b) the Member in question is notified and does not object. The procedures set forth in Annex VI shall apply to investigations on the premises of a firm. Subject to the requirement to protect confidential information, the authorities shall make the results of any such investigations available, or shall provide disclosure thereof pursuant to para 8, to the firms to which they pertain and may make such results available to the applicants.

12.7   In cases in which any interested Member or interested party refuses access to, or otherwise does not provide, necessary information within a reasonable period or significantly impedes the investigation, preliminary and final determinations, affirmative or negative, may be made on the basis of the facts available.

12.8   The authorities shall, before a final determination is made, inform all interested Members and interested parties of the essential facts under consideration which form the basis for the decision whether to apply definitive measures. Such disclosure should take place in sufficient time for the parties to defend their interests.

12.9   For the purposes of this agreement, 'interested parties' shall include:

   (i) an exporter or foreign producer or the importer of a product subject to investigation, or a trade or business association a majority of the members of which are producers, exporters or importers of such product; and

   (ii) a producer of the like product in the importing Member or a trade and business association a majority of the members of which produce the like product in the territory of the importing Member.

   This list shall not preclude Members from allowing domestic or foreign parties other than those mentioned above to be included as interested parties.

12.10   The authorities shall provide opportunities for industrial users of the product under investigation, and for representative consumer organisations in cases where the product is commonly sold at the retail level, to provide information which is relevant to the investigation regarding subsidisation, injury and causality.

12.11   The authorities shall take due account of any difficulties experienced by interested parties, in particular small companies, in supplying information requested, and shall provide any assistance practicable.

12.12   The procedures set out above are not intended to prevent the authorities of a Member from proceeding expeditiously with regard to initiating an investigation, reaching preliminary or final determinations, whether affirmative or negative, or from applying provisional or final measures, in accordance with relevant provisions of this agreement.

Article 13 – Consultations

13.1 As soon as possible after an application under Article 11 is accepted, and in any event before the initiation of any investigation, Members the products of which may be subject to such investigation shall be invited for consultations with the aim of clarifying the situation as to the matters referred to in para 2 of Article 11 and arriving at a mutually agreed solution.

13.2 Furthermore, throughout the period of investigation, Members the products of which are the subject of the investigation shall be afforded a reasonable opportunity to continue consultations, with a view to clarifying the factual situation and to arriving at a mutually agreed solution.

13.3 Without prejudice to the obligation to afford reasonable opportunity for consultation, these provisions regarding consultations are not intended to prevent the authorities of a Member from proceeding expeditiously with regard to initiating the investigation, reaching preliminary or final determinations, whether affirmative or negative, or from applying provisional or final measures, in accordance with the provisions of this agreement.

13.4 The Member which intends to initiate any investigation or is conducting such an investigation shall permit, upon request, the Member or Members the products of which are subject to such investigation access to non-confidential evidence, including the non-confidential summary of confidential data being used for initiating or conducting the investigation.

Article 14 – Calculation of the amount of a subsidy in terms of the benefit to the recipient

For the purpose of Part V, any method used by the investigating authority to calculate the benefit to the recipient conferred pursuant to para 1 of Article 1 shall be provided for in the national legislation or implementing regulations of the Member concerned and its application to each particular case shall be transparent and adequately explained. Furthermore, any such method shall be consistent with the following guidelines:

(a) government provision of equity capital shall not be considered as conferring a benefit, unless the investment decision can be regarded as inconsistent with the usual investment practice (including for the provision of risk capital) of private investors in the territory of that Member;

(b) a loan by a government shall not be considered as conferring a benefit, unless there is a difference between the amount that the firm receiving the loan pays on the government loan and the amount the firm would pay on a comparable commercial loan which the firm could actually obtain on the market. In this case, the benefit shall be the difference between these two amounts;

(c) a loan guarantee by a government shall not be considered as conferring a benefit, unless there is a difference between the amount that the firm receiving the guarantee pays on a loan guaranteed by the government and the amount that the firm would pay on a comparable commercial loan absent the government guarantee. In this case, the benefit shall be the difference between these two amounts adjusted for any differences in fees;

(d) the provision of goods or services or purchase of goods by a government shall not be considered as conferring a benefit unless the provision is made for less than adequate remuneration, or the purchase is made for more than adequate remuneration. The adequacy of remuneration shall be determined in relation to prevailing market conditions for the good or service in question in the country of provision or purchase (including price, quality, availability, marketability, transportation and other conditions of purchase or sale).

Article 15 – Determination of injury

15.1 A determination of injury for purposes of Article VI of GATT 1994 shall be based on positive evidence and involve an objective examination of both (a) the volume of the subsidised imports and the effect of the subsidised imports on prices in the domestic market for like products; and (b) the consequent impact of these imports on the domestic producers of such products.

15.2 With regard to the volume of the subsidised imports, the investigating authorities shall consider whether there has been a significant increase in subsidised imports, either in absolute terms or relative to production or consumption in the importing Member. With regard to the effect of the subsidised imports on prices, the investigating authorities shall consider whether there has been a significant price undercutting by the subsidised imports as compared with the price of a like product of the importing Member, or whether the effect of such imports is otherwise to depress prices to a significant degree or to prevent price increases, which otherwise would have occurred, to a significant degree. No one or several of these factors can necessarily give decisive guidance.

15.3 Where imports of a product from more than one country are simultaneously subject to countervailing duty investigations, the investigating authorities may cumulatively assess the effects of such imports only if they determine that (a) the amount of subsidisation established in relation to the imports from each country is more than *de minimis* as defined in para 9 of Article 11 and the volume of imports from each country is not negligible and (b) a cumulative assessment of the effects of the imports is appropriate in light of the conditions of competition between the imported products and the conditions of competition between the imported products and the like domestic product.

15.4 The examination of the impact of the subsidised imports on the domestic industry shall include an evaluation of all relevant economic factors and indices having a bearing on the state of the industry, including actual and potential decline in output, sales, market share, profits, productivity, return on investments, or utilisation of capacity; factors affecting domestic prices; actual and potential negative effects on cash flow, inventories, employment, wages, growth, ability to raise capital or investments and, in the case of agriculture, whether there has been an increased burden on government support programmes. This list is not exhaustive, nor can one or several of these factors necessarily give decisive guidance.

15.5 It must be demonstrated that the subsidised imports are, through the effects of subsidies causing injury within the meaning of this agreement. The demonstration of a causal relationship between the subsidised imports and the injury to the domestic industry shall be based on an examination of all relevant evidence before the authorities. The authorities shall also examine any known factors other than the subsidised imports which at the same time are injuring the domestic industry, and the injuries caused by these other factors must not be attributed to the subsidised imports. Factors which may be relevant in this respect include, *inter alia*, the volumes and prices of non-subsidised imports of the product in question, contraction in demand or changes in the patterns of consumption, trade restrictive practices of and competition between the foreign and domestic producers, developments in technology and the export performance and productivity of the domestic industry.

15.6 The effect of the subsidised imports shall be assessed in relation to the domestic production of the like product when available data permit the separate identification of that production on the basis of such criteria as the production process, producers' sales and profits. If such separate identification of that production is not possible, the effects of the subsidised imports shall be assessed by the examination of the production of the narrowest group or range of products, which includes the like product, for which the necessary information can be provided.

15.7 A determination of a threat of material injury shall be based on facts and not merely on allegation, conjecture or remote possibility. The change in circumstances which would create a situation in which the subsidy would cause injury must be clearly foreseen and imminent. In making a determination regarding the existence of a threat of material injury, the investigating authorities should consider, *inter alia*, such factors as:

(i) nature of the subsidy or subsidies in question and the trade effects likely to arise there from;

(ii) a significant rate of increase of subsidised imports into the domestic market indicating the likelihood of substantially increased importation;

(iii) sufficient freely disposable, or an imminent, substantial increase in, capacity of the exporter indicating the likelihood of substantially increased subsidised exports to the importing Member's market, taking into account the availability of other export markets to absorb any additional exports;

(iv) whether imports are entering at prices that will have a significant depressing or suppressing effect on domestic prices, and would likely increase demand for further imports; and

(v) inventories of the product being investigated.

No one of these factors by itself can necessarily give decisive guidance but the totality of the factors considered must lead to the conclusion that further subsidised exports are imminent and that, unless protective action is taken, material injury would occur.

15.8 With respect to cases where injury is threatened by subsidised imports, the application of countervailing measures shall be considered and decided with special care.

Article 16 – Definition of domestic industry

16.1 For the purposes of this agreement, the term 'domestic industry' shall, except as provided in para 2, be interpreted as referring to the domestic producers as a whole of the like products or to those of them whose collective output of the products constitutes a major proportion of the total domestic production of those products, except that when producers are related to the exporters or importers or are themselves importers of the allegedly subsidised product or a like product from other countries, the term 'domestic industry' may be interpreted as referring to the rest of the producers.

16.2 In exceptional circumstances, the territory of a Member may, for the production in question, be divided into two or more competitive markets and the producers within each market may be regarded as a separate industry if (a) the producers within such market sell all or almost all of their production of the product in question in that market, and (b) the demand in that market is not to any substantial degree supplied by producers of the product in question located elsewhere in the territory. In such circumstances, injury may be found to exist even where a major portion of the total domestic industry is not injured, provided there is a concentration of subsidised imports into such an isolated market and provided further that the subsidised imports are causing injury to the producers of all or almost all of the production within such market.

16.3   When the domestic industry has been interpreted as referring to the producers in a certain area, ie a market as defined in para 2, countervailing duties shall be levied only on the products in question consigned for final consumption to that area. When the constitutional law of the importing Member does not permit the levying of countervailing duties on such a basis, the importing Member may levy the countervailing duties without limitation only if (a) the exporters shall have been given an opportunity to cease exporting at subsidised prices to the area concerned or otherwise give assurances pursuant to Article 18, and adequate assurances in this regard have not been promptly given, and (b) such duties cannot be levied only on products of specific producers which supply the area in question.

16.4   Where two or more countries have reached under the provisions of para 8(a) of Article XXIV of GATT 1994 such a level of integration that they have the characteristics of a single, unified market, the industry in the entire area of integration shall be taken to be the domestic industry referred to in paras 1 and 2.

16.5   The provisions of para 6 of Article 15 shall be applicable to this article.

Article 17 – Provisional measures

17.1   Provisional measures may be applied only if:

(a)   an investigation has been initiated in accordance with the provisions of Article 11, a public notice has been given to that effect and interested Members and interested parties have been given adequate opportunities to submit information and make comments;

(b)   a preliminary affirmative determination has been made that a subsidy exists and that there is injury to a domestic industry caused by subsidised imports; and

(c)   the authorities concerned judge such measures necessary to prevent injury being caused during the investigation.

17.2   Provisional measures may take the form of provisional countervailing duties guaranteed by cash deposits or bonds equal to the amount of the provisionally calculated amount of subsidisation.

17.3   Provisional measures shall not be applied sooner than 60 days from the date of initiation of the investigation.

17.4   The application of provisional measures shall be limited to as short a period as possible, not exceeding four months.

17.5   The relevant provisions of Article 19 shall be followed in the application of provisional measures.

Article 18 – Undertakings

18.1   Proceedings may be suspended or terminated without the imposition of provisional measures or countervailing duties upon receipt of satisfactory voluntary undertakings under which:

(a)   the government of the exporting Member agrees to eliminate or limit the subsidy or take other measures concerning its effects; or

(b)   the exporter agrees to revise its prices so that the investigating authorities are satisfied that the injurious effect of the subsidy is eliminated. Price increases under such undertakings shall not be higher than necessary to eliminate the amount of the subsidy. It is desirable that the price increases be less than the amount of the subsidy if such increases would be adequate to remove the injury to the domestic industry.

18.2   Undertakings shall not be sought or accepted unless the authorities of the importing Member have made a preliminary affirmative determination of subsidisation and injury caused by such subsidisation and, in case of undertakings from exporters, have obtained the consent of the exporting Member.

18.3   Undertakings offered need not be accepted if the authorities of the importing Member consider their acceptance impractical, for example if the number of actual or potential exporters is too great, or for other reasons, including reasons of general policy. Should the case arise and where practicable, the authorities shall provide to the exporter the reasons which have led them to consider acceptance of an undertaking as inappropriate, and shall, to the extent possible, give the exporter an opportunity to make comments thereon.

18.4 If an undertaking is accepted, the investigation of subsidisation and injury shall nevertheless be completed if the exporting Member so desires or the importing Member so decides. In such a case, if a negative determination of subsidisation or injury is made, the undertaking shall automatically lapse, except in cases where such a determination is due in large part to the existence of an undertaking. In such cases, the authorities concerned may require that an undertaking be maintained for a reasonable period consistent with the provisions of this agreement. In the event that an affirmative determination of subsidisation and injury is made, the undertaking shall continue consistent with its terms and the provisions of this agreement.

18.5 Price undertakings may be suggested by the authorities of the importing Member, but no exporter shall be forced to enter into such undertakings. The fact that governments or exporters do not offer such undertakings, or do not accept an invitation to do so, shall in no way prejudice the consideration of the case. However, the authorities are free to determine that a threat of injury is more likely to be realised if the subsidised imports continue.

18.6 Authorities of an importing Member may require any government or exporter from whom an undertaking has been accepted to provide periodically information relevant to the fulfilment of such an undertaking, and to permit verification of pertinent data. In case of violation of an undertaking, the authorities of the importing Members may take, under this agreement in conformity with its provisions, expeditious actions which may constitute immediate application of provisional measures using the best information available. In such cases, definitive duties may be levied in accordance with this agreement on products entered for consumption not more than 90 days before the application of such provisional measures, except that any such retroactive assessment shall not apply to imports entered before the violation of the undertaking.

Article 19 – Imposition and collection of countervailing duties

19.1 If, after reasonable efforts have been made to complete consultations, a Member makes a final determination of the existence and amount of the subsidy and that, through the effects of the subsidy, the subsidised imports are causing injury, it may impose a countervailing duty in accordance with the provisions of this article unless the subsidy or subsidies are withdrawn.

19.2 The decision whether or not to impose a countervailing duty in cases where all requirements for the imposition have been fulfilled, and the decision whether the amount of the countervailing duty to be imposed shall be the full amount of the subsidy or less, are decisions to be made by the authorities of the importing Member. It is desirable that the imposition should be permissive in the territory of all Members, that the duty should be less than the total amount of the subsidy if such lesser duty would be adequate to remove the injury to the domestic industry, and that procedures should be established which would allow the authorities concerned to take due account of representations made by domestic interested parties whose interests might be adversely affected by the imposition of a countervailing duty.

19.3 When a countervailing duty is imposed in respect of any product, such countervailing duty shall be levied, in the appropriate amounts in each case, on a non-discriminatory basis on imports of such product from all sources found to be subsidised and causing injury, except as to imports from those sources which have renounced any subsidies in question or from which undertakings under the terms of this agreement have been accepted. Any exporter whose exports are subject to a definitive countervailing duty but who was not actually investigated for reasons other than a refusal to cooperate, shall be entitled to an expedited review in order that the investigating authorities promptly establish an individual countervailing duty rate for that exporter.

19.4 No countervailing duty shall be levied on any imported product in excess of the amount of the subsidy found to exist, calculated in terms of subsidisation per unit of the subsidised and exported product.

Article 20 – Retroactivity

20.1 Provisional measures and countervailing duties shall only be applied to products which enter for consumption after the time when the decision under para 1 of Article 17 and para 1 of Article 19, respectively, enters into force, subject to the exceptions set out in this article.

20.2 Where a final determination of injury (but not of a threat thereof or of a material retardation of the establishment of an industry) is made or, in the case of a final determination of a threat of injury, where the effect of the subsidised imports would, in the absence of the provisional measures, have led to a determination of injury, countervailing duties may be levied retroactively for the period for which provisional measures, if any, have been applied.

20.3 If the definitive countervailing duty is higher than the amount guaranteed by the cash deposit or bond, the difference shall not be collected. If the definitive duty is less than the amount guaranteed by the cash deposit or bond, the excess amount shall be reimbursed or the bond released in an expeditious manner.

20.4 Except as provided in para 2, where a determination of threat of injury or material retardation is made (but no injury has yet occurred) a definitive countervailing duty may be imposed only from the date of the determination of threat of injury or material retardation, and any cash deposit made during the period of the application of provisional measures shall be refunded and any bonds released in an expeditious manner.

20.5 Where a final determination is negative, any cash deposit made during the period of the application of provisional measures shall be refunded and any bonds released in an expeditious manner.

20.6 In critical circumstances where for the subsidised product in question the authorities find that injury which is difficult to repair is caused by massive imports in a relatively short period of a product benefiting from subsidies paid or bestowed inconsistently with the provisions of GATT 1994 and of this agreement and where it is deemed necessary, in order to preclude the recurrence of such injury, to assess countervailing duties retroactively on those imports, the definitive countervailing duties may be assessed on imports which were entered for consumption not more than 90 days prior to the date of application of provisional measures.

Article 21 – Duration and review of countervailing duties and undertakings

21.1 A countervailing duty shall remain in force only as long as and to the extent necessary to counteract subsidisation which is causing injury.

21.2 The authorities shall review the need for the continued imposition of the duty, where warranted, on their own initiative or, provided that a reasonable period of time has elapsed since the imposition of the definitive countervailing duty, upon request by any interested party which submits positive information substantiating the need for a review. Interested parties shall have the right to request the authorities to examine whether the continued imposition of the duty is necessary to offset subsidisation, whether the injury would be likely to continue or recur if the duty were removed or varied, or both. If, as a result of the review under this paragraph, the authorities determine that the countervailing duty is no longer warranted, it shall be terminated immediately.

21.3 Notwithstanding the provisions of paras 1 and 2, any definitive countervailing duty shall be terminated on a date not later than five years from, its imposition (or from the date of the most recent review under para 2 if that review has covered both subsidisation and injury, or under this paragraph), unless the authorities determine, in a review initiated before that date on their own initiative or upon a duly substantiated request made by or on behalf of the domestic industry within a reasonable period of time prior to that date, that the expiry of the duty would be likely to lead to continuation or recurrence of subsidisation and injury. The duty may remain in force pending the outcome of such a review.

21.4 The provisions of Article 12 regarding evidence and procedure shall apply to any review carried out under this article. Any such review shall be carried out expeditiously and shall normally be concluded within 12 months of the date of initiation of the review.

21.5 The provisions of this article shall apply *mutatis mutandis* to undertakings accepted under Article 18.

Article 22 – Public notice and explanation of determinations

22.1 When the authorities are satisfied that there is sufficient evidence to justify the initiation of an investigation pursuant to Article 11, the Member or Members the products of which are subject to such investigation and other interested parties known to the investigating authorities to have an interest therein shall be notified and a public notice shall be given.

22.2 A public notice of the initiation of an investigation shall contain, or otherwise make available through a separate report, adequate information on the following:

(a) the name of the exporting country or countries and the product involved;

(b) the date of initiation of the investigation;

(c) a description of the subsidy practice or practices to be investigated;

(d) a summary of the factors on which the allegation of injury is based;

(e) the address to which representations by interested Members and interested parties should be directed; and

(f) the time limits allowed to interested Members and interested parties for making their views known.

22.3 Public notice shall be given of any preliminary or final determination, whether affirmative or negative, of any decision to accept an undertaking pursuant to Article 18, of the termination of such an undertaking, and of the termination of a definitive countervailing duty. Each such notice shall set forth, or otherwise make available through a separate report, in sufficient detail the findings and conclusions reached on all issues of fact and law considered material by the investigating authorities. All such notices and reports shall be forwarded to the Member or Members the products of which are subject to such determination or undertaking and to other interested parties known to have an interest therein.

22.4 A public notice of the imposition of provisional measures shall set forth, or otherwise make available through a separate report, sufficiently detailed explanations for the preliminary determinations on the existence of a subsidy and injury and shall refer to the matters of fact and law which have led to arguments being accepted or rejected. Such a notice or report shall, due regard being paid to the requirement for the protection of confidential information, contain in particular:

(i) the names of the suppliers or, when this is impracticable, the supplying countries involved;

(ii) a description of the product which is sufficient for customs purposes;

(iii) the amount of subsidy established and the basis on which the existence of a subsidy has been determined;

(iv) considerations relevant to the injury determination as set out in Article 15;

(v) the main reasons leading to the determination.

22.5 A public notice of conclusion or suspension of an investigation in the case of an affirmative determination providing for the imposition of a definitive duty or the acceptance of an undertaking shall contain, or otherwise make available through a separate report, all relevant information on the matters of fact and law and reasons which have led to the imposition of final measures or the acceptance of an undertaking, due regard being paid to the requirement for the protection of confidential information.

In particular, the notice or report shall contain the information described in para 4, as well as the reasons for the acceptance or rejection of relevant arguments or claims made by interested Members and by the exporters and importers.

22.6 A public notice of the termination or suspension of an investigation following the acceptance of an undertaking pursuant to Article 18 shall include, or otherwise make available through a separate report, the non-confidential part of this undertaking.

22.7 The provisions of this article shall apply *mutatis mutandis* to the initiation and completion of reviews pursuant to Article 21 and to decisions under Article 20 to apply duties retroactively.

Article 23 – Judicial review

Each Member whose national legislation contains provisions on countervailing duty measures shall maintain judicial, arbitral or administrative tribunals or procedures for the purpose, *inter alia*, of the prompt review of administrative actions relating to final determinations and reviews of determinations within the meaning of Article 21. Such tribunals or procedures shall be independent of the authorities responsible for the determination or review in question, and shall provide all interested parties who participated in the administrative proceeding and are directly and individually affected by the administrative actions with access to review.

PART VI – INSTITUTIONS

Article 24 – Committee on subsidies and countervailing measures and subsidiary bodies

24.1   There is hereby established a Committee on Subsidies and Countervailing Measures composed of representatives from each of the Members. The committee shall elect its own Chairman and shall meet not less than twice a year and otherwise as envisaged by relevant provisions of this agreement at the request of any Member. The committee shall carry out responsibilities as assigned to it under this agreement or by the Members and it shall afford Members the opportunity of consulting on any matter relating to the operation of the agreement or the furtherance of its objectives. The WTO Secretariat shall act as the secretariat to the committee.

24.2   The committee may set up subsidiary bodies as appropriate.

24.3   The committee shall establish a Permanent Group of Experts composed of five independent persons, highly qualified in the fields of subsidies and trade relations. The experts will be elected by the committee and one of them will be replaced every year. The PGE may be requested to assist a panel, as provided for in para 5 of Article 4. The committee may also seek an advisory opinion on the existence and nature of any subsidy.

24.4   The PGE may be consulted by any Member and may give advisory opinions on the nature of any subsidy proposed to be introduced or currently maintained by that Member. Such advisory opinions will be confidential and may not be invoked in proceedings under Article 7.

24.5   In carrying out their functions, the committee and any subsidiary bodies may consult with and seek information from any source they deem appropriate. However, before the committee or a subsidiary body seeks such information from a source within the jurisdiction of a Member, it shall inform the Member involved.

PART VII – NOTIFICATION AND SURVEILLANCE

Article 25 – Notifications

25.1   Members agree that, without prejudice to the provisions of para 1 of Article XVI of GATT 1994, their notifications of subsidies shall be submitted not later than 30 June of each year and shall conform to the provisions of paras 2 through 6.

25.2   Members shall notify any subsidy as defined in para 1 of Article 1, which is specific within the meaning of Article 2, granted or maintained within their territories.

25.3   The content of notifications should be sufficiently specific to enable other Members to evaluate the trade effects and to understand the operation of notified subsidy programmes. In this connection, and without prejudice to the contents and form of the questionnaire on subsidies, Members shall ensure that their notifications contain the following information:

(a)   form of a subsidy (ie grant, loan, tax concession, etc);

(b)   subsidy per unit or, in cases where this is not possible, the total amount or the annual amount budgeted for that subsidy (indicating, if possible, the average subsidy per unit in the previous year);

(c) policy objective and/or purpose of a subsidy;

(d) duration of a subsidy and/or any other time limits attached to it;

(e) statistical data permitting an assessment of the trade effects of a subsidy.

25.4 Where specific points in para 3 have not been addressed in a notification, an explanation shall be provided in the notification itself.

25.5 If subsidies are granted to specific products or sectors, the notifications should be organised by product or sector.

25.6 Members which consider that there are no measures in their territories requiring notification under para 1 of Article XVI of GATT 1994 and this agreement shall so inform the Secretariat in writing.

25.7 Members recognise that notification of a measure does not prejudge either its legal status under GATT 1994 and this agreement, the effects under this agreement, or the nature of the measure itself.

25.8 Any Member may, at any time, make a written request for information on the nature and extent of any subsidy granted or maintained by another Member (including any subsidy referred to in Part IV), or for an explanation of the reasons for which a specific measure has been considered as not subject to the requirement of notification.

25.9 Members so requested shall provide such information as quickly as possible and in a comprehensive manner, and shall be ready, upon request, to provide additional information to the requesting Member. In particular, they shall provide sufficient details to enable the other Member to assess their compliance with the terms of this agreement. Any Member who considers that such information has not been provided may bring the matter to the attention of the committee.

25.10 Any Member who considers that any measure of another Member having the effects of a subsidy has not been notified in accordance with the provisions of para 1 of Article XVI of GATT 1994 and this article may bring the matter to the attention of such other Member. If the alleged subsidy is not thereafter notified promptly, such Member may itself bring the alleged subsidy in question to the notice of the committee.

25.11 Members shall report without delay to the committee all preliminary or final actions taken with respect to countervailing duties. Such reports shall be available in the Secretariat for inspection by other Members. Members shall also submit, on a semi-annual basis, reports on any countervailing duty actions taken within the preceding six months. The semi-annual reports shall be submitted on an agreed standard form.

25.12 Each Member shall notify the committee (a) which of its authorities are competent to initiate and conduct investigations referred to in Article 11, and (b) its domestic procedures governing the initiation and conduct of such investigations.

Article 26 – Surveillance

26.1 The committee shall examine new and full notifications submitted under para 1 of Article XVI of GATT 1994 and para 1 of Article 26 of this agreement at special sessions held every third year. Notifications submitted in the intervening years (updating notifications) shall be examined at each regular meeting of the committee.

26.2 The committee shall examine reports submitted under para 11 of Article 25 at each regular meeting of the committee.

PART VIII – DEVELOPING COUNTRY MEMBERS

Article 27 – Special and differential treatment of developing country members

27.1 Members recognise that subsidies may play an important role in economic development programmes of developing country Members.

27.2 The prohibition of para 1(a) of Article 3 shall not apply to:

(a) developing country Members referred to in Annex VII;

(b) other developing country Members for a period of eight years from the date of entry into force of the WTO Agreement, subject to compliance with the provisions in para 4.

27.3   The prohibition of para 1(b) of Article 3 shall not apply to developing country Members for a period of five years, and shall not apply to least developed country Members for a period of eight years, from the date of entry into force of the WTO Agreement.

27.4   Any developing country Member referred to in para 2(b) shall phase out its export subsidies within the eight year period, preferably in a progressive manner. However, a developing country Member shall not increase the level of its export subsidies and shall eliminate them within a period shorter than that provided for in this paragraph when the use of such export subsidies is inconsistent with its development needs. If a developing country Member deems it necessary to apply such subsidies beyond the eight year period, it shall not later than one year before the expiry of this period enter into consultation with the committee, which will determine whether an extension of this period is justified after examining all the relevant economic, financial and development needs of the developing country Member in question. If the committee determines that the extension is justified, the developing country Member concerned shall hold annual consultations with the committee to determine the necessity of maintaining the subsidies. If no such determination is made by the committee, the developing country Member shall phase out the remaining export subsidies within two years from the end of the last authorised period.

27.5   A developing country Member which has reached export competitiveness in any given product shall phase out its export subsidies for such product(s) over a period of two years. However, for a developing country Member which is referred to in Annex VII and which has reached export competitiveness in one or more products, export subsidies on such products shall be gradually phased out over a period of eight years.

27.6   Export competitiveness in a product exists if a developing country Member's exports of that product have reached a share of at least 3.25% in world trade of that product for two consecutive calendar years. Export competitiveness shall exist either (a) on the basis of notification by the developing country Member having reached export competitiveness, or (b) on the basis of a computation undertaken by the Secretariat at the request of any Member. For the purpose of this paragraph, a product is defined as a section heading of the Harmonised System Nomenclature. The committee shall review the operation of this provision five years from the date of the entry into force of the WTO Agreement.

27.7   The provisions of Article 4 shall not apply to a developing country Member in the case of export subsidies which are in conformity with the provisions of paras 2 through 5. The relevant provisions in such a case shall be those of Article 7.

27.8   There shall be no presumption in terms of para 1 of Article 6 that a subsidy granted by a developing country Member results in serious prejudice, as defined in this agreement. Such serious prejudice, where applicable under the terms of para 9, shall be demonstrated by positive evidence, in accordance with the provisions of paras 3 through 8 of Article 6.

27.9   Regarding actionable subsidies granted or maintained by a developing country Member other than those referred to in para 1 of Article 6, action may not be authorised or taken under Article 7 unless nullification or impairment of tariff concessions or other obligations under GATT 1994 is found to exist as a result of such a subsidy, in such a way as to displace or impede imports of a like product of another Member into the market of the subsidising developing country Member or unless injury to a domestic industry in the market of an importing Member occurs.

27.10   Any countervailing duty investigation of a product originating in a developing country Member shall be terminated as soon as the authorities concerned determine that:

(a)   the overall level of subsidies granted upon the product in question does not exceed 2% of its value calculated on a per unit basis; or

(b)   the volume of the subsidised imports represents less than 4% of the total imports of the like product in the importing Member, unless imports from developing country Members whose individual shares of total imports represent less than 4% collectively account for more than 9% of the total imports of the like product in the importing Member.

27.11   For those developing country Members within the scope of para 2(b) which have eliminated export subsidies prior to the expiry of the period of eight years from the date of entry into force of the WTO Agreement, and for those developing country members referred to in Annex VII, the number in para 10(a) shall be 3% rather than 2%. This provision shall apply from the date that the elimination of export subsidies is notified to the committee, and for so long as export subsidies are not granted by the notifying developing country Member. This provision shall expire eight years from the date of entry into force of the WTO Agreement.

27.12 The provisions of paras 10 and 11 shall govern any determination of *de minimis* under para 3 of Article 15.

27.13 The provisions of Part III shall not apply to direct forgiveness of debts, subsidies to cover social costs, in whatever form, including relinquishment of government revenue and other transfer of liabilities when such subsidies are granted within and directly linked to a privatisation programme of a developing country Member, provided that both such programme and the subsidies involved are granted for a limited period and notified to the committee and that the programme results in eventual privatisation of the enterprise concerned.

27.14 The committee shall, upon request by an interested Member, undertake a review of a specific export subsidy practice of a developing country Member to examine whether the practice is in conformity with its development needs.

27.15 The committee shall, upon request by an interested developing country Member, undertake a review of a specific countervailing measure to examine whether it is consistent with the provisions of paras 10 and 11 as applicable to the developing country Member in question.

PART IX – TRANSITIONAL ARRANGEMENTS

Article 28 – Existing programmes

28.1 Subsidy programmes which have been established within the territory of any Member before the date on which such a Member signed the WTO Agreement and which are inconsistent with the provisions of this agreement shall be:

(a) notified to the committee not later than 90 days after the date of entry into force of the WTO Agreement for such Member; and

(b) brought into conformity with the provisions of this agreement within three years of the date of entry into force of the WTO Agreement for such Member and until then shall not be subject to Part II.

28.2 No Member shall extend the scope of any such programme, nor shall such a programme be renewed upon its expiry.

Article 29 – Transformation into a market economy

29.1 Members in the process of transformation from a centrally planned into a market, free enterprise economy may apply programmes and measures necessary for such a transformation.

29.2 For such Members, subsidy programmes falling within the scope of Article 3, and notified according to para 3, shall be phased out or brought into conformity with Article 3 within a period of seven years from the date of entry into force of the WTO Agreement. In such a case, Article 4 shall not apply. In addition during the same period:

(a) Subsidy programmes falling within the scope of para 1(d) of Article 6 shall not be actionable under Article 7;

(b) With respect to other actionable subsidies, the provisions of para 9 of Article 27 shall apply.

29.3 Subsidy programmes falling within the scope of Article 3 shall be notified to the committee by the earliest practicable date after the date of entry into force of the WTO Agreement. Further notifications of such subsidies may be made up to two years after the date of entry into force of the WTO Agreement.

29.4 In exceptional circumstances, Members referred to in para 1 may be given departures from their notified programmes and measures and their time frame by the committee if such departures are deemed necessary for the process of transformation.

PART X – DISPUTE SETTLEMENT

Article 30

The provisions of Articles XXII and XXIII of GATT 1994 as elaborated and applied by the Dispute Settlement Understanding shall apply to consultations and the settlement of disputes under this agreement, except as otherwise specifically provided herein.

PART XI – FINAL PROVISIONS

Article 31 – Provisional application

The provisions of para 1 of Article 6 and the provisions of Article 8 and Article 9 shall apply for a period of five years; beginning with the date of entry into force of the WTO Agreement. Not later than 180 days before the end of this period, the committee shall review the operation of those provisions, with a view to determining whether to extend their application, either as presently drafted or in a modified form, for a further period.

Article 32 – Other final provisions

32.1 No specific action against a subsidy of another Member can be taken except in accordance with the provisions of GATT 1994, as interpreted by this agreement.

32.2 Reservations may not be entered in respect of any of the provisions of this agreement without the consent of the other Members.

32.3 Subject to para 4, the provisions of this agreement shall apply to investigations and reviews of existing measures, initiated pursuant to applications which have been made on or after the date of entry into force for a Member of the WTO Agreement.

32.4 For the purposes of para 3 of Article 21, existing countervailing measures shall be deemed to be imposed on a date not later than the date of entry into force for a Member of the WTO Agreement, except in cases in which the domestic legislation of a Member in force at that date already included a clause of the type provided for in that paragraph.

32.5 Each Member shall take all necessary steps, of a general or particular character, to ensure, not later than the date of entry into force of the WTO Agreement for it, the conformity of its laws, regulations and administrative procedures with the provisions of this agreement as they may apply to the Member in question.

32.6 Each Member shall inform the committee of any changes in its laws and regulations relevant to this agreement and in the administration of such laws and regulations.

32.7 The committee shall review annually the implementation and operation of this agreement, taking into account the objectives thereof. The committee shall inform annually the Council for Trade in Goods of developments during the period covered by such reviews.

32.8 The Annexes to this agreement constitute an integral part thereof.

Annex I

Illustrative list of export subsidies

(a) The provision by governments of direct subsidies to a firm or an industry contingent upon export performance.

(b) Currency retention schemes or any similar practices which involve a bonus on exports.

(c) Internal transport and freight charges on export shipments, provided or mandated by governments, on terms more favourable than for domestic shipments.

(d) The provision by governments or their agencies either directly or indirectly through government-mandated schemes, of imported or domestic products or services for use in the production of exported goods, on terms or conditions more favourable than for provision of like or directly competitive products or services for use in the production of goods for domestic consumption, if (in the case of products) such terms or conditions are more favourable than those commercially available on world markets to their exporters.

(e) The full or partial exemption remission, or deferral specifically related to exports, of direct taxes or social welfare charges paid or payable by industrial or commercial enterprises.

(f) The allowance of special deductions directly related to exports or export performance, over and above those granted in respect to production for domestic consumption, in the calculation of the base on which direct taxes are charged.

(g) The exemption or remission, in respect of the production and distribution of exported products, of indirect taxes in excess of those levied in respect of the production and distribution of like products when sold for domestic consumption.

(h) The exemption, remission or deferral of prior-stage cumulative indirect taxes on goods or services used in the production of exported products in excess of the exemption, remission or deferral of like prior-stage cumulative indirect taxes on goods or services used in the production of like products when sold for domestic consumption, provided, however, that prior-stage cumulative indirect taxes may be exempted, remitted or deferred on exported products even when not exempted, remitted or deferred on like products when sold for domestic consumption, if the prior-stage cumulative indirect taxes are levied on inputs that are consumed in the production of the exported product (making normal allowance for waste). This item shall be interpreted in accordance with the guidelines on consumption of inputs in the production process contained in Annex II.

(i) The remission or drawback of import charges in excess of those levied on imported inputs that are consumed in the production of the exported product (making normal allowance for waste); provided, however, that in particular cases a firm may use a quantity of home market inputs equal to, and having the same quality and characteristics as, the imported inputs as a substitute for them in order to benefit from this provision if the import and the corresponding export operations both occur within a reasonable time period, not to exceed two years. This item shall be interpreted in accordance with the guidelines on consumption of inputs in the production process contained in Annex II and the guidelines in the determination of substitution drawback systems as export subsidies contained in Annex III.

(j) The provision by governments (or special institutions controlled by governments) of export credit guarantee or insurance programmes, of insurance or guarantee programmes against increases in the cost of exported products or of exchange risk programmes, at premium rates which are inadequate to cover the long term operating costs and losses of the programmes.

(k) The grant by governments (or special institutions controlled by and/or acting under the authority of governments) of export credits at rates below those which they actually have to pay for the funds so employed (or would have to pay if they borrowed on international capital markets in order to obtain funds of the same maturity and other credit terms and denominated in the same currency as the export credit), or the payment by them of all or part of the costs incurred by exporters or financial institutions in obtaining credits, in so far as they are used to secure a material advantage in the field of export credit terms. Provided, however, that if a Member is a party to an international undertaking on official export credits to which at least 12 original Members to this agreement are parties as of 1 January 1979 (or a successor undertaking which has been adopted by those original Members), or if in practice a Member applies the interest rates provisions of the relevant undertaking, an export credit practice which is in conformity with those provisions shall not be considered an export subsidy prohibited by this agreement.

(l) Any other charge on the public account constituting an export subsidy in the sense of Article XVI of GATT 1994.

Annex II

Guidelines on consumption of inputs in the production process

I

1 Indirect tax rebate schemes can allow for exemption, remission or deferral of prior-stage cumulative indirect taxes levied on inputs that are consumed in the production of the exported product (making normal allowance for waste). Similarly, drawback schemes can allow for the remission or drawback of import charges levied on inputs that are consumed in the production of the exported product (making normal allowance for waste).

2 The Illustrative List of Export Subsidies in Annex I of this agreement makes reference to the term 'inputs that are consumed in the production of the exported product' in paras (h)

and (i). Pursuant to para (h), indirect tax rebate schemes can constitute an export subsidy to the extent that they result in exemption, remission or deferral of prior-stage cumulative indirect taxes in excess of the amount of such taxes actually levied on inputs that are consumed in the production of the exported product. Pursuant to para (i), drawback schemes can constitute an export subsidy to the extent that they result in a remission or drawback of import charges in excess of those actually levied on inputs that are consumed in the production of the exported product. Both paragraphs stipulate that normal allowance for waste must be made in findings regarding consumption of inputs in the production of the exported product. Paragraph (i) also provides for substitution, where appropriate.

II

In examining whether inputs are consumed in the production of the exported product, as part of a countervailing duty investigation pursuant to this agreement, investigating authorities should proceed on the following basis:

1   Where it is alleged that an indirect tax rebate scheme, or a drawback scheme, conveys a subsidy by reason of over-rebate or excess drawback of indirect taxes or import charges on inputs consumed in the production of the exported product, the investigating authorities should first determine whether the government of the exporting Member has in place and applies a system or procedure to confirm which inputs are consumed in the production of the exported product and in what amounts. Where such a system or procedure is determined to be applied, the investigating authorities should then examine the system or procedure to see whether it is reasonable, effective for the purpose intended, and based on generally accepted commercial practices in the country of export. The investigating authorities may deem it necessary to carry out, in accordance with para 6 of Article 12, certain practical tests in order to verify information or to satisfy themselves that the system or procedure is being effectively applied.

2   Where there is no such system or procedure, where it is not reasonable, or where it is instituted and considered reasonable but is found not to be applied or not to be applied effectively, a further examination by the exporting Member based on the actual inputs involved would need to be carried out in the context of determining whether an excess payment occurred. If the investigating authorities deemed it necessary, a further examination would be carried out in accordance with para 1.

3   Investigating authorities should treat inputs as physically incorporated if such inputs are used in the production process and are physically present in the product exported. The Members note that an input need not be present in the final product in the same form in which it entered the production process.

4   In determining the amount of a particular input that is consumed in the production of the exported product, a 'normal allowance for waste' should be taken into account, and such waste should be treated as consumed in the production of the exported product. The term 'waste' refers to that portion of a given input which does not serve an independent function in the production process, is not consumed in the production of the exported product (for reasons such as inefficiencies) and is not recovered, used or sold by the same manufacturer.

5   The investigating authority's determination of whether the claimed allowance for waste is 'normal' should take into account the production process, the average experience of the industry in the country of export, and other technical factors, as appropriate. The investigating authority should bear in mind that an important question is whether the authorities in the exporting Member have reasonably calculated the amount of waste, when such an amount is intended to be included in the tax or duty rebate or remission.

Annex III

Guidelines in the determination of substitution drawback systems as export subsidies

I

Drawback systems can allow for the refund or drawback of import charges on inputs which are consumed in the production process of another product and where the export of this latter product contains domestic inputs having the same quality and characteristics as those substituted for the imported inputs. Pursuant to para (i) of the Illustrative List of Export Subsidies in Annex I, substitution drawback systems can constitute an export subsidy to the extent that they result in an excess drawback of the import charges levied initially on the imported inputs for which drawback is being claimed.

II

In examining any substitution drawback system as part of a countervailing duty investigation pursuant to this agreement, investigating authorities should proceed on the following basis:

1   Paragraph (i) of the Illustrative List stipulates that home market inputs may be substituted for imported inputs in the production of a product for export provided such inputs are equal in quantity to, and have the same quality and characteristics as, the imported inputs being substituted. The existence of a verification system or procedure is important because it enables the government of the exporting Member to ensure and demonstrate that the quantity of inputs for which drawback is claimed does not exceed the quantity of similar products exported, in whatever form, and that there is not drawback of import charges in excess of those originally levied on the imported inputs in question.

2   Where it is alleged that a substitution drawback system conveys a subsidy, the investigating authorities should first proceed to determine whether the government of the exporting Member has in place and applies a verification system or procedure. Where such a system or procedure is determined to be applied, the investigating authorities should then examine the verification procedures to see whether they are reasonable, effective for the purpose intended, and based on generally accepted commercial practices in the country of export. To the extent that the procedures are determined to meet this test and are effectively applied, no subsidy should be presumed to exist. It may be deemed necessary by the investigating authorities to carry out, in accordance with para 6 of Article 12, certain practical tests in order to verify information or to satisfy themselves that the verification procedures are being effectively applied.

3   Where there are no verification procedures, where they are not reasonable, or where such procedures are instituted and considered reasonable but are found not to be actually applied or not applied effectively, there may be a subsidy. In such cases, a further examination by the exporting Member based on the actual transactions involved would need to be carried out to determine whether an excess payment occurred. If the investigating authorities deemed it necessary, a further examination would be carried out in accordance with para 2.

4   The existence of a substitution drawback provision under which exporters are allowed to select particular import shipments on which drawback is claimed should not of itself be considered to convey a subsidy.

5   An excess drawback of import charges in the sense of para (i) would be deemed to exist where governments paid interest on any moneys refunded under their drawback schemes, to the extent of the interest actually paid or payable.

Annex IV

Calculation of the total ad valorem subsidisation (para 1(a) of Article 6)

1   Any calculation of the amount of a subsidy for the purpose of para 1(a) of Article 6 shall be done in terms of the cost to the granting government.

2   Except as provided in paras 3 through 5, in determining whether the overall rate of subsidisation exceeds 5% of the value of the product, the value of the product shall be calculated as the total value of the recipient firm's sales in the most recent 12-month period, for which sales data is available, preceding the period in which the subsidy is granted.

3   Where the subsidy is tied to the production or sale of a given product, the value of the product shall be calculated as the total value of the recipient firm's sales of that product in the most recent 12 month period, for which sales data is available, preceding the period in which the subsidy is granted.

4   Where the recipient firm is in a start-up situation, serious prejudice shall be deemed to exist if the overall rate of subsidisation exceeds 15% of the total funds invested. For purposes of this paragraph, a start-up period will not extend beyond the first year of production.

5   Where the recipient firm is located in an inflationary economy country, the value of the product shall be calculated as the recipient firm's total sales (or sales of the relevant product, if the subsidy is tied) in the preceding calendar year indexed by the rate of inflation experienced in the 12 months preceding the month in which the subsidy is to be given.

6   In determining the overall rate of subsidisation in a given year, subsidies given under different programmes and by different authorities in the territory of a Member shall be aggregated.

7   Subsidies granted prior to the date of entry into force of the WTO Agreement, the benefits of which are allocated to future production, shall be included in the overall rate of subsidisation.

8   Subsidies which are non-actionable under relevant provisions of this agreement shall not be included in the calculation of the amount of a subsidy for the purpose of para 1(a) of Article 6.

Annex V

Procedures for developing information concerning serious prejudice

1   Every Member shall cooperate in the development of evidence to be examined by a panel in procedures under paras 4 through 6 of Article 7. The parties to the dispute and any third country Member concerned shall notify to the DSB, as soon as the provisions of para 4 of Article 7 have been invoked, the organisation responsible for administration of this provision within its territory and the procedures to be used to comply with requests for information.

2   In cases where matters are referred to the DSB under para 4 of Article 7, the DSB shall, upon request, initiate the procedure to obtain such information from the government of the subsidising Member as necessary to establish the existence and amount of subsidisation, the value of total sales of the subsidised firms, as well as information necessary to analyse the adverse effects caused by the subsidised product. This process may include, where appropriate, presentation of questions to the government of the subsidising Member and of the complaining Member to collect information, as well as to clarify and obtain elaboration of information available to the parties to a dispute through the notification procedures set forth in Part VII.

3   In the case of effects in third country markets, a party to a dispute may collect information, including through the use of questions to the government of the third country Member, necessary to analyse adverse effects, which is not otherwise reasonably available from the complaining Member or the subsidising Member. This requirement should be administered in such a way as not to impose an unreasonable burden on the third country Member. In particular, such a Member is not expected to make a market or price analysis specially for that purpose. The information to be supplied is that which is already available or can be readily obtained by this Member (eg most recent statistics which have already been gathered by relevant statistical services but which have not yet been published, customs data concerning imports and declared values of the products concerned, etc). However, if a party to a dispute undertakes a detailed market analysis at its own expense, the task of the person or firm conducting such an analysis shall be facilitated by the authorities of the third country Member and such a person or firm shall be given access to all information which is not normally maintained confidential by the government.

4   The DSB shall designate a representative to serve the function of facilitating the information-gathering process. The sole purpose of the representative shall be to ensure the timely development of the information necessary to facilitate expeditious subsequent multilateral review of the dispute. In particular, the representative may suggest ways to most efficiently solicit necessary information as well as encourage the cooperation of the parties.

5   The information-gathering process outlined in paras 2 through 4 shall be completed within 60 days of the date on which the matter has been referred to the DSB under para 4 of Article 7. The information obtained during this process shall be submitted to the panel established by the DSB in accordance with the provisions of Part X. This information

should include, *inter alia*, data concerning the amount of the subsidy in question (and, where appropriate, the value of total sales of the subsidised firms), prices of the subsidised product, prices of the non-subsidised product, prices of other suppliers to the market, changes in the supply of the subsidised product to the market in question and changes in market shares. It should also include rebuttal evidence, as well as such supplemental information as the panel deems relevant in the course of reaching its conclusions.

6   If the subsidising and/or third country Member fails to cooperate in the information-gathering process, the complaining Member will present its case of serious prejudice, based on evidence available to it, together with facts and circumstances of the non-cooperation of the subsidising and/or third country Member. Where information is unavailable due to non-cooperation by the subsidising and/or third country Member, the panel may complete the record as necessary relying on best information otherwise available.

7   In making its determination, the panel should draw adverse inferences from instances of non- cooperation by any party involved in the information-gathering process.

8   In making a determination to use either best information available or adverse inferences, the panel shall consider the advice of the DSB representative nominated under para 4 as to the reasonableness of any requests for information and the efforts made by parties to comply with these requests in a cooperative and timely manner.

9   Nothing in the information-gathering process shall limit the ability of the panel to seek such additional information it deems essential to a proper resolution to the dispute, and which was not adequately sought or developed during that process. However, ordinarily the panel should not request additional information to complete the record where the information would support a particular party's position and the absence of that information in the record is the result of unreasonable non-cooperation by that party in the information-gathering process.

Annex VI

Procedures for on-the-spot investigations pursuant to para 6 of Article 12

1   Upon initiation of an investigation, the authorities of the exporting Member and the firms known to be concerned should be informed of the intention to carry out on-the-spot investigations.

2   If in exceptional circumstances it is intended to include non-governmental experts in the investigating team, the firms and the authorities of the exporting Member should be so informed. Such non-governmental experts should be subject to effective sanctions for breach of confidentiality requirements.

3   It should be standard practice to obtain explicit agreement of the firms concerned in the exporting Member before the visit is finally scheduled.

4   As soon as the agreement of the firms concerned has been obtained, the investigating authorities should notify the authorities of the exporting Member of the names and addresses of the firms to be visited and the dates agreed.

5   Sufficient advance notice should be given to the firms in question before the visit is made

6   Visits to explain the questionnaire should only be made at the request of an exporting firm In case of such a request the investigating authorities may place themselves at the disposal of the firm; such a visit may only be made if (a) the authorities of the importing Member notify the representatives of the government of the Member in question, and (b) the latter do not object to the visit.

7   As the main purpose of the on-the-spot investigation is to verify information provided or to obtain further details, it should be carried out after the response to the questionnaire has been received, unless the firm agrees to the contrary and the government of the exporting Member is informed by the investigating authorities of the anticipated visit and does not object to it; further, it should be standard practice prior to the visit to advise the firms concerned of the general nature of the information to be verified and of any further information which needs to be provided, though this should not preclude requests to be made on-the-spot for further details to be provided in the light of information obtained.

8   Enquires or questions put by the authorities or firms of the exporting Members and essential to a successful on-the-spot investigation should, whenever possible, be answered before the visit is made.

Annex VII

Developing country Members referred to in para 2(a) of Article 27

The developing country Members not subject to the provisions of para 1(a) of Article 3 under the terms of para 2(a) of Article 27 are:

(a)   Least-developed countries designated as such by the United Nations which are Members of the WTO.

(b)   Each of the following developing countries which are Members of the WTO shall be subject to the provisions which are applicable to other developing country Members according to para 2(b) of Article 27 when GNP per capita has reached $1,000 per annum: Bolivia, Cameroon, Congo, Côte d'Ivoire, Dominican Republic, Egypt, Ghana, Guatemala, Guyana, India, Indonesia, Kenya, Morocco, Nicaragua, Nigeria, Pakistan, Philippines, Senegal, Sri Lanka and Zimbabwe.

CHAPTER 9

TRADE IN INTELLECTUAL PROPERTY

INTRODUCTION

International trade in goods and services incorporating intellectual property rights has increased dramatically over the past 50 years. Advances in areas such as medicine, information technology, television and the internet have driven demand for products such as pharmaceuticals, films, music and computer hardware and software. Companies have recognised the power of branding as an advantage in international trade. At the same time, many of those same technological advances have made it far easier for third parties to act as free riders - producing and marketing copies of successful products without the need to spend significant amounts on research, development and marketing.

International agreements attempting to resolve some of the problems associated with international trade in goods and services incorporating intellectual property rights have existed for over 100 years, for example, the Paris Convention for the Protection of Industrial Property (1883), the Berne Convention for the Protection of Literary and Artistic Works (1886). Although those agreements have been substantially revised numerous times to take into account technological and philosophical changes during the last century, the rate at which technological progress has accelerated meant that it was difficult to ensure that those agreements provided adequate protection for owners of intellectual property rights.

As such, the last decade has seen the development of a number of new treaties regulating intellectual property rights. These include: the WIPO Copyright Treaty (1996), the WIPO Performances and Phonograms Treaty (1996) (each maintained by the World Intellectual Property Organisation) and the Agreement on Trade-Related Aspects of Intellectual Property Rights 1994 (TRIPS Agreement), which forms Annex 1C of the Agreement Establishing the World Trade Organisation.

Given the number of treaties regulating international trade in intellectual property rights, this chapter will only examine the major components of the TRIPS Agreement. That Agreement has been selected for a number of reasons:

1   The TRIPS Agreement forms part of the World Trade Organisation (WTO) treaty system along with the General Agreement on Tariffs and Trade (GATT) and the General Agreement on Trade in Services (GATS), which are covered elsewhere in this book.

2   The TRIPS Agreement incorporates substantial components of the Paris Convention and the Berne Convention.

3   The TRIPS Agreement applies to a large number of Member States.

4   Unlike the other major treaties, the TRIPS Agreement incorporates a binding dispute resolution process through the WTO Dispute Settlement Body (DSB).

5   Analysis of all of the major treaties would be beyond the scope of this chapter.

A list of references to the other major agreements regulating intellectual property rights is included at the end of this chapter.

THE TRIPS AGREEMENT

Background

Prior to the signing of the TRIPS Agreement in 1994 during the WTO Uruguay Round negotiations (which began in 1986), a number of discrete treaties regulated separate intellectual property rights, for example, the Berne Convention and Uniform Copyright Convention regulated copyright, the Paris Convention regulated patents and trade marks, etc. Negotiations to amend and update those agreements were difficult and time consuming. This complexity was deepened by the fact that the signatories to each of those treaties differed and there were no provisions for dispute resolution by independent bodies.

Intellectual property rights create a natural tension between economically developed countries and those still pursuing industrialisation. Throughout modern history, the majority of creators and owners of intellectual property rights have traditionally been found in the most economically advanced countries of their time. Those creators and owners have sought to protect their rights (and profit margins) against imitators who have not had to incur the same level of investment in research, development and marketing. As intellectual property rights, such as patents, trade marks and copyrights are monopolies granted by governments in individual countries, those rights have also been limited by the geographic borders of those countries. An increasingly globalised world has led to the owners of intellectual property rights attempting to export their products to markets located in other countries. Those other countries often have not provided the same level of recognition of, or protection for, intellectual property rights (for example, until recently, India did not permit patents on pharmaceuticals and, when newly formed, the USA did not permit copyrights to be held by non-citizens (a situation not rectified until the turn of the 20th century)).[1] Less developed countries have justified limiting the grant of intellectual property rights on the grounds of national interest and the need to 'catch up' as soon as possible. This loss of revenue and market share has frequently led to trade disputes which the existing intellectual property rights treaties, such as the Berne and Paris Conventions, had been ineffective at resolving.

For example, the Government of the USA has used the so called 'Special 301' provisions of its trade laws to impose and threaten trade sanctions upon countries that did not provide sufficiently strong levels of protection for American intellectual property rights, or who denied fair market access to American persons that relied on intellectual property rights.[2] In 2003, 'Special 301' was used to continue the imposition of US$75 million of sanctions imposed during the prior year on Ukrainian products due to that country's lax intellectual property laws.[3]

In an attempt to overcome the perceived weaknesses in dispute resolution and breadth of membership inherent in the pre-existing intellectual property rights Conventions, intellectual property rights owners in the US lobbied their government

---

1   Office of Technological Assessment, 'Intellectual property rights in an age of electronics and information', 1989, p 32, available at: www.wws.princeton.edu/cgi-bin/byteserv.prl/~ota/disk2/1986/8610_n.html (last visited 20 February 2004).
2   19 USC Sec 2411, see usinfo.state.gov/products/pubs/intelprp/301.htm.
3   www.ustr.gov/reports/2003/execsummary.pdf.

in an attempt to have intellectual property rights included on the agenda of the WTO Uruguay Round. The inclusion of intellectual property in the WTO Rounds was perceived as a means by which developed countries, led by the US and EU, could leverage rights of trade access to their primary industry markets (keenly sought by less developed countries) against enhanced protection of intellectual property rights in those same less developed countries.[4]

Effectively, the US and EU held out the granting of enhanced, consistent intellectual property rights around the world as the cost of access to raw material markets such as fruits and vegetables. The ability to resolve disputes multilaterally under the DSB of the WTO was seen as another significant benefit by developed countries – any breaches of TRIPS obligations by less developed countries could be countered by sanctions imposed not only on intellectual property products created or owned by interests within that less developed country (likely to be a relatively small punishment), but also upon raw commodities or services (often a far more effective punishment).

This is not to say, however, that the TRIPS Agreement is strictly one-sided in favour of developed countries. The Preamble for the TRIPS Agreement recognises '... the underlying public policy objectives of national systems for the protection of intellectual property, including developmental and technological objectives ... [and] ... also the special needs of the least-developed country members in respect of maximum flexibility in the domestic implementation of laws and regulations in order to enable them to create a sound and viable technological base ...'. Article 1.1 also states: 'Members shall be free to determine the appropriate method of implementing the provisions of this Agreement within their own legal system and practice.' Article 7 provides that: 'the protection and enforcement of intellectual property rights should contribute to the promotion of technological innovation and to the transfer and dissemination of technology, to the mutual advantage of producers and users of technological knowledge and in a manner conducive to social and economic welfare, and to a balance of rights and obligations.'

Under Art 8, 'Members may, in formulating or amending their laws and regulations, adopt measures necessary to protect public health and nutrition, and to promote the public interest in sectors of vital importance to their socio-economic and technological development' or 'to prevent the abuse of intellectual property rights by right holders or the resort to practices which unreasonably restrain trade or adversely affect the international transfer of technology', provided that such measures are consistent with the provisions of the TRIPS Agreement.

These Articles create opportunities for less developed countries to reduce some of the negative impacts which will be felt by their economies as a consequence of enacting domestic legislation which implements their TRIPS obligations.

---

4   Correa, C and Yusuf, A (eds), *Intellectual Property and International Trade*, 1998, London: Kluwer Law International, p 8.

SCOPE OF THE TRIPS AGREEMENT

The TRIPS Agreement establishes minimum standards for the protection of intellectual property rights in the areas of:

1   copyright;
2   trade marks;
3   geographical indications;
4   patents, industrial designs;
5   integrated circuit layout designs; and
6   undisclosed information (often known as confidential information or trade secrets).

It applies basic principles of the WTO system, such as the national treatment principle and the most-favoured-nation (MFN) principle to intellectual property rights, incorporates references to a number of other intellectual property treaties and requires that signatories develop adequate enforcement regimes under their own legal systems. The TRIPS Agreement then enables signatories to bring compliance disputes against other signatories to the WTO DSB. Finally, it provides transitional arrangements for less and least developed countries to amend their laws to comply with their obligations under the TRIPS Agreement.[5]

National treatment and most-favoured-nation status

Article 3.1 of the TRIPS Agreement provides that:

> Each member shall accord to the nationals of other members treatment no less favourable than that it accords to its own nationals with regard to the protection of intellectual property, subject to the exceptions already provided in, respectively, the Paris Convention (1967), the Berne Convention (1971), the Rome Convention or the Treaty on Intellectual Property in Respect of Integrated Circuits. In respect of performers, producers of phonograms and broadcasting organisations, this obligation only applies in respect of the rights provided under this Agreement. Any member availing itself of the possibilities provided in Article 6 of the Berne Convention (1971) or paragraph 1(b) of Article 16 of the Rome Convention shall make a notification as foreseen in those provisions to the Council for TRIPS.

National treatment has a lengthy history in intellectual property treaties and has assisted in the harmonisation process of intellectual property laws across many countries. One of the differences between the national treatment principle under Art 3 of the TRIPS Agreement when compared to pre-existing intellectual property treaties is the object which must be treated equally. Under the GATT and GATS, products and services must not be discriminated against based upon their country of origin as compared to domestic products or services. Continuing with this WTO theme, under the TRIPS Agreement, the national treatment principle also applies to works subject to intellectual property rights. In comparison, under the Berne and Paris conventions, the

---

5   WTO, 'Understanding the WTO: intellectual property protection and enforcement', 2004, available at: www.wto.org/english/thewto_e/whatis_e/tif_e/agrm7_e.htm (last visited 20 February 2004).

national treatment principle applies to entities holding intellectual property rights rather than to the works themselves. This enabled foreign rights holders to complain about discrimination as compared to nationals under a domestic law, whereas under the TRIPS Agreement, only governments (and not the rights holders themselves) can be involved directly in the dispute settlement process.

Given the minimum standards established by the TRIPS Agreement and the extent to which intellectual property laws have been harmonised in many countries, the nationality principle will be more important in situations where Member States have enacted domestic legislation which goes beyond those minimum standards.[6] One example of this is the amendments which were made to s 104 of US patent laws to remove the discrimination against overseas patent holders based upon the date of invention as compared to the date of filing of a patent application within that country.[7]

Most-favoured-nation (MFN) status

Article 4 of the TRIPS Agreement provides that: 'with regard to the protection of intellectual property, any advantage, favour, privilege or immunity granted by a member to the nationals of any other country shall be accorded immediately and unconditionally to the nationals of all other members.' Unlike the nationality principle, the most-favoured-nation principle has not been historically included in treaties regulating intellectual property rights. It has however, been a basic principle of WTO agreements such as the GATT and GATS. The most-favoured-nation principle requires that any advantage, etc, provided by a Member State to nationals of other Member States must automatically be made available to nationals of all other signatories to the TRIPS Agreement. The most-favoured-nation principle is also discussed in more detail in Chapter 7.

Of particular interest under Art 4 of the TRIPS Agreement are the exemptions to the most-favoured-nation principle permitted for:

1   bi-lateral agreements which entered into force prior to the TRIPS Agreement;

2   advantages deriving from international agreements on judicial assistance and law enforcement of a general nature;

3   reciprocal treatment laws permitted under the Berne Convention and the Paris Convention; and

4   advantages for performers, producers of phonograms and broadcasting organisations to the extent the rights of those entities are not regulated by the TRIPS Agreement.

Article 5 of the TRIPS Agreement exempts Member States from being in breach of their obligations under Arts 3 and 4 of the TRIPS Agreement in situations where those Member States have amended their domestic laws as a result of signing and implementing multilateral agreements that relate to the acquisition or maintenance of

---

6   Correa, *op cit*, pp 15–16.
7   European Community, 'Protection of intellectual property', available at: europa.eu.int/en/agenda/eu-us/pub/tbr95/chap2/c2s7.wd (last visited 20 February 2004).

intellectual property rights under the auspices of the WIPO, such as the WIPO Copyright Treaty and WIPO Performances and Phonograms Treaty.

Copyright

Section 1 of Part II of the TRIPS Agreement establishes rules in relation to copyright. Article 9.1 states that: 'Members shall comply with Articles 1 through 21 of the Berne Convention (1971) and the Appendix thereto. However, members shall not have rights or obligations under this Agreement in respect of the rights conferred under Article 6 *bis* of that Convention or of the rights derived therefrom.' As the TRIPS Agreement establishes minimum standards, Member States that are already signatories to the Berne Convention 1971 remain fully bound by all of their obligations under that Convention. TRIPS Agreement Member States that had not previously signed the Berne Convention (or who had only signed a version prior to the 1971 version) must enact domestic legislation that complies with the first 21 articles of that 1971 Convention, excluding Art 6 *bis*, which established moral rights.

Article 9.2 states that 'copyrights extend to expressions and not to ideas, procedures, methods of operation or mathematical expressions'. All TRIPS Member States must establish domestic legal systems which recognise the rights of authors of 'literary and artistic works'[8] to control the translation,[9] reproduction,[10] performance,[11] broadcast,[12] public recitation[13] and adaptation[14] of their works. Member States must also protect sound recordings[15] and cinematographic works,[16] permit the fair use[17] of copyrighted works and give authors the rights to seize infringing copies of their works.[18]

Interestingly, Art 14 of the TRIPS Agreement establishes certain specific minimum rights to protect performers, producers of phonograms and broadcasting organisations similar to those contained in the 1961 Rome Convention for the Protection of Performers, Producers of Phonograms and Broadcasting Organisations (which is not included by reference in the TRIPS Agreement in a manner akin to the 1971 Berne Convention). TRIPS Member States are specifically permitted by Art 14.6 to retain their domestic implementations of the Rome Convention.

The TRIPS Agreement permits copyright (as a literary work) and trade secret protections for computer software but does not require patent protection.[19] This does not mean, however, that patent protection for computer software is prohibited. If a

---

8   Article 2 of the Berne Convention (1971).
9   Article 8 of the Berne Convention (1971).
10   Article 9 of the Berne Convention (1971).
11   Article 11 of the Berne Convention (1971).
12   Article 11*bis* of the Berne Convention (1971).
13   Article 11ter of the Berne Convention (1971).
14   Article 12 of the Berne Convention (1971).
15   Article 13 of the Berne Convention (1971).
16   Article 14 of the Berne Convention (1971).
17   Article 10 of the Berne Convention (1971).
18   Article 16 of the Berne Convention (1971).
19   Articles 10.1 and 39 of the TRIPS Agreement.

computer program satisfies the criteria for patentability set out in a Member State's domestic implementation of the TRIPS Agreement, it may be patented in that jurisdiction. Databases that constitute intellectual creations, through the selection or arrangement of the data contained within them, are also protected.[20]

Copyrights must, at a minimum, be protected for at least 50 years from the end of the calendar year in which the work was authorised for publication.[21] Many works will be protected for much longer than this minimum term as, under Art 7(1) of the Berne Convention (which is incorporated by reference to Art 9 of the TRIPS Agreement), protection is available for those works for a term of the life of the author plus 50 years.

Trade marks and geographical indications

Article 16.1 of the TRIPS Agreement provides that: 'the owner of a registered trade mark shall have the exclusive right to prevent all third parties not having the owner's consent from using in the course of trade identical or similar signs for goods or services which are identical or similar to those in respect of which the trade mark is registered where such use would result in a likelihood of confusion.' The onus of proving that confusion does not exist falls upon the user of an identical sign to sell goods or services identical to those sold under the registered mark. The rights granted under Art 16.1 do not prejudice any existing prior rights, nor do they affect the possibility of Member States making rights available on the basis of use. However, registration of trade marks must be possible without prior use of those marks within that jurisdiction. Owners of trade marks for services must be granted rights equal to those granted to owners of trade marks for goods. Noticeably absent from the TRIPS Agreement is a prohibition on the parallel importation of trade marked goods or services.

Article 15.1 defines a trade mark as 'any sign, or any combination of signs, capable of distinguishing the goods or services of one undertaking from those of other undertakings'. These marks are specified to include words containing personal names, letters, numerals, figurative elements and combinations of colours as well as any combination of such signs. Where signs are not inherently capable of distinguishing the relevant goods or services, Member States may make the ability to register depend on distinctiveness acquired through use. Member States are also permitted to require, as a condition of registration, that signs be visually perceptible (although some Member States have also permitted trade marks based upon distinctive sounds or smells).

Under Art 6 *bis* of the Paris Agreement, well known trade marks are protected through prohibitions on the registration of marks and use of marks which conflict with well known trade marks. Such well known trade marks are granted additional protection under Art 16.2 and 16.3 of the TRIPS Agreement. The use of well known marks in other classes of goods and services must not be permitted if such use would suggest a connection with the goods or services of the owner of the well known mark and such use would cause damage to that owner.

---

20   Article 10.2 of the TRIPS Agreement.
21   Article 12 of the TRIPS Agreement.

Descriptive (or generic) marks may be the subject of fair use within TRIPS Member States, but the interests of the registered owners of those marks and third parties must be taken into account.[22]

Trade marks must be protected for a minimum of seven years and be subject to perpetual renewal.[23] If a trade mark is not used for at least three uninterrupted years in a Member State which requires such usage to maintain registration, that registration may be cancelled unless the trade mark owner can show that non-use was due to valid obstacles beyond their control. Such obstacles are defined to include import restrictions or other government controls on the goods or services for which the mark is used.[24] The use of a trade mark by another person who is subject to the control of the owner of the registered trade mark (for example, through a licence agreement) is use for the purposes of renewal.[25]

Member States may not impose special requirements such as the combined use of another trade mark before permitting the use of a trade mark for goods or services.[26] However, in the *Indonesian Autos Dispute*, the Dispute Settlement Body analysed Art 20 and found that the Indonesian Government's requirement that vehicles produced under its 'National Car Program' must be co-branded was not in breach of the TRIPS Agreement. The fact that the National Car Program provided benefits such as lower tariffs, etc, was not sufficient to cause a breach as vehicles could be sold in Indonesia outside of that Program without the requirement to use the co-branded mark.[27]

Under Art 21, compulsory licensing of trade marks is prohibited but Member States may impose other conditions on the licensing or assignment of trade marks. Trade marks may, however, be sold separately from businesses to which they belong.

The European Union was heavily involved in negotiations for the protection of geographical indications, which are of particular importance to French and Italian wine producers. Those negotiators were successful in achieving the inclusion of specific protection for such indications in Art 21 of the TRIPS Agreement. Article 21.1 defines a geographical indication as 'an indication which identifies a good as originating in the territory of a member, or a region or locality in that territory, where a given quality, reputation or other characteristic of the good is essentially attributable to its geographical origin'. Member States must enact laws that enable the owners of such indications to prevent the use of those indications by others whose products did not originate within the territory, region or locality to which the geographical indication relates.[28] Producers of wines and spirits from geographical regions are provided with additional protection against the use of indications with suffixes such as '-type' or '-style', etc, through the requirement for them to have standing to seek legal sanctions within the laws of Member States to prevent and prohibit such misuse.[29] Article 24

---

22 Article 17 of the TRIPS Agreement.
23 Article 18 of the TRIPS Agreement.
24 Article 19.1 of the TRIPS Agreement.
25 Article 19.2 of the TRIPS Agreement.
26 Article 20 of the TRIPS Agreement.
27 Geuze, M and Wager, H, 'WTO dispute settlement practice relating to the TRIPS Agreement', (1999) *Journal of International Economic Law*, 347 at 370.
28 Article 21.1 of the TRIPS Agreement.
29 Article 23 of the TRIPS Agreement.

requires Member States to commit to future negotiations to implement protections for geographical indications, but provides an exception for entities already using continuously such geographical indications for at least 10 years prior to 15 April 1994.[30]

Industrial designs

Articles 25 and 26 of the TRIPS Agreement require Member States to protect industrial designs that are created independently and are new or original. Protection is not required to be given to designs principally dictated by technical or functional requirements or to those that are too similar to pre-existing designs. Member States must provide legal means for the registered owners of industrial designs to prevent the making, selling or importing of articles bearing or embodying a design which is a copy, or substantially a copy, of the protected design, when such acts are undertaken for commercial purposes by persons who do not have the consent of that registered owner. Registered industrial designs must be protected for a minimum of 10 years.

Patents

Article 2 of the TRIPS Agreement requires all Member States to comply with Arts 1–12 and 19 of the Paris Convention for the Protection of Industrial Property (1967). However, the TRIPS Agreement also contains mechanisms that provide substantially greater protection for patent holders than existed under the Paris Convention. Under Art 27.1, patents 'shall be available for any inventions, whether products or processes, in all fields of technology, provided that they are new, involve an inventive step and are capable of industrial application'. This requirement restricts the power of less developed countries to prohibit the patentability of entire sectors of their economies. Discriminations in the laws of Member States based upon the place of invention, the field of technology and whether products are imported or locally produced are also prohibited.[31] Patent holders must also have the right to be able to supply exclusively a market with imported products (which prevents Member States from acquiring compulsorily domestic manufacturing knowledge).[32] Member States must also provide patent protection for 20 years from the date of filing of the application for the patent (this provision required the US to amend its laws to extend patent protection from 17 to 20 years).[33] Disclosure of patent claims is required under Art 29.1. If a patent is denied or revoked, avenues must be available within Member States for judicial review of that decision.[34]

Article 27.2 and 27.3 contains important exceptions to the broad concept of what is patentable as defined by Art 27.1. Article 27.2 provides that: 'Members may exclude from patentability inventions, the prevention within their territory of the commercial

---

30 Article 24.4 of the TRIPS Agreement.
31 In the Canadian Pharmaceutical Patents dispute, the DSB refused to import and apply definitions of 'discrimination' developed under the GATT into its analysis of the term under Art 28.1 of the TRIPS Agreement. See WT/DS/114/R available at www.wto.org.
32 Article 28.1 of the TRIPS Agreement.
33 See Article 33 of the TRIPS Agreement and the amendment made to 35 USC, s 154.
34 Article 32 of the TRIPS Agreement.

exploitation of which is necessary to protect *ordre public* or morality, including to protect human, animal or plant life or health or to avoid serious prejudice to the environment, provided that such exclusion is not made merely because the exploitation is prohibited by their law.' Member States may also exclude from patentability diagnostic, therapeutic and surgical methods for treating humans or animals. Plants and animals (except for micro-organisms) may be excluded from patentability but Member States must create *effective sui generis* systems for the protection of plant varieties, or utilise a combined system of patents and *sui generis* protection.[35] These exceptions were the subject of lengthy debate and were insisted upon by negotiators from less developed countries to counter the breadth of Art 27.1. 'Ordre public' is not clearly defined in international law and is likely to be one of the issues that will be the subject to review by the DSB in the future.[36]

Article 28.1 requires Member States to create legal systems which provide the owner of a patent within that Member State with the exclusive right to prevent third parties not having the owner's consent from the acts of: making, using, offering for sale, selling, or importing the product for those purposes. Owners of patented processes must have the exclusive right to prevent third parties not having the owner's consent from the act of using the process, and from the acts of: using, offering for sale, selling, or importing for these purposes at least the product obtained directly by that process. The exclusive rights conferred under Art 28.1 and 28.2 are expressed by a footnote within the TRIPS Agreement itself to be subject to the explicit exclusion of the concept of exhaustion from the TRIPS Agreement under Art 6.

Article 30 permits Member States to create exceptions to the exclusive rights granted under Art 27.1. However, such exclusions must be limited, must not conflict unreasonably with the normal exploitation of the patent and must not prejudice unreasonably the legitimate interests of the patent owner (taking into account the legitimate interests of third parties).[37] For example, Member States could provide for exceptions based upon private, non-commercial acts, research, experimentation on the invention, or for parallel imports of the patented goods or methods.[38]

Article 31 imposes 12 separate limitations on Member States that wish to draft laws granting exceptions under Art 30. These limitations include requirements that each application for a limitation be considered separately, attempts must have been unsuccessfully made to seek approval for the use from the patent holder on reasonable terms and conditions, the use must be non-exclusive and non-assignable. Any products produced must be predominantly sold in the domestic markets of that Member State and adequate remuneration must be paid to the rights holder. The adequacy of such remuneration must also be subject to judicial review. These requirements do not apply if an exception is permitted under Art 30 as a result of a determination of anti-competitive conduct by the holder of the patent.

---

35 Article 27.3 of the TRIPS Agreement.
36 Correa, C, *Intellectual Property Rights, the WTO and Developing Countries*, 2000, London: Zed Books, pp 62–67.
37 For an extensive discussion of the requirements of Art 30, see the decision of the Dispute Settlement Panel in the Canadian Pharmaceutical Patents dispute WT/DS/170/R at www.wto.org.
38 Correa, *op cit*, pp 75–76.

Integrated circuits

Article 35 of the TRIPS Agreement imposes on Member States an obligation to comply with Arts 2–7, 12 and para 3 of Art 16 of the Treaty on Intellectual Property in Respect of Integrated Circuits (1989). Article 36 requires Member States to create laws which provide holders of registered integrated circuit designs with the power to prevent unauthorised persons from 'importing, selling, or otherwise distributing for commercial purposes a protected layout-design, an integrated circuit in which a protected layout-design is incorporated, or an article incorporating such an integrated circuit only in so far as it continues to contain an unlawfully reproduced layout-design'. In the event that a person did not know and had no reasonable grounds to know, when acquiring an integrated circuit or article incorporating such an integrated circuit, that it incorporated an unlawfully reproduced layout-design, that person is permitted to import sell or otherwise distribute that integrated circuit or article.[39] If a Member State wishes to issue a compulsory licence for an integrated circuit, Art 37.2 requires that the provisions of Art 31(a)–(k) apply *mutatis mutandis*. The minimum term of protection for integrated circuit designs is 10 years from the date of registration in Member States that require registration, and 10 years from the date of first commercial exploitation anywhere in the world in Member States where registration is not required.[40]

Undisclosed information

Article 39 of the TRIPS Agreement provides protection for undisclosed information (often known as trade secrets) and information provided to governments or governmental agencies. Member States are required to enact legislation that permits the holders of trade secrets to prevent those secrets from being 'disclosed to, acquired by, or used by others without their consent in a manner contrary to honest commercial practices'.[41] Such information must not be generally known or readily accessible to persons within the relevant field, have commercial value and have been the subject of reasonable efforts by its holder to be kept secret. Under Art 39.3, undisclosed test data provided to government agencies for the purposes of testing (for example, pharmaceuticals and agricultural chemicals) must not be disclosed unless such disclosure is necessary to protect the public interest or steps have been taken to counteract unfair commercial use.

Transitional arrangements

Under Art 65 of the TRIPS Agreement, Member States were given a minimum of one year from the date of entry into force of the Agreement to implement or amend their domestic laws to comply with their obligations under the Agreement. Developing country Member States were permitted five years to comply and could delay the application of patent obligations for previously unprotected fields of technology for an

---

39 Article 37.1 of the TRIPS Agreement.
40 Article 38 of the TRIPS Agreement.
41 Article 39.2 of the TRIPS Agreement.

additional five years. Except for obligations under Arts 3–5, least developed Member States could delay their implementation of the TRIPS Agreement for up to 10 years and could receive assistance from developed Member States to achieve such implementation.[42] Under Art 67, developed Member States agreed to provide, on request and on mutually agreed terms and conditions, technical and financial co-operation in favour of developing and least developed Member States including 'assistance in the preparation of laws and regulations on the protection and enforcement of intellectual property rights as well as on the prevention of their abuse, and to provide support regarding the establishment or reinforcement of domestic offices and agencies relevant to those matters, including the training of personnel'.[43]

Enforcement

Article 41 of the TRIPS Agreement obliges Member States to create domestic laws which contain '… enforcement procedures to permit effective action against any act of infringement of intellectual property rights covered by this Agreement, including expeditious remedies to prevent infringements and remedies which constitute a deterrent to further infringements'. Such laws must be designed to 'avoid the creation of barriers to legitimate trade and to provide for safeguards against their abuse'.

Those domestic procedures must be fair and equitable, without unnecessary complication, cost or delay, nor involve overly onerous time limits.[44] Decisions should (but are not required to) contain reasons, be made in writing, and copies should be provided to the relevant parties. The parties must have been provided with the opportunity to be heard on all matters of evidence used in making the decision.[45] Member States must provide avenues of judicial review for administrative decisions and appeals on at least legal issues when disputes are resolved by courts. Criminal prosecutions are not required to be subject to appeal under the TRIPS Agreement.[46]

Articles 42–49 of the TRIPS Agreement set out broad principles for fair and equitable procedures, evidence, injunctions, damages, other remedies, rights of information and indemnification for the defendant and administrative procedures. The TRIPS Agreement does not attempt to specify exactly how a Member State will provide the means to enable intellectual property owners to enforce their TRIPS Agreement rights within the legal system of that Member State, it merely specifies the broad goals that such legal systems must achieve.

Article 41.5 of the TRIPS Agreement provides an important protection for least and less developed Member States. It provides that Member States are not required to redirect judicial resources towards the protection of the rights of intellectual property owners as compared to the rights of persons under the general law of that Member State. Thus, a Member State with an under-resourced judicial system that results in lengthy delays in hearing disputes is not required to create special intellectual property

---

42 Article 66 of the TRIPS Agreement.
43 Article 67 of the TRIPS Agreement.
44 Article 41.2 of the TRIPS Agreement.
45 Article 41.3 of the TRIPS Agreement.
46 Article 41.4 of the TRIPS Agreement.

courts, nor to transfer its scarce judicial resources towards reducing delays in hearing intellectual property disputes as compared to other legal disputes.

Article 50 requires that Member States create methods for intellectual property rights owners to seek preliminary (and *ex parte*) orders from domestic courts to protect their rights. Such intellectual property rights owners must also be able to petition the customs offices of Member States to stop the release into that Member State of goods that the rights owner reasonably believes are 'pirated copyright goods' or which contain 'counterfeit trade marks'.

'Pirated copyright goods' are defined in footnote 14(b) to the TRIPS Agreement as 'any goods which are copies made without the consent of the right holder or person duly authorised by the right holder in the country of production and which are made directly or indirectly from an article where the making of that copy would have constituted an infringement of a copyright or a related right under the law of the country of importation'. Goods which contain 'counterfeit trade marks' are defined in footnote 14(a) as 'any goods, including packaging, bearing without authorisation a trade mark which is identical to the trade mark validly registered in respect of such goods, or which cannot be distinguished in its essential aspects from such a trade mark, and which thereby infringes the rights of the owner of the trade mark in question under the law of the country of importation'.

Article 61 of the TRIPS Agreement requires that Member States must enact criminal offences for wilful trade mark counterfeiting or copyright piracy on a commercial scale. Punishments should include imprisonment and/or fines equivalent to punishments imposed for offences of corresponding gravity.

Dispute Settlement Body (DSB)

Disputes about whether a Member State has complied with its obligations under the TRIPS Agreement may only be brought by other Member States (and not by intellectual property rights holders themselves). To better enable Member States to determine whether other Member States are in compliance with their treaty obligations, Art 63 requires that each Member State must publish its laws implementing the TRIPS Agreement and provide copies of those laws to the TRIPS Council. If a Member State believes that another Member State has not complied with its obligations under the TRIPS Agreement, it may only take action by bringing a dispute before the WTO DSB.[47]

Interestingly, the vast majority of TRIPS Agreement disputes have been between two highly developed Member States. Of the less developed Member States, only India, Pakistan and Indonesia have had to defend their compliance with their TRIPS Agreement obligations. The USA had initiated 11 disputes, the European Union four and Canada one. No less developed countries had initiated disputes at the time of writing.[48]

---

47 Article 64 of the TRIPS Agreement.
48 See list of disputes set out in 'WTO TRIPS Agreement Analytic Index', available at www.wto.org/english/res_e/booksp_e/analytic_index_e/trips_03_e.htm.

In 1996, a WTO DSB panel was established to resolve a dispute between the US and India concerning India's compliance with its obligations under Art 70.8 and 70.9 of the TRIPS Agreement.[49] The panel found that India's administrative processes were insufficient to ensure that pharmaceutical and agricultural chemical patent holders were able to lodge applications for patents that would be backdated upon the expiry of India's five year transition period under Art 65. India had also failed to provide sufficient legal means for those patent holders to exclusively market their products during that five year period, as required by Art 70.9. This panel decision was appealed by India, but the Appellate Body upheld the conclusions of the panel.[50]

After this decision, the European Union also initiated a dispute against India on the same grounds.[51] This was done because a Member State must receive a decision in its favour before it can take action (for example, impose countervailing tariffs on the exports of the defending Member State) under the TRIPS Agreement.[52] Whilst the panel heard the European Union's arguments after the panel that heard the US' claim had published its decision on the same issues, the EC–India panel stated that it did not consider itself bound by the decision of the US–India panel. It would, however, take that decision into account.[53]

As was discussed earlier in the section relating to trade marks, the US initiated a dispute against Indonesia over Arts 3 and 20, and of the TRIPS Agreement in relation to Indonesia's National Car Programme[54] (in the context of a much larger dispute involving the GATT and other international agreements). The panel found that the US was unable to show that Indonesia had breached its obligations in relation to national treatment under the TRIPS Agreement and therefore the complaint was dismissed.

In a dispute initiated in 1999, the European Community Union alleged that Canada had breached its obligations under Arts 27.1, 28 and 33 of the TRIPS Agreement,[55] as it did not provide full protection for pharmaceutical patents over the entire life of those patents. In particular, Canadian legislation permitted a third party to use another party's patents without consent prior to the expiry of that patent for the purposes of preparing for later access to the Canadian market after the expiry of the other party's patent rights (including the right to stockpile those patented products in the last six months of the patent's life).

In a later dispute,[56] delays in granting patents under Canadian law resulted in Canada being found to be in breach of Art 33 of the TRIPS Agreement. The panel found that patent holders would have faced additional expenses and time delays in the event that a patent examiner rejected a patent application and thus, as Art 33 granted 20 years protection from the date of filing, such delays between filing and

---

49   See WTO Panel Report WT/DS/50/R available at www.wto.org.
50   See WT/DS50/AB/R available at www.wto.org.
51   See documents available at WT/DS/79/R, available at www.wto.org.
52   Geuze, *op cit*, at 350.
53   *Ibid* at 351.
54   See WT/DS/59/R available at www.wto.org.
55   See WT/DS/114/R available at www.wto.org and Geuze, *op cit*, at 374–75.
56   See WT/DS/170/R available at www.wto.org

grant of the patent would have reduced the protection period for patents.[57] The panel rejected Canada's contention that the procedures set out in Art 62.2 of the TRIPS Agreement would have permitted a lesser 'effective period' of protection for patents. On appeal, the Appellate Review Board upheld the decision of the panel and stated, 'a harmonious interpretation of Article 33 and Article 62.2 must regard these two treaty provisions as distinct and separate Articles containing obligations that must be fulfilled distinctly and separately'.[58]

CONCLUSION

The TRIPS Agreement integrates intellectual property rights within the scope of the WTO. It extends those rights to many countries that previously had much weaker intellectual property regimes and creates a strong dispute resolution process, something that had been lacking in previous intellectual property treaties. Whilst the Agreement could be argued to favour net exporters of intellectual property rights, it does contain a number of provisions designed to protect the interests and public policies of Member States, especially those still seeking to 'catch up' technologically.

The TRIPS Agreement has expanded the geographic spread of minimum levels of protection for intellectual property rights, but has not necessarily created consistency around the world. Developed countries have, in some situations, amended their laws to exceed the levels of protection required by the TRIPS Agreement, whereas less developed countries have taken advantage of the compliance time periods to implement minimum standards at a slower rate. The extent to which less and least developed countries will attempt to further minimise changes to their laws through the exceptions and protections provided in Arts 7 and 8 of the TRIPS Agreement is unclear. It is an issue that is likely to be the subject of the WTO dispute settlement process provided for under the TRIPS Agreement.

In an unexpected twist, highly developed countries have mainly used the dispute resolution process established by the TRIPS Agreement as a negotiating tool to resolve trade disputes between themselves.[59] Most such disputes have been settled. In contrast, disputes between developed and less developed countries over compliance with the TRIPS Agreement (whilst fewer in number) have been more likely to be resolved by Panel decisions.

The TRIPS Agreement is still in the process of implementation by Member States and its efficacy is not yet clear. The specific exclusion of the concept of exhaustion from regulation highlights the degree to which Member States differ on important issues. Only the passage of further time will tell whether the TRIPS Agreement achieves the goals of its proponents.

---

57 'WTO TRIPS Agreement Analytical Index', at www.wto.org/english/res_e/booksp_e/analytic_index_e/trips_03_e.htm.
58 See WT/DS/170/ABR available at www.wto.org.
59 Kumar, A, 'Dispute Settlement Body (WTO): battleground of developed countries', available at www.indlaw.com (last visited 8 April 2004).

MAJOR AGREEMENTS

There are many treaties regulating intellectual property rights. For copies of these treaties, see WIPO: Treaties and Contracting Parties at www.wipo.int/treaties/en/index.html.

Intellectual property treaties

Copyright

- Berne Convention for the Protection of Literary and Artistic Works
- WIPO Copyright Treaty
- WIPO Performances and Phonograms Treaty
- Rome Convention for the Protection of Performers, Producers of Phonograms and Broadcasting Organisations
- Convention for the Protection of Producers of Phonograms Against Unauthorised Duplication of Their Phonograms
- Brussels Convention Relating to the Distribution of Programme-Carrying Signals Transmitted by Satellite

Patent and trade marks

- Paris Convention for the Protection of Industrial Property
- Patent Law Treaty
- Trademark Law Treaty
- Madrid Agreement for the Repression of False and Deceptive Indications of Source on Goods
- Nairobi Treaty on the Protection of the Olympic Symbol

Integrated circuits

- Washington Treaty on Intellectual Property in Respect of Integrated Circuits

Global protection system treaties

Trade marks

- Madrid Agreement Concerning the International Registration of Marks
- Lisbon Agreement for the Protection of Appellations of Origin and their International Registration

Patents

- Patent Co-operation Treaty
- Budapest Treaty on the International Recognition of the Deposit of Micro-organisms for the Purposes of Patent Procedure

Industrial designs

• Hague Agreement Concerning the International Deposit of Industrial Designs

Classification treaties

Trade marks

• Nice Agreement Concerning the International Classification of Goods and Services for the Purposes of the Registration of Marks
• Vienna Agreement Establishing an International Classification of the Figurative Elements of Marks

Patents

• Strasbourg Agreement Concerning the International Patent Classification

Industrial designs

• Locarno Agreement Establishing an International Classification for Industrial Designs

TUTORIAL QUESTIONS

1   Which areas of intellectual property rights are regulated under the TRIPS Agreement? Which areas were not included? Why?

2   Why did developed countries push for the inclusion of intellectual property rights in the WTO agenda? What problems had those countries previously faced when trying to negotiate bilateral treaties?

3   What exceptions are available to TRIPS Member States when implementing the TRIPS Agreement into their domestic intellectual property laws? Why were concessions given to less developed countries and least developed countries?

4   If the TRIPS Agreement sets out minimum standards of protection for intellectual property rights, in what circumstances do you think that Member States should provide higher protection? Give examples.

5   Why was the concept of exhaustion of intellectual property rights excluded specifically from the dispute settlement process under the TRIPS Agreement (Art 6)?

6   Do you think the less developed countries will benefit or be disadvantaged by the TRIPS Agreement? Consider arguments for and against your position, giving examples.

7   Should less developed countries be able to require the granting of compulsory licences over patents granted to companies based in developed countries for research conducted into plants or animals found within those less developed countries?

8   Why were geographical indications singled out for protection under the TRIPS Agreement? Which countries and which industries lobbied hard for their inclusion?

9 How does the TRIPS Agreement interact with pre-existing treaties covering intellectual property rights?

10 How does the inclusion of rights over 'undisclosed information' under Art 39 of the TRIPS Agreement affect less developed countries? If the majority of such undisclosed information is produced by entities in developed countries, what benefits would less developed countries receive by providing protection to such information if it will rarely ever be disclosed legally or enter the public domain (see further, patents)?

11 What options are available to Member States to control anti-competitive licensing practices under the TRIPS Agreement?

12 Why was it necessary to expand upon the patent protections provided under the Paris Convention (1967)? What industries do you think will most benefit from the additional rights granted under the TRIPS Agreement?

FURTHER READING

Anderson, R, 'The interface between competition policy and intellectual property in the context of the international trading system' (1998) *Journal of International Economic Law*, Vol 1, No 4, 655.

Beier, F-K and Schricker, G (eds), *From GATT to TRIPs: the Agreement on Trade-Related Aspects of Intellectual Property Rights*, 1996, Weinheim, Germany: VCH

Blakeney, M, *Trade Related Aspects of Intellectual Property Rights: a Concise Guide to the TRIPs Agreement*, 1996, London: Sweet & Maxwell.

Campbell, D and Cotter, S, *International Intellectual Property Law: Global Jurisdictions*, 1996, New York: J Wiley & Sons.

Correa, C, *Intellectual Property Rights, the WTO and Developing Countries: The TRIPS Agreement and Policy Options*, 2000, London: Zed Books.

Correa, C and Yusuf, A (eds), *Intellectual Property and International Trade*, 1998, London: Kluwer Law International.

D'Amato, A and Long, D, *International Intellectual Property Law*, 1997, London: Kluwer Law International.

Department of Foreign Affairs and Trade, *Intellectual Property, A Vital Asset for Australia: Background Briefing on the Review of the TRIPS Agreement (Agreement on Trade-Related Aspects of Intellectual Property Rights)*, 2000, Canberra, Australia.

Gervais, D, *The TRIPS Agreement: Drafting History and Analysis*, 1998, London: Sweet & Maxwell.

Geuze, M and Wager, H, 'WTO dispute settlement practice relating to the TRIPS Agreement' (1999) *Journal of International Economic Law* 347–84.

Kumar, A, 'Dispute Settlement Body (WTO): battleground of developed countries', available at www.indlaw.com (last visited 8 April 2004).

Leonardos, G, 'TRIPS' trademark, geographical indications and trade secret provisions: a Latin American perspective', available at www.leonardos.com.br/Textos/pdf/EctaComplete_.pdf (last visited 27 April 2004).

Maskus, K, *Intellectual Property Rights in the Global Economy*, 2000, Washington: Institute for International Economics.

Office of Technological Assessment, 'Intellectual Property Rights in an Age of Electronics and Information', 1986, available at www.wws.princeton.edu/cgi-bin/byteserv.prl/~ota/disk2/1986/8610_n.html (last visited 20 February 2004).

Reichman, J, 'Securing compliance with the TRIPS Agreement after USA v India' (1998) *Journal of International Economic Law*, Vol 1, No 4, 585.

Revesz, J, *Trade-related Aspects of Intellectual Property Rights*, 1999, Productivity Commission Staff Research Paper, Canberra: AGPS.

Rozek, R, 'The WTO dispute settlement mechanism: TRIPS rulings and the developing countries: prospects after Seattle' (2001) *Journal of World Intellectual Property*, Vol 4, No 2, 271.

Sell, S, *Private Power, Public Law: the Globalization of Intellectual Property Rights*, 2003, New York: CUP.

South Centre, 'The TRIPS Agreement, a guide for the south', available at www.southcentre.org/publications/trips/toc.htm (last visited 15 March 2004).

Vandoren, P, 'The TRIPS Agreement: a rising star?' (2001) *Journal of World Intellectual Property*, Vol 4, No 3, 307.

Watal, J, *Intellectual Property Rights in the WTO and Developing Countries*, 2001, Boston: Kluwer Academic Publishers.

World Trade Organisation, 'TRIPS Agreement Analytic Index', available at www.wto.org/english/res_e/booksp_e/analytic_index_e/trips_01_e.htm through to /trips_04_e.htm (last visited 20 February 2004).

Yambrusic, E, *Trade Based Approaches to the Protection of Intellectual Property*, 1992, New York: Oceana Publications.

APPENDIX

ANNEX 1C TO THE AGREEMENT ESTABLISHING THE WORLD TRADE ORGANISATION

AGREEMENT ON TRADE-RELATED ASPECTS OF INTELLECTUAL PROPERTY RIGHTS

PART I – GENERAL PROVISIONS AND BASIC PRINCIPLES

PART II – STANDARDS CONCERNING THE AVAILABILITY, SCOPE AND USE OF INTELLECTUAL PROPERTY RIGHTS

1   Copyright and related rights
2   Trademarks
3   Geographical indications
4   Industrial designs
5   Patents
6   Layout-designs (topographies) of integrated circuits
7   Protection of undisclosed information
8   Control of anti-competitive practices in contractual licences

PART III – ENFORCEMENT OF INTELLECTUAL PROPERTY RIGHTS

1   General obligations
2   Civil and administrative procedures and remedies
3   Provisional measures
4   Special requirements related to border measures
5   Criminal procedures

PART IV – ACQUISITION AND MAINTENANCE OF INTELLECTUAL PROPERTY RIGHTS AND RELATED INTER PARTES PROCEDURES

PART V – DISPUTE PREVENTION AND SETTLEMENT

PART VI – TRANSITIONAL ARRANGEMENTS

PART VII – INSTITUTIONAL ARRANGEMENTS; FINAL PROVISIONS

AGREEMENT ON TRADE-RELATED ASPECTS OF INTELLECTUAL PROPERTY RIGHTS

Members,

Desiring to reduce distortions and impediments to international trade, and taking into account the need to promote effective and adequate protection of intellectual property rights, and to ensure that measures and procedures to enforce intellectual property rights do not themselves become barriers to legitimate trade;

Recognizing, to this end, the need for new rules and disciplines concerning:

(a) the applicability of the basic principles of GATT 1994 and of relevant international intellectual property agreements or conventions;

(b) the provision of adequate standards and principles concerning the availability, scope and use of trade-related intellectual property rights;

(c) the provision of effective and appropriate means for the enforcement of trade-related intellectual property rights, taking into account differences in national legal systems;

(d) the provision of effective and expeditious procedures for the multilateral prevention and settlement of disputes between governments; and

(e) transitional arrangements aiming at the fullest participation in the results of the negotiations;

Recognizing the need for a multilateral framework of principles, rules and disciplines dealing with international trade in counterfeit goods;

Recognizing that intellectual property rights are private rights;

Recognizing the underlying public policy objectives of national systems for the protection of intellectual property, including developmental and technological objectives;

Recognizing also the special needs of the least-developed country Members in respect of maximum flexibility in the domestic implementation of laws and regulations in order to enable them to create a sound and viable technological base;

Emphasizing the importance of reducing tensions by reaching strengthened commitments to resolve disputes on trade-related intellectual property issues through multilateral procedures;

Desiring to establish a mutually supportive relationship between the WTO and the World Intellectual Property Organization (referred to in this Agreement as 'WIPO') as well as other relevant international organizations;

Hereby agree as follows:

PART I – GENERAL PROVISIONS AND BASIC PRINCIPLES

Article 1 – Nature and scope of obligations

1   Members shall give effect to the provisions of this Agreement. Members may, but shall not be obliged to, implement in their law more extensive protection than is required by this Agreement, provided that such protection does not contravene the provisions of this Agreement. Members shall be free to determine the appropriate method of implementing the provisions of this Agreement within their own legal system and practice.

2   For the purposes of this Agreement, the term 'intellectual property' refers to all categories of intellectual property that are the subject of Sections 1 through 7 of Part II.

3   Members shall accord the treatment provided for in this Agreement to the nationals of other Members.[60] In respect of the relevant intellectual property right, the nationals of other Members shall be understood as those natural or legal persons that would meet the criteria for eligibility for protection provided for in the Paris Convention (1967), the Berne Convention (1971), the Rome Convention and the Treaty on Intellectual Property in Respect of Integrated Circuits, were all Members of the WTO members of those conventions.[61] Any Member availing itself of the possibilities provided in paragraph 3 of Article 5 or paragraph 2 of Article 6 of the Rome Convention shall make a notification as foreseen in those provisions to the Council for Trade-Related Aspects of intellectual property rights (the 'Council for TRIPS').

Article 2 – Intellectual property conventions

1   In respect of Parts II, III and IV of this Agreement, Members shall comply with Articles 1 through 12, and Article 19, of the Paris Convention (1967).

2   Nothing in Parts I to IV of this Agreement shall derogate from existing obligations that Members may have to each other under the Paris Convention, the Berne Convention, the Rome Convention and the Treaty on Intellectual Property in Respect of Integrated Circuits.

---

60   When 'nationals' are referred to in this Agreement, they shall be deemed, in the case of a separate customs territory member of the WTO, to mean persons, natural or legal, who are domiciled or who have a real and effective industrial or commercial establishment in that customs territory.

61   In this Agreement, 'Paris Convention' refers to the Paris Convention for the Protection of Industrial Property; 'Paris Convention (1967)' refers to the Stockholm Act of this Convention of 14 July 1967. 'Berne Convention' refers to the Berne Convention for the Protection of Literary and Artistic Works; 'Berne Convention (1971)' refers to the Paris Act of this Convention of 24 July 1971. 'Rome Convention' refers to the International Convention for the Protection of Performers, Producers of Phonograms and Broadcasting Organizations, adopted at Rome on 26 October 1961. 'Treaty on Intellectual Property in Respect of Integrated Circuits' (IPIC Treaty) refers to the Treaty on Intellectual Property in Respect of Integrated Circuits, adopted at Washington on 26 May 1989. 'WTO Agreement' refers to the Agreement Establishing the WTO.

Article 3 – National treatment

1   Each Member shall accord to the nationals of other Members treatment no less favourable than that it accords to its own nationals with regard to the protection[62] of intellectual property, subject to the exceptions already provided in, respectively, the Paris Convention (1967), the Berne Convention (1971), the Rome Convention or the Treaty on Intellectual Property in Respect of Integrated Circuits. In respect of performers, producers of phonograms and broadcasting organizations, this obligation only applies in respect of the rights provided under this Agreement. Any Member availing itself of the possibilities provided in Article 6 of the Berne Convention (1971) or paragraph 1(b) of Article 16 of the Rome Convention shall make a notification as foreseen in those provisions to the Council for TRIPS.

2   Members may avail themselves of the exceptions permitted under paragraph 1 in relation to judicial and administrative procedures, including the designation of an address for service or the appointment of an agent within the jurisdiction of a Member, only where such exceptions are necessary to secure compliance with laws and regulations which are not inconsistent with the provisions of this Agreement and where such practices are not applied in a manner which would constitute a disguised restriction on trade.

Article 4 – Most-favoured-nation treatment

With regard to the protection of intellectual property, any advantage, favour, privilege or immunity granted by a Member to the nationals of any other country shall be accorded immediately and unconditionally to the nationals of all other Members. Exempted from this obligation are any advantage, favour, privilege or immunity accorded by a Member:

(a) deriving from international agreements on judicial assistance or law enforcement of a general nature and not particularly confined to the protection of intellectual property;

(b) granted in accordance with the provisions of the Berne Convention (1971) or the Rome Convention authorizing that the treatment accorded be a function not of national treatment but of the treatment accorded in another country;

(c) in respect of the rights of performers, producers of phonograms and broadcasting organizations not provided under this Agreement;

(d) deriving from international agreements related to the protection of intellectual property which entered into force prior to the entry into force of the WTO Agreement, provided that such agreements are notified to the Council for TRIPS and do not constitute an arbitrary or unjustifiable discrimination against nationals of other Members.

Article 5 – Multilateral agreements on acquisition or maintenance of protection

The obligations under Articles 3 and 4 do not apply to procedures provided in multilateral agreements concluded under the auspices of WIPO relating to the acquisition or maintenance of intellectual property rights.

Article 6 – Exhaustion

For the purposes of dispute settlement under this Agreement, subject to the provisions of Articles 3 and 4 nothing in this Agreement shall be used to address the issue of the exhaustion of intellectual property rights.

Article 7 – Objectives

The protection and enforcement of intellectual property rights should contribute to the promotion of technological innovation and to the transfer and dissemination of technology, to the mutual advantage of producers and users of technological knowledge and in a manner conducive to social and economic welfare, and to a balance of rights and obligations.

---

62   For the purposes of Arts 3 and 4, 'protection' shall include matters affecting the availability, acquisition, scope, maintenance and enforcement of intellectual property rights as well as those matters affecting the use of intellectual property rights specifically addressed in this Agreement.

Article 8 – Principles

1 Members may, in formulating or amending their laws and regulations, adopt measures necessary to protect public health and nutrition, and to promote the public interest in sectors of vital importance to their socio-economic and technological development, provided that such measures are consistent with the provisions of this Agreement.

2 Appropriate measures, provided that they are consistent with the provisions of this Agreement, may be needed to prevent the abuse of intellectual property rights by right holders or the resort to practices which unreasonably restrain trade or adversely affect the international transfer of technology.

PART II – STANDARDS CONCERNING THE AVAILABILITY, SCOPE AND USE OF INTELLECTUAL PROPERTY RIGHTS

Section 1 – Copyright and related rights

Article 9 – Relation to the Berne Convention

1 Members shall comply with Articles 1 through 21 of the Berne Convention (1971) and the Appendix thereto. However, Members shall not have rights or obligations under this Agreement in respect of the rights conferred under Article *6bis* of that Convention or of the rights derived there from.

2 Copyright protection shall extend to expressions and not to ideas, procedures, methods of operation or mathematical concepts as such.

Article 10 – Computer programs and compilations of data

1 Computer programs, whether in source or object code, shall be protected as literary works under the Berne Convention (1971).

2 Compilations of data or other material, whether in machine readable or other form, which by reason of the selection or arrangement of their contents constitute intellectual creations shall be protected as such. Such protection, which shall not extend to the data or material itself, shall be without prejudice to any copyright subsisting in the data or material itself.

Article 11 – Rental rights

In respect of at least computer programs and cinematographic works, a Member shall provide authors and their successors in title the right to authorize or to prohibit the commercial rental to the public of originals or copies of their copyright works. A Member shall be excepted from this obligation in respect of cinematographic works unless such rental has led to widespread copying of such works which is materially impairing the exclusive right of reproduction conferred in that Member on authors and their successors in title. In respect of computer programs, this obligation does not apply to rentals where the program itself is not the essential object of the rental.

Article 12 – Term of protection

Whenever the term of protection of a work, other than a photographic work or a work of applied art, is calculated on a basis other than the life of a natural person, such term shall be no less than 50 years from the end of the calendar year of authorized publication, or, failing such authorized publication within 50 years from the making of the work, 50 years from the end of the calendar year of making.

Article 13 – Limitations and exceptions

Members shall confine limitations or exceptions to exclusive rights to certain special cases which do not conflict with a normal exploitation of the work and do not unreasonably prejudice the legitimate interests of the right holder.

Article 14 – Protection of performers, producers of phonograms (sound recordings) and broadcasting organizations

1 In respect of a fixation of their performance on a phonogram, performers shall have the possibility of preventing the following acts when undertaken without their authorization: the fixation of their unfixed performance and the reproduction of such fixation. Performers shall also have the possibility of preventing the following acts when undertaken without

their authorization: the broadcasting by wireless means and the communication to the public of their live performance.

2 Producers of phonograms shall enjoy the right to authorize or prohibit the direct or indirect reproduction of their phonograms.

3 Broadcasting organizations shall have the right to prohibit the following acts when undertaken without their authorization: the fixation, the reproduction of fixations, and the rebroadcasting by wireless means of broadcasts, as well as the communication to the public of television broadcasts of the same. Where Members do not grant such rights to broadcasting organizations, they shall provide owners of copyright in the subject matter of broadcasts with the possibility of preventing the above acts, subject to the provisions of the Berne Convention (1971).

4 The provisions of Article 11 in respect of computer programs shall apply *mutatis mutandis* to producers of phonograms and any other right holders in phonograms as determined in a Member's law. If on 15 April 1994 a Member has in force a system of equitable remuneration of right holders in respect of the rental of phonograms, it may maintain such system provided that the commercial rental of phonograms is not giving rise to the material impairment of the exclusive rights of reproduction of right holders.

5 The term of the protection available under this Agreement to performers and producers of phonograms shall last at least until the end of a period of 50 years computed from the end of the calendar year in which the fixation was made or the performance took place. The term of protection granted pursuant to paragraph 3 shall last for at least 20 years from the end of the calendar year in which the broadcast took place.

6 Any Member may, in relation to the rights conferred under paragraphs 1, 2 and 3, provide for conditions, limitations, exceptions and reservations to the extent permitted by the Rome Convention. However, the provisions of Article 18 of the Berne Convention (1971) shall also apply, *mutatis mutandis*, to the rights of performers and producers of phonograms in phonograms.

Section 2 – Trademarks

Article 15 – Protectable subject matter

1 Any sign, or any combination of signs, capable of distinguishing the goods or services of one undertaking from those of other undertakings, shall be capable of constituting a trademark. Such signs, in particular words including personal names, letters, numerals, figurative elements and combinations of colours as well as any combination of such signs, shall be eligible for registration as trademarks. Where signs are not inherently capable of distinguishing the relevant goods or services, Members may make registrability depend on distinctiveness acquired through use. Members may require, as a condition of registration, that signs be visually perceptible.

2 Paragraph 1 shall not be understood to prevent a Member from denying registration of a trademark on other grounds, provided that they do not derogate from the provisions of the Paris Convention (1967).

3 Members may make registrability depend on use. However, actual use of a trademark shall not be a condition for filing an application for registration. An application shall not be refused solely on the ground that intended use has not taken place before the expiry of a period of three years from the date of application.

4 The nature of the goods or services to which a trademark is to be applied shall in no case form an obstacle to registration of the trademark.

5 Members shall publish each trademark either before it is registered or promptly after it is registered and shall afford a reasonable opportunity for petitions to cancel the registration. In addition, Members may afford an opportunity for the registration of a trademark to be opposed.

Article 16 – Rights conferred

1 The owner of a registered trademark shall have the exclusive right to prevent all third parties not having the owner's consent from using in the course of trade identical or similar signs for goods or services which are identical or similar to those in respect of

which the trademark is registered where such use would result in a likelihood of confusion. In case of the use of an identical sign for identical goods or services, a likelihood of confusion shall be presumed. The rights described above shall not prejudice any existing prior rights, nor shall they affect the possibility of Members making rights available on the basis of use.

2   Article 6*bis* of the Paris Convention (1967) shall apply, *mutatis mutandis*, to services. In determining whether a trademark is well-known, Members shall take account of the knowledge of the trademark in the relevant sector of the public, including knowledge in the Member concerned which has been obtained as a result of the promotion of the trademark.

3   Article 6*bis* of the Paris Convention (1967) shall apply, *mutatis mutandis*, to goods or services which are not similar to those in respect of which a trademark is registered, provided that use of that trademark in relation to those goods or services would indicate a connection between those goods or services and the owner of the registered trademark and provided that the interests of the owner of the registered trademark are likely to be damaged by such use.

Article 17 – Exceptions

Members may provide limited exceptions to the rights conferred by a trademark, such as fair use of descriptive terms, provided that such exceptions take account of the legitimate interests of the owner of the trademark and of third parties.

Article 18 – Term of protection

Initial registration, and each renewal of registration, of a trademark shall be for a term of no less than seven years. The registration of a trademark shall be renewable indefinitely.

Article 19 – Requirement of use

1   If use is required to maintain a registration, the registration may be cancelled only after an uninterrupted period of at least three years of non-use, unless valid reasons based on the existence of obstacles to such use are shown by the trademark owner. Circumstances arising independently of the will of the owner of the trademark which constitute an obstacle to the use of the trademark, such as import restrictions on or other government requirements for goods or services protected by the trademark, shall be recognized as valid reasons for non-use.

2   When subject to the control of its owner, use of a trademark by another person shall be recognized as use of the trademark for the purpose of maintaining the registration.

Article 20 – Other requirements

The use of a trademark in the course of trade shall not be unjustifiably encumbered by special requirements, such as use with another trademark, use in a special form or use in a manner detrimental to its capability to distinguish the goods or services of one undertaking from those of other undertakings. This will not preclude a requirement prescribing the use of the trademark identifying the undertaking producing the goods or services along with, but without linking it to, the trademark distinguishing the specific goods or services in question of that undertaking.

Article 21 – Licensing and assignment

Members may determine conditions on the licensing and assignment of trademarks, it being understood that the compulsory licensing of trademarks shall not be permitted and that the owner of a registered trademark shall have the right to assign the trademark with or without the transfer of the business to which the trademark belongs.

Section 3 – Geographical indications

Article 22 – Protection of geographical indications

1   Geographical indications are, for the purposes of this Agreement, indications which identify a good as originating in the territory of a Member, or a region or locality in that territory, where a given quality, reputation or other characteristic of the good is essentially attributable to its geographical origin.

2 In respect of geographical indications, Members shall provide the legal means for interested parties to prevent:

   (a) the use of any means in the designation or presentation of a good that indicates or suggests that the good in question originates in a geographical area other than the true place of origin in a manner which misleads the public as to the geographical origin of the good;

   (b) any use which constitutes an act of unfair competition within the meaning of Article 10*bis* of the Paris Convention (1967).

3 A Member shall, *ex officio* if its legislation so permits or at the request of an interested party, refuse or invalidate the registration of a trademark which contains or consists of a geographical indication with respect to goods not originating in the territory indicated, if use of the indication in the trademark for such goods in that Member is of such a nature as to mislead the public as to the true place of origin.

4 The protection under paragraphs 1, 2 and 3 shall be applicable against a geographical indication which, although literally true as to the territory, region or locality in which the goods originate, falsely represents to the public that the goods originate in another territory.

Article 23 – Additional protection for geographical indications for wines and spirits

1 Each Member shall provide the legal means for interested parties to prevent use of a geographical indication identifying wines for wines not originating in the place indicated by the geographical indication in question or identifying spirits for spirits not originating in the place indicated by the geographical indication in question, even where the true origin of the goods is indicated or the geographical indication is used in translation or accompanied by expressions such as 'kind', 'type', 'style', 'imitation' or the like.[63]

2 The registration of a trademark for wines which contains or consists of a geographical indication identifying wines or for spirits which contains or consists of a geographical indication identifying spirits shall be refused or invalidated, *ex officio* if a Member's legislation so permits or at the request of an interested party, with respect to such wines or spirits not having this origin.

3 In the case of homonymous geographical indications for wines, protection shall be accorded to each indication, subject to the provisions of paragraph 4 of Article 22. Each Member shall determine the practical conditions under which the homonymous indications in question will be differentiated from each other, taking into account the need to ensure equitable treatment of the producers concerned and that consumers are not misled.

4 In order to facilitate the protection of geographical indications for wines, negotiations shall be undertaken in the Council for TRIPS concerning the establishment of a multilateral system of notification and registration of geographical indications for wines eligible for protection in those Members participating in the system.

Article 24 – International negotiations; exceptions

1 Members agree to enter into negotiations aimed at increasing the protection of individual geographical indications under Article 23. The provisions of paragraphs 4 through 8 below shall not be used by a Member to refuse to conduct negotiations or to conclude bilateral or multilateral agreements. In the context of such negotiations, Members shall be willing to consider the continued applicability of these provisions to individual geographical indications whose use was the subject of such negotiations.

2 The Council for TRIPS shall keep under review the application of the provisions of this Section; the first such review shall take place within two years of the entry into force of the WTO Agreement. Any matter affecting the compliance with the obligations under these provisions may be drawn to the attention of the Council, which, at the request of a Member, shall consult with any Member or Members in respect of such matter in respect of

---

63 Notwithstanding the first sentence of Art 42, members may, with respect to these obligations, instead provide for enforcement by administrative action.

which it has not been possible to find a satisfactory solution through bilateral or plurilateral consultations between the Members concerned. The Council shall take such action as may be agreed to facilitate the operation and further the objectives of this Section.

3   In implementing this Section, a Member shall not diminish the protection of geographical indications that existed in that Member immediately prior to the date of entry into force of the WTO Agreement.

4   Nothing in this Section shall require a Member to prevent continued and similar use of a particular geographical indication of another Member identifying wines or spirits in connection with goods or services by any of its nationals or domiciliaries who have used that geographical indication in a continuous manner with regard to the same or related goods or services in the territory of that Member either (a) for at least 10 years preceding 15 April 1994 or (b) in good faith preceding that date.

5   Where a trademark has been applied for or registered in good faith, or where rights to a trademark have been acquired through use in good faith either:

(a) before the date of application of these provisions in that Member as defined in Part VI; or

(b) before the geographical indication is protected in its country of origin;

measures adopted to implement this Section shall not prejudice eligibility for or the validity of the registration of a trademark, or the right to use a trademark, on the basis that such a trademark is identical with, or similar to, a geographical indication.

6   Nothing in this Section shall require a Member to apply its provisions in respect of a geographical indication of any other Member with respect to goods or services for which the relevant indication is identical with the term customary in common language as the common name for such goods or services in the territory of that Member. Nothing in this Section shall require a Member to apply its provisions in respect of a geographical indication of any other Member with respect to products of the vine for which the relevant indication is identical with the customary name of a grape variety existing in the territory of that Member as of the date of entry into force of the WTO Agreement.

7   A Member may provide that any request made under this Section in connection with the use or registration of a trademark must be presented within five years after the adverse use of the protected indication has become generally known in that Member or after the date of registration of the trademark in that Member provided that the trademark has been published by that date, if such date is earlier than the date on which the adverse use became generally known in that Member, provided that the geographical indication is not used or registered in bad faith.

8   The provisions of this Section shall in no way prejudice the right of any person to use, in the course of trade, that person's name or the name of that person's predecessor in business, except where such name is used in such a manner as to mislead the public.

9   There shall be no obligation under this Agreement to protect geographical indications which are not or cease to be protected in their country of origin, or which have fallen into disuse in that country.

Section 4 – Industrial designs

Article 25 – Requirements for protection

1   Members shall provide for the protection of independently created industrial designs that are new or original. Members may provide that designs are not new or original if they do not significantly differ from known designs or combinations of known design features. Members may provide that such protection shall not extend to designs dictated essentially by technical or functional considerations.

2   Each Member shall ensure that requirements for securing protection for textile designs, in particular in regard to any cost, examination or publication, do not unreasonably impair the opportunity to seek and obtain such protection. Members shall be free to meet this obligation through industrial design law or through copyright law.

Article 26 – Protection

1   The owner of a protected industrial design shall have the right to prevent third parties not having the owner's consent from making, selling or importing articles bearing or

embodying a design which is a copy, or substantially a copy, of the protected design, when such acts are undertaken for commercial purposes.

2   Members may provide limited exceptions to the protection of industrial designs, provided that such exceptions do not unreasonably conflict with the normal exploitation of protected industrial designs and do not unreasonably prejudice the legitimate interests of the owner of the protected design, taking account of the legitimate interests of third parties.

3   The duration of protection available shall amount to at least 10 years.

Section 5 – Patents

Article 27 – Patentable subject matter

1   Subject to the provisions of paragraphs 2 and 3, patents shall be available for any inventions, whether products or processes, in all fields of technology, provided that they are new, involve an inventive step and are capable of industrial application.[64] Subject to paragraph 4 of Article 65, paragraph 8 of Article 70 and paragraph 3 of this Article, patents shall be available and patent rights enjoyable without discrimination as to the place of invention, the field of technology and whether products are imported or locally produced.

2   Members may exclude from patentability inventions, the prevention within their territory of the commercial exploitation of which is necessary to protect *ordre* public or morality, including to protect human, animal or plant life or health or to avoid serious prejudice to the environment, provided that such exclusion is not made merely because the exploitation is prohibited by their law.

3   Members may also exclude from patentability:

(a) diagnostic, therapeutic and surgical methods for the treatment of humans or animals;

(b) plants and animals other than micro-organisms, and essentially biological processes for the production of plants or animals other than non-biological and microbiological processes. However, Members shall provide for the protection of plant varieties either by patents or by an effective sui generis system or by any combination thereof. The provisions of this subparagraph shall be reviewed four years after the date of entry into force of the WTO Agreement.

Article 28 – Rights conferred

1   A patent shall confer on its owner the following exclusive rights:

(a) where the subject matter of a patent is a product, to prevent third parties not having the owner's consent from the acts of: making, using, offering for sale, selling, or importing[65] for these purposes that product;

(b) where the subject matter of a patent is a process, to prevent third parties not having the owner's consent from the act of using the process, and from the acts of: using, offering for sale, selling, or importing for these purposes at least the product obtained directly by that process.

2   Patent owners shall also have the right to assign, or transfer by succession, the patent and to conclude licensing contracts.

Article 29 – Conditions on patent applicants

1   Members shall require that an applicant for a patent shall disclose the invention in a manner sufficiently clear and complete for the invention to be carried out by a person skilled in the art and may require the applicant to indicate the best mode for carrying out the invention known to the inventor at the filing date or, where priority is claimed, at the priority date of the application.

---

64 For the purposes of this Article, the terms 'inventive step' and 'capable of industrial application' may be deemed by a member to be synonymous with the terms 'non-obvious' and 'useful' respectively.

65 This right, like all other rights conferred under this Agreement in respect of the use, sale, importation or other distribution of goods, is subject to the provisions of Art 6.

2 Members may require an applicant for a patent to provide information concerning the applicant's corresponding foreign applications and grants.

Article 30 – Exceptions to rights conferred

Members may provide limited exceptions to the exclusive rights conferred by a patent, provided that such exceptions do not unreasonably conflict with a normal exploitation of the patent and do not unreasonably prejudice the legitimate interests of the patent owner, taking account of the legitimate interests of third parties.

Article 31 – Other use without authorization of the right holder

Where the law of a Member allows for other use[66] of the subject matter of a patent without the authorization of the right holder, including use by the government or third parties authorized by the government, the following provisions shall be respected:

(a) authorization of such use shall be considered on its individual merits;

(b) such use may only be permitted if, prior to such use, the proposed user has made efforts to obtain authorization from the right holder on reasonable commercial terms and conditions and that such efforts have not been successful within a reasonable period of time. This requirement may be waived by a Member in the case of a national emergency or other circumstances of extreme urgency or in cases of public non-commercial use. In situations of national emergency or other circumstances of extreme urgency, the right holder shall, nevertheless, be notified as soon as reasonably practicable. In the case of public non-commercial use, where the government or contractor, without making a patent search, knows or has demonstrable grounds to know that a valid patent is or will be used by or for the government, the right holder shall be informed promptly;

(c) the scope and duration of such use shall be limited to the purpose for which it was authorized, and in the case of semi-conductor technology shall only be for public non-commercial use or to remedy a practice determined after judicial or administrative process to be anti-competitive;

(d) such use shall be non-exclusive;

(e) such use shall be non-assignable, except with that part of the enterprise or goodwill which enjoys such use;

(f) any such use shall be authorized predominantly for the supply of the domestic market of the Member authorizing such use;

(g) authorization for such use shall be liable, subject to adequate protection of the legitimate interests of the persons so authorized, to be terminated if and when the circumstances which led to it cease to exist and are unlikely to recur. The competent authority shall have the authority to review, upon motivated request, the continued existence of these circumstances;

(h) the right holder shall be paid adequate remuneration in the circumstances of each case, taking into account the economic value of the authorization;

(i) the legal validity of any decision relating to the authorization of such use shall be subject to judicial review or other independent review by a distinct higher authority in that Member;

(j) any decision relating to the remuneration provided in respect of such use shall be subject to judicial review or other independent review by a distinct higher authority in that Member;

(k) Members are not obliged to apply the conditions set forth in subparagraphs (b) and (f) where such use is permitted to remedy a practice determined after judicial or administrative process to be anti-competitive. The need to correct anti-competitive practices may be taken into account in determining the amount of remuneration in such cases. Competent authorities shall have the authority to refuse termination of authorization if and when the conditions which led to such authorization are likely to recur;

---

66 'Other use' refers to use other than that allowed under Art 30.

(l) where such use is authorized to permit the exploitation of a patent ('the second patent') which cannot be exploited without infringing another patent ('the first patent'), the following additional conditions shall apply:

(i) the invention claimed in the second patent shall involve an important technical advance of considerable economic significance in relation to the invention claimed in the first patent;

(ii) the owner of the first patent shall be entitled to a cross-licence on reasonable terms to use the invention claimed in the second patent; and

(iii) the use authorized in respect of the first patent shall be non-assignable except with the assignment of the second patent.

Article 32 – Revocation/forfeiture

An opportunity for judicial review of any decision to revoke or forfeit a patent shall be available.

Article 33 – Term of protection

The term of protection available shall not end before the expiration of a period of twenty years counted from the filing date.[67]

Article 34 – Process patents: burden of proof

1   For the purposes of civil proceedings in respect of the infringement of the rights of the owner referred to in paragraph 1(b) of Article 28, if the subject matter of a patent is a process for obtaining a product, the judicial authorities shall have the authority to order the defendant to prove that the process to obtain an identical product is different from the patented process. Therefore, Members shall provide, in at least one of the following circumstances, that any identical product when produced without the consent of the patent owner shall, in the absence of proof to the contrary, be deemed to have been obtained by the patented process:

(a) if the product obtained by the patented process is new;

(b) if there is a substantial likelihood that the identical product was made by the process and the owner of the patent has been unable through reasonable efforts to determine the process actually used.

2   Any Member shall be free to provide that the burden of proof indicated in paragraph 1 shall be on the alleged infringer only if the condition referred to in subparagraph (a) is fulfilled or only if the condition referred to in subparagraph (b) is fulfilled.

3   In the adduction of proof to the contrary, the legitimate interests of defendants in protecting their manufacturing and business secrets shall be taken into account.

Section 6 – Layout-designs (topographies) of integrated circuits

Article 35 – Relation to the IPIC Treaty

Members agree to provide protection to the layout-designs (topographies) of integrated circuits (referred to in this Agreement as 'layout-designs') in accordance with Articles 2 through 7 (other than paragraph 3 of Article 6), Article 12 and paragraph 3 of Article 16 of the Treaty on Intellectual Property in Respect of Integrated Circuits and, in addition, to comply with the following provisions.

Article 36 – Scope of the protection

Subject to the provisions of paragraph 1 of Article 37, Members shall consider unlawful the following acts if performed without the authorization of the right holder:[68] importing, selling, or otherwise distributing for commercial purposes a protected layout-design, an integrated

---

67 It is understood that those members that do not have a system of original grant may provide that the term of protection shall be computed from the filing date in the system of original grant.

68 The term 'right holder' in this Section shall be understood as having the same meaning as the term 'holder of the right' in the IPIC Treaty.

circuit in which a protected layout-design is incorporated, or an article incorporating such an integrated circuit only in so far as it continues to contain an unlawfully reproduced layout-design.

Article 37– Acts not requiring the authorization of the right holder

1   Notwithstanding Article 36, no Member shall consider unlawful the performance of any of the acts referred to in that Article in respect of an integrated circuit incorporating an unlawfully reproduced layout-design or any article incorporating such an integrated circuit where the person performing or ordering such acts did not know and had no reasonable ground to know, when acquiring the integrated circuit or article incorporating such an integrated circuit, that it incorporated an unlawfully reproduced layout-design. Members shall provide that, after the time that such person has received sufficient notice that the layout-design was unlawfully reproduced, that person may perform any of the acts with respect to the stock on hand or ordered before such time, but shall be liable to pay to the right holder a sum equivalent to a reasonable royalty such as would be payable under a freely negotiated licence in respect of such a layout-design.

2   The conditions set out in subparagraphs (a) through (k) of Article 31 shall apply *mutatis mutandis* in the event of any non-voluntary licensing of a layout-design or of its use by or for the government without the authorization of the right holder.

Article 38 – Term of protection

1   In Members requiring registration as a condition of protection, the term of protection of layout-designs shall not end before the expiration of a period of 10 years counted from the date of filing an application for registration or from the first commercial exploitation wherever in the world it occurs.

2   In Members not requiring registration as a condition for protection, layout-designs shall be protected for a term of no less than 10 years from the date of the first commercial exploitation wherever in the world it occurs.

3   Notwithstanding paragraphs 1 and 2, a Member may provide that protection shall lapse 15 years after the creation of the layout-design.

Section 7 – Protection of undisclosed information

Article 39

1   In the course of ensuring effective protection against unfair competition as provided in Article 10*bis* of the Paris Convention (1967), Members shall protect undisclosed information in accordance with paragraph 2 and data submitted to governments or governmental agencies in accordance with paragraph 3.

2   Natural and legal persons shall have the possibility of preventing information lawfully within their control from being disclosed to, acquired by, or used by others without their consent in a manner contrary to honest commercial practices[69] so long as such information:

   (a)   is secret in the sense that it is not, as a body or in the precise configuration and assembly of its components, generally known among or readily accessible to persons within the circles that normally deal with the kind of information in question;

   (b)   has commercial value because it is secret; and

   (c)   has been subject to reasonable steps under the circumstances, by the person lawfully in control of the information, to keep it secret.

---

69   For the purpose of this provision, 'a manner contrary to honest commercial practices' shall mean at least practices such as breach of contract, breach of confidence and inducement to breach, and includes the acquisition of undisclosed information by third parties who knew, or were grossly negligent in failing to know, that such practices were involved in the acquisition.

3   Members, when requiring, as a condition of approving the marketing of pharmaceutical or of agricultural chemical products which utilize new chemical entities, the submission of undisclosed test or other data, the origination of which involves a considerable effort, shall protect such data against unfair commercial use. In addition, Members shall protect such data against disclosure, except where necessary to protect the public, or unless steps are taken to ensure that the data are protected against unfair commercial use.

Section 8 – Control of anti-competitive practices in contractual licences

Article 40

1   Members agree that some licensing practices or conditions pertaining to intellectual property rights which restrain competition may have adverse effects on trade and may impede the transfer and dissemination of technology.

2   Nothing in this Agreement shall prevent Members from specifying in their legislation licensing practices or conditions that may in particular cases constitute an abuse of intellectual property rights having an adverse effect on competition in the relevant market. As provided above, a Member may adopt, consistently with the other provisions of this Agreement, appropriate measures to prevent or control such practices, which may include for example exclusive grantback conditions, conditions preventing challenges to validity and coercive package licensing, in the light of the relevant laws and regulations of that Member.

3   Each Member shall enter, upon request, into consultations with any other Member which has cause to believe that an intellectual property right owner that is a national or domiciliary of the Member to which the request for consultations has been addressed is undertaking practices in violation of the requesting Member's laws and regulations on the subject matter of this Section, and which wishes to secure compliance with such legislation, without prejudice to any action under the law and to the full freedom of an ultimate decision of either Member. The Member addressed shall accord full and sympathetic consideration to, and shall afford adequate opportunity for, consultations with the requesting Member, and shall cooperate through supply of publicly available non-confidential information of relevance to the matter in question and of other information available to the Member, subject to domestic law and to the conclusion of mutually satisfactory agreements concerning the safeguarding of its confidentiality by the requesting Member.

4   A Member whose nationals or domiciliaries are subject to proceedings in another Member concerning alleged violation of that other Member's laws and regulations on the subject matter of this Section shall, upon request, be granted an opportunity for consultations by the other Member under the same conditions as those foreseen in paragraph 3.

PART III – ENFORCEMENT OF INTELLECTUAL PROPERTY RIGHTS

Section 1 – General obligations

Article 41

1   Members shall ensure that enforcement procedures as specified in this Part are available under their law so as to permit effective action against any act of infringement of intellectual property rights covered by this Agreement, including expeditious remedies to prevent infringements and remedies which constitute a deterrent to further infringements. These procedures shall be applied in such a manner as to avoid the creation of barriers to legitimate trade and to provide for safeguards against their abuse.

2   Procedures concerning the enforcement of intellectual property rights shall be fair and equitable. They shall not be unnecessarily complicated or costly, or entail unreasonable time-limits or unwarranted delays.

3   Decisions on the merits of a case shall preferably be in writing and reasoned. They shall be made available at least to the parties to the proceeding without undue delay. Decisions on the merits of a case shall be based only on evidence in respect of which parties were offered the opportunity to be heard.

4   Parties to a proceeding shall have an opportunity for review by a judicial authority of final administrative decisions and, subject to jurisdictional provisions in a Member's law

concerning the importance of a case, of at least the legal aspects of initial judicial decisions on the merits of a case. However, there shall be no obligation to provide an opportunity for review of acquittals in criminal cases.

5   It is understood that this Part does not create any obligation to put in place a judicial system for the enforcement of intellectual property rights distinct from that for the enforcement of law in general, nor does it affect the capacity of Members to enforce their law in general. Nothing in this Part creates any obligation with respect to the distribution of resources as between enforcement of intellectual property rights and the enforcement of law in general.

Section 2 – Civil and administrative procedures and remedies

Article 42 – Fair and equitable procedures

Members shall make available to right holders[70] civil judicial procedures concerning the enforcement of any intellectual property right covered by this Agreement. Defendants shall have the right to written notice which is timely and contains sufficient detail, including the basis of the claims. Parties shall be allowed to be represented by independent legal counsel, and procedures shall not impose overly burdensome requirements concerning mandatory personal appearances. All parties to such procedures shall be duly entitled to substantiate their claims and to present all relevant evidence. The procedure shall provide a means to identify and protect confidential information, unless this would be contrary to existing constitutional requirements.

Article 43 – Evidence

1   The judicial authorities shall have the authority, where a party has presented reasonably available evidence sufficient to support its claims and has specified evidence relevant to substantiation of its claims which lies in the control of the opposing party, to order that this evidence be produced by the opposing party, subject in appropriate cases to conditions which ensure the protection of confidential information.

2   In cases in which a party to a proceeding voluntarily and without good reason refuses access to, or otherwise does not provide necessary information within a reasonable period, or significantly impedes a procedure relating to an enforcement action, a Member may accord judicial authorities the authority to make preliminary and final determinations, affirmative or negative, on the basis of the information presented to them, including the complaint or the allegation presented by the party adversely affected by the denial of access to information, subject to providing the parties an opportunity to be heard on the allegations or evidence.

Article 44 – Injunctions

1   The judicial authorities shall have the authority to order a party to desist from an infringement, *inter alia* to prevent the entry into the channels of commerce in their jurisdiction of imported goods that involve the infringement of an intellectual property right, immediately after customs clearance of such goods. Members are not obliged to accord such authority in respect of protected subject matter acquired or ordered by a person prior to knowing or having reasonable grounds to know that dealing in such subject matter would entail the infringement of an intellectual property right.

2   Notwithstanding the other provisions of this Part and provided that the provisions of Part II specifically addressing use by governments, or by third parties authorized by a government, without the authorization of the right holder are complied with, Members may limit the remedies available against such use to payment of remuneration in accordance with subparagraph (h) of Article 31. In other cases, the remedies under this Part shall apply or, where these remedies are inconsistent with a Member's law, declaratory judgments and adequate compensation shall be available.

---

70 For the purpose of this Part, the term 'right holder' includes federations and associations having legal standing to assert such rights.

Article 45 – Damages

1   The judicial authorities shall have the authority to order the infringer to pay the right holder damages adequate to compensate for the injury the right holder has suffered because of an infringement of that person's intellectual property right by an infringer who knowingly, or with reasonable grounds to know, engaged in infringing activity.

2   The judicial authorities shall also have the authority to order the infringer to pay the right holder expenses, which may include appropriate attorney's fees. In appropriate cases, Members may authorize the judicial authorities to order recovery of profits and/or payment of pre-established damages even where the infringer did not knowingly, or with reasonable grounds to know, engage in infringing activity.

Article 46 – Other remedies

In order to create an effective deterrent to infringement, the judicial authorities shall have the authority to order that goods that they have found to be infringing be, without compensation of any sort, disposed of outside the channels of commerce in such a manner as to avoid any harm caused to the right holder, or, unless this would be contrary to existing constitutional requirements, destroyed. The judicial authorities shall also have the authority to order that materials and implements the predominant use of which has been in the creation of the infringing goods be, without compensation of any sort, disposed of outside the channels of commerce in such a manner as to minimize the risks of further infringements. In considering such requests, the need for proportionality between the seriousness of the infringement and the remedies ordered as well as the interests of third parties shall be taken into account. In regard to counterfeit trademark goods, the simple removal of the trademark unlawfully affixed shall not be sufficient, other than in exceptional cases, to permit release of the goods into the channels of commerce.

Article 47 – Right of information

Members may provide that the judicial authorities shall have the authority, unless this would be out of proportion to the seriousness of the infringement, to order the infringer to inform the right holder of the identity of third persons involved in the production and distribution of the infringing goods or services and of their channels of distribution.

Article 48 – Indemnification of the defendant

1   The judicial authorities shall have the authority to order a party at whose request measures were taken and who has abused enforcement procedures to provide to a party wrongfully enjoined or restrained adequate compensation for the injury suffered because of such abuse. The judicial authorities shall also have the authority to order the applicant to pay the defendant expenses, which may include appropriate attorney's fees.

2   In respect of the administration of any law pertaining to the protection or enforcement of intellectual property rights, Members shall only exempt both public authorities and officials from liability to appropriate remedial measures where actions are taken or intended in good faith in the course of the administration of that law.

Article 49 – Administrative procedures

To the extent that any civil remedy can be ordered as a result of administrative procedures on the merits of a case, such procedures shall conform to principles equivalent in substance to those set forth in this Section.

Section 3 – Provisional measures

Article 50

1   The judicial authorities shall have the authority to order prompt and effective provisional measures:

(a)   to prevent an infringement of any intellectual property right from occurring, and in particular to prevent the entry into the channels of commerce in their jurisdiction of goods, including imported goods immediately after customs clearance;

(b)   to preserve relevant evidence in regard to the alleged infringement.

2   The judicial authorities shall have the authority to adopt provisional measures *inaudita altera parte* where appropriate, in particular where any delay is likely to cause irreparable harm to the right holder, or where there is a demonstrable risk of evidence being destroyed.

3   The judicial authorities shall have the authority to require the applicant to provide any reasonably available evidence in order to satisfy themselves with a sufficient degree of certainty that the applicant is the right holder and that the applicant's right is being infringed or that such infringement is imminent, and to order the applicant to provide a security or equivalent assurance sufficient to protect the defendant and to prevent abuse.

4   Where provisional measures have been adopted *inaudita altera parte*, the parties affected shall be given notice, without delay after the execution of the measures at the latest. A review, including a right to be heard, shall take place upon request of the defendant with a view to deciding, within a reasonable period after the notification of the measures, whether these measures shall be modified, revoked or confirmed.

5   The applicant may be required to supply other information necessary for the identification of the goods concerned by the authority that will execute the provisional measures.

6   Without prejudice to paragraph 4, provisional measures taken on the basis of paragraphs 1 and 2 shall, upon request by the defendant, be revoked or otherwise cease to have effect, if proceedings leading to a decision on the merits of the case are not initiated within a reasonable period, to be determined by the judicial authority ordering the measures where a Member's law so permits or, in the absence of such a determination, not to exceed 20 working days or 31 calendar days, whichever is the longer.

7   Where the provisional measures are revoked or where they lapse due to any act or omission by the applicant, or where it is subsequently found that there has been no infringement or threat of infringement of an intellectual property right, the judicial authorities shall have the authority to order the applicant, upon request of the defendant, to provide the defendant appropriate compensation for any injury caused by these measures.

8   To the extent that any provisional measure can be ordered as a result of administrative procedures, such procedures shall conform to principles equivalent in substance to those set forth in this Section.

Section 4 – Special requirements related to border measures[71]

Article 51 – Suspension of release by customs authorities

Members shall, in conformity with the provisions set out below, adopt procedures[72] to enable a right holder, who has valid grounds for suspecting that the importation of counterfeit trademark or pirated copyright goods[73] may take place, to lodge an application in writing with competent authorities, administrative or judicial, for the suspension by the customs authorities

---

71   Where a member has dismantled substantially all controls over movement of goods across its border with another member with which it forms part of a customs union, it shall not be required to apply the provisions of this Section at that border.

72   It is understood that there shall be no obligation to apply such procedures to imports of goods put on the market in another country by or with the consent of the right holder, or to goods in transit.

73   For the purposes of this Agreement:

   (a)   'counterfeit trademark goods' shall mean any goods, including packaging, bearing without authorisation a trade mark which is identical to the trade mark validly registered in respect of such goods, or which cannot be distinguished in its essential aspects from such a trade mark, and which thereby infringes the rights of the owner of the trademark in question under the law of the country of importation;

   (b)   'pirated copyright goods' shall mean any goods which are copies made without the consent of the right holder or person duly authorised by the right holder in the country of production and which are made directly or indirectly from an article where the making of that copy would have constituted an infringement of a copyright or a related right under the law of the country of importation.

of the release into free circulation of such goods. Members may enable such an application to be made in respect of goods which involve other infringements of intellectual property rights, provided that the requirements of this Section are met. Members may also provide for corresponding procedures concerning the suspension by the customs authorities of the release of infringing goods destined for exportation from their territories.

Article 52 – Application

Any right holder initiating the procedures under Article 51 shall be required to provide adequate evidence to satisfy the competent authorities that, under the laws of the country of importation, there is *prima facie* an infringement of the right holder's intellectual property right and to supply a sufficiently detailed description of the goods to make them readily recognizable by the customs authorities. The competent authorities shall inform the applicant within a reasonable period whether they have accepted the application and, where determined by the competent authorities, the period for which the customs authorities will take action.

Article 53 – Security or equivalent assurance

1   The competent authorities shall have the authority to require an applicant to provide a security or equivalent assurance sufficient to protect the defendant and the competent authorities and to prevent abuse. Such security or equivalent assurance shall not unreasonably deter recourse to these procedures.

2   Where pursuant to an application under this Section the release of goods involving industrial designs, patents, layout-designs or undisclosed information into free circulation has been suspended by customs authorities on the basis of a decision other than by a judicial or other independent authority, and the period provided for in Article 55 has expired without the granting of provisional relief by the duly empowered authority, and provided that all other conditions for importation have been complied with, the owner, importer, or consignee of such goods shall be entitled to their release on the posting of a security in an amount sufficient to protect the right holder for any infringement. Payment of such security shall not prejudice any other remedy available to the right holder, it being understood that the security shall be released if the right holder fails to pursue the right of action within a reasonable period of time.

Article 54 – Notice of suspension

The importer and the applicant shall be promptly notified of the suspension of the release of goods according to Article 51.

Article 55 – Duration of suspension

If, within a period not exceeding 10 working days after the applicant has been served notice of the suspension, the customs authorities have not been informed that proceedings leading to a decision on the merits of the case have been initiated by a party other than the defendant, or that the duly empowered authority has taken provisional measures prolonging the suspension of the release of the goods, the goods shall be released, provided that all other conditions for importation or exportation have been complied with; in appropriate cases, this time-limit may be extended by another 10 working days. If proceedings leading to a decision on the merits of the case have been initiated, a review, including a right to be heard, shall take place upon request of the defendant with a view to deciding, within a reasonable period, whether these measures shall be modified, revoked or confirmed. Notwithstanding the above, where the suspension of the release of goods is carried out or continued in accordance with a provisional judicial measure, the provisions of paragraph 6 of Article 50 shall apply.

Article 56 – Indemnification of the importer and of the owner of the goods

Relevant authorities shall have the authority to order the applicant to pay the importer, the consignee and the owner of the goods appropriate compensation for any injury caused to them through the wrongful detention of goods or through the detention of goods released pursuant to Article 55.

Article 57 – Right of inspection and information

Without prejudice to the protection of confidential information, Members shall provide the competent authorities the authority to give the right holder sufficient opportunity to have any goods detained by the customs authorities inspected in order to substantiate the right holder's claims. The competent authorities shall also have authority to give the importer an equivalent opportunity to have any such goods inspected. Where a positive determination has been made on the merits of a case, Members may provide the competent authorities the authority to inform the right holder of the names and addresses of the consignor, the importer and the consignee and of the quantity of the goods in question.

Article 58 – Ex officio *action*

Where Members require competent authorities to act upon their own initiative and to suspend the release of goods in respect of which they have acquired *prima facie* evidence that an intellectual property right is being infringed:

(a) the competent authorities may at any time seek from the right holder any information that may assist them to exercise these powers;

(b) the importer and the right holder shall be promptly notified of the suspension. Where the importer has lodged an appeal against the suspension with the competent authorities, the suspension shall be subject to the conditions, *mutatis mutandis*, set out at Article 55;

(c) Members shall only exempt both public authorities and officials from liability to appropriate remedial measures where actions are taken or intended in good faith.

Article 59 – Remedies

Without prejudice to other rights of action open to the right holder and subject to the right of the defendant to seek review by a judicial authority, competent authorities shall have the authority to order the destruction or disposal of infringing goods in accordance with the principles set out in Article 46. In regard to counterfeit trademark goods, the authorities shall not allow the re-exportation of the infringing goods in an unaltered state or subject them to a different customs procedure, other than in exceptional circumstances.

Article 60 – De minimis *imports*

Members may exclude from the application of the above provisions small quantities of goods of a non-commercial nature contained in travellers' personal luggage or sent in small consignments.

Section 5 – Criminal procedures

Article 61

Members shall provide for criminal procedures and penalties to be applied at least in cases of wilful trademark counterfeiting or copyright piracy on a commercial scale. Remedies available shall include imprisonment and/or monetary fines sufficient to provide a deterrent, consistently with the level of penalties applied for crimes of a corresponding gravity. In appropriate cases, remedies available shall also include the seizure, forfeiture and destruction of the infringing goods and of any materials and implements the predominant use of which has been in the commission of the offence. Members may provide for criminal procedures and penalties to be applied in other cases of infringement of intellectual property rights, in particular where they are committed wilfully and on a commercial scale.

PART IV – ACQUISITION AND MAINTENANCE OF INTELLECTUAL PROPERTY RIGHTS AND RELATED *INTER PARTES* PROCEDURES

Article 62

1   Members may require, as a condition of the acquisition or maintenance of the intellectual property rights provided for under Sections 2 through 6 of Part II, compliance with reasonable procedures and formalities. Such procedures and formalities shall be consistent with the provisions of this Agreement.

2   Where the acquisition of an intellectual property right is subject to the right being granted or registered, Members shall ensure that the procedures for grant or registration, subject to compliance with the substantive conditions for acquisition of the right, permit the granting or registration of the right within a reasonable period of time so as to avoid unwarranted curtailment of the period of protection.

3   Article 4 of the Paris Convention (1967) shall apply *mutatis mutandis* to service marks.

4 Procedures concerning the acquisition or maintenance of intellectual property rights and, where a Member's law provides for such procedures, administrative revocation and *inter partes* procedures such as opposition, revocation and cancellation, shall be governed by the general principles set out in paragraphs 2 and 3 of Article 41.

5 Final administrative decisions in any of the procedures referred to under paragraph 4 shall be subject to review by a judicial or quasi-judicial authority. However, there shall be no obligation to provide an opportunity for such review of decisions in cases of unsuccessful opposition or administrative revocation, provided that the grounds for such procedures can be the subject of invalidation procedures.

PART V – DISPUTE PREVENTION AND SETTLEMENT

Article 63 – Transparency

1 Laws and regulations, and final judicial decisions and administrative rulings of general application, made effective by a Member pertaining to the subject matter of this Agreement (the availability, scope, acquisition, enforcement and prevention of the abuse of intellectual property rights) shall be published, or where such publication is not practicable made publicly available, in a national language, in such a manner as to enable governments and right holders to become acquainted with them. Agreements concerning the subject matter of this Agreement which are in force between the government or a governmental agency of a Member and the government or a governmental agency of another Member shall also be published.

2 Members shall notify the laws and regulations referred to in paragraph 1 to the Council for TRIPS in order to assist that Council in its review of the operation of this Agreement. The Council shall attempt to minimize the burden on Members in carrying out this obligation and may decide to waive the obligation to notify such laws and regulations directly to the Council if consultations with WIPO on the establishment of a common register containing these laws and regulations are successful. The Council shall also consider in this connection any action required regarding notifications pursuant to the obligations under this Agreement stemming from the provisions of Article 6ter of the Paris Convention (1967).

3 Each Member shall be prepared to supply, in response to a written request from another Member, information of the sort referred to in paragraph 1. A Member, having reason to believe that a specific judicial decision or administrative ruling or bilateral agreement in the area of intellectual property rights affects its rights under this Agreement, may also request in writing to be given access to or be informed in sufficient detail of such specific judicial decisions or administrative rulings or bilateral agreements.

4 Nothing in paragraphs 1, 2 and 3 shall require Members to disclose confidential information which would impede law enforcement or otherwise be contrary to the public interest or would prejudice the legitimate commercial interests of particular enterprises, public or private.

Article 64 – Dispute settlement

1 The provisions of Articles XXII and XXIII of GATT 1994 as elaborated and applied by the Dispute Settlement Understanding shall apply to consultations and the settlement of disputes under this Agreement except as otherwise specifically provided herein.

2 Subparagraphs 1(b) and 1(c) of Article XXIII of GATT 1994 shall not apply to the settlement of disputes under this Agreement for a period of five years from the date of entry into force of the WTO Agreement.

3 During the time period referred to in paragraph 2, the Council for TRIPS shall examine the scope and modalities for complaints of the type provided for under subparagraphs 1(b) and 1(c) of Article XXIII of GATT 1994 made pursuant to this Agreement, and submit its recommendations to the Ministerial Conference for approval. Any decision of the Ministerial Conference to approve such recommendations or to extend the period in paragraph 2 shall be made only by consensus, and approved recommendations shall be effective for all Members without further formal acceptance process.

PART VI – TRANSITIONAL ARRANGEMENTS

Article 65 – Transitional arrangements

1 Subject to the provisions of paragraphs 2, 3 and 4, no Member shall be obliged to apply the provisions of this Agreement before the expiry of a general period of one year following the date of entry into force of the WTO Agreement.

2 A developing country Member is entitled to delay for a further period of four years the date of application, as defined in paragraph 1, of the provisions of this Agreement other than Articles 3, 4 and 5.

3 Any other Member which is in the process of transformation from a centrally-planned into a market, free-enterprise economy and which is undertaking structural reform of its intellectual property system and facing special problems in the preparation and implementation of intellectual property laws and regulations, may also benefit from a period of delay as foreseen in paragraph 2.

4 To the extent that a developing country Member is obliged by this Agreement to extend product patent protection to areas of technology not so protectable in its territory on the general date of application of this Agreement for that Member, as defined in paragraph 2, it may delay the application of the provisions on product patents of Section 5 of Part II to such areas of technology for an additional period of five years.

5 A Member availing itself of a transitional period under paragraphs 1, 2, 3 or 4 shall ensure that any changes in its laws, regulations and practice made during that period do not result in a lesser degree of consistency with the provisions of this Agreement.

Article 66 – Least-developed country members

1 In view of the special needs and requirements of least-developed country Members, their economic, financial and administrative constraints, and their need for flexibility to create a viable technological base, such Members shall not be required to apply the provisions of this Agreement, other than Articles 3, 4 and 5, for a period of 10 years from the date of application as defined under paragraph 1 of Article 65. The Council for TRIPS shall, upon duly motivated request by a least-developed country Member, accord extensions of this period.

2 Developed country Members shall provide incentives to enterprises and institutions in their territories for the purpose of promoting and encouraging technology transfer to least-developed country Members in order to enable them to create a sound and viable technological base.

Article 67 – Technical cooperation

In order to facilitate the implementation of this Agreement, developed country Members shall provide, on request and on mutually agreed terms and conditions, technical and financial cooperation in favour of developing and least-developed country Members. Such cooperation shall include assistance in the preparation of laws and regulations on the protection and enforcement of intellectual property rights as well as on the prevention of their abuse, and shall include support regarding the establishment or reinforcement of domestic offices and agencies relevant to these matters, including the training of personnel.

PART VII – INSTITUTIONAL ARRANGEMENTS; FINAL PROVISIONS

Article 68 – Council for trade-related aspects of intellectual property rights

The Council for TRIPS shall monitor the operation of this Agreement and, in particular, Members' compliance with their obligations hereunder, and shall afford Members the opportunity of consulting on matters relating to the trade-related aspects of intellectual property rights. It shall carry out such other responsibilities as assigned to it by the Members, and it shall, in particular, provide any assistance requested by them in the context of dispute settlement procedures. In carrying out its functions, the Council for TRIPS may consult with and seek information from any source it deems appropriate. In consultation with WIPO, the Council shall seek to establish, within one year of its first meeting, appropriate arrangements for cooperation with bodies of that Organization.

Article 69 – International cooperation

Members agree to cooperate with each other with a view to eliminating international trade in goods infringing intellectual property rights. For this purpose, they shall establish and notify contact points in their administrations and be ready to exchange information on trade in infringing goods. They shall, in particular, promote the exchange of information and cooperation between customs authorities with regard to trade in counterfeit trademark goods and pirated copyright goods.

Article 70 – Protection of existing subject matter

1   This Agreement does not give rise to obligations in respect of acts which occurred before the date of application of the Agreement for the Member in question.

2   Except as otherwise provided for in this Agreement, this Agreement gives rise to obligations in respect of all subject matter existing at the date of application of this Agreement for the Member in question, and which is protected in that Member on the said date, or which meets or comes subsequently to meet the criteria for protection under the terms of this Agreement. In respect of this paragraph and paragraphs 3 and 4, copyright obligations with respect to existing works shall be solely determined under Article 18 of the Berne Convention (1971), and obligations with respect to the rights of producers of phonograms and performers in existing phonograms shall be determined solely under Article 18 of the Berne Convention (1971) as made applicable under paragraph 6 of Article 14 of this Agreement.

3   There shall be no obligation to restore protection to subject matter which on the date of application of this Agreement for the Member in question has fallen into the public domain.

4   In respect of any acts in respect of specific objects embodying protected subject matter which become infringing under the terms of legislation in conformity with this Agreement, and which were commenced, or in respect of which a significant investment was made, before the date of acceptance of the WTO Agreement by that Member, any Member may provide for a limitation of the remedies available to the right holder as to the continued performance of such acts after the date of application of this Agreement for that Member. In such cases the Member shall, however, at least provide for the payment of equitable remuneration.

5   A Member is not obliged to apply the provisions of Article 11 and of paragraph 4 of Article 14 with respect to originals or copies purchased prior to the date of application of this Agreement for that Member.

6   Members shall not be required to apply Article 31, or the requirement in paragraph 1 of Article 27 that patent rights shall be enjoyable without discrimination as to the field of technology, to use without the authorization of the right holder where authorization for such use was granted by the government before the date this Agreement became known.

7   In the case of intellectual property rights for which protection is conditional upon registration, applications for protection which are pending on the date of application of this Agreement for the Member in question shall be permitted to be amended to claim any enhanced protection provided under the provisions of this Agreement. Such amendments shall not include new matter.

8   Where a Member does not make available as of the date of entry into force of the WTO Agreement patent protection for pharmaceutical and agricultural chemical products commensurate with its obligations under Article 27, that Member shall:

(a) notwithstanding the provisions of Part VI, provide as from the date of entry into force of the WTO Agreement a means by which applications for patents for such inventions can be filed;

(b) apply to these applications, as of the date of application of this Agreement, the criteria for patentability as laid down in this Agreement as if those criteria were being applied on the date of filing in that Member or, where priority is available and claimed, the priority date of the application; and

(c) provide patent protection in accordance with this Agreement as from the grant of the patent and for the remainder of the patent term, counted from the filing date in accordance with Article 33 of this Agreement, for those of these applications that meet the criteria for protection referred to in subparagraph (b).

9   Where a product is the subject of a patent application in a Member in accordance with paragraph 8(a), exclusive marketing rights shall be granted, notwithstanding the provisions of Part VI, for a period of five years after obtaining marketing approval in that Member or until a product patent is granted or rejected in that Member, whichever period is shorter, provided that, subsequent to the entry into force of the WTO Agreement, a patent application has been filed and a patent granted for that product in another Member and marketing approval obtained in such other Member.

Article 71 – Review and amendment

1   The Council for TRIPS shall review the implementation of this Agreement after the expiration of the transitional period referred to in paragraph 2 of Article 65. The Council shall, having regard to the experience gained in its implementation, review it two years after that date, and at identical intervals thereafter. The Council may also undertake reviews in the light of any relevant new developments which might warrant modification or amendment of this Agreement.

2   Amendments merely serving the purpose of adjusting to higher levels of protection of intellectual property rights achieved, and in force, in other multilateral agreements and accepted under those agreements by all Members of the WTO may be referred to the Ministerial Conference for action in accordance with paragraph 6 of Article X of the WTO Agreement on the basis of a consensus proposal from the Council for TRIPS.

Article 72 – Reservations

Reservations may not be entered in respect of any of the provisions of this Agreement without the consent of the other Members.

Article 73 – Security exceptions

Nothing in this Agreement shall be construed:

(a)   to require a Member to furnish any information the disclosure of which it considers contrary to its essential security interests; or

(b)   to prevent a Member from taking any action which it considers necessary for the protection of its essential security interests;

    (i)   relating to fissionable materials or the materials from which they are derived;

    (ii)   relating to the traffic in arms, ammunition and implements of war and to such traffic in other goods and materials as is carried on directly or indirectly for the purpose of supplying a military establishment;

    (iii)   taken in time of war or other emergency in international relations; or

(c)   to prevent a Member from taking any action in pursuance of its obligations under the United Nations Charter for the maintenance of international peace and security.

CHAPTER 10

INTERNATIONAL COMMERCIAL ARBITRATION

THE ISSUES

The ongoing growth in international trade, promoted by the breaking down of barriers to trade and investment, advances in communications and the ongoing industrialisation of developing countries, has resulted in a progressive increase in the range and number of international business transactions. These transactions are usually between business entities domiciled in different States (and in some cases involve a State as a principal). Resolution of disputes arising in the course of these commercial relationships can be made particularly difficult by the fact of this difference in domicile. Whereas transactions between residents of the same State can readily be litigated in the national court system, applying the municipal law is more difficult where the parties have their place of business in different states.

For convenience of exposition it will be assumed in what follows that the dispute is between two parties, the plaintiff and the defendant, although it is recognised that in practice a dispute may involve more than two parties.

There are two obvious problems in litigation between residents of different States. One party may not wish to litigate in the other party's courts, because of a perception that they may be biased in favour of the latter. Likewise, the first party may not wish to have the dispute decided by the law of the forum, because it is unfamiliar. Should the party persevere and obtain judgment against the defendant, enforcement against its assets within the State may be comparatively straightforward. What, however, of the situation where the plaintiff has sought to circumvent these problems and has sued in its own jurisdiction? A third problem presents itself. Assuming that it obtains a verdict in its favour, how does it enforce this verdict against the assets in the defendant's jurisdiction? If there is no treaty between the two States of the parties' respective domicile for the mutual recognition and enforcement of one another's court judgments, then the plaintiff may not have any means of enforcing the judgment. Thus, there can be fundamental obstacles to enforcing the judgment of a court outside its own State.

These three difficulties inherent in international commercial litigation – lack of perceived neutrality on the part of the courts, an unfamiliar law and difficulties of enforcement – can be overcome by resort to international commercial arbitration. Such is the attraction of this dispute resolution mechanism that it is now the most common formal means of resolving international commercial disputes.

CONTRASTING MEDIATION, LITIGATION AND ARBITRATION

Mediation and arbitration are two dispute resolution mechanisms commonly grouped together as subsets of the dispute settlement process known as alternative dispute resolution, or ADR. The real contrast is between mediation on the one hand, and arbitration and litigation on the other, given that the latter two are much more closely related, conceptually, than either is to mediation.[1]

Mediation centres on the notion of a mediator agreed upon by the disputants, chairing a discussion between them as they attempt to negotiate their dispute. Mediation provides a structured forum for the negotiation of a settlement. It is entirely voluntary at all times. The parties must agree to undertake mediation, and either can withdraw from the process at any time. No agreement reached during mediation is binding, unless it is embodied in a contract. The process is confidential, cheap and quick, relative to arbitration and litigation. As Moens notes the mediator, as neutral facilitator, differs from an arbitrator in two respects in particular: (i) the mediator does not have coercive authority; and (ii) the mediator 'aims to sow the seeds of doubt about the impregnability of each side's case and to leave each disputant with the impression that he or she is not entirely in the right'.[2]

Litigation involves the adjudication of the dispute in a court. Judicial trials of an issue are arbitral – they lead to a binding decision and therefore may be described as determinative. This decision is final, subject to appellate review by a higher court. Grounds for appeal must be established, such as that the trial miscarried because of error of law. Appeal purely on the facts may not be readily available, or if it is there may be a high threshold for the appellant (such as where the appellate grounds of review require the appellant to show that the decision on the facts was perverse). Once a plaintiff has embarked upon litigation, the defendant has no control over proceedings, other than to offer a defence or to settle. The parties do not have a choice of judge, nor do they control the court's timetable. The judge will be dealing with the case along with numerous other cases. Only when it comes to the trial proper will be parties get the undivided attention of the judge. A party wishing to delay proceedings may have ample opportunity to do so, by seeking interlocutory orders and the like. The parties have no control over the law of procedure to be applied, nor do they control the substantive law. The law to be applied will be the law of the forum (unless the law of the forum permits the parties to have the matter tried under the law specified by them in a dispute resolution provisions in any contract to be litigated). The trial must proceed in a judicial manner. The procedure to be followed can be exacting, depending on the jurisdiction and the level of court. Proceedings are not confidential. The right of appeal may be a negative – it can add to delay and expense.

In summary, and depending on the efficiency of the courts in the particular jurisdiction, litigation can have certain benefits. It provides for a decision that is *prima facie* final, subject only to appeal; and it provides for a trial according to the rule of law. Negatively, it can be a slow and expensive process, it lacks confidentiality, and the parties lack control over key aspects, such as choice of law and choice of judge. Other drawbacks have been noted above, insofar as transnational disputes are concerned – lack of perceived neutrality and enforcement of the court's judgment beyond the borders of the forum.

Arbitration like mediation is a private dispute resolution process. An arbitration can only take place pursuant to an agreement between the disputants. This agreement may be found in arbitral provisions in the contract that has given rise to the dispute or in

---

1   Moens, G, 'Reflections on commercial dispute resolution' 7 *ADR Bulletin* 3, 41, discussing Fulton, MJ, *Commercial Alternative Dispute Resolution*, 1989, Sydney: Law Book Co.

2   Moens, *op cit* at 44 – sourcing the quotation comprising (ii) from Fulton, *op cit* at 79.

some other antecedent agreement; or it may be the product of an agreement between the parties after the dispute has arisen. The arbitrator or arbitral panel (where there is more than one arbitrator – typically three) derive their authority and jurisdiction from this agreement of the parties. The arbitration can be of a domestic or a transnational dispute.

The parties through their agreement control significant aspects of the process, subject to any applicable law, most obviously the law of the jurisdiction where the arbitration takes place. (Typically this law is facilitative rather than subversive of the arbitral agreement.) The parties will control the structure of the process (for example, how proceedings are initiated and conducted, and the composition of the arbitral tribunal), and the applicable procedural and substantive law. They will appoint the arbitrator or arbitrators, and the arbitrator will focus on their case with a greater deal of exclusivity than will be possible for a judge in a court system.

The arbitration is determinative, in that the arbitrator's decision is *prima facie* binding (subject to any grounds of judicial review). In this aspect the arbitration mimics litigation in the regular court system. Like the latter, the arbitration is to be decided according to law (whichever law that the parties have agreed upon). The arbitrator must proceed in a judicial manner, but the procedure will be less intricate and more flexible than is commonly the case in the courts. In the typical case the arbitral agreement (subject to any overriding law of the place of arbitration) will severely limit judicial review. Where this is allowed it will be based on error of law and not of fact. This limitation on appeals may be attractive to the parties, because it carries with it the promise of a relatively quick and less expensive road to a final determination.

Arbitration should be quicker than litigation, given the relative simplicity of procedure and the fact that the arbitral tribunal can concentrate with a greater degree of exclusivity upon the case than can a judge in a court. The process may be cheaper, but this is not always the case. The parties must after all fully fund the cost of the infrastructure, whereas the judicial infrastructure in the regular court system is mostly publicly funded.

Where the arbitration concerns an international dispute, there is the advantage previously noted – the perceived neutrality of the arbitral panel as opposed to (the typical case where) the court shares the nationality of one of the parties. Another advantage is the greater scope for enforcement of the arbitral award as opposed to the court's judgment. It is very difficult to enforce the judgment of a court outside of its jurisdiction, in the absence of a treaty between the State where the court has rendered judgment and the State where enforcement is sought, providing for the mutual recognition and enforcement of one another's court decisions. It is a fact that there is no general international treaty providing for this mutual recognition and enforcement of judicial determinations. There are, however, significant treaties that have been widely ratified by many nations and underwritten by domestic laws, providing for the recognition and enforcement of international commercial arbitral awards. In this key aspect, the arbitral award is advantaged in comparison with the court judgment. A third advantage of international arbitration is apparent – the parties get to agree on the applicable law, both the procedural law governing the arbitration and the substantive law governing the dispute. This will typically not be possible where the matter is tried in a court. The court will apply the law of its jurisdiction, which may be unfamiliar to one of the parties.

In summary, the arbitration as contrasted to judicial proceedings in a regular court provides a number of advantages. The parties have greater control over proceedings, enjoying what has been called 'party autonomy'[3] (although once these are under way they can only be terminated by agreement of the parties); they choose the applicable law; they choose the arbitral tribunal; appellate grounds are limited (which assists in a quicker resolution of the dispute); proceedings are confidential; the arbitral proceedings are quicker if not cheaper; the decision-making tribunal is *ex facie* more neutral; and enforcement of the arbitral award can be more readily achieved.

TYPES OF ARBITRATION

One classification divides arbitrational processes into two types – institutional and *ad hoc*.

Institutional arbitration – the International Chamber of Commerce (ICC) Rules

Arbitrations are said to be institutional when they are conducted through the medium of a permanent organisation, such as the International Chamber of Commerce (ICC), or the London Court of International Arbitration (LCIA). Other such organisations include the American Arbitration Association and the Stockholm Chamber of Commerce, and the Australian Centre for International Commercial Arbitration.

Also of note is the Convention on the Settlement of Investment Disputes between States and Nationals of Other States (the Washington Convention, 1965), which provides for the International Centre for Settlement of Investment Disputes (ICSID).

These organisations typically have rules that govern the arbitral process in some detail, and an administrative structure, or secretariat. They provide arbitral services that facilitate the conduct of the procedure. Their rules will govern such matters as the commencement and conduct of the arbitration, and the fees to be charged by the service provider and the arbitrators. The parties may have contracted in the agreement that comes to be disputed, or otherwise, for resort to one of these institutional regimes.

The ICC is the most commonly resorted to institution. The ICC Rules of Arbitration notes in the Foreword (to the 1998 Rules) that the work of the arbitral tribunals formed under its auspices is monitored by the ICC Court, which meets weekly.[4] The Court organises and supervises arbitration under these Rules. The Rules have been specially designed for international cases, but can be used in domestic cases. The ICC has propounded a standard arbitration clause for inclusion by parties to an international transaction, in their contract.

The Rules deal with such matters as the role of the International Court of Arbitration (it does not itself settle disputes – it has the function of ensuring the application of the Rules: Art 2). The arbitration is commenced by the submission of a Request for arbitration to the ICC's Secretariat, with relevant detail including the

---

3   Moens, *op cit* at 43.
4   www.iccwbo.org. The rules are at www.iccarbitration.org.

parties and the dispute. The Secretariat is to send a copy of the Request to the Respondent for its Answer. In these respects, the ICC functions as a court registry, and is a pivot for a process of pleading intended to identify the issues for arbitration. Provision is made for counterclaims by the Respondent. If the parties agree to submit the matter to arbitration under the Rules, they are deemed to have submitted to the Rules (Art 6). As in a court, if the arbitration has been commenced, it is to continue, even if a party refuses or fails to take part in it (Art 6.3). The legal basis for this compulsion is the agreement between the parties for arbitration under the Rules.

Provision is made for the appointment of an arbitral panel (a sole arbitrator or three arbitrators, their confirmation, challenges to their appointment and replacement (Arts 8ff)). The Court has the power to appoint arbitrators in the absence of agreement by the parties.

The place and course of arbitral proceedings are regulated by the Rules (Arts 19ff). The parties typically choose significant matters such as the place of arbitration, language and the applicable rules of law (if the parties cannot agree the Court selects those most appropriate). The Arbitral Tribunal is to draw up Terms of Reference, which are to be signed or approved by the Court. Provision is made for establishing the facts of the case by written submissions, other documents and if necessary oral testimony (Art 20). Expert witnesses may be appointed (Art 20.3–4). When it is necessary to conduct a hearing the tribunal is to summon the parties. It may proceed in the absence of a party if the party fails to appear without reasonable excuse (Art 21). The tribunal may order interim or conservatory measures on the request of a party. In appropriate circumstances a party may apply to a competent judicial authority (usually a court, for these (Art 23)).

Awards are dealt with in Arts 24ff. The tribunal must render its final award within six months of a defined event such as the date of the final signature by the tribunal or as party on the Terms of Reference (Art 24). The ICC Court may extend this limit. Where there is more than one arbitrator the award is by majority decision. The award is to state the reasons for decision (Art 25). There may be an award by consent, where the parties reach a settlement (Art 26). The tribunal is to submit the draft award to the ICC Court for scrutiny. The Court may lay down modifications and, without affecting the tribunal's liberty of decision, may also draw its attention to points of substance. No award can be rendered until approved by the Court as to its form (Art 27).

Provision is made for the notification by the Secretariat of the text of the award to the parties provided that the costs of the arbitration have been duly paid to the ICC by the parties or one of them (Art 28). Provision is also made for the correction and interpretation of the award (Art 29), and costs (Art 30). Broadly, the Court is to fix the administrative costs and the fees and expenses of the arbitrators as soon as practicable,[5] but provision is made for adjustment of this amount, given that the proceedings as they unfurl may be more complex. The final award is to fix the global costs of the arbitration – ICC administrative costs, fees and expenses of arbitrators, expert witness fees and expenses, and the costs of legal representation for the parties; and to decide which of the parties shall bear them and in what proportion (Art 31).

---

5   Appendix III to the ICC Rules of Arbitration provides for scales for administrative expenses and arbitrator's fees, calculated by reference to the sum in dispute.

Ad hoc arbitration – the UNCITRAL Model Law

Ad hoc arbitration is a process of arbitration that is independent of one of the arbitration service providers. It will occur where the parties have not, in the contract in dispute or otherwise, agreed to submit their dispute for arbitration under the auspices and (where applicable) rules of one of the arbitration organisations.

If they cannot agree upon arbitration, then the obvious alternative mechanism for dispute resolution will be the courts.

Alternatively, the parties will, after a dispute has arisen, agree to submit their dispute to arbitration. They will need to agree upon the rules of arbitration and all other aspects of the arbitration, such as place of arbitration and rules of law to be applied, both procedural and substantive. They will need to put the infrastructure in place themselves, selecting the arbitral panel, agreeing on costs and fees, etc.

It will simplify matters if the parties agree in the contract in dispute or otherwise, that their dispute is to be decided according to an established set of arbitral rules. One possibility is for them to agree that their dispute should be arbitrated according to a statute governing arbitration in the State of one of them. For the reasons noted earlier, this may not suit both parties.

The alternative is for them to agree upon arbitration according to rules which are independent of either parties' State. One such regime is the UNCITRAL Model Law on International Commercial Arbitration, which was adopted by the United Nations Commission in International Trade Law on 21 June 1985. In this case they will not need to settle the rules of arbitration, although they will still need collectively to organise the infrastructure for the arbitration. The UNCITRAL rules provide for international arbitration in the complete sense, in that not only does the dispute have a transnational aspect, but the rules applied to the arbitration are of transactional application.

The UNCITRAL rules are the best known of these international commercial arbitration rules.

Article 1 applies the Model Law (the Law) to international commercial arbitration. 'International' is defined – it covers cases where, *inter alia*, the parties have their businesses in different States; or the place of arbitration as determined in or pursuant to the arbitration agreement is situated outside the State in which the parties have their places of business; or the parties have expressly agreed that the subject-matter of the arbitration agreement relates to more than one country (Art 1(3)). The term 'commercial' is to be interpreted so as to cover matters arising from all relationships of a commercial nature, whether contractual or not.

Article 5 provides that the role of the State's courts (most obviously the State where the arbitration is to be conducted) cannot intervene except where provided by the Law. Self-evidently, the Law cannot effectively limit judicial intervention in this way unless the Law is enacted into the domestic law of the State in question, and thereby given force of law. This has been done in many States – about 45. If an action concerning the dispute is brought before a court, notwithstanding an agreement between the parties for arbitration pursuant to the Law, the court is on the request of a party to refer the parties to arbitration unless it finds that the agreement is null and void, inoperative or incapable of being performed (Art 8(1)). Consistent with the agreement, a party may seek from the court an interim measure of protection (Art 8(2)).

The arbitral agreement must be in writing, although the writing can consist of a collection of documents, including telecommunications, which record the agreement (Art 7(2)).

Article 10 prescribes the number of arbitrators. The parties are free to choose this, but failing agreement the number is to be three. The parties are free to appoint the arbitrator or arbitrators, but where they cannot agree provision is made. If need be, the court or other authority[6] is to appoint them (Art 11). Provision is made for challenges to arbitrators' appointments. If the panel cannot satisfactorily resolve this, the matter is referred to the court or other authority (Art 13). If an arbitrator becomes *de jure* or *de facto* unable to act his mandate terminates if he withdraws from office or if the parties agree on the termination. Otherwise the court may decide the issue (Art 14). Provision is made for appointment of a substitute arbitrator (Art 15).

As it will be noted, the Law does preserve a role for judicial intervention in cases where matters of significance cannot be agreed upon by the party and the Law itself cannot provide a satisfactory resolution of the issue. This is particularly apparent in matters involving the setting up of the infrastructure, issues which can be dealt with by the arbitral organisation in institutional arbitration. Essentially, the court's role is facilitative of the arbitral process.

The arbitral tribunal is competent to rule on its own jurisdiction, including any objections with respect to the existence or validity of the arbitral agreement. A decision that an agreement containing an arbitral clause is null and void does not in itself invalidate the arbitral clause (Art 16). The tribunal has the power to order interim measures of protection in respect of the subject matter of the dispute (Art 17).

Provision is made for the conduct of the arbitral proceedings. Parties are to be treated equally and given a full opportunity to present their case (Art 18). This reflects that arbitral proceedings, though not judicial in nature, are to be conducted in a quasi-judicial manner. The parties are free to agree on the procedure to be followed by the tribunal, but failing agreement the tribunal will, subject to the Law, conduct the arbitration in such manner as it considers appropriate. This power extends to determining the admissibility, relevance and weight of evidence (Art 19).

The parties may agree upon the place of arbitration, otherwise the tribunal will determine it having regard to appropriate circumstances (Art 20). The parties are to agree on the language of the arbitration, failing which the tribunal will determine the language (Art 22).

The parties are to prepare statements of claim and defence. These may be amended during proceedings unless the tribunal considers this to be inappropriate (Art 23).

Unless the parties agree otherwise, the tribunal shall decide whether to hold oral hearings for the presentation of evidence or for oral argument, or whether the proceedings shall be conducted on the basis of documents and other materials. All statements, documents or other materials supplied to be tribunal by a party shall be supplied to the other party. Any other material which the tribunal may rely upon shall be made available to the parties (Art 24).

---

6   See Art 6. Each State enacting the Law as law within its jurisdiction must include appropriate specifications. See, for example, the International Arbitration Act 1974 (Cth) s 18 – if the place of arbitration is a State the court is the Supreme Court of the State, and if it is a Territory it is the Supreme Court of the Territory.

The arbitration is to continue notwithstanding an act of default by a party such as non-communication of a statement or claim or defence or failure to appear at a hearing or to produce documentary evidence, where no sufficient cause for this failure is shown (Art 25).

Unless the parties agree otherwise, the tribunal can appoint an expert or experts to report to it on specific issues or supply other information, including by way of participation in a hearing (Art 26). The tribunal or party with its approval may seek the court's assistance in taking evidence (Art 27).

The tribunal is to decide the dispute according to the rules of law chosen by the parties as applicable to the substance of rhe dispute. Where the parties refer to the law of a State as being applicable, this designation shall be taken as referring to the substantive law of the State and not (merely) its conflict of laws rules. If there is no such agreement by the parties, the arbitral tribunal is to apply the conflict of laws rules it considers applicable to determine the applicable substantive law (Art 28(1)–(2)).[7]

The tribunal shall decide matters *ex aequo et bono* or as *amiable compositeur* only if the parties have expressly agreed on this (Art 28(3)). This may be appropriate where the law otherwise applicable would compel a result that is unwelcome to the parties. When the tribunal acts in this mode it does not apply the law of any forum but decides matters in accordance with equity (in the non-technical sense[8]) and justice. This does not preclude the tribunal from looking at exemplars of equity and justice in domestic legal systems and international law.

The tribunal is to decide in accordance with the terms of the contract and to take into account the usages of the trade (that is, the norms and practices and conventions) applicable to the transaction (Art 28(4)).

Decision-making by the tribunal is by majority, where there is more than one arbitrator (Art 29).

The parties may settle their dispute at any stage during arbitration, in which case the tribunal is to record the settlement in an arbitral award on agreed terms (Art 30).

The award is to be in writing and signed by the arbitrator or arbitrators. It is to state the reasons for the decision (unless the parties have agreed that no reasons are to be given, or it is an award on agreed terms) (Art 31). The proceedings are terminated by the final award, or withdrawal of the claim or agreement of the parties. They are also terminated when the tribunal finds that continuation is unnecessary or impossible (Art 32).

Provision is made for correction and interpretation of the award. The correction goes only to non-substantive matters. A party, with the agreement of the other party, may request the tribunal to interpret a point or part of the award. A party may (unless otherwise agreed by the parties) request the tribunal to make an additional award as to claims presented in the proceedings but omitted from the award.

---

7   For example, if the parties agree that the arbitration is to be held in Sydney, and the contract in dispute involves parties in Australia and Singapore, the Australian conflict of laws rules would identify Australian law (federal and New South Wales) as the applicable substantive law. In any event, the specification of a country of arbitration would carry with it an implied agreement that the law of this place should apply, in the absence of any contrary intention.

8   Ie, the sense in which the term is understood in a common law jurisdiction, as denoting the judge-made principles and rules descended from the English Court of Chancery.

Provision is made in Art 34 for recourse against the award. A party may apply to a court to set aside the award in specified cases, such as where a party to the arbitration agreement was under an incapacity, or the award is not valid under the law to which the parties have subjected it or under the law of the State of arbitration, or lack of proper notice of the arbitration to a party, or on the ground that the award deals with a dispute not contemplated by or falling within the terms of the submission to arbitration, or the composition of the tribunal was not as agreed by the parties, or the subject matter was not capable of settlement by arbitration under the law of the State of arbitration or the award conflicts with the public policy of this State.

Provision is made in Arts 35–36 for the recognition and enforcement of awards. The award is declared to be binding, irrespective of the country in which it was made. Application may be made to a competent court (in a State which has adopted the UNCITRAL Model Law) for enforcement of the award. The applicant must supply the duly authenticated original award or a certified copy.

Pursuant to Art 36, recognition and enforcement of the arbitral award may be refused only on certain grounds. These include the grounds set out in Art 34 above, concerning bases for seeking the setting aside of an award by a court. An additional ground for refusing enforcement is that the award has not yet become binding on the parties or has been set aside or suspended by a court of the country in which, or under the law of which, that award was made (Art 36(1)(a),(v)).

Articles 35 and 36 differ in that in the context of the former, a party will seek to pre-empt enforcement of the award by applying to a court to have it set aside; whereas Art 36 will be invoked in a case where the party disputing its validity is Respondent to an action by the successful party for the enforcement of the award.

Articles 35 and 36 parallel the key provisions in the New York Convention (the Convention on the Recognition and Enforcement of Foreign Arbitral Awards) which has been adopted into the law of about 130 countries and is examined in Chapter 11 of this book. These provisions in UNCITRAL and the New York Convention permit judicial review of arbitral awards, but at the same time confine its scope. In particular the unsuccessful party to arbitration does not have a general right to judicial review of the award on the basis of the facts or error of law on the part of the tribunal. Review is confined to those grounds for review specified in these two regimes. The parties may be taken to have been attracted to this limitation on judicial review by their agreement to arbitration in circumstances attracting the operation of one or both of these regimes. As noted earlier, limiting the role of the courts may have the effect of simplifying and expediting the resolution of the dispute, and in some cases but not all, getting this done more cheaply.

HOW DO PARTIES COME TO BE BOUND BY INTERNATIONAL ARBITRATION REGIMES?

The parties to an international contract or other commercial relationship may come under an obligation to settle their dispute by arbitration as a result of their agreement. How does this arbitral process come to be governed by one or another of the international arbitral regimes?

One obvious way is to specify this regime in a clause in their arbitral agreement. If they specify arbitration, then in the normal course they will specify additional matters such as the applicable rules. Such an agreement can only be enforced if the law of the State where the arbitration is to take place, and/or where the arbitral award is to be enforced, recognise this election.

Another possibility is that the law of the forum imposes an obligation upon the parties to conduct their arbitration pursuant to one of the recognised arbitral regimes. Any such stipulation will centre on one of the international treaty regimes, such as the UNCITRAL Model Law. It will not mandate use of private rules associated with an arbitral organisation such as the ICC. The imposition of the regime may be mandatory. If it is mandatory the parties may be given the right to opt out of it. Alternatively, it may only be imposed when the parties have nominated it (in which case the parties can, if they have nominated it, normally opt out of it by unanimous agreement at a later time).

ROLE OF THE NATIONAL LAW

The law of the State where the agreement is to be carried out, or an award made under it recognised and enforced in the courts of the State, will need to recognise and apply the regime. This will happen where the State has ratified the convention for the regime and given it the force of law in domestic legislation. The domestic legislation implementing the rules in each case will have to contain ancillary details such as how arbitral awards are to be enforced in the State.

In such a case, as reflected above, national law may apply the international arbitral regime irrespective of the parties' wishes, or it may apply it where they enliven it through an agreement that specifies that their arbitration will proceed according to one of these regimes (or they fail to opt out).

If the parties do not specify arbitration, then normally they will be free to litigate the dispute in the courts of the subject State. It will only be where the parties have specified arbitration, and the dispute is an international one according to the relevant definition, that the issue of the applicability of the regime arises.

The international arbitration provisions in the Australian federal statute, the International Arbitration Act 1974 (Cth), are perhaps representative. Australia has ratified the New York Convention and adopted the UNCITRAL Model Law.

The Act by s 16 gives the UNCITRAL Model Law the force of law, subject to the Act. The Law itself provides in Art 1(2) that it does not apply fully in the subject State if the arbitration was outside the State.[9] The UNCITRAL regime applies *prima facie* to foreign arbitrations, but by s 21 of the Act, the parties can opt out of the regime by unanimous written agreement. It follows that provided the other tests are satisfied the parties will be bound by the regime unless they expressly opt out of it. This agreement can be in the contract in dispute or it can be entered into at a later stage.

---

9 Article 1(3) provides that the provisions of this Law, except Arts 8, 9, 35 and 36, apply only if the place of arbitration is the territory of this State. This is logical – if the award is sought to be enforced (necessarily, after it is rendered) in State X being a State other than where it was rendered, the details of the arbitral process, such as Arts 10ff, will have no application in State X.

The Law limits judicial review of the arbitral process as has been noted.[10]

The International Arbitration Act 1974 sets out, in Schedule I, the text of the New York Convention on the Recognition and Enforcement of Foreign Arbitral Awards. It does not specify in a discrete section that it has the force of law, but the provisions in Part II, headed 'Enforcement of foreign awards' in substance do this. By s 3(1), a 'foreign award' is 'an arbitral award made, in pursuance of an arbitration agreement, in a country other than Australia, being an arbitral award in relation to which the Convention applies'. It follows that these provisions do not apply to awards rendered within Australia, even if they are international in nature.[11]

Enforcement is only available under the Act (and in turn the Convention as enacted in substance by it) in defined cases, including where the procedure in relation to an arbitration agreement is governed, by an express term in the agreement or otherwise, by the law of a Convention country (that is, one which has ratified the Convention), or where a party to the agreement is domiciled or ordinarily resident in a Convention country (including Australia) (s 1).

Section 8 provides that a foreign award is binding by virtue of this Act for all purposes on the parties (subs (1)), and that it may be enforced in a court of a State or Territory in accordance with the law of that State or Territory (subs (2)).[12] It also provides for limited judicial review of the award in the same terms as are provided in Art V of the Convention dealing with challenges to recognition and enforcement (such as that the subject matter of the difference is not capable of settlement by arbitration under the law of the subject country, or enforcement would be contrary to public policy).

Where Part II of the Act (which applies the Convention) is applicable, the recognition and enforcement provisions in the Law do not apply (s 20).

ROLE OF THE NATIONAL COURTS

The courts of the State where an arbitral agreement is sought to be enforced, and an award made under it enforced, have the role in relation to these matters that is conferred on them by the law of the State.

As a general observation, domestic law typically does respect the arbitral process, and confines the grounds for judicial review of the process and of resulting awards.

More specifically, where the UNCITRAL Model Law is recognised and made part of the law of a State, the grounds for judicial review of the process and of the award

---

10 See as well s 19 of the Act, which provides that without limiting the generality of subparas 34(2)(b)(ii) and 36(1)(b)(ii) of the Law, it is hereby declared for the avoidance of doubt that an award is in conflict with the public policy of Australia if the making of the award was induced or affected by corruption, or a breach of the rules of natural justice occurred in connection with the making of the award.

11 In which case the enforcement may be sought under the UNCITRAL Model Law as applied by the Act, or in a case where the Law is not applicable, under a State or Territorial arbitration statute. As noted the UNCITRAL provisions on the recognition and enforcement of foreign arbitral awards mirror those in the New York Convention.

12 Consistent with s 7(1), by s 8(4) the award cannot be enforced under s 8(1)–(2) where at the time enforcement is sought the country where the award was made was not a Convention country, unless at this time the applicant is domiciled or ordinarily resident in Australia.

are limited. The court can be approached in defined circumstances for orders facilitating the arbitral process.

Where awards are concerned, the grounds for judicial review, both under the recognition and enforcement regimes in the Law and the New York Convention, are limited. These regimes do not permit a general right of review, or appeal, on the facts or the law. This is consistent with the rationale for arbitration (that is, that disputes can be settled more quickly), and where international disputes are concerned, in a State-neutral forum applying laws agreed upon by parties.

TUTORIAL QUESTIONS

Note: some of these tutorial questions are based on actual examination questions, set by the Chartered Institute of Arbitrators for people who propose to qualify as an Associate Member of the Institute (ACIArb).

1   You receive a letter from a firm of solicitors inviting you to accept appointment as arbitrator. The letter contains no other details. What information would you request before deciding whether to accept the appointment?

2   Describe the grounds on which a party may challenge an award.

3   Describe briefly what the following mean:
    (i)   Consent award.
    (ii)   Interim award.
    (iii) Final award.

4   You are conducting the arbitration hearing of a contractual dispute between a Claimant farmer and a Respondent veterinary surgeon, held at the farm of the Claimant. On the morning of the second day, the Claimant says that when the Respondent left the previous evening, he left two gates open and a lot of stock wandered off. It took the farmer several hours to retrieve them and he missed the milk collection, but much worse, passing traffic injured a cow, two sheep and a pig. The Respondent denies all liability. The Claimant then asks you to include this dispute in the reference. What do you do?

5   What is the general principle on which an arbitrator awards costs? When might the arbitrator depart from it?

6   An award should set out certain information before it deals with the dispute itself. What should this information ideally comprise?

7   List and discuss five substantive requirements of a valid and enforceable award.

8   Is any and all evidence allowable at an arbitration hearing? Explain any forms or categories of evidence which should not be permitted by arbitrators.

FURTHER READING

Berger, KP, *Arbitration Interactive*, 2002, Frankfurt am Main: Peter Lang.

Binder, P, *International Commercial Arbitration in UNCITRAL Model Law Jurisdictions*, 2000, London: Sweet & Maxwell.

Born, GB, *International Commercial Arbitration*, 2nd edn, 2001, Ardsley, NY: Transnational Publishers/The Hague: Kluwer Law International.

Broches, A, *Commentary on the UNCITRAL Model Law on International Commercial Arbitration*, 1990, Deventer: Kluwer.

Burnett, R, *The Law of International Business Transactions*, 3rd edn, 2004, Sydney: Federation Press.

Carbonneau, TE, *Cases and Materials on the Law and Practice of Arbitration*, 3rd edn, 2002, Yonkes, NY: Juris Publishing.

Carr, I and Kidner, R, *Statutes and Conventions on International Trade Law*, 1993, London: Cavendish Publishing.

Chukwumerije, O, *Choice of Law in International Commercial Arbitration*, 1994, Westport, CT: Quorum Books.

Coe, J, *International Commercial Arbitration: American Principles and Practice in a Global Context*, 1997, Irving-on-Hudson, NY: Transnational Publishers.

D'Arcy, L, Murray, C and Cleave, B, *Schmitthoff's Export Trade: The Law and Practice of International Trade*, 10th edn, 2000, London: Sweet & Maxwell.

Garnett, R, Gabriel, H, Waincymer, J and Epstein, J, *A Practical Guide to International Commercial Arbitration*, 2000, Dobbs Ferry, NY: Oceana Publications.

Garrett, A, *Practical Guide to International Commercial Arbitration*, 2000, Dobbs Ferry, NY: Oceana Publications.

Hill, J, *International Commercial Disputes*, 1998, London: LLP Reference Publishing.

Huber, SK and Trachte-Huber, WE, *Arbitration: Cases and Materials*, 1998, Cincinnati, OH: Anderson Publishing.

Lookofsky, JM, *Transnational Litigation and Commercial Arbitration: A Comparative Analysis of American, European, and International Law*, 1992, Ardsley, NY: Transnational Juris Publications.

Lord, R and Salzedo, S, *Guide to the Arbitration Act 1996*, 1996, London, Cavendish Publishing.

Redfern, A and Hunter, M, *Law and Practice of International Commercial Arbitration*, student edition, 4th edn, 2004, London: Sweet & Maxwell.

Sarcevic, P, *Essays on International Commercial Arbitration*, 1989, London: Graham and Trotman.

Schaffer, R, Earle, B and Agusti, F, *International Business Law and its Environment*, 4th edn, 1999, Cincinnati, OH: West Educational Publishing, Ch 4.

Todd, P, *Cases and Materials on International Trade Law*, 2003, London: Sweet & Maxwell.

Van Den Berg, A, *The New York Arbitration Convention of 1958*, 1981, The Hague: Kluwer

Van Houtte, H, *The Law of International Trade*, 1995, London: Sweet & Maxwell.

Internet resources

http://www.lib.uchicago.edu/~llou/forintlaw.html   International Commercial Arbitration: Resources in Print and Electronic format, University of Chicago Law School, D'Angelo Law Library.

www.worldbank.org   ICSID materials.

www.iccwbo.org/court   ICC Court of International Arbitration materials.

www.Lcia.com   London Centre for International Arbitration.

www.pca.cpa.org   Permanent Court of Arbitration at The Hague.

www.uncitral.org   UNCITRAL instruments.

www.jus.uio.no/lm/index.html   Lex Mercatoria – international law and e-commerce site.

www.jurisint.org   Juris International – international conventions, etc.

www.asil.org/resource/pill.htm   ASIL guide to Electronic Resources for International Law.

www.laweye.de   Eye on International Business Law.

www.cisg.law.pace.edu   Pace University site on Vienna Convention – CSIG.

APPENDIX

UNCITRAL MODEL LAW ON INTERNATIONAL COMMERCIAL ARBITRATION

(United Nations document A/40/17, Annex I)

(As adopted by the United Nations Commission on International Trade Law on 21 June 1985)

CHAPTER I – GENERAL PROVISIONS

Article 1 – Scope of application*

1   This Law applies to international commercial** arbitration, subject to any agreement in force between this State and any other State or States.

2   The provisions of this Law, except Articles 8, 9, 35 and 36, apply only if the place of arbitration is in the territory of this State.

3   An arbitration is international if:

    (a) the parties to an arbitration agreement have, at the time of the conclusion of that agreement, their places of business in different States; or

    (b) one of the following places is situated outside the State in which the parties have their places of business:

        (i)   the place of arbitration if determined in, or pursuant to, the arbitration agreement;

        (ii) any place where a substantial part of the obligations of the commercial relationship is to be performed or the place with which the subject-matter of the dispute is most closely connected; or

    (c) the parties have expressly agreed that the subject-matter of the arbitration agreement relates to more than one country.

---

* Article headings are for reference purposes only and are not to be used for purposes of interpretation.

** The term 'commercial' should be given a wide interpretation so as to cover matters arising from all relationships of a commercial nature, whether contractual or not. Relationships of a commercial nature include, but are not limited to, the following transactions: any trade transaction for the supply or exchange of goods or services; distribution agreement; commercial representation or agency; factoring; leasing; construction of works; consulting; engineering; licensing; investment; financing; banking; insurance; exploitation agreement or concession; joint venture and other forms of industrial or business co-operation; carriage of goods or passengers by air, sea, rail or road.

---

1   For the purposes of paragraph (3) of this article:

    (a) if a party has more than one place of business, the place of business is that which has the closest relationship to the arbitration agreement;

    (b) if a party does not have a place of business, reference is to be made to his habitual residence.

2   This Law shall not affect any other law of this State by virtue of which certain disputes may not be submitted to arbitration or may be submitted to arbitration only according to provisions other than those of this Law.

Article 2 – Definitions and rules of interpretation

For the purposes of this Law:

(a) 'arbitration' means any arbitration whether or not administered by a permanent arbitral institution;

(b) 'arbitral tribunal' means a sole arbitrator or a panel of arbitrators;

(c) 'court' means a body or organ of the judicial system of a State;

(d) where a provision of this Law, except Article 28, leaves the parties free to determine a certain issue, such freedom includes the right of the parties to authorize a third party, including an institution, to make that determination;

(e) where a provision of this Law refers to the fact that the parties have agreed or that they may agree or in any other way refers to an agreement of the parties, such agreement includes any arbitration rules referred to in that agreement;

(f) where a provision of this Law, other than in Articles 25(a) and 32(2)(a), refers to a claim, it also applies to a counter-claim, and where it refers to a defence, it also applies to a defence to such counter-claim.

Article 3 – Receipt of written communications

1   Unless otherwise agreed by the parties:

   (a) any written communication is deemed to have been received if it is delivered to the addressee personally or if it is delivered at his place of business, habitual residence or mailing address; if none of these can be found after making a reasonable inquiry, a written communication is deemed to have been received if it is sent to the addressee's last-known place of business, habitual residence or mailing address by registered letter or any other means which provides a record of the attempt to deliver it;

   (b) the communication is deemed to have been received on the day it is so delivered.

2   The provisions of this article do not apply to communications in court proceedings.

Article 4 – Waiver of right to object

A party who knows that any provision of this Law from which the parties may derogate or any requirement under the arbitration agreement has not been complied with and yet proceeds with the arbitration without stating his objection to such non-compliance without undue delay or, if a time-limit is provided therefore, within such period of time, shall be deemed to have waived his right to object.

Article 5 – Extent of court intervention

In matters governed by this Law, no court shall intervene except where so provided in this Law.

Article 6 – Court or other authority for certain functions of arbitration assistance and supervision

The functions referred to in Articles 11(3), 11(4), 13(3), 14, 16(3) and 34(2) shall be performed by ... [Each State enacting this model law specifies the court, courts or, where referred to therein, other authority competent to perform these functions.]

CHAPTER II – ARBITRATION AGREEMENT

Article 7 – Definition and form of arbitration agreement

1   'Arbitration agreement' is an agreement by the parties to submit to arbitration all or certain disputes which have arisen or which may arise between them in respect of a defined legal relationship, whether contractual or not. An arbitration agreement may be in the form of an arbitration clause in a contract or in the form of a separate agreement.

2   The arbitration agreement shall be in writing. An agreement is in writing if it is contained in a document signed by the parties or in an exchange of letters, telex, telegrams or other means of telecommunication which provide a record of the agreement, or in an exchange of Statements of claim and defence in which the existence of an agreement is alleged by one party and not denied by another. The reference in a contract to a document containing an arbitration clause constitutes an arbitration agreement provided that the contract is in writing and the reference is such as to make that clause part of the contract.

Article 8 – Arbitration agreement and substantive claim before court

1   A court before which an action is brought in a matter which is the subject of an arbitration agreement shall, if a party so requests not later than when submitting his first Statement on the substance of the dispute, refer the parties to arbitration unless it finds that the agreement is null and void, inoperative or incapable of being performed.

2   Where an action referred to in paragraph (1) of this article has been brought, arbitral proceedings may nevertheless be commenced or continued, and an award may be made, while the issue is pending before the court.

Article 9 – Arbitration agreement and interim measures by court

It is not incompatible with an arbitration agreement for a party to request, before or during arbitral proceedings, from a court an interim measure of protection and for a court to grant such measure.

CHAPTER III – COMPOSITION OF ARBITRAL TRIBUNAL

Article 10 – Number of arbitrators

1   The parties are free to determine the number of arbitrators.

2   Failing such determination, the number of arbitrators shall be three.

Article 11 – Appointment of arbitrators

1   No person shall be precluded by reason of his nationality from acting as an arbitrator, unless otherwise agreed by the parties.

2   The parties are free to agree on a procedure of appointing the arbitrator or arbitrators, subject to the provisions of paragraphs (4) and (5) of this article.

3   Failing such agreement,

(a) in an arbitration with three arbitrators, each party shall appoint one arbitrator, and the two arbitrators thus appointed shall appoint the third arbitrator; if a party fails to appoint the arbitrator within thirty days of receipt of a request to do so from the other party, or if the two arbitrators fail to agree on the third arbitrator within thirty days of their appointment, the appointment shall be made, upon request of a party, by the court or other authority specified in Article 6;

(b) in an arbitration with a sole arbitrator, if the parties are unable to agree on the arbitrator, he shall be appointed, upon request of a party, by the court or other authority specified in Article 6.

4   Where, under an appointment procedure agreed upon by the parties,

(a) a party fails to act as required under such procedure, or

(b) the parties, or two arbitrators, are unable to reach an agreement expected of them under such procedure, or

(c) a third party, including an institution, fails to perform any function entrusted to it under such procedure, any party may request the court or other authority specified in article 6 to take the necessary measure, unless the agreement on the appointment procedure provides other means for securing the appointment.

5   A decision on a matter entrusted by paragraph (3) or (4) of this article to the court or other authority specified in Article 6 shall be subject to no appeal. The court or other authority, in appointing an arbitrator, shall have due regard to any qualifications required of the arbitrator by the agreement of the parties and to such considerations as are likely to secure the appointment of an independent and impartial arbitrator and, in the case of a sole or third arbitrator, shall take into account as well the advisability of appointing an arbitrator of a nationality other than those of the parties.

Article 12 – Grounds for challenge

1   When a person is approached in connection with his possible appointment as an arbitrator, he shall disclose any circumstances likely to give rise to justifiable doubts as to his impartiality or independence. An arbitrator, from the time of his appointment and throughout the arbitral proceedings, shall without delay disclose any such circumstances to the parties unless they have already been informed of them by him.

2   An arbitrator may be challenged only if circumstances exist that give rise to justifiable doubts as to his impartiality or independence, or if he does not possess qualifications agreed to by the parties. A party may challenge an arbitrator appointed by him, or in whose appointment he has participated, only for reasons of which he becomes aware after the appointment has been made.

Article 13 – Challenge procedure

1   The parties are free to agree on a procedure for challenging an arbitrator, subject to the provisions of paragraph (3) of this article.

2   Failing such agreement, a party who intends to challenge an arbitrator shall, within fifteen days after becoming aware of the constitution of the arbitral tribunal or after becoming aware of any circumstance referred to in Article 12(2), send a written Statement of the

reasons for the challenge to the arbitral tribunal. Unless the challenged arbitrator withdraws from his office or the other party agrees to the challenge, the arbitral tribunal shall decide on the challenge.

3   If a challenge under any procedure agreed upon by the parties or under the procedure of paragraph (2) of this article is not successful, the challenging party may request, within thirty days after having received notice of the decision rejecting the challenge, the court or other authority specified in Article 6 to decide on the challenge, which decision shall be subject to no appeal; while such a request is pending, the arbitral tribunal, including the challenged arbitrator, may continue the arbitral proceedings and make an award.

Article 14 – Failure or impossibility to act

1   If an arbitrator becomes *de jure* or *de facto* unable to perform his functions or for other reasons fails to act without undue delay, his mandate terminates if he withdraws from his office or if the parties agree on the termination. Otherwise, if a controversy remains concerning any of these grounds, any party may request the court or other authority specified in Article 6 to decide on the termination of the mandate, which decision shall be subject to no appeal.

2   If, under this article or Article 13(2), an arbitrator withdraws from his office or a party agrees to the termination of the mandate of an arbitrator, this does not imply acceptance of the validity of any ground referred to in this article or Article 12(2).

Article 15 – Appointment of substitute arbitrator

Where the mandate of an arbitrator terminates under Articles 13 or 14 or because of his withdrawal from office for any other reason or because of the revocation of his mandate by agreement of the parties or in any other case of termination of his mandate, a substitute arbitrator shall be appointed according to the rules that were applicable to the appointment of the arbitrator being replaced.

CHAPTER IV – JURISDICTION OF ARBITRAL TRIBUNAL

Article 16 – Competence of arbitral tribunal to rule on its jurisdiction

1   The arbitral tribunal may rule on its own jurisdiction, including any objections with respect to the existence or validity of the arbitration agreement. For that purpose, an arbitration clause which forms part of a contract shall be treated as an agreement independent of the other terms of the contract. A decision by the arbitral tribunal that the contract is null and void shall not entail *ipso jure* the invalidity of the arbitration clause.

2   A plea that the arbitral tribunal does not have jurisdiction shall be raised not later than the submission of the Statement of defence. A party is not precluded from raising such a plea by the fact that he has appointed, or participated in the appointment of, an arbitrator. A plea that the arbitral tribunal is exceeding the scope of its authority shall be raised as soon as the matter alleged to be beyond the scope of its authority is raised during the arbitral proceedings. The arbitral tribunal may, in either case, admit a later plea if it considers the delay justified.

3   The arbitral tribunal may rule on a plea referred to in paragraph (2) of this article either as a preliminary question or in an award on the merits. If the arbitral tribunal rules as a preliminary question that it has jurisdiction, any party may request, within thirty days after having received notice of that ruling, the court specified in article 6 to decide the matter, which decision shall be subject to no appeal; while such a request is pending, the arbitral tribunal may continue the arbitral proceedings and make an award.

Article 17 – Power of arbitral tribunal to order interim measures

Unless otherwise agreed by the parties, the arbitral tribunal may, at the request of a party, order any party to take such interim measure of protection as the arbitral tribunal may consider necessary in respect of the subject-matter of the dispute. The arbitral tribunal may require any party to provide appropriate security in connection with such measure.

CHAPTER V – CONDUCT OR ARBITRAL PROCEEDINGS

Article 18 – Equal treatment of parties

The parties shall be treated with equality and each party shall be given a full opportunity of presenting his case.

Article 19 – Determination of rules of procedure

1   Subject to the provisions of this Law, the parties are free to agree on the procedure to be followed by the arbitral tribunal in conducting the proceedings.

2   Failing such agreement, the arbitral tribunal may, subject to the provisions of this Law, conduct the arbitration in such manner as it considers appropriate. The power conferred upon the arbitral tribunal includes the power to determine the admissibility, relevance, materiality and weight of any evidence.

Article 20 - Place of arbitration

1   The parties are free to agree on the place of arbitration. Failing such agreement, the place of arbitration shall be determined by the arbitral tribunal having regard to the circumstances of the case, including the convenience of the parties.

2   Notwithstanding the provisions of paragraph (1) of this article, the arbitral tribunal may, unless otherwise agreed by the parties, meet at any place it considers appropriate for consultation among its members, for hearing witnesses, experts or the parties, or for inspection of goods, other property or documents.

Article 21 – Commencement of arbitral proceedings

Unless otherwise agreed by the parties, the arbitral proceedings in respect of a particular dispute commence on the date on which a request for that dispute to be referred to arbitration is received by the respondent.

Article 22 – Language

1   The parties are free to agree on the language or languages to be used in the arbitral proceedings. Failing such agreement, the arbitral tribunal shall determine the language or languages to be used in the proceedings. This agreement or determination, unless otherwise specified therein, shall apply to any written Statement by a party, any hearing and any award, decision or other communication by the arbitral tribunal.

2   The arbitral tribunal may order that any documentary evidence shall be accompanied by a translation into the language or languages agreed upon by the parties or determined by the arbitral tribunal.

Article 23 – Statements of claim and defence

1   Within the period of time agreed by the parties or determined by the arbitral tribunal, the claimant shall State the facts supporting his claim, the points at issue and the relief or remedy sought, and the respondent shall State his defence in respect of these particulars, unless the parties have otherwise agreed as to the required elements of such Statements. The parties may submit with their Statements all documents they consider to be relevant or may add a reference to the documents or other evidence they will submit.

2   Unless otherwise agreed by the parties, either party may amend or supplement his claim or defence during the course of the arbitral proceedings, unless the arbitral tribunal considers it inappropriate to allow such amendment having regard to the delay in making it.

Article 24 – Hearings and written proceedings

1   Subject to any contrary agreement by the parties, the arbitral tribunal shall decide whether to hold oral hearings for the presentation of evidence or for oral argument, or whether the proceedings shall be conducted on the basis of documents and other materials. However, unless the parties have agreed that no hearings shall be held, the arbitral tribunal shall hold such hearings at an appropriate stage of the proceedings, if so requested by a party.

2   The parties shall be given sufficient advance notice of any hearing and of any meeting of the arbitral tribunal for the purposes of inspection of goods, other property or documents.

3   All Statements, documents or other information supplied to the arbitral tribunal by one party shall be communicated to the other party. Also any expert report or evidentiary document on which the arbitral tribunal may rely in making its decision shall be communicated to the parties.

Article 25 – Default of a party

Unless otherwise agreed by the parties, if, without showing sufficient cause,

(a) the claimant fails to communicate his Statement of claim in accordance with Article 23(1), the arbitral tribunal shall terminate the proceedings;

(b) the respondent fails to communicate his Statement of defence in accordance with Article 23(1), the arbitral tribunal shall continue the proceedings without treating such failure in itself as an admission of the claimant's allegations;

(c) any party fails to appear at a hearing or to produce documentary evidence, the arbitral tribunal may continue the proceedings and make the award on the evidence before it.

Article 26 – Expert appointed by arbitral tribunal

1   Unless otherwise agreed by the parties, the arbitral tribunal

(a) may appoint one or more experts to report to it on specific issues to be determined by the arbitral tribunal;

(b) may require a party to give the expert any relevant information or to produce, or to provide access to, any relevant documents, goods or other property for his inspection.

2   Unless otherwise agreed by the parties, if a party so requests or if the arbitral tribunal considers it necessary, the expert shall, after delivery of his written or oral report, participate in a hearing where the parties have the opportunity to put questions to him and to present expert witnesses in order to testify on the points at issue.

Article 27 – Court assistance in taking evidence

The arbitral tribunal or a party with the approval of the arbitral tribunal may request from a competent court of this State assistance in taking evidence. The court may execute the request within its competence and according to its rules on taking evidence.

CHAPTER VI – MAKING AWARD AND
TERMINATION OF PROCEEDINGS

Article 28 – Rules applicable to substance of dispute

1   The arbitral tribunal shall decide the dispute in accordance with such rules of law as are chosen by the parties as applicable to the substance of the dispute. Any designation of the law or legal system of a given State shall be construed, unless otherwise expressed, as directly referring to the substantive law of that State and not to its conflict of laws rules.

2   Failing any designation by the parties, the arbitral tribunal shall apply the law determined by the conflict of laws rules which it considers applicable.

3   The arbitral tribunal shall decide *ex aequo et bono* or as *amiable compositeur* only if the parties have expressly authorized it to do so.

4   In all cases, the arbitral tribunal shall decide in accordance with the terms of the contract and shall take into account the usages of the trade applicable to the transaction.

Article 29 – Decision making by panel of arbitrators

In arbitral proceedings with more than one arbitrator, any decision of the arbitral tribunal shall be made, unless otherwise agreed by the parties, by a majority of all its members. However, questions of procedure may be decided by a presiding arbitrator, if so authorized by the parties or all members of the arbitral tribunal.

Article 30 – Settlement

1   If, during arbitral proceedings, the parties settle the dispute, the arbitral tribunal shall terminate the proceedings and, if requested by the parties and not objected to by the arbitral tribunal, record the settlement in the form of an arbitral award on agreed terms.

2   An award on agreed terms shall be made in accordance with the provisions of Article 31 and shall State that it is an award. Such an award has the same status and effect as any other award on the merits of the case.

Article 31– Form and contents of award

1   The award shall be made in writing and shall be signed by the arbitrator or arbitrators. In arbitral proceedings with more than one arbitrator, the signatures of the majority of all members of the arbitral tribunal shall suffice, provided that the reason for any omitted signature is Stated.

2   The award shall State the reasons upon which it is based, unless the parties have agreed that no reasons are to be given or the award is an award on agreed terms under Article 30.

3   The award shall State its date and the place of arbitration as determined in accordance with Article 20(1). The award shall be deemed to have been made at that place.

4   After the award is made, a copy signed by the arbitrators in accordance with paragraph (1) of this article shall be delivered to each party.

Article 32 – Termination of proceedings

1   The arbitral proceedings are terminated by the final award or by an order of the arbitral tribunal in accordance with paragraph (2) of this article.

2   The arbitral tribunal shall issue an order for the termination of the arbitral proceedings when:
    (a) the claimant withdraws his claim, unless the respondent objects thereto and the arbitral tribunal recognizes a legitimate interest on his part in obtaining a final settlement of the dispute;
    (b) the parties agree on the termination of the proceedings;
    (c) the arbitral tribunal finds that the continuation of the proceedings has for any other reason become unnecessary or impossible.

3   The mandate of the arbitral tribunal terminates with the termination of the arbitral proceedings, subject to the provisions of Articles 33 and 34(4).

Article 33 – Correction and interpretation of award; additional award

1   Within thirty days of receipt of the award, unless another period of time has been agreed upon by the parties:
    (a) a party, with notice to the other party, may request the arbitral tribunal to correct in the award any errors in computation, any clerical or typographical errors or any errors of similar nature;
    (b) if so agreed by the parties, a party, with notice to the other party, may request the arbitral tribunal to give an interpretation of a specific point or part of the award. If the arbitral tribunal considers the request to be justified, it shall make the correction or give the interpretation within thirty days of receipt of the request. The interpretation shall form part of the award.

2   The arbitral tribunal may correct any error of the type referred to in paragraph (1)(a) of this article on its own initiative within thirty days of the date of the award.

3   Unless otherwise agreed by the parties, a party, with notice to the other party, may request, within thirty days of receipt of the award, the arbitral tribunal to make an additional award as to claims presented in the arbitral proceedings but omitted from the award. If the arbitral tribunal considers the request to be justified, it shall make the additional award within sixty days.

4   The arbitral tribunal may extend, if necessary, the period of time within which it shall make a correction, interpretation or an additional award under paragraph (1) or (3) of this article.

5   The provisions of Article 31 shall apply to a correction or interpretation of the award or to an additional award.

CHAPTER VII – RECOURSE AGAINST AWARD

Article 34 – Application for setting aside as exclusive recourse against arbitral award

1 Recourse to a court against an arbitral award may be made only by an application for setting aside in accordance with paragraphs (2) and (3) of this article.

2 An arbitral award may be set aside by the court specified in Article 6 only if:

(a) the party making the application furnishes proof that:

(i) a party to the arbitration agreement referred to in Article 7 was under some incapacity; or the said agreement is not valid under the law to which the parties have subjected it or, failing any indication thereon, under the law of this State; or

(ii) the party making the application was not given proper notice of the appointment of an arbitrator or of the arbitral proceedings or was otherwise unable to present his case; or

(iii) the award deals with a dispute not contemplated by or not falling within the terms of the submission to arbitration, or contains decisions on matters beyond the scope of the submission to arbitration, provided that, if the decisions on matters submitted to arbitration can be separated from those not so submitted, only that part of the award which contains decisions on matters not submitted to arbitration may be set aside; or

(iv) the composition of the arbitral tribunal or the arbitral procedure was not in accordance with the agreement of the parties, unless such agreement was in conflict with a provision of this Law from which the parties cannot derogate, or, failing such agreement, was not in accordance with this Law; or

(b) the court finds that:

(i) the subject-matter of the dispute is not capable of settlement by arbitration under the law of this State; or

(ii) the award is in conflict with the public policy of this State.

3 An application for setting aside may not be made after three months have elapsed from the date on which the party making that application had received the award or, if a request had been made under Article 33, from the date on which that request had been disposed of by the arbitral tribunal.

4 The court, when asked to set aside an award, may, where appropriate and so requested by a party, suspend the setting aside proceedings for a period of time determined by it in order to give the arbitral tribunal an opportunity to resume the arbitral proceedings or to take such other action as in the arbitral tribunal's opinion will eliminate the grounds for setting aside.

CHAPTER VIII – RECOGNITION AND ENFORCEMENT OF AWARDS

Article 35 – Recognition and enforcement

1 An arbitral award, irrespective of the country in which it was made, shall be recognized as binding and, upon application in writing to the competent court, shall be enforced subject to the provisions of this article and of Article 36.

2 The party relying on an award or applying for its enforcement shall supply the duly authenticated original award or a duly certified copy thereof, and the original arbitration agreement referred to in Article 7 or a duly certified copy thereof. If the award or agreement is not made in an official language of this State, the party shall supply a duly certified translation thereof into such language.***

*** The conditions set forth in this paragraph are intended to set maximum standards. It would, thus, not be contrary to the harmonization to be achieved by the model law if a State retained even less onerous conditions.

Article 36 – Grounds for refusing recognition or enforcement

1 Recognition or enforcement of an arbitral award, irrespective of the country in which it was made, may be refused only:

(a) at the request of the party against whom it is invoked, if that party furnishes to the competent court where recognition or enforcement is sought proof that:

  (i) a party to the arbitration agreement referred to in Article 7 was under some incapacity; or the said agreement is not valid under the law to which the parties have subjected it or, failing any indication thereon, under the law of the country where the award was made; or

  (ii) the party against whom the award is invoked was not given proper notice of the appointment of an arbitrator or of the arbitral proceedings or was otherwise unable to present his case; or

  (iii) the award deals with a dispute not contemplated by or not falling within the terms of the submission to arbitration, or it contains decisions on matters beyond the scope of the submission to arbitration, provided that, if the decisions on matters submitted to arbitration can be separated from those not so submitted, that part of the award which contains decisions on matters submitted to arbitration may be recognized and enforced; or

  (iv) the composition of the arbitral tribunal or the arbitral procedure was not in accordance with the agreement of the parties or, failing such agreement, was not in accordance with the law of the country where the arbitration took place; or

  (v) the award has not yet become binding on the parties or has been set aside or suspended by a court of the country in which, or under the law of which, that award was made; or

(b) if the court finds that:

  (i) the subject-matter of the dispute is not capable of settlement by arbitration under the law of this State; or

  (ii) the recognition or enforcement of the award would be contrary to the public policy of this State.

2   If an application for setting aside or suspension of an award has been made to a court referred to in paragraph (1)(a)(v) of this article, the court where recognition or enforcement is sought may, if it considers it proper, adjourn its decision and may also, on the application of the party claiming recognition or enforcement of the award, order the other party to provide appropriate security.

CHAPTER 11

ENFORCEMENT OF INTERNATIONAL COMMERCIAL ARBITRATION AWARDS – THE NEW YORK CONVENTION

INTRODUCTION

If the arbitration of disputes arising from an international contract or other legal relationship has ended with the rendering of an award, and the party against which the award is made refuses to honour the award, then the question arises as to which law governs the recognition and enforcement of this award. Ultimately, the law governing enforcement is that of the State in which enforcement is sought, which will be a State where the losing party has assets. If the State has implemented the New York Convention on the Recognition and Enforcement of Foreign Arbitral Awards of 1958 ('the Convention'), recognition and enforcement will be according to the terms of this Convention.

In practice, the Convention – as adopted into municipal law – is the main vehicle for the recognition and enforcement of international arbitration awards. The Convention has been ratified by more than 130 countries, including all of the major trading nations.

The recognition and enforcement regime provided for in the Convention aims to provide straightforward and effective procedures for the enforcement of international arbitral awards. It aims to promote uniformity in the principles and processes applying to enforcement, irrespective of the country in which enforcement is sought. The place of enforcement will be chosen according to the location of recoverable assets, rather than the legal system of this State. It is therefore important that the award be readily transportable from State to State without legal or other complications. The Convention intends that the arbitral award be final and not subject to review by the courts in the country of recognition and enforcement. This after all, is what the parties are to be taken to have intended in subscribing to an arbitral agreement. Accordingly, the Convention limits the grounds (or defences) that a party resisting enforcement can plead, although it does not entirely preclude judicial review. The list of grounds for refusing recognition and enforcement is an exhaustive one. There is no provision in the Convention for a general review of the award on the merits, by a court in the country where enforcement is sought.

The courts have manifested a pro-enforcement bias in hearing challenges to recognition and enforcement, having regard to the parties' agreement to arbitration and to the objectives of the Convention. Even where a court finds a defence to be established, it has discretion to reject the challenge and to order enforcement.

The Convention deals with the 'recognition and enforcement' of awards. If a court enforces an award, necessarily it will have recognised it. Infrequently recognition alone will be sought. This might happen, for example, where an award has been rendered, and the award is pursuant to the arbitral agreement, final and binding. Notwithstanding this, a party seeks to litigate afresh issues settled in the arbitration and embodied in the resulting award. The other party could plead the *res judicata* principle, that is, that the issue has been conclusively and finally resolved as between them by the agreed tribunal, and that it is not open to a subsequent court or other tribunal to rehear the matter.

The statutes implementing the Convention in each State by and large reproduce the terms of the Convention. They must, however, make provision for additional matters. One of these is the precise procedure for enforcement of the award through the vehicle of the State's legal system. The chosen models vary. One model is provision for registering the award in the designated court, so that it may be enforced as a judgment of the court. Or provision may be made for application to the court for an order of enforcement, or for the entering of a judgment mirroring the terms of the award. Provision may be made for the range of enforceable remedies that an arbitrator can grant. Provision may be made for suing on the award as if was a debt, or suing for a breach of its terms as a breach of contract.

The implementation statute may need to deal with the meaning of the term 'commercial', where the State in question has at the time of ratification, declared that it will apply the Convention only to differences arising out of legal relationships which are considered as commercial under the State's law, pursuant to Art I(3). The statute may deal with the circumstances in which an award is not to be considered as a 'domestic' award, for the purposes of Art I(1). The statute may deal with the situation when some other legal regime, such as the UNICTRAL Model Law on Commercial Arbitration applies to recognition and enforcement of international commercial awards, instead of the Convention.[1]

Other arbitration conventions or instruments may also be relevant. The International Centre for the Settlement of Investment Disputes (ICSID) was established by the Washington Convention. The ICSID provides for the arbitration of disputes between a State and a national of another State. It is not commonly resorted to.

The UNCITRAL[2] Model Law on Commercial Arbitration, which was adopted by the United Nations Commission on International Trade Law (UNICTRAL) in 1985, has a wider scope than the New York Convention, although its provisions dealing with recognition and enforcement more or less mirror those of the Model Law. It will be for the State that ratifies and implements the Model Law along with the New York Convention to stipulate in statute law when each regime is to apply. Where recognition and enforcement is concerned, not a lot in practice will depend upon which regime applies, given that the defences to recognition and enforcement are uniform across the two of them.

The terms of the New York Convention will now be examined.

RESERVATIONS – RECIPROCITY; COMMERCIAL IN NATURE

Article I(3) of the New York Convention provides that a signatory State may declare stipulated reservations when acceding to the Convention. First, it may declare that it will apply the Convention to the recognition and enforcement of awards made only in the territory of another contracting State. Secondly, it may declare that it will apply the

---

1   Eg, in Australia the International Arbitration Act 1974 (Cth) provides that the Convention governs the enforcement of foreign arbitral awards, but the Model Law applies to local awards made in respect of international disputes, except where the parties have expressly opted out of the Model Law.

2   United Nations Commission on International Trade Law.

Convention only to differences arising out of legal relationships, whether contractual or not, which are considered as commercial under the national law of the State making such a declaration.

As to the first, it has been held by a US court that this principle of reciprocity is concerned with the State in which the arbitration will occur and whether that State is a signatory to the Convention – not whether both parties are nationals of signatory States.[3]

Where the commercial reservation is concerned, the Convention does not define the meaning of the term 'commercial'. Where a State has declared this reservation, the implementing statute may define the scope of 'commercial'.[4] It has been held in a US case, in reliance upon the implementation statute, that seafarers' contracts of employment are excluded from the scope of a 'commercial' dispute for the purposes of the Convention (the US having declared the commercial reservation).[5] In another American case it was held that for the purposes of the Convention a dispute between corporate shareholders regarding the proceedings of a stock transaction was one arising from a commercial relationship.

CONVENTION DEALS WITH INTERNATIONAL ARBITRAL AWARDS AND NON-DOMESTIC AWARDS

The Convention, Art I(1) provides, applies to the recognition and enforcement of awards which are (i) made in the State other than the State where the recognition and enforcement of such awards are sought, and arising out of differences between persons, whether physical or legal; or (ii) not considered as domestic awards in the State where their recognition and enforcement are sought.

The intent of the Article is to confine the application of the Convention to awards that have a genuine international element. The first category of awards covers the standard case where the award is sought to be enforced in a State other than the State where the award was rendered. By definition, such an award has an international element. In practice (although it is not obligatory) the adversaries will be domiciled in different States.

The second category consists of awards that are not considered domestic in the country of enforcement, even though, for example, the place of rendition and enforcement may be the same. This is illustrated in the US case of *Bergesen v Joseph Muller Corporation* (1983),[6] where the award was held to be within the scope of the Convention, although the US was the State both of arbitration and enforcement. The foreign element arose from the fact that the parties were domiciled in foreign countries. Although the Convention did not define 'non-domestic', the concept was to be construed broadly, having regard to the goal of the Convention to encourage

3   *EAST Inc v M/V Alaia* (1989) 876 F 2d 1168 (5th Cir).
4   See, eg, *Food Corp of India v Mardestine Compania Naviera* (1979) IV Yearbook Commercial Arbitration; *Sumimoto Corp v Parakopi Compania Maritima SA* (1979) 477 F Supp 737 (SD NY).
5   *Jaranilla v Megasea Maritime Ltd* (2001) 171 F Supp 2d 644, 646.
6   (1983) 710 F 2d 928. Consideration of the US statute implementing the Convention fortified this conclusion – at 933–34.

the recognition and enforcement of commercial arbitration agreements in international contracts, and applying 'that purpose to this case involving two foreign entities leads to the conclusion that this award is not domestic'.[7] In another US case, the court considered an arbitral agreement which was entered into between US parties and related solely to matters occurring in the US, but which provided for arbitration in London. Enforcement in New York was contemplated should an award be rendered. Consideration of the US statute implementing the Convention led the court to conclude that the arbitral agreement lacked the requisite foreign element, with the result that any award resulting from the agreement would not be within Art I(1) of the Convention, and thus not able to be enforced pursuant to the Convention.[8]

SUBJECT MATTER MUST BE CAPABLE OF SETTLEMENT BY ARBITRATION

Article II(1) provides that each contracting State is to recognise an agreement in writing under which the parties undertake to submit to arbitration any or all differences which have arisen or which may arise between them in respect of a defined legal relationship, whether contractual or not, concerning a matter capable of settlement by arbitration.

The requirements as to form are examined in 'The Article IV requirements as to form in respect of an application for enforcement' below.

The requirement that the subject matter be capable of arbitration is a requirement that it be legally arbitrable, that is, it must be arbitrable under the law of the country of enforcement: 'it seems ... that "capable" means legally capable – for any matter can theoretically be arbitrated or compromised ...'[9] Assuming that the matter has been arbitrated, it is a ground for refusing recognition and enforcement of a resulting award that the difference is not capable of settlement by arbitration under the law of the country of enforcement (Art V2(a)). This defence is examined in 'The Article V grounds for resisting recognition and enforcement' below.

DISPUTE TO BE ARBITRATED, UNLESS AGREEMENT NULL AND VOID, INOPERATIVE OR INCAPABLE OF BEING PERFORMED

Article II(3) provides that the court of a Contracting State, when seized of a matter in respect of which the parties have made an arbitral agreement, shall, at the request of one of the parties, refer the parties to arbitration, unless it finds that the agreement is null and void, inoperative or incapable of being performed.

This issue – essentially the validity of the agreement to arbitrate – logically will be raised prior to arbitration. If it is not raised, or it is raised unsuccessfully by a party, and this party later disputes the recognition and enforcement of the arbitral award, the

---

7   *Ibid* at 932.
8   *Jones v Sea Tow Services Freeport NY Inc* (1994) 30 F 3d 360 (2nd Cir).
9   *Mitsubishi Motors Corp v Soler Chrysler-Plymouth* (1983) 723 F 2d 155, 164.

issue of validity will have to be disputed pursuant to one of the Art V defences. It might, for example, be contended that the agreement being invalid, the arbitrator acted beyond jurisdiction in terms of Art V(1)(c).

Arbitrator's jurisdiction to decide validity of arbitral agreement

Before considering the factors bearing upon the determination of validity, it will be convenient to consider whether an arbitrator has the power to decide on the validity of the arbitral agreement that appoints him or her. Two basic agreements are discernible in the arbitration context – the underlying contract embodying the transaction between the parties, and the agreement to submit to arbitration any disputes arising from this underlying contract and its performance. In practice the arbitral agreement will usually be provided for in a clause in the underlying contract.

The starting point in resolving this issue – in essence whether the arbitrator can determine whether or not he or she has jurisdiction – is to recognise that one party to a contract cannot compel another to submit to arbitration, unless the parties have agreed to submit any dispute to arbitration. Thus, the arbitration agreement must be valid and in existence at the time of the purported submission to arbitration.

It follows that the court will have jurisdiction to determine the threshold issue, that is, whether or not a valid arbitral agreement is in existence at the relevant time. This was confirmed in, for instance, the US case of *Apollo Computer Inc v Berg* (1989).[10] A party sought a permanent stay of arbitral proceedings, contending that there was no agreement to arbitrate between the parties. The court found that the parties had agreed to submit issues to arbitration. As to the contention that, given this foundation agreement, it was no longer valid at the time when arbitration was sought, this secondary issue fell to be determined by the arbitrator. This was because the foundation arbitral agreement provided for arbitration pursuant to the Rules of Arbitration of the International Chamber of Commerce (ICC). Pursuant to these rules, the ICC's Court of Arbitration had determined that the arbitration should proceed because it was satisfied as to the *prima facie* existence of the arbitration agreement. The ICC rules further provided for the delegation to the arbitrator decisions involving the (continued) existence and validity of a *prima facie* agreement to arbitrate.[11]

Where, as will usually be the case, the arbitral agreement is contained in a clause in the underlying contract, and it is contended that the contract is invalid, does this logically mean that the court will decide the issue both of the validity of the agreement to arbitrate and of the underlying contract, because in deciding the threshold issue the court is necessarily deciding the larger issue? The courts have resisted taking control of both issues, and confined themselves to determining no more than is needed to resolve the arbitrator's jurisdiction. They have done this by severing (or separating) the arbitral clause from the underlying agreement, and determining the validity of this clause only, and (assuming the clause is found to be valid), leaving the issue of the validity of the overall agreement to the arbitrator. This is consistent with respecting the

---

10   (1989) 886 F 2d 469 (1st Cir).
11   Likewise, see *Filanto SpA v Chilewich International Corp* (1992) 789 F Supp 1229 (SD NY), holding that it is for the court to decide whether the arbitral agreement exists, and if it does, it is for the arbitrator to decide issues regarding the existence of the underlying contract.

parties' agreement that substantive issues should be submitted to arbitration rather than the courts. (Of course sometimes a court's determination that the arbitral clause is valid, will be supported by reasoning that is sufficiently persuasive to deter a party from raising the issue of the validity of the overall contract during arbitration.)

The process of severing the arbitral clause from the overall agreement is illustrated in the US case of *Societe Nationale Algerienne Pour La Recherche, La Production, Le Transport, La Transformation et La Commercialisation des Hydocarbures v Distrigas Corporation* (1987).[12] The clause, the court held, necessarily had to be separated in a dispute as to the validity of the overall contract, because 'allowing an arbitration clause to be automatically invalidated along with the principal agreement would be akin to destroying "precisely what the parties had sought to create" as a dispute resolution device'.[13] Accordingly, the court confined its attention to the validity of the arbitral clause, determining it to be valid and referring the dispute to arbitration.

In *Twi Lite International Inc v Anam Pacific Corp* (1996)[14] a US court considered that notwithstanding that the overall contract was alleged to have been vitiated by fraud, the arbitral clause in it would be severed so as to compel the referral of the substantive claim, that the principal contract was null and void, to the arbitrator for decision. Furthermore, none of the fraud claimed related to the arbitral provisions.

In the Australian case of *QH Tours Ltd v Ship Design and Management (Aust) Pty Ltd* (1991)[15] the court was concerned with a domestic arbitration agreement, but the principles are logically applicable to an international agreement subject to the Convention. The court considered a challenge to an arbitral clause in a principal contract, with the party resisting arbitration contending that because of the nature of the remedy it sought – an order that the contract be declared to be void *ab initio* pursuant to the Trade Practices Act 1974 (Cth) – the arbitrator was without jurisdiction. For the arbitrator to determine the dispute and award the remedy sought, if this was indeed the outcome of the projected arbitration, would necessarily mean that the contract including the arbitral clause would be determined to be void *ab initio*. As such, it was contended, in this circumstance the arbitrator was logically without jurisdiction. The court held that the arbitral clause could be severed from the overall agreement. Given that the clause existed, it operated to compel arbitration. The plaintiff's challenge to the validity of the clause was based on a technical rather than a substantive complaint. To accede to it would undermine the arbitral process that the parties had contracted for.[16] Foster J commented that having 'regard to the specific nature of an arbitration clause ... generally speaking, it can be regarded as severable from the main contract with the result that, logically, an arbitrator, if otherwise empowered to do so, can declare the main contract void *ab initio* without at the same time destroying the basis of his power to do so'.[17]

---

12 (1987) 80 BR 606, 612.

13 *Ibid* at 609, citing *Lummus Co v Commonwealth Oil Refining Co Inc* (1960) 280 F 2d 915, 924 (1st Cir), cert denied, 364 US 911. See also *Filanto SpA v Chilewich International Corp* (1992) 789 F Supp 1229 (SD NY).

14 (1996) WL 637843 (ND Cal).

15 (1991) 33 FCR 227.

16 *Ibid* at 234–37, applying *Heyman v Darwins Ltd* [1942] AC 356.

17 *Ibid* at 240.

Agreement null and void

Arbitration may be resisted on the basis that the arbitral agreement is null and void, inoperative, or incapable of being performed. If the parties' agreement to arbitrate is ineffective, then there is no legal basis for the arbitration. Limitations on the arbitrator's jurisdiction to determine the threshold issue of the arbitral agreement have just been noted.

It has been said of the 'null and void, inoperative or incapable of being performed' clause that it is to be construed narrowly,[18] having regard to the objectives of the Convention, which are to promote arbitration as a dispute resolution mechanism where the parties have contracted for this, and the presumption in favour of arbitration manifested by the signatory countries in their decision to accede to the Convention. In one case a claim that the contract had been procured by fraud, and was therefore null and void, was ineffective in stalling arbitration. The arbitral clause, it was held, was properly to be severed from the main agreement, and the matter referred to arbitration on the substantive claim of fraud.[19]

In an American case it was commented that the clause 'must be interpreted to encompass only those situations – such as fraud, mistake, duress, and waiver – that can be applied neutrally on an international scale'.[20]

If an arbitral agreement imposes a time limit on resort to arbitration, and this time has expired, *prima facie* the agreement would be inoperative. Cases in which a party has contended arbitration was time barred are examined in the discussion of the Art V(1)(c), below.

THE ARTICLE IV REQUIREMENTS AS TO FORM IN RESPECT OF AN APPLICATION FOR ENFORCEMENT

Article IV(1) provides that a party applying to a court for recognition and enforcement of an award must supply at the time of application (a) the duly authenticated original award or a duly certified copy thereof; and (b) the original agreement referred to in Art II (that is, the arbitration agreement or an agreement containing an arbitration provision) or a duly certified copy thereof. Article IV(2) requires the production of a certified translation of these documents where the originals are in a language other than that of the country of enforcement.

Article II(2) provides that the term 'agreement in writing' shall include an arbitral clause in a contract or an arbitration agreement, signed by the parties, or contained in an exchange of letters or telegrams. A US court has held that notwithstanding the words 'shall include' this provision is exhaustive as to what satisfies 'an agreement in writing'.[21]

---

18 *Twi Lite International Inc v Anam Pacific Corp* (1996) WL 637843, where it was claimed that the contract containing the arbitral clause was procured by fraud; *Oriental Commercial and Shipping Co Ltd v Rosseel* (1985) NV, 609 F Supp 75 (SD NY).

19 *Twi Lite International Inc v Anam Pacific Corp, ibid.*

20 *Ledee v Ceramiche Ragno* (1982) 684 F 2d 184,187 (1st Cir); *Mitsubishi Motors Corp v Soler Chrysler-Plymouth, op cit; Oriental Commercial and Shipping Co Ltd v Rosseel, opcit.*

21 However, the court in *Chloe Z Fishing Co Inc v Odyssey Re (London) Ltd* (2000) 109 F Supp 2d 1236 (SD Cal), holding that Art II(2) prescribes a mandatory, not a minimum requirement.

This court held that arbitral clauses in marine insurance policies (in this case protection and indemnity policies) satisfied the Art II(2) requirement and thus in turn Art IV(1).[22] In the court's view, detailed review of the conduct of the parties in negotiating the policies demonstrated that they had manifested their consent to the arbitral clauses within the meaning of the 'exchange of letters or telegrams' within the meaning of Art II(2). This conduct included the submission by their brokers before each renewal year of the assureds' request for quotation by way of a document known as a 'slip', to the insurers. Each slip contained details of the proposed policy, and the insurer effected a contract of insurance by affixing their stamp to the broker's slip and endorsing it. The broker's slip and the insurer's certificate of insurance constituted an exchange of letters evidencing an assent to contract. These documents were not in the traditional sense 'letters', but the Convention concept was not to be construed so restrictively. It would be unworkable unless it was read expansively as referring to written communications including documents like these, and other forms of communication such as faxes, telexes and e-mails.[23] In summary, the court held that a valid agreement in writing between the parties under the Convention had come into existence.

Furthermore, although the slip and certificate did not include the arbitral clause, they incorporated it by reference to the policy containing it.

A US court held that the Art V(1)(a) requirement that the party seeking enforcement must provide a duly authenticated original award or a duly certified copy of this is satisfied when the party submits (at the minimum) a certified copy of the award. It does not require that this party produce either a duly authenticated original or a duly certified copy of a duly authenticated original. Such a reading of the Article was unduly restrictive: copies 'of the award and the agreement which have been certified by a member of the arbitration panel provide a sufficient basis upon which to enforce the award ...'.[24]

Enforcement was refused in an Italian case when the claimant failed to produce the award and agreement as required by Art IV.[25]

THE ARTICLE V GROUNDS FOR RESISTING RECOGNITION AND ENFORCEMENT

Overview

Article V lists the grounds for refusing recognition and enforcement of an award. Logically, these grounds will be invoked only after an award has been rendered. Article V(1) sets out the five grounds that may be invoked by the party resisting enforcement. Article V(2) provides for two additional grounds for refusing recognition

---

22 *Ibid.*

23 Likewise, see *Compagnie de Navigation et Transports SA v MSC-Mediterranean Shipping Co* (1996) XXI Yearbook Commercial Arbitration 690, 697 (Switzerland), minimising the need for a signature having regard to modern forms of communication.

24 *Bergesen v Joseph Muller Corp* (1983) 710 F 2d 928 at 934.

25 *Vicere Livio (Italy) v Prodexport (Romania)* (1981) VII Yearbook Commercial Arbitration 345.

and enforcement, where the court can act of its own motion. Collectively, and informally, these grounds may be referred to as the seven 'defences' to enforcement. Article V envisages that that the party against which the award has been made will take proceedings before a competent authority (in practice a court) for a ruling against enforcement, in the State where the prevailing party seeks to enforce the award.

The Preamble to Art V(1) provides that recognition and enforcement of an award may be refused, at the request of the party against whom it is invoked, only if that party furnishes to the competent authority where the recognition and enforcement is sought, proof of the facts grounding one of the defences listed thereafter.

The Preamble to Art V(2) provides that recognition and enforcement of an arbitral award may also be refused if the competent authority in the country where recognition and enforcement is sought is satisfied that the facts grounding one of the grounds for refusal listed thereafter, are fulfilled.

The courts hearing challenges to enforcement, have consistently referred to the pro-enforcement bias inherent in the Convention. It has been commented in an American decision that the goal of the Convention was to encourage the recognition and enforcement of international arbitral agreements (and their underlying contracts) and unify the standards by which these agreements are observed, and awards made pursuant to them enforced in signatory countries.[26] This international regulatory regime would be significantly compromised if the courts in individual countries too readily construed or applied it in such a manner as to create uncertainty as to the binding effect of international arbitral awards duly rendered. Another US court commented that the 'expansion of American business and industry will hardly be encouraged if, notwithstanding solemn contracts, we insist on a parochial concept that all disputes must be resolved under our laws and in our courts ... We cannot have trade and commerce in world markets and international waters exclusively on our terms, governed by our law, and resolved in our courts'.[27] The pro-enforcement bias is reflected in cases that have rejected challenges to enforcement based upon the public policy defence, even though the award or underlying contract is contrary to the law of the country of enforcement.

The court has a discretion not to refuse recognition and enforcement of an award, even if a defence is established. This is made clear in the Preambles to Art V(1) and V(2) (recognition and enforcement 'may' be refused). Rejecting a challenge to enforcement in, for instance, circumstances where the party resisting enforcement has established a defence, but in circumstances raising technical rather than substantive issues, would be consistent with the pro-enforcement bias informing application of the Convention.[28] The failure of a party to object before or during arbitration to the matter

---

26 *Sumitomo Corporation v Parakopi Compania Maritima SA* (1979) 477 F Supp 737 (SD NY); *Seven Seas Shipping (UK) Ltd v Tondo Limitada* (1979) 99 CIV 1164 (DLC).

27 *The Bremen v Zapata Off-Shore Co* (1972) 407 US 1, cited in *Societe Nationale Algerienne Pour La Recherche, La Production, Le Transport, La Transformation et La Commercialisation des Hydocarbures v Distrigas Corporation* (1987) 80 BR 606, 612.

28 See *China Nanhai Oil Joint Service Corp v Gee Tai Holdings Co Ltd* (1995) XX Yearbook Commercial Arbitration 671 at 678–79 (objection to an award because the arbitrators were drawn from list A and not list B; defence established but rejected in exercise of the court's discretion). See also *Chromalloy Aeroservices v The Arab Republic of Egypt* (1996) 939 F Supp 907, 909 (DDC).

subsequently complained of by this party will be influential in a court exercising its discretion not to refuse enforcement. In conventional terms, the party may be described as being estopped from relying upon the defence that has been established.[29]

The seven grounds for resisting recognition and enforcement of an award, which are provided for in Art V, are exhaustive.[30] This is made clear by the use of the word 'only' in the Preamble to Art V(1), and limitation of the court's authority to refuse recognition and enforcement, pursuant to Art V(2), to two grounds. In short, the Convention explicitly limits the defences to those provided for in it. This is consistent with the objectives of the Convention, which include providing a uniform framework for, and relative certainty in, enforcement proceedings, no matter where they are sought.

An Australian judge has commented *obiter*, that bearing on mind the wording of the relevant implementing statute in Australia, the court has a residual discretion to refuse to enforce an award, even where none of the defences stipulated in the Convention has been established. In effect it was contended that the grounds for refusing recognition and enforcement were not limited to those stipulated in Art V. This contention may be queried on the basis that had the Australian legislature intended so radical a change in the operation of the Convention in Australia, this would have been provided for expressly in the statute.[31]

It has been commented by an American court that the effect of the Convention is that the enforcement court is not to conduct a review of the arbitrator's findings, in the absence of extraordinary circumstances. In particular, a mistake of law or fact is insufficient to refuse confirmation of an arbitral award.[32] This is consistent with the Convention's objective in making the arbitrator's decision final, with no appeal being permitted to a court on the merits. For the situation to be otherwise would greatly undermine an arbitral regime, whether it be that provided for by the Convention or otherwise. Review of the decision is only permitted, if at all, to the extent provided for by the Art V defences. None of these provides for a general review on the merits.

29 *China Nanhai* decision, *ibid.*

30 *Karaha Bodas Company LCC v Perusahaan Pertambangan Minyak Dan Gas Bumi Negara* (2001) 190 F Supp 2d 936, 943 (SD Texas); *Parsons & Whitmore Overseas Co Inc v Societe Generale de l'Industrie du Papier (RAKTA)* (1974) 508 F 2d 969,973 (CANY); *Yusuf Ahmed Alghanim & Sons WLL v TOYS 'R' US Inc* (1977) 126 F 3d 15 (2nd Cir).

31 *Resort Condominiums International Inc v Bowell* (1993) 118 ALR 655 at 675,678 (SC Qld). The judge, Lee J, held that the alleged award was not an arbitral award within the scope of the Convention, being in the nature of interlocutory orders and not a final award. Even if it was an award, he considered that he had a residual discretion to refuse recognition independently of the Convention defences that were provided for in the implementing statute. This was because this statute, the International Arbitration Act 1974 (Cth), s 8(5), provided that the court 'may, at the request of the party against whom it is invoked, refuse to enforce the award if that party proves that' [the defences in Art V(1)(a) are listed in the remainder of s 8(5)]. Lee J saw it to be significant that the term 'only' was not used in this Preamble to s 8(5), in contrast to Art V(1)(a), the Preamble to which states that recognition and enforcement may be refused '... only if the party' [proves one of the defences enumerated below]. See the comment by Okezie Chukwumerije, 'Enforcement of foreign awards in Australia: the implications of Resort Condominiums' (1994) *Aust Dispute Resolution J* 237.

32 *Karaha Bodas* decision, *op cit.*

The party resisting enforcement pursuant to Art V(1) has the burden of proof imposed upon it to sustain the defence pleaded. This is made explicit by the Preamble to Art V(1), providing that this party must 'furnish ... proof' of the matters grounding the defence. The Preamble to Art V(2) is to like effect, providing that the competent authority may refuse enforcement where it 'finds' that the grounds for refusal exist; language consistent with a requirement that proof of these grounds must exist.[33]

Incapacity; agreement invalid

Article V(1)(a) provides that recognition and enforcement of the award may be refused where the applicant party proves that the parties to the arbitration agreement were, under the law applicable to them, under some incapacity, or the said agreement is not valid under the law to which the parties have subjected it or, failing any indication thereon, under the law of the country where the award was made.

The defence has not been invoked very often.

It would be unlikely in practice that a party to a contract with an international dimension, would be under an incapacity. On occasions the defence of sovereign immunity has been invoked, with it being contended by a party against which enforcement of an award is sought that it is immune from the processes of the enforcement court because it enjoys State immunity as a State or a State agency. In a US case, Libya successfully raised a claim of State immunity to defeat enforcement of an arbitral award against it, but in reliance upon Art V(2)(a) of the Convention (rather than Art V(1)(a)), it being contended that the dispute was not arbitrable.[34] This case will be dealt with in more detail in the review of Art V(2)(a), below. The facts were exceptional, pivoting upon the enactment of laws in Libya that nationalised oil assets. More typically, in the instance of conventional contracts entered into by the entity and a private party, a claim of State immunity will be defeated on the basis that the entity has waived its immunity by agreeing to submit disputes to arbitration.[35]

The second branch of Art V(1)(a) logically would not be invoked very often. If a party believes that the agreement to arbitrate is invalid under the law of the arbitration agreement or the forum in which the award is made, this submission would normally be raised earlier, prior to the marking of an award. Article II(3) provides in substance that the court of the State in which arbitration is sought shall refer the dispute to arbitration unless it finds that the agreement is null and void, inoperative or incapable of being performed. Presumably a party that contests the validity of the agreement would seek a stay of arbitration in the court, on the basis that the agreement to arbitrate is 'null and void', or 'inoperative' or 'incapable of being performed', grounds of stay which are broad enough to comprehend a plea of

---

33 That the party resisting enforcement bears the burden of proof has been confirmed by the courts many times – for example, see *Karaha Bodas* decision, *op cit*.

34 *Libyan American Oil Co v Socialist People's Libyan Arab Jamahirya* (1980) 482 F Supp 1175.

35 See *ibid* at 1178, citing *Ipitrade International, SA v Federal Republic of Nigeria* (1978) 465 F Supp 824 (DDC). See also the discussion of the issue in the decision of an arbitration panel in *SPP (Middle East) Ltd, Hong Kong v Arab Republic of Egypt* (1983) IX Yearbook Commercial Arbitration 111. The panel rejected Egypt's claim of sovereign immunity, endorsing the view that it would be anomalous to conclude that a State because of its supreme position and qualities, should be unable to give a binding promise, at 119.

invalidity. If there is substance in the plea, in the normal course an application for a stay would succeed. The invalidity of the agreement to arbitrate could also be raised during the course of arbitration, assuming that the issue was not raised prior to this time under Art II(3). A party to an agreement to arbitrate sought to stay arbitration proceedings in the US case of *Twi Lite International Inc v Anam Pacific Corp* (1996).[36] The plaintiff contended that its agreement to the arbitration clause was null and void because it had been procured by fraud, was unconscionable and was voidable on the grounds of fraud and misrepresentation. The contention was found to be unpersuasive on the facts, especially having regard to the pro-enforcement bias implicit in the Convention. The matter was referred to arbitration. The court noted also that while the court would review an arbitration clause alleged to have been procured by fraud, because this was envisaged by Art II(3), it would have been inappropriate for the court to review the underlying contract to determine whether it had been procured by fraud. This latter issue was one for the arbitrator, should be it be raised during arbitration.[37]

The defence would therefore only be invoked in unusual situations, such as where the party pleading it had not previously raised it, and was not cognisant of grounds for the plea prior to arbitration; or after having unsuccessfully raised it during arbitration, was confident that the arbitrator had ruled wrongly on the issue.

A party unsuccessfully attempted to invoke Art V(1)(a) in an Italian case, it being argued that the applicable law (US law and the Convention as implemented by it) did not recognise an arbitration clause which was printed on the back of certain purchase orders which were at the centre of the disputed transactions.[38]

A decision of the Administrative Tribunal of Syria by implication dealt with Art V(1)(a). The contest was one between a French company and a Syrian ministry. The parties had submitted their contractual dispute to arbitration in Geneva, with the French party prevailing. Enforcement was refused in Syria, on the basis that the ministry had not sought authorisation from the Syrian Council of State before agreeing to arbitration, as required by Syrian law. Accordingly, the arbitral award was 'non-existent'.[39]

Party not given proper notice; or otherwise unable to present case

Article V(1)(b) provides that a party may resist recognition or enforcement of an award on the basis that the party was not given proper notice of the appointment of the arbitrator or of the arbitration proceedings, or was unable otherwise to present his case.

The defence, or rather cluster of defences, are concerned with procedural irregularity sufficient to amount to a denial of due process or natural justice. The courts have construed the provision restrictively. An American court has commented

---

36 (1996) WL 637843 (ND Cal).

37 Citing *Prima Paint Corporation v Flood & Conklin Manufacturing Co* (1967) 388 US 395, 404.

38 *Bobbie Brooks Inc (US) v Lanificio Walter Banci sas (Italy)* (1978) IV Yearbook Commercial Arbitration 289 at 290–91 (Court of Appeal, Florence).

39 *Fougerolle SA (France) v Ministry of Defence of the Syrian Arab Republic* (1990) XV Yearbook Commercial Arbitration 515 .

that the defence 'essentially sanctions the application of the forum State's standards of due process'.[40] It has been said that enforcement 'may be denied only if there was a procedural infirmity that rendered the proceedings fundamentally unfair and caused prejudice to the complaining party'.[41] The procedural irregularity must be more than merely technical. If the party had an opportunity to raise the perceived procedural unfairness during the arbitration and declined to do so, then normally this will preclude application of the defence in enforcement proceedings.

A challenge to enforcement based upon an alleged lack of notice failed in the American case of *Geotech Lizenz AG v Evergreen Systems Inc* (1988).[42] The party resisting enforcement – Evergreen – did not participate in the arbitration. It was, however, appraised of every step of the arbitration process, and given every opportunity to participate, and fully appraised of the perils of non-appearance. Its non-participation was a matter of choice. Further, the fact that the arbitration was held in Switzerland whereas Evergreen was domiciled in the US, did not justify its non-participation on the ground that this would have been inconvenient. Evergreen had entered into an agreement after arms length negotiations, nominating Switzerland as the forum of arbitration in the event of dispute. Likewise, in an Italian case, the absence of a party from the arbitration was held not to warrant non-enforcement of the award.[43] The party resisting enforcement was an Italian company, and the arbitration was held in the US. The court found that the company had been informed of the pending arbitration, and that it had refused explicitly to participate in the process.[44]

A claim by a party resisting enforcement, that a relevant procedural irregularity occurred when the arbitrators would not disclose the identity of a 'secret expert' was rejected in the US case of *International Standard Electric Corporation v Bridas Sociodad Anonima Petrolera Industrial Y Comercial* (1990).[45] The expert testified on aspects of New York State law. The party contended that the expert might have a conflict of interest. The court found the possibility theoretical and speculative. The complaint did not address a matter of substance. Moreover, it was very relevant that the party had not complained of the matter during arbitration, when substantive arguments, if any, could have been put to the arbitral panel.[46]

Enforcement was refused in another US case, on the basis that the party resisting enforcement had improperly been denied an opportunity to present its case to the arbitral tribunal. At a pre-hearing conference, the party was told to submit audited accounts receivable ledgers rather than a vast collection of invoices. Later, another arbitrator questioned the method of proof, in response to which the party explained that it was proceeding according to an earlier understanding. This arbitrator subsequently found against the party on the ground of lack of clear proof, without having made it clear that the actual invoices were required to substantiate its claim.

40　*Iran Aircraft Industries v AVCO Corporation* (1992) 980 F 2d 141 at 145 (2nd Cir).
41　*Karaha Bodas Co LLC v Perusahaan Pertambangan Minyak Dan Gas Bumi Negara*, op cit at 949, citing *Hammermills* (1992) WL 122712 at *5.
42　(1988) 697 F Supp 1248 (EDNY).
43　*Bobbie Brooks Inc (US) v Lanificio Walter Banci sas (Italy)*, op cit.
44　*Ibid* at 291.
45　(1990) 745 F Supp 172.
46　*Ibid* at 180.

The party had proceeded on the basis that the audited accounts were adequate for the purposes of arbitration. As such, it had not been given an opportunity to be heard 'at a meaningful time and in a meaningful manner'.[47]

In the American case of *Karaha Bodas Co LLC v Perusahaan Pertambangan Minyak Dan Gas Bumi Negara* (2001),[48] enforcement was challenged on the basis that the arbitral tribunal failed to grant it a continuance in order that it could prepare a response to new allegations made by the opposing party, and that it was unfairly denied discovery on a material issue. The challenge was unsuccessful, with the court finding that the party had ample time to prepare its case, and that it had not been unfairly denied discovery. The hurdle for the defence was high: the 'issue is not whether this court would have granted the discovery or continuance. The issue is whether the procedures employed met the minimum requirements of fairness'.[49] In any event, the procedural issues were well within the reasonable exercise of the arbitral tribunal's discretion, and its decisions did not prevent the party 'from having a meaningful hearing [that did] not rise to the level of fundamental unfairness necessary to deny enforcement of the arbitration award'.[50]

Issue not within terms of arbitration, or award deals with matter not within scope of arbitration

Article V(1)(c) provides that recognition or enforcement of an award may be refused on the grounds that the award deals with a difference not contemplated by, or not falling within, the terms of submission to arbitration, or it contains decisions on matters beyond the scope of submission to arbitration, provided that, if the decisions on matters submitted to arbitration can be separated from those not so submitted, that part of the award which contains decisions on matters submitted to arbitration may be recognised and enforced. The two branches of the defence overlap. The first allows contentions that the issues raised were beyond the scope of the arbitration agreement, while the second allows submissions that some of these matters were beyond scope.

In substance, the Article provides a defence that the award does not relate to matters that the parties have agreed may be submitted to arbitration. If this is so, then the arbitral authority has exceeded its jurisdiction, either wholly or in part. The instrument for determining this issue of arbitrability is the parties' arbitral agreement (or more usually, arbitration clause within the underlying contract). The Article then, creates a defence that a particular issue was not arbitrable according to the terms of this agreement.

As such, the Article is to be distinguished from Art V(2)(a) providing for non-recognition or enforcement where the dispute is not arbitrable under the law of the country where recognition or enforcement is sought.

An attempt to stay arbitration proceedings was rejected in the US case of *Twi Lite International Inc v Anam Pacific Corp* (1996).[51] Although the case was one where a stay

---

47 *Iran Aircraft Industries v AVCO Corporation, op cit*, citing *Mathews v Eldrige* (1976) 424 US 319 at 333 (S Ct); *Armstrong v Manzo* (1965) 380 US 545 at 552.
48 (2001) 190 F Supp 936 (SD Texas).
49 *Ibid* at 951 n 15.
50 *Ibid* at 952.
51 (1996) WL 637843 (ND Cal).

was sought, rather than one involving a challenge to enforcement of an award, it is instructive. The issues in dispute were numerous, and included a claim of misappropriation of trade secrets. One of the plaintiff's claims was that the issue in question was beyond the scope of the arbitration provision. It was held that the clause was sufficiently broad to cover the issue, providing as it did for the arbitration of all disputes that may arise between the parties, out of or in connection with the (underlying) agreement or for the breach thereof.

The court in *Twi Lite* drew a distinction from another case where a clause was found to be insufficiently broad to encompass the dispute in question, which was a claim of misappropriation of trade secrets, an issue not dealt with in the contract. In this latter case, the arbitral clause covered disputes 'arising out of' the agreement, but omitted reference to claims 'relating to' an agreement. The court construed the phrase 'arising out of' as applying only to disputes 'relating to the interpretation and performance of the contract itself', and not a collateral issue such as a claim of misappropriation of trade secrets.[52]

If the award deals partly with issues which are properly arbitrable pursuant to the agreement to arbitrate, and partly with those which are not, then in terms of the Article, the award may be enforced in respect of the first category of issues, provided (as would normally be the case) the two categories of finding can properly be separated.

If a party contends that the matter was not within the terms of the arbitration because the arbitration clause is no longer valid, or operative (if ever it was), this would ordinarily be a matter for assessment pursuant to Art II(3), and would be resolved prior to submission to arbitration, or alternatively, would be raised during arbitration with a view to procuring a determination from the arbitral panel that it is without jurisdiction. However, in the US case of *Henry v Murphy* (2002),[53] a party resisted enforcement of an award on the basis that the arbitrator was barred by a time clause, without having raised this issue before or during arbitration. The arbitration by agreement was heard in Ireland and proceeded pursuant to Irish law. The Irish statute of limitations imposed a six year limitation on arbitration proceedings. The arbitration took place beyond this time. Enforcement of the award was sought under the New York Convention. The statute of limitations defence was rejected by the court of enforcement on the basis that the party seeking to invoke it had not raised it before or during arbitration.[54]

Composition of arbitral authority, or arbitral procedure not in accordance with the agreement or law of country of arbitration

Article V(1)(d) provides for non-recognition or enforcement where the composition of the arbitral authority or the arbitral procedure was not in accordance with the

---

52 *Trace Research Corp v National Environmental Services Co* (1994) 42 F 3d 1292 (9th Cir).

53 (2002) US Dist Lexis 227.

54 In contrast, a party resisting enforcement of an award in the English case of *Ford and Co Ltd v Compagnie Furness (France)* (1922) 12 Ll L Reports 281, on the same ground, ie, that the arbitration was time-barred, was successful. This party had raised the issue prior to arbitration, and had declined to participate in it. The case predated the New York Convention, but the outcome would logically be the same had it applied to enforcement.

agreement of the parties, or failing such agreement, was not in accordance with the law of the country where the arbitration took place.

In a Hong Kong, case enforcement of an award made in China was resisted on the basis that the arbitral panel was not composed of arbitrators on the Beijing list as specified in the agreement to arbitrate, but rather, with arbitrators drawn from the Shenzhen list. Enforcement was permitted in reliance upon the court's residual discretion, the party resisting enforcement having participated in the arbitration knowing of the non-conformity with the agreement and not having complained of this.[55]

It is to be noted that where complaint is made of a substantive procedural irregularity amounting to a denial of due process, the defence provided for in Art V(1)(b) is applicable.

If it is contended that the arbitral panel was wrongly constituted because there was no valid agreement to arbitrate in the first place, resort would be had to Art II(1) or (3).

Award not yet binding on parties, or has been set aside or suspended in country of award

Article V(1)(e) provides that recognition and enforcement of an award may be refused where the award has not yet become binding on the parties, or has been set aside or suspended by a competent authority of the country in which, or under the law of which, the award was made.

According to the cases, an award is binding when it is contractually binding on the parties, pursuant to the terms of their agreement to arbitrate, the arbitration process having run its course and the award having been rendered. It does not cease to be binding merely because (in the event of non-compliance by a burdened party) some further step has to be taken to have it enforced by a court; or because recourse may still be had to the court by way of proceedings to resist enforcement. In the words of a US court, the 'terms "final" and "binding" merely refer to a contractual intent that the issues joined and resolved in the arbitration may not be tried *de novo* in any court ... even a "final" and "binding" arbitral award is subject to the defences to enforcement provided for in the New York Convention...'.[56]

In an Italian case, an award rendered in the US was enforced in Italy. According to the court, the award was binding when it is no longer open to attack in arbitral proceedings, according to the law where enforcement is sought.[57]

In the US case of *Fertilizer Corp of India v IDI Management Inc* (1981),[58] an award made in India was sought to be enforced in the US. It was contended that the award was not yet binding on the parties, because it had not been reviewed by an Indian court for errors of law. The award was currently before the Indian courts for ruling on

---

55 *China Nanhai Oil Joint Service Corp v Gee Tai Holdings Co Ltd* (1995) XX Yearbook Commercial Arbitration 671 at 679.

56 *Iran Aircraft Industries v AVCO Corp, op cit*, citing *I/Sstavborg v National Metal Converters Inc* (1974) 500 F 2d 424, 427 (2nd Cir)

57 *Bobbie Brooks Inc (US) v Lanificio Walter Banci sas (Italy), op cit*.

58 (1981) 517 F Supp 948 (SD Ohio).

a range of issues. The court held that an award was not precluded from being binding merely because it is appealable, or even under current challenge before a court. Further, Indian law recognised it to be such – not only binding on the parties when made, but having a *res judicata* effect, which could be relied upon in litigation of the same subject matter between the parties. In the court's view, an award was binding if it could be said that recourse could not be had to another (appellate) arbitral tribunal. The possibility of recourse to a court does not prevent it from being binding in terms of the Article, because otherwise an obstructive loser could delay enforcement by bringing or threatening to bring proceedings to have the award set aside or suspended.[59] Notwithstanding this conclusion as to the scope of the first branch in the Art V(1)(e) defence, the court stayed enforcement proceedings pending the outcome of the Indian litigation, pursuant to Art VI. This aspect of the case will be further commented upon in 'Adjournment of enforcement proceedings pursuant to Article VI, where application made to have award set aside or suspended' below.

In a Dutch case likewise, it has been held that an award does not cease to be binding merely because an action has been initiated to set it aside. The award had been made in France. The party resisting enforcement commenced proceedings in a French court. The Dutch court granted leave to enforce the award, having regard to the purpose of the Convention to enhance the recognition and enforcement of awards subject to a minimum number of conditions.[60]

The second branch of the Art V(1)(e) defence permits the discretionary refusal of recognition or enforcement where the award has been set aside or suspended by a competent authority in the country where recognition and enforcement is sought. It is to be distinguished from Art VI permitting adjournment of enforcement proceedings where application for the setting aside or suspension of an award by this competent authority referred to in Art V(1)(e).

The decision of the court in the country where enforcement is sought, to decline enforcement, is discretionary, whenever any of the Art V defences are made out. This is made clear by the Preamble to Art V. In the US case of *Chromalloy Aeroservices v The Arab Republic of Egypt* (1996),[61] the award had been rendered in Egypt, and enforcement was sought in the US. The arbitral agreement precluded appeal to an Egyptian court. Notwithstanding this, the party against which the award had been made appealed to an Egyptian court, which suspended it and subsequently made an order for its nullification. The US court made an order for the enforcement of the award, in exercise of its discretion to enforce it notwithstanding fulfilment of the requirements of the defence provided for in the second branch of Art V(1)(e). It was relevant that the party resisting enforcement had provided no evidence that corruption, fraud or undue means was used in procuring the award, or that the arbitrators exceeded their powers in any way. It was also relevant that US law presumed that arbitral awards were binding. It was further relevant that the US courts had manifested a pro-enforcement bias in relation to awards made under the New York Convention – there 'are no reported cases in which a court of the United States has faced a situation, under the Convention, in which the court of a foreign nation has

---

59   *Ibid* at 958, noting the comments of Professor Gerald Aksen, General Counsel of the American Arbitration Association.

60   *SPP (Middle East) Ltd (Hong Kong) v The Arab Republic of Egypt, op cit*, at 489–90.

61   (1996) 939 F Supp 907 (DDC).

nullified an otherwise valid arbitral award'.[62] Considerations of comity between nations favoured non-enforcement, but the objectives of the Convention favoured enforcement. It was relevant that Egypt had made a 'solemn promise to abide by the results of the arbitration'.[63]

The Convention does not, for the purpose of Art V(1)(e), specify or otherwise limit the grounds upon which the court of the State of rendition may set aside the award, thus potentially triggering an application for non-recognition or enforcement under the Article. It is for this reason that the court from which an order for enforcement is sought will logically need to be vigilant against attempts to stymie enforcement of awards which have been set aside on insubstantial grounds. This approach is reflected in the *Chromalloy* case, above.

A US court has held that in an action to set aside an award as contemplated by Art V(1)(e), the applicable law controlling the application and its determination is that of the rendering State.[64]

Article VI may be noted in relation to Art V(1)(e). Article VI provides for the adjourning of enforcement proceedings where an application has been made to the court for the setting aside or suspension of an award in the country in which, or under the law of which, that award was made. Article VI is commented upon below, at 'Adjournment of enforcement proceedings pursuant to Article VI, where application made to have award set aside or suspended'.

Award not arbitrable under the law of the country of enforcement

It is provided in Art V(2)(a) and (b) that the competent authority (usually the court) in the country of enforcement may (of its own motion) refuse to recognise and enforce an award in defined cases. Refusal is discretionary.

Pursuant to Art V(2)(a), this may be done where the subject matter of the difference is not capable of settlement under the law of the country of enforcement. 'Capable' has been described as meaning 'legally capable', because 'any matter can in theory be arbitrated or compromised'.[65]

The issue was touched upon in the US case of *Parsons & Whitmore Overseas Co Inc v Societe Generale de l'industrie du Papier (RAKTA)* (1974).[66] In the court's opinion, the party resisting enforcement did not raise a substantial issue of arbitrability. The claim that the national interest of the US, as the State of enforcement, in some way made the dispute non-arbitrable, was rejected, with it being commented that there 'is no special national interest in judicial, rather than arbitral, resolution of the breach of contract claim underlying the award in this case'.[67] The court commented *obiter* that a US court

62   *Ibid* at 911.
63   *Ibid* at 912ff. In *Hilmarton Ltd v Omnium de traitement et de valorisation (OTV) Revue de l'arbitrage* (1994) (see extracts in (1995) XX Yearbook Commercial Arbitration 663), an award which had been set aside in Switzerland was enforced by a French court.
64   *Yusuf Ahmed Alghanim & Sons WLL v TOYS 'R' US Inc, op cit.* Likewise, see *International Standard Electric Corp v Bridas Sociodad Anomina Petrolera, Industrial Y Comercial* (1990) 745 F Supp 172, 178.
65   *Mitsubishi Motors Corp v Soler Chrysler-Plymouth Inc, op cit.*
66   (1974) 508 F 2d 969 (CANY).
67   *Ibid* at 975.

might be expected to decline enforcement of an award involving arbitration of an anti-trust claim in view of domestic arbitration cases which have determined that this issue is not arbitrable, and must be determined by the judiciary. On the other hand, 'it may well be that the special considerations and policies underlying "a truly international agreement"[68] ... call for a narrower view of non-arbitrability in the international rather than the domestic context'.[69] In the later case of *Mitsubishi Motors Corp v Soler Chrysler-Plymouth Inc* (1983),[70] the court held that an international arbitration could not arbitrate on US anti-trust issues, commenting that 'decisions as to anti-trust regulation of business are too important to be lodged in arbitrators chosen from the business community – particularly those from a foreign community that has had no experience with or exposure to our law and values'.[71] The US interest in judicial resolution of anti-trust issues could not be described as 'parochial' in the sense of being 'petty provincialism'.[72]

In a Belgian case, enforcement of an award made in Switzerland was refused on the basis that Belgian law precluded an agreement for the submission of a dispute to arbitration before the end of the contract from which it arose, with the result that the dispute was not arbitrable.[73] This might be thought to reflect an unduly parochial attitude towards application of the Convention. The parties had, after all, agreed that any arbitration was to be conducted in Switzerland pursuant to Swiss law. In favour of the decision, the underlying contract was one for the granting of a motor vehicle sales franchise wholly or partially within Belgian territory, a class of contract which was closely regulated by Belgian law, a feature of which was the vesting of a right in the concessionaire to invoke the protection of Belgian law, except where he has renounced the right by an agreement, after the end of the contract, pursuant to which the concession was granted.

In an American case, enforcement of a foreign arbitral award in a US court was refused on the basis that the dispute was not arbitrable, and by application of the act of State doctrine (viz, sovereign immunity). It was not arbitrable because of the application of the doctrine of sovereign State immunity. The party resisting enforcement was a State that had nationalised certain oil assets, which act had given rise to the subject of arbitration. In the view of the court, expropriation of the assets of an alien within the boundaries of the sovereign State are considered to be classic acts of State immune from judicial scrutiny.[74] If it was so immune, it would likewise be non-arbitrable, and the court could not review any arbitral award pertaining to the topic.

68 Citing *Scherk v Alberto-Culver Co* (1974) 42 USLW 4911, 4914.
69 *Parsons & Whitmore Overseas Co Inc v Societe Generale de L'Industry du Papier (RAKTA)* (1994) 50B F 2d 969 at 974 (CANY)
70 (1983) 723 F 2d 155.
71 *Ibid* at 162.
72 *Ibid* at 163.
73 *Audi-NSU Auto Union AG (FR Germ) v SA Adelin Petit & Cie (Belgium)* (1979) V Yearbook International Arbitration 257 (Court of Appeal of Liege).
74 *Libyan American Oil Co v Socialist People's Libyan Arab Jamahirya* (1980) 482 F Supp 1175 at 1178–1179.

Public policy

Article V(2)(b) provides that recognition and enforcement of an arbitral award may be refused if the competent authority in the country where recognition and enforcement is sought finds that recognition and enforcement would be contrary to the public policy of that country.

The ground is more commonly invoked than most of the grounds, but with indifferent success. The courts have given the clause a restricted scope, defeating attempts to treat it as a 'catch-all' defence comprehending grounds of resistance to enforcement not specifically enumerated in the preceding clauses in Art V.

The public policy defence has been described as one which should be 'construed narrowly',[75] so that the enforcement of awards may be denied on this basis 'only where enforcement would violate the forum State's most basic notions of morality and justice'.[76] It was said in an Indian case that the public policy exception was enlivened only where enforcement would be contrary to '(i) fundamental policy of Indian law; or (ii) the interests of India; or (iii) justice or morality'.[77] An English judge commented that the public policy principles captured in essence 'principles of morality of general application'.[78] US authority holds that the defence applies 'only where enforcement would violate [the forum State's] most basic notions of morality and justice'.[79] In Germany it has been commented that for the arbitral proceeding to deviate from domestic rules is not necessarily sufficient to ground the public policy defence – what is needed is 'an infringement of international public policy'; the arbitral proceedings must 'have been affected by a serious shortcoming touching upon fundamental principles of economic and constitutional life'.[80] A Swiss court commented that a procedure in arbitral proceedings would not ground the public policy defence unless it was such a violation of Swiss law as to amount to 'a violation of fundamental principles of our legal system, which would contrast in an unbearable manner with our feelings of justice'.[81] In an Ontario case it was commented that the award must 'be contrary, not merely to Ontario law, but contrary to the essential morality of the community in Ontario'.[82]

---

75 *Parsons & Whitmore Overseas Co Inc v Societe Generale de L'Industry Du Papier (RAKTA), op cit,* per Joseph Smith J, citing *Loucks v Standard Oil Co* (1918) 224 NY 99, 111. See too *Mitsubishi Motors Corp v Soler Chrysler-Plymouth, op cit; Renusagar Power Co Ltd (India) v General Electric Co (US)* (1995) XX Yearbook Commercial Arbitration 681 at 701 (Supreme Court of India); *Henry v Murphy* (2002) US Dist Lexis 227 at 11 (confirming the judicial bias in favour of narrow construction).

76 *Parsons & Whittemore Overseas Co Inc v Societe Generale de L'Industry Du Papier (RAKTA), ibid.*

77 *Renusagar Power Co Ltd (India) v General Electric Co (US), op cit.*

78 *Lemeda Trading Co Ltd v African Middle East Petroleum Co Ltd* [1988] QB 448 at 461, per Phillips J, cited in *Westacre Investments Inc v Jugoimport-SDPR Holding Co Ltd* [1999] 3 All ER 864 at 874, per Waller LJ.

79 *Waterside Ocean Navigation Co v International Navigation Ltd* (1984) 737 F 2d 150, 152 (2nd Cir); *Europcar Italia SpA v Maiellano Tours Inc* (1998) 156 F 3d 310, 315 (2nd Cir); *Henry v Murphy, op cit* at 11.

80 *Seller (Nationality not indicated) v Buyer (Nationality not indicated)* (1992) XVII Yearbook Commercial Arbitration 503 at 505 (Federal Supreme Court, Germany); similarly, see *German (FR) Charterer v Romanian Shipowner* (1987) XII Yearbook Commercial Arbitration 489 at 490 (Federal Supreme Court, Germany).

81 *KS AG v CC SA* (1995) XX Yearbook Commercial Arbitration 762 at 763–64 (Execution and Bankruptcy Chamber, Canton Tessin, Switzerland).

82 *Arcata Graphics Buffalo Ltd v The Movie (Magazine)* (1993) Ont Sup CJ Lexis 530 (Ontario Court of Justice.

It is generally accepted that the mere fact that the recognition or enforcement of the award (or for that matter, the contract upon which it is based) is contrary to the law of the forum State, does not *per se* ground the public policy exception.[83] Municipal law is of course infinitely variable in its details across the range of States, and a technical or even a substantive illegality of a parochial kind ought not to render an award unenforceable as a matter of form, otherwise the enforcement of awards would be seriously compromised. Thus, the usual approach of the courts has been to look to international norms in public policy, and to minimise the significance of inconsistencies within local law.

The Italian Court of Appeal in Florence enforced an award made in the USA under the rules of the American Arbitration Association, notwithstanding a challenge to enforcement based on the fact that the arbitrators' reasons for decision were not stated in the award. The public policy defence was not enlivened by the fact that the statement of reasons in an adjudicator's decision was a principle in the Italian constitution – 'the fact that reasoning constitutes a principle of the Italian constitution is not important because what is fundamental in Italian law of procedure may not be considered as such by foreign legislative and judicial authorities'.[84]

In the Indian case of *Renusagar Power Co Ltd (India) v General Electric Co (US)* (1995),[85] the Supreme Court of India refused to stay enforcement of an award on the public policy ground, rejecting claims that the award violated technical provisions in Indian legislation. The court remarked that in any event that 'contravention of the law alone will not attract the bar of public policy and something more than contravention of the law is required'.[86] Enforcement would be refused, as noted above, if such enforcement would be contrary to the fundamental policy of the law, or the interests of India, or justice or morality.[87]

In the English Court of Appeal case of *Westacre Investments Ltd v Jugoimport-SDPR Holding Co Ltd* [1999],[88] the enforcement of an award made in Switzerland in relation to a contract governed by Swiss law, was challenged on the basis that the contract was unenforceable in England, because one of its terms involved the purchasing of personal influence over government officials. The court held by majority that because the arbitrators had considered and rejected this bribery claim, and there was no fresh evidence adduced on the issue, it was inappropriate for the court to go behind the award and investigate the claim afresh.[89] Further, there was nothing to suggest incompetence on the part of the arbitrators, nor was there reason to suspect collusion or bad faith in the obtaining of the award.[90] The third member of the court would have investigated the claim afresh.

---

83   *Bobbie Brooks Inc (US) v Lanificio Walter Banci sas (Italy), op cit*; *Renusagar Power Co Ltd (India) v General Electric Co (US), op cit*; *Westacre Investments Inc v Jugoimport-SDPR Holding Co Ltd, op cit, per* Waller J; *Seller (Nationality not indicated) v Buyer, (Nationality not indicated)* (1992) XVII Yearbook Commercial Arbitration 503 at 505 (Federal Supreme Court, Germany); *KS AG v CC SA, op cit.*
84   *Bobbie Brooks Inc (US) v Lanificio Walter Banci sas (Italy), op cit.*
85   (1995) XX Yearbook Commercial Arbitration 681 at 701.
86   *Ibid* at 701.
87   *Ibid* at 702.
88   [1999] 3 All ER 864.
89   Mantell and Hirst LJJ, at 887, 888.
90   *Ibid* at 887, *per* Mantell LJ.

An English court refused to stay enforcement on the public policy ground, rejecting a claim that the public policy of England was violated where the two parties were each citizens of countries between which a State of war had existed from a date after formation of the contract, on the claimed basis that such a change in the political situation would have dissolved the contract by operation of a rule of English common law or international law.[91]

An Australian court held that an alleged arbitral award was not an award within the meaning of the Convention, because it was in the nature of interlocutory orders rather than a final award. Even if it were an award, public policy would preclude its enforcement, because the orders comprised in this award were as drafted orders of a type that would not be made in Queensland, particularly without undertakings as to appropriate security and because of other reasons, but also because of double vexation and practical difficulties in interpretation and enforcement.[92]

The public policy defence was rejected in a Swiss case, it having been contended that Swiss public policy had been violated because one of the members of the arbitral tribunal did not sign the award, a requirement imposed neither by Swiss law nor the Convention.[93] In a German decision, the participation of a legal consultant in the arbitral proceedings, including drafting the award, though not a member of the arbitral panel, did not enliven the defence. This was so even if the activity of a consultant in this role would have required the express agreement of the parties in a German domestic arbitration (an issue which had not been settled).[94] In another German case, it was insufficient that one of the parties had appointed the arbitrator, rather than the appointment being a jointly agreed one. The respondent had not shown any violation of the arbitrator's duty of neutrality, nor that the arbitrator had a relationship with the party that appointed him which would have raised any concerns.[95]

The public policy defence has also been employed as a catch-all defence, in order to ground a defence that cannot be comprehended under the other more specific grounds for refusing recognition and enforcement in Art V (which Article exhaustively defines the grounds for refusal). For example, a line of American cases has seen it invoked in situations where it has been argued that the award was rendered in 'manifest disregard' of the law (a defence to enforcement in the domestic arbitration context impliedly provided for in the Federal Arbitration Act, specifically 9 USC 10).[96]

91 *Dalmia Dairy Industries Ltd v National Bank of Pakistan* [1978] 2 Lloyd's Reports 223.
92 *Resort Condominiums International Inc v Bolwell* (1993) 111 ALR 655 at 680 (SC Qld).
93 *KS AG v CC SA, op cit.*
94 *Seller (Nationality not indicated) v Buyer (Nationality not indicated), op cit.*
95 *German (FR) Charterer v Romanian Shipowner, op cit.*
96 See *Parsons & Whitmore Overseas Co Inc v Societe Generale de L'Industry Du Papier (RAKTA), op cit,* citing a *dictum* in *Wilko v Swan* (1953) 346 US 427. Its invocation in the *Parsons* case was unproductive. See also *Yusuf Ahmed Alghanim & Sons, WLL v TOYS 'R' US Inc (HK), op cit,* where the manifest disregard of the law defence was unsuccessfully invoked in a case governed by the New York Convention.

ADJOURNMENT OF ENFORCEMENT PROCEEDINGS PURSUANT TO ARTICLE VI, WHERE APPLICATION MADE TO HAVE AWARD SET ASIDE OR SUSPENDED

Article V provides that if an application for the setting aside or suspension of the award has been made to a competent authority (usually, the court), referred to in Art V(1)(e), the authority before which the award is sought to be relied upon may, if it considers it proper, adjourn the decision on the enforcement of the award and may also, on the application of the party claiming enforcement of the award, order the other party to give suitable security.

Article V(1)(e) provides *inter alia*, that enforcement may be refused where it has been set aside or suspended by a competent authority of the country in which, or under the law of which, the award was made. Given the provision of this ground of refusal, it is logical to provide for the adjournment of enforcement proceedings where application has been made to this competent authority for the setting aside or suspension of the award.

Article VI was invoked in the US case of *Fertilizer Corp of India v IDI Management Inc* (1981).[97] Enforcement was sought in the US of an award made in India. At the time enforcement was sought, the losing party had commenced proceedings before an Indian court challenging the award, on the basis that arbitrators had exceeded their jurisdiction by awarding consequential damages despite an express clause in the contract to the contrary. The court noted that it had an unfettered grant of discretion under Art VI. The court noted that the objectives of the Convention were to liberalise enforcement procedures, limit defences and place the burden of proof upon the party opposing enforcement. By implication, these considerations disposed the court towards applying a stringent standard to adjourning the proceedings. However, the court granted the adjournment sought, 'in order to avoid the possibility of an inconsistent result'.[98] Accordingly, the matter would be adjourned until the Indian court had rendered its decision.

The decision may be contrasted with that in the Dutch case of *SPP (Middle East) Ltd (Hong Kong) v The Arab Republic of Egypt*,[99] and cases dealing with Art V(1)(e), where a court enforced an award notwithstanding that the award had been set aside by a court in the place of rendition (see 'Award not yet binding on parties, or has been set aside or suspended in country of award' above). Consideration of the purposes of the Convention would favour not adjourning proceedings. On the other hand, the presence of Art VI in the Convention cannot be ignored. The Convention clearly envisages that adjournment may be appropriate in certain circumstances. The substantive merits of the case made, at least on a *prima facie* view, by the party challenging the award in the place of rendition logically will inform the exercise of the discretion under Art VI. Furthermore, a refusal to adjourn proceedings might not (all things being equal) save time or expense. If proceedings had not been adjourned in the *Fertilizer* case, presumably the US court would had to have heard arguments directed

---

97   (1981) 517 F Supp 948 (SD Ohio).
98   *Ibid* at 962.
99   See above, 'Award not yet binding on parties, or has been set aside or suspended in country of award'.

INTERNATIONAL TRADE AND BUSINESS

towards establishing the same defence under Art V that was to be heard by the Indian court.

FURTHER READING

Aksen, G, 'American arbitration accession arrives in the age of Aquarius: United States implements United Nations Convention on the Recognition and Enforcement of Foreign Arbitral Awards' (1971) 3 Sw ULR 1.

Bernini, G, 'The enforcement of foreign arbitral awards by national judiciaries: a trial of the New York Convention's ambit and workability' in Schultsz, J, and van den Berg, A, *The Art of Arbitration: Essays on International Arbitration*, 1982, Netherlands: Kluwer, pp 51ff.

Binder, P, *International Commercial Arbitration in UNCITRAL Model Law Jurisdictions*, 2000, London: Sweet & Maxwell, Ch 8.

Coe, J, *International Commercial Arbitration: American Principles and Practice in a Global Context*, 1997, Irving-on-Hudson, NY: Transnational Publishers.

Chukwumerije, O, 'Enforcement of foreign awards in Australia: the implications of resort condominiums' (1994) *Aust Dispute Resolution J* 237.

Gaillard, G, 'Enforcement of a nullified foreign award' (1997) 218 NYLJ 3.

Garnett, R, 'The current status of international arbitration agreements in Australia' (1999) 15 *Journal of Contract Law*.

Islam, R, *International Trade Law*, 1999, Sydney: Law Book Co, Ch 8.2.

Kaplan, N, 'A case by case examination of whether national courts apply different standards when assisting arbitral proceedings and enforcing awards in international cases as contrasting with domestic disputes. Is there a worldwide trend towards supporting an international arbitration culture?' in Van den Berg, A (ed), *International Dispute Resolution*, 1996, The Hague: Kluwer Law International, pp 187ff.

Kolkey, D, 'Attacking arbitral awards: rights of appeal and review in international arbitrations' (1988) 22 *International Law* 693.

Paulsson, J, 'Rediscovering the New York Convention: further reflections on Chromalloy', (1997) 1 *Mealey's Int'l Arb Rep* 20.

Ratnapala, S and Haller, L, 'International commercial arbitration' in Moens, G and Gillies, P (eds), *International Trade and Business: Law Policy and Ethics*, 1998, London: Cavendish, Ch 11.

Redfern, A, and Hunter, M, *Law and Practice of International Commercial Arbitration*, 3rd edn, 1999, London: Sweet & Maxwell, Ch 10.

Sarcevic, P, *Essays on International Commercial Arbitration*, 1989, London: Graham & Trotman, Ch 9.

Schaffer, R, Earle, B and Agusti, F, *International Business Law and its Environment*, 4th edn, 1999, Cincinnati, Ohio: West Educational Publishing Co, Ch 4.

Schultsz, J, 'Recognition and enforcement of foreign arbitral awards without a convention being applicable' in Schultsz, J, and Van den Berg, A, *The Art of Arbitration: Essays on International Arbitration*, 1982, Netherlands: Kluwer, pp 295ff.

Taherzadeh, M, 'International arbitration and enforcement in US Federal Courts' (2000) 22 *Hous J Int'l L* 371.

Van den Berg, A, *The New York Arbitration Convention of 1958*, 1981, The Hague: Kluwer.

Volz, J, and Haydock, R, 'Foreign arbitral awards: enforcing the award against the recalcitrant loser' (1996) 21 *Wm Mitchell L rev* 867.

APPENDIX

UNITED NATIONS CONVENTION ON THE RECOGNITION AND ENFORCEMENT OF FOREIGN ARBITRAL AWARDS – NEW YORK, 10 JUNE 1958

Article I

1 This Convention shall apply to the recognition and enforcement of arbitral awards made in the territory of a State other than the State where the recognition and enforcement of such awards are sought, and arising out of differences between persons, whether physical or legal. It shall also apply to arbitral awards not considered as domestic awards in the State where their recognition and enforcement are sought.

2 The term 'arbitral awards' shall include not only awards made by arbitrators appointed for each case but also those made by permanent arbitral bodies to which the parties have submitted.

3 When signing, ratifying or acceding to this Convention, or notifying extension under Article X hereof, any State may on the basis of reciprocity declare that it will apply the Convention to the recognition and enforcement of awards made only in the territory of another Contracting State. It may also declare that it will apply the Convention only to differences arising out of legal relationships, whether contractual or not, which are considered as commercial under the national law of the State making such declaration.

Article II

1 Each Contracting State shall recognize an agreement in writing under which the parties undertake to submit to arbitration all or any differences which have arisen or which may arise between them in respect of a defined legal relationship, whether contractual or not, concerning a subject matter capable of settlement by arbitration.

2 The term 'agreement in writing' shall include an arbitral clause in a contract or an arbitration agreement, signed by the parties or contained in an exchange of letters or telegrams.

3 The court of a Contracting State, when seized of an action in a matter in respect of which the parties have made an agreement within the meaning of this article, at the request of one of the parties, refer the parties to arbitration, unless it finds that the said agreement is null and void, inoperative or incapable of being performed.

Article III

Each Contracting State shall recognize arbitral awards as binding and enforce them in accordance with the rules of procedure of the territory where the award is relied upon, under the conditions laid down in the following articles. There shall not be imposed substantially more onerous conditions or higher fees or charges on the recognition or enforcement of arbitral awards to which this Convention applies than are imposed on the recognition or enforcement of domestic arbitral awards.

Article IV

1 To obtain the recognition and enforcement mentioned in the preceding article, the party applying for recognition and enforcement shall, at the time of the application, supply:

(a) the duly authenticated original award or a duly certified copy thereof;

(b) the original agreement referred to in Article II or a duly certified copy thereof.

2 If the said award or agreement is not made in an official language of the country in which the award is relied upon, the party applying for recognition and enforcement of the award shall produce a translation of these documents into such language. The translation shall be certified by an official or sworn translator or by a diplomatic or consular agent.

Article V

1   Recognition and enforcement of the award may be refused, at the request of the party against whom it is invoked, only if that party furnishes to the competent authority where the recognition and enforcement is sought, proof that:

(a) the parties to the agreement referred to in Article II were, under the law applicable to them, under some incapacity, or the said agreement is not valid under the law to which the parties have subjected it or, failing any indication thereon, under the law of the country where the award was made; or

(b) the party against whom the award is invoked was not given proper notice of the appointment of the arbitrator or of the arbitration proceedings or was otherwise unable to present his case; or

(c) the award deals with a difference not contemplated by or not falling within the terms of the submission to arbitration, or it contains decisions on matters beyond the scope of the submission to arbitration, provided that, if the decisions on matters submitted to arbitration can be separated from those not so submitted, that part of the award which contains decisions on matters submitted to arbitration may be recognized and enforced; or

(d) the composition of the arbitral authority or the arbitral procedure was not in accordance with the agreement of the parties, or, failing such agreement, was not in accordance with the law of the country where the arbitration took place; or

(e) the award has not yet become binding on the parties, or has been set aside or suspended by a competent authority of the country in which, or under the law of which, that award was made.

2   Recognition and enforcement of an arbitral award may also be refused if the competent authority in the country where recognition and enforcement is sought finds that:

(a) the subject matter of the difference is not capable of settlement by arbitration under the law of that country; or

(b) the recognition or enforcement of the award would be contrary to the public policy of that country.

Article VI

If an application for the setting aside or suspension of the award has been made to a competent authority referred to in Article V(1)(e), the authority before which the award is sought to be relied upon may, if it considers it proper, adjourn the decision on the enforcement of the award and may also, on the application of the party claiming enforcement of the award, order the other party to give suitable security.

Article VII

1   The provisions of the present Convention shall not affect the validity of multilateral or bilateral agreements concerning the recognition and enforcement of arbitral awards entered into by the Contracting States nor deprive any interested party of any right he may have to avail himself of an arbitral award in the manner and to the extent allowed by the law or the treaties of the country where such award is sought to be relied upon.

2   The Geneva Protocol on Arbitration Clauses of 1923 and the Geneva Convention on the Execution of Foreign Arbitral Awards of 1927 shall cease to have effect between Contracting States on their becoming bound and to the extent that they become bound, by this Convention.

Article VIII

1   This Convention shall be open until 31 December 1958 for signature on behalf of any Member of the United Nations and also on behalf of any other State which is or hereafter becomes a member of any specialized agency of the United Nations, or which is or hereafter becomes a party to the Statute of the International Court of Justice, or any other State to which an invitation has been addressed by the General Assembly of the United Nations.

2   This Convention shall be ratified and the instrument of ratification shall be deposited with the Secretary-General of the United Nations.

Article IX

1   This Convention shall be open for accession to all States referred to in Article VIII.

2   Accession shall be effected by the deposit of an instrument of accession with the Secretary-General of the United Nations.

Article X

1   Any State may, at the time of signature, ratification or accession, declare that this Convention shall extend to all or any of the territories for the international relations of which it is responsible. Such a declaration shall take effect when the Convention enters into force for the State concerned.

2   At any time thereafter any such extension shall be made by notification addressed to the Secretary-General of the United Nations and shall take effect as from the ninetieth day after the day of receipt by the Secretary-General of the United Nations of this notification, or as from the date of entry into force of the Convention for the State concerned, whichever is the later.

3   With respect to those territories to which this Convention is not extended at the time of signature, ratification or accession, each State concerned shall consider the possibility of taking the necessary steps in order to extend the application of this Convention to such territories, subject, where necessary for constitutional reasons, to the consent of the Governments of such territories.

Article XI

In the case of a federal or non-unitary State, the following provisions shall apply:

(a) With respect to those articles of this Convention that come within the legislative jurisdiction of the federal authority, the obligations of the federal Government shall to this extent be the same as those of Contracting States which are not federal States.

(b) With respect to those articles of this Convention that come within the legislative jurisdiction of constituent States or provinces which are not, under the constitutional system of the federation, bound to take legislative action, the federal Government shall bring such articles with a favourable recommendation to the notice of the appropriate authorities of constituent States or provinces at the earliest possible moment.

(c) A federal State Party to this Convention shall, at the request of any other Contracting State transmitted through the Secretary-General of the United Nations, supply a Statement of the law and practice of the federation and its constituent units in regard to any particular provision of this Convention, showing the extent to which effect has been given to that provision by legislative or other action.

Article XII

1   This Convention shall come into force on the ninetieth day following the date of deposit of the third instrument of ratification or accession.

2   For each State ratifying or acceding to this Convention after the deposit of the third instrument of ratification or accession, this Convention shall enter into force on the ninetieth day after deposit by such State of its instrument of ratification or accession.

Article XIII

1   Any Contracting State may denounce this Convention by a written notification to the Secretary-General of the United Nations. Denunciation shall take effect one year after the date of receipt of the notification by the Secretary-General.

2   Any State which has made a declaration or notification under Article X may, at any time thereafter, by notification to the Secretary-General of the United Nations, declare that this Convention shall cease to extend to the territory concerned one year after the date of the receipt of the notification by the Secretary-General.

3   This Convention shall continue to be applicable to arbitral awards in respect of which recognition and enforcement proceedings have been instituted before the denunciation takes effect.

Article XIV

A Contracting State shall not be entitled to avail itself of the present Convention against other Contracting States except to the extent that it is itself bound to apply the Convention.

Article XV

The Secretary-General of the United Nations shall notify the States contemplated in Article VIII of the following:

(a) signatures and ratifications in accordance with Article VIII;

(b) accessions in accordance with Article IX;

(c) declarations and notifications under Articles I, X and XI;

(d) the date upon which this Convention enters into force in accordance with Article XII;

(e) denunciations and notifications in accordance with Article XIII.

Article XVI

1   This Convention, of which the Chinese, English, French, Russian and Spanish texts shall be equally authentic, shall be deposited in the archives of the United Nations.

2   The Secretary-General of the United Nations shall transmit a certified copy of this Convention to the States contemplated in Article VIII.

INDEX